The Times.

Nº 32,543.

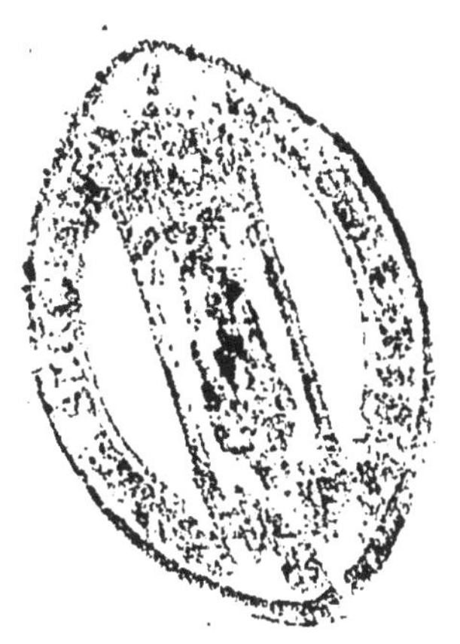

Ouvrages de M. A. Elwall :

Dictionnaire classique anglais-français et français-anglais, rédigé sur un plan méthodique, à l'usage des élèves des établissements d'instruction publique et des gens du monde, par *M. A. Elwall* : 16e édition ; 1 fort vol. in-8°. — *rel. toile*, 12 f. Chaque partie se vend séparément.

Dictionnaire classique anglais-français : 16e édition ; in-8°. — *rel. toile*, 6 f. 50 c.

Dictionnaire classique français-anglais : 16e édition ; in-8°. — *rel. toile*, 6 f. 50 c.

Petit Dictionnaire classique anglais-français et français-anglais, rédigé spécialement en vue de l'étude de la langue anglaise dans les divers établissements d'instruction publique, à l'usage des cours élémentaires, par *M. A. Elwall* : 11e édition ; 1 fort vol. grand in-18 de 1200 pages à 2 colonnes, imprimé en caractères anglais. — *rel. toile*, 5 f.

Premières Notions de Grammaire anglaise, suivies de lectures, à l'usage des Classes élémentaires, par *M. A. Elwall* : 4e édition ; in-12. — *cart.* 60 c.

Tableau synoptique des principaux sons dans la prononciation de la langue anglaise, et *règles générales de l'accent tonique*, par *M. A. Elwall* ; 4 pages in-8° jésus. — *l'exempl.* 15 c.

Éléments de Prononciation et d'Accentuation anglaises, avec exercices pratiques, par *M. A. Elwall* : 3e édition ; in-12. — *br.* 30 c.

Recueil de Morceaux choisis (*anecdotes, descriptions, fables, contes*, etc.), en anglais, suivis de *Petits Thèmes d'imitation*, à l'usage de la division élémentaire, avec notes et vocabulaires par *M. A. Elwall* : 5e édition ; in-12. — *cart.* 1 f. 20 c.

Cours théorique et pratique de Langue anglaise, à l'usage des Classes de grammaire, contenant des notions générales de grammaire et un choix gradué et facile de versions, de thèmes et de conversations, suivi de deux vocabulaires spéciaux, par *M. A. Elwall* : 8e édition ; 1 vol. in-12. — *cart.* 1 f. 50 c.

Éléments de Grammaire anglaise, par *Siret* : nouvelle édition, entièrement refondue, par *M. A. Elwall* ; 1 vol. in-12. — *cart.* 1 f. 50 c.

Cours gradué de Thèmes anglais, précédé de notions sur la formation des mots, à l'usage des Classes de grammaire, par *M. A. Elwall* : 17e édition ; 1 vol. in-12, — *cart.* 2 f.

Cours gradué de Versions anglaises, précédé de notions de prononciation anglaise, à l'usage des Classes de grammaire, par *M. A. Elwall* : 4e édition ; 1 vol. in-12, — *cart.* 2 f.

Morceaux choisis des Classiques anglais, Prose et Vers, à l'usage des Classes supérieures (troisième, seconde, rhétorique, mathématiques élémentaires), avec remarques, notes et introduction historique, par *M. A. Elwall* : 8e édition ; 1 vol. in-12. — *cart.* 3 f.

Dialogues, Conversations et Questions en français et en anglais, suivis d'interrogations sur la grammaire, la littérature, la géographie et l'histoire d'Angleterre, des États-Unis et de l'Australie, par *MM. Elwall* et *East* : 2e édition ; 1 vol. grand in-32. — *rel. toile*, 2 f.

Extraits des Récits d'un grand-père, de Walter Scott, avec notes explicatives, par *M. A. Elwall* ; 1 vol. in-12. — *cart.* 2 f.

Morceaux choisis des romans historiques de Walter Scott, avec sommaires analytiques et notes explicatives, par *M. A. Elwall* ; 1 vol. in-12. — *cart.* 2 f. 50 c.

Traité de Prosodie anglaise, comprenant toutes les règles de la versification, avec des exemples, par *M. A. Elwall* ; in-12. — *br.* 1 f.

THE TIMES

No. 32,543

AN ABSTRACT OF THE ENGLISH LIFE, MANNERS, CUSTOMS, LAWS AND TRADE OF THE PRESENT DAY

PRÉPARÉ ET ANNOTÉ
POUR LES CLASSES SUPÉRIEURES DES HAUTES ÉCOLES DE COMMERCE
ET DE L'ENSEIGNEMENT SECONDAIRE SPÉCIAL EN FRANCE
ET DANS TOUS PAYS OÙ L'ON PARLE LE FRANÇAIS

PAR

ALFRED ELWALL

PROFESSEUR A L'ÉCOLE SUPÉRIEURE DES MINES ET AU LYCÉE HENRI IV
CHEVALIER DE LA LÉGION D'HONNEUR.

PARIS

IMPRIMERIE ET LIBRAIRIE CLASSIQUES

MAISON JULES DELALAIN ET FILS

DELALAIN FRÈRES, Successeurs

56, RUE DES ÉCOLES.

PRÉFACE

Une mort cruelle et presque subite est venue arracher M. Alfred Elwall à ses études, et interrompre ce travail auquel il allait mettre la dernière main. Tout au plus a-t-il eu la consolation de voir avant de mourir la première épreuve de cet ouvrage et de savoir que son entreprise serait par suite menée à bonne fin.

C'est donc à son fils qu'est revenue la lourde responsabilité de revoir ces notes nombreuses pendant la correction des épreuves; j'y ai donné tous mes soins. Grâce à l'attention apportée par l'auteur dans son premier travail, ma tâche a été grandement facilitée.

Il est maintenant un devoir dont je tiens à m'acquitter. Je dois remercier M. le professeur Frédérick Landmann de l'École supérieure de Commerce de Leipzig, qui le premier a eu l'idée de ce livre si original et si moderne, et qui voulut bien permettre que l'application de son idée fût faite en France. Je remercie également l'administration du *Times*, qui, ayant d'abord autorisé M. Elwall à choisir et à publier tel ou tel numéro de ce journal, a bien voulu, avec une bonne grâce qui ne s'est jamais démentie, répondre ensuite à toutes les demandes de renseignements que l'auteur s'est parfois vu obligé de lui adresser.

Quant au livre lui-même, m'appartient-il de dire que le nom dont il est signé, si aimé dans l'Université, si connu par de nombreux travaux, est un trop sûr garant du soin et de l'intelligence avec lesquels il a été fait, pour qu'il ait besoin d'une autre recommandation?

GEORGE ELWALL.

Novembre 1889.

CONTENTS OF THIS DAY'S PAPER.

HISTORIQUE DU JOURNAL *THE TIMES*.

On New Year's day, 1788, was published in Printing-House-Square[1], the first number of *The Times*[2]. There was little in the surrounding externals of the event to mark the date as a memorable one. Two centuries earlier, the year 1588 had been recorded as an *Annus mirabilis*[3], in which England was delivered from the peril of foreign invasion[4]; one century earlier, another deliverance had rescued the nation from the thraldom of a selfish and unpatriotic despotism[5]. But a hundred years ago, though the world was tottering on the edge of a tremendous cataclysm, statesmen and publicists were able to congratulate themselves on the state of Europe, and even on the state of France. Louis XVI was still firmly seated on his throne; the meeting of the States-General was only the dream of a few advanced politicians; Pitt[6]

1. *Printing-House-Square*, ou Place de l'Imprimerie, à Londres, immeuble qui appartient en toute propriété au *Times*, et où se fait tout le travail de cet immense journal. — 2. Dans l'année 1785, Mr. John Walter fonda à Londres " *The Daily Universal Register* ", auquel il donna, le 1er janvier 1788, le titre de " *The Times, or Daily Universal Register* ", pour éviter la confusion avec une quantité d'autres feuilles qui alors portaient le nom de " *Register* ". Très peu de temps après, le journal, rejetant son sous-titre, parut avec des armes royales imprimées entre les deux mots *The Times*, comme cela a lieu encore aujourd'hui. John Walter, avec l'aide d'un typographe, Henri Johnson, avait inventé un nouveau genre de caractères, appelé *Logotype*, qui imprimaient des mots tout entiers, dont il se servit pour faire imprimer le *Times*, mais il n'en resta pas là. Grâce à l'énergie infatigable de son fondateur, le journal occupa bientôt une position des plus honorables; il contenait les articles les mieux écrits et les plus nombreuses annonces, et pouvait se vendre 0 fr. 30, quand les autres ne se vendaient que 0 fr. 25. Le fondateur, John Walter, mourut en 1812; mais, dès l'année 1798, il s'était déjà associé son fils cadet, à qui, depuis 1803, il avait laissé toute la direction. Ce fils, qui fut pendant longtemps membre de la Chambre des Communes, continua de diriger le journal jusqu'à sa mort, en 1847, avec la même énergie, et c'est sous lui et sous son fils aîné que le *Times* est devenu le premier journal du monde. Le *Times* paraît de bonne heure le matin, à l'exception du dimanche. Il publie, en outre, tous les deux jours, " *The Mail* ", et, de plus, une édition hebdomadaire, " *The Times' Weekly edition* ". Le *Times* emploie dans ses ateliers environ 400 personnes, et, chaque matin, il est tiré, selon les besoins, de 80 000 à 100 000 exemplaires de 16 et assez souvent de 24 pages grand in-folio, imprimées en 6 colonnes d'un texte serré. Mais tout cela est si habilement arrangé que chacun peut trouver à l'instant la partie du journal qui l'intéresse le plus, ou celle qu'il a besoin de consulter. — 3. *Annus mirabilis*, l'année mémorable; *mirabilis*, merveilleux. — 4. Celle de l'*Invincible Armada* (en 1588), envoyée par Philippe d'Espagne, sous les ordres du Prince de Parme. Elle fut complètement dispersée, tant par la bravoure des marins anglais que par les tempêtes qui l'assaillirent après sa défaite. — 5. Le despotisme de Jacques II, qui dut quitter l'Angleterre en 1688 et céder la couronne à sa fille Mary, qui avait épousé Guillaume d'Orange (Guillaume III). — 6. William (Pitt le jeune) fut premier ministre de l'Angleterre, de 1783 à 1801.

was a peace minister, with large and liberal views of fiscal and parliamentary reform; and NAPOLEON was a young and obscure officer of artillery. We doubt whether the historian of the future will recognize in the annals of 1788 any event more noteworthy than the establishment of *The Times*. The career of this journal during the century that lies behind us forms, we are bold to say, no insignificant or unconspicuous part of the history of Great Britain. Our record extends far enough back to justify us in speaking on this point with a certain amount of freedom. *The Times* as its founder[1] described it, even before it assumed the name, was intended to be " uninfluenced by party, uncontrolled by power, and attached solely to the public interest ". To that ideal the conductors of the paper have steadily adhered during one hundred years thronged with change and chances, through all revolutions of political power, of literary expression, and of popular taste. How remarkable the transformation is, our readers may judge for themselves by the extracts we print this morning[2] from the first few numbers of *The Times* issued a hundred years ago. Yet a plain-dealing spirit of independence is recognizable, we hope and believe, through every variation of circumstance and costume. We have fought for great causes, victorious or vanquished; we have endeavoured to represent, not unsuccessfully, as we are proud to think, the solid sense, the steady patriotism, and the practical instincts of the great body of the people of the United Kingdom, without distinction of class. *The Times* has never been and never will be the organ of a party, however triumphant, or the mouthpiece of a political leader, however autocratic. We are entitled to affirm that this attitude of unfettered criticism has left its mark for good on the amazing development of the British nation during the past hundred years. The position of primacy in the journalism of the world long since established by *The Times* is acknowledged, not throughout the United Kingdom only, but in foreign countries. In Europe, in America, in India and the colonies, *The Times* is universally recognized as having a right to speak in the name of England. That high privilege, involving[3] duties even higher, we may confidently assert, will never be abused; but will be maintained, according to the traditions of the paper, by the enterprise, the independence and the resolution that have been crowned hitherto with success.

1. John Walter, dont nous avons parlé plus haut, fut d'abord marchand de charbon de terre, puis assureur maritime; mais la capture par les Français d'une flotte de navires marchands lui causa une telle perte, qu'il dut entrer en association avec l'imprimeur Henry Johnson, dans Printing-House-Square (voy. page 1, note 2). — 2. Nous ne croyons pas qu'il soit nécessaire de donner ces extraits. — 3. *Involving*, entraînant, *imposant* (des devoirs).

Since the poet Cowper[1], in an oft quoted verse, spoke of

> " *The* folio of four pages, happy work,
> Which not even critics criticize, "

the Press has become a power — some may even be inclined to say the greatest power — in the State. The British Constitution has gradually shifted its basis, and now rests mainly as acute observers have pointed out, on " government by discussion ". Parliamentary debates are almost overshadowed[2] by the controversies conducted in the newspapers, or in speeches which without the aid of the newspapers might as well not be delivered at all. It was not unimportant, under these conditions, that the tradition of honourable independence, the paramount obligations of national duty, the dignity of public censorship should have been maintained; as we trust, *The Times* has always been able to maintain them, against the temptations of passing gain, of political partisanship, or of social influences. It has been the function of this journal, so far as its conductors have from time to time understood it, to express the prevailing convictions of the best part of the British people[3]. In stimulating the courage and the endurance of the nation during the long struggle with Napoleon[4], in furthering PITT's policy of Union with Ireland[5], in denouncing the slave-trade[6], in supporting the cause of parliamentary reform[7], in advocating the just claims of the Roman catholics[8] and the removal of Irish grievances when those grievances were substantial, in opposing the disruptionist Irish policy begun by O'CONNELL[9], and revived by Mr. PARNELL[10] and Mr GLAD-

1. William Cowper [kaou'-per *ou* kou'-per], poète anglais (1731-1800); les vers cités sont tirés du poème intitulé *The Task* (livre IV), où Cowper fait une description du journal. — 2. *Overshadowed*, jeté dans l'ombre. — 3. *Of the British people*, du peuple anglais. *British* se dit de tous les habitants du Royaume-Uni de la Grande-Bretagne et de l'Irlande; on dit : *the British government, the British fleet, etc.*, alors qu'on dit en français : le gouvernement *anglais*, la flotte *anglaise*. — 4. Le *Times* publia contre Napoléon des articles tellement violents que Napoléon lui-même demanda aux juristes anglais s'il ne pouvait poursuivre ce journal devant les tribunaux. — 5. Jusqu'en 1801, l'Irlande avait eu son parlement à elle qui siégeait à Dublin. Pitt fit passer une loi, acceptée par le parlement irlandais, qui établit la réunion (*the Union*) avec le parlement anglais, comme cela avait déjà eu lieu (en 1706) pour l'Ecosse. C'est le Rappel de l'Union que demandent aujourd'hui encore, sous le nom de *Home Rule*, le parti nationaliste irlandais. — 6. *The slave-trade*, la traite des esclaves fut abolie dans toutes les possessions anglaises par une loi passée en 1833. L'agitation en faveur de l'abolition de l'esclavage, créée par Wilberforce, fut vigoureusement soutenue par *The Times;* le commerce des esclaves avait été déclaré illégal dès l'année 1807. — 7. La réforme du parlement, c'est-à-dire une meilleure et plus juste distribution des sièges au parlement, n'a eu lieu qu'en 1832. — 8. L'émancipation des catholiques, c'est-à-dire leur admission à siéger au parlement et à remplir les postes civils ou militaires du royaume, n'a été votée qu'en 1829, bien que Pitt l'eût déjà proposée en 1801. — 9. Daniel O'Connell, surnommé " le Libérateur ", lutta longtemps et vivement pour obtenir le " Rappel de l'Union " (voy. note 5). Il fut accusé de sédition et condamné à la prison en 1844; il fut libéré après appel à la Chambre des Pairs; mais, dès ce moment, son influence s'affaiblit. Il mourut en 1847. — 10. CHARLES STEWART PARNELL, chef actuel du parti nationaliste en Irlande, fils

STONE[1], in condemning the fatuity of those who were determined to uphold Protection[2] against the popular will, in curbing the frenzy[9] of the railway mania[3], in speaking out in behalf of English opinion when Russian or French aggression[4] had to be faced, in exposing and censuring the departmental blundering which led to the disasters of the Crimean campaign[5] *The Times* strove ever and unflinchingly[10] to do what seemed to be its duty. It must be acknowledged, even by those who have differed from its policy, that its support or its opposition has always been an important factor in the movement of events. Yet though this journal stood by PEEL[6] against both Whigs[7] and Protectionists, and though at a later period it sustained PALMERSTON[8] against RUSSELL, DERBY,

d'un propriétaire irlandais, né en 1846, à Avondale, dans le comté de Wicklow, aidé de M. GLADSTONE, qui l'a autrefois combattu comme premier ministre, cherche à obtenir une indépendance *complète* pour l'Irlande et le partage des terres entre les Irlandais. L'Autriche ne saurait exister sans la Hongrie et la Bohême : l'Angleterre, sans l'Irlande, ne serait plus l'Angleterre. — 1. M. W. GLADSTONE, connu comme littérateur et financier de premier ordre, et à qui ses admirateurs ont donné le surnom du GRAND OLD MAN, a eu une très grande influence sur toute la politique européenne. Il a été trois fois et longtemps premier ministre. Aujourd'hui encore, comme chef de l'Opposition et malgré son âge avancé (il est né en 1809), il est plein d'énergie et d'activité, et son éloquence n'a perdu rien de sa vigueur. Beaucoup de ses anciens admirateurs ont cessé de le suivre dans la campagne qu'il entreprend aujourd'hui, avec les députés irlandais, en faveur du *Home-rule*, nom nouveau pour le Rappel de l'Union avec l'Angleterre (voir notes 5, 9 et 10, page 3). — 2. PROTECTION, c'est-à-dire les droits prohibitifs établis, en 1815, par les CORN LAWS sur les blés étrangers. *The Times* n'était pas seulement un ardent avocat de l'abolition de ces lois, mais il fut le premier à donner la nouvelle de l'abolition projetée dès le 4 décembre 1845. La loi qui la consacrait fut promulguée en 1846, sous le ministère de SIR ROBERT PEEL, convaincu de la nécessité de cette mesure, dont il avait été longtemps l'adversaire acharné. — 3. *The railway mania*, la rage des spéculations sur les chemins de fer. Lors de l'introduction des chemins de fer, les insertions du *Times* doublèrent, et dans une seule semaine, du 11 au 18 octobre 1845, elles rapportèrent la somme de 167 500 francs. Ce profit énorme n'empêcha pas le *Times* de tonner contre la rage qui s'était emparée de tout le monde pour obtenir des actions. La baisse qui suivit bientôt amena la ruine d'un grand nombre de gens, et justifia les dénonciations toutes désintéressées du *Times*. Le désir d'obtenir des actions dans les chemins de fer n'était pas moins ardent en France, où l'on vendait à la Bourse jusqu'à la promesse d'une action non encore émise ni souscrite. — 4. Contre la marche en avant de la Russie dans les Balkans et dans l'Asie, et sous Napoléon III, contre la fameuse lettre de menaces d'invasion écrite par un certain nombre de colonels de l'armée française, à la suite du fameux attentat d'Orsini, en 1858. C'est aux articles du *Times*, à cette époque, qu'il faut attribuer la création des régiments de volontaires, création qui existe toujours et se maintient avec le même enthousiasme. — 5. Ce sont les lettres de M. H. Russell, correspondant du *Times* en Crimée, en 1854, qui amena la chute du ministère Aberdeen, et une complète réforme dans le service de l'administration de l'armée anglaise. — 6. Sir Robert Peel, un des plus grands ministres que l'Angleterre ait jamais eus (voy. note 2), était fils d'un grand manufacturier d'Angleterre, dont le père avait servi comme contremaître dans cette même manufacture. — 7. Les *Whigs* et les *Torys*, noms des deux grands partis politiques du Royaume-Uni, se sont changés depuis 1830 en *Liberals* et *Conservatives*, libéraux et conservateurs, comme les *Repealers* ou *Unionists* sont devenus *Home-rulers* ou autonomes. — 8. Palmerston, etc. Ce sont les noms des premiers ministres (présidents du conseil) depuis 1830. Voici les différents ministères qui, depuis 1835, ont gouverné l'Angleterre sous la reine Victoria : Lord Melbourne (Whig-Libéral), 1835-1841 ; Sir Robert Peel (Conservateur-Tory), 1841-1846 ; Lord John Russell, 1846-1852 ; Earl (comte) of Derby (Conservateur), 1852 ; comte d'Aberdeen (coalition), 1852-1855 ; Lord Palmerston (Libéral), 1855-1858 ; Earl of Derby (Conservateur), 1858-1859 ; Lord Palmerston (Libéral), 1859-1865 ; Lord John Russell (le comte Russell,

9) le délire 10 intrépidement

DISRAELI, GLADSTONE and COBDEN [1], it was never bound to the triumphal car of these great men, even when they appeared to be the authentic exponents[2] for the time of the opinions of the middle classes of these kingdoms. PEEL and PALMERSTON, though in the main they were regarded by the conductors of *The Times* as the best representatives of national conviction and sentiment, were criticised from time to time, when occasion arose, in our columns, as severely as Melbourne, Stanley, and Newcastle [3]. The system of anonymity [4], which is sometimes ignorantly attacked, has been a main security for the power, exercised always in the public interest, of speaking the truth without fear or favour. A long succession of men of the highest distinction and of the most brilliant abilities — many of them not even known by name to the public — have, under these conditions, been able to contribute to the power and reputation of *The Times*, and in return to add infinitely to the weight and effect of their work on the opinion and destinies of the nation. Nor, in a plain statement of historical facts, is it possible to omit a reference to the advantages derived by this journal from continuity[5] of policy and conduct during the eventful years of the present century — advantages due to the steady, liberal, energetic, and sensible administration of its affairs since 1803 by the son and grandson of its founder.

The progress achieved by *The Times* since the era of the Napoleonic[6] wars has, no doubt, been largely the result of the contempt for patronage[7] and favour shown when its conductors refused, not only to accept Ministerial assistance[8], but even to secure immunity against official obstruction, on terms in any way compromising the independence of the paper. But there are material as well as moral conditions of success. We are justified in asserting that from the very outset the conductors of *The Times* have been eager to try every new method which could possibly be made available in the collection and the circulation of news or in the various processes of printing and publishing. We believe that in every one of the improvements, which have made the newspa-

Libéral), 1865-1866; Benjamin Disraeli (Conservateur), 1868; W. E. Gladstone (Libéral), 1868-1874; Disraeli (Earl Beaconsfield), 1874-1880; W. E. Gladstone, 1880-1885; Marquis de Salisbury (Conservateur), 1885-1886; W. E. Gladstone, 1886; Marquis de Salisbury (Conservateur), 1886-18.... — 1. Cobden fut, avec John Bright, un des grands auteurs du Rappel de la loi des Céréales, et, plus près de nos jours, de l'introduction du Libre-Échange. — 2. *Exponents*, interprètes. — 3. Newcastle, le très inhabile ministre de la guerre pendant la guerre de Crimée. — 4. *Anonymity*, l'anonymie, c'est-à-dire l'absence des noms des auteurs au bas des articles des journaux. — 5. Voyez note 2, page 1. — 6. *The Napoleonic wars*, les guerres de Napoléon Ier. — 7. *Patronage*, patronage, protection. Le *Times* s'est constamment refusé à recevoir aucune obligation de la part du gouvernement, et a souvent eu à souffrir de grands ennuis à cause de sa défense obstinée de son indépendance, plus spécialement en 1805, quand le gouvernement faisait arrêter sa correspondance étrangère. — 8. *Ministerial assistance*, c'est-à-dire des subsides fournis par les fonds secrets.

per press of the present day what it is, this journal has led and shown the way to all its contemporaries. The employment, for the purposes of the press, of the railway and the telegraph[1], which the journals of some great continental capitals have scarcely as yet begun to use at all, was seized upon in the very infancy of those wonderworking changes for the development of the infancy of *The Times*. The uninstructed public can form no conception of the amount of labour, the expenditure of money, and the coordination of materials involved in the collection of the foreign and domestic news published in our columns on any single day of the week. Furthermore there are mechanical developments with which a newspaper of the first rank ought to keep abreast ; and in this respect *The Times* has been able to act as a pioneer for the Press of the whole civilized world, mainly because the conductors of this journal have steadily refused from the very beginning to place their work and the immense interests involved in it at the mercy of a selfish and exclusive system of trade-unionism[2]. The application of steam[3] power in printing, the multiplication of forms by stereotyping[4], the invention of the « Walter Press[5] », and the introduction into practical use of composing machines[6], have been the most striking successive steps in the direction of speed, efficiency, and economy. The difficulties with which every advance of the kind has had to contend cannot be appreciated by the outer world, and, possibly, may not be acknowledged by those who have derived equal benefit with ourselves from our victory over them. Happily, there are portions of the work done by *The Times* during the past century which have received a more generous recognition. Leaving on one side political questions, we can point with unalloyed satisfaction to the duties we have discharged towards the public in safeguarding commercial and financial integrity, at no little risk and cost. A tablet[7] over the door of the printing

1. Le *Times* a à lui des fils télégraphiques de Berlin et de Paris, et reçoit, malgré des frais énormes, des colonnes entières de télégrammes de toutes les parties du monde. — 2. *Trade-unionism.* Les associations ouvrières des typographes s'opposèrent de toutes leurs forces à l'introduction de la presse à vapeur et de la « composing machine ». — 3. C'est en 1814 que le *Times* inscrivit sur un de ses numéros « Voici le premier journal imprimé à la vapeur »; ce fut le premier succès éclatant des inventeurs laborieux de la presse mécanique au service du *Times*, les Allemands Kœnig et Bauer. — 4. *Forms by stereotyping*, le clichage. Quand la première composition est terminée et mise en forme, il en est pris une empreinte; avec celle-ci on obtient un cliché, qui est placé sous un cylindre, et le tirage commence. — 5. La presse mécanique Walter imprime en une heure 24 000 feuilles des deux côtés; 3 300 mètres de papier courent sur un rouleau, *contre* le cliché, autour d'un cylindre qui fait 900 révolutions par minute. — 6. *Composing machines*, machines à composer, avec lesquelles on composait, pour 368 francs, huit pages d'annonces, qui, faites à la main, coûtaient 850 francs. — 7. *Tablet*, plaque de marbre. En 1840, M. O'Reilly, correspondant parisien du *Times*, que le hasard avait mis sur les traces d'une bande d'escrocs, et qui n'avait épargné aucuns frais pour découvrir leurs desseins, fit connaître leur intention d'obtenir des sommes énormes d'argent sur les places du continent, à l'aide de fausses lettres de crédit. Un des

house in Printing-House-Square testifies to the gratitude of the merchants and bankers of the city of London for one service of this kind we were able to render to the cause of honesty in business. So long as *The Times* retains its position in the ranks of the newspaper Press, its conductors will pursue the same course, disdaining the coarse arts of calumny and prurient gossip, and strictly respecting the sanctities of private life, but attacking imposture, unveiling fraud, and branding corrupt relations with crime, whether the world of trade or the world of politics be the scene of the outrage upon law. While animated by this resolve, we need entertain no fear that *The Times* will lose any part of its unique influence, its wide authority, or its representative character. The position from which we must not descend was once forcibly depicted in the House of Commons by a brilliant orator and a versatile man of letters[1] : — « If I desire, » he said, « to leave to remote posterity some memorial of existing British civilization, I would prefer, not our docks, not our railways, not our public building, not even the palace in which we hold our sittings : I would prefer a file of *The Times*. »

Monday, January 2nd, 1888.

---

complices, nommé par le *Times* lors de la révélation, eut l'audace d'intenter une action au *Times* pour diffamation, et obtint un *farthing* (2 centimes) de dommages-intérêts. La chose tout entière coûta au *Times* une somme de £ 5 000 (125 000 francs). Les négociants de Londres ouvrirent une souscription pour parfaire cette somme, mais le *Times* refusa de la recevoir ; sur quoi, la corporation de Londres fit dresser deux plaques commémoratives, l'une dans les salles des assureurs du Lloyd, et l'autre à l'entrée de l'imprimerie du *Times*. — 1. *A man of letters*, un homme de lettres, Sir Bulwer Lytton, auteur de *Les derniers jours de Pompéi*, d'*Eugène Aram*, et d'une foule d'autres ouvrages, frère de Lord Lytton, ancien vice-roi des Indes, aujourd'hui ambassadeur de Sa Majesté Britannique à Paris, qui est lui-même un poète des plus distingués et l'auteur de *English and French*, comparaison des plus justes et des plus bienveillantes entre les deux peuples.

The Times.

No. 32,543. LONDON, WEDNESDAY, NOV. 14, 1888. PRICE 3d.

BIRTHS.

On the 3d Oct., at Beaconsfield-Parade, Melbourne, Australia[1], the wife of CHARLES W. ATKINS of a son[2].

On the 20th Oct., at Wynberg, near Cape Town, South Africa, the wife of CAPTAIN L. FLEETWOOD BARTON, 1st Battalion The Royal Scots[3], of a daughter.

On the 7th Nov.. at Bognor[4], the wife of CAPTAIN CHARLES STUART, s.s.[5] Inanda, formerly of the s. s. Dabulamanzi, of a daughter.

On the 8th Nov., at Rayapuram, Madras, the wife of FRANCIS W. LETHBRIDGE (The Buffs[6], on service with the 9th Regt. M.N.I.), of a daughter.

On Friday, the 9th Nov., the wife of the REV.[7] F. W. CRICK, M.A., the Grammar School[8], Kibworth, of a son.

On the 9th Nov., at Stoke Newington, the wife of F. S. VANE BENNETT, of a son.

On the 9th inst.[9], at Carstairs House[10], the wife of JOSEPH MONTEITH, of a daughter.

On the 10th Nov., at Mabfield, Victoria-road, Waterloo, near Liverpool, the wife of FRED EATON, of a daughter.

On the 10th inst., at Spennymoor, Durham, the wife of ROBERT S. ANDERSON, M.D.[11], of a son.

On the 10th inst., at Burnside, Rutherglen, the wife of ROBERT FINDLAY, Esq.[12], of a daughter.

On the 10th inst., at 15, Lansdown-place, Cheltenham, the wife of MAJOR T. E. HARMAN, of a daughter.

On Sunday, the 11th Nov., at Bury, Lancashire, Mrs.[13] R. G. RANDALL, of a son.

On the 11th Nov., at 50, Forest-road West[14], Nottingham, the wife of CHARLES H. ROGERS, of a daughter.

On the 11th Nov., at 7, Park-view, Wigan, the wife of HARRIS BIGG-WITHER, of a daughter.

On the 11th Nov., at Trevenna, Sidcup, the wife of ARTHUR HUGHES, of a son.

On the 11th Nov., at Saxonhurst, Rock Ferry, Cheshire[15], the wife of FRANCIS H. KENDALL, of a son.

On the 11th inst., at 1, Fulwood-park, Liverpool, the wife of W. F. MOORE, of a daughter.

On the 11th inst., at Selhurst, South Norwood, the wife of J. H. HARRISON, of a son.

---

1. On remarquera le soin avec lequel les Anglais font annoncer dans les journaux anglais les événements de famille, à quelque distance de la métropole que ces événements aient lieu. — 2. *Of a son*, d'un fils; sous-entendu *brought to bed*, accouchée. — 3. *The Royal Scots*, les Écossais royaux, régiment de l'armée anglaise. — 4. *Bognor*, dans le Pays de Galles. — 5. *S. s. Inanda*, du navire à vapeur l'Inanda. — 6. *The Buffs* (pourpoints de peau de chamois), nom d'un régiment d'infanterie. *M. N. I.*, Madras Native Infantry. *Native*, indigène. — 7. *Rev.* pour *Reverend*, titre donné aux ecclésiastiques dans les pays anglais. Ce titre doit être toujours suivi du prénom ou des lettres initiales du prénom, comme ici *the Rev. F. W. Crick* (et non *the Rev. Crick*). En écrivant, on commence par *Reverend Sir*. *M. A.*, Magister Artium, titre universitaire équivalent à celui de licencié ès lettres, en France. — 8. *The Grammar School*, lycée ou collège. — 9. *On the 9th inst.*, le 9 du courant. — 10. *At Carstairs House*, au château de Carstairs. — 11. *M. D.*, Medicinæ Doctor, docteur en médecine. — 12. *Esq.*, abrév. d'*Esquire*, titre de respect ajouté à la suite du nom dans les adresses des lettres à tous ceux qui ont un certain rang dans la société, ou qui exercent une profession libérale, etc. Il signifie *écuyer* ou *porte-écu d'un chevalier*, et se donnait autrefois aux aspirants chevaliers, et plus tard aux fils puînés des familles nobles. Il faut avoir soin de comprendre le prénom ou au moins l'initiale du prénom dans l'adresse : *Robert* (ou *R.*) *Findlay, Esq.* — 13. *Mrs.* (abréviation de *Mistress*, prononcez miss'-iz), madame. — 14. *West*, West postal district, à Londres. — 15. *Cheshire*, comté de Chester, comme *Lancashire*, plus haut, comté de Lancaster. *Shire*, comté.

On the 11th inst., at The Lindens, 36, Abbey-road, N. W[1], the wife of BEN DAVIES, of a daughter.

On the 12th inst., at Chicago, Ills., U. S. A.[2], the wife of JAMES B. CLOSE, Esq., of a son.

On the 12th inst., at 18, Beaumont-street, Oxford, the wife of OCTAVIUS BEATTY, M.A., LL.B.[3], of the Middle Temple, Barrister-at-law[4], of a daughter.

On the 13th inst., at 12a, Kensington Palace-gardens, the wife of F. E. R. FRYER, Esq., of a son.

MARRIAGES.

On the 15th Aug. at St. Mary's Church, Brisbane, by the Ven. Archdeacon Dawes, assisted by the Rev. Barton Parks, LOUIS RALSTON HUXTABLE, M. B.[5], son of Charles Henry Huxtable, Esq., of Hobart[6] to LILIE, eldest daughter of the late Hon. WILLIAM HENRY WALSH, Brisbane[7].

On the 17th Oct., 1888, at the Cathedral, Spanish Town, Jamaica, W. I.[8], by the Rev. W. Kemp Bussell and the Rev. G. W. Downer, SURGEON C. W. THIELE, M. B., Army Medical Staff, eldest son of Charles Thiele, Esq., Bermuda, to MABEL LUCILLE, youngest daughter of the late Honble. ISAAC LEVY, of St. Jago Park, Spanish Town, Jamaica.

On the 7th inst., at the Synagogue, Upper Berkeley-street, by the Rev. Professor Marks, assisted by the Rev. A. Lowy JACQUES D. MYERS, nephew of Mr. and Mrs. Daniel Myers, of 44, Myddelton-square, to ROSE FLORENCE, eldest daughter of ALBERT T. BOSS, of Cumberland House, Clifton-gardens.

On the 7th. inst., at St. Peter's, Streatham, by the Rev. E. D. Cree, uncle of the bride, assisted by the Rev. J.J. Stockley and the Rev. W. A. Harrison, ROBERT T. PEAKE, of Penang[9], second son of Robert W. Peake, of Spring Grove, Isleworth, to ADA E. TAYLOR, of St. Seiriols, Knollys-road, Streatham, daughter of the late John Taylor, of Albert-square, Clapham.

On the 12th Nov., at St. John's, Allen-street, Kensington, by the Rev. C. Moinet, M. A., ROBERT BRUCE BOSWELL, M. A. Oxon.[10], to WINDLAY, daughter of the late J. BRUCE, of Bower, Caithness, and niece of F. W. C. Cumming, of Devonshire-terrace, Kensington.

On the 12th Nov., at the Cathedral, Cape Town, KENNETH CHARLES, fourth son of PETER BAIRNSFATHER, Esq., of Dumbarrow, J. P.[11] and Deputy Lieutenant, Forfarshire, to JULIE EDITH, second daughter of JAMES FARMER, Esq., J. P., of Kinkell, St. Andrews, 5, and 6, Porchestergate, W.[12] (By telegram.)

On the 13th inst., at the parish church of St. Marylebone, by the Rev. Grant E. Thomas, M. A., B.C.L.[13], the REV. E. J. OWEN, Curate of Maker, Cornwall, to JESSIE BEATRICE, third daughter of CAPTAIN AUGUSTUS PATERSON, late 42d Royal Highlanders[14].

DEATHS.

On the 19th Oct., at Cape Town[15], JAMES, eldest son of the late JAMES

1. *N. W.*, the North Western postal district, à Londres. — 2. *Ills., U. S. A.* Illinois, United States of America. — 3. *LL. B., Legum Baccalaureus*, Bachelor of Laws, à peu près notre licencié en droit. — 4. *Barrister-at-law*, avocat plaidant. Pour obtenir le droit de passer cet examen, il faut avoir pris douze inscriptions (avoir fait trois années d'études) dans une des (*Inns of Court*) Écoles de droit à Londres et être âgé de 21 ans. C'est parmi les *barristers* que sont choisis les juges. — 5. *M. B.*, Medicinæ baccalaureus, bachelier en médecine. — 6. *Hobart* ou *Hobart-Town*, capitale de la Tasmanie ou de la Terre de Van Diemen. — 7. *Brisbane*, capitale du *Queensland*, Australie du Sud. — 8. *W. I., West Indies*, les Indes Occidentales ou les Antilles. — 9. *Penang* ou Ile du Prince-de-Galles, à l'entrée du détroit de Malacca. — 10. *Oxon.*, c'est-à-dire *Oxoniensis*, d'Oxford. — 11. *J. P., Justice of the Peace*, juge de paix, c'est-à-dire magistrat nommé par la couronne et chargé des premières instructions. Ces fonctions sont gratuites. — 12. *W.*, Western postal district, à Londres. — 13. *B. C. L.*, Bachelor of Civil Law. — 14. Régiment des *Highlanders* ou montagnards écossais. — 15. *Cape-Town*, la ville du Cap (de Bonne-Espérance).

Mc[1] EWAN, of London, and Melbourne, Australia, aged 36.

On the 6th Nov., at Deanscroft, Forest-hill, aged 61 years, ELLEN, the beloved wife of HENRY ELWORTHY, formerly of Wellington, Somerset.

On the 7th Nov. at his residence, Southport, Lancashire, JOSEPH MAUDE BELLASIS, third son of the late G. H. Bellasis, Esq., of Holly Hill, Bowness, Windermere, aged 77 years.

On the 7th Nov., at her son's house, Litcham Rectory, Norfolk, aged 73, EMMA SOPHIA, widow of the late REV. CHARLES H. BINGHAM, Incumbent[2] of Ramsey, Hunts.[3].

On the 7th Nov., at her mother's residence, KATE FLORENCE POPE, aged 29 years, wife of Percy Pope, M.R.C.S.[4], L.R.C.P., and daughter of the late Robert Peckham, Solicitor, and of Mrs. Peckham, of Cromwell-road, Teddington.

On the 7th inst., at Rock House, Cintra-park, Upper Norwood, S.E.[5], GEORGE TAYLOR, M.D., F.R.C.S.[6], J.P., in his 70th year.

On the 7th inst., at Ewell, Surrey, CHARLES JAMES SHARPE, aged 45 years.

On the 8th Nov., at Ullingswick Rectory, Herefordshire, MARY ANNE, wife of the REV. J. M. WARE, aged 58 years.

On the 8th Nov., at Prospect, Ballycassidy, county Fermanagh[7], CHARLES W. H. RICHARDSON, late Lieut. 73d Regt. aged 47 years.

On the 8th inst., at Tunbridge-Wells, ELIZABETH, last surviving daughter of the late JOHN POYNDER, Esq., aged 74 years.

On the 8th inst., at Greenbank, Harrow, FLORENCE AMELIA, widow of the late EDWARD JOHN DENT-GARDNER, aged 37. Funeral To-day (Wednesday), Kensal-green, at 2 o'clock.

On the 8th inst., in the Hotel du Lion, Milan, Italy, GORDON, the beloved and only child of C. TARNEY and VERA ARCHER, very deeply regretted.

On the 8th inst., on board the s.s.[8] Kaikoura, on his passage home from New Zealand. WILLIAM PRATT CARD, younger son of Henry Benson Card, Esq., Head Postmaster of Colchester District, and grandson of the late Rev. Dr. Henry Card, Vicar of Malvern, in the 31st year of his age.

On the 9th Nov., at Ilfracombe, JAMES HUGHES, of 328, Camdenroad, London N.[9], aged 71 years.

On the 9th Nov., at The Lawn, Southport, LT.[10]-GENERAL HENRY GRIERSON, aged 71 years. Friends will please accept this, the only intimation.

On the 9th inst., at Cockington, Torquay, HELENA W. A. BARROWS, widow of the late Col. William Barrows, J.P. for counties Stafford and Worcester, aged 58. Friends, kindly accept this, the only intimation.

On Saturday, the 10th Nov., at Kirby, Douglas, Isle of Man, JOHN DRINKWATER-LAWE, youngest son of Sir William L. Drinkwater, First Deemster[11] of the Isle of Man, aged 34.

On the 10th Nov., at Powderham-crescent, Exeter, after a lingering illness, PEARSON BARRY HAYWARD, aged 50..

On the 10th Nov., at Brighton, after a few days' illness, FANNY MACAULAY, aged 39, daughter of Zachary Macaulay, and only surviving sister of Lord Macaulay[12].

---

1. *Mc Ewan*, pour *Mac Ewan*. *Mac*, mot gaélique ou celtique qui signifie *fils*, se met devant un très grand nombre de noms patronymiques écossais et irlandais. — 2. *Incumbent*, curé actuel. — 3. *Hunts.*, abrév. de *Huntingdonshire*, ou comté de Huntingdon, au centre de l'Angleterre. — 4. *M. R. C. S.*, Membre du Collège Royal des Chirurgiens. *L. R. C. P.*, Licentiate of the Royal College of Physicians. — 5. South Eastern postal district (London). — 6. *F. R. C. S.*, *Fellow of the Royal College of Surgeons*, agrégé en chirurgie. — 7. *County Fermanagh*, en Irlande. — 8. *S. s.*, steam-ship. — 9. *London N.*, North postal district (de Londres). — 10. *LT.*, lieutenant. — 11. *First Deemster*, juge principal. L'île de Man, petite île située dans la Mer d'Irlande. — 12. *Lord Macaulay*, orateur, historien et critique, mort en 1859. Ses

On Sunday, 11th Nov., OLIVE MARJORY, the baby daughter of the REV. W. P. and Mrs. JAY, Christ Church Vicarage, Watney-street, E.[1].

On the 11th Nov., suddenly, at 51, Mildmay-grove, LUCY, widow of the late JAMES P. SNELL. No flowers, by request.

On the 11th Nov., 1888, at Highgate, N., EDWARD HENRY, third son of the late MAJOR MARKHAM S. KITTOE, 6th Regt. N.I.[2], and of Coddenham, Suffolk, aged 42 years. R.I.P.[3].

On the 11th Nov., at 13, Northbrook-road, Lee, S.E.[4], JANE ELIZABETH, widow of JOHN MOLLETT, late[14] of Austin Friars, and Gold Hill, Bucks.[5], in the 84th year of her age.

On the 11th Nov., at Charmouth, Dorsetshire, MAJOR-GENERAL CLAUDE MALET DUCAT, late Bombay Staff Corps[6], aged 55 years.

On the 11th inst., PHILIP JACOB SAHLER, of Southfield Park, Harrow Weald, Middlesex, after a prolonged illness, in his 79th year. German papers, please copy[7].

PERSONAL[8], &c.

MARY JANE COMRIE is requested to COMMUNICATE with the undersigned, when she will hear of something to her advantage. If dead, any one sending proof of her death to the undersigned will be well rewarded. Last heard of five years ago. She was the widow of Staff Surgeon Peter Comrie, R.N.[9] Scotch, American, and Australian papers, please copy[10]. Harcourt and Son, 13, Moorgate-street, London, E.C.[11], Solicitors.

TIPPER-BATE. — If Mrs. PHŒBE TIPPER will APPLY by letter to the undersigned she may hear of something to her advantage. If dead her personal representatives may apply. Mrs. Tipper was a daughter of Samuel Bate, late of the Woolpack Inn, Stourbridge, and she sailed to Baltimore, U.S.[12], some time previous to 1863.

BERNARD KING and SONS,
Solicitors,
Stourbridge, England.

BANK of ENGLAND. — No. 12,890. — Application having been made to the Governor of the Bank of England to direct the re-transfer[13] from the Commissioners for the Reduction of the National Debt of the sum of £132 11s. 11d. Consolidated £3 per Cent. Annuities, which at one time stood in the names of DAVID PRICE, Gardener, and JANE PRICE, Spinster, both of Balham-place, Balham-hill, Clapham, and which was transferred to the said Commissioners in consequence of the dividends thereon having remained unreceived since the 5th July, 1859. — Notice is hereby given that on the expiration of three months from this date (November 14th), the said Stock will be re-transferred into their names and the dividends thereon paid to William Martin Price, administrator to the said Jane Price, Spinster, deceased, who was the survivor, he having claimed the same, unless some

Essais de critique et le Ier volume de son *Histoire d'Angleterre* sont compris dans le programme de l'enseignement secondaire. — 1. *E.*, East postal district (de Londres). — 2. *N. I.*, *Native Infantry*, infanterie indigène. — 3. *R. I. P.*, Requiescat in pace. — 4. *S. E.*, South-East postal district (de Londres). — 5. *Bucks.* pour *Buckinghamshire*, comté de Buckingham, au centre de l'Angleterre. — 6. *Late Bombay Staff Corps*, ancien officier d'État-Major du corps de Bombay (Indes orientales). — 7. *German papers, please copy*, journaux allemands, veuillez copier. C'est une invitation aux journaux allemands d'insérer cette mort. — 8. Cette colonne s'appelle aussi « *The Agony column* », parce qu'on s'y informe des parents et des proches qui ont disparu, qui se sont enfuis, etc., etc. — 9. *R. N.*, *Royal Navy*, de la marine royale. — 10. Voyez note 7. — 11. *E. C.*, East Central postal district, à Londres. — 12. *U. S.*, United States (of America). — 13. *Re-transfer*, restitution. Quand les coupons de rentes sont restés sans être réclamés, on les verse, en même temps que les titres, dans le Trésor public, quitte à les rendre au propriétaire légitime, s'il vient à les réclamer.
14. autrefois à (établi, résidant à) ancien résidant de.

other claim thereto shall in the meantime be made and sustained.

JAMES CURRY Deceased. — JAMES CURRY, late of Taunton, Somerset, Gentleman, by his will dated 18th May 1876 (and proved in the following year) gave unto his wife a life interest in his real and personal ESTATE, and upon her decease directed the same to be converted into money, and the proceeds to be divided as therein set out between his children, viz., Jane (the wife of Ebenezer Rolls), Caroline (the wife of William Wensley), John Curry Harriett (the wife of William Tiner) and the child or children of his late son James Curry. The Widow of the deceased having died, the Trustees have converted the estate into money. The above-named BENEFICIARIES, or their REPRESENTATIVES are requested to send their names and addresses to the undersigned with the view of the proceeds of the said sale being distributed according to the Trusts of the Testator's Will.

REED and COOK Sols.[1] 12, Paul-street, Taunton and Town Clerk's office, Bridgewater.

JOSEPH DARNTON Pursuant to a Judgment of the High Court of Justice, Chancery Division, England, made in an Action of Marsland v.[2] Guest 1886 M. No 295 dated the 6th day of February 1886 and of an order in the said Action dated the 30th day of October 1888 dispensing with service of Notice of the said Judgment upon Joseph Darnton hereinafter named and any person claiming by, through or under him the said JOSEPH DARNTON, if living, or, if dead, any person or persons claiming by, through or under him, is or are hereby required to come in and establish his or their respective claims to a share of the property to which the action relates, at the Chambers of Mr. Justice Stirling, Royal Courts of Justice, Strand, London, on or before the 4th day of April 1889 or in default thereof he or they will after the expiration of the time so limited be bound by the proceedings in the said action as if he or they had on the date of the said order dispensing with service been served with notice of the said Judgment. The said Joseph Darnton formerly of Ardwick, Manchester, left England many years ago and is alleged to have resided at Sydney in the Colony of New South Wales and to have died there. Thursday the 11th day of April 1889 at 2 of the clock in the afternoon at the said Chambers is appointed for hearing and adjudicating upon the claims.

Dated this 5th day of November 1888.

H. F. CHURCH, Chief Clerk.
CUNLIFFES & DAVENPORT,
43, Chancery Lane W. C[3].
Agents for Claye & Son Manchester
Plaintifs Solicitors.

IN the HIGH COURT of JUSTICE. Probate, Divorce, and Admiralty Division (Divorce). To WILLIAM JAMES HAMLYN, late of Woburn Place Russell Square in the County of Middlesex Take Notice that a CITATION bearing date the 27th day of April 1888, has issued at the instance of Elizabeth Crawley Hamlyn of The Berners Hotel Berners-street in the County of Middlesex citing you to appear within 8 days after service and publication hereof, and to answer the Petition filed by the said Elizabeth Crawley Hamlyn praying for a dissolution of marriage and such Citation contains an intimation that in default of your so doing the Court will proceed to hear the said Petition proved in due course of law and to pronounce sentence thereon, your absence notwithstanding, and a further intimation that for the purpose aforesaid, you are to attend in person or by your Solicitor at

1. *Sols., Solicitors*, avoués. — 2. *Marsland v. Guest, M. versus G.*, c'est-à-dire dans une action intentée par M. à G. — 3. *W. C.*, West Central post district. On voit qu'il est d'habitude d'ajouter aux adresses des lettres dans Londres des initiales indiquant le district spécial de Londres, où se trouve la rue, la place, etc.

the Divorce Registry at Somerset House, Strand, in the County of Middlesex, and there to enter an appearance in a book provided for that purpose, without which you will not be allowed to address the Court in person or by Counsel at any stage of the proceedings in the Cause.
ROBT. A. PRITCHARD, Registrar.
S. G. C. SANSOM, 162, Kennington Road S. E. Solicitor for the said Elizabeth Crawley Hamlyn.

LOST, on Saturday, 10th November, from Queen'smews, Bayswater, a SMALL IRISH TERRIER, crop ears and short tail, deep red coat, with rather bowed fore-legs. Weight from 10 lb. to 12 lb. Whoever will bring the same to 9a, Porchester terrace, shall be handsomely REWARDED.

ROYAL MATERNITY CHARITY. Instituted 1757. — Patron, Her MAJESTY The QUEEN. — The Committee RETURN their grateful THANKS for a timely GRANT of TEN GUINEAS[1] from the Trustees of Berman's Charity.
JEREMIAH LONG, Secretary.
Charity's House, 31, Finsbury-square, Nov. 12, 1888.

DENTAL HOSPITAL of LONDON, Leicester-square. President — H. R. H.[2] the DUKE of CAMBRIDGE. K. G.[3] —The Managing Committee gratefully ACKNOWLEDGE the RECEIPT of FIVE GUINEAS, as an Annual Subscription, from Edward Grey, Esq., in aid of the funds of this recently enlarged, unendowed Charity.
J. FRANCIS PINK, Secretary.

NORTH LONDON or UNIVERSITY COLLEGE HOSPITAL, Gower-street, W.C., supported by voluntary contributions. — The Committee gratefully ACKNOWLEDGE the RECEIPT of a DONATION of £21[4] towards the Rebuilding Fund from the Trustees of Berman's Charity.
NEWTON H. NIXON, Secretary.

ST. MARY'S HOSPITAL, W.[5], entirely dependent on voluntary contributions. — The Governors gratefully ACKNOWLEDGE the RECEIPT of the following NEW ANNUAL SUBSCRIPTIONS, viz. :— G. A. Tonge, Esqr. £2 2s[6] and Captain E. B. Pusey, £5 5s.
THOMAS RYAN, Secretary.
November 13, 1888.

THE SURGICAL AID SOCIETY.— The Committee thankfully ACKNOWLEDGE the RECEIPT of NEW ANNUAL SUBSCRIPTION of £3 3s. from Horace Peel, Esq.
W. M. TRESIDDER, Secretary.
Offices, Salisbury-square, Fleet-street, E.C.

LEE CONSERVANCY[7]. — Notice is hereby given, that all persons who desire to CLAIM, under the provisions

---

1. *Ten guineas*, dix guinées. La guinée, qui n'existe plus comme pièce d'or, valait une livre sterling plus un shelling, c'est-à-dire 26 fr. 25. Les professions libérales, et même les personnes qui louent des appartements meublés, se font payer ordinairement en guinées plutôt qu'en livres sterling, mettant ainsi en action le refrain de la vieille chanson :

I'd rather have a guinea
Than a one poundnote.

— 2. *H. R. H.*, *His Royal Highness*, Son Altesse Royale. — 3. *K. G.*, *Knight of the Garter*, Chevalier de la Jarretière. C'est le principal ordre de chevalerie dans la Grande-Bretagne. Il fut institué par Édouard III, en 1349. — 4. £ *pound sterling*, 25 fr. £. *s. d.* s'écrivent pour *pounds*, *shillings* et *pence*. Les Italiens, inventeurs de *la tenue des livres*, écrivaient en haut des colonnes de comptabilité *L. s. d.*, *Lire* (ou *libri*), *soldi*, *denari*, et les Anglais, en adoptant cette comptabilité, en ont adopté les abréviations. Les Français écrivaient de même *L. s. d.*, ou *livres*, *sols*, *deniers*. — 5. *W.*, West postal district. — 6. £ 2. 2 *s.*, £ 5. 5 *s*; c'est absolument la même chose que *two guineas* et *five guineas*. Du reste, pour la valeur des monnaies anglaises, on peut consulter la *Grammaire anglaise* par A. Elwall. — 7. *The Lee Conservancy*, Commission pour la protection des pêcheries dans la rivière Lee (Irlande).

of the « Lee Conservancy Acts, 1868 and 1874 », to have their names INSERTED in the LIST of ELECTORS of REPRESENTATIVES of LANDOWNERS for the purpose of the ELECTION of CONSERVATORS, in March 1889, are required to deliver a statement of their respective claims to the Lee Conservancy Board, at their office, No. 12, Finsbury-circus, London, E. C., on or before the 31st day of December, 1888. A person whose name already stands in the list of electors is not required again to send in a claim. Forms of claim to be obtained of the undersigned.

Dated this 5th day of November, 1888.

By order of the Lee Conservancy Board,
GEO. CORBLE, Clerk.

CHANGE of NAME.—Notice is hereby given, that I, Philip Alexander Solomon Philips, of No. 34, Bedford-place, Russell-square, in the County of Middlesex, Art Student, who have heretofore been called or known by the name of PHILIP ALEXANDER SOLOMON, by a deed poll[1] under my hand and seal, dated the 12th day of November, 1888, and intended to be forthwith enrolled in the Chancery Division of Her Majesty's High Court of Justice in England, have ASSUMED, taken and adopted the SURNAME of PHILIPS; and that I shall, in all deeds, documents, and writings, and in all other future instruments which I may hereafter execute, sign, or write, and in all actions, suits, and other proceedings, at law or otherwise, to or in which I am a party or may be otherwise interested, subscribe, affix, sign, and use the name of Philip Alexander Solomon Philips.—Dated the 12th day of November, 1888.

PHILIP A. S. PHILIPS.

Witness—Lionel H. Barnard, Solicitor; Queen Anne-chambers, No. 112, Poultry, E. C.[2].

IN PARLIAMENT. — Session 1889. London Coal and Wine Duties Continuance Act[3]. Notice is hereby given, that it is intended to APPLY to Parliament in the ensuing Session for an ACT to continue the London Coal and Wine Duties or some of them, and to alter such duties, and to confer, vary, or extinguish exemptions therefrom, and to provide for the appropriation and application thereof to such public improvements, open spaces, and works, or in such manner as may be prescribed by Parliament; and for the purposes aforesaid it is intended to amend and enlarge the powers and provisions of the several London Coal and Wine Duties Acts, including, amongst others, the London Coal and Wine Duties Continuance Acts, 1861, 1863, and 1868.

Dated this 8th day of November 1888.

G. PRIOR GOLDNEY, Remembrancer[4], Guildhall[5], London, E. C.

J. E. WAKEFIELD, Clerk of the Metropolitan Board of Works, Spring Gardens, S. W.

NOTICE. — EDWARD STANFORD begs to inform his numerous customers and the public generally that he has REMOVED from 55, Charing-cross to new and extensive premises at 26 and 27, Cockspur-street, 20 doors westward from his former house. His geographical and mounting departments[6], formerly at 13 and 14, Long-acre, have also been removed to the same address. Edward Stanford's stock includes all

1. *By a deed poll*, par un acte simple. *A deed poll* diffère d'un *deed indented*, en ce que ce dernier est fait en double, que les bords sont échancrés de manière à s'adapter l'un dans l'autre et qu'il est signé de deux parties contractantes. Le *deed poll* est un acte d'une personne qui agit en son nom personnel. — 2. *E. C.*, East Central postal district. — 3. Loi pour continuer la perception des droits d'entrée à Londres (droits d'octroi) sur la houille et le vin. — 4. *Remembrancer*, greffier-archiviste. — 5. *Guildhall*, l'hôtel de ville. *Guild*, corporations; *hall*, salle, salle des corporations. — 6. *Mounting department*, ateliers pour le montage des cartes.

the Ordnance and Geological Survey Maps, for the sale of which he is the sole official agent in England and Wales. All communications should be addressed Edward Stanford, 26 and 27, Cockspur-street, Charing-cross, London, S. W.[1].

NEW COUNTY BOUNDARIES, &c. — The published MAPS of the ORDNANCE SURVEY[2] are the most suitable delineating Unions, Parishes, and other Local Government Divisions, and are all obtainable, in any form preferred, from EDWARD STANFORD, Sole Agent by appointment in England and Wales, 26 and 27, Cokspur-street, Charing-cross, London, S. W.

NOTICE. — The BUSINESS of J. WHITE, of Regent-street, is NOT, and has not at any time been, for DISPOSAL as reported, the proprietor having no intention of relinquishing it. — J. White, 252 and 254, Regent-street, 22, 23 and 24, Argyll-street.

MOSER'S DETECTIVE AGENCY, 31, Southampton-street, Strand, W. C. Agents in the principal towns and cities at home and abroad. Telegraphic address, Shadows, London.

FUNERALS.

FUNERALS. — JAY'S[3] for FUNERALS.

FUNERALS by PETER ROBERTSON.

FUNERALS. — GLAZIER and SONS, 193, Tottenham-court-road, W., and 1, Park-side, Hyde-park-corner, S. W.

REFORMED FUNERALS. — The FUNERAL COMPANY was established in 1843 for funeral economy and reform. Offices 28, New Bridge-street, E. C., and 82, Baker-street, W.
ALEXIS BONO, General Manager.

MEMORIAL BRASSES and BRONZES. — Illustrated lists, or special designs and estimates free of cost. — FRANK SMITH and Co. 13, Southampton-street, Strand, London.

ALTAR CROSSES, Candlesticks, Vases, Flagons, Chalices, and Patens. Inspection invited. Designs free[4]. — FRANK SMITH and Co.

SURPLICES and CASSOCKS, both clergy and choir, ready for immediate use. Patterns and prices on application. — FRANK SMITH and Co.

CHURCH FURNISHERS by Royal Warrant to H. R. H.[5] the Prince of Wales. — ALTAR COVERS, Textile Fabrics, Wood and Metal Work. Catalogues free[6]. — FRANK SMITH and Co., 13, Southampton-street, Strand, London. W. C.

CHURCH ORGAN for sale (new). Price £ 250. Grand toned instrument, 17 feet high, 10 ft. wide, 7 ft. deep. Pitchpine case, suited for congregation of 800. Guarantee given. Inspection invited. W. Samuel, 62, Montagne-road, Dalston.

ABERDEEN GRANITE MONUMENTS, &c. — ALEX. MACDONALD and Co., Limited (late A. Macdonald, Field and Co.), Quarries and Works, Peterhead and Aberdeen. Premises in London, 373, Euston-road, where numerous examples of monumental and architectural work may be seen. For information as to designs and delivery of work at any locality

1. *S. W.*, South Western postal district. — 2. *Maps of the Ordnance Survey*, cartes topographiques du Ministère de la guerre. *The Ordnance department*, le bureau de l'artillerie. — 3. *Jay's (Establishment) for funerals.* — 4. *Designs free*, on envoie sur demande les dessins et modèles francs de port. — 5. *H. R. H.*, *His Royal Highness*, Son Altesse Royale. — 6. *Free*, franc de port.

apply to Granite Works. Aberdeen : or 373, Euston-road, N. W.

TO EXECUTORS[1]. — Old GOLD, old Silver, old Jewellery. Highest price given. Valuations for probate[2] or family division. — WATERSTON and SON, 12, Pall-mall east (adjoining the National Gallery[3]), London, S. W.

TO EXECUTORS and others. — VALUATIONS made of JEWELLERY, Plate, &c., for probate, or Purchased for cash, by Messrs. HANCOCKS and Co., Jewellers and Silversmiths by Royal Warrant to the Queen, Empress of India[4], 39, Bruton-street, corner of New Bond-street, W.

VALUATIONS.—Messrs. PHILLIPS, SON, and NEALE respectfully announce that they undertake, with an experienced staff, VALUATIONS for PROBATE and other purposes. They also assess fire claims[5] and arrange compensation cases. Address Auction Rooms, 73, New Bond-street, London, W. Telephone No 3,670.

VALUATIONS of JEWELS and PLATE, &c. — SPINK and SON, Goldsmiths and Silversmiths, 2, Gracechurch-street, Cornhill, E. C. (under the patronage of H. M.[6] The Queen), beg respectfully to state that they have made the accurate VALUATION or PURCHASE of valuable JEWELS and SILVER PLATE, &c., a speciality for many years. Valuations for bankers, solicitors, executors, and others. Appointments made in London or country, Established 1772.

ENTERTAINMENTS[7], &c.

ROYAL ACADEMY of MUSIC, Tenterden-street, W. — NEXT FORTNIGHTLY CONCERT, Nov. 17, at 8.

For Syllabus[8] of Metropolitan and Local Examinations[9], 1889, and other information apply to the Secretary.

ROYAL CHORAL SOCIETY (Royal Albert-hall).

Patron — Her MAJESTY The QUEEN.

President — H. R. H.[10] the DUKE of EDINBURGH, K. G.

Conductor — Mr. BARNBY.

Cowen's RUTH on Wednesday, Nov. 28th, at 8.

Artists : — Miss Anna Williams, Miss Agnes Larkcom, Madame Belle Cole; Mr. Barton Mc Guckin, and Mr. Watkin Mills. Organist, M. Hodge. Prices 7 s. 6 d., 5 s., 4 s., 3 s., and gallery promenade 1 s.[11].

Ten Concerts will be given during the season, eight being by subscription.

Prices for the Subscription Concerts — 42 s., 32 s., 24 s., and 20 s.

ROYAL COLLEGE of MUSIC, Kensington-gore,[12]

1. *To Executors*, aux exécuteurs testamentaires. — 2. *Probate*, attestation de la valeur des bijoux légués par testament. *Family division*, partage entre les différents membres de la famille. *The Court of Probate* est un tribunal institué pour l'enregistrement et l'examen (*proof*, preuve) des testaments. — 3. *The National Gallery*, c'est une exposition permanente de peinture. — 4. *Empress of India*, c'est le nouveau titre décerné à la reine Victoria, il y a quelques années seulement, mais elle ne l'emploie que dans les actes qui concernent l'administration des Indes. Cela rappelle un peu la couronne impériale offerte à Jules César :

> " And he shall wear his crown in every place,
> By sea and land, save here in Italy. "

— 5. *They assess fire claims*, agissent comme experts dans les réclamations pour incendie. — 6. *H. M.*, Her Majesty. — 7. *Entertainments*, amusements. — 8. *Syllabus*, programme. — 9. *Metropolitan and Local Examinations*, examens faits à Londres et en province. — 10. Voy. note 2, page 13. — 11. Pour la valeur des monnaies, voy. *Grammaire anglaise* par Elwall, page 199. 12. Pointe du Kens.

S. W.[1] Incorporated by Royal Charter, 1883.
President — H. R. H. the PRINCE of WALES, K. G.
Director — Sir George Grove, D. C. L.[2], LL. D.[3].

NEXT COLLEGE CONCERT, To-morrow (Thursday); 15th. inst., at 7.30 p. m.

Pianoforte trio in C minor (Mendelssohn); organ sonata No 3 (Mendelssohn); two (M. S.) songs, Thos. Chapman (student); piano solo, Forest Scenes (Schumann); recitation (Adelaide Proctor); violin solo (Vieuxtemps); air (Schira); string quartet in C minor (Beethoven).

Associate Examination (A. R. C. M.)[4].

The examination for 1889 is fixed for April 9th and 10th. The list of pieces may now be obtained.

Open Free Scholarships[5].

Fifteen Open Free Scholarships will be competed for in March.

Last day for receiving applications January 20th.

Forms of application and particulars may be obtained from the Registrar, Mr. George Watson, at the College.

CHARLES MORLEY, Honorary Secretary.

ROYAL ALBERT-HALL.

MADAME ADELINA PATTI.

MADAME ADELINA PATTI will make her LAST APPEARANCES in London previous to her departure for America at two grand orchestral concerts at the Royal Albert-hall on Tuesdays, Nov. 20th and Dec. 11th, at 8 o'clock.

MADAME ADELINA PATTI. — Royal Albert-hall.—Madame ADELINA PATTI will SING Qui la voce (I Puritani) (Bellini), song Let the bright seraphim (Handel[6]), and duet Quis est Homo (Stabat Mater) (Rossini), on Tuesday evening next.

MADAME ADELINA PATTI. — Royal Albert-hall.—Madame TREBELLI will SING gavotte In veder l'amata (Mignon) (Thomas), aria Vieni che poi sereno (Glück), and in the duet with Madame Adelina Patti, on Tuesday evening next.

MADAME ADELINA PATTI. — Royal Albert-hall.—Mr. EDWARD LLOYD will SING aria Fra Poco (Lucia di Lammermoor) (Donizetti), and song Wake from thy Grave, Giselle (Loder), on Tuesday evening next.

MADAME ADELINA PATTI. — Royal Albert-hall. — SIGNOR FOLI will SING air She alone charmeth my sadness (La Reine de Saba) (Gounod), and aria Chi mi dira (Marta) (Flotow), on Tuesday evening next.

MADAME ADELINA PATTI. — Royal Albert-hall.—Miss NETTIE CARPENTER will PLAY solo violin Fantasia on Faust. (Sarasate), solos violin (a), Andante from the 2d Concerto (Wieniawski) (b), Mazurka (Zarzycki), on Tuesday evening next.

MADAME ADELINA PATTI. — Royal Albert-hall. — Full Orchestra, Mr. Ganz, Conductor. — The ORCHESTRA will PLAY overture Euryanthe (Weber) allegretto moderato from the Unfinished Symphony (Schu-

---

1. *Kensington*, quartier de Londres dans le South-Western postal district. — 2. *D. C. L.*, *Doctor of Common Law*, docteur du droit coutumier. — 3. *LL. D.*, *Legum Doctor*, docteur en droit (docteur des deux droits, coutumier et écrit). — 4. *A. R. C. M.*, Associate of the Royal College of Music. — 5. *Open free scholarships*, bourses entières pour lesquelles tous les candidats sont admis à concourir. — 6. Handel ou Hændel, grand musicien, auteur de nombreux opéras et surtout d'oratorios, né à Halle (Saxe) en 1684, vécut à Londres depuis 1712 jusqu'à sa mort en 1759, et fut enterré à l'abbaye de Westminster. Les Anglais le regardent comme musicien anglais.

bert), overture Merry Wives of Windsor (Nicolai), Entr'acte from La Colombe (Gounod), and overture Le Domino Noir (Auber), Tuesday evening next, at 8. Tickets, 12s. 6d., 10s. 6d., 7s., 5s., 3s., and 2s.; boxes, two to five guineas, at the Royal Albert-hall; of N. Vert; usual agents'; and at St. James's-hall. — N. Vert, 6, Cork-street, W.[1]

MONDAY POPULAR CONCERTS, St. James's-hall.—SECOND CONCERT of the SEASON on Monday evening next, November 19, at 8.30[2]. Executants — Madame Néruda, Mlle Janotha; MM. L. Ries, Hollander, and Piatti. Vocalist — Miss Elsa. Accompanist — Dr. Engel. Programmes and tickets at Chappell and Co.'s, New Bond-street; and at the hall.

SATURDAY POPULAR CONCERTS, St. James's-hall. — FIRST CONCERT of the SEASON on Saturday afternoon next, November 17, 1888. Programme : — Mendelssohn's string quintet in B flat[3], nocturne in E, and barcarolle in F sharp, for pianoforte alone, by Chopin; Brahms's Sonato in A, Op. 100, for pianoforte and violin; and Beethoven's pianoforte trio in D major, Op. 70, No. 1. Executants — Madame Néruda (Lady Hallé), Sir Charles Hallé, MM. L. Ries, Straus, Gibson, and Piatti. Vocalist, Miss Liza Lehmann. Accompanist, Mr. Frantzen. Commence at 3. Stalls, 7s. 6d.; balcony, 3s.; admission, 1s. Subscription to stalls, £ 5 for 20 concerts. Programmes and tickets at Chappell and Co.'s, Bond-street; Tree's, St. James's-hall Ticket office; and of the usual concert agents.

LONDON BALLAD CONCERTS.

LONDON BALLAD CONCERTS, St. James's-hall. — Twenty-third Season. — The FIRST EVENING CONCERT will be given on Wednesday, November 21st, at 8. Artists — Mrs. Mary Davies, Madame Bertha Morre, and Mlle Antoinette Trebelli, Madame Antoinette Sterling and Madame Belle Cole; Mr. Sims Reeves and Mr. Charles Banks, Signor Foli, Mr. Barrington Foote, and Mr. Maybrick. Violin, Madame Néruda. Mr. Eaton Fanning's Select Choir of 25 voices. Conductor, Mr. Sidney Naylor. Stalls, 7s. 6d.; balcony, 3s.; area, 4s. and 2s.; orchestra and gallery, 1s.; family tickets to admit four to stalls, price 25s. Tickets to be had of Basil Tree, St. James's-hall; the usual Agents; and Boosey and Co., 295, Regent-street.

THE FIRST MORNING BALLAD CONCERT will take place on Wednesday, November 28th, at 3. — Boosey and Co., 295, Regent-street, W.

LONDON SYMPHONY CONCERTS. — Mr. Henschel, Conductor. — The series of the third season, 1888-89, will comprise 10 EVENING CONCERTS, to take place at St. James's-hall on the following Tuesdays : — Nov. 20, 27; Dec. 4, 11; Jan. 15, 22, 29; Feb. 5, 12, 19, and in addition (not included in the subscription) two Afternoon Concerts on Wednesdays, Dec. 19 and Feb. 27. Subscription : — Reserved seats[4] for the series of 10 concerts, £2 15s. and £1 10s.

LONDON SYMPHONY CONCERTS. — FIRST CONCERT (THIRD SERIES), Tuesday evening next, Nov. 20, at 8.30. Programme : — A Faust overture (Wagner), Symphony in A, No. 7 (Beethoven), ballet music from Rosa-

1. On remarquera ces cinq annonces toutes différentes pour la même représentation le même soir. — 2. 8.30, : eight thirty *ou* half past eight o'clock *ou* thirty minutes past eight. C'est depuis l'introduction des chemins de fer et du télégraphe que la première forme, la plus brève, s'est introduite dans la langue. — 3. *B flat*, si bémol; *F sharp*, fa dièze. Les notes A, B, C, D, E, F, G correspondent aux notes françaises : *la, si, do, ré, mi, fa, sol.* — 4. *Reserved seats*, places prises en location.

munde (Schubert), overture Scherzo, and Finale op. 52 (Schumann), New Suite, op. 46 (first time) (Grieg). Tickets :— Reserved seats, 7s. 6d. and 4s. ; unreserved[1] seats, 2s. and 1s., of the usual agents, and at St. James's-hall. — N. Vert, 6, Cork-street, W.

ACADEMY of MUSIC, 16, Chepstow-place, W. — Operatic Training School[2]; Richard Temple (Savoy), Operatic Professor. CONCERT at the Academy, Thursday, Nov. 29th, 3 p. m.[3]. Under study for public and private performance, Mozart's Figaro and a modern comic opera. Pupils for principal and minor parts, also chorus, now received. A few Resident Pupils accommodated. — Robert Goldbeck, Director.

HERR WALDEMAR MEYER has the honour to announce TWO GRAND ORCHESTRAL CONCERTS, under the immediate patronage of H. R. H. PRINCESS MARY, DUCHESS of TECK[4], at St. James's-hall, Thursday, November 22d., and Wednesday, December 12th, to commence each evening at 8 o'clock. Orchestra of 70 performers. Leader, Mr. A. Burnett. — Conductor, Prof. C. Villiers Stanford.

HERR WALDEMAR MEYER'S FIRST CONCERT. — Programme : — Symphony in D major[5] (No. 1) (Mozart); violin concerto (Brahms), Herr Waldemar Meyer; suite de pièces (Ries), Herr Waldemar Meyer; ballad overture, The Dowie Dens o' Yarrow (Hamish MacCunn); violin concerto (Mendelssohn), Herr Waldemar Meyer; overture, Namensfeier (Beethoven). — Admission : — 10s. 6d., 7s. 6d., 3s., and 1s. Tickets at all Libraries, Musicsellers', and of Basil Tree, Ticket office, St. James's-hall, Piccadilly, W.

The Concerts under the Management of Mr. W. B. Healey.

MADAME ANNETTE ESSIPOFF will give a PIANOFORTE RECITAL[6], at St. James's-hall, on Thursday, Nov. 29, at 3 o'clock. Tickets, 7s. 6d., 3s., and 1s., at St. James's-hall, and the usual agents. — N. Vert, 6, Cork-street, W.

MISS ROSA KENNEY'S RECITAL, Steinway-hall, To-morrow (Thursday), at half past 2 p. m. Artists — Mesdames Edith Wynne, Ada Cavendish, P. Boucicault, M. Kenney, W. Everard, A. Boucicault, M. Marras. Tickets at 10, Vereker-road, and the hall.

TOBIAS A. MATTHAY. — ANNUAL PIANOFORTE RECITAL, Princes'-hall, Piccadilly, To-morrow (Thursday), at 3. Stalls 5s., balcony 1s., of usual Agents, at the hall, and at 40, Manor-street, Clapham, S. W.

TOBIAS A. MATTHAY. — PIANOFORTE RECITAL. — Ballade in D (Brahms); Romance D min. (Schumann); Lyrische Stückchen, Op. 43 (Grieg); Etude in C (Rubinstein); Sonata, D min., Op. 31 (Beethoven); Moods of a Moment (Matthay); Scherzo, Op. 20 (Chopin); La Gondola (Henselt); Genrebild No. 4 (Goetz); La Fileuse (Raff); Valse Caprice (Nunn); Rhapsody, C sharp (Liszt).

LAST DAY PERFORMANCE BUT ONE.

THIS AFTERNOON (Wednesday), at 3, the MOORE and BURGESS MINSTRELS will give a grand DAY PERFORMANCE of their new and extraordinarily successful ENTERTAINMENT, at the St. James's-hall, Piccadilly. Doors open at 2.30, com-

1. *Unreserved*, pris au guichet ou à la porte. — 2. Classes préparatoires pour l'Opéra. — 3. 3 *p. m.* à 3 heures de l'après-midi ou du soir; *p. m.*, post méridiem, après-midi. — 4. Marie, duchesse de Teck, fille de la duchesse de Cambridge et petite-cousine de la reine. — 5. *In D major*, en ré majeur. Les notes de musique sont marquées en anglais A, B, C, D, E, F, G, au lieu de *la, si, do, ré, mi, fa, sol.* — 6 *A pianoforte recital*, un concert de piano.

mence at 3. No fees. Last six performances at the St. James's-hall till Christmas.

LAST SIX PERFORMANCES of the MOORE and BURGESS MINSTRELS' PERFORMANCE until Christmas. Last six performances of the immensely successful programme.

MOORE and BURGESS MINSTRELS, St. James's-hall, every night, at 8. — Illuminated DAY PERFORMANCES TO-DAY (Wednesday), and Saturday, at 3. Last six performances until Boxing-day [1], when they re-open in the newly-decorated St. James's Grand Hall with an entirely new and gigantic programme. — Fauteuils, 5s.; stalls, 3s.; area, 2s.; gallery (equal to the dress circle seats in the West-end theatres), 1s. No fees of any description. Tickets and places can be secured of Basil Tree, Ticket office, St. James's-hall, from 9.30 till 7.

LAST SIX PERFORMANCES of the MOORE and BURGESS MINSTRELS' immensely successful ENTERTAINMENT, at St. James's-hall, till Boxing-day. Reappearance of Mr. Eugene Stratton with his enormously successful song, The Whistling Coon [2] (1,200th time), at every performance. He will also give his last new song and dance, I lub a lubly gal [3], I do (written and composed by Mr. Brandon Thomas); Mr. Eddie Quinn's wonderful and charming solo on the American Sleigh Bells; Mr. Sam Raeburn in a banjo [4] caprice of quaint parodies and Messrs. Morton and Sadler the funny American exponents [5] of song and dance, &c. — St. James's-hall, TO-NIGHT, at 8. Day Performances To-day (Wednesday) and Saturday, at 3 as well.

THE MOORE and BURGESS MINSTRELS. — The highly successful burlesque entitled CLOTHILDE, or The Bruised Heart, in which Mr. Eugene Stratton and the company will appear at every performance. The press and the public say that this is the best burlesque of the season. — St. James's-hall, TO-NIGHT, at 8. Day Performances To-day (Wednesday) and Saturday, at 3. Last six performances till Christmas.

ROYAL, Holborn. — Always a Grand Company. — ALEXANDER'S PANTOMIMIC COMPANY, G. H. Macdermott, J. W. Rowley, Ada Convers, Rezne and Robine, Florence Dorling, De Voy, Le Clerq and Co., Billee Barlow, Gower Godfrey, Katie Seymour, A. Forrest, Tom Bass, Nelly Bennett, and others. — Prices from 6d. to £2 2s. Every evening at 7.30. Saturday Matinées, 2.30.

MR. and Mrs. GERMAN REED'S ENTERTAINMENT, under the management of Mr. Alfred German Reed and Mr. Corney Grain, TO-NIGHT at 8. Monday, Wednesday and Friday, at 8; Tuesday, Thursday, and Saturday, at 3. — St. George's-hall, Langham-place. Stalls, 5s. and 3s.; admission, 2s. and 1s. No fees [6].

TALLY HO [7]! TO-NIGHT, at 8. — Written by Malcolm Watson, music by Alfred J. Caldicott. Characters by Miss Fanny Holland, Miss Kate Tully, Mr. Ernest Laris, Mr. Walter Browne, and Mr. Alfred German Reed. Monday, Wednesday, and Friday, at 8; Tuesday, Thursday, and Saturday, at 3.

JOHN BULL ABROAD, TO-NIGHT, at 9.30, an entirely new Musical

1. *Boxing-day*, le lendemain de Noël, jour où l'on envoie les étrennes ou cadeaux de Noël, de *box*, cadeau, d'où *Christmas-box*. — 2. *The whistling coon*, le raton siffleur, titre de chanson. — 3. C'est parler nègre pour *I love a lovely girl*. — 4. *A banjo caprice*, un caprice sur le *banjo*, instrument à six cordes qu'on joue avec les doigts. — 5. *Exponent*, interprète. — 6. *No fees*, pas de gratifications à donner, on ne donne rien aux ouvreuses. — 7. *Tally-ho!* taïaut! cri de chasse.

Sketch by Mr. Corney Grain. Monday, Wednesday, and Friday evenings; Tuesday, Thursday, and Saturday afternoons. Mr. and Mrs. German Reed's Entertainment, St. George's-hall, Langham-place, W.

MASKELYNE, COOKE, and Entire EGYPTIAN-HALL COMPANY on TOUR, Free Trade-hall. Manchester, third week. Will return to their Home of Mystery[1] Dec. 17, with new wonders for the Christmas programme.

HERCAT, Egyptian-hall, daily, at 3 and 8. — HERCAT'S MYSTERY of SHE concludes the programme at 4.45 and 9.45. Prior to the production of this great illusion, Hercat's magical melange and ventriloquial entertainment continue to surprise and amuse crowded audiences of the elite of London society. Hercat's fame had preceded him, and England is now thoroughly endorsing the Yankee opinion that he has no equal as an illusionist, ventriloquist, and humourist. Admission from 5s to 1s. Seats booked at the Box-office and all Libraries. — W. Morton, Manager.

CRYSTAL PALACE[2]. — Admission TO-DAY, 10 to 8.30, 1s. Vocal and Instrumental Concert, 3.30 (free)[3]. Vocalists — Miss Florence Christie, Miss Edith Robiolo, and Mr. Edward Nottingham. Violin — Miss Duckham. The renowned Crystal Palace Orchestra. Conductor, Mr. August Manns.

CRYSTAL PALACE. — DR. SABUNJIE'S ENTERTAINMENT, A Trip Round the World, with dissolving views, TO-DAY, at 4.0 and 6.30 (6d. and 1s.).

Variety Entertainment, 5.45 (free), including Griffitha Brothers and their Blondin Donkey, and the Delevantis; Picture Gallery and Museum, open all day (free); panorama (1s.).

CRYSTAL PALACE.—Evening Play, the late Charles Reade's celebrated Adelphi drama, IT'S NEVER TOO LATE TO MEND, THIS EVENING, at 7.30, under direction of Mr. Oscar Barrett. Seats, 1s. to 5s.[4]; 1,000 seats at 1s. For cast[5] see under clock.

CRYSTAL PALACE.—Mr. EDWARD TERRY and his COMPANY from Terry's Theatre, To-morrow (Thursday), at 3.0, in Mr. Pinero's enormously successful domestic drama, SWEET LAVENDER. Seats 1s. to 5s.

PROMENADE CONCERTS. — CRYSTAL PALACE. — Every Thursday and Saturday evening. Free. To-morrow, at 7.0. Band of the Royal Horse Guards (by permission of Col. the Hon. Oliver Montague). Conductor, Mr. Charles Godfrey, R. A. M.[6] On Saturday, at 7.0. band of Grenadier Guards (by permission of Col. the Hon.[7] W. S. D. Home). Conductor, Lieut. Dan Godfrey. Vocalists this week : — Miss Clara Leighton and Mr. Iver McKay, Miss Alice Gomes and Mr. W. H. Burgon. Accompanist, Mr. A. J. Eyre.

PROMENADE CONCERT. — CRYSTAL PALACE. — Miss CLARA LEIGHTON will SING The Minstrel Boy (Moore) and Robin Adair, To-Morrow (Thursday) evening, at 7.0.

1. *Their Home of Mystery,* leur demeure mystérieuse, c'est-à-dire leur théâtre où ils font leurs tours de magie. — 2. *Le palais de Crystal,* construit d'abord à Londres par sir Joseph Poxton, jardinier-architecte, pour la première Grand Exhibition, fut ensuite acheté par une compagnie et transporté à une heure de distance de Londres, à Norwood, où, placé au milieu d'un magnifique jardin avec de grandes eaux, il sert à donner des fêtes de tout genre, feux d'artifices superbes, etc. Prix d'un billet de saison, 1 guinée (26. 50); prix d'une seule entrée, 1 shelling. — 3. *Free,* gratis, c'est-à-dire quand on a une fois payé le prix d'entrée au palais. — 4. Les prix marqués ainsi sont en sus du prix d'entrée au palais. — 5. *For cast,* pour le programme. — 6. *R. A. M.,* de l'Académie royale de musique. — 7. *The Honourable,* titre donné aux fils puînés des pairs d'Angleterre.

PROMENADE CONCERT. — CRYSTAL PALACE. — Mr. IVER Mc KAY will SING The Macgregor's Gathering (Lee) and Let me Like a Soldier Fall, Maritana (Wallace), To-Morrow (Thursday) evening, at 7.

CRYSTAL PALACE. — THE GOLDEN LEGEND (Sir Arthur Sullivan's dramatic cantata) will be performed at Saturday's Concert, Nov. 17, at 3. The renowned Crystal Palace Orchestra and the Crystal Palace Choir. Conductor[1], Mr. August Manns. Organ.[2], Mr. A. J. Eyre. Numbered seats, 2s. 6d., may now be booked.

CRYSTAL PALACE.—Mr. EDWARD LLOYD, Mr. Andrew Black, and Mr. Barrington Foote will SING in THE GOLDEN LEGEND, Saturday next, at 3. Numbered seats, 2s. 6d.

OLYMPIA. — The WINTER EXHIBITION.

Heated and ventilated throughout. Lighted by electricity on the latest approved principle.

A GRAND CHRISTMAS FAIR of all nations, with special attractions, will be held on December 1st to February 23d., 1889.

Full particulars will be duly announced.

Prospectus and applications for space of Secretary, Winter Exhibition, Olympia, Kensington, London.

OLYMPIA. — CHRISTMAS FAIR. Toy Makers and Toy Importers, English and Foreign, will be allotted space free in best positions.

Plans, and full particulars of the Secretary.

OLYMPIA. — PROMENADE CONCERTS.

The MESSIAH, Christmas Eve.
Orchestra of 70 performers.
Chorus of 300.

FOURTH GREAT TERRIER SHOW TO-DAY (Wednesday), Thursday, and Friday, Nov. 14, 15, 16. Volunteer Tournament and Fête[3] (by permission of H. R. H. the Duke of Cambridge) To-Morrow (Thursday), Friday, and Saturday, Nov. 15, 16, 17.—ROYAL AQUARIUM, S. W.

ROYAL AQUARIUM. — JOSEPH DARBY, the Champion Jumper of the World; Les Deux Voleurs, by Jones and Kitchen's Continental Pantomime Company, Barretto, Wilson, and Hall's Gymnastic Company, Dutch Daly, Frederick's Performing Cats, Miss Cora Cardignan, Sismondi and Vivian, Prof. Cross (Phrenologist), the Beckwiths (Swimming), &c. La Belle Fatma, the Beauty of Tunis, &c. Admission 1s.; children 6d., including the unreserved seats. Ask for railway tickets including admission. Every afternoon at 3, and every evening at 8.

BLONDIN. — Notice. — Blondin will perform every evening at 9.5, and this afternoon and every Wednesday and Saturday afternoon only at 4.45. Notice. — Blondin performs all his original and celebrated feats on the high rope, which have made his name a household word for the past 55 years.

THE PRINCES CINDERELLA. — Sixth Annual Series. — FIRST DANCE, November 22. Particulars may be had upon application to the Secretary, Chelsea Hospital for Women, Fulham-road, S. W.

THE ZOOLOGICAL SOCIETY'S GARDENS, Regent's-park, are

---

1. *Conductor*, chef d'orchestre. — 2. *Organ*, organiste. C'est en imitation de l'orgue du Crystal Palace qu'on a installé le grand orgue dans la salle du Trocadéro, à Paris. — 3. Tournoi et fête donnés par les volontaires. Le duc de Cambridge est général en chef de l'armée anglaise.

OPEN DAILY (except Sundays), from 9 a. m. till sunset. Admission 1s.; on Mondays, 6d. Children always 6d.

NIAGARA in LONDON. — Open every day, all the year round, 10 to 10. One shilling. Fogs defeated. Electric light (100 000 candles), home-made, always ready. Building warmed throughout.

NIAGARA in LONDON. — Colossal Pictorial Realization of the great Falls by M. Philippoteaux, painter of the Siege of Paris. Largest picture in the world with original effects. Electric light. Daily, from 10 to 10, 1s. No fees.

NIAGARA in LONDON. — Pleasant lounge, music. American Museum (decorated by Bell). Refreshments by Beguinot. York-street, Westminster, St. Jame's-park Station. Praised by entire Press. Half a million visitors in six months.

MADAME TUSSAUD and SONS'. — Present EMPEROR of GERMANY; also the late Frederick III. Portrait models of King Milan of Servia, Mr. C. S. Parnell, M. P., and Mr. Davitt, M. P., General Boulanger. Superb new Court trains, as worn at the Court of St. James's. Over 400 portrait models. Orchestra, 3 afternoon; and evening, 7.30. Open 10 a. m. till 10 p. m. Admission 1s., under 12 years 6d. Refreshments at popular prices.

CHAMBER of HORRORS. — The most notorious criminals of the century. — MADAME TUSSAUD'S.

HERR L. EMIL BACH will PLAY, at the Association des Artistes Musiciens, in Brussels, on the 24th inst., his CAPRICCIO and CONCERTO by Liszt with orchestra; and in Antwerp on the 26th. Pleyel Wolff and Co.'s Concert Grand Piano.

AT LACON and OLLIER'S, 168, New Bond-street, the best BOXES and STALLS at every THEATRE and CONCERT can always be had. Lacon and Ollier are sole agents for Crosse's celebrated Anglo-Hungarian Band, and they also provide choice entertainments for private parties. — No. 168, New Bond-street.

LE PETIT ORCHESTRE de SALON. —This celebrated band, comprising solo instrumentalists from the Royal Italian Opera, and including the celebrated Hungarian cymbalo, can now be engaged for matinées, soirées, balls, etc. — Alfred Hays, 26, Old Bond-street, W., and 4, Royal Exchange-buildings.

MITCHELL'S ROYAL LIBRARY. — THE ARMADA. DRURY-LANE THEATRE. — A BOX[1] to hold eight persons for one guinea. Boxes, Stalls, and all Reserved Seats for every Theatre and entertainment in London and Paris, also Entertainments provided for Drawing Rooms, Receptions, etc. Private theatricals and concerts arranged, also bands for private, county, and hunt balls. — Mitchell's Royal Library, 33, Old Bond-street (City office, 51, Threadneedle-street), and 15, Boulevard des Italiens, Paris.

FANCY BALLS and THEATRICALS. — Tableaux. — Special Notice. — SIMMONS'S, the celebrated Court Costumier, old-established show rooms, NOT REMOVED from only address, King-street, Covent-garden. Costumes for Hire or to Order. Portable Theatres. Direct letters Simmons's, King-street, Covent-garden.

SPORTING[2].

PHEASANTS and PARTRIDGES. — Large numbers of ADULT PHEASANTS for SALE, for turning out, at low prices. Orders for Hungarian Partridges, for delivery in the autumn or

1. *A box*, une loge. — 2. Chasses, etc.

next spring, now being booked[1]. — JOHN BAILY and SON, 116, Mount-street, London, W.

TO HUNTING MEN.— To be LET, for season, four miles from Windsor, two from Ascot, and in the middle of the Queen's and Garth's country, SEVEN LOOSE BOXES[2], forage and saddle rooms, together with paddock. Apply to Mr. Mason, Estate Agent, Windsor.

SHOOTING SHIRTS. — F. LACK and SON are now prepared to supply their SPECIALITÉ SPORTING SHIRT, so strongly recommended by Medicinæ Doctor in the Field[3]. The material is as soft as silk, warm as flannel, and will not shrink. Invaluable to all sportsmen. For hunting we make a special shape, preventing the shirt rising. — F. Lack and Son, 90, Strand.

GUNS. — Several Second-hand, very little used, to be SOLD, at greatly reduced prices. Also several high-class Rifles. Apply Joseph Lang and Son, 22, Cokspur-street, Pall-mall, S. W.

GYMNASTICS and SPORTS. — PIGGOTT BROS.[4], and Co., Gymnasia for clubs and colleges, Portable Gymnastics, can by tried on the premises. Football[5], Boxing, and Fencing requisites. Write for Sports Catalogue, post free.— 59, 58, 57, Bishopsgate without, London.

GYMNASTIC APPLIANCES[6] at HALF PRICE. — Horizontal bars, 25s. complete; parallel bars, substantial make, 40s.; the guinea portable gymnasium, 16s. 6d.; dumb-bells, 1½d. lb.; Indian clubs, 4½d. lb.; boxing-gloves, 4s. 6d. set. Catalogue gratis. — S. GOFF, 17, King-street, Covent-garden.

NURSES[7] PRIVATE HOSPITALS, &c.

NURSING SISTERS of S. JOHN the DIVINE.—TRAINED MEDICAL, Surgical, and Monthly NURSES supplied. Private rooms for patients at S. John's Morden-hill, Lewisham. Apply to Superior, 68, Drayton-gardens, South Kensington.

THE WIGMORE TRAINED NURSES' INSTITUTE. — Resident skilled and experienced NURSES, for Medical, Surgical, Monthly, Mental, and Fever Cases, SUPPLIED, at a minute's notice. Address Miss Carty, 32, Wigmore-street, London, W.

VICTORIA HOSPITAL PRIVATE NURSING INSTITUTION, Chelsea, S. W. — TRAINED NURSES can be obtained for medical, surgical, and infectious cases. Apply to the Lady Superintendent.

GENERAL NURSING INSTITUTE, 5, Henrietta-street, Covent-Garden, W. C. Established 1862.

Solely under Medical Direction.

SKILLED MEDICAL, Surgical, Mental, and Monthly Hospital-trained NURSES are SUPPLIED at a moment's notice from this Institute, being resident in the Home; also Male Attendants and Nurses specially for Fever cases, etc. Applications to Secretary or Lady-Superintendent. Telegraphic address, Nursing Institute, London.

LONDON HOSPITAL PRIVATE NURSING INSTITUTION, Whitechapel-road, E.[8] — Thoroughly trained NURSES, for medical, surgical, mental, and fever cases, can be immediately obtained from the Matron.

LONDON HOSPITAL TRAINING SCHOOL for NURSES, White-

1. *Now being booked*, on reçoit dans ce moment. — 2. *Seven loose boxes*, sept stalles détachées (pour chevaux). — 3. *In the Field*, dans le journal de ce nom. — 4. Piggott Frères et Cie. — 5. *Football*, jeu de ballon. On se propose de parler de ce jeu tout au long un peu plus loin. — 6. Appareils. — 7. Garde-malade. — 8. *E.*, East postal district.

chapel, E. — NURSING LECTURES are given every Wednesday, at 8 p. m. The first course, on the General Details of Nursing, by Miss Luckes, Matron to the Hospital, began in August. The second course, on Elementary Anatomy and Surgical Nursing, by Frederick Treves, Esq., F. R. C. S.[1], Surgeon to the Hospital, will begin on Wednesday, Nov. 21st. The third course, on Elementary Physiology and Medical Nursing, by James Anderson, Esq., M. D., F. R. C. P.[2], will begin in March. A limited number of ladies are admitted on payment of half a guinea for each course. Apply to the Matron.

ST. HELENA HOME. — Private patients received and treated by their own medical attendant. Trained nurses sent out on application to the Lady Superintendent, 1, Grove-end-road, London, N. W. Telegraphic address, Helena, London.

ST. THOMAS'S HOME, Palace-Road, Lambeth. — Medical and surgical cases of both sexes received upon payment. Terms, including medical treatment, nursing, and board, 8s. a day. Special cases excepted. Application should be made to the Resident Medical Officer, either personally at 12 o'clock, or by letter.

MAGNETIC MASSAGE. Medical-Gymnastics, &c., by Mr. E. BRAARUP, late Medical Manager of Zander Institution. Patients attended at their residences. Apply 32, Westbourne-place, Eaton-square. At home 12-2[3]. Consultations free.

MASSAGE in SKILLED HANDS, and the celebrated MAITLAND MEDICAL and the EKNOS[4] ELECTRIC VAPOUR BATHS (patented), for Liver, Rheumatism, Nervous Exhaustion, &c. Treatment of corpulence a specialité.— Mrs. Maitland, 31, Grosvenor-street, W. hours 10 till 5. Consultations 11 till 2 (except Saturdays). Lessons given. Resident patient received.

ART EXHIBITIONS, &c.

DORÉ'S[5] GREAT PICTURE. — VALE OF TEARS.

AN altogether exceptional and pathetic interest attaches to the latest addition to the Doré-Gallery — The VALE of TEARS — the last work produced by the vanished hand of the great Alsatian. It is a rendering of « Come unto me all ye that travail and are heavy laden, and I will give you rest. » The back-ground of the picture represents The Vale of Tears, a shadowy valley flanked by an enormous crag. At the entrance stands the Saviour clothed in white, bearing a cross. The Divine figure is surrounded by a shadowy light, symbolizing Hope even in the Vale of Tears. It is filled by a number of typical figures, representing the weary and heavy laden ones. Every class of human suffering is represented. The king, glorious in cloth of gold, turns a wan, despairing, beseeching face to Christ. The aged and feeble, the maimed, the halt, and the blind, and the hated and despised leper, all look to Christ, for the rest which earth denies them. It is a beautiful and touching subject to have been the outcome of the great artist's very last thoughts. — Society. ON VIEW at the Doré-Gallery, No 35, New Bond-street, with his other celebrated pictures. 10 to 6. Admission 1s.

---

1. *F. R. C. S.*, Fellow (agrégé) of the Royal College of Surgeons. — 2. *F. R. C. P.*, Fellow of the Royal College of Physicians. — 3. *At home* 12-2, chez lui, de midi à 2 heures. — 4. *Eknos*, du grec ἔκνοος, égaré, en délire. — 5. *Gustave Doré*, grand artiste français, mort à Paris en 1887, a obtenu en Angleterre une très grande estime. Il y a peint un très grand nombre de ses meilleurs tableaux. En France, Gustave Doré est estimé surtout comme dessinateur.

DORÉ'S CHRIST LEAVING the PRÆTORIUM, Christian Martyrs, Dream of Pilate's Wife, Night of the Crucifixion, Christ Entering Jerusalem, House of Caiaphas, Moses before Pharaon, « Ecce Homo », The Ascension. The Day Dream, &c., are still ON VIEW at the Doré Gallery, 35, New Bond-street.

ANNO DOMINI, by E. LONG, R. A.[1] — « A picture to which we may point when a foreign critic tells us that high art is extinct in England. » — Saturday Review. ON VIEW, with Jephthah's Vow, Zeuxis, &c., at 168, New Bond-street. 10 to 6. 1s.

ARTHUR TOOTH and SONS' ANNUAL AUTUMN EXHIBITION of high-class PICTURES by British and Continental Artists is NOW OPEN at their Galleries, Nos 5 and 6, Haymarket, opposite Her Majesty's Theatre. Admission, 1s.

ARTHUR TOOTH and SONS' ANNUAL AUTUMN EXHIBITION includes :

FRANK HOLL, R.A.'S PICTURE BESIEGED.

L. DEUTSCH'S new PICTURE. LA JEUNE FAVORITE.

PETER GRAHAM. R. A.'S new PICTURE, RISING MISTS.

P. A. J. DAGNAN-BOUVERET'S new PICTURE, LE PARDON, BRETAGNE.

H. W. B. DAVIS, R.A.'S. PICTURE, DEWY EVE.

LÉON LHERMITTE'S new PICTURE, LA VEILLÉE.

B. W. LEADER. A.R.A.'S PICTURE, STRATFORD LOCK.

JOSEF ISRAELS' new PICTURE, A GLEANER of the SHORE.

C. BURTON BARBER'S new PICTURE, MISCHIEF.

AT ARTHUR TOOTH and SONS' GALLERIES, 5 and 6, Haymarket, S. W.

CHOICE ETCHINGS and ENGRAVINGS, in the proof states[2] after Sir E. Landseer, R. A., Sir J. E. Millais, R. A., Sir F. Leighton, P. R. A.[3], Sir J. Reynolds, P. R. A., L. Alma Tadema, R. A., B. Rivière, R. A., George Mason, A. R. A., Fred. Walker, A. R. A., B. W. Leader, A.R.A.[4], V. Oole, A.R.A., G. J. Pinwell, Corot, Millet, Rembrand, and others, always ON VIEW at ARTHUR TOOTH and SONS' GALLERIES, 5 and 6, Haymarket.

THE ANNUAL WINTER EXHIBITION of OIL-PAINTINGS by artists of the British and foreign schools is NOW OPEN at THOMAS McLEAN'S GALLERY, 7, Haymarket (next the theatre). Admission including catalogue, 1s.

ROSA BONHEUR'S[5] NEW PICTURE of " Pasture in the Pyrenees, " the most important work by this artist that has been in England for many years, is included in this Exhibition.

THERE are also new and important PICTURES by Peter Graham, R.A., E. Van Marke, Henry Moore, A. R. A.,

1. *R. A.*, Royal Academy *ou* Royal Academician. — 2. A l'état d'épreuves. Les premières épreuves tirées des gravures sur acier et sur cuivre se vendent plus cher que les feuilles tirées plus tard. — 3. *P. R. A.*, President of the Royal Academy. — 4. *A. R. A.*, Associate of the Royal Academy. — 5. Mlle Rosa Bonheur, artiste français, chevalier de la Légion d'honneur, célèbre pour ses peintures d'animaux et d'agriculture.

E. de Blas, Zubes, Birkett Foster, T. S. Cooper, R. A.

ETCHINGS and ENGRAVINGS, in the finest proof and print states, always ON VIEW at the Publisher's THOMAS McLEAN, 7, Haymarket (next the theatre).

AT THOMAS McLEAN'S GALLERY, 7, Haymarket (next the theatre).

NINETEENTH CENTURY ART SOCIETY, The Conduit-street Galleries. — The AUTUMN EXHIBITION NOW OPEN, from 10 to 6.
FREEMAN and MARRIOTT, Secretaries.

INSTITUTE of PAINTERS in OIL COLOURS, Piccadilly, W. — The ANNUAL EXHIBITION is NOW OPEN, from 10 till 5. Admission 1s. The Galleries will be illuminated at dusk and on dark days.
W. T. BLACKMORE, Secretary.

SHAKESPEARE'S HEROINES, now ON VIEW, at the Graphic Gallery, 14, Brook-street (two doors from New Bond-street).

FRENCH GALLERY, 129, Pall-mall. — PROF. H. SIEMIRADZKI'S great work, The PIRATES CAVE, and other Pictures by British and Foreign Artists, now ON VIEW. Admission 1s.

GROSVENOR GALLERY. — FIRST EXHIBITION of PASTELS NOW OPEN from 10 a. m. to 6 p. m. Admission, 1s.

HANOVER GALLERY, 47, New Bond-street. — Winter Exhibition. — ON VIEW, The RETURN of the FLOCK, by ROSA BONHEUR, also Works by J. T. Millet, Verboeckhoven, Diaz, Corot, Daubigny, Dupré, etc. Admission, one shilling, including catalogue. —. HOLLENDER and CREMETTI, Proprietors.

JAPANESE GALLERY, 28, New Bond-street. — The COLLECTION of JAPANESE and CHINESE ART and CURIOS[1]. is of the very highest class, and is also the most complete and extensive to select from in this country.

PARIS SALON. — ANNUAL EXHIBITION of the most remarkable PAINTINGS from this year's Salon NOW OPEN at the Continental Gallery, 157, New Bond-street. Admission, one shilling, including catalogue.

EXHIBITION of SUSSEX SCENERY, by A. F. Grace, A. W. Weedon, and Reginald Jones (also a collection of Screens On View). Hunting, Racing, Coaching, and Yachting, by eminent artists. — BURLINGTON GALLERY, 27, Old Bond-street.

EARLY ENGLISH PAINTERS. — SHEPHERD'S WINTER EXHIBITION includes choice works by Old Crome, John Constable, R. A., George Vincent, J. S. Cotman, Sir Joshua Reynolds, George Morland, David Cox, R. P. Bonnington, &c. — Shepherd's Gallery, 27, King-street, St. James's-square.

WATER-COLOUR DRAWINGS, by the principal Artists. — A collection of important works is now OPEN at the FINE ART SOCIETY'S, 143, New Bond-street.

OUR COUNTRY and OUR COUNTRY FOLK. A series of Drawings, by A. Hopkins, R. W. S.[2], and C. Robertson, R. W. S. F. R. P. E., ON VIEW at Messrs. DOWDESWELLS, 160, New Bond-street. Admission, one shilling, including catalogue.

1. *Curios.*, abrév. de *curiosities.* — 2. *R. W. S.*, Royal Water Colour Society. *Water colour*, aquarelle.

THE BATHERS, by the late FRED. WALKER, A. R. A. Messrs. Thos Agnew and Sons have the honour to announce that the ARTIST'S PROOFS of the etching by Mr. Macbeth are now being PUBLISHED. — 39, Old Bond-street, W.

MEZZOTINT ENGRAVINGS, by COUSENS, Dickenson, Earlom Green, Hodges, Jones, McArdell, Meyer, Reynolds, Spilsbury, Turner, Watson, Ward, and other eminent engravers. A LOAN COLLECTION on VIEW at J. and W. Vokins' Gallery, 14, Great Portland-street, W. Admission free.

BRUCK LAJOS' celebrated PICTURE, The QUARTETT (a Rehearsal), representing the four eminent artists, viz. : — Herrn Johachim, Ries, Straus, and Signor Piatti, rehearsing a quartett. This remarkable picture now ON VIEW at L. H. Lefèvre's Gallery, 1a, King-street, St. James's, S. W. Admission by address card, 10 to 5.

AN important ETCHING of the above by LEOPOLD LOWENSTAM will shortly be issued. A limited number of impressions only. Particulars of the Publisher, L. H. Lefèvre 1a, King-street, St. James, S. W.

PHOTOGRAPHIC SOCIETY'S EXHIBITION, 5a, Pall-mall east, open daily, from 10 to 5. 1s. Monday, Wednesday and Saturday evening. 7 to 10, 6 d. Optical lantern, Monday evening. Closes Wednesday evening, November 14th.

PHOTOGRAPHIC SOCIETY EXHIBITION. — Note. — FALLOWFIELD'S SPECIAL PLATE SUNK MOUNTS, with India tint for Platinotypes. Illustrated catalogue, 160 pages, of every photographic requisite, ready in stock, post free.—Jonathan Fallowfield, Photo. Stores, Lower-marsh, Lambeth.

PAINTING, by an Old Master — Mlle de Montespan by Mignard—to be SOLD, cheap. For particulars apply, by letter, A. B. care of The Briars. Eastbourne.

FOR SALE. TWO LARGE PICTURES, by Thomas Phillips, R.A., 1822, and Snyders respectively. For further particulars apply Alpha. Willington, Burton-on-Trent.

TO M. P.'s[1].—For SALE. PAIR of PARLIAMENTARY PICTURES, by Landseer[2], representing Bright and Cobden[3] in the Repeal of Corn Laws, coming into power; Lord Derby and Disraeli, government going out of power. Price £75. Apply to Henry Graves, Oak-lodge, Purley, Surrey.

MISCELLANEOUS.

CARTERS' — The CHEAPEST and BEST BULBS.

CARTERS' GUINEA BOX contains 1,250 BULBS, and is sent, packing and carriage free, to any station in England and Wales on receipt of cheque or postal order for 20s. It comprises the pick of the world[4], as follows :—

50 Hyacinths, named, in 9 colours	100 Crocus, yellow
50 Tulips, double early	50 Anemones
50 Tulips, single early	100 Daffodils
100 Narcissus poeticus	50 Ranunculus, Persian
50 Narcissus biflorus	50 Spanish Iris
50 Scilla campanulata	50 Snowdrops
100 Crocus, white	100 Winter aconites
100 Crocus, purple	86 Star of Bethlehem
100 Crocus, striped	14 Muscari botryoides

Half the box, 11s, carriage free; one quarter 7s., carriage free. Carters, Seedsmen by Royal Warrant to H. M.

---

1. *To M. P.'s*, aux membres du Parlement. — 2. *Landseer*, peintre anglais fort estimé, connu surtout par ses tableaux d'animaux. — 3. Bright et Cobden, les grands chefs de l'agitation en faveur de l'abolition des droits sur les céréales. Voy. *Historique*, page 5, note 1. — 4. *The pick of the world*, ce qu'il y a de mieux au monde. *To pick*, cueillir, choisir.

the Queen and H.R.H. the Prince of Wales, 237 and 238, High Holborn, London, W. C.

THE ANGLO-FRENCH NATURAL FLOWER COMPANY, 62, Avenue de la Gare, Nice, France, will forward all through the winter months to any part of the United Kingdom, delivered free on receipt of post-office order, boxes or bouquets containing beautiful fresh choice FLOWERS. Prices 2s., 6s., 7s. 6d., 10s. 6d., up to £3, according to size of boxes. Orange Blossoms always in stock. Bouquets of very choice flowers price 5s., 7s. 6d., 10s. 6d., up to £5, according to size. Roses, violets, orange blossom, camelias, pinks, hyacinths, lillies of the valley, &c., are the flowers usually made up in boxes and bouquets. Price lists on application (free by post), giving sizes of bouquets and boxes.

NOTICE. — SPECIAL SALE of CLOCKS, Watches, Chains, and Bronzes.

LUND and BLOCKLEY beg to announce that during November and December there will be a REDUCTION of 15 per cent. for cash off all WATCHES and CHAINS, and 25 per cent for cash off marked prices of Clocks and Bronzes.—Lund and Blockley (late-Viner). Est.[1] 1801. By appointment to The Queen. — No. 41, Pall-mall, London, S. W.

STREETERS' DIAMONDS.

MOUNTED, from £5 to £5,000.

STREETERS', the Pearl Merchants.

PEARLS direct from their Pearling Fleet[2].

STREETERS', the Gem Merchants.

PRECIOUS STONES direct from the Mines.

THE 18-CARAT STANDARD JEWELLERY, introduced by Mr. STREETER in 1850, is still the lowest quality of gold manufactured, exported, and kept in stock by this firm. — Streeter and C°, 18, New Bond-street, W.

HOTELS, &c.

APARTMENTS. — SMITH'S PRIVATE HOTEL[3] 70 and 72, Porchester-terrace, Hyde-park. Handsomely furnished suites of drawing and dining rooms. Excellent cuisine and attendance. Terms strictly moderate. Vacant[4] on 20th inst.

BURR'S HOTEL, Queen-square, London, W. C., near British Museum. Restful quiet here[5]. Bed room, breakfast, gas, attendance, 5s.; lunch, dinner, &c., extra, if had[6]. Or pension 5s. or 7s. per day. First-class. Room for 50 visitors.

BOLTON MANSIONS HOTEL, 11, 12, 13, Bolton-gardens west, South Kensington. 100 appartments, unequalled for luxury and comfort. Spacious reception, coffee, ball, billiard, smoke, and private sitting rooms. Excellent cuisine under chef. Moderate terms for visitors on pension. Night porter.

BUCKINGHAM PALACE HOTEL. Buckingham-gate, London, S.W.—

1. *Est.* 1801, established in 1801: — 2. *Their pearling fleet,* leur flottille pour la pêche des perles. — 3. *Private hotel,* hôtel-pension. — 4. *Vacant on 20th inst.*, il y aura des appartements libres le 20 courant. — 5. *Restful quiet here,* on y trouve calme et tranquillité. — 6. *Extra, if had,* se payent à part quand on les prend.

Delightfully situated, facing the Royal Palace, close to the Royal parks, and near Victoria Station. Very reduced terms for appartments and board. Table d'hôte, 5s. Hydraulic lift[1] to all floors. Fine public rooms. Under same management as the Burlington Hotel, Cork-street and Old Burlington-street, London, W.—GEORGE COOKE, Manager.

HYDE-PARK HOTEL, Hyde-park-place, overlooking the park and Park-lane. Every modern comfort and convenience. Table d'hôte daily, at separate tables, open to non-residents. Very moderate charges.

LONDON. — SOUTH KENSINGTON HOTEL, Queen's-gate-terrace, S.W.[2] is situated in the healthiest and most fashionable part of London, close to Kensington-gardens and Hyde-park, and contains 200 rooms, elegantly furnished, hydraulic lift, most improved sanitary arrangements, and every home comfort. Suites of appartments for wedding breakfasts, dinner parties, &c.—JAMES BAILEY, proprietor (and of Bailey's Hotel, Gloucester-road, S.W.).

LONDON-HOTEL VICTORIA, Limited, Northumberland-avenue, Charing-cross, W. C., one of the most magnificent hotels in Europe.

500 rooms, superbly furnished. Electric lights. Four lifts.

Table d'hôte, open to non-residents, separate tables for large or small parties from 6 to 8.30, the most perfect dinner in London, price 5s.

HENRY LOGAN, Manager.

MANSION HOTEL, Richmond-hill. Winter terms from 7s. per day, board and residence included. No extras. Table d'hôte from 7 to 8.30. Excellent cuisine. Finest wines at moderate prices. Handsome suites of dining, drawing, billiard, and smoking rooms.

NORRIS'S PRIVATE HOTEL, Addison-road Station, Kensington, W. Easy access to all parts of London. Private suites for families, also bed rooms, with use of coffee room and drawing room. Moderate tariff.

NORWOOD (UPPER).—The QUEEN'S HOTEL. Near the Crystal Palace. Patronized by the late Emperor and Empress of Germany. Recommended by the most eminent physicians. Special additional bed rooms for bachelors. Commodious drawing, billiard, and smoking rooms. Table d'hôte at 7 o'clock. Winter terms.

CHATSWORTH-PARK, Derbyshire. — BASLOW HYDRO[3] overlooking Chatsworth-park, sheltered from east winds[4], combines home comforts with hotel luxuries, complete system of baths first-class table. Table d'hôte 6.30. Omnibus meets trains at Rowsley. Reduced winter terms from 35s. per week. Address Manager, Baslow, via Chesterfield.

HASTINGS. — ALBANY HOTEL, Robertson-terrace, facing the sea. Sheltered position. Home comforts. Superior cuisine. Moderate tariff or boarding terms.

HASTINGS HYDROPATHIC.—Charming Residence, beautifully situated, picturesque grounds. Baths include Turkish, with sea-water plunge. Billiards, tennis, quoits. Excellent cooking. Liberal table. Home comforts. Moderate charges.

MATLOCK BATH, Derbyshire. — ROYAL HOTEL and Hydropathic Baths. Celebrated winter ressort, shel-

1. *Hydraulic lift to all floors*, ascenseur hydraulique à tous les étages. — 2. *S. W.*, south Western postal district. — 3. *Hydro*, établissement d'hydrothérapie (de Baslow). — 4. *East winds*, ce sont les vents de l'est qu'on craint le plus en Angleterre, ils viennent de la Norvège, en traversant la mer du Nord. En France, au contraire, les vents d'est sont regardés comme les meilleurs et les plus agréables.

tered from all cold winds. Hotel heated throughout. Inclusive terms, £3 per week, with the use of baths, from October until March.—J.A. HINTON, proprietor.

OXFORD.—MITRE HOTEL, one of the most economical first class hotels in the kingdom.

OATLANDS-PARK HOTEL, Walton-on-Thames, Surrey, 17 miles from Waterloo Station. South aspect. Hotel warmed throughout. The park and grounds are lovely. A desirable winter residence, with every home comfort. Present boarding terms[1] 10s. 6d. per day. Suites of appartments at greatly reduced prices. Table d'hôte at 7 p. m. Billiard room (two tables). Excellent stabling. The hotel omnibus meets the 8.50 and 9.34 a. m. up trains[2] from Walton and the 5.20 p. m. down train from Waterloo Station.—H. GADJE, Manager.

WORTHING.—The ROYAL HOTEL (Sea-house). First class hotel, in unrivalled position, facing the sea and the pier. Moderate terms.

AUSTRALIA.—ROBERTS' HOTEL. George and Market streets, Sydney, is LIGHTED by ELECTRICITY, and possesses every modern convenience and comfort. For apartments, address the Secretary.

ANDALUSIA. Spain. — HOTEL COLUMBUS
Huelva
WINTER SEASON.

Average Temperature.	Midday.	Midnight.
December	59·20	51·50 Fahrenheit[3].

The Hotel is fitted throughout with the most complete English sanitars appliances, also with hot and cold, fresh and sea water baths.

The most comfortable and conomical hotel in the peninsula. Extensive gardens, billiards, lawn tennis, carriagés, and horses.

Luggage can be booked through from Madrid, and after October from Lisbon, viâ the New Zafra, to Huelva Line.

Huelva Hotel Company, Limited, 11, Old Jewry-chambers, London, E. C.

COSTEBELLE, Hyeres (Peyrons' Hotel). — HOTEL de l'ERMITAGE and GRAND HOTEL de COSTEBELLE, OPENED for the season 1st. October. A. Pyron, proprietor. Telegraphic address, Ermitage, Hyeres.

MADEIRA.—REIDS' HOTELS.—Oldest established. Every comfort. Drainage on latest principles by Banner Company. All steamers met. Address Reid, Madeira.

MADEIRA. — CARDWELL'S HOTELS. — These hotels are situated in the most beautiful part of the island, and command unrivalled views of the sea and mountain scenery; within easy distance of the town of Funchal[4], being on the only level road in the island, which extends a distance of nearly six miles along the sea shore. The buildings are replete with every convenience. The sanitary arrangements in every sense are of the most perfect description.

NICE. — HOTEL des ANGLAIS. — This first-class hotel, facing the sea, and under English management, RE-OPENED for the season on the 1st. October, 1888. There is a lift for the use of visitors.

R. BAKER HAYS, Secretary.
No. 11, Abchurch-lane, London, E. C.

1. *Boarding terms*, prix de pension. — 2. *The* 8.50 *and* 9.34 *a. m. up trains*, les trains montant (vers Londres) de 8.50 et de 9.34 du matin. *a. m.*, ante meridiem, avant midi. Voy. note 3, page 19. — 3. Pour la réduction des degrés Fahrenheit en centigrades, voy. *Grammaire Elwall*, page 204. Le point glace de Fahrenheit est à 32°, et 9° F = 5° centigrades. — 4. *Funchal*, prononcez foun'-châl, capitale de l'île de Madère.

A PHYSICIAN, who has travelled extensively in malarial countries[1], wishes to go abroad for the winter in MEDICAL CHARGE of INVALIDS, or with a party of sportsmen. Address M. D., care of W. D. Johnson, 6, Duke-street, Adelphi.

TO PATRONS, &c. — A clergyman, possessing large private means, desires SMALL BENEFICE or ADVOWSON[2]. Spacious house indispensable. Address Vicar, cure of Mr. Chapham, Albert-square, Manchester.

BARCELONA EXHIBITION. — The GOLD MEDAL for HAVANA CIGARS exhibited at the Barcelona Exhibition has been awarded to JUAN CUETO and Co., the sole Manufacturers of the brands[3], Flor de Naves and Don Quixote de Mancha, for excellence of tobacco and superiority of make.

WEEKLY NEWSPAPER and PRINTING BUSINESS for SALE, in one of the largest towns in South Wales. A good opportunity for an energetic young man with a capital of about £600. Address H. Z., care of J. W. Vickers, 5, Nicholas-lane, E. C.

BOOKCASE. — WANTED, a well-made BOOKCASE, about 5ft. wide by about 6ft. 6 high. Good locks, good bolts. Address B. C., care of Mr. Channon, 96, Brompton-road.

BOOKS BOUGHT. — To Executors, Sollicitors, &c. — HENRY SOTHERAN and Co., 36, Piccadilly, and 136, Strand, Second-hand Booksellers, PURCHASE LIBRARIES, or Smaller Collections of Books, in town or country, and give the utmost value in cash. Experienced valuers sent. Removals without trouble or expense to vendors. Established 1816. Telegraphic address, Bookmen, London.

CATALOGUES GRATIS. — Cheap and good SECOND-HAND BOOKS. — H. SOTHERAN and Co., well-known as being the largest purchasers of private collections at auctions, are enabled to offer to book buyers unusual advantages. Public libraries liberally treated with. Est. 1816. — 136, Strand, by Waterloo-bridge.

ANTIQUITIES. — Mr. DAVIS, expert, purchaser, and valuer of works of art, is desirous of PURCHASING ANTIQUITIES, Works of Art, and high-class pictures of the English, French, and Dutch schools. Valuations made for probate[4]. — 147, New Bond-street, London.

MEDALS and COINS WANTED, of every description, either in gold, silver, or bronze. Single medals and coins or collections purchased, and high prices given for any fine or scarce specimens. — Spink and Son, Numismatists and Medallists, 2, Gracechurch-street, London. Established 1772.

OLD SILVER for PRESENTS. — SPINK and SON, Goldsmiths and Silversmiths, 2, Gracechurch-street, Cornhill, E. C.[5], respectfully invite an inspection of their choice STOCK of genuine OLD ENGLISH SILVER, at moderate cash prices, with 10 per cent. discount. Under the patronage of H. M. The Queen. Established 1772.

TO be SOLD, for £21 (cost £47), a GENTLEMAN'S GOLD KEYLESS WATCH[6], by C. Frodsham, Strand; an excellent instrument, quite unimpaired by wear. Written guarantee. May be seen at Wales and McCulloch's, 22, Ludgate-hill.

---

1. *In malarial countries,* dans des pays où il y a la *malaria* des pays marécageux. — 2. *Advowson,* cure. — 3. *The brands,* les marques. — 4. *Probate,* voy. note 8, p. 15. — 5. *E. C.,* East central postal district (de Londres). — 6. *A keyless watch,* une montre à remontoir.

TWO PAIRS of perfectly pure, white, flawless DIAMONDS for SALE, for single stone ear-rings, weight 3 1/2 carats and 7 1-16 carats per pair respectively. Being unmounted can be examined thoroughly and purchased very reasonably, there being no intermediate profit. — Bryce Wright, Mineralogist and Expert in Gems, the Museum, 26, Savile-row, W.

NEW GAMES. — PATCHESI, a splendid game for two or more players, price 1s., 2s. 6d., 5s., 8s. 6d., 10s. 6d.; Chopsticks, causing endless fun, 3s. 6d., 5s., 7s. 6d.; Sigma, just out, 1s.; Royal Reversi, 7s. 6d. and 12s. 6d.; Peel Puzzles[1], 1s. 6d.; John Bull Puzzle, 6d.; Zoological Loto, 4s., 7s. 6d., 10s. 6d.; Cannonade, 10s. 6d., 14s., 21s., 31s. 6d., and up[2]. Catalogue free. Of all dealers, Wholesale, JACQUES[3] and SON, London.

CHRISTMAS CARDS. — A PACKET of SIXTY first-class CARDS for 2s. 9d. post free. Being the clearance of a manufacturer's remainder, a limited number only can be supplied at this price. — H. S. WARR, Stationer, 63, High Holborn.

CHRISTMAS GREETINGS. — Patterns of these new and fashionable Complimentary Cards for Christmas are now ready, and will be sent post free (specially printed). A most complete collection, amongst them many striking novelties. — PARKINS and GOTTO, Court Stationers, Oxford-street, London.

PARKINS and GOTTO, COURT STATIONERS,
54, Oxford-street, London.

NOTICE.

JAS SHOOLBRED and Co.'s SALE of

FANCY GOODS, Toys, &c., for CHRISTMAS PRESENTS will commence on

MONDAY, Nov. 19th.

TOTTENHAM-HOUSE,
Tottenham-court-road.

TO be SOLD, in consequence of death, a MERLIN[4] INVALID CHAIR (Carter's), with indiar-ubber wheels and sliding foot-rest[5]. Moves very easily, and is in good condition. Price 3 1/2 guineas. Also to be Disposed Of, good Leg-Rest. — C., 37, West-square, Southwark.

GENTLEMAN, shortly going to India, wishes to DISPOSE OF his splendid real RUSSIAN OVERCOAT, trimmed and lined throughout with costly fur; only worn a few times; will fit any one. Cost 40 guineas in Petersburg last year; accept 15 guineas only. Address Arnold, 1, St. Aubyn's-road, Upper Norwood, London.

A GENTLEMAN'S NEW FUR-LINED OVERCOAT. Price only £10. Great bargain. Fine blue military cloth, lined throughout, richest real musquash fur[6], with deep, handsome fur collar, cuffs, and facings, five pockets lined chamois leather, fit chest 42in.[7], length 52in. Suit officer or medical man. Will be sent on approval by the makers, Perry and Co., 8, Mason's-avenue, City.

1. *Puzzle,* jeu de patience. — 2. *And up* ou *upwards*, et au-dessus. — 3. Si je ne me trompe, Jacques est l'inventeur du jeu de *croquet*. — 4. *A Merlin invalid chair*, une chaise de malade de Merlin. — 5. *Foot-rest* ou *leg-rest*, appui pour les jambes. — 6. *Musquash fur*, fourrure de rat musqué. — 7. 42 *inches*, 42 pouces. *Fit chest*, entre dans une caisse de 42 pouces de large sur 52 pouces de long. Voy. *Grammaire Elwall*, p. 202.

SHIPPING[1].

PENINSULAR and ORIENTAL COMPANY (carrying Her Majesty's Mails) to INDIA, CHINA, the STRAITS, AUSTRALIA, CEYLON, EGYPT, MALTA, and GIBRALTAR. Accelerated through services[2] as under: OVERLAND ROUTE to INDIA, the EAST, and AUSTRALIA.

BOMBAY and KURRACHEE by P. and O.[3] from LONDON and BRINDISI, every week. Dates of Departure: —

	Tons.	London.	Naples.	Brindisi.
Brindisi	.. 3,553	.. Nov. 15	—	—
Bengal	.. 4,499	.. Nov. 22	—	Dec. 3
Nepaul	.. 3,549	.. Nov. 29	Dec. 7	—
Peninsular	.. 5,500	.. Dec. 7	—	Dec. 17

CALCUTTA DIRECT, by P. and O., from LONDON, every fortnight. Dates of departure as follows: —

	Tons.	London.	Naples.	Brindisi.
Nepaul	3,554	Thurs., Nov. 29	Dec. 7	—
Chusan	4,496	Thurs., Dec. 13	Dec. 21	—
Rosetta	3,525	Fri., Dec. 28	—	Jan. 7
Coromandel	4,499	Thurs., Jan. 10	—	—

CEYLON DIRECT, by P. and O. from LONDON, every week.

CHINA, STRAITS, and JAPAN, by P. and O. — The P. and O. COMPANY despatch a STEAMER for the above ports from London every alternate Thursday, from Brindisi every alternate Monday.

AUSTRALIA DIRECT from LONDON, by P. and O., calling at Brindisi every fortnight. Dates of departure as follows: —

	Tons.		London.	Brindisi.
Oceana	6,362	7,000 h. p.[4]	Fri., Nov. 16	Nov. 26
Carthage	5,013	5,500 h. p.	Thurs. Nov. 29	Dec. 10
Rome	5,011	5,000 h. p.	Thurs., Dec. 13	Dec. 24
Arcadia	6,362	7,000 h. p.	Fri., Dec. 28	Jan. 7

GIBRALTAR, Malta, Brindisi, Port-Said, and Ismailia. — P. and O. COMPANY despatch weekly from London one of their large and well-appointed STEAMERS for the above ports. Cheap single and return tickets[5], also to Malta, viâ Brindisi.

NAPLES; Southern Italy, viâ Naples. — The P. and O. STEAMERS leave London on Nov. 29 and Dec. 13 for NAPLES.

ALEXANDRIA by P. and O. FORTNIGHTLY SERVICES leaving VENICE every alternate Friday afternoon; Brindisi every alternate Monday morning; London, calling at Gibraltar, Malta, and Brindisi, every fortnight.

AUSTRALIA and BACK for 100 guineas first saloon; £65 second saloon, by PENINSULAR and ORIENTAL steamers fortnightly.

AUSTRALIA, NEW ZEALAND, TASMANIA, by the P. and O. COMPANY'S steamers (carrying Her Majesty's mails) from London. Departures every fortnight. Electric lighting; music and smoking saloons; very superior cuisine. The Company's fine steamer CARTHAGE, 5,013 tons, 5,000-horse power. Captain, E. G. STEAD, will leave LONDON for SYDNEY, MELBOURNE, ADELAIDE, and ALBANY, on the 29th November. This ship is fitted with all the most modern improvements, and has accomodation for first and second class saloon passengers equal to any afloat. Fares from £30 to £70. Return tickets £65 to £105. First and second class passengers only carried.

CHEAP RETURN TICKETS to the EAST. — The P. and O. COMPANY issue RETURN TICKETS at reduced fares to India, China, Japan, Australia, Tasmania, New Zealand, Mediterranean Ports, and Egypt.

1. *Shipping*, navigation. — 2. *Through services*, service du point de départ au point extrême d'arrivée. — 3. *P. and O., Peninsular and Oriental Company*, compagnie très puissante dont les magnifiques navires à vapeur desservent la Péninsule du sud de l'Europe et tout l'Orient. *Kurrachee*, port du Sind, province de Bombay. — 4. *H. p., horse-power* : 7 000 *h. p.*, de la force de 7 000 chevaux. — 5. *Return tickets*, billets d'aller et de retour.

PENINSULAR and ORIENTAL COMPANY. For passage and freight apply at 122, Leadenhall-street, and 25, Cockspur-street, London. Freight Brokers, Escombe Bros. and Co., Liverpool, Manchester, Glasgow, and London. — Parcels 4d. per lb.[1].

BRITISH INDIA STEAM NAVIGATION COMPANY (Limited[2]). — Mail and Passenger STEAMERS to ZANZIBAR, Kurrachee, Malabar, Coast Ports, and Persian Gulf, Colombo, Madras, and Calcutta, with liberty to call at any ports in the Mediterranean, British India Association Steamers (Ld.) to India — Queenslands Royal Mail Line to Java and Queensland Ports. Loading berth, Royal Albert Docks.

Kurrachee and Bombay.		Colombo[3], Madras and Calcutta.		Queensland, viâ Batavia.	
Kangra	Nov. 24	Pundua	Nov. 15	Taroba.	Nov. 20
Henzada	Dec. 21	*India	Nov. 22	Merkara	Dec. 11
Huzara	Jan. 18	Navarino	Dec. 6	Jumna	Jan. 8
Kerbela	Feb. 15	Goorkha	Dec. 20	Dacca	Feb. 5

*Calling at Trincomalee.

Every comfort for a tropical voyage. Passengers and cargo booked by the Company's steamers to all important points in India, Burmah, Persian Gulf, Java, Sumatra, and Queensland.

Apply to Gray, Dawes, and Co., 13, Austinfriars; or Gellatly, Hankey, Sewell, and Co., 51, Pall-mall, and 109, Leadenhall-street, E.C.

COLOMBO, Madras, and Calcutta, viâ Suez Canal, transshipping to Coromandel and Burmese Ports by BRITISH INDIA STEAM NAVIGATION COMPANY'S STEAMERS, fortnightly, from Royal Albert Docks. Apply as above.

ZANZIBAR, viâ Suez Canal. — BRITISH INDIA STEAM NAVIGATION COMPANY'S SERVICE from London. For dates of sailing see detailed advertisement, or apply as above.

ANCHOR LINE. — INDIAN SERVICE. Surgeons and stewardesses[4] carried. Every comfort. Punkahs[5], &c.

Liverpool to Bombay direct.

Nubia	3,551 t.	Nov. 17	Asia	3,660 t.	Dec. 15
Arabia	3,544 t.	Dec. 1	Armenia	3,395 t.	Jan. 19

Liverpool to Calcutta direct.

Britannia	3,069 t.	Nov. 23	Roumania	3,387 t.	Dec. 17

Fares as low as other lines. Grindlay and Co, 55, Parliament-street; Henderson Brothers, 8, Regent-street, and 18, Leadenhall-street.

HALL LINE. — LIVERPOOL TO BOMBAY, KURRACHEE, and the PUNJAB.

For BOMBAY direct.

Kirby Hall[6], 27th Nov. | Wernetli Hall, 4th Jan., 1889.
Locksley Hall, 20th Dec.

For KURRACHEE and the PUNJAB direct.

Rufford Hall, 15th Dec. | Branksome Hall, 23d Jan., 1889.

Note. — Passengers and parcels are booked through, viâ Kurrachee, to all the principal stations on the North-Western Railway of India, Rates on application. Surgeon and stewardess carried.

Apply to Henry S. King and Co., 65, Cornhill, and 450, Pall-mall; or to Robert Alexander and Co., 9 and 11, Fenchurch-avenue, E.C., and 19, Tower-buildings north, Liverpool.

CALCUTTA, viâ Suez Canal. — HARRISSON LINE. From Liverpool direct. Fast steamers. Regular sailings. Next departure, the steamer ELECTRICIAN, from Morpeth Dock, on Monday, Nov. 19. Apply to Thos. and Jas[7]. Harrison, Liverpool.

1. *4d. per lb.*, four pence per pound; c'est 40 c. par demi-kilo. — 2. *Limited*, c'est-à-dire dont les actionnaires ne sont responsables que jusqu'au montant des actions qu'ils ont souscrites et non pour toute leur fortune. — 3. *Colombo*, capitale de l'île de Ceylan, Indes anglaises. — 4. *Stewardesses*, fémin. plur. de *Steward*, femmes chargées spécialement du service des voyageuses. — 5. *Punkah*, mot hindou, sorte d'éventail énorme suspendu au plafond et mis en mouvement pour ventiler les appartements. — 6. *Hall*, château. — 7. *Thos. and Jas. Harrison*, pour Thomas et James Harrison.

CALCUTTA. — STAR LINE of STEAMERS from LIVERPOOL, calling at COLOMBO, to land passengers only and embarking passengers, viâ Naples, at Suez :

Vega	Tuesday, Dec. 4	Mira	Tuesday, Jan. 22
Capella	Friday, Dec. 28	Pallas	Saturday, Feb. 16

These steamers take saloon passengers[1] only, are fitted with icehouse, punkahs, &c., and carry a surgeon, stewardess, and European crew. For terms, &c., apply to J. B. Westray and Co., 112, Fenchurch-street, E.C.; Grindlay and Co., 55, Parliament-street, S.W.; or to Rathbone, Brothers, and Co., 21, Water-street, Liverpool.

CITY STEAMERS for CALCUTTA and BOMBAY.

LIVERPOOL to CALCUTTA direct :—

City of Venice, Wed., Nov. 14	City of Oxford, Wed., Nov. 28

LIVERPOOL to BOMBAY and KURRACHEE.

City of Dublin, Sat., Dec. 22

Highest class speed. Splendid accommodation. Surgeon and stewardess carried. Crews entirely European.

For plans, freight, &c., apply to Montgomerie and Workman, 36, Gracechurch-street, E. C.; Allan, Brothers, and Co., James-street, Liverpool; or to the Owners[2], George Smith and Sons, Glasgow.

GELLATLY, HANKEY, SEWELL, and Co. despatch STEAMERS[3] from Royal Albert Dock :—

Destination.	Viâ Suez Canal.	To Sail.
Kurrachee, Bombay.	Kangra	Nov. 29
Colombo, Madras, Calcutta.	Pundua	Nov. 15
	India..	Nov. 22
Queensland Ports	Taroba	Nov. 20
	Merkara	Dec. 11
Marseilles, Mediterranean, China, and Japan		Nov. 18
		Nov. 25
		Dec. 2
Mahe, King Georges Sound, Adelaide, Melbourne, Sydney.	Messageries Maritimes de France	Dec. 9
Obock, Aden, Zanzibar, Madagascar Ports, Mauritius, and Reunion	Messageries Maritimes de France	Nov. 25

For freight or passage apply to Gellatly, Hankey, Sewell, and Co., No. 51, Pall-mall, S.W., and 109, Leadenhall-street, London, E.C.

CLAN[4] LINE STEAMERS to INDIA. Reduced Rates for Return Tickets.

COLOMBO, MADRAS and CALCUTTA.

†Clan Macpherson	Sails Nov. 17
Clan Drummond	Sails Dec. 1
Clan Buchanan	Sails Dec. 15
Clan Mackenzie	Sails Dec. 29

BOMBAY.

Clan Singlair	Sails Nov. 22
Clan Monroe	Sails Dec. 11
Clan Macdonald	Sails Dec. 31
Clan Graham	Sails Jan. 14

†Cabins amidships, and fitted throughout with the electric light.

Regular fortnightly sailings from Liverpool. Specially built for the Indian trade, fitted with all improvements. Separate two-berth cabins. Moderate fares, and reduced rates for families, &c.

For particulars apply to Wheatley and Co., 23, Regent-street, W.; or CAYZER, IRVINE, and Co., Leadenhall-buildings, E.C.

RANGOON[5] DIRECT, viâ Suez.—The magnificent screw[6] steamer CASTLEDALE, 100A1[7], 2,358 tons register, will be despatched from Victoria Dock, London, about November 23d. For freight, &c., apply to P. Henderson and Co., 15, St. Vincent-place, Glasgow;

1. *Saloon passengers*, voyageurs de première classe. — 2. *To the Owners*, aux armateurs. *Owner*, propriétaire. — 3. *Despatch steamers*, navires à vapeur portant les dépêches. — 4. *Clan line*, " clan line ". *Clan*, mot gaélique, signifiant enfants, famille, et qui désignait en Ecosse une tribu ou collection de familles, portant ordinairement le même nom et obéissant au même chef, et qu'on supposait tous descendus d'un commun ancêtre. Les noms qui suivent le mot *clan* sont tous des noms écossais. — 5. *Rangoon*, capitale de la province de Pégou, dans la Birmanie britannique, sur la côte est du golfe de Bengale. — 6. *Screw steamer*, navire à vapeur à hélice. *Screw*, vis, hélice. — 7. 100A1. C'est le titre de navire à vapeur de *première classe* donné au *Lloyd's* à Londres comme certificat d'enregistrement, établissant la qua-

C. Howard and Son, 17, Philpot-lane, London, E.C.; or to Livingston, Briggs, and Co., 22, Great St. Helen's, London, E. C.

BATAVIA, CHERIBON, SAMARANG, and SOURABAYA[1]. — The ROTTERDAM LLOYD'S MAIL STEAMERS will leave Southampton regularly every fortnight for above ports direct, taking cargo for all transshipment ports.

Utrecht	2,227 tons	Nov. 20
Soerabaja	2,227 tons	Dec. 4

For freight or passage apply to Escombe, Brothers, and Co., 3, East-India-avenue, London; 88, King-street, Manchester; 14, Water-street, Liverpool; 51, St. Vincent-street, Glasgow; and Queen's-terrace, Southampton.

STEAM for the STRAITS[2] and CHINA weekly, viâ Marseilles (overland[3]) and Algiers. — Passengers by Ocean Steamship Company's vessels can leave London on Wednesday, proceeding overland to Marseilles and thence to Algiers by Transatlantic Company's express boat, to join OCEAN STEAMSHIP COMPANY'S STEAMER leaving Algiers on Saturday. First-class tickets through from London to Singapore £40; to Hongkong, £45; to Shanghai, £50. Apply to Alfred Holt, 1, India-buildings, Liverpool.

STEAM for the STRAITS SETTLEMENTS[4] and CHINA.—The OCEAN STEAMSHIP COMPANY'S VESSELS will be despatched for PENANG, Singapore, Hongkong, and Shanghai, as follows: —

Stentor, from Liverpool, Nov. 16.
Patroclus, from Liverpool, Nov. 24.
Deucalion, from Liverpool, Nov. 30.
Jason, from Liverpool, Dec. 8.
Dardanus, from Liverpool, Dec.

Sleeping rooms and saloons on deck. Surgeon, stewardess, and European crew. First-class fare to the Straits, £40; to Hongkong, £45; to Shanghai, £50. Apply to John Swire and Sons, 19, Billiter-street, London; or to Alfred Holt, 1, India-buildings, Liverpool.

JAPAN-CHINA.—OCCIDENTAL and ORIENTAL STEAMSHIP COMPANY. STEAMERS leave San Francisco as follows: —

Oceanic ..	Wednesday, Nov. 28	Belgic	Tuesday, Jan. 8
Gaelic ..	Tuesday, Dec. 18	Arabic	To follow

First-class accommodation. Superior table. Through bookings from England. For passage apply to Ismay, Imrie, and Co., 10, Water-street, Liverpool; 34, Leadenhall-street, London; Thomas Cook and Son, Ludgate-circus, London; or Company's agents at 41, Broadway, New York; 237, Broadway, New York; 839, Broadway, New York; R. R. Building, corner 4th, and Townsend streets, San Francisco. — T. H. Goodman, General Passenger Agent, Leland Stanford, President.

UNION LINE (for South African Gold Fields). — CAPE of GOOD HOPE, NATAL, and EAST AFRICAN ROYAL MAIL STEAMERS. — The UNION STEAMSHIP COMPANY'S

lité du navire. Lloyd, nom du propriétaire d'un café à Londres, *Lloyd's Coffee house*, près de la Bourse, vers l'an 1688, où se réunissaient tous ceux qui avaient des relations d'affaires avec la navigation; c'est là qu'aujourd'hui l'on rencontre à certaines heures les assureurs de navires et de cargaisons. C'est pour ainsi dire la Bourse de la navigation. Le Bureau Veritas, à Paris, en est une imitation ainsi que le Lloyd autrichien (note sur Plimpsoll's Act). — 1. Villes de l'île de Java, possession hollandaise dans la Malaisie, dont Batavia est la capitale. — 2. *The Straits*, c'est le détroit de Malacca qu'on désigne ainsi, avec ceux de la Sonde, etc., etc., qui permettent le passage de la mer des Indes dans l'Océan Pacifique. — 3. *Overland*, c'est-à-dire par terre de Calais à Marseille, pour éviter le long voyage sur mer par l'Océan Atlantique (surtout le golfe de Gascogne), le détroit de Gibraltar et la Méditerranée jusqu'à Marseille. — 4. *The straits settlements*, c'est-à-dire pour Sumatra, Malacca Bornéo, etc.

ROYAL MAIL STEAMERS will sail as follows for the SOUTH AFRICAN PORTS and DELAGOA BAY, calling at LISBON and MADEIRA.

Steamers.	Hamburg.	Southampton.	Lisbon.
Spartan	9th Nov.	Friday, Nov. 16	Monday, Nov. 19
Athenian	23d Nov.	Friday, Nov. 30	Monday, Dec. 3
Tartar	7th Dec.	Friday, Dec. 14	Monday, Dec. 17

Return tickets issued to Madeira and South Africa.

Apply to the Union Steamship Company, Limited, Oriental-place, Southampton, or No. 11, Leadenhall-street, London.

TO LISBON in 2 ½ DAYS and MADEIRA in 4 ½ DAYS from ENGLAND, at reduced fares, by the UNION STEAMSHIP COMPANY'S ROYAL MAIL STEAMERS, leaving Southampton every alternate Friday.

Apply to the Union Steamship Company, Limited, Oriental-place, Southampton, and 11, Leadenhall-street, London. Direct communication between Madeira, Teneriffe, Canary Islands, and the Azores.

CASTLE LINE (for the Gold Fields of South Africa).—CAPE COLONY, NATAL, EAST AFRICA, MAURITIUS, and MADAGASCAR. — The CASTLE COMPANY'S ROYAL MAIL STEAMERS load in East India Dock Basin, London, and sail as follows: —

Steamers.	From London.	From Darmouth.
†Garth Castle	Wednesday, Nov. 21	Fri., Nov. 23
*Roslin Castle	Wednesday, Dec. 5	Fri., Dec. 17
†Hawarden Castle	Wednesday, Dec. 19	Fri., Dec. 2

*Viâ Lisbon and Las Palmas for South Africa.
†Viâ Lisbon and Madeira for South and East Africa.

Mauritius, &c.—Next steamer leaves London 26th December.

Return tickets issued to all ports.

Apply to Donald Currie and Co., 3 and 4, Fenchurch-street, E. C.

LISBON in 60 hours, Grand Canary (Las Palmas), Madeira in 4 ½ days. Excellent winter climate. — Regular service from London and Darmouth by the ROYAL MAIL STEAMERS of the CASTLE LINE. Apply to Donald Currie and Co., 4, Fenchurch-street, London, E.C. Note.—Regular communication between Lisbon and Madeira and the Azores, Canary Islands, Teneriffe, &c.

AUSTRALIA, NEW ZEALAND, TASMANIA. — ORIENT LINE FORTNIGHTLY SERVICE.—The following STEAMSHIPS, belonging to the ORIENT and PACIFIC COMPANIES, leave London as under, Plymouth one day later, Naples nine days later, for ALBANY, ADELAIDE, MELBOURNE, and SYDNEY direct, with Her Majesty's mails, taking passengers for all ports in Australasia: —

Oroya	6,184 tons	7,000-h. p.	Nov. 23
Orizaba	6,184 tons	7,000-h. p.	Dec. 7
Liguria	4,688 tons	4,200-h. p.	Dec. 21
Austral	5,588 tons	7,000-h. p.	Jan. 4
Iberia	4,702 tons	4,200-h. p.	Jan. 18
Ormuz	6,116 tons	8,500-h. p.	Feb. 1

The steamers will call at Colombo until further notice.

Loading berth[1], Tilbury Docks.

Cheap single and return tickets.

Managers, F. Green and Co., 13, Fenchurch-avenue; and Anderson, Anderson, and Co., 5, Fenchurch-avenue, London, E. C.

For freight or passage apply to the latter firm[2]; or to the West-end Agents, Grindlay and Co., 55, Parliament-street, S.W.

GIBRALTAR, Naples, Port Said, Suez, and Colombo[3] by ORIENT LINE every fortnight. Through tickets to Cairo and Alexandria, and cheap circular tickets for tours in the Mediterranean. Steamers among the largest and fastest afloat. High-class cuisine; electric lighting; hot and cold baths; good ventilation and every comfort. Apply as above[4].

---

1. *Loading berth*, lieu de chargement. — 2. *To the latter firm*, à cette dernière maison. — 3. *Colombo*, capitale de l'île de Ceylan. — 4. *As above*, comme dans l'annonce ci-dessus.

AUSTRALIA and BACK[1] by ORIENT LINE every fortnight.— First saloon for 100 guineas; second saloon, £65. Apply as above.

AUSTRALIA by OVERLAND ROUTE.—ORIENT LINE.—Passengers leaving London not later than Friday, Nov. 16th, by the 8 p. m. train, conveying the Australian mails, can overtake the s.s.[2] Lusitania at Naples, leaving there on the 19th Nov. for Australia, viâ Suez Canal. For through tickets, including railway fare and fee for voiture de luxe, apply as above.

ABERDEEN LINE.—Passage to Australia.—The favourite clipper ship[3] PATRIARCH, 1,339 tons register, will be despatched from the East India Docks on the 27th November, taking saloon and second-class passengers to SYDNEY, and at through rates[4] to other Australian ports. Carries a surgeon. For particulars apply to Geo. Thompson and Co., 24, Leadenhall-street, E. C.

AUSTRALIA. — The ABERDEEN LINE.

Port.	Vessel.	Tons reg.[5]	Date.
Melbourne	Clynder.. ..	1,117	Nov.23
Sydney	Patriarch ..	1,339	Nov.27
Melbourne and Sydney	Damascus (s.)[6]	3,709	Dec.31

Apply to Geo. Thompson and Co., 24, Leadenhall-street, E. C.

AUSTRALIA, viâ Capé.—The splendid steamship REGIUS, 3,232 tons, 2,500 h.p., to leave about Nov. 20th for ADELAIDE, Melbourne, and Sydney. Saloon passengers only. Large state rooms. A doctor carried. Fare 40 guineas. For plans and all particulars apply to Allport and Hughes, 7.

Leadenhall-street; and John Porter and Co., 15, Great St. Helen's, E. C.

AUSTRALIA.—The well-known favourite passenger steamer HANKOW will be despatched from London, December 1st, for ADELAIDE[7], Melbourne, and Sydney. Passengers booked to all Australian and New Zealand ports. Surgeon and stewardess carried. Piano, ladies' boudoir, smoking room, and every convenience for saloon passengers. Fares from 40 guineas. For full particulars apply to Wm. Milburn and Co., Billiter avenue, London.

AUSTRALIA.—FAST MAIL STEAMERS of the NORDDEUTSCHER LLOYD[8], from Southampton every 28 days, viâ Columbo. Passengers can join the steamer at Genoa nine days later. Cuisine after the model of the very best Continental hotels. Electric lighting and perfect ventilation. Next sailing: — S. s. Hohenzollern, December 2.

Apply to the General Agents, Keller, Wallis and Co., 32, Cockspur-street, Charing-cross; 5., Fenchurch-street, City, and at Southampton; also to Philipps and Graves. Botolph-house, Eastcheap, E. C.

AUSTRALIA and NEW ZEALAND, viâ America. — The UNION STEAMSHIP COMPANY of NEW ZEALAND, Limited, ROYAL MAIL STEAMERS. SAN FRANCISCO to AUCKLAND and SYDNEY, viâ Honolulu[9] monthly. Through passage rates from Europe to all Colonial ports. Next steamer leaves

1. *And back*, et de retour. Ce voyage est aujourd'hui fort recommandé pour la santé par les médecins anglais. — 2. *S. s.*, *steam ship*. — 3. *Clipper ship*, navire à voiles construit pour une marche rapide. — 4. *At through rates*, à tarif entier. — 5. *Tons reg.*, *tons registered*, mesure d'espace pour navire = 100 pieds cubiques anglais = 2.8 m. cubes. — 6. Le *Clynder* et le *Patriarch* sont des navires à voiles; le *Damascus* est un navire à vapeur (*s.* steam). — 7. *Adelaïde*, ville capitale de l'Australie du sud. Cette province est bien la plus agricole de toutes celles de l'Australie. — 8. De la compagnie du Lloyd de l'Allemagne du Nord. *The Lloyd* est une compagnie de navigation qui emprunte son nom au Lloyd's anglais dont nous avons parlé à la note 7, page 36. — 9. Honolulu, port principal des îles Sandwich, environ 10 000 habitants.

San Francisco 15th December. Berths secured and particulars obtained from the office of the Company, 18, Walbrook, E.C., and Thomas Cook and Son, Ludgate-circus, E. C.

AUSTRALIA. — The AUSTRALIAN MUTUAL SHIPPING COMPANY, Limited, will despatch the undermentioned high-class iron VESSELS from the East India Docks : Sydney and

Newcastle	Moel Tryvan	1,639	100A1	Dec. 10
Melbourne	Moel Eilian	1,081	*AA [1]	Dec. 5

For freight or passage apply to the Managers, Wincott, Cooper, and Co., 3, Brabant-court, Philpot-lane, E. C.

AUSTRALIA, &c.—LONDON LINE of STEAM and SAILING SHIPS.

Port.	Vessel.	Loading.	Date.
Fremantle. ..	Elderslie, s.s..	London.	Nov. 15
Fremantle. ..	Bessel.. ..	London.	Dec. 15
Brisbane.. ..	Scottish Chief.	Liverpool.	Nov. 5
Maryborough..	J. C. Warns..	London.	Dec. 5
Adelaide. . ..	Anna	Liverpool.	Nov. 15
Melbourne. ..	Winefred. ..	London.	Sailed.
Sydney.. ..	Edinburgh ..	London.	Nov. 15
Sydney.. ..	Corolla.. ..	Liverpool.	Nov. 20
Rockhampton .	Dunelm.. ..	London.	Dec. 5

C. Bethell and Co., 110, Fenchurch-street, London.

AUSTRALIA, NEW ZEALAND, and TASMANIA. — The P. and O. COMPANY'S STEAMERS, carrying Her Majesty's Mails, leave London for SYDNEY, MELBOURNE, ADELAIDE, and ALBANY direct, every fortnight, starting from London as soon after noon as the tide permits. Loading berth [2] Royal Albert Docks.

Nov. 16	Oceana	Capt. Tomlin	6,362 t.	7,000h.p.
Nov. 29	Carthage	Capt. Stead	5,013 t.	5,000 —
Dec. 13	Rome	Capt. Adamson	5,011 t.	5,000 —
Dec. 28	Arcadia	Capt. Andrews	6,362 t.	7,000 —
Jan. 10	Valetta	Capt. Orman	4,919 t.	5,000 —
Jan. 25	Britannia	Capt. Hector	6,257 t.	7,000 —

First saloon, £60 to £70.
Second saloon, £30 to £37.
Return tickets, £65 to £105.
First and second saloon passengers only carried.

Offices, 122, Leadenhall-street, and 25, Cockspur-street.

STEAM, LONDON to AUSTRALIA, viâ Teneriffe and Cape of Good Hope. — The ABERDEEN LINE, s.s. DAMASCUS, 3,709 tons, will leave the Royal Albert Docks on December 31st for MELBOURNE and SYDNEY, taking passengers for all Australian and New Zealand Ports. The accommodation for first and third classe passengers is very superior, and an experienced surgeon will be carried. Fares from 15 guineas. For freight or passage apply to Geo. Thompson and Co., 24, Leadenhall-street, London, E. C.

STEAM. — First-class Steamers are despatched, viâ Antwerp, Bremen, or Southampton, to the undermentioned ports, and through tickets from London issued at the fares stated.

ADELAIDE and MELBOURNE, £14 14s.; Sydney, £14 14s.; Hobart, £15 5s.; Brisbane, £15 15s.; Colombo, £35 1s.; Singapore, £38 1s.; Hongkong, £43 16s.; Shanghai, £50 1s.; Nagazaki, £54 1s.; Hiogo, £51 11s.; Yokohama, £50 1s.; Baltimore, £6 10 s.; Corunna, £4 15s.; Lisbon, Bahia, Rio de Janeiro, Santos, Montevideo, and Buenos Ayres, £8; New York, from Southampton, £13 10s.

From London direct to Gothenburg, £2 2s.; Bremen, 15s.; Rotterdam, 11s.; with low fares through to the Rhine; Amsterdam, cargo only.

The fares named are the cheapest, but are increased according to accommodation. For further particulars and passage tickets apply to Phillipps and Graves, Botolph-house, 12, Eastcheap, London, E.C.

QUEENSLAND, viâ Torres Straits [3]. — The QUEENSLAND ROYAL

1. **AA1.*, first class certificate renewed by the surveyors of Lloyd's after long navigation of the ship. Voy. note 7, page 36. — 2. Voy. note 1, page 38. — 3. Détroit de Torrès ou d'Endeavour, dans l'Océan équinoxial, entre la Nouvelle-Guinée et l'Australie, parsemé d'îlots et de récifs.

MAIL LINE STEAMERS, carrying the Queensland mails, leave London for BRISBANE, calling at Thursday Island, Cooktown, Townsville, Bowen, Mackay, and Rockhampton.

Steamer.	Tons.	Commander.	Date of Sailing.
Taroba	4,938	A. Morris.	20th Nov.
Merkara	3,079	J. Smith	11th Dec.
Jumna	5,179	W. A. Burkett	Jan. 8
Dacca	3,909	J. Stone	Feb. 5

These steamers are fitted with all the latest improvements, electric lighted throughout, and present a favourable opportunity for saloon passengers proceeding to the Colony. For freight and passage apply to Gray, Dawes, and Co., 13. Austinfriars; or Gellatly, Hankey Sewell, and Co., 109, Leadenhall-street, London.

NEW ZEALAND and AUSTRALIA, viâ Teneriffe, Cape of Good Hope, and Hobart. Shortest tropical passage. — Postal Service, under contract with the Government of New Zealand. — The NEW ZEALAND SHIPPING COMPANY (Limited) will despatch from Albert Docks, London, the following full-powered ROYAL MAIL STEAMERS, conveying all classes of passengers to above ports. Plymouth Departure two days later :—

Nov. 15	Ruapehu	4,163 t.	Port Chalmer and ports.
Dec. 13	Kaikoura	4,474 t.	Lyttelton and ports.
Jan. 10	Tongariro	4,163 t.	Wellington and ports.

Return tickets at reduced rates.

These steamers are supplemented by the frequent despatch of fine clipper sailing ships to the principal ports in the colony. Loading berth, No. 2 jetty, South-West India Dock.

For freight, passage, or further information apply to the Company's Agents. Tyser and Co., 138, Leadenhall-street, London, E. C.; or to the West-end Agents, Guion and Co., 5, Waterloo-place, Pall-mall, S. W.

NEW ZEALAND, TASMANIA, AUSTRALIA, calling at Teneriffe, Cape Town, and at Hobart, to land passengers for Tasmania and Australia (through booking). — SHAW, SAVILL, and ALBION COMPANY, Limited, despatch their magnificent full-powered ROYAL MAIL STEAMERS from London (Royal Albert Dock) to NEW ZEALAND every four weeks. The next departures are :—

Tainui	5,031 tons	Auckland and Wellington	Nov. 29
Doric	4,784 tons	Wellington and Lyttelton	Dec. 27
Arawa	5,026 tons	Otago and Lyttelton	Jan. 24

From Plymouth two days later. By this favourite route the intense heat of the Red Sea is escaped. Reduced fares. Very superior second saloon accommodation at specially low rates. Cheap return tickets. The Company's well-known first-class sailing ships are also despatched at regular intervals from the East India Docks. Apply to P. Henderson and Co., Glasgow; and Shaw, Savill, and Albion Company, Limited, 34, Leadenhall-street, or to their West-end office [1], 51, Pall-mall, London.

MELBOURNE EXHIBITION. — Return fare [2] first saloon, 100 guineas; second saloon, £60 to £65.—Magnificent ROYAL MAIL STEAMERS. Complete tour round the world, visiting Teneriffe, Cape Town, Hobart, Australia, Zealand, and Rio de Janeiro. Favourite route. No Red Sea discomfort. Apply Shaw, Savill, and Albion Company. Limited, 34, Leadenhall-street, E. C.

GUION ROYAL and U. S [3]. MAIL STEAMERS. — LIVERPOOL to NEW YORK, every Saturday. Superior accommodation for all classes, at low rates. ARIZONA, Nov, 17, at 3 p. m. — Guion and Co., 5, Waterloo-place, Pall-mall, London (telephone 3,768); 21, Water-street, 11, Rumford-street, Liverpool.

NEW YORK direct from LONDON.— WILSON HILL LINE STEAMERS Weekly. Saloon amidships, £9. Apply

1. *West-end office*, bureaux dans les districts de l'ouest de Londres, la partie fashionable. — 2. *Return fare*, comme *return ticket*, voyage aller et retour. — 3. *U. S.*, *United States*, c'est-à-dire américains.

Allan Brothers, 103, Leadenhall-street, E.C.

NEW YORK. — Shortest Route from London, passage 7 1/2 days — NORDDEUTSCHER LLOYD EXPRESS MAIL STEAMERS, from Southampton. High-class cuisine and appointments. Electric light. Low winter fares.

Lahn, Nov. 15	Aller, Nov. 22	Ems, Dec. 2
Werra, Nov. 18	Saale, Nov. 29	Trave, Dec. 6

Special train from Waterloo Station every sailing day at 12.25. Apply to the General Agents, Keller, Wallis, and Co., 32, Cockspur-street, Charing-cross, or 5, Fenchurch-street, City; and at Southampton; or to Philipps and Graves, Botolph-house, Eastcheap, E.C.

INMAN[1] LINE. — The INMAN and INTERNATIONAL COMPANY'S ROYAL MAIL STEAMERS, LIVERPOOL to NEW YORK, every Wednesday, viâ Queenstown.

City of Richmond.. Wednesday, Nov. 14
City of Berlin.. .. Wednesday, Nov. 21

Saloon, second cabin, and steerage[2] accommodation of highest class. Apply to Richardson, Spence, and Co., Liverpool; R. H. Graefe, 9, Rue Scribe, Paris: Eives and Allen, 99, Cannon-street, and 76, Leadenhall-street and at Company's office, 13, Pall-mall, London.

WHITE STAR LINE ROYAL MAIL STEAMERS. — LIVERPOOL to NEW YORK, every Wednesday: —

Celtic.. Wed., Nov. 14 | Germanic.. Wed., Nov. 21

The splendid vessels of this line are all of the largest class, uniform in model and arrangements, and unsurpassed in the completeness of their appointments. Saloon and state room amidships. Steerage passage at low rates (including rail ticket from London to Liverpool). Apply to Ismay, Imrie and Co., 34, Leadenhall-street, London, E. C., and 10, Water-street, Liverpool.

CUNARD LINE. — ROYAL MAIL STEAMERS. —. LIVERPOOL to NEW YORK and BOSTON, viâ Queenstown.

Gallia	Nov. 17	Scythia. ..	Nov. 15
Umbria.. ..	Nov. 24	Pavonia. ..	Nov. 22

Saloon fares: — 12, 15, 18, and 21 guineas and £26. Return tickets, 25, 30, and 35 guineas and £45. Intermediate passage, £7 7s. and £8 8s. Return tickets 14 and 15 guineas. Steerage at low rates.

Passengers booked through to China, Japan, Australia, &c.

LIVERPOOL to the MEDITERRANEAN. — First class steamers are despatched about every 10 days, calling at all the principal ports.

For freight or passage apply to the Cunard Steamship Company, Limited — in Liverpool, No. 8, Water-street; or in London, 6, St. Helen's-place, E. C., and No. 28, Pall-mall, S. W.

CANADA. — DOMINION[3] ROYAL MAIL LINE. — LIVERPOOL to HALIFAX and PORTLAND. — VANCOUVER, Nov. 15. Apply to Flinn, Main, and Montgomery, Liverpool and Bristol. For agents' names see Friday's paper.

PACIFIC LINE to BRAZIL, RIVER PLATE[4], and WEST COAST of SOUTH AMERICA, calling at Bordeaux, Corunna, Carril, Vigo and Lisbon. — The PACIFIC STEAM NAVIGATION COMPANY'S STEAMERS are appointed to sail from Liverpool, as under, with Her Majesty's mails: —

Cotopaxi, Wed., Nov. 14, 2 p. m.	Araucania, Wed., Dec. 12, 2 p. m.
Aconcagua, Wed., Nov. 28, 2 p. m.	Sorata, Thurs., Dec. 27, 1 p. m.

1. *Inman*, nom du fondateur de cette ligne. — 2. *Steerage passengers*, voyageurs d'entrepont, voyageurs de 3e classe. — 3. On appelle *Dominion* la réunion des différentes provinces de l'Amérique anglaise, c'est-à-dire le Haut et le Bas Canada, la Nouvelle-Écosse et le Nouveau-Brunswick, formée en 1867. En 1873, le *Dominion* s'est augmentée des autres provinces anglaises, le Manitoba, les Pays de la Baie d'Hudson, la Colombie britannique et l'Ile du Prince Edouard. — 4. *The River Plate*, le Rio de la Plata *ou* Rivière d'argent, donne son nom

Loading berth, Morpeth Dock, Birkenhead. For terms of passage or freight apply at the Company's offices, 31, James-street, Liverpool; in Glasgow, to James Dunn and Sons, 24, St. Vincent-place; and in London, to N. Griffiths, Tate, and Co., 5 and 7, Fenchurch-street. — A. M. SAUNDERSON, Manager and Secretary.

RIVER PLATE DIRECT. — LAMPORT and HOLT LINE. — First-class PASSENGER STEAMERS will be despatched from Southampton to Montevideo and Buenos Ayres direct as under (through tickets issued to Rosario) : —

Pleiades, 16th Nov. | Maskeline, 2nd Dec.

Fares : — Cabin, £35; return, £52 10s.; steerage, £10.

For passage apply to Arthur Holland and Co., 2, East India-avenue, London, E. C.; or to Lamport and Holt, Liverpool.

RIO de JANEIRO and MADEIRA. — LAMPORT and HOLT LINE. — The first-class and fast passenger steamer OLBERS will be despatched from Southampton on the 9th December direct to RIO DE JANEIRO, calling at Madeira.

Fares. — Rio de Janeiro, cabin, £30; steerage, £10. Madeira, cabin, £12; return, £20.

For passage apply to Arthur Holland and Co., 2, East India-avenue, London, E. C.; or Lamport and Holt, Liverpool.

ROYAL MAIL STEAM PACKET COMPANY, under contract for Her Majesty's mails to the West Indies [1], Brazil, and River Plate. From Southampton : —

Stmr.	Tons	To Sail.	Ports.
Para ..	3,805	Nov. 15	West Indies, Jacmel [2], Port-au-Prince, Havana, Mexico, Savanilla, Colon, and Pacific Ports.
Trent ..	2,912	Nov. 22	Carril, Vigo, Lisbon, Pernambuco, Maceio, Bahia, Rio de Janeiro, Santos, Montevideo, and Buenos Ayres (Rosario).
Derw'nt	2,471	Nov. 24	Barbados, St. Lucia, St. Vincent, Grenada, Trinidad, Venezuela, Savanilla, Carthagena, Colon, Limon, Greytown, and Pacific Ports.
Moselle	3,280	Nov. 29	West Indies, Venezuela, Jacmel, Savanilla, Colon, Limon, Greytown, and Pacific Ports.
La Plata	3,210	Dec. 6	Vigo, Lisbon, St. Vincent (Cape Verds), Pernambuco, Bahia, Rio de Janeiro, Montevideo, and Buenos Ayres (Rosario).

Return, tourist, and family tickets issued. Apply at the Company's offices, 18, Moorgate-street, London; Albert-square, Manchester; and Southampton; or Henderson Bros., 8, Regent-street, S. W.

SEA VOYAGES for HEALTH or PLEASURE, from three to twelve months, by the ROYAL MAIL STEAM PACKET COMPANY'S STEAMERS from Southampton. Return tickets to the West Indies for £40; to Brazil, £45; and to the River Plate, £52 10s.

Apply at the Company's offices, 18, Moorgate-street, London; or to Henderson Brothers, 8, Regent-street, S. W. Cuba, Mexico, Venezuela, Spanish Main, and Isthmus of Panama comprised in Itineraries.

LISBON. — Winter Residence in Portugal. — The magnificent STEAMERS of the ROYAL MAIL STEAM PACKET COMPANY leave Southampton every alternate Thursday. Return tickets issued. For particulars apply to J. M. Lloyd, 18, Moorgate-street, London, E. C.

WEST INDIES, MEXICO and PACIFIC PORTS. — The WEST

à la *République argentine*, cap. Buénos-Ayres, dans l'Amérique du Sud. — 1. *The West Indies*, les Indes Occidentales, c'est-à-dire les Antilles. — 2. Jacmel, port sur la côte sud de l'île d'Haïti.

INDIA and PACIFIC COMPANY'S ROYAL MAIL STEAMERS sail regularly from LIVERPOOL to VENEZUELA, Colombia, Mexico, the West India Islands, and Colon, taking cargo and passengers for all ports on the Pacific coast.

For freight, passages, and all information apply at the Company's Agency in London, St. George's-house, Eastcheap; or in Liverpool, at the Head office, The Temple, Dale-street.

STEAM to ITALY. — Regular Line of Screw Steamers, loading in the Wapping Basin, London Dock. — The splendid fast steamships of this line are despatched punctually for GENOA, Leghorn, Naples, Messina, and Palermo. Next departure s.s. ADRIA, 844 tons register, 200-h.p. To clear[1] Friday, 16th November. For freight apply to M'Cracken, Fenwick, and Co., 38, Fenchurch-street, London.

LONDON to LISBON, MADRID (by rail, viâ Lisbon), GIBRALTAR, MALAGA, and CADIZ. — The undermentioned STEAMERS will be despatched from the London Docks : —

Malaga ..	100A1	1,614	J. Russell	Nov. 15
Cadiz ..	100A1	1,400	T. Drummond	Nov. 22
Gibraltar.	100A1	1,412	J. C. Harvey	Nov. 29

Through passenger tickets issued from London to Madrid. For freight or passage apply to the owners, John Hall, jun., and Co., 1, New London-street, E. C.; or to the West-end Agents, G. W. Wheatley and Co., 23, Regent-street, S. W.

WILSON LINE of ROYAL MAIL PASSENGER STEAMERS for NORWAY and SWEDEN, with saloons and sleeping accommodation amidships, sail from HULL every Tuesday to Stavanger and Bergen, every Friday to Christiansand and Christiania; Thursday, 22d Nov., and fortnightly to Drontheim; every Wednesday and Saturday morning to Gothenburg. From LONDON, every Thursday to Christiania; alternate Thurdays to Christiansand. For programmes, with full particulars, apply to Thos. Wilson, Sons, and Co., Hull; Gellatly, Hankey, Sewell, and Co., 51, Pall-mall, S. W.; Guion and Co., 5, Waterloo-place, S. W.; and W. E. Bott and Co., 1, East India-avenue, London, E. C.

SPECIAL WINTER FARES, of the General Steam Navigation Company.

BORDEAUX from London. First class, £2; fore cabin[2], £1 10s. Return :.— First class, £3; fore cabin, £2 5s.

BIARRITZ (viâ Bordeaux) from London. First class throughout, £3 0s. 7d.; second class, £2 5s. 6d.

ARCACHON (viâ Bordeaux) from London. First class throughout, £2 3s. 10d.; second class, £1 12s. 11d.

PAU (viâ Bordeaux) from London. First class throughout, £3 3s.; second class, £2 7s. 3d.

CANNES (viâ Bordeaux) from London. First class throughout, £6 2s. 3d.; second class, £4 11s. 8d.

NICE (viâ Bordeaux) from London. First class throughout, £6 5s. 4d.; second class, £4 14s.

MARSEILLES (viâ Bordeaux) from London. First class throughout, £5 3s. 1d.; second class, £3 17s. 4d.

MADRID (viâ Bordeaux) from London. First class throughout, £6 1s. 6d.; second class, £4 11s. 1d.

BARCELONA (viâ Bordeaux) from London. First class throughout, £5 8s. 1d.; second class, £4 1s. 2d. Return : — First class, £7 7s.; second class, £4 11s. 6d.

---

1. *To clear Friday*, doit prendre vendredi (à la douane) son certificat de départ. — 2. *Fore cabin*, cabine à l'avant, c'est-à-dire 2e classe.

HAMBURG (viâ Thames). First class, £1; second class, 15s. Return :— First class, £1 11s. 6d.; second class, £1.

HAMBURG (viâ Harwich). First class, £1 7s. 6d.; second class, £1. Return :— First class, £2; second class, £1 10s.

BERLIN (viâ Thames and Hamburg) from London. First class throughout, £2 8s.; second class, £1 15s. 11d.

Express, viâ Liverpool-street Station and Harwich, first class throughout, £2 15s. 6d.; second class, £2 0s. 11d.

HANOVER (viâ Thames and Hamburg) from London. First class throughout, £1 17s. 9d.; second class, £1 8s. 3d.

Express, viâ Liverpool-street Station and Harwich, first class throughout, £2 5s. 3d.; second class, £1 13s. 3d.

COPENHAGEN (viâ Hamburg) from London (Express, viâ Liverpool-street Station and Harwich). First class throughout, £2 18s. 3d.; second class, £2 6s. 2d. Return :— First class, £4 6s. 3d.; second class, £3 9s. 4d.

OSTEND. First class, 7s. 6d.; second class, 5s. Return :— First class, 12s. 6d.; second class, 7s. 6d.

BRUSSELS (viâ Ostend) from London. First class throughout, 15s. 2d.; second class, 10s. 9d.

COLOGNE (viâ Ostend) from London. First class throughout, £2 2s. 3d.; second class, £1 11s. Return :— First class, £3 7s.; second class, £2 9s. 6d.

FOR further particulars of the above apply to the General Steam Navigation Company, 55, Great Tower-street, or No. 14, Waterloo-place, London.

MADEIRA, CANARY ISLANDS, and the AZORES. — For particulars as to SAILINGS and FARES, Single and Return, apply for circular to THOS. COOK and SON, Ludgate-circus; 35, Piccadilly; 99, Gracechurch-street, &c.

ALGIERS, Cannes, Nice, Mentone, Rome, and all parts of the world.— For CONVEYANCE of LUGGAGE, Merchandise, &c., by quickest and cheapest routes, apply to DAVIES, TURNER, and Co. (estd. 1870), 52, Lime-street, and 113a, Regent-street.

INDIA, Australia, New Zealand, Canada, &c. — PASSAGES ENGAGED, Baggage Received and Shipped, Goods Forwarded, Insurance effected. Price lists of deck chairs[1], P. and O.[2] and other companies' regulation trunks, and all necessaries for voyage and residence abroad. Apply to S. W. SILVER and Co., Sun-court, 67, Cornhill, London, E.C.

TASMANIA, Australia, New Zealand, India, China, Japan, West Indies, and South African Colonies. — STEAMERS for all above ports at regular intervals. Goods shipped and insured.

Passages engaged. For rates[3] and dates apply to STALEY, RADFORD, and Co., 2, Fenchurch-avenue, Lime-street, E. C.

SALOON PASSENGERS to AUSTRALIA and NEW ZEALAND, America, Canada, Cape, Brazil, India, will receive every information, cabin plans, tickets, on application to ALFRED JAKINS and Co., Licensed Passage Brokers, 96, Leadenhall-street, E. C., and 6, Camden-road, N. W. Wire Jakins, London.

HORSES, CARRIAGES, &c.

HORSES. — Rugby Horse Fair. — Jas. Pearl, 44, Worship-street,

1. *Deck chairs*, sièges sur le pont. — 2. *P. and O.*, Peninsular and Oriental. — 3. *For rates and dates*, pour les tarifs et les dates des départs.

Finsbury-square, E. C., begs to inform the public that his HORSES from the above Fair will be on SHOW[1] Wednesday, Nov. 14, and following days.— N. B. — Well-selected seasoned[2] stepping horses for riding and driving always on show to be let for any period.

HORSES. — J. MILLER, 67, Seymour-place, Bryanston-square, W., begs to inform the nobility and gentry he has several PAIRS of CARRIAGE and BROUGHAM HORSES; also some Single-harness Horses, with superior action[3] fit for immediate use, to be LET, on Hire, for any period.

HORSES, with unrivalled high action[4]. — Messrs. M. and W. MILTON, of 6, Park-lane, Piccadilly, Dealers in high-class, high-stepping[5] English and Irish HORSES only, beg to inform the nobility and gentry that they have several Pairs. Also Single Horses and Cobs[6]. Prices moderate. Horses let on job[7].

JOB HORSES. — Messrs. M. and W. MILTON, 6, Park-lane, Piccadilly, W., SUPPLY superior, high-stepping[8] Pairs and Single Horses of quality, by the month or year. Terms moderate.

A Sixteen-stone[9] high-class IRISH HUNTER for SALE-Chestnut Gelding[10], rising six years, 16 hands[11]; a magnificent and highly-bred horse, of great quality, with the most perfect manners and temper, a clever fencer and excellent hack[12], and can go in any country, quiet in harness, sound. Subject to veterinary examination and a reasonable trial previous to purchase. Apply to Henry Down, Esq., Woodfield, Woburn Sands, Beds[13].

BAY MARE, 15.3, quiet to ride and drive, and has been hunted[14]. Been in constant use for over 10 months. Price 30 guineas. Apply to Coachman, 22. Drayson-mews, Hornton-street, High-street, Kensington.

FOR SALE, a strong, useful BAY COB[15], six years, 14.2, quiet to ride and drive; also a Four-wheel Dogcart[16] to suit same, and set of harness, both new. — W. Statham, The Redings, Totteridge, N.

GELDING, Shamrock[17], for SALE, at a moderate figure; he is a Dappled Bay, black points, 16 hands, has great quality and strength combined, is one of the grandest goers in England, of a kind and good temper, no vice or blemish, quiet in any kind of harness and a good riding horse, capable of drawing a brougham or landau in a hilly country; his manners are perfect; the owner will warrant him in every way; his age is 7 last May, Trial had. Apply No. 103, Stanhope-street, Regent's-park (near Gower-street Station).

THOROUGH-BRED BAY MARE, Mermaid[18], eight years, 15[19]. Late property Lt. S. H. Pollen at Sandhurst. Perfect manners quiet to ride and drive, fine action, and fast. Owner gone to

---

1. *On show*, à voir. — 2. *Seasoned*, habitués, bien dressés. — 3. *With superior action*, belles actions. — 4. *High action*, hautes actions. — 5. *High-class, high-stepping horses*, des chevaux *steppers* de première classe. — 6. *Cob*, bidet, cheval de selle fort et à jambes courtes..— 7. *Let on job*, de louage. — 8. *High-stepping*, qui lèvent haut les pieds et ont un pas allongé. — 9. *Sixteen-stone*, 101 kil. 6. *The stone* vaut 6 kilog. 35, c'est un poids qui sert à évaluer ce que pèse un cavalier. Le cheval ci-dessus peut porter 16 stones. — 10. *Gelding*, cheval hongre. — 11. *Rising* 16 *hands*, de la taile de 1 m. 62. The *hand*, mesure réservée à indiquer la taille des chevaux, égale 0 m. 102. — 12. *Hack*, cheval de route (du français *haquenée*). — 13. *Beds*, for Bedfordshire, comté de Bedford. — 14. *Has been hunted*, a été monté comme cheval de chasse. — 15. Voyez note 6 ci-dessus. — 16. *Dogcart*, petite voiture à deux ou à quatre roues, avec deux sièges dos à dos et un caisson destiné à porter des chiens; se dit en français *docart* ou *dog-cart*, prononcez doc-art. — 17. *Shamrock*, trèfle, nom du cheval. Le *Shamrock* est l'emblème national de l'Irlande. — 18. *Mermaid*, sirène, nom de la jument. — 19. 15 *hands*. Voy. note 11 ci-dessus.

India. Take £50. Write Pollen, May's Advertising offices, No. 162, Piccadilly.

TO REAL JUDGES of HORSES and DEALERS. — Lady (going abroad) requires immediate purchaser for exceedingly handsome CHESTNUT COB (gelding), six years, 14.3. Perfectly sound, fast, grand action, very free, but perfect mouth and manners. Only £55. — 3, Osborne-mews, Windsor.

ALDRIDGE'S[1], London (Established 1753). — SALES by AUCTION of HORSES and CARRIAGES, every Wednesday and Saturday, at 10.30 o'clock precisely. — The SALE THIS DAY (Wednesday), Nov. 14, will include upwards of 225 Brougham and Phaeton Horses from Messrs. Wolfe and Son, Messrs. Ward and Sons, and other jobmasters, with hacks and harness horses, cobs, ponies and cart horses, from noblemen, gentlemen and the trade; also new and second-hand Carriages, harness, etc. Sales and valuations in town or country. No dealing allowed on the part of any one connected with establishment. —W. and S. FREEMAN, Proprietors.

HOBBS'S COMMISSION STABLES, Canterbury-terrace, Elgin-avenue, Maida-vale, W. (established 1870.)— For the SALE of medium-priced HORSES and COBS. — Each horse is sold with a guarantee subject to seven days' trial. Every facility is offered for trial previous to purchase. Hunters can be tried in the paddocks over fences. The following, with several others, are now on view :

Match pair[2], short-legged, compact made, Bay Geldings 15 hands 2, 7 and 8 years old, ride and drive, fast; one a good hunter. 80 guineas.

Match pair, short-legged, compact made Bay Geldings, 5 and 6 years old, both good hunters. 90 guineas. Up to great weight.

Black-brown Mare, well bred, 15 hands, 3, 6 years old, good hack and huntress, carries a lady. At first reasonable offer.

Remarkably handsome Chestnut Cob Gelding, 6 years old, 15 hands, ride and drive up to 18 stone[3] fast, safe walker, invaluable for elderly gentleman. 50 guineas.

Handsome Bay Hack, 6 years old, 15 hands 1, perfect in all paces, and carries a lady, and good hunter. 30 guineas.

Handsome Black-brown Cob Gelding, 6 years old, 14 hands, ride and drive, fast, with action. 30 guineas.

Handsome Chestnut Cob Mare, 6 years old, 14 hands, perfect hack, up to 14 stone. 25 guineas.

THURSDAYS' SALES at TATTERSALL'S[4]. Albert-gate. — Messrs. TATTERSALL beg to give notice that they will hold EXTRA SALES on the Thursdays in November.

TANDEM TEAM and HARNESS. — To be SOLD, by AUCTION, by Messrs. TATTERSALL, near Albert-gate, Hyde-park, on Thursday next, TWO GREY MARES — one has been regularly driven as leader, and is very fast; the other is an iron grey, well bred; driven as wheeler, and been regularly hunted this season : carrying 14 stone, and is very fast. They will stand in the 18-stall stable.

HORSES. — WILLIAM SEWELL, Veterinary Surgeon, F.R.C.V.S.[5], respectfully offers his services and experience to assist gentlemen in search of horses, and examine as to soundness and general qualifications. Tattersall's and other sales attended. — 53 Elizabeth-street, Eaton-square, London, S. W.

---

1. *Aldridge's stables and coach houses.* — 2. *Match pair*, paire de chevaux pareils. — 3. Voy. note 9, page 46. — 4. *Tattersall's*, grand établissement pour l'achat et la vente des chevaux. Il y a aujourd'hui, à Paris, un établissement du même nom. — 5. *F. R. C. V. S.*, Fellow of the Royal College of Veterinary surgeons.

ALDERNEY[1], Jersey, and Guernsey COWS.—P. H. FOWLER, Importer, Watford. Herts[2] (two minutes' walk from the station), has always on SALE a large herd of newly-calved COWS and HEIFERS; also Pedigree Young Bulls[3]. P.H.F. delivers free by rail to all parts. Descriptions forwarded.

MORGAN and Co., Limited. — BROUGHAMS of every size and description new and second-hand, the largest selection in London. — Long-acre[4] and Old Bond-street.

THE MINIATURE PATENT LANDAU, built specially to suit one horse or pair of cobs for a hilly country.

THE MINIATURE PATENT LANDAU, to be obtained only at the Company's Manufactory and Show Rooms, 100, 101, 102, 103, 104, 128, 129, 15, 15a, 116, Long-acre; and 10, Old Bond-street.

TO be SOLD, by order of Executors, an elegant PATENT LANDAU, Special Brougham, Victoria, Mail Phaeton, Brougham, patent Cee-spring[5] Sandringham[6] Cabriolet, Polo Cart[7], Waggonettes, and double and single Harness. Apply at the Builders, MORGAN and Co., Limited, 100, 101, 102, 103, 104, 115, 115a, 116, 128, and 129, Long-acre.

NO. 10, OLD BOND-STREET, W.

MORGAN and Co., Limited, Sole Patentees and Manufacturers of CEE-SPRING CARRIAGES without perch.

MORGAN and Co., Limited, 10, Old Bond-street, W., are instructed to SELL a PATENT CEE-SPRING LANDAU. Princess Victoria, and Single Brougham[8], the property of Lord W. The carriages have never been used, and are offered at a liberal reduction.

VICTORIA CARRIAGE WORKS[9]. Three Years' System. — 25, Long-acre, W.C.

THE THREE YEARS' SYSTEM[10]. — CARRIAGES of every description SOLD on this system for an extra charge of 5 per cent., at the Victoria Carriage Works, 25, Long-acre, W. C. Builders to the Royal Family.

HEADED WAGGONETTES[11], the lightest carriages of the kind built. — TWO of these SPECIALITIES for hilly country work have been sent in for SALE, and are now on view at the builders. Prices exceedingly low to an immediate purchaser. The owners can be referred to. — Victoria Carriage Works, 24 and 25, Long-acre, W. C.

BROUGHAM, very compact and light, and exceptionnally well finished in every detail. This natty little carriage is scarcely soiled, and the owner is disposing of it at an enormous sacrifice. A bargain seldom seen. —Victoria Carriage Works, 24 et 25, Long-acre, W.C.

1. *Alderney*, île d'Aurigny. — 2. *Herts.* pour *Hertforshire*, comté de Hertford. Prononcez Hœr'fend. — 3. *Pedigree young bulls*, de jeunes taureaux dont la généalogie est connue. — 4. *Long-acre*, rue de Londres. — 5. *Cee-spring*, avec des ressorts. — 6. *Sandringham*, résidence du prince de Galles. — 7. *Polo cart*, voiture pour le polo, ressemblant à une voiture de maître, malgré son nom de *cart*, charrette. Le *polo* est un jeu de balle (jeu de paume) qui se joue à cheval avec des raquettes, et le cheval sur lequel on le joue est attelé en tandem à la voiture. — 8. *Brougham*, coupé, ainsi appelé d'après lord Brougham, grand chancelier d'Angleterre, mort en 1858, jurisconsulte, littérateur et homme de science, auteur de *Vies d'écrivains et de savants* et d'ouvrages scientifiques, en outre de ses travaux sur la constitution et les lois de l'Angleterre. *Single Brougham*, coupé construit d'une manière spéciale pour une seule personne. — 9. *Works*, ateliers. — 10. *Three years' system*, payable par termes en trois ans. — 11. *Headed waggonnette*, waggonnette couverte. C'est une voiture ou-

CARRIAGE BAZAAR, Baker-street and King-street, Portman-square, W.

UPWARDS of 800 New and Second-hand CARRIAGES, of all inscriptions, on SALE, by Commission, at the Carriage Bazaar, Baker-street, W. — E. T. DAVIS, Manager. Also new and second-hand Harness and Saddlery of all descriptions.

NEW and SECOND-HAND CARRIAGES and HARNESS are also SOLD by Public AUCTION[1] on every other Tuesday throughout the year, at the Carriage Bazaar, Baker-street, W. The next Sale, Tuesday, November 20, at 12 o'clock.

GENTLEMEN having CARRIAGES or HARNESS to DISPOSE OF will find the Baker-street Carriage Bazaar an excellent market. Carriages also warehoused. Prospectus post free. — E. T. DAVIS, Manager.

THE next PERIODICAL SALE of CARRIAGES by AUCTION, at the Baker-street Carriage Bazaar, will take place on Tuesday, November 20th, at 12 o'clock. Carriages for this sale should be sent in on or before the previous Thursday to insure insertion in the catalogue.—E. T. DAVIS, Manager.

BURLINGTON CARRIAGE COMPANY. Established 1840. 315-317, Oxford-street, W. A specific[2] three years' guarantee with every carriage. Cash, or payments to suit purchaser.

SIXTY GUINEAS. — VICTORIA, by noted builder, in perfect, sound condition. For cash or deferred payment system[3]. At Burlington Carriage Company, 315-317, Oxford-street, W.

REMOVABLE HEADED WAGGONETTE, convertible into Stanhope[4] (three complete carriages in one), india-rubber bearings[5], brake[6] and every requirement. Suitable for hilly district. Special bargain.—Burlington Carriage Company, 315-317, Oxford-street, W.

TO COUNTY GENTLEMEN. — SMALL, compact FAMILY OMNIBUS, exceptionnally light and easy draught; built for hilly country work; fitted with brake, single and pair fittings[7], removable roof, seats and every requisite; offered at a very tempting price, as owner must make a speedy sale; builders would arrange for deferred payments.— Burlington Carriage Company, 315-317, Oxford-street, W.

ONE-HORSE COUNTRY LANDAU, 110 guineas, built a short time since for over 200 guineas. Has every requisite, patent break, patent head, close couplings[8], wings, &c., also fittings for pair. Condition equal to new. Most exceptional bargain.—At Builders', who give guarantee, Burlington Carriage Company, 315-317, Oxford-street, W.

NOTE. — SPECIAL STATION BROUGHAM[9]. This newly-introduced Brougham eclipses all others in style, completeness, finish, and lightness with strength, fitted with patent lever break, removable luggage rail, hickory wheels[10], &c. Price 90 guineas, or 33 guineas per annum on three years' system. An inspection in-

verte à 4 roues, avec les sièges placés de côté comme un omnibus et pouvant contenir depuis 4 jusqu'à 8 ou 10 personnes selon sa grandeur. — 1. *By public auction*, en vente publique, à l'encan. — 2. *Specific*, explicatif. — 3. *Deferred payment system*, payement à termes réguliers, à tempérament. — 4. *Stanhope*, voiture découverte à deux roues. — 5. *Bearings*, coussinets. — 6. *Brake*, appareil d'enrayure, s'écrit aussi *break*, comme plus loin. — 7. *Single and pair fittings*, ajustements pour un ou deux chevaux. — 8. *Close couplings*, raccords bien faits. — 9. *Station Brougham*, coupé muni au-dessous d'un appareil pour les bagages. — 10. *Hickory wheels*, roues en bois de noyer (d'Amérique).

vited at the builders', Burlington Carriage Company, 315-317, Oxford-street, W.

W. and F. THORN'S BROUGHAMS.

BROUGHAMS, BROUGHAMS.

W. and F. THORN'S SPECIALITY.

BROUGHAMS of EVERY DESCRIPTION.

W. and F. THORN'S SPECIALITY.

MESSRS. W. and F. THORN beg to inform the public that BROUGHAMS are their special study. They keep three sizes of every description ready to finish to choice[1] in three weeks, and over 50 new and second-hand ones finished and ready for delivery. Weights from 7 1/2 cwt.[2], and prices from £60.—W. and F. Thorn, 19, Great Portland-street, W., and Ranelagh-house, Lower Grosvenor-place, S. W. Three years' system, for sale, or hire with option to purchase if required.

JOB HORSES. — Messrs. W. and F. THORN have made arrangements to SUPPLY COACHMEN, Horses, Harness, Stabling, Fodder, and every accessory, and are prepared to build or finish to choice any description of carriage, for an inclusive charge[3], for the London season, month, or year. Particulars on application, No 19, Great Portland-street, Oxford-circus, W. This is by far the best and cheapest way to keep an establishment.

W. and F. THORN have FOUR STATION BROUGHAMS finished and ready for delivery. Send for drawings and particulars, as built by them for H. R. H. the Prince of Wales. 90 guineas cash.

W. and F. THORN have a nearly new PRIVATE OMNIBUS, with roof seat and luggage rails[4] and brake, for SALE. Great bargain. — Ranelagh-house, Lower Grosvenor-place, S. W. Two new ones building.

MESSRS. W. and F. THORN have for SALE, at reduced prices for cash, LIGHT ONE-HORSE LANDAU, several excellent pair-horse landaus[5], circular fronted brougham, fitted with brake, basket, pole, and shafts, square-fronted double brougham, single-seated brougham, stanhope waggonette, all in excellent order, On view at 19, Great Portland-street, Oxford-circus, W.

W. and F. THORN'S BROUGHAMS.

BARGAINS in CARRIAGES.— SECOND-HAND VICTORIAS. Two Miniature Landaus (for one horse). Four Miniature Single Broughams. Two Miniature Double Broughams. No reasonable offer refused. At the Makers, ROGERS', 365, Oxford-street.

LAURIE and MARNER solicit an inspection of their stock of new and second-hand CARRIAGES, all of the best finish, and with the latest improvements. Any can be hired with option of purchase.—Manufactory, 311, Oxford-street, London.

PRIVATE HANSOM[6] for SALE. — India-rubber tyres[7]. Very light and

1. *To choice*, sur devis de l'acheteur. — 2. 7 1/2 *cwt.* (*hundredweight*). Le *cwt.* ou quintal vaut environ 50 kilos. Voy. *Gramm. Elwall*, p. 201. — 3. *An inclusive charge*, un prix sans extras. — 4. *With luggage rails*, à galerie pour bagages. — 5. *Pair-horse landau*, à deux chevaux. — 6. *Hansom* ou *Hansom cab*, cabriolet à deux grandes roues pour deux personnes assises très bas ; le cocher est assis par derrière tout en haut. Il communique avec les voyageurs par une petite trappe en haut. Ce sont les côtes si nombreuses à Paris qui ont jusqu'ici empêché ce genre de voiture de réussir dans cette ville. — 7. *India-rubber tyres* (ou mieux *tires*), bandes (de roue) en caoutchouc.

elegant; also Harness. Price £38. Apply to Medicus, care of Whippy and Co., 35 and 36, North Audley-street, W.

PORTMAN CARRIAGE WORKS. — The Premises Sold.—STOCK, to effect clearance, 50 per cent. under cost price, consisting of broughams, landaus, new and second-hand Victorias, and every description of carriages. — 13, Orchard-street, W.

BRAINSBY and SONS have for SALE a handsome private OMNIBUS, fitted with all the latest improvements, brake, pole and bar[1], roof seat, sliding windows, and mirror. A bargain seldom to be met with.—48 and 49, Long-acre, W.C.

WINTER SEASON.—THRUPP and MABERLY, 425, Oxford-street, have a beautiful MINIATURE BROUGHAM for SALE, painted and lined quiet and tasty colours. It is nearly new and is hung on long easy springs. It can be used with one horse or a pair. Price only 95 guineas, or be hired for winter with option to buy.

HART'S NIKEMA[2]—a Cee and under-spring[3] Carriage, without a perch. Acknowledged the greatest invention of the age. Hundreds of testimonials testifying its supremacy. An invaluable luxury for those requiring ease in riding.

HART.—The PATENT THAUMA[4] WAGGONETTE, the wonder of the age, fitted with dividing sliding seats and patent folding step, obviating the necessity of mounting the wheels[5]. Only to be obtained of the Patentees.—79, New Bond-street.

HART.—A Light MINIATURE LANDAU for one horse, equal to new, having been used once only. 90 guineas; cost building 165. For further particulars apply at Builder's, 79, New Bond-street. Carriages to be let, with option of purchase.

NOTICE.—High-class CARRIAGES. —Upwards of 250 new and second-hand to be SOLD at reasonable offers, comprising broughams, light landaus, Victorias, waggonettes, Stanhope, and spider[6], other phaetons, drags[7], breaks, one and pair horse omnibuses, buggies, gigs. Established 1820. Patronized by Royalty.— H. G. Dunstan, 193, 195, 197, et 199, Marylebone-road, W.

HARNESS (PAIR)[8], full-size, London made, hand-stitched, plated mounts, equal to new (property of a lady), will be SOLD unusually cheap.—F., Phipps and Co.'s, 104, High Holborn.

GOFF'S Three-guinea GENT.'S SADDLE[9], warranted real pigskin, only 25s.; Weymouth, Pelham, and snaffle Bridles[10], complete, 3s. 3d., 4s. 6d., 5s. 9d.; Harness, pony[11], £2 15s.; cob, £3 15s.; full-size, £4 10s.—S. Goff, 17, King-street, Covent-garden; also 32, Brompton-road. Catalogues gratis.

GOFF'S MUNSTER HORSE RUG (registered) is made by patent machinery to shape of horse; very warm, durable, and smart looking. Price, bound and strapped, 12s. 6d., Testimonials 1,000 stables. Manufactured solely by S. Goff and Co., 17, King-street, Covent-garden.

1. *Pole and bar*, timon et barre. — 2. *Nikema*, mot grec, victoire gagnée, de νίκη, victoire. — 3. *Cee and under-spring*, à ressort c et ressorts en-dessous. On appelle ressort c ou en c les ressorts des voitures à 8 ressorts, dont 4 sont en c et 4 à pincette. — 4. *Thauma*, la merveille, du mot grec θαῦμα. — 5. *Of mounting the wheels*, de mettre le pied sur les roues pour monter. — 6. *Spider phaeton*, voiture ouverte à quatre roues, très haute et d'une construction élégante, ainsi appelée à cause de sa légèreté (*spider*, araignée). — 7. *Drag*, voiture basse à deux roues. — 8. *Harness (Pair)*, harnais pour attelage de deux chevaux. — 9. *Gent's saddle*, selle pour cavalier (*gent's*, *gentleman's*). — 10. *Snaffle bridle*, bridon. — 11. *Harness, pony, cob*, harnais pour poney, pour bidet.

TWO-STALL[1] STABLE and COACH-HOUSE, with man's rooms over, to be LET. Rent £36 per annum. Apply No. 5, Courtfield-mews, Courtfield-gardens, South Kensington, S. W.

DEVONSHIRE-MEWS[2], Portland-place. — STABLING to be LET, comprising two stalls, loose box, harness room, coach-house, and dwelling rooms, &c. Apply to Mr. Robert Reid, No. 51, Great Marlborough-street, W.

EDUCATIONAL.

EDUCATION in DRESDEN. — The Fräulein[3] Hopp RECEIVE a limited number of YOUNG LADIES, and offer the highest educational advantages, together with the comforts of an English home. Highest references. Apply Moor-park, Ludlow.

EDUCATION.—35, Emperor's-gate, South Kensington.—Refined and attractive educational home life for YOUNG LADIES. Religious and moral training and mental culture. Royal Academy examinations. Special attention to music, languages, literature, and painting. Address principal.

EDUCATION. — WANTED, to PLACE a YOUNG LADY in a good SCHOOL, where her services in superintendence of household would be some equivalent for her maintenance and improvement of education. Age 27. Thoroughly domesticated. Apply, stating terms, which must be moderate, T. E., 11, Rutland-street, Hampstead-road, N. W.

EDUCATION.—ONGAR.GRAMMAR SCHOOL[4], 20 miles from London. Special training for mercantile pursuits. A Preparatory Class for Little Boys. 20 acres[5] of ground. Gravel soil. 200 feet above sea level. Pure milk from own dairy farm. Diet unlimited. Grand tepid swimming bath. Cricket, tennis[6], fishing. Terms 30 guineas inclusive; reduction for brothers. Principal, Dr. CLARK. Places may be secured for next term, commencing Jan. 16.

EDUCATION. — TAPLOW GRAMMAR SCHOOL, 20 miles from London. 30 guineas. No extras. No charge for laundress or books. Extensive premises, well adapted and healthfully situate; 30 acres of ground for out-door recreation; tepid swimming bath, &c. Detached infirmary. Pure milk and vegetables from school farm. Preparatory department. Principal has been a successful tutor many years. No corporal punishment. No quarter's notice. Best diet, without limit. Address to the principal.

EDUCATION. — Choice of Schools, Tutors, and Families (gratis) in England, France, Germany, Belgium, &c. Prospectuses and full particulars sent (without charge) to parents by Griffiths, Smith, and Powell, Educational Agents (established 1833), No. 34, Bedford-street, Strand. Articled Pupils Wanted, £20 to £30.

EDUCATION. — Madame AUBERT RECOMMENDS English and Foreign SCHOOLS and EDUCATIONAL HOMES, Governesses, Class Teachers, Repetitrices, Music and Art Teachers. Matrons introduced. Schools transferred.—166, Regent-street, W.

1. *Two stall*, à deux stalles, c'est-à-dire pour deux chevaux. — 2. *Mews*, écuries. A Londres, dans les grands quartiers, *the mews* sont bâties dans de petites rues derrière les hôtels. — 3. *The Fräulein*, les demoiselles. — 4. *Grammar school*, équivaut à nos collèges, quelquefois à nos lycées. — 5. *Acre*, mesure de surface, = 40 ares 47, un peu plus que l'ancien arpent. — 6. *Cricket, tennis*, jeux ordinaires dans les écoles anglaises et qu'on s'efforce d'introduire aujourd'hui dans nos lycées. On en trouvera la description et les règles plus loin dans le volume.

A WIDOW LADY wishes to take entire CHARGE of two LITTLE GIRLS (sisters), to educate with her own daughters. Good schools and every advantage offered. Good references given and required. Address Mrs. D., Parkhouse's Library, Tiverton, Devon.

ONE or more PUPILS RECEIVED into a good German family where purest German is spoken. Highest references given and required. Address Borncucann, Bad Kreuznach, Prussia.

PROFESSOR of FRENCH, with 12 years' residence in England, RECEIVES ENGLISH PUPILS in Paris, and prepares them in foreign languages for all examinations. For particulars apply to Messrs. Mertens and Co., 3, Cross-lane, London, E.C.

RIVIERA.—A married English gentleman, residing on the Western Riviera, will undertake the EDUCATION of three or four backward or delicate BOYS. Comfortable home, moderate terms, references. Address R. H. San Remo.

REQUIRED, TUITION, Board, and Lodging, for a gentleman's son, 17 years old, where a first-rate technical training, with a view to a future career in applied science may be secured, also modern languages, and also sufficient supervision of personal habits, manners, &c. The preference will be given to a place having a few other boys similar to above. Address P. W. E., care of Jones Yarrell and Co., 8, Bury-street, St. Jame's, S. W.

CLERKS—CIVIL SERVICE[1], £80 to £400. Age 14-30. Ladies under 20. Private and Postal CLASSES for coming exams.[2], all grades. Largest staff[3] and best results extant. 750 passes, 30 firsts. Write or call. Practical Guide Free. — Mr. Skerry, 21, Chancery-lane, London.

COLONEL PALMER, late Royal Artillery, is forming a SMALL CLASS of OFFICERS for the MILITIA COMPETITIVE EXAMINATIONS in 1889. During the present year, 1888, out of three sent up, Lieutenants H. S. Carey and E. Mansel were successful. — 4, Perham-road, West Kensington, S. W.

ARMY. — Tutors in England and on the Continent. — Messrs. Askin, Gabbitas, and Killik file prospectuses of successful TUTORS, and are prepared to forward (gratis) particulars of the same to those seeking information with regard to this special branch of tuition. Address, 38, Sackville-street, Piccadilly, W.

MR. H. ROCHE begs to announce that his FRENCH CLASSES for YOUNG LADIES have just RECOMMENCED at 23, Somerset-street, Portman-square, W., and at No. 29, Brompton-square, S. W.

SHORTHAND[4] (PITMAN'S). — METROPOLITAN SCHOOL, 27, Chancery-lane.—Soc. of Arts and Pitman's Certificates. Half for the United Kingdom were ours. Business men taught any time they can call (separate school). Send your son here for business acquirements on leaving school. Bookkeeping, Banking (by a Chartered Accountant), Writing, &c. Prospectus post free.

BOOKKEEPING, Writing. — SMITH and SMART, 19, Wormwood-street, Bishopsgate-street, City, and 7, New Oxford-street, guarantee proficiency in a few easy private lessons. Arithmetic and Shorthand. Lessons by post. Est.[5] 1840.

1. *The civil service*, les fonctions administratives, surtout dans les Indes. — 2. *Exams.*, *examinations*, examens. — 3. *Largest staff*, personnel (de professeurs). — 4. *Shorthand*, la sténographie. — 5. *Est.*, established.

DANCING.—Mr. and Mrs. NICHOLAS HENDERSON are now holding Morning and Evening LESSONS and CLASSES. Adults (ladies and gentlemen) wholly unacquainted with dancing taught in a few easy private lessons. The valse, minuet, gavotte, &c. Four lessons one guinea. — 19, Newman-street, W.

DANCING. — Mr. BLAND and DAUGHTERS, having the honour of instructing the nobility and gentry, give LESSONS daily in the New Valse and all the modern dances. Four private lessons one guinea, any time by appointment. Assemblies. Prospectus, 77, New Oxford-street, W. C. (late of Golden-square).

MADAME STAINTON TAYLOR'S CLASSES for DEPORTMENT[1], Dancing, and Physical Exercices at her residence for families of position. Private valse lessons to gentlemen. Class on Saturday afternoon for Girls attending High Schools. — No. 35, Colcherne-road, Redcliffe-square, South Kensington.

THE LONDON ACADEMY of DANCING (founded 1863), Cavendish Rooms, Mortimer-street, Cavendish-square. The most complete and rapid system of instruction and practice. — 12 classes every week. Special private tuition and practice. — Prospectus, Edward Humphrey, Principal.

CHIOSSO'S RATIONAL GYMNASTICS. — The only system of physical culture for ladies, gentlemen, and children of all ages, temperament, or condition. Cases received, visited. Fencing, boxing, sabres. Only address The London Gymnasium and School of Arms (Est. 1855), 7, Argyll-street, Regent-street, W.

A LADY wishes to take, for next Midsummer, a good BOARDING SCHOOL for GIRLS, in a healthy suburb of London. Apply, by letter, stating situation, price, &c., M., R112, Address and Inquiry office. The Times Office, E. C.

FOR TRANSFER[2], high-class GIRLS' DAY SCHOOL, at the West-end. 40 pupils. Very good position. Satisfactory reasons for retiring. (622.) Address Messrs. Biver, 298, Regent-street, W.

FOR TRANSFER, GIRLS' SCHOOL (Seaside), 23, boarders and day pupils, at fair terms. Income £1,500. No premium for goodwill. Furniture at valuation (716.) —Messrs. Biver, 298, Regent-street, W.

PUBLICATIONS.

THE LOCAL GOVERNMENT ACT[3]. — Now ready, the SERIES of EXPLANATORY ARTICLES which have recently appeared in The Times, price 6d., bound in cloth. Apply to the

1. *Classes for deportment*, classes de maintien (esthétique). — 2. *For transfer*, à céder. — 3. *The Local government act.* C'est une loi passée dans la présente année (1888). C'est une des lois les plus importantes, une des plus grandes réformes et des plus libérales qu'on ait faites depuis bien longtemps en Angleterre. La loi a été adoptée, après de longues et sérieuses délibérations, et approuvée par les libéraux, quoique présentée par les conservateurs. Cette loi retire une grande partie des pouvoirs exercés jusqu'ici par les magistrats (*Justices of the Peace*, J. P.) choisis par la couronne parmi les grands propriétaires terriens, pour les remettre entre les mains d'un *County Council* (*ou* conseil du comté) élu pour les trois quarts, et dont le quatrième quart est choisi parmi les conseillers élus (*three fourths elected and one fourth selected*). La loi actuelle ne s'applique pour le présent qu'à l'Angleterre et au pays de Galles. Chaque comté a son conseil, mais Londres et un assez grand nombre de villes (52) sont regardées comme des comtés, et ce sont leurs conseils municipaux qui formeront aux trois quarts leur *County Council.* Les pouvoirs des County Councils sont très étendus sur les finances, l'administration, les travaux publics, etc. Ils partagent avec les magistrats, au moyen de commissions mixtes, certains autres pouvoirs tels que l'assistance pu-

Publisher, The Times Office. Printing-house-square, London.

THE SPECIAL COMMISSION[1]. — Now ready, Paris, I., II., and III., of THE TIMES REPORT of the PROCEEDINGS before the Special Commission, price 6d. each. Apply to the Publisher, The Times Office, Printing-house-square, London.

PARNELLISM and CRIME. — REPRINTS of the TWO SERIES of ARTICLES published under this title, of the Facsimile Page from the Irish World, of the Alleged Facsimile Letter of Mr. Parnell on the Phœnix Park Murders, and of the articles entitled " Behind the Sciences in America," are now on sale, and may be had by application to the Publisher, price 1d. each. Also the above in one volume, bound in cloth, price 1s.—The Publisher, The Times Office, Printing-house-square, E.C.

O'DONNELL v. WALTER. — A full REPORT of this case, reprinted from The Times, is now ready, price two pence. Apply to the Publisher, The Times Office, Printing-house-square.

A VISIT to the STATES[2]. — The two Series of Letters under this title, from The Times' Special Correspondent, are now ready, bound in cloth, Price 1s. each volume.—The Publisher, The Times Office, Printing-house-square, E. C.

THE TIMES PARLIAMENTARY DEBATES, arranged in a convenient form for binding, will be issued every Monday during the sitting of Parliament. Price 1s., or 25s. per annum, post free. Annual subscription for bound volumes—half-bound in morocco leather, £3 10s.; cloth, lettered, £2 10s. Apply to the Publisher, The Times Office, Printing-house-square, E. C.

THE TIMES PARLIAMENTARY DEBATES. — This week's number contains Reports of the Debates in Committee of Supply, the African Slave Trade, the Education Estimates, &c. Price 1s. Apply to the Publisher, The Times Office, Printing-house-square, E.C.

MISS BRADDON'S ANNUAL, The MISLETOE BOUGH, now ready, price 1s., illustrated with 36 Original Drawings by F. H. Townsend, W. Parkinson, J. B. Partridge and Hal Ludlow. The largest, the best, and the most popular Annual. London, Simpkin, Marshall, and Co.

REMINISCENCES of J. L. TOOLE, the Comedian. Related by Himself and chronicled by JOSEPH HATTON. Second edition now ready, in 2 vols, demi 8vo. Illustrated by Alfred Bryan and W. H. Margetson. Price 30s. " A most agreable and entertaining book. " —Ers.[3] Hurst and Blackett (Limited). 13, Great Marlborough-street.

MR. MITCHELL has arranged with Messrs. Remington and Co. for a constant supply of the MAPLESON MEMOIRS[4], copies of which can now

blique et la police du comté; mais la direction de la police elle-même, la nomination et la révocation des officiers de police et les ordres qui sont donnés en cas d'émeute, etc., restent entièrement entre les mains des magistrats. — 1. *The special commission.* Le *Times* avait publié des lettres (*Parnellism and Crime*) qu'il prétendait être écrites de la main même de M. Parnell (voy. *Historique*, note 10, page 3), par lesquelles celui-ci se trouvait incriminé de quasi-complicité dans des meurtres politiques commis en Irlande. La loi anglaise permet à un homme accusé de diffamation d'en faire la preuve en justice. La loi française ne le permet que lorsque la personne diffamée est fonctionnaire du gouvernement. Un premier procès eut lieu, mais n'aboutit pas. Le gouvernement fut alors autorisé par le Parlement à nommer une commission spéciale, formée de trois des juges les plus estimés du royaume, pour examiner l'affaire. Cette affaire est terminée; le *Times* a reconnu la fausseté des lettres. — 2. *To the* (*United*) *States* (*of America*). — 3. *Ers., editors.* — 4. Mémoires de nos jours, livre qui a eu un grand succès cette année en Angleterre.

be obtained at the Royal Library, 33, Old Bond-street, and at his City office, 51, Threadneedle-street, E. C.

THE UNIVERSAL REVIEW. Edited by HARRY QUILTER. On November 15th, price Half-a-crown.

Contents: —

Competitive Examination. Sir John Lubbock, Walter Wren, Professor Ray Lankester, the Editor.

A Sculptor and A Shrine. Samuel Butler.

The last Word on Political Economy. Professor Brentano (University of Vienna).

Richard Jefferies. Edward Garnett.

Suum Cuique. H. Arthur Kennedy.

The Progress of Woman. Part I. In Politics, Mrs. Henry Fawcett; In Literature, Lucas Malet; In Scholarship, Miss Clough (Newnham); In Medicine, Mrs. Scharlieb, M. B.

One of the Forty. Alphonse Daudet.

A Decorative Society. Harry Quilter.

Recent Literature.

Illustrations (full-page): —

Dawn. Miss Ethel King.

Sleep. Mrs. Henrietta Rae.

Jack. Miss Nettie Huxley.

Imogen. Madame Canziani (née Stau).

A Study. Mrs Jopling.

Woman's Place. Mrs. Perugini.

A Study in Jena. Miss A. C. Channer.

David and Goliath. H. A. Kennedy.

Judith. Heywood Summer.

The Arts and Crafts. Walter Crane.

The Man with the Staff. Tabachetti.

And 15 smaller illustrations.

FIFTEEN POUNDS in PRIZES for DRESSING DOLLS[1].—For particulars of this most interesting competition see TRADE, FINANCE, and RECREATION, which is to be had at all railway bookstall, or will be sent post free 2d. stamps[2].—35, Marklane, E. C.

GOLDEN OPPORTUNITY.—Increase your income £2 to £10 per week. See TRADE, FINANCE, and RECREATION. Of all Newsvendors or Railway Bookstalls, or post free., 2d. — No. 35, Mark-lane, E. C.

HOME-MADE CHRISTMAS PRESENTS, and other Practical Papers for Amateurs, with working diagrams.—See Wednesday's issue of the BAZAAR, which also contains many other interesting articles and hundreds of announcements of all kinds of Property for Exchange, Wanted, or for Sale by private persons. Price 2d., at all newsagents' and bookstalls; by post, 2½d. Office No. 170, Strand, London.

HAPPY DAYS. A little Illustrated Pamphlet of 32pp.[3], of interest to all men, women, and children. Post free. Address Publisher, John M. Richards, 46, Holborn-viaduct. London, E. C.

STAMMERING: its Treatment. By B. BEASLEY (who cured himself after suffering nearly 40 years). Post free for 13 stamps from the Author, Green Bank College, Hall-green, near Birmingham.

TO STOUT PEOPLE.—Sunday Times says:— "M. Russell's aim is to eradicate, to cure the disease, and that his treatment is the true one seems beyond all doubt. The medicine he prescribes does not lower, but builds up and tones the system. Book (116 pages), with recipe and notes how to pleasantly and rapidly cure obesity (average reduction in first week is 3lb.[4]), post free eight stamps. — F. C. RUSSELL, Woburn-house, Store-street, Bedford-square, London, W. C.

GRIEG'S, MOSZKOWSKI'S, and other NEW PUBLICATIONS in Peters' Edition.—See MONTHLY MUSICAL RECORD for November and Peters' Catalogue. Augener, Sole Agent,

1. *For dressing dolls*, pour la toilette des poupées. — 2. 2*d. stamps*, timbres de 2 *pence*, 20 centimes. — 3. 32 *pp.*, 32 pages. — 4. 3*lb.*, three pounds, 1 kil. 300 environ.

36, Newgate-street, E. C., and 1, Foubert's place, W.

SCHOOL FESTIVALS.—CANTATAS for ladies' voices, suitable for public performance :—Abt's Christmas, Cinderella, Little Red Riding Hood, Snow White, and Reinecke's Little Rose Bud, Snow Drop, Cinderella, and Bethlehem, each 3s. net. — AUGENER'S School Department, address, 86, Newgate-street.

LOVE'S GOLDEN DREAM WALTZ.

LOVE'S GOLDEN DREAM. By THEO. BONHEUR. Splendidly illustrated. This most charming waltz must become the success of the season and the rage of London. Performed with overwhelming applause at all the Exhibitions, Promenade Concerts, &c. 2s. net. Band and military parts now ready. London Music Publishing Company (Limited), 54, Great Marlborough-street, W.

ADVERTISEMENTS INSERTED in The Times and all London and country newpapers, and in the London Gazette (published by authority), by HENRY GREEN, Advertisement Agent and Contractor, 117, Chancery-lane.

SELL (established 1869).—ADVERTISEMENTS received for insertion in The Times, Standard, Telegraph, Daily News and all London and Country Daily and Weekly Newspapers. Advice given and estimates supplied free of charge for any line of advertising by Mr. Henry Sell, Editor of "Sell's Dictionary of the World's Press and Advertiser's Reference Book" (1,350 pp.), price 2s.—Sell's Advertising Agency (Limited), 167 and 168, Fleet-street (ground floors), London, E. C. Telegraphic address, Sell, London.

New Story by the Author of "Gideon's Rock," &c.

DIAMONDS in DARKNESS : The "Good Words" Christmas Story for 1888. By KATHERINE SAUNDERS, Author of "Gideon's Rock", &c. With Illustrations by William Small. Now ready, price 6d. Isbister and Co. (Limited), 56, Ludgate-hill, London, E. C.

Sixth edition, 1s. post free.

PAINLESS and IMMEDIATE CURE of HŒMORRHOIDS and PROLAPSUS. By G. EDGELOW, M.D.—H. Renshaw, 356, Strand.

12th edition. 1s.; post free for 12 stamps.

THE HUMAN HAIR : why it falls off or turns gray, and the remedy. By PROFESSOR HARLEY PARKER. Sold by C. Mills and Co., 21, Claverton-street, S. W. "Everybody should read this little book."— Scotsman.

Second edition, price 2s. 6d.

THE ANATOMY of NERVOUSNESS and NERVOUS EXHAUSTION. By H. CAMPBELL, M. D. Leading subjects : — Brain Fag[1], Sleeplessness, Irritable Temper, Uncertain Will, Misery, Panic, Melancholy, Craving for Stimulants, Nevralgia, Spinal Irritation and Exhaustion, Hysteria, Noises and Heaviness in Head, Sexual Disturbances, Nervous Dispepsia, Irritable Heart, Shyness, Blushes, &c. Treatment : — Diet, change, holidays, baths, medicine, nerve vibration, electricity, massage, &c.—H. Renshaw, 356, Strand.

CARVED OAK PULPIT.—For SALE, very fine OAK PULPIT, in perfect condition. Suit any church. For full particulars J. Ichenhauser, Carved Oak Specialist, 68, New Bond-street, W.

CARVED OAK PANELLING[2].—A quantity of fine OAK PANEL-

1. *Brain fag*, surmenage du cerveau. — 2. *Panelling*, panneaux.

LING, suit[1] dining room, entrance hall, or library. For full particulars J. Ichenhauser, Carved Oak Specialist, 68, New Bond-street, W.

SUITE of QUEEN ANNE CHAIRS.—SUITE of eight very picturesque QUEEN ANNE CHAIRS, covered in antique repoussé Cordovan[2] leather. For full particulars J. Ichenhauser, Carved Oak Specialist, 68, New Bond-street, W.

OLD NUREMBERG PANELLED ROOM.—Beautiful, complete PANELLING of a ROOM, comprising also panelled celling, at present in Nuremberg; most interesting and desirable. Photograph and fuller particulars at J. Ichenhauser's, Carved Oak Specialist, 68, New Bond-street, W.

MR. LITCHFIELD'S SPECIAL ANNOUNCEMENT to ART COLLECTORS.— A very interesting and valuable collection of OLD ENGLISH PORCELAIN, comprising 200 (two hundred) genuine specimens, mostly marked, and including some of the choicest productions of the famous Chelsea, Bow, Derby, Worcester, and other factories well known to collectors.

THE CHELSEA included the famous vase, formerly owned by Mr. W. King and subsequently purchased at the Leicester Hibbert sale, at Christie's; also about 50 of the most rare specimens of English fabrics, collected by the late Mr. W. Wareham and purchased at his sale at about half their value.

THE COLLECTION has been carefully catalogued by Mr. Litchfield, who will be responsible for the descriptions and date assigned to every specimen, and it has been arranged in a special room, where it may be seen and examined.

ADAMS, contemporary with Wedgwood (1 specimen), Bow (11), Bristol (10), Chelsea (49), Derby and Chelsea Derby (29), Nantgarw (2), Neale ditto, contemporary with Wedgwood (5), Rockingham (2), Salopian[3] (4), Spode (2), Wedgwood (15), Worcester (Wall, crescent, square mark, Grainger, Chamberlain, Flight and Bair, and transfer periods), forming a complete collection in itself, with different colourings, marks, and characteristics, from 1751 to 1793 (70 specimens), also 40 specimens of Battersea enamel, including some rare forms and colourings. On view at LITCHFIELD'S, Nos. 28 and 30, Hanway-street, Oxford-street, London.

NOTICE.—Mr. LITCHFIELD is anxious to PURCHASE, at good prices, exceptional specimens of OLD ENGLISH PORCELAIN, and he values and catalogues amateurs' collections. Only address.

Litchfield's, 28 and 30, Hanway-street, Oxford-street, London.

BEAUTIFUL OLD CARVED OAK PANELLING for SALE. The richly-carved oak panelling for a room, style Flemish Renaissance in 1600, about 50ft. run[4], 7ft. high, with cornice and skirting[5] complete; also about 60 loose panels, similar design, for making up to suit the architectural features of purchaser's room, and a richly-carved door to match.

The above is temporarily arranged in Mr. LITCHFIELD'S Antique Furniture and Rare Porcelain Warehouse, 28 and 30, Hanway-street, Oxford-street, London, W.

ALSO THREE fine OLD STAINED GLASS WINDOW from a Carthusian convent, dated 1541. One is on view, and photographs of the others may be seen at Mr. LITCHFIELD'S Antique Furniture and Rare Porcelain

---

1. *Suit* pour *will suit*, conviendra à. — 2. *In Cordovan leather*, en cuir de Cordoue (en Espagne). — 3. *Salopian*, du Shropshire. — 4. 50*ft. run*, d'une longueur de 50 pieds; *run*, course. — 5. *Skirting*, bordure, encadrements.

Warehouse, Nos. 28 and 30, Hanway-street, Oxford-street, W.

AMATEUR LITHOGRAPHY.—This is a new invention for manifold copying, which possesses notable advantages over the many devices which have been before the public for the last 10 years. It is, in fact, the introduction of lithography into general use. The operator writes or draws upon a small lithographic stone or a special zinc plate with an ordinary pen and flowing black ink. There is a fixed flexible cover with an elastic plate, which so operates upon the written surface as to transfer a copy to the copying paper. The apparatus is as good for drawings, plans, sketches, diagrams, &c., as it is for writing, and there is practically no limit to the number of copies that may be pulled. The copies come off clean and without blemish, and may be made on any paper. No previous training is needed. This is an invention carrying amateur copying or printing to great lengths in range of utility. The AMATEUR LITHOGRAPHER can be had of all Stationers, or direct from the Manufacturers, 16, Queen Victoria-street, London, E.C., where a free trial is allowed. Particulars and specimen of work sent free on application.

CAUTIONS AND NOTICES.

CAUTION. — BRAND and Co.'s ESSENCE of BEEF, Turtle Soup, and other specialities for invalids. Beware of imitations. No connexion with any other establishment. Sole address, 11, Little Stanhope-street, Mayfair, W. Established 1835.

CAUTION. — NIXEY'S REFINED BLACK LEAD[1]. Used without waste or dust. Sold everywhere. Ask for Nixey's Black Lead, and see that you have it. Caution.—There are several spurious and worthless imitations. —W. G. Nixey, the largest Black Lead Manufacturer in the world.—Soho-square, London.

CAUTION. — A. S. LLOYD'S EUXESIS[2], for shaving without soap, water, or brush.—R. HOVENDEN and SONS, having purchased under an administration suit the business of the late A. S. Lloyd, with the receipt, trade mark, and goodwill of the celebrated Euxesis, the public are cautioned that the original and genuine Euxesis bears only the address of the original manufactory, No. 27, Glasshouse-street, Regent-street.

NOTICE. — OETZMANN and Co. — FURNITURE. Nos. 67, 69, 71, 73, 75, 77, and 79, Hampstead-road (near Tottenham-court-road).

NOTICE. — OETZMANN and Co. — £5 5s.—BED ROOM FURNISHED complete for £5 5s. For illustration and full detailed list see page 152 in Illustrated Catalogue, post free on application.

NOTICE. — OETZMANN and Co. — New Design. — The WELBECK ASH[3] BED-ROOM SUITE. 3ft. 9in. wardrobe, with plate-glass door and drawer, marble-top and tile-back double washstand, with towel rails and pedestal cupboard attached, 3ft. 3in. dressing chest, jewel drawers and toilet glass attached, three strong cane-seat chairs. £11 15s. complete.

NOTICE. — OETZMANN and Co. — New Designs. — The WINDSOR CARPETS, artistic, all-wool, bordered, and fringed. Seamless carpets, 8ft. by 7ft. 6in., 18s. Illustrated price list of other sizes post free.

NOTICE. — OETZMANN and Co. — ART CRETONNES, our special

1. *Black lead*, mine de plomb, graphite. — 2. *Euxesis*, du grec εὖ, bien, et ξέω, polir. — 3. *Welbeck ash*, en bois de frêne.

designs, by Lewis F. Day. The Versailles, reversible design[1], 6 3/4d.[2] per yard; the Indian Butterfly, reversible design, 9 3/4d. per yard; the Calyx, reversible design, 10 3/4d. per yard; the Poppy design, 1s. 0 1/2d. per yard; the Pomegranate, 1s. 0 1/2d. per yard. Patterns post free.

NOTICE. — OETZMANN'S ILLUSTRATED CATALOGUE, the best furnishing guide extant, containing coloured and other illustrations, with full particulars and prices of every article required in complete house furnishing. Post free on application. — Oetzmann and Co., Hampstead-road.

NOTICE. — OETZMANN and Co., Cabinetmakers, Upholsterers, and Complete House Furnishers, Hampstead-road (near Tottenham-court-road and Gower-street Station). Shilling cab fares[3] from Charing-cross, Euston, King's-cross, St. Pancreas, and Waterloo Stations, Regent-circus, and Piccadilly.

NOTICE.—DINNEFORD'S FLUID MAGNESIA. — This well-known remedy for acidity, heartburn, and indigestion can now be procured at all the principal pharmacies of Europe.

NOTICE.—COLLINSON and LOCK'S HOUSE-HOLD DECORATIONS in MARBLE, Wood, Plaster, and other Materials, 76 to 80, Oxford-street, W.

NOTICE.—M. F. DENT, 33 and 34, Cockspur-street, Charing-cross (sole address), Watch, Clock, and Chronometer Maker to the Queen, to the Crowns of Europe, and to the Lords Commissioners of the Admiralty. Price lists on application.

NOTICE.—THOMAS GOODE and Co., South Audley-street, W., Artists and Designers in CHINA and GLASS, invite a visit to their unrivalled collection and a comparison of their prices with those of any co-operative stores[4].

NOTICE. — PEARLS and OLD JEWELS BOUGHT for cash. A special demand now enables M. J. W. BENSON to offer owners the most tempting prices to realise. 10 a. m. to 3 p. m.[5].—25 Old Bond-street, W.

NOTICE. — OUTFITS to INDIA, China, and the Colonies. Estimates, with list of necessary articles for every appointment, will be forwarded on application to THRESHER and GLENNY, Outfitters (next door to Somerset-house), Strand, W. C.

NOTICE. — MORTLOCK'S, Oxford-street.—SALE of DINNER SERVICES still progressing. More reductions made to clear house previous to rebuilding. Many services offered at half price. Innumerable oddments[6], &c., at merely nominal sums.—466, 468, 470, Oxford-street.—Mortlock's.

NOTICE. — DOULTON WARE[7]. — As inferior imitations of their celebrated ART POTTERY are being introduced, Messrs. DOULTON beg to inform the public that their Art manufactures invariably bear an impressed stamp "Doulton, Lambeth," or "Doulton Burslem".

NOTICE. — The Lancet says of ATKINSON'S PERFECT TRUSS[8]. — "An important improvement. The practical surgeon will see the great advantages presented in this truss." Particulars

1. *Reversible design*, dessin qu'on peut retourner, dessin sans envers (bon des deux côtés). — 2. 6 3/4 *d.*, *six pence three farthings*, 64 centimes. *The farthing* ou *quart du penny* vaut un peu plus que le centime. — 3. *Shilling cab fares*, la course en voiture n'est que d'un shelling des endroits nommés chez Oetzmann. — 4. *Co-operative stores*, magasin coopératif, société coopérative. — 5. *From* 10 *in the morning to* 3 *in the afternoon*, voy. note 3, p. 19. — 6. *Oddments*, pièces dépareillées. — 7. *Ware*, pour *earthenware*, poterie. — 8. *Truss*, trousse de chirurgien.

gratis of inventor and maker, B. F. Atkinson, No. 7, Mill-street, Hanover-square, W.

NOTICE.—DEFRIES' SAFETY WATER WHITE[1] OIL. The purest and finest burning oil in England. Delivered carriage paid in London postal district, for five gallons and upwards, 1s. per gallon; two, three, or four galls, 1s. 2d. per gall. Terms cash on or before delivery. Full price allowed for returned cans.

NOTICE.—DEFRIES' SAFETY LAMP and OIL COMPANY, Limited, 43 and 44, Holborn-viaduct.

NOTICE.—Britannia accepts Erin's[2] offering and appreciates it. Peace, love, and concord achieved by LUNHAM'S MILD-CURED BREAKFAST BACON and HAMS. Patronized by H. R. H. the Prince of Wales for his use. The only bacon and hams consumed by him on his voyage to India. Such a treat for the breakfast table no household should be without them. Sold by all leading purveyors of provisions in the United Kingdom, and every piece branded Lunham. Lunham, Premier.

NOTICE.—Shaftesbury-avenue Marble, Fine Art, and Furniture Galleries (late King-street, Soho, W.). — GEORGE SINCLAIR begs to call the attention of his customers to the extension of his premises, in which is displayed an immense STOCK of CHIMNEY-PIECES, in wood, marble, and stone, Grates, Dog Stoves, Fenders, Fire Brasses, Cabinets, Tables, Chairs, Couches, Secretaire, Pictures (ancient and modern), Busts, Pedestals, Clocks, Bronzes, Vases, Wall-Lights[3], Candelabra, and Art Decorations generally. An inspection sollicited.

NOTICE.—ALFRED WEBB MILES and COMPANY (established 1841) respectfully inform gentlemen that their establishment is full to positive repletion with every description of FASHIONABLE MATERIALS for the WINTER, consisting of Beavers, Vicunas, Elastic Twilled Coatings, Dress and Morning Suiting, &c.; also the new Fabrics and Styles in Scotch and West of England manufacture for their world-famed Trousers at 13s., 16s., and one guinea per pair, or two pairs for 25s., 30s., and 40s. respectively. Only address, 12, 10, and 8, Brook-street, Hanover-square, London. Patterns and self-measurement forms upon application.

NOTICE.—ALFRED WEBB MILES and COMPANY'S SHOW ROOMS contain the best and most varied assortment of OVERCOATS, in all the fashionable styles for winter, for the approval of gentlemen, at moderate prices, as illustrated by their celebrated Treble Elastic Warwick Overcoats, at two guineas, which have given such universal satisfaction; Blue and Black Beaver Overcoats, Covert-coats, Dress Inverness Capes, Beaufort Sacs, Furlined Overcoats, Ulsters, &c., of first-class materials, make, and style, ready for immediate use, or as models to order from. N.B.—Only address, 12, 10 and 8, Brook-street, Hanover-square, London, W. Telegrams. Webb Miles, London. Telephone 3,929.

SPECIAL NOTICE.—PIMMS' NATIVE OYSTERS[4].—Messrs. Pimms and Co. beg respectfully to inform their patrons that the season 1888-9 for their finest selected native oysters has commenced. Oysters specially selected for invalids and packed into quarter barrels, containing three dozen, can be despatched to all parts of the United Kingdom.

1. *Water white*, blanche comme de l'eau. — 2. *Britannia*, l'Angleterre ; *Erin*, l'Irlande. Cela devrait signifier que M. Lunham importe ses porcs de l'Irlande, mais rien ne le prouve. — 3. *Wall-lights*, appliques, candélabres appliqués contre le mur. — 4. *Native oysters*, huîtres anglaises.

Price list on application to Pimms', 3, 4, and 5, Poultry[1], London, E. C.

SPECIAL NOTICE.—BRAND and Co., Purveyors of specialities for invalids to H.R.H. the Prince of Wales and original manufacturers of Essences of Beef (green label) and other of such specialities, have NOT REMOVED from their sole address, No. 11, Little Stanhope-street, Mayfair, W.

NOTICE OF REMOVAL. — GEO. CORDING, Waterproofer[2], has REMOVED from 62, Piccadilly, corner of Albemarle-street, to 125, Regent-street.

NEGRETTI and ZAMBRA'S OPERA, Race, and Field GLASSES[3], in sling cases[4] complete, two and three guineas.

NEGRETTI and ZAMBRA'S SEA-SIDE and TOURISTS' TELESCOPES, Binocular Telescopes for Deer-stalking, Yachting, &c. New illustrated price list free on application.

NEGRETTI and ZAMBRA'S STANDARD METEOROLOGICAL INSTRUMENTS, Barometers, Thermometers, Anemometers, Rain Gauges, &c., as supplied to the Royal Observatory, Meteorological Office, &c.

NEGRETTI and ZAMBRA, Opticians to The Queen, British and Foreign Governments, &c. The accuracy of all instruments guaranteed. The trade and shippers supplied. — Holborn-viaduct, E. C. Branches—45, Cornhill; 122, Regent-street. Photographic studio, Crystal Palace. Telephone No. 6,583.

WEAK and DEFECTIVE SIGHT. — SPECTACLES scientifically adapted to remedy impaired vision by Mr. ACKLAND, Surgeon, daily, at Horne and Thornwaite's, Opticians to the Queen, 416, Strand, London. The weak-sighted should read Ackland's Hints on Spectacles, 6d. post free.

SIR JULIUS BENEDICT wrote: — "I have tried the principal London opticians without success, but your SPECTACLES suit admirably; the clearness of your glasses, compared with others, is really surprising." — To Mr. H. LAURANCE, Oculist-Optician, 1a, Old Bond-street, W., and 6, Poultry, E. C. Spectacles scientifically adapted. Pamphlet free.

FANCY DRESS.—Complete DRESSES of CHINESE MANDARIN and LADY, for SALE. Quite new.—E. C. S., Dashwood-house, 9, New Broad-street, E. C.

BILLIARDS. — A full-sized CLUB TABLE[5], 95 guineas, by the greatest London makers, for £45; made in most costly manner; best ever played on. Used only two months. With all the fittings. Can be seen and tried. — 35, Surrey-street, Strand.

BILLIARDS. — THREE handsome full-sized TABLES, in wainscot oak, pollard oak, and walnut; also several tables in mahogany, a little used, price from 25 guineas. 100 tables in stock from 10 guineas to 150 guineas. — WRIGHT and Co.'s Show Rooms, 162 to 164, Westminster-bridge-road, London, 13 Prize Medals.

DEALS[6], &c., Oats[7], &c.: — 2 by 4, at 1/2d. per foot run[8]; floorings, matched boards, &c., at low prices. Good Oats, 14s. 9d. per quarter, 304lb., ex docks. Catalogues post free. — The CHEAP WOOD COMPANY, 95, Bishopsgate-street within, E.C.

---

1. *Poultry*, quartier de Londres. — 2. *Waterproofer*, fabricant de vêtements imperméables; *waterproof*, à l'épreuve de l'eau; comme *fireproof*, à l'épreuve du feu. — 3. Lorgnettes pour l'opéra, les courses ou la campagne. — 4. *In sling cases*, en étuis avec courroie. — 5. Grand billard pour cercle. — 6. *Deals*, planches pour parquets, etc. *Deal*, bois blanc, sapin. — 7. *Oats*, avoine. — 8. *Per foot run*, par pied en longueur.

LAW REPORT[1], *Nov.* 13.

HOUSE OF LORDS[2].

(*Present* — *The* LORD CHANCELLOR[3], LORD WATSON, *and* LORD MACNAGHTEN.)

LILLEY V.[4] HAMILL AND OTHERS.

This was an appeal from a judgment of the Court of Appeal affirming a decision of the Lord Chief Justice sitting without a jury.

Mr. Henn Collins, Q.C[5]., and Mr. Hindmarsh appeared for the appellant; and Mr. Murphy, Q. C., Mr. Lumley Smith, Q. C., and Mr. Percy Gye for the respondents.

It appeared that Mr. Hamill, senior, the respondent, being the registered owner of a large number of shares in the Colorado United Mining Company, had a son, a young man about 21, who was living with him in Colorado, to whom he intrusted the certificates of ownership, which showed that Hamill, senior, was the registered owner of these shares, and he also gave his son some blank transfers[6] sealed by his seal. The son came over to England for the purpose of forming a syndicate for the purchase of his father's shares, but failing in that object he, in excess of his authority, raised money upon certain of the shares from, among other persons, a Mr. Greene, who deposited with the appellant certain certificates and documents purporting to be transfers of 2,000 of the shares as security for an advance. The respondent, on discovering the transaction, gave notice to the company not to transfer the shares in question, and brought the present action[7] to recover possession of the certificates and transfers, and also for an injunction to restrain the appellant from dealing with such shares and documents. The Lord Chief Justice found in favour of the respondent, and his decision was affirmed[8] by the Court of Appeal, who held that the appellant had made the advance without

1. *Law Report*, compte rendu des tribunaux. — 2. La Chambre des pairs, où siègent *d'office* les lords magistrats, juges des trois hautes cours de justice, forme le tribunal suprême de justice et d'appel en Angleterre dans les causes civiles et dans certaines causes criminelles. — 3. *The Lord* (*High*) *Chancellor* est le chef de la justice en Angleterre, principal conseiller légal de la couronne et président de la Chambre des pairs. Il est aussi président de la Haute Cour de justice (*chancery*), et de la Cour d'appel, tuteur de tous les orphelins, des idiots et des lunatiques, et visiteur des hôpitaux. Dickens, dans son roman de *Bleak House*, donne une certaine idée des fonctions multiples du lord chancelier. Quand il se retire d'office, il reçoit une pension de 125 000 francs, mais il ne saurait plus plaider et doit toujours ses conseils et son assistance à la couronne. — 4. *v.*, *versus*, contre. — 5. *Q. C.*, *Queen's Council;* c'est un titre accordé par la couronne à un avocat distingué, équivalant à peu près à *conseiller intime;* il peut plaider en toutes causes, même contre la couronne, mais alors il a besoin d'une autorisation spéciale. — 6. *Blank transfers*, transferts signés en blanc. — 7. *To bring an action*, intenter une action. — 8. *Affirmed*, confirmée.

having made sufficient inquiries as to the nature of the transaction and as to the authority of young Hamill to transfer the shares.

At the conclusion of the arguments for the appellant,

Their LORDSHIPS, without calling upon the counsel for the respondents to argue the case, delivered judgment, affirming[1] the decision of the Court of Appeal, on the ground that the issue being upon the appellant[2] he had failed to satisfy their Lordships that he had made sufficient inquiries as to the authority of young Mr. Hamill to transfer the shares before making the advance to Mr. Greene upon the security of the transfer.

Judgment affirmed and appeal dismissed with costs[3].

SUPREME COURT OF JUDICATURE.

COURT OF APPEAL.

(*Before the* MASTER *of the* ROLLS[4], LORD JUSTICE FRY, *and* LORD LOPES JUSTICE.)

OAKLEY V. BOULTON, MAYNARD, AND COMPANY.

This was an appeal by the plaintiff from the judgment of Mr. Justice Hawkins at the trial of the action without a jury. The plaintiff, Richard Banner Oakley, sued upon two (out of three) bills of exchange, dated December 9, 1886, each for £166 13s. 4d., payable four months after date, and accepted in the name of the defendant firm. The defendant firm consisted at the time of two partners, Condamine and Henry, and the bills were accepted by Condamine, and Henry, who was the real defendant, pleaded that the bills were accommodation bills[5], that Condamine had no authority to accept them for the firm, but accepted them for his own purposes, of which the plaintiff was aware, and that the plaintiff was not the drawer. The facts were as follows :—The plaintiff carried on business in Holborn as the Æolus Water Spray General Ventilating and Electrical Engineering Company, but formerly was connected with the Co-operative Credit Bank. In December, 1886, Braithwaite, a commission agent, came to the plaintiff from Armstrong and Co. (under which name one Bauerman carried on business as a financial broker) with two of the bills in question, and asked him to discount them. At that time the bills were accepted, but there was no drawer's name on

---

1. *Affirming*, confirmant. — 2. Que c'était au plaignant de faire la preuve. — 3. *Appeal dismissed with costs*, l'appel débouté avec frais. — 4. *The Master of the Rolls*, conservateur des archives. Ce sont des fonctions de grande importance et qui donnent une haute position. Cette dignité remonte jusqu'à l'an 1205 au moins, car on la trouve mentionnée dans les chroniques de cette époque. Il est juge *in chancery* (causes civiles) et il siège comme président dans la Haute Cour de Justice et à la Cour d'appel. — 5. *Accommodation bills*, billets de complaisance.

them. Braithwaite stated to the plaintiff that the acceptors wanted the bills discounted in order to purchase a wine business in the west of London, and that Armstrong and Co. were trying to discount them. The plaintiff thereupon, on December 14, wrote to the defendant firm in effect as follows : “ I understand that under an arrangement with Armstrong and Co. you have accepted three bills in blank at four months each for £166 13s. 4d., of which the enclosed is one. Please say if they are in order, and authorize me to fill in my name or the name of my firm as drawer, and return the bill to me so that I may operate.” To this the following answer was sent : — “ We have no objection to your firm's name being filled in as drawer of the bills, which are quite in order.” This letter, as appeared in evidence, was in the handwriting of Condamine. The plaintiff applied to the London Association for the Protection of Trade as to the defendant firm[1] and heard in answer that they were a respectable firm, but owing to the bad state of the wine trade were in a declining state. The plaintiff, after making these inquiries, filled in his own name, “ Richard Oakley, ” as drawer, and gave Braithwaite £144 8s. 11d. for each of the bills. Armstrong and Co., it appeared, gave Condamine £100 in cash and certain acceptances of third parties. The plaintiff now sued the defendant upon the two bills so discounted. The plaintiff stated in evidence that until an interview with Henry on January 8, 1887, he did not know that the bills were accepted by Condamine in fraud of Henry. Neither Bauerman nor Condamine were called at the trial. Mr. Justice Hawkins gave judgment for the defendant (4 *The Times* Law Reports[2], 379).

Mr. Henry Kisch appeared for the plaintiff. Mr. John Montefiore, for the defendant, was not called upon.

The COURT dismissed the appeal.

The MASTER of the ROLLS said that the acceptances were in a firm name, in which firm there were two partners. The only authority one partner would have, to sign acceptances would be to sign on firm business for firm purposes[3]. Condamine accepted in the firm's name for his own purposes. Therefore the acceptances were fraudulent. Section 30 of the Bills of Exchange Act[4], 1882, provided that (assuming the plaintiff was the drawer) where an acceptance was fraudulent the burden lay on the holder to prove that he gave value for the bill *bonâ fide*. To be done *bonâ fide* it must be

1. *Applied..... as to the defendant firm*, demanda des renseignements sur la position de la maison de commerce du défendeur. *The London Association for the protection of Trade*, c'est une association formée des premières maisons de commerce de la ville de Londres ; elle tient un registre qui donne des renseignements sur l'honorabilité et la position commerciale des différentes maisons. — 2. Outre le journal, l'administration du *Times* publie à part les comptes rendus des débats du Parlement (Parliamentary Debates) et les procès devant les différents tribunaux (*The Times* Law Reports). — 3. *On firm business for firm purposes*, pour les affaires de la maison de commerce et dans les intérêts de cette maison. — 4. *The Bills of Exchange Act*, la loi (passée en 1882) sur les effets de commerce.

done honestly. The *onus*[1] therefore lay upon the plaintiff to prove that he gave value honestly for the bills. Now, the facts were that the bills were brought to the plaintiff in a strange form, not like ordinary trade bills. Some explanation was required. The plaintiff wrote to the defendant firm, and received in answer a letter signed in the same handwriting as the acceptances. The plaintiff did not give value for them as ordinary trade bills, but charged about 40 per cent. per annum, which showed that he thought there was some risk. But the great point against the plaintiff was that when the acceptances were shown to be fraudulent he never called Bauerman or Condamine at the trial to explain the circumstances. Both of them should properly have been called by the plaintiff. Therefore there were against the plaintiff, on whom the burden of proof lay, the suspicious form in which the bills came to him and his not having called Bauerman and Condamine. Under these circumstances, the acceptances being fraudulent, it was open to the Judge to say[2] that the plaintiff had not proved that he gave value honestly for the bills. Upon that ground, therefore, the judgment was right. The other objection was this—when the instruments were brought to the plaintiff they were not negotiable instruments, as there was no drawer. The plaintiff had to prove his authority to fill in the name of the drawer so as to make them negotiable instruments. The authority given to the plaintiff was to fill in the name of the plaintiff's firm. The plaintiff inserted his own name as drawer. He did not follow the authority, and therefore he never made them negotiable instruments, and could not sue the defendant upon them. This was decided in " Hogarth v. Latham and Co. " (3, Q.B. D[3]., 643). Upon this ground also the judgment was right.

The LORDS JUSTICES concurred.

(*Before* LORDS JUSTICES COTTON, LINDLEY, *and* BOWEN.)

IN RE[4] THE ANGLO-ITALIAN AND COLONIAL INDUSTRIAL AND COMMERCIAL INSTITUTION (LIMITED)—COLONEL GREY'S CASE.

This was an appeal from the refusal by Mr. Justice Kay of an application

1. *The onus therefore lay upon the plaintiff to....*, c'était donc au plaignant à..... (*Onus*, mot latin, veut dire charge, fardeau.) — 2. *It was open to the judge to say*, le juge était autorisé à dire. — 3. *Q. B. D.*, *Queen's Bench decision*, ainsi décidé par la Cour du Banc de la Reine. C'est une des trois grandes cours de justice en Angleterre. Elle tire son nom de cette formule *coram ipso rege* (en présence du roi, ou *ipsâ reginâ*, de la reine), qu'elle emploie dans ses actes et de l'usage où étaient anciennement les rois d'y siéger en personne. Sa juridiction s'étend sur tous les tribunaux inférieurs et sur toutes les corporations. Elle connaît de beaucoup de causes civiles et criminelles, des attentats à la paix publique, etc., etc. Les trois grandes cours de justice en Angleterre sont : *the Court of Chancery*, *the Court of Queen's Bench*, *the Court of appeal* (voy. note 3, page 63), qui se subdivisent en dix-neuf tribunaux séparés, siégeant dans le palais appelé *The New Law Courts*, dans le Strand. *The Central Hall* ou *Salle des pas perdus*, a 230 pieds de long, 80 pieds de haut et 48 pieds de large. Ce sont les juges de ces différents tribunaux qui vont présider les *Quarter sessions* ou assises trimestrielles, les uns chargés des causes civiles, les autres des causes criminelles. — 4. *In re*, dans l'affaire de.

by Colonel Grey to rectify the register of shareholders in this company, now being wound up[1], by altering the date at which he ceased to be a holder of shares in the company from the 14th of August, 1883, to a date in January or February, 1883, or some other date more than a year previous to the commencement of the winding up of the company on the 14th of July, 1884. The company was registered in January, 1882, with a nominal capital of £5,000,000, in shares of £10 each. Colonel Grey was allotted 500 shares in the company, and in January, 1883, was anxious to get rid of them. Malgarini, who was the promoter of the company, offered to buy the shares, which were transferred to him by an undated[2] transfer, which was stated by Colonel Grey to have been executed by him on the 24th of January, 1883. It appeared that in spite of inquiries made by Colonel Grey and, as he stated, the instructions for registration given by him at the company's office on the 9th of May, 1883, the transfer, the date of which as of the 8th of August was filled in by the secretary, was not registered until the 14th of August, 1883; both the date of transfer and of registration being thus within a year of the winding up, so as, assuming these dates to be correct, to leave Colonel Grey liable for the shares. The case made in support of the application was that the delay in registering the transfer arose from the default of the company, and that without being actually told that the transfer which was executed in January, 1883, had been registered, he had been assured that the matter was all right. Mr. Justice Kay in June last upon the evidence held that the date of August 8, 1883, was the right date of the transfer, and refused the application to rectify the register by antedating the registration. From this decision, which left Colonel Grey liable as a contributory for the 500 shares, the present appeal was brought.

Mr. H. Burton Buckley, Q. C.[3], and Mr. Rolls Warrington appeared in support of the appeal; Mr. Marten, Q. C., and Mr. T. L. Wilkinson, for the liquidator, were not called on.

LORD JUSTICE COTTON, in affirming the decision of Mr. Justice Kay, said that he did not intend to express any opinion upon the question when the transfer was actually executed. What was incumbent on Colonel Grey in order to relieve himself from liability as a contributory, was to show that he had given directions to the officers of the company to register the transfer before the 14th of July, 1883; for a transferor remained liable for his shares until a complete transfer had been made, and no transfer was complete unless and until it had been entered upon the register of the company. Upon the evidence, to which his Lordship referred, Colonel Grey unfortunately had not discharged the onus[4] of showing that he had given such directions to the

---

1. *Now being wound up*, maintenant en liquidation. — 2. *An undated transfer*, un acte de cession sans date. — 3. *Q. C.* Voy. note 5, p. 63. — 4. *Onus*. Voy. note 1, p. 66.

officers of the company as would have compelled them to register before the 14th of July, 1883. The appeal must therefore be dismissed.

LORD JUSTICE LINDLEY concurred. Upon the evidence Colonel Grey had not ceased to be a member more than a year before the commencement of the winding up, and he had not discharged the burden of proving that he had got his transfer registered at an earlier period or that the absence of registration within proper time arose from the default of the company or their officers. He would assume that the transfer was, as Colonel Grey stated, executed in January, 1883, but certainly there was nothing then done by him to put the company in default for not registering. It must be borne in mind, too, that the Companies Act, 1867, contained a clause (section 26) which expressly enabled a transferor to insist upon and enforce registration by the company of his transfer.

LORD JUSTICE BOWEN agreed, but wished to call attention to the abuse of cross-examination in this case before the special examiner. The point was a very short one, but the cross-examination had occupied no less than three days. Some explanation might be given, but as matters stood he should suggest that a direction should be given to the Taxing Master[1] to look into the question as to the propriety or otherwise of the costs of this cross-examination.

Mr. MARTEN, Q.C., suggested that cross-examinations were often spread over what might seem a long period in order to suit the convenience of counsel.

HIGH COURT OF JUSTICE.

CHANCERY DIVISION[2].

(*Before* MR. JUSTICE KAY.)

IN RE THE FAURE ELECTRIC ACCUMULATOR COMPANY (LIMITED).

This case raised two questions of the highest importance to directors of limited liability companies, one being a question which has often been discussed—namely, whether directors are in the position of trustees[3] for their company and, as such, subject to the liabilities of ordinary trustees. The other question was one which now came before the Court for the first time for direct decision—namely, whether directors are justified in paying out of the moneys of their company brokerage[4] or commission to brokers or other agents for "placing," or inducing the public to take shares,—a practice which it is believed very commonly prevails. It will be seen from his Lordship's judgment that such a practice is illegal. The company now in

---

1. *The Taxing Master,* le vérificateur des frais de justice, l'expert. — 2. Voy. note 3, p. 63. — 3. *Trustee,* fidéi-commissaire. — 4. *Brokerage,* courtage.

question—the Faure Electric Accumulator Company (Limited)—was registered on February 13, 1882, for the purpose of purchasing and working[1] certain patents for the storage[2] of electricity, the invention of a M. Faure. The patents were then the property of a company registered in Belgium under the name of " La Force et la Lumière ". The capital of the Faure Company was £1,000,000 in 80,000 ordinary shares of £10 each and £200,000 deferred shares[3] of £1 each. On June 19, 1884, the company went into voluntary liquidation, and in July following an order was made continuing the winding up under the supervision of the Court. The matter now came before the Court on a summons by the liquidators of the company under section 165 of the Companies Act, 1862, asking (1) for a declaration that Simon Philippart, Sir Arthur Otway, Sir Charles Clifford, Charles Seymour Grenfell, Harvey Ranking, and Edward Ponsonby, the first directors of the company, had committed a breach of trust and misfeasance[4] towards the company either in allotting 19,872 shares to one William Morris a nominee of Philippart's, or, alternatively, for allowing 18,500 of such shares to be transferred by Morris to Philippart with the knowledge that Philippart would be unable to pay the £8 per share then remaining uncalled thereon; and (2) for a declaration that the directors were in any event jointly and severally liable to make good to the assets[5] of the company sums of £937 10s. and £1,547 15s., making together £2,485 5s., being the amount of brokerage on the 19,872 shares. There were two other claims, but they were dropped when the summons came on for hearing. The directors all acted from the date of their appointment by the articles of association until December 19, 1882, when, at a board meeting held on that day, they executed an assignment of the Faure Company's patents to a company called the English Storage Company, and then resigned. This intention of resigning had been communicated by Sir Arthur Otway, the chairman of the board[6], to a general meeting of shareholders held on December 4, when he stated as his reason for resignation the passing of a resolution at a previous meeting of the company on November 6, sanctioning a scheme by M. Philippart for the purchase by the company of interests in foreign electric patents, and for establishing companies in England or abroad for working such patents, and which scheme had not met with the approval of Philippart's co-directors. The other facts of the case are stated in his Lordship's judgment. The arguments, which occupied the greater part of four days, were concluded on Wednesday last, when his Lordship reserved judgment, which he delivered this morning.

Sir Horace Davey, Q.C., and Mr. Grosvenor Woods appeared for the

1. *Of working*, d'exploiter. — 2. *Storage*, accumulation. — 3. *Deferred shares*, des actions à payer plus tard.—4. *Misfeasance*, expression légale, mal faisance, dommage.—5. *The assets*, l'actif. — 6. *The board*, le conseil d'administration.

liquidators; Mr. Ince, Q.C., Mr. Buckley, Q.C., and Mr. Woodroffe for the late directors, other than M. Philippart; and Mr. John Henderson and Mr. Merrick for M. Philippart.

MR. JUSTICE KAY said: — The liquidators of this company, which is being wound up, have taken out the present summons[1] against certain gentlemen who were formerly directors of the company, under section 165 of the Companies Act[2], 1862, seeking to make them personally liable for alleged misfeasances as such directors. No imputation whatever is made upon the honesty or honourable conduct of any of these gentlemen, but it is alleged that they have committed breaches of trust[3] in making certain payments out of the moneys of the company and in permitting the transfer of certain of its shares. These questions involve a consideration of what is the real position of the directors of a joint-stock trading company[4]. With respect to the capital of the company which is under their management, it has been said that they are "quasi-trustees[5]" for the company (" Flitcraft's Case, 21 Ch. D.[6], 534). In that and other respects they are "to a certain extent trustees" (" Lindley on Partnership[7], " p. 587). In the language of Lord Romilly in "York and North Midland Railway Company v. Hudson" "The directors are persons selected to manage the affairs of the company for the benefit of the shareholders; it is an office of trust, which, if they undertake, it is their duty to perform fully and entirely." They certainly are not trustees in the sense of those words as used with reference to an instrument of trust such as a marriage settlement or a will. One obvious distinction is that the property of the company is not legally vested in them. Another and perhaps still broader difference is that they are the managing agents[8] of a trading association, and such control as they have over its property and such powers as by the constitution of the company are vested in them are confided to them for purposes widely different from those which exist in the case of such ordinary trusts as I have referred to and which require that a larger discretion should be given to them. Perhaps the nearest analogy to their position would be that of the managing agent of a mercantile house to whom the control of its property and very large powers for the management of its business were confided; but there is no analogy which is absolutely perfect. Their position is peculiar because of the very great extent of their powers and the absence of control except the action of the shareholders of the company. However, it is quite obvious that to apply to directors the strict rules

1. *Summons*, assignation. *To take out a summons against*, assigner, citer. — 2. *The Companies Act*, loi sur les associations (commerciales). — 3. *A breach of trust*, un abus de confiance. — 4. *A joint-stock trading company*, compagnie commerciale par actions. — 5. "Quasi-trustees", de quasi-fidéi-commissaires. — 6. *Ch. D.*, *Décision of the court of Chancery*. — 7. *Lindley on partnership*, ouvrage sur les associations par le très honorable sir N. Lindley (né en 1828), un des *Lords justices* de la cour d'appel, fils du Dr John Lindley, professeur de botanique à Oxford. — 8. *Managing agents*, directeurs gérants.

of the Court of Chancery with respect to ordinary trustees[1] might fetter their action to an extent which would be exceedingly disadvantageous to the companies they represent. In the " Forest of Dean Mining Company " (10 Ch. D., 451) Sir G. Jessel, Master of the Rolls[2] said, " Directors have sometimes been called trustees or commercial trustees, and sometimes they have been called managing partners[3]. It does not much matter what you call them as long as you understand what their true position is, which is that they are really commercial men managing a trading concern for the benefit of themselves and of all the other shareholders in it. . . . .
They are no doubt trustees of assets[4] which have come into their hands or which are under their control, but they are not trustees of a debt due to the company. The company is the creditor, and, as I said before, they are only the managing partners." In " Smith v. Anderson " (15 Ch. D., 275) Lord Justice James said, " The distinction between a director and a trustee[5] is an essential distinction founded on the very nature of things. A trustee is a man who is the owner of the property and deals with it as principal, as owner, and as master, subject only to an equitable obligation to account to some persons to whom he stands in the relation of trustee and who are his *cestuis que trust*[6]. The same individual may fill the office of director and also be a trustee having property, but that is a rare, exceptional, and casual circumstance. The office of director is that of a paid servant of the company. A director never enters into a contract for himself, but he enters into contracts for his principal—that is, for the company of whom he is a director, and for whom he is acting. He cannot sue on such contracts, nor be sued on them unless he exceeds his authority. That seems to me to be the broad distinction between *trustees and directors*." If directors apply money of the company for purposes so outside its powers that the company could not sanction such application, they may be made personally liable as for a breach of trust. On the other hand, if they apply the money of the company or exercise any of its powers in a manner which is not *ultra vires*[7], then a strong and clear case of misfeasance must be made out to render them liable. Lord Hatherley, in " Overend and Gurney Co. v. Gibb " (" L.R." 5, H.L. 487), intimates that in such a case their conduct must amount to *crassa negligentia*. In " Marzetti's Case " (28 W.R., 541), a definite test is applied. Lord Justice James said :—" A director should not be held liable upon any very strict rules such as those, in my opinion, too strict rules which were laid down by the Court of Chancery to make unfortunate trustees liable[8].

1. *Ordinary trustees*, mandataires ordinaires. — 2. *Master of the Rolls*, voy. note 4, page 64. — 3. *Managing partners*, associés gérants. — 4. *They are no doubt trustees of assets*, ils sont sans aucun doute administrateurs du capital qui... — 5. Ici *trustee* signifie encore *fidéi-commissaire*, ou plutôt un usufruitier. — 6. *Cestuis que trust*, vieux français, signifiant ceux en faveur desquels il tient un fidéi-commis. — 7. *Ultra vires*, plus que n'accordent les pouvoirs ou les droits qui leur sont concédés. — 8. *A trustee* est donc une personne à qui est confiée

Directors are not to be made liable on those strict rules which have been applied to trustees." And he intimates that the negligence for which a director would be held liable must be such as would make a managing director of a business liable to his employers. Lord Justice Brett said the director must be "guilty of such negligence as would make him liable in an action. Mere imprudence is not such negligence; want of judgment is not; it must be such negligence as would make a man liable in point of law;" and with this Lord Justice Cotton concurs. That is the law which must be applied to the circumstances of this case. The Faure Electric Accumulator Company was formed on the 13th of February, 1882, for the purpose of making and carrying out an agreement for the purchase of certain patents[1] and to carry on the business of electricians, and other matters. The capital was £1,000,000, divided into 80,000 ordinary shares of £10 each, and 200,000 deferred shares[2] of £1 each. Article 92 authorized the directors, out of the funds of the company, to pay the necessary legal and other expenses of and incident to the promotion, formation, and registration of the company, and all other preliminary expenses of the company. Article 28 provided, "No transfer of shares not being fully paid up shall be registered unless and until the transferree[3] is approved by the board of directors, and the board at their discretion may decline to register any transfer of shares upon which the company has a lien[4]." On the 15th of February, 1882, the company entered into an agreement for the purchase of certain patents under which large payments had to be made in shares of the company; 20,128 shares of £10 each were subsequently allotted to the general public, and in this manner all the original £10 share capital was issued, except about 20,000 shares. It appears that the company got into litigation in May of that year with another company who, they alleged, were infringing their patents. M. Philippart[5], who, it seems, was very familiar with the working of their patents, attended in that month at a meeting of the board, accompanied by a Mr. Pincoffs, a London stockbroker, who acted as his interpreter. Philippart was a holder both of original and deferred shares. He had made himself very active in the company's affairs; and upon the 22d of May, 1882, he wrote to the board offering to take up the unsubscribed capital of the first issue, that is, the £10 shares, by taking 5,000 shares himself and 5,000 by his friends, on condition that his friends should have the option, till the 15th of June, of taking up the remaining 10,000 shares, and that he, Philippart,

la direction de certaines valeurs ou propriétés pour le profit d'un tiers. La loi à laquelle on fait ici allusion et que la cour de *Chancery* a appliquée si sévèrement est *the Law on the Liability of Trustees* (loi sur la responsabilité des fidéi-commissaires), passée en 1888. — 1. *Patent*, brevet. — 2. *Deferred shares*, actions payables à une époque ultérieure. — 3. *Transferree*, cessionnaire. — 4. *Lien*, gage; c'est aussi le droit de retenir comme gage. — 5. *M. Philippart*, spéculateur belge et grand actionnaire de nombreuses compagnies diverses, a été déclaré en faillite en 1883.

should be elected a director, and that no brokerage should be paid in respect of the allotment[1] of these shares. This was considered at a board meeting, on the next day, May 23, and declined. On that day Pincoffs wrote to the company :—"I beg to offer to place 7,500 shares of your company at par[2] upon condition of your giving my client the option of taking the remaining 12,382 unapplied-for shares[3] at par until the 23rd of June next, and subject to the usual brokerage of 2s. 6d. per share to myself." The board appeared to have taken the advice of their solicitors, who advised them by a letter, which is in evidence, that there was no objection in law to the acceptance of these terms, provided the board were satisfied with the allottees[4], and that the brokerage was paid by the company and not deducted from the price of issue. Thereupon the board assented to the proposal, and later in the day a letter was handed to them from Mr. W. Morris, a stockbroker, stating that he was willing to take 7,500 shares at par and pay £2 a share at once, provided he had the option of taking at par, on or before the 23rd of June, the balance of the unallotted shares amounting to about 12,500, and that the board would allow 5s. per share commission on the whole number of shares taken by him, the commission on the 7,500 to be paid at once; the commission on the shares to be paid to Mr. Pincoffs. It is stated in the evidence that Morris was known to the directors to be a stockjobber[5] of very large means[6]. A formal application followed, and on that same 23rd of May the directors allotted 7,500 £10 shares to Morris, and paid £937 to Pincoffs as commission. Subsequently, about the 17th of June, they allotted the remaining 12,382 £10 shares to Morris and paid £1,547 15s. as commission to Pincoffs. They received from Morris £2 a share on these allotments, that is, nearly £40,000. In the meantime the board, on the 24th of May, 1882, had received notice of a charge[7] by Philippart to Seavar on all his shares in the company, and on the 30th of May, 1882, they had notice of an injunction[8] as to the deferred shares of Philippart in the company. They referred this to their solicitor, who wrote on the 7th of June, 1882 :—"The directors should consider whether in the circumstances any transfers of shares to M. Philippart should be registered before being fully paid." On the 30th of June, 1882, Philippart was elected a director of the company. On the 27th of September, 1882, the company had notice of two charging orders[9] on Philippart's shares for £420 and £1,355 respectively. Morris seems to have been at this time in communication with the board, being called in by them to advise, he having a large stake in the company. It

1. *Allotment*, répartition. — 2. *At par*, au pair. — 3. *Unapplied-for shares*, actions non encore souscrites. — 4. *The allottees*, ceux à qui on assigne les actions, les cessionnaires. — 5. *Stockjobber*, agioteur. — 6. *Of very large means*, de grandes ressources. — 7. *A charge*, un ordre. — 8. *Injunction*, arrêt de sursis; aussi instructions, défense. — 9. *Charging order*, saisie-arrêt ou opposition.

appears that he was desirous to transfer the shares he held; and on the 11th of October, 1882, the board sanctioned and subsequently passed a transfer of about 19,528 shares from Morris to Philippart. The transfer was completed on the 18th of October. Shortly afterwards the directors against whom this claim is made resigned. A call of £1 a share had been made, and on the 3rd of January, 1883, Philippart and his brother directors forfeited his shares, which were then about 18,500 in number, for non-payment of that call. Subsequently two other calls of £1 a share were made. On the 10th of April, 1883, Philippart became bankrupt. In July, 1884, a winding-up order[1] was made; 30s. a share has been called up in the liquidation. The debts of the company, which were admitted have all been paid. Claims to a large amount are outstanding[2] which the liquidator is resisting, and there are, I am told, some costs of the liquidation still to be provided for. The claims[3] made by this summons[4] are: first, damages for the alleged misfeasance of the former directors in allotting 7,500 shares on the 25th of May, 1882, and 12,372 shares on the 19th of June, 1882, to Morris, as nominee of Philippart, or in allowing 18,500 of such shares to be transferred on the 18th of October, 1882, to Philippart; and secondly, that they may be ordered to repay the sums paid to Pincoffs for brokerage on such allotment, with interest. The summons also contains two other claims, which have not been opened before me, and which of course must be refused. I will deal with these claims in the order in which they are made. It has not been attempted at the bar[5] to urge that the directors are liable in respect of the allotment to Morris. Morris was a very substantial[6] person, and I have no reason to doubt that the allotment to him was an advantage to the company. He paid £2 a share, and was liable for the uncalled £8 on all the shares allotted to him. The stress of the argument on the first point related to the transfer to Philippart, as to which the case is put, as I understand, in two ways. It is urged that the directors did not in fact "approve" Philippart as a transferree under art. 28. That is, although they allowed the transfer to him, they did not exercise the judgment and discretion which they were bound to exercise according to that article. And the second contention upon this point is that if they did, the transaction was so utterly improper that it amounted to a gross breach of duty for which they may be rendered liable. The first of these two arguments rests mainly upon a passage in the cross-examination of one of the directors. He states that he recollects the attention of the Board being drawn on the 11th of October, 1882, to the large number of shares which it was proposed that Morris should transfer to Philippart, and he says the matter was well considered, and the directors came to the conclusion

1. *A winding-up order*, un ordre de liquidation. — 2. *Are outstanding*, sont en suspens. — 3. *Claims*, réclamations. — 4. *Summons*, citation. *Summons* est un singulier. — 5. *At the bar*, à la barre du tribunal. — 6. *Substantial*, solvable. Voy. note 6, page 73.

that the transfer should be passed, as there was no valid objection. This gentleman, who said that at this distance of time he found it very difficult to recollect what took place, added :—" I cannot say whether a discussion of any duration took place on it. No one threw a doubt on the prudence of sanctioning such transfer. We were told by our solicitor at that meeting that as there was no valid objection we had no option in the matter. I believe the solicitor was present at that meeting. At all events it was at a meeting at which the solicitor happened to be present." Another of these gentlemen gives pretty much the same account, and says the solicitor advised them to sanction the transfer, and said they must do so, and could not help themselves. If it is right to rely on the imperfect recollection of these gentlemen of a transaction which took place five-and-a-half years before, I must say that these extracts produce in my mind exactly the contrary effect to that for which they were cited. I should infer *primâ facie*[1] from the mere circumstance of the transfer that, rightly or wrongly, the directors did in fact approve the transferree[2], and these statements of the directors confirm that view. They show that the matter was discussed, and that the advice of the solicitor of the company was taken upon it. But the argument has rather been upon the other point—whether such approval was a misfeasance for which the directors are liable. They have made an affidavit[3] in which they say that when they sanctioned the transfer from Morris to Philippart they did not know or believe that he would be unable to pay the amount uncalled—*i. e.*[4], £8 a share. Looking at the matter in the light of the later occurrences, the failure of Philippart to pay the calls on his shares, his bankruptcy, and the ruin and winding up of the company under his management, it is easy to see that the transfer was an act much to be regretted; but, anything like corrupt or dishonest dealing being out of the question, the difficulty is—Can the Court, putting itself as completely as is now possible in the position of the directors in October, 1883, say that their conduct in then sanctioning this transfer was so grossly improper that they must be made liable personally for the consequences? They have been cross-examined at enormous length for eight days, and their depositions, without the questions, cover 35 pages of printed matter. I have read with care all portions of them which relate to this transaction and a great deal besides. The case made against them may be shortly summed up thus :— On the 23rd of May, 1882, the directors had declined to allot to Philippart the £20,000 unallotted £10 shares. They did not particularly like his manner, which was overbearing. They or some of them knew that he had been engaged in large financial operations abroad, and had failed some time previously. It had been brought

1. *Primâ facie*, à la première apparence, c'est-à-dire tout d'abord. — 2. Voy. note 3, page 72. — 3. *Affidavit*, déclaration *par écrit* faite devant un magistrat, attestation en justice. — 4. *i. e.*, *id est*, c'est-à-dire.

to their attention that there were judgments against him and charging orders[1] upon the other shares which he then held in this company, and their solicitor had suggested that they should hesitate to allow any shares to be transferred to him unless they were fully paid. Nevertheless, on the 30th of June, 1882, he was elected a director, and on the 11th of October, at a meeting of the Board at which he attended part of the time, this transfer was approved. On the other hand, the directors say that they understood that, although he had failed for a very large amount before this company was formed, he was " up again[2] " and had made a largish sum of money. The judgments against him had been brought to his attention, and he had said they were all nonsense, and he was not going to be blackmailed[3]. They understood—though not, it would seem, according to their present recollection, from any very definite information—that he was being backed[4] by some of the most powerful people in France, and had considerable means of his own. They found that the Faure accumulators, the subject of their patents, were very difficult to manage, and that Philippart had an intimate knowledge of their construction which would be of great use to the company, and therefore principally, and also because of his activity as a shareholder, he was made a director. I have no doubt that when the question concerning the transfer of Morris's shares to him arose it seemed to them that they had no valid reason for not approving him as a tranferree. They knew, of course, as men of business, that he could not possibly obtain the transfer from Morris without satisfying the very large sum of £40,000 which Morris had actually paid to the company. He did this to some extent by transferring other shares in the company to Morris, but he must have provided a large sum in cash. Anything like corruption or dishonesty on the part of the directors being out of the question, I am unable to treat them as responsible for the consequences of permitting this transfer. Even if the act was, with the knowledge which they had at the time, a grave error of judgment, that is not a ground upon which the Court could properly hold them liable. Upon the second point I have felt much more difficulty. It was said in argument against the directors that the payment of brokerage to Pincoffs was analogous to issuing the shares at a discount. The analogy seems to me imperfect. In "*In re* Almada and Tirito Company, and Allen's Case " (36, "W.R., " 593), the Court of Appeal held that issuing shares at a discount was *ultra vires*[5], because it would in effect be altering the amount of the capital of the company in a manner not authorized by the Joint Stock Companies Act[6], and was equivalent to returning part of the capital to the

1. Voy. note 9, page 73. — 2. " *Up again* ", de nouveau debout, c'est-à-dire qu'il s'était relevé. *Largish*, assez grand. Les deux expressions sont *familières*. — 3. *He was not going to be blackmailed*, il n'allait pas se laisser extorquer de l'argent. — 4. *Backed*, appuyé, soutenu. — 5. Voy. note 7, page 71. — 6. Loi pour la réglementation des compagnies par actions.

allottee. Payment of brokerage to a person not the shareholder implies a receipt from the shareholder of the full amount payable on the shares, and then an application either of part of the money so received or other money of the company in paying the brokerage. The real question is whether such an application of capital is within the power of the company. If the payment be completely *ultra vires*, then the directors who made it are liable as for a breach of trust, unless the case comes within that rather exceptional class which I had to consider in " Tomkinson v. South-Eastern Railway Company" (35, Ch. D.[1], 675), where the payments were treated as being within the general power of the directors as managers, although not in the strictest sense payments for any of the objects mentioned in the memorandum. In this case there is nothing whatever in the memorandum of association which would justify such a payment except the words " to do all such other things as the company may deem incidental[2] or conducive to the attainment of any of the aforesaid objects of the company." The " aforesaid objects " do not include the issue of the company's shares. But it is argued that the first thing which a newly-formed company has to do is to invite and encourage persons to take shares. For this purpose, it is said, they may print and issue prospectuses and they may advertise. Why should they not employ agents to travel about the country and invite persons to join? If they may, such agents must be paid for their services; and where is the difference between that and giving a commission to some one, like a broker who has a large number of clients whom he may induce to take shares in the company? I am not satisfied that such employment of agents would be legitimate; but, if it were, it seems to me that there is a difference, and an important one. Payment of what is called brokerage for placing shares is not really payment for work and labour. It is a commission—that is, a bonus to A to use his influence to make B, C, and D shareholders. Put the simplest case. A says to the directors, " I know a wealthy man whom I can persuade to take 10,000 of your shares; give me £2,000 and I will induce him to do so." Would that be a legitimate payment? This practice, so far as it exists, has grown up from the launching of bubble companies[3] which could not be brought out without the aid of speculators, who insist on being paid a bonus or commission for their help. In the case of an enterprise which is favourably received by the public not a penny need be spent in this way. It is only companies which are unsound, or at any rate unpopular, which resort to such devices. In this very case four of the five directors in their joint affidavit state that when Pincoffs' offer was made the company's shares were unsaleable at par, and that, accordingly, they thought

1. *Ch. D., Chancery decision*; jugement de la Cour de Chancery. — 2. *Incidental*, comme appartenant à. — 3. *The launching of bubble companies*, la création de compagnies frauduleuses. *Bubble*, bulle d'air.

it beneficial to accept his terms. That is a distinct statement that, unless speculators were paid out of the company's capital to place the shares, there was no chance of issuing them. In my opinion such a course of proceeding is calculated to lead to a great amount of evil in the commercial world. It ought to be discouraged. These are considerations which must be regarded in determining whether such a payment is *ultra vires*. Another consideration is this. The question does not depend on the amount paid unless it were so large as to suggest *mala fides*[1]. If 2s. 6d. a share may be paid, why not 5s., 10s., or £1 ? The more needy[2] the company the greater must be the payment. The more hopeless the enterprise the larger would be this kind of outlay? The terms of Morris's letter of the 23rd of May, 1882, in which he insisted on the payment of a commission to Pincoffs, suggest a suspicion that the commission would be some pecuniary advantage to him. It is but a suspicion. I have no evidence that such was the case, but I refer to it as an obvious danger which would result from such a practice. A commission to Morris would, in effect, be issuing shares at a discount[3]. Giving a commission to brokers may in this way be a roundabout mode of returning part of the capital to the allottee[4]. The capital of the company is placed under the control of the directors for the purpose of carrying on the business of a trading concern. In any expenditure concerning its proper business the Court treats them as having a large discretion. A moderate expenditure in launching the company—that is, in introducing it to the notice of the public to invite them to join—though not part of the trading business, may be treated as conducive thereto. It is not easy to draw a definite line as to every payment of this kind. But a company cannot employ the capital which has been subscribed for the purposes of its business in making payments to induce persons to take shares to such persons themselves. Can it be legitimate to make such payments to another who has influence over them? Is that such an application of the capital of the company as a general meeting could sanction ? Suppose such a meeting called, and the directors were to say to it, " We have tried all the ordinary means of inducing the public to take shares and failed. By paying a bonus[5] to influential members of the Stock Exchange or influential solicitors or bankers we can get them to persuade their clients to take further capital. Sanction our doing this. " Could a general meeting validly decide that the capital subscribed to carry on the business of the company should be so applied ? Without using the word in any offensive sense the objection to such payments is that they partake of the nature of a bribe[6]. The broker or agent is paid to give advice

1. *Mala fides*, mots latins, la mauvaise foi. — 2. *The more needy... the greater must be...*, plus... est besogneuse... plus... doit être grand. Voy. *Gramm. Elwall*, n° 222. — 3. *At a discount*, au rabais. — 4. *The allottee*, le cessionnaire. — 5. *A bonus*, une prime, un boni. — 6. *A bribe*, corruption par dons.

and the persuasion is presumably, he would not do that without such payment. Suppose the broker to say candidly, " I think badly of the prospects of your company. I would not take a share in it myself, but pay me, and I will find you some foolish people who will do so under my persuasion ". Would that be a legitimate thing to do? Yet something of this kind is necessarily involved in every such case. In my opinion, the payments to Pincoffs of 2s. 6d. for every share taken by Morris were *ultra vires*[1], that is, they were an application[2] of the subscribed capital which could not be sanctioned by a general meeting. I have dealt with this question entirely on principle. The actual point does not seem to have arisen before for decision. Two cases have been referred to, which have some bearing[3] upon it. In " Lydney, &c., Co. v. Bird " (31 Ch. D.[4], 329), Bird and Co., iron merchants, had given a guarantee before the company was formed to Messrs. Allaway in consideration of a commission of £10,800, by which they purported to " guarantee and provide for the subscription required from the public to complete the capital, " and to make other payments. The company was registered on the 30th of December, 1871, and subsequently, on the 9th of January, 1872, the agreement as to the guarantee was adopted and modified to this extent—that the guarantee was given by William Bird alone, and £5,000 of the £10,800 was to be paid to him as a consideration for his giving the guarantee, the remainder of the £10,800 being retained by James Bird, a former partner in the firm, of which William Bird had ceased to be a member. The action was brought against William Bird and James Bird to recover the £10,800. The Court of Appeal (33 Ch. D., 85) held that James Bird was liable for the whole £10,800 subject to just allowances, and on the question whether he could be allowed the £5,000 he had paid to William Bird the Court said :—" It appears to us wholly wrong to make the company pay for the issue of its own shares. No part of the capital of the company could be properly so applied. To allow James Bird the £5,000 paid by him to William Bird for his guarantee would be in effect to make the company misapply its capital. " Those words are large enough to include the present case, and I must observe that they occur in a considered judgment delivered for the Court by Lord Justice Lindley[5], who has paid very great attention to this branch of the law. But I do not rely on them too much, because distinctions may be drawn between the guarantee in that case and the agreement for commission in this. I have therefore preferred to rest my decision upon the reasons which I have given. On the other hand, reference is made to " Bagnall v. Carlton " (6 Ch. D., 371), which was a suit against certain promoters[6] of a company seeking to set aside an agreement

1. Voy. note 7, page 71. — 2. *An application*, un emploi. — 3. *Some bearing*, quelque rapport. — 4. *Chancery decision*, voy. note 1, p. 77. — 5. Voy. note 6, page 70. — 6. *Promoters*, lanceurs.

for the purchase by the company of certain property and asking repayment of the purchase moneys after deducting such sum as should be declared by the Court to be a fair allowance for commission and expenses. The Court held that the company, who were plaintiffs, were bound by the offer made in their pleadings to allow something to the defendants by way of commission for their trouble in promoting the company, Lord Justice James saying that it was clear that the defendants were not entitled to commission in any way whatever except by reason of the offer made in the bill. No question was raised as to such a payment being beyond the powers of the company, and I do not see how there could have been any such question, because the Court was imposing on the plaintiff company[1] certain terms as the price of the relief it was granting, and the order of the Court would be sufficient whether the payment was within the company's powers or not. It seems to me impossible to treat that case as a decision of this question. I must declare that the respondents, the directors who made these payments to Pincoffs, are jointly and severally liable to repay the same to the company, with interest at 4 per cent. per annum since the moneys were paid. It has been suggested that the Court should follow the example set by Vice-Chancellor Wickens in "Pickering v. Stephenson" ("L. R." 14, Eq.[2] 322), by declining to order repayment by the directors. In that case, and in "Studdert v. Grosvenor" (23 Ch. D., 528), in which it was followed, the amount was very small and the interest of the applicant in that small amount was almost infinitesimal. Here the amount is considerable, and the liquidators who apply represent the whole body of shareholders, whose liability will be lessened if this money is recovered. The respondents, other than Philippart, against whom no relief is asked because he is insolvent, and Mr. Ponsonby, who was not a director till after the allotment of these shares, must be ordered jointly and severally to repay the amounts paid to Pincoffs with interest at 4 per cent. I must refuse the summons with costs[3] as to all the claims except the second which I allow with costs, such costs to be set off[4]. I must direct the Taxing Master[5] to allow to Mr. Ponsonby any separate costs which may have been incurred—that is, any increase of the costs by making him a respondent. The liquidator may take any costs out of the estate which will remain after the set off, except that I must direct the Taxing Master to disallow any costs of the cross-examination[6] which he may consider excessive.

1. *The plaintiff company*, la compagnie plaignante. — 2. *L. R.* 14, *Eq.* Equity. La cour de la chancellerie (*the Court of Chancery*) siège aussi comme Cour d'équité, et, à ce titre, elle a pour devoir de suppléer à l'insuffisance de la loi ou d'en modérer la trop grande sévérité. — 3. *With costs*, avec dépens. — 4. *To be set off*, être réservés. — 5. *The Taxing Master*, le vérificateur des frais, l'expert. Voy. note 1, page 68. — 6. *To disallow any costs of the cross-examination*, de refuser les frais de l'interrogation contradictoire (*ou* contre-examen par l'avocat de la partie adverse).

QUEEN'S BENCH DIVISION[1].

(*Before* Mr. Justice Wills *and* Mr. Justice Grantham.)

IN THE MATTER OF THE EXTRADITION ACTS, 1870 AND 1873, AND OF EDDIE GUÉRIN, A PRISONER IN HOLLOWAY GAOL, UNDER AN EXTRADITION WARRANT.

This was an extradition case[2] in the course of which two highly important questions arose; the one, as to the legality of the practice in Metropolitan police-courts of the magistrate disposing of a case only part of the evidence in which he has himself heard, part having been previously heard by another magistrate; the other, as to the nationality of persons born in America of British or Irish birth. The case out of which these points arose was as follows: —The prisoner, Eddie Guerin, was brought before Sir James Ingham at Bow-street on July 24, charged with the larceny of a great number of notes of great value from the " guichet " or wicket window of the Lyon's Bank in France; and his extradition, for trial upon that charge, was demanded by the French Government under the Extradition Act of 1870 (33 and 34 Vict.[3]). Sir James Ingham heard the evidence on July 24, 25, 26, 27, and 28, also on September 6, when the depositions of several witnesses were taken in support of the case for the application. Dispute arising as to Guerin's nationality (it being asserted on his behalf that he was an American, against him that he was a British subject), owing to the difficulty of securing witnesses upon this part of the case, some delay ensued. Sir James took his holiday in the ordinary course, and on the next day to which the hearing had been remanded—viz., September 27, and again on the subsequent days of the hearing—viz., October 4, 11, 22, and 25, Mr. Vaughan heard the evidence for and against the man's nationality. But—and here arose the matter now complained of as an irregularity which vitiated the whole process in the Court below—the evidence taken before Sir James Ingham was not repeated before Mr. Vaughan, nor were the witnesses previously examined called again, or their evidence read over to them for their adoption on the adjournment before the first magistrate—a course which, Mr. Poland stated, was, in his experience, the custom in criminal cases on such a change of magistrate. It is not, how-

1. Voy. note 3, page 66. — 2. Les lois sur l'extradition, c'est-à-dire sur la remise d'un étranger accusé de tout crime de droit commun entre les mains des officiers de justice de son propre pays, n'ont été admises dans le Royaume-Uni qu'en 1870 et en 1873. La remise de *Guérin*, accusé d'avoir volé la Banque de Lyon, a soulevé une question de la plus haute importance quant à la légalité d'un mandat d'extradition délivré par un magistrat de la police métropolitaine, quand il n'a entendu lui-même qu'une partie des témoignages produits contre l'accusé. Bien qu'on ait dans l'espèce confirmé le mandat sous la considération que les témoins entendus devant le magistrat de Londres ont suffisamment prouvé la culpabilité apparente de l'accusé, il a été regardé comme irrégulier et blâmable de la part d'un magistrat de délivrer un mandat d'extradition sur des témoignages qui n'ont pas été donnés devant lui. — 3. Les 33e et 34e années du règne de la reine Victoria. Les lois sont désignées en Grande-Bretagne par l'année du règne pendant laquelle elles ont été promulguées.

ever, to be supposed that the previous evidence was not read by Mr. Vaughan; the complaint was that, not having seen and heard the witnesses himself, he had not had the opportunity of judging of their credibility by their demeanour. Further evidence was heard by Mr. Vaughan himself—that, viz., of two witnesses who alleged that Guerin was born in Hoxton, in the house of a Mr. Walker, and had been dropped in the garden while a baby and had had in consequence a flat nose since, and that Guerin had also lost by some accident the tips of two fingers of his left hand; and also the evidence of a witness from Chicago, who alleged that Guerin was born in Chicago, and had long lived there. On this evidence Mr. Vaughan held that Guerin was not a British subject, and that, there being a *primâ facie* proof of guilt of the larceny against him (among others this, that in his room in London was found a Lyon's railway luggage ticket, dated on the day of the robbery, and among the articles of luggage to which the ticket referred two pairs of gloves the ends of which were filled up with wadding, as might be used by hands maimed of the finger tips), the extradition order must go[1] and issued it accordingly. The prisoner's release under this warrant was now sought for on the above-stated ground. The article of the Extradition Treaty relied on was as follows:—

"Extradition Treaty with France.

"Article II.

"Native born or naturalized subjects of either country are excepted from extradition. In the case, however, of a person, who since the commission of the crime or offence of which he is accused, or for which he has been convicted, has become naturalized in the country whence the surrender is sought, such naturalization shall not prevent the pursuit, arrest, and extradition of such person, in conformity with the stipulations of the present treaty[2]."

The ATTORNEY-GENERAL[3] (Mr. R. S. Wright and Mr. Danckwerts with him) appeared to show cause against a rule which had been recently obtained by Mr. Poland for an order of *habeas corpus*[4] to the Governor of Holloway

1. *The extradition order must go*, le mandat d'extradition devait être délivré. — 2. L'extradition n'a été réellement accordée que le 27 janvier 1889. On avait pu prouver que Guérin n'était pas naturalisé Anglais. — 3. *The Attorney-General* (*for the Crown*) correspond à peu près au *Procureur de la République* devant les tribunaux de France. Toutefois, il a en Angleterre d'autres fonctions de la plus haute importance. Il est le premier conseiller légal de la couronne et, depuis 1673, est toujours membre du Parlement. Il reçoit sa nomination du ministère en exercice et quitte ses fonctions quand ce ministère se retire. Le traitement attaché à cette dignité est 175 000 francs (£ 7 000), mais il lui est permis, en outre, de plaider dans des causes particulières, pourvu que ce ne soit pas contre les intérêts de la couronne. L'*Attorney-General* actuel est sir Richard Webster; il a plaidé pour *the Times* dans le procès Parnell v. the Times. — 4. *An order* (ou *a writ*) *of habeas corpus*, un mandat d'élargissement, ou dans tous les cas de comparution immédiate devant un magistrat. *Habeas corpus* sont les premiers mots de la formule latine que les magistrats anglais doivent employer, d'après un statut de 1673, pour donner l'ordre d'élargir un prisonnier. Ce statut est regardé comme la principale sauvegarde des libertés anglaises. Il ordonne que tout prévenu doit

Gaol to release Guerin on the grounds of the above stated irregularity in the hearing in the Court below, and in the course of his argument in support of the warrant remarked upon the inconvenience of holding in accordance with Mr. Poland's contention, as remands were so commonly asked for and granted, and different magistrates were in the habit of sitting on different days. He cited the case of " Regina v. Huguet[1] " (12 Cox C. C. 551[2]) where Mr. Vaughan took the first part of the evidence and Sir Thomas Henry the latter part; and it was objected that Sir Thomas ought not to look at the previous evidence, and that he having done so his committal was invalid, but held that, there being sufficient evidence before him apart from the previously heard evidence, the committal was good; also the case of " Regina v. De Vidil, " (9 Cox C. C. 4), where it was held under the circumstances of that case that a deposition was admissible, though taken before two Justices, who were not the two who subsequently committed—a decision of Mr. Justice Blackburn.

Mr. Poland (Mr. Gill with him) urged that there was no evidence of the commission of the crime in France. Grave inconvenience and grave mischief might arise if, as was claimed here, one magistrate could commit upon evidence heard before another. If this were permissible in the case of two magistrates, it would be in the case of six hearing different portions of the evidence on six different days. There had been eleven hearings of this case. The prisoner had been in custody since the 24th of July, and was committed for trial on the 25th of October by Mr. Vaughan. From September 6 till that day Mr. Vaughan had no title of evidence before himself; the only evidence was that taken before Sir James Ingham on earlier days. One magistrate could not act on evidence laid before another; this was inconsistent with elementary rules of justice. [Mr. Justice Wills.—Was there oral evidence before Mr. Vaughan against Guerin? Mr. Danckwerts.—Undoubtedly, my Lord, and the Attorney-General expressly reserved his right to argue upon that if the Court is against him upon the main point here—viz., that if no evidence were heard by Mr. Vaughan, the warrant was bad.] Only in the cases of death, insanity, and being kept out of the way by the accused were depositions readable. In " Reg. v. Austen " (" Dearsley's C. C., " 612), where a witness had gone abroad after examination, it was held

comparaître publiquement devant un magistrat dans les vingt-quatre heures de son emprisonnement pour en apprendre les motifs et pour en contester, s'il y a lieu, la validité. S'il y réussit, il est aussitôt remis en liberté. Cette loi soumet l'usage de l'emprisonnement préventif à un contrôle et en empêche l'abus. Le Parlement seul peut, dans les temps de trouble, en suspendre l'action. La liberté individuelle avait été garantie par une clause de la Grande Charte (*Magna Charta*), même contre un ordre du roi, mais, jusqu'au XVIIe siècle, la prérogative royale était si vaguement limitée et la puissance royale si grande, que des personnes furent souvent détenues en prison illégalement. Cela est impossible depuis l'*Habeas corpus* de 1673. — 1. *Regina v. Huguet*, la reine contre Huguet. — 2. *Cox C. C.*, *Cox's (collection of) Chancery Court (causes)*.

that the deposition was not admissible. "Reg. v. De Vidil" (9 "Cox C. C.[1]," 4) was the only scrap of authority for the course here sought to be defended, which, if allowed, would be a most serious innovation, and one of infinite danger to the administration of justice to prisoners. As to the evidence of the prisoner's nationality here, in "Reg. v. Wilson" ("L.R." 3, Q.B.D.[2], 42) the British nationality was admitted, and it was held that the treaty was incorporated with the Act, and that no British subject could be surrendered to the Swiss Government. [The COURT here relieved Mr. Poland from further argument in support of the right of the Court to review the magistrate's decision upon the fact of nationality, holding that it was a collateral matter, giving foundation to the magistrate's jurisdiction, and therefore clearly reviewable by this Court.]

MR. JUSTICE WILLS.—That being so, Mr. Wright, would it not be desirable, presuming as I do that this Court has the power so to do, to direct that the issue of nationality[3] in this case should be tried, if necessary, before a jury?

Mr. R. S. WRIGHT.—The Court without doubt, my Lord, has the power to direct such an issue, and the thing was done. In the case of "Mary Ellen Andrews" (8 "L.R.," Q.B.D., 153), it was held that a person who has been duly appointed under Car. 2, c. 24, s. 8[4], by the will of a father to be guardian of his child, stands *in loco parentis*[5], and, having therefore a legal right to the custody of the child, may, in order to obtain possession of such child, claim a writ of *habeas corpus*, which a common-law Court has no discretion to refuse if the applicant be such person and the child too young to choose for itself. Where, however, the validity of the testamentary appointment is disputed, the Court will direct an issue[6] to be tried by a jury in order to establish the same.

Mr. POLAND, resuming.—Nothing short of a statutory enactment[7] to that effect could give such a power. [MR. JUSTICE GRANTHAM.—As a matter of practice, is not this actually done daily?] My experience is that, in the case of rehearings before another magistrate, the practice is to reswear the witnesses, read their evidence, and receive their adoption of it on its being read over in their hearing as their evidence. The power to commit when the evidence was "completed as aforesaid" meant completed in accordance with section 17, prescribing the ordinary process of law—viz., oral evidence and depositions read over, and caution to the accused. As to the argument drawn from the form of warrant[8] (form "H. and D."), in 11

1. Voir note 2, page 83. — 2. *Q. B. D.*, Queen's Bench Decision. — 3. *The issue of nationality*, la question de nationalité. — 4. *Car.* 2, *c.* 24, *s.* 8, Carolus secundus, Charles II, chap. 24, section 8. — 5. *In loco parentis*, au lieu et place de père ou de mère. — 6. *An issue*, un point de fait. — 7. *Statutory enactment*, ordre basé sur une loi. — 8. *Form of warrant* (*form H. and D.*), *in* 11 *and* 12 *Vic.*, *c.* 4, forme de mandat dans la loi adoptée les années 11 et 12 de Victoria, chapitre 4.

and 12 Vic., c. 4, whereby a witness is " to be brought before me on . . at . . . or before such other justice of the peace for the same county as may then be there, to testify . . . ." this, like a similar provision in chapter 42, merely means to be dealt with according to the due course of law. The same observation arose upon the form of remand (Q 1)[1]; and upon the words :—" Before such justice as may then be there to answer further, " the meaning was that if the justice who heard the case before was not sitting at the adjournment, the prisoner was not to be discharged, but remanded till such justice should be sitting and dispose of the case. As to the case of " R. v. Jeffreys[2] " (22 *L. T.*[3], 936), that was in his favour as far as it went, for that was a case of a bastardy order (held in " R. v. Barry " to be a civil proceeding), and as such declared good. As to " R. v. Huguet " (12 Cox. C. C.[4], 557), that also, so far from being against him, was in his favour, the majority of the Court being in favour of the view he was now presenting.

Mr. Stevenson Moore appeared on behalf of the French Republic and the Bank of France.

Without calling on Mr. R. S. Wright to reply, the Court, after a long and elaborate argument, yielded to an application by Mr. Poland for a translation of the French depositions as to the luggage and identification of the prisoner as the man seen waiting about the railway office at the time of the robbery, and for time to consider their effect. The Court hereupon stated that they had perused them in the French, and were much impressed with the opinion that they clearly disclosed a *primâ facie*[5] case against Guerin, but would defer their decision upon that portion of the case till Thursday next, when they would hear Mr. Poland, if he wished, upon that part. Having distinctly made up their mind on the rest of the case, they would at once give their judgment upon it.

Mr. Justice Wills said the question was one of great importance and of very wide application, needing most careful consideration. If he entertained any doubt he would reserve his judgment for further consideration, but he did not. The first question in point of logical order was—Did the treaty apply to such as Guerin? That depended on whether he could bring himself within the exception of the treaty—viz., that native-born subjects of either country were excepted from its operation. The *onus*[6] of proving himself within the exception lay on Guerin. There are only two ways of acquiring or possessing the *status*[7] of a British subject—(1) naturalization; (2) birth. He could not distinguish between " natural born ", the words used

1. *The form of remand* (*Q* 1), la forme de l'ordre de renvoi (à une autre audience et indiquant par suite un renvoi au lieu de détention). — 2. *R. v. Jeffreys*, Regina versus Jeffreys, la reine contre Jeffreys. — 3. 22 *L. T.*, *Law Times*. Voir *Historique du Times*, p. 1. — 4. Voy. note 2, page 83. — 5. *A primâ facie case*, argument péremptoire. On remarquera que la loi anglaise emploie beaucoup d'expressions latines. — 6. *The onus of proving himself*, la charge de prouver qu'il est.... — 7. *The status*, la condition et, par suite, les droits.

in the statute[1], and "native born," the words used in the treaty, nor did he think any distinction was contemplated; native means native from the circumstance of his birth. There were contradictory affidavits; there must therefore be an issue to determine the fact of the nationality of Guerin—the only means which were at the disposal of this Court to inform itself upon such a matter of fact. Here some depositions were taken before Sir James Ingham, and then the rest were heard by Mr. Vaughan. He had seen enough already of these depositions to make it most probable that the eventual effect upon his mind would be that there was ample evidence to justify the magistrate's order. It was contrary to all his ideas and experience of justice for one magistrate to take up an inquiry commenced before another. Every prisoner was entitled to the decision of a magistrate as to whether a *primâ facie* case was made out. This decision, in truth, was not final, but he is entitled to the decision of the magistrate upon it. The proceeding, though not final, is a judicial proceeding, and can only be satisfactorily conducted by one who has heard the case throughout, and seen and heard for himself the witnesses and their demeanour. The principle of the Common Law was clear upon the matter. If there be any statutory infringement[2] upon this rule of natural justice, the Court must, of course, obey it. There were some statutes to that effect, specially enabling depositions taken before one magistrate in specified cases to be admissible evidence before another; in such cases *cadit quæstio*[3]; but this was not one. Here there had been eleven different hearings. There may, therefore, according to the argument adressed to the Court, have been eleven different magistrates engaged on the part-hearing of parts of this case. The remand "before the justice who part heard or some other justice" was a provision to meet the case of the first magistrate dying or resigning. In civil cases even one Judge or magistrate could only take up a case commenced before another by consent. Of course, a still more strict rule applied in criminal cases. 11-12 Vict., c. 43[4], bears importantly upon this[5]. In the sections of adjournment and in the forms of commitment[8] the same language was found used with respect to the hearing before the magistrate; in both cases, the case was to be conducted in accordance with the ordinary rules and forms of justice. The similarity and almost identity of the language used raised a fair[6], if not powerful, inference that in both cases there must be no departure from the ordinary rules of just procedure. This being so upon the statute, there was nothing in the decided cases[7] to

1. *In the statute*, dans la loi. — 2. *Any statutory infringement*, quelque infraction à la loi. — 3. *Cadit quæstio*, la question tombe, c'est-à-dire la question est résolue. — 4. 11-12 *Vict.*, c. 43. Comme nous l'avons dit plus haut, les lois sont désignées en Grande-Bretagne par l'année du règne pendant laquelle elles ont été promulguées. D'autre part, l'ensemble des lois pendant la même session est considéré comme formant un seul tout, subdivisé en chapitres, chaque loi représentant un chapitre. — 5. *Bears importantly upon this*, s'y rapporte d'une manière effective.— 6. *A fair inference*, une très juste conclusion ou conséquence.— 7. *In*

8. renvoi à une commission d'examen

the contrary. In " R. v. Vidil " (9 Cox), Mr. Justice Blackburn admitted the deposition of a witness taken before a magistrate who had not committed[5], but only heard the first part of the evidence against the prisoner under section 17. For one magistrate to act on evidence taken before another was wholly different, and this case was no authority for such a course. As to " R. v. Huguet " (12 Cox C. C.), the late Chief Baron spoke vigorously of the irregularity of a course of conduct such as that adopted here, but the decision of the majority of the Court, Barons Martin and Pollock, was that, without the evidence then there irregularly taken, there was other evidence taken regularly before the magistrate which was sufficient to support the order complained of. The clear distinction between " R. v. Jeffries " (27 *L.T.*, 786[1]) and this case was that that was a civil and not a criminal case. As to " R. v. Bertrand, " (1 P. C. App. C., 535), the case where on a second trial for murder, and some of the witnesses having been resworn and their evidence read over to them from the Judge's notes, and a new trial held on appeal from New South Wales[2], the case was not quite the same as this, but it was deeply interesting because of the vigorous denunciation by Mr. Justice Coleridge in that case of the course there adopted. Mr. Poland had read that learned Judge's words in the judgment :—

" The most careful note must often fail to convey the evidence fully in some of its most important elements, those for which the open oral examination[3] of the witness, in presence of prisoner, Judge, and jury, is so justly prized. It cannot give the look or manner of the witness, his hesitation, his doubt, or variations of language, his confidence or precipitancy, his calmness or consideration ; it cannot give the manner of the prisoner, when that has been important upon the statement of anything of particular moment. Nor could the Judge properly take on him to supply any of these defects, who, indeed, will not necessarily be the same on both trials. It is, in short, or it may be, the dead body of the evidence, without its spirit, which is supplied, when given openly and orally, by the ear and eye of those who receive it. "

That language of Sir John Taylor Coleridge clearly and forcibly exposed the radical objections to such a course as was here complained of. With respect to the power of the Court to review the finding of the magistrate upon a collateral matter like nationality in this case, it was a matter of principle that, where a matter of fact was cardinal to[4] the existence of a magistrate's jurisdiction, it was the right of the Court to inquire into the sufficiency

---

the decided cases, dans les causes sur lesquelles le jugement a été prononcé. — 1. (27 *L. T.*, 786), *Law Times*, v. note 3, p. 85. — 2. *New South Wales*, la Nouvelle Galles du Sud, la plus ancienne colonie anglaise en Australie, dont la capitale est Sydney. Cette colonie fut fondée en 1788, comme établissement pénal. — 3. *The open oral examination*, l'interrogatoire oral et public. Nous ferons remarquer ici que cet interrogatoire en France n'a lieu que devant le juge d'instruction, excepté pour les questions peu importantes de troubles, désordres, etc. — 4. *Where a matter of fact was cardinal to...*, là où un point de fait était

5. Déposé

of the evidence upon which the magistrate acted, as being a matter on which his jurisdiction to hear the case at all was based. He was, as he had intimated, strongly of impression upon the evidence already before this Court that there was abundantly sufficient evidence in the French depositions justifying the magistrate's decision upon the nationality of Guerin; but as Mr. Poland requested that the French deposition might be translated for his more careful inspection, this opportunity would be granted him, and the Court would hear him, if he desired to address to them any argument thereupon, again upon that point next Thursday.

MR. JUSTICE GRANTHAM concurred.

The result of the judgment, therefore, is that the magistrate's order extraditing the prisoner is affirmed, as being based on sufficient evidence actually heard by himself at the adjournment; but the practice of any magistrate's acting on evidence not heard before himself in any criminal case stands condemned by judicial censure as irregular and contrary to natural justice.

(*Sittings in Bankruptcy*[1], *before* MR. JUSTICE CAVE.)

EX PARTE RAWLINGS—RE DAVIS[2].

This was an application by the trustee under the failure of Messrs. J. and H. Davis for a declaration that he was entitled to the benefit of certain hiring agreements[3] specified in an assignment dated May 9, 1887, and executed in favour of Mr. W. Pipe, formerly carrying on business as a furniture dealer in Whitfield-street, Tottenham-court-road.

Mr. E. C. Willis, Q. C., and Mr. Rose Innes appeared for the trustee in support of the application; and Mr. Sidney Woolf for the respondent.

The bankrupts formerly traded in Tottenham-court-road as furniture dealers, and a large portion of their business consisted of letting out furniture on the hire-purchase system[4]. By the assignment in question, after reciting certain of these hiring agreements and that the hirers were indebted to Davis and Co. in various sums of money and that Davis and Co. were indebted to Pipe in £600, Davis and Co. assigned to Pipe all moneys which might be then or at any time thereafter become due in respect of the agreements and their rights and remedies thereunder, the same being accepted *pro tanto*[5] on account of the debt due to Pipe. The assignment was not

---

le point principal pour que la juridiction pût exister. — 1. *In Bankruptcy*, dans la Cour des faillites. *A bankrupt* n'est pas nécessairement un banqueroutier; c'est un simple failli, un commerçant déclaré en faillite. Le titre de *banqueroutier* est donné au failli qui est convaincu de fraude. — 2. *Ex parte*: ce terme est expliqué comme suit par M. C. Sweet dans son *Law Dictionary:* Dans son sens premier, se rapportant à une demande en justice, *ex parte* signifie que la demande est faite par une personne qui, n'étant point partie, a cependant un intérêt dans l'instance où elle peut être introduite. Dans son sens plus habituel, *ex parte* signifie que la demande est soutenue par une partie en l'absence de l'autre. *Re Davis*, affaire Davis. — 3. *Hiring agreements*, contrats de louage. — 4. *The hire-purchase system*, vente (locative) à terme. L'objet loué devient la propriété du locataire après un certain temps. — 5. *Pro tanto*, pour autant, c'est-à-dire pour leur valeur réelle.

registered under the Bills of Sale Act[1]. There were three questions involved in the application, but the only point necessary to notice was whether the assignment became void against the trustee in bankruptcy by reason of non-registration[2].

MR. JUSTICE CAVE, after hearing the arguments of counsel and referring to the terms of the assignment, gave judgment to the effect that the right of Davis and Co. under the agreements was to receive the moneys coming due from the hirers. This right was a *chose in action*, and the assignment, of which notice had been given to the hirers, did not require registration under the Bills of Sale Act. The case was not within the mischief of that Act[3], and the application must be dismissed, with costs.

WESTERN AUSTRALIA[4].—The revenue of Western Australia during the past year amounted to £377,903 and the expenditure to £456,897, large sums having been spent in public works, especially in railways. The estimated population was 42,488. The imports were valued at £832,213 and the exports at £604,656. There was an increase in the area of cultivated land over the previous year of 19,236 acres[5], the total amount under cultivation being 105,582 acres, while in all kinds of farming stock[6] the increase was very considerable. During the year, concludes the administrative report, the colony made a substantial advance in settlement. " The extension of the railways, the improvements, which were very marked, in the principal towns, the satisfactory increase in stock of various classes and in the area of cultivated land, as well as the continued good reports from the prospectors of the auriferous lands, are matters which the colonists may be congratulated upon."

ST. VINCENT[7].—The Blue-book of St. Vincent for the past year describes it as the very worst year the colony has ever experienced. The revenue was £23,661 and the expenditure £29,720, while the public debt amounts to £9,920. The value of the imports was £80,000, being 10 per cent. less than the previous year, and 20 per cent. less than the year before that while the exports were valued at £85,000, the staples[8] being sugar and arrowroot[9].

---

1. *The Bills of Sale Act*, la loi sur les contrats (ou les comptes) de vente. — 2. *Non-registration*, défaut d'enregistrement. — 3. *Was not within the mischief of that Act*, ne subissait pas l'effet dommageable de cette loi. — 4. *Western Australia*, l'Australie occidentale, c'est-à-dire la région comprenant la moitié occidentale de l'Australie au delà du 129° degré de longitude E. La capitale est *Perth*. Les ressources de cette colonie sont énormes, mais elles ne sont pas encore développées. On y trouve des mines de plomb, de cuivre, d'or, de houille, d'étain, de zinc et de fer, des forêts d'une valeur incalculable, de grandes étendues de pâturages, et des pêcheries de perles. Le sol dans bien des endroits convient à la culture de la vigne, des oliviers et des vers à soie. — 5. *An acre*, mesure agraire d'environ 40 ares $^1/_2$ (40 ares 4671). L'hectare vaut donc à peu près 2 *acres* et demi. — 6. *Farming stock*, bétail, animaux de ferme. — 7. *St. Vincent*, une des Antilles (Iles sous le Vent). — 8. *The staples*, les denrées principales. — 9. *Arrowroot*, substance farineuse et nutritive, surtout pour les enfants et les estomacs faibles; elle porte le même nom en français. Les Indiens l'employaient, dit-on, autrefois pour guérir les blessures faites par les flèches empoisonnées (*arrow*, flèche; *root*, racine).

80 per cent. of the sugar goes to the United States, but all the other exports to Great Britain. The population is estimated at 45,000.

RUSSIAN TRADE IN CENTRAL ASIA.—A telegram from Kizil Arvat, dated the 7th inst., states that in consequence of the advantages presented by the Trans-Caspian Railway many merchants in Bokhara have substituted for their imports from India the route *viâ* Bushire, Persia, and Askabad, for the old one through Afghanistan. During the months of June and July 1,781,400 roubles[1] worth of Russian merchandise from Bokhara for Afghanistan was exported, and 2,961,103 roubles worth was imported from Afghanistan.

MONEY-MARKET and CITY INTELLIGENCE[2].

PRINTING-HOUSE-SQUARE,
Tuesday Evening.

The demand for loans[3] was again small, and the discount inquiry is still on a very small scale. Bill rates[4], in the marked absence of business, were, however, unchanged, the return of the Bank of England notes taken for Russia some weeks ago having had, apparently, no effect, owing probably to the general impression that about an equal amount of gold will be withdrawn shortly for South America. On 'Change[5], bills on France and Belgium were in good demand. The chief feature, however, was a considerable recovery[6] in the Russian exchange[7], owing to the announcement of the new loan. Cheques on Paris changed hands at 25f. 30c. and 25f. 31c., and those on Germany at 20m. 38pf.[8] and 20m. 40pf. We subjoin our usual table:—

Loans.		Discount (Bank Bills)[11].			Bank of England Rate of Discount[13].	
Day to day[9].	For short periods[10].	3 mths.[12]	4 mths.	6 mths.	At present	Changed on Oct. 4
$1\frac{1}{4}\ \frac{1}{2}$ p.c.	$2\frac{1}{4}$ p.c.	$3\frac{1}{8}$ p.c.	3 p.c.	3 p.c.	5 p.c.	from 4 p.c.

The announcement made by our Philadelphia Correspondent that a "war of rates[14]" had again broken out among the New York-Chicago Trunk

1. Le *rouble*, monnaie russe, devait valoir 4 francs; mais le rouble *papier* ne vaut réellement aujourd'hui qu'environ 2 francs, ou moins encore. — 2. *Money-market and City intelligence*, bulletin financier et nouvelles commerciales. — 3. *Loan*, emprunt, prêt. — 4. *Bill rates*, l'escompte sur effets. — 5. *On 'Change*, à la Bourse (*Change* pour *the Exchange*). — 6. *Recovery*, reprise. — 7. *In the Russian exchange*, dans le change sur la Russie. — 8. 20 *m.* 38 *pf.*, 20 marks 38 pfennigs; le *mark* vaut 1 fr. 25 et se divise en 100 pfennigs; le pfennig valant un peu plus que le centime. — 9. *Day to day*, du jour au lendemain. — 10. *For short periods*, à court terme. — 11. *Discount (Bank Bills)*, escompte sur les effets émis par les grandes banques de premier ordre. — 12. 3 *mths.* $3\frac{1}{8}$ p. c., 3 months, $3\frac{1}{8}$ per cent. Les Anglais comptent par huitièmes ou *eights*, parce que la livre sterling se divise en huit *half-crowns;* voy. Gramm. Elwall. — 13. *Rate of discount*, taux d'escompte de la Banque d'Angleterre. — 14. *A war of rates*, une guerre de tarifs.

lines[1] produced a heavy fall in all American Railroad securities[2], and some other stocks were flat in sympathy with them. No satisfactory explanation of this "bolt out of the blue[3]," which has naturally affected the market all the more because it was quite unexpected, is forth-coming. The best-informed people are disposed to think that the trouble has arisen out of the uncompleted sale of the South Pennsylvania line to the Pennsylvania by the New York Central. The two principal parties to this transaction were quite agreed about it, but it will be remembered that as soon as preparations were made for carrying out the bargain the Courts[4] were called upon by a small section of the shareholders who are interested in getting a competing line made to Pittsburg to declare it illegal, which, on hearing the evidence, they did. Since then the line has not been completed, but is has not, of course, been handed over to the Pennsylvania, and the same minority of shareholders, some of whom are very wealthy, have been doing all they can to force the directors to finish it. It appears to us that if this is the whole ground for quarrrel between the Pennsylvania and the New York Central there ought to be no quarrel at all, and we shall expect to hear before long that the "war" has been put an end to by the good sense of the two great companies and the remonstrances of the other members of what used to be called the "Trunk Lines' Pool[5]." But it is said by many people that the present trouble is due to Mr. Roberts's[6] hostility to rate agreements of any kind, which has caused a certain amount of friction among the Trunk lines for some time past. If it should turn out to be the fact that the attitude of the president of the Pennsylvania Railroad Company is the chief cause of the want of harmony among the Trunk lines which has so suddenly and disagreeably manifested itself again, it will become necessary to consider whether the ungrudging support which Mr. Roberts has hitherto received from the majority of English shareholders in the Pennsylvania should be withdrawn. It will be wise, however, to wait for further information before adopting any conclusion as to who is to blame for what has occurred.

The Market for Home Government Securities[7] has been a trifle firmer to day, owing to the low value of money. New Consols[8] closed at $97\frac{1}{8}$ $97\frac{1}{4}$ for money and $97\frac{1}{4}$ $97\frac{3}{8}$ for the account, a rise of 1-16 to $\frac{1}{8}$. Two-and-a-Half per Cents. at 94 and Old Consols[9] at 101 were unaltered. Indian Government

1. *Trunk-lines*, lignes principales. — 2. *Securities*, valeurs. — 3. "*This bolt out of the blue*", cette sortie subite de l'état de calme; c'est un américanisme. — 4. *The Courts*, les tribunaux. — 5. *The Trunk Lines' Pool*, les grands actionnaires. *Pool*, masse. — 6. M. Roberts, président de la compagnie « la Pennsylvanie ». — 7. *Home Government Securities*, bons de trésor du gouvernement anglais. — 8. *New Consols*, les 2 3/4 p. %. C'est par une loi passée en 1888 que M. Goschen, ministre des finances (*Chancellor of the Exchequer*) a réduit de 1/4 p. % l'intérêt jusqu'en 1903, et de 1/2 p. % à partir de cette époque. La réduction a été généralement acceptée par les porteurs de rente et la réduction a eu son effet depuis le mois d'avril 1889. — 9. *Old Consols*, ce sont les fonds qui n'ont pas été convertis. Ils ne montent qu'à £ 40,000 000 (un milliard de francs), et le gouvernement a été libre de les payer à partir

Securities were not much dealt in. The Three per Cents. fell $\frac{1}{8}$ to 97$\frac{1}{4}$, but the Three-and-a-Half per Cents. were $\frac{1}{8}$ higher at 106 106$\frac{1}{4}$. Colonial Government Securities were inclined to be rather firmer.

The Home Railway Market was, for the most part, neglected, and prices were, as a rule, dull, the amount of business entered into for the new account being very small. London and North-Western was rather in demand and rose $\frac{1}{2}$ to 169, London and South-Western $\frac{1}{2}$ to 139$\frac{1}{2}$, Great Western $\frac{1}{4}$ to 151, and Midland $\frac{1}{8}$ to 133$\frac{5}{8}$. On the other hand, North-Eastern Consols fell $\frac{1}{4}$ to 157$\frac{5}{8}$, South-Eastern Deferred[1] $\frac{1}{4}$ to 108$\frac{3}{8}$, Chatam $\frac{1}{8}$ to 23$\frac{3}{8}$, and Brighton Deferred $\frac{1}{8}$ to 129$\frac{5}{8}$. The Scotch stocks were also lower.

The traffic receipts of the undermentioned railways for the past week show the following changes when compared with those of the corresponding period of last year :—Increases.—Great Eastern, £2,578 ; Metropolitan, £746 ; Metropolitan District, £110.

In the Canadian Railway Market the Grand Trunk Company's[2] stocks opened flat on the reported " rate war[3] " and prices fell away rapidly. Some recovery[4] afterwards took place and the market was very unsettled until the close, when the tone was flat and prices were at the lowest points of the day. The Ordinary declined 7-16 to 10$\frac{5}{8}$, the First Preference[5] 1$\frac{5}{8}$ to 66$\frac{1}{8}$, the Second Preference 2$\frac{1}{8}$ to 45$\frac{5}{8}$, the Third Preference 1$\frac{1}{8}$ to 25$\frac{5}{8}$, and the Guaranteed 1$\frac{1}{2}$ to 70$\frac{1}{4}$. Canadian Pacific shares were also depressed and left off 1 lower at 56$\frac{1}{8}$.

The American Railroad Market has, as already mentioned, been seriously affected by the surprising announcement that the Vanderbilt[6] roads have been compelled to respond to the " secret cutting of rates[7] " which, it is said, has for some time past been obstinately persisted in by the Pennsylvania Railroad Company. The outbreak of a " war of rates " is all the more extraordinary at the present juncture because, with the expected early closing of the canals, the heavy traffic which must result from the largest corn crop ever known, and the accumulation of traffic delayed for want of increased

---

du mois de juillet 1889, par portions qui ne doivent pas être moindres de £ 500 000 (20 000 000 de francs) à la fois. La dette nationale d'Angleterre, à la fin de la guerre en 1815, montait à la somme énorme de £ 885 000 000 (*ou* 22 milliards 125 millions de francs) ; elle n'est plus aujourd'hui que de £ 705 millions et demi ou 17 milliards de francs environ. D'après l'amortissement mis en réserve, cette dette, *à moins de complications européennes*, doit s'éteindre en 57 ans environ. La dette nationale de France est actuellement de plus de 23 milliards. — 1. *Deferred*, voy. note 2, page 72. — 2. *The Grand Trunk Company*, grande ligne du Canada avec un grand nombre d'embranchements, appelée aussi *The Canadian Pacific Railway Company*. Ce chemin de fer part de Montréal à l'est jusqu'à l'île de Vancouver à l'ouest ; il offre une différence de 720 milles (ou 1158 kilomètres) de moins avec la route par Liverpool à New-York et San Francisco, et tout le parcours se trouve sur terre britannique. Le premier train est arrivé à Vancouver le 24 mai 1887. — 3. Voyez note 14, p. 90. — 4. *Recovery*, reprise. — 5. *Preference shares*, actions privilégiées. — 6. *M. Vanderbilt*, Américain colossalement riche, grand fondateur et actionnaire de plusieurs chemins de fer dans les États-Unis d'Amérique. — 7. *Cutting of rates*, baisse des tarifs.

supplies of rolling stock[1], it might be supposed that there would be work enough for all the roads. Further details are wanting, however, to explain this strange business, and there are already rumours that negotiations are now proceeding with the object of restoring harmony, but the immediate result of the news was that both speculators and holders[2] have sold heavily all descriptions of stock, and the final prices were within a shade[3] the lowest points of the day. It is a considerable time since such a general and material decline has taken place in this department. The last quotations show a fall of $3\frac{1}{2}$ in Lake Shore[4] to $102\frac{1}{8}$; $2\frac{1}{2}$ in Erie Preferred to 64; 2 in New York Central to 111; $1\frac{7}{8}$ in Louisville and Nashville to 59; $1\frac{3}{4}$ each in Union Pacific to 65, Northern Pacific Preferred to $61\frac{1}{2}$, Denver Preferred to $47\frac{1}{2}$, and Erie Common to $27\frac{3}{4}$; 1 to $1\frac{1}{4}$ in Pennsylvania to $55\frac{1}{8}$, Illinois Central to 119, "St. Paul" to $66\frac{7}{8}$, Central Pacific to $35\frac{5}{8}$, Denver Common to $17\frac{1}{2}$, Norfolk and Western Preferred to 52, and "Ontarios" to $15\frac{1}{2}$; and $\frac{1}{2}$ to $\frac{3}{4}$ in Ohio and Mississippi to $22\frac{3}{4}$, Wabash Preferred to $27\frac{1}{8}$, and Philadelphia and Reading to $24\frac{3}{8}$. All the usually active bonds were likewise offered—there being a fall of $1\frac{7}{8}$ in New York, Pennsylvania, and Ohio "Firsts" to $39\frac{1}{4}$, $1\frac{1}{2}$ in "Wabash Generals" to $42\frac{3}{4}$, $1\frac{1}{4}$ in "Erie Seconds" to $102\frac{3}{4}$, and $\frac{5}{8}$ in Philadelphia and Reading New "First Fives" to $91\frac{5}{8}$.

The Mexican Railway stocks have been weak, and closed $\frac{1}{2}$ to 1 lower, the Ordinary at $46\frac{1}{2}$, the First Preference at $120\frac{1}{4}$, and the Second Preference at $77\frac{1}{4}$. Mexican Central Four per Cents. declined $\frac{7}{8}$ to $67\frac{1}{8}$. There was not much business doing in Argentine Railway securities, but the tone was firm. Business was also quiet in the Mining Market. British Broken Hill rose $\frac{1}{8}$ to $3\frac{3}{8}$, and Don Pedro and Nundydroog 1-16 each to $1\frac{1}{2}$ and 2. In Copper shares, Mason and Barry fell $\frac{1}{8}$ to 11 11-16, and Cape and Copiapo 1-16 each to $6\frac{3}{8}$ and 5 1-16 respectively; but Tharsis and Panulcillo rose 1-16 each to $6\frac{3}{8}$ and 2 11-16. Diamond shares were weaker, De Beers falling $\frac{1}{2}$ to $16\frac{5}{8}$, South African Exploration $\frac{3}{8}$ to $18\frac{1}{8}$, and Jagersfontein $\frac{1}{4}$ to $14\frac{7}{8}$. In South African Gold shares Moodies fell $\frac{1}{8}$ to $1\frac{1}{2}$, but Sheba rose 1-16 to $1\frac{3}{8}$. In the Miscellaneous Market, Brewery shares were steady. The shares of the Salt Union rose $\frac{1}{8}$ to $4\frac{3}{4}$. Those of Spratt's Patent fell $\frac{5}{8}$ to $9\frac{7}{8}$, and those of Bell's Asbestos $\frac{1}{4}$ to $13\frac{3}{8}$. Gas Light and Coke "A" stock rose 1 to 248.

The tone in the Foreign Market has been dull all day, and business was

---

1. *Rolling stock*, matériel de roulage. — 2. *Holders*, porteurs. — 3. *Within a shade*, à une nuance près. — 4. Les noms qui suivent sont tous des chemins de fer dans les États-Unis. Peut-être serait-il curieux ici de donner une chronologie des chemins de fer dans le monde : je l'emprunte aux *Annales industrielles*. Les premiers chemins de fer ont été ouverts : En Angleterre, 25 septembre 1825 ; en Autriche, 30 septembre 1828 ; en France, 1er octobre 1828 ; aux États-Unis, 1829 ; en Belgique et en Allemagne, 1835 ; en l'île de Cuba, 1837 ; en Russie, 1838 ; en Italie, 1839 ; en Suisse, 1844 ; dans l'île de la Jamaïque, 1845 ; en Espagne, 1848 ; au Canada, 1850 ; au Mexique et au Pérou, 1850 ; en Suède, 1851 ; au Chili, 1852 ; aux Indes, 1853 ; en Norvège, 1853 ; en Portugal et au Brésil, 1854 ; en Australie, 1854 et 1855 ; dans la Colombie, 1855 ; en Égypte, 1856 ; dans le Natal, 1860 ; et en Turquie, 1860.

again very small in volume, as operators are still holding aloof from fresh transactions, owing chiefly to prices on the Continental Bourses being reported lower. The stocks connected with Egypt declined $\frac{1}{8}$ to $3\frac{3}{8}$, "Unified" closing at 80 11-16, the Daira bonds at $76\frac{3}{4}$, the Five per Cent. Preference stock at $100\frac{5}{8}$, the Turkish "Defence" loan at $93\frac{1}{2}$, and the 1871 issue at $81\frac{1}{2}$. The Turkish "Group" issues were also weaker, "Group" I. closing at $27\frac{3}{4}$, a fall of $\frac{1}{4}$, while "Groups" II., III., and IV. were 1-16 to 3-16 lower at $16\frac{1}{8}$, $15\frac{1}{8}$, and 15 5-16 respectively, and Ottoman Bank shares fell 1-16 to 11 1-16. Suez Canal shares, however, were slightly higher at $88\frac{1}{8}$. Hungarian Gold Four per Cent. Rentes and Russian stock of 1873 were decidedly depressed, and fell 7-16 each to 83 13-16 and 100 13-16 respectively, and the Greek bonds of 1881 and 1884 and the Monopoly Loan declined $\frac{3}{8}$ and $\frac{1}{2}$ to $82\frac{7}{8}$ and $72\frac{1}{4}$ respectively. Spanish Four per Cents. fell $\frac{1}{4}$ on Paris sales, their last price being 72 9-16, while Italian Rente at $95\frac{5}{8}$, Mexican Converted stock at $39\frac{3}{4}$, and Portuguese stock at $63\frac{1}{2}$ declined $\frac{1}{8}$ to $\frac{1}{4}$. Peruvian Five and Six per Cents. were pressed for sale[1] by an operator having accounts open for the rise in other departments[2]. It was alleged, also, that the negotiations respecting the "Grace contract[3]" had failed, and the rumour is believed in well-informed quarters to be well founded. Their last prices were $\frac{3}{8}$ lower than those of last night at $15\frac{1}{2}$ and $17\frac{1}{2}$ respectively. Among other South American stocks Argentine National Cedulas "A" and "B" and Buenos Ayres Cedulas "I" fell $\frac{1}{4}$ each to $60\frac{1}{4}$, 60, and $61\frac{1}{4}$ respectively, but Uruguayan "Unified" and the Six per Cent. loan of 1886 again advanced $\frac{1}{4}$ each to $74\frac{1}{2}$ and $88\frac{1}{2}$ respectively. The Brazilian loan of 1888 was also $\frac{1}{4}$ higher at $95\frac{1}{2}$.

No transactions in gold were reported at the Bank. The Hawarden Castle[4], from the Cape, has arrived with £18,266, composed almost entirely of native gold, while the Coromandel, due on the 18th inst., is bringing £65,000 in sovereigns[5] from Sydney, £35,000 in sovereigns from Melbourne, and £7,040 in gold from Hongkong.

The Bombay exchange was easier at 1s. 4 15-32d., and the Shanghai rate fell $\frac{1}{8}$d. to 4s. $3\frac{3}{4}$d. The Silver Market was very inactive, there being no change in the quotations of either bars or Mexican dollars. Rupee Paper is also unaltered.

At the Metal Exchange Chili bar copper[6] closed at £78 2s. 6d. to £78 12s. 6d. cash, and £79 to £79 10s. three months; and G. M. B.[7] at

1. *Pressed for sale*, mis en vente. — 2. *For the rise in other departments*, à la hausse sur d'autres valeurs. — 3. *The "Grace contract"* fait allusion à une tentative de compromis qui n'aboutit pas. — 4. *Le Château d'Hawarden*, navire ainsi nommé d'après la résidence de M. Gladstone. C'est là que le célèbre homme d'État déjà très âgé (il a eu quatre-vingts ans cette année (1889) s'amuse à abattre des arbres pour entretenir ses forces. — 5. *In sovereigns*, en souverains, c'est-à-dire en pièces d'or. — 6. *Chili bar copper*, cuivre en barres du Chili. — 7. *G. M. B.* C'est par leurs initiales que l'on désigne le plus souvent les grandes banques ou les maisons de commerce très connues à la Bourse.

£78 2s. 6d. to £78 12s. 6d. cash, and £79 to £79 10s. three months. Straits tin[1] closed at £101 to £101 10s. cash, and £101 15s. to £102 5s. three months.

Our Paris Correspondent telegraphs that the Bourse to-day was influenced by the weakness of the German Stock Exchanges, but prices left off at about the level of the close yesterday. Three per Cents. opened at 82f. 97c., and after touching 83f. 2c. and 82f. 95c., left off at 82f. 97c. —a fall of 3c. on the closing price of yesterday. Redeemable[2] opened and left off at 86f., unchanged since yesterday. Four-and-a-Half per Cents. opened at 104f. 60c. and left off at 104f. 65c.—a fall of 2c. since yesterday. Suez Canal shares began at 2,227f. 50c., and closed at 2,230f.—a fall of 2f. 50c. since yesterday. Drafts at sight on London[3], 25f. 30½c.—a fall of ½c. Four o'Clock Prices.—Four-and-a-Half per Cents., 104f. 65c.; Three per Cents., 83f.; Italian, 96f. 72c.; Spanish External, 73½; Egyptian Unified, 410f.; Turkish, 15f. 40c.; Ottoman Bank, 530f.; Panama, 252f. 50c.; Rio Tinto, 677f.

At the meeting of the court of directors of the London and St. Katharine Docks Company, held to-day, Mr. C. M. Norwood was elected chairman, and Mr. W. E. Hubbard deputy-chairman.

We regret to have to announce the death of Mr. William Quilter, which occurred last night at his residence, No. 28, Norfolk-street, Park-lane. The deceased, who had been in failing health for some time, was the founder of the firm of Quilter, Ball, and Co., of which he was the senior partner for upwards of 50 years. He was, at the foundation of the Institute of Accountants[4], elected the first president, and continued to hold that office for some years. He was in his 81st year.

Subjoined is Messrs. Mocatta and Goldsmid's Circular :—

" There was rather more demand for silver for India last week, and the price advanced from 43d. at the date of our last Circular to 43⅛d.[5] on the 7th inst., at which it remained for a few days, but in consequence of weaker Indian exchanges it relapsed to 43 1-16d. on the 10th, when the consignments by the Chili steamer were sold, and yesterday a small amount by the Moselle realized only 43d., which is to-day's quotation. There has been no change in Mexican dollars, a few transactions having taken place at the previous rate. There has been no export demand for bar gold except for small orders for India, and most of the arrivals have been bought by the Bank, amounting to about £227,000. On the other hand, £1,089,000 in sovereigns has been withdrawn for South America."

We have received the following notices :—

1. *Straits tin*, l'étain des détroits, c'est-à-dire des colonies britanniques de la Malaisie.— 2. *Redeemable*, le 3 p. % amortissable. — 3. *Drafts at sight on London*, chèques à vue sur Londres. — 4. *The Inst. of Accountants*, l'Institut des comptables. — 5. 43 *d.* ⅛, 43 pence et ⅛ de penny.

Messrs. Baring Brothers and Co. are prepared to deliver part paid scrip certificates[1] of the City of Montreal Three per Cent. Loan in exchange for letters of allotment[2].

The Consul-General for Paraguay has notified to the Council of Foreign Bondholders[3] that he has received the remittance for the payment of the coupon due January 1, 1889, on the Paraguay Bonds of 1886.

THE ENGLISH ROMAN CATHOLIC BISHOPS AND THE POPE.

The following address to the Pope has been drawn up by the English Roman Catholic bishops :—

" Most Holy Father,—The undersigned bishops of England have learnt with great sorrow and indignation that new laws have been proposed and are about to be carried in the Italian Parliament against the bishops, the clergy, and the faithful of Italy, under the pretext of repressing attacks against authority, whether by word or by writing. The authority to be protected by these laws is the authority of a revolution that by violence has possessed itself of the city of Rome. Henceforth whosoever shall venture to write or to speak in defense of the rights of the Holy See and of the Catholic world is to be punished by fine and imprisonment. There is no exception made in favour of any person, howsoever eminent or sacred may be his dignity. The venerable and sovereign person of your Holiness, whose absolute liberty in the exercise of your primacy over the Catholic world was said to be guaranteed, is not exempted from these penal laws. To proclaim to the people of Christendom that Rome is the capital of the Catholic world will be an offence against the authority which by force has established itself within its walls, and would be a contravention of those laws. That which is lawful to all Catholics throughout the world in every free nation will henceforth be unlawful only in Italy, and above all for those whose rights are despised and violated.

" We, who live in a land where the Catholic Church enjoys full liberty, are profoundly aggrieved and offended at seeing the injustice and the violence with which the sacred rights of the head of the Church are obstructed and violated in the very centre and in the very seat of its supreme authority. Already the filial devotion of all Catholic pastors and people in all parts of the world, and also the free and healthy public opinion of all civi-

1. *Part paid scrip certificates,* certificats d'actions souscrites non entièrement libérées. — 2. *Letters of allotment,* lettres annonçant la répartition. — 3. *Bondholders,* obligataires, porteurs d'obligations. Remarquez les mots : *shares,* actions ; *scrip,* certificats d'actions et, par suite, actions, obligations, valeurs ; *debentures,* bons, obligations ; *bonds,* obligations, bons du Trésor ; *railway bonds,* obligations de chemin de fer.

lized nations, has rebuked and condemned this penal legislation. And we also add our protest to that of the civilized world, declaring, together with all Catholics, our detestation of such great injustice. We offer fervent prayers to the Divine head of the Church that He may bring to naught[1] these and all other attemps against the liberty and independence of His vicar upon earth, and we humbly implore for ourselves and for England the Apostolical Benediction.

"November 10, 1888."

AGRICULTURAL PRODUCE.

(From the *London Gazette.*)

An Account showing the quantities of certain kinds of Agricultural Produce imported into the United Kingdom in the week ended Nov. 10, 1888, together with the quantities imported in the corresponding week of the previous year :—

		Quantities.	
		1887.	1888.
Animals, living :—			
Oxen, bulls, cows, and calves	Number.	3,711	5,293
Sheep and lambs..	»	15,976	20,634
Swine..	»	110	486
Dead Meat :—			
Bacon	Cwt.[2]	46,319	39,952
Beef, salted and fresh	»	14,792	24,782
Ham	»	7,919	10,497
Meat unenumerated, salted and fresh	»	728	604
D°, preserved	»	10,435	13,561
Mutton, fresh	»	9,810	16,344
Pork, salted (not ham) and fresh ..	»	10,469	12,201
Poultry and game..	Value £	6,985	4,986
Rabbits	Cwt.	4,286	3,329
Butter..	»	22,665	31,851
Margarine..	»	25,720	19,910
Cheese..	»	24,440	26,195
Eggs	Great Hundred[3].	226,413	197,554
Lard	Cwt.	7,619	19,162
Vegetables :—			
Onions, raw..	Bushels[4].	114,019	88,538
Potatoes.	Cwt.	39,515	18,245
Unenumerated	Value £	9,004	10,165
Corn, Grain, Meal, and Flour[5] :—			
Wheat	Cwt.	659,646	1,057,579

1. *To bring to naught*, réduire à néant, anéantir. — 2. Nous avons déjà dit que le *cwt.* ou *hundredweight* égale à peu près 50 kilos ; voy. Gramm. Elwall, page 201. — 3. *Great hundred*, c'est-à-dire 112 livres pour cent livres. — 4. *Bushel*, boisseau, à peu près 36 litres. — 5. *Meal and flour*, farine. Les deux mots sont à peu près synonymes ; *flour* indiquant une farine plus fine.

		Quantities.	
		1887.	1888.
Barley	Cwt.	296,510	486,980
Oats..	»	661,203	540,394
Peas..	»	56,431	48,157
Beans	»	43,945	50,657
Maize	»	413,096	318,124
Wheat Meal and Flour..	»	368,931	314,485

JOHN COURROUX.

Statistical Office, Custom-house, London, Nov. 12.

Honours to General Prjevalski[1]. — The Municipal Council of St. Petersbourg voted unanimously on the 6th inst. that a portrait of the late general should be placed in the free reading room of the town, and that two of the new primary schools to be opened next year should bear the explorer's name. A special service, at which prayers were offered up for the soul of the deceased officer, and which was attended by the chief military authorities, was held on the same day at the chapel of the staff major.

STOCKS[2] and RAILWAY and OTHER SHARES.

Printing-house-square,
Tuesday Evening.

The next Settlement[3] in Consols will begin on November 30 and end on December 3. The next Settlement in Railway and Foreign Stocks, etc., will begin on the 27th and end on the 29th inst.

The following is a statement of the opening and closing quotations of the under-mentioned securities, together with the quotations[4] at which they closed last night, and the prices at which they were "made up"[5] at the last Settlement.

[N. B. — In the case of railway and other companies whose issues quoted here are of more than one kind, the prices given relate to the "Ordinary" stock of shares, unless otherwise specified[6]. In the case of all securities the closing quotations are the latest obtained up to half-past 4 on all days except Saturday, when the latest prices are those obtained at 2.

1. Le général Prjevalski, explorateur russe. — 2. Fonds publics et actions de chemins de fer et autres. — 3. *The next Settlement*, la prochaine liquidation (à la Bourse). *Foreign stocks*, fonds étrangers. — 4. *Quotations*, la cote. — 5. *Made up*, compensé. — 6. Comme je ne trouve pas grand intérêt à lire la liste entière des valeurs cotées à la Bourse de Londres où il n'y a pas de cote officielle, c'est-à-dire limitée à un certain nombre de valeurs autorisées, je ne donne ici que les plus importantes ou du moins les plus intéressantes.

For movements in prices which may take places after these hours reference must be made to our City Article.]

BRITISH AND INDIAN GOVERNMENT STOCKS AND BRITISH CORPORATION SECURITIES[1].

Last making up price[2].	Name of Security.	Closing Prices last night.		To-day's Prices. Opening.		To-day's Prices. Closing.	
97 1/2	2 3/4 p.c. Consols (1903)[3]..	97	97 1/8	97	97 1/8	97 1/8	97 1/4
—	D°, Acc.[4] (Dec.)	97 1/4		97 3-16	97 5-16	97 1/4	97 3/8
94 1/4	2 1/2 p.c. (1905)	93 7/8	94 1/8	93 3/4	94 1/4	93 7/8	94 1/8
103	Excheq'r Bills[5], Mar.	5s. dis.	par	5s. dis.	par	5s. dis.	par
—	D°, June	8s. dis.	8s. dis.	8s. dis.	8s. dis.	8s. dis.	8s. dis.
—	Bank of Eng. Stock..	317	321	317	321	317	320
106	India, 3 1/2 p.c.	105 7/8	106 1/8	105 3/4	106 1/4	106	106 1/4
97 1/2	D°, 3 p.c.	97 1/4	97 1/2	97	97 1/2	97 1/8	97 3/8
111 3/4	Met. Bd. Wks., 3 1/2 p.c.[6]	112	112 1/4	111 3/4	112 1/4	111 3/4	112 1/4

BRITISH RAILWAY STOCKS[7].

Last making up price	Name of Security	Closing Prices last night		Opening		Closing	
68 1/8	Great Eastern	68 1/8	68 3/8	68 1/8	68 3/8	68 1/8	68 3/8
115 3/4	Great Northern, Ord.[8]	115 1/2	116 1/2	115 1/2	116 1/2	115 1/2	116 1/2
150 1/2	Great Western	150 5/8	150 7/8	150 1/2	151	150 7/8	151 1/8
143	Lon. & Brighton, Ord.	143	145	142	144	142	144
129 1/4	D°, Deferred	129 3/8	129 5/8	129 1/2	129 3/4	129 1/4	129 1/2
168 1/4	Lond. & N.-Western..	168 3/8	168 5/8	168 1/4	168 3/4	168 7/8	169 1/8
139	Lond. & S.-Western..	138 1/2	139 1/2	138 1/2	139 1/2	139	140
76	Metropolitan..	75 3/4	76 1/4	76	76 1/2	75 3/4	76 1/4
33 1/2	Metropolitan District	33	33 1/2	33 1/4	33 3/4	33	33 1/2
133 1/4	Midland	133 3/8	133 5/8	133 1/4	133 3/4	133 1/2	133 3/4

CANADIAN RAILWAY SECURITIES.

Last making up price	Name of Security	Closing Prices last night		Opening		Closing	
57	Canadian Pacific Sh.[9]	57	57 1/4	56 1/2	57	56	56 1/4
107	D°, 1st Mort. Bds.[10]	107 1/2	108 1/2	106 1/2	107	106 1/2	107 1/2
11 1/8	Grand Trunk Shares	11	11 1/8	11	11 1/8	10 1/2	10 3/4
67 7/8	D°, 1st Preference	67 5/8	67 7/8	67 5/8	67 7/8	66	66 1/4

AMERICAN RAILWAY SECURITIES.

Last making up price	Name of Security	Closing Prices last night		Opening		Closing	
37	Central Pacific	36 7/8	37 1/8	36 1/2	37	35 3/4	36
68	Chic., Mil., & St. Paul	67 3/4	68	67 1/4	67 3/4	66 5/8	66 7/8
29 1/2	N. Y., L. Erie, & W.	29 1/4	29 1/2	28 1/4	28 1/2	27 3/4	28
66 1/2	D°, Preferred	66 1/4	66 3/4	66 1/4	66 3/4	63 3/4	64 1/4
16 1/2	N. Y., Ontario, & W.	16 1/4	16 1/2	16	16 1/2	15 3/4	16
23 1/2	Ohio & Mis'ppi., Shrs.	23 1/4	23 3/4	22 3/4	23 1/4	22 1/4	22 3/4
25	Phil. & Read. $50 Shs.	25	25 1/4	24 1/2	24 3/4	24 1/8	24 3/8
66 3/4	Union Pacific..	66 5/8	66 7/8	65 3/4	66 1/4	64 7/8	65 1/8

1. *British corporation securities*, valeurs municipales. — 2. *Making up price*, prix de compensation. — 3. (1903), c'est-à-dire réductible à 2 1/2 p. % en 1903. — 4. *Acc.* c'est-à-dire *Account.* — 5. *Exchequer bills*, bons du Trésor. — 6. *Metropolitan Board of Works*, Conseil général des travaux publics de Londres. — 7. *British Railway Stocks*, actions des chemins de fer britanniques. — 8. *Ord.* c'est-à-dire *Ordinary stock.* — 9. *Sh.* = *shares*, actions. — 10. *Mort. Bds.* c'est-à-dire *Mortgage Bonds.*

OTHER FOREIGN RAILWAY SECURITIES.

Last making up price.	Name of Security.	Closing Prices last night.		To-day's Prices. Opening.		To-day's Prices. Closing.	
47 1/2	Mexican	47 3/8	47 5/8	47	47 1/2	46 3/8	46 5/8
120 1/2	D°, 1st Preference	120 1/2	121	120	120 1/2	120	120 1/2
77 1/2	D°, 2d Preference	77 1/2	78	77 1/4	77 3/4	77	77 1/2
68	Mexican Cent.[1], 4 p.c.	67 3/4	68 1/4	67 1/4	67 3/4	67	67 1/4
17 1/4	Ottoman Shares	17	17 1/2	17	17 1/2	17	17 1/4
9	Sth. Austrian Shares	8 7/8	9 1/8	8 7/8	9 1/8	8 3/4	9
	TELEGRAPH AND TELEPHONE SECURITIES.						
46 1/2	Anglo-Amer. Teleg.	46	47	46	47	46	47
77 3/4	D°, Preferred	77 1/2	78 1/2	77	78	77 1/2	78 1/2
15 1/2	D°, Deferred	15 1/4	15 3/4	15 1/4	15 3/4	15 1/4	15 3/4
9 3/4	Direct U. S. Cable	9 5/8	9 7/8	9 5/8	9 7/8	9 5/8	9 7/8
12 3/8	Eastern Telegraph	12 3/8	12 5/8	12 1/4	12 1/2	12 3/8	12 5/8
13 1/4	Eastern Extension	13 1/8	13 3/8	13 1/8	13 3/8	13 1/8	13 3/8
13 5/8	United Telephone	13 5/8	13 7/8	13 5/8	13 7/8	13 5/8	13 7/8
13 7/8	West. & Brazil Teleg.	13 7/8	14 1/8	13 3/4	14	13 3/4	14
	MINES.						
6 5-16	Cape Copper. £2 Shs	6 3/8	6 1/2	6 3/8	6 1/2	6 5-16	6 7-16
26 5-16	Rio Tinto	26 3/8	26 3/4	26 1/2	26 5/8	26 5/8	26 3/4
6 3/8	Tharsis	6 1/4	6 3/8	6 3/8	6 1/2	6 5-16	6 7-16
	MISCELLANEOUS SECURITIES.						
11 1/8	Imp. Ottoman Bank	11 1-16	11 3-16	11	11 1/4	11	11 1/8
88	Suez Canal Shares	87 3/4	88 1/4	87 3/4	88 1/4	88	88 1/4
	FOREIGN GOVERNMENT SECURITIES.						
80 7/8	Egypt., Unified, 4 p.c.	81 1-16	81 3-16	80 7/8	81	80 5/8	80 3/4
100 3/8	D°, Prefer., 5 p.c.	100 3/8	100 5/8	100 3/8	100 5/8	100 1/4	100 1/2
102 1/4	D°, State Do.[2], 5 p.c.	102 1/4	102 1/2	102 1/4	102 3/4	102	102 1/2
76 3/4	D°, Daira, 4 p.c.	77	77 1/4	76 3/4	77	76 5/8	76 7/8
104 1/4	French, 4 1/2 p.c.	104 1/2	105	104 1/2	104 3/4	104 1/2	104 3/4
84 1/4	Hungary Gold, 4 p.c.	84 1/8	84 3/8	84	84 1/4	83 3/4	84
95 5/8	Italy, 5 p.c.	95 5/8	95 7/8	95 1/2	95 3/4	95 1/2	95 3/4
63 5/8	Portugal, 3 p.c.	63 5/8	63 7/8	63 1/2	63 3/4	63 3/8	63 5/8
101 1/4	Russia, 1873	101 1/8	101 3/8	101	101 1/4	100 3/4	100 7/8
72 5/8	Spain, 4 p.c.	72 3/4	72 7/8	72 11-16	72 13-16	72 9-16	72 11-16
82	Turkey, 4 1/4 p.c. 1871	81 3/4	82 1/4	81 1/2	82	81 1/4	81 3/4
93 3/4	D°, 5 p.c., Defence	93 1/2	94	93 1/2	94	93 1/4	93 3/4
27 3/4	D°, "Group I". (A)	27 3/4	28 1/4	27 3/4	28 1/4	27 1/2	28
15 5/8	D°, "Group IV". (D)	15 3/8	15 1/2	15 1/4	15 1/2	16 1/4	15 3/8
—	United States, 4 p.c.	129 1/2	130 1/2	129 1/2	130 1/2	129 1/2	130 1/2

The following are the changes recorded in the Official List up to 3 p. m. :—

HOME CORPORATION STOCKS (Free of Duty [3]). — Croydon ROSE 1/2 to 109 1/2 10 1/2; and Liverpool 1/4 to 110 1/2 11.

FOREIGN GOVERNMENT SECURITIES. — An ADVANCE of 2 in Dutch (Three-and-a-Half per Cent. Bonds) to 100 2; 1 each in ditto (ex 12 guilders) to 76 8, ditto (Three-and-a-Half

1. *Mexican Central.* — 2. *Egypte domaniales.* — 3. *Free of duty*, exempt de l'impôt mobilier.

per Cent. Certificates) to 99 101, Buenos Ayres (1870 and 1873) to 99 101, Guatemala (Four per Cent. Bonds) to 59 61; and $^1/_2$ in Ecuador to $23^1/_2$ $4^1/_2$. A FALL of 1 each in Greek (Six per Cent., 1888, scrip all paid) to 92 4, and Venezuela to 52 4.

HOME RAILWAY. — East London ROSE 1 to $11^1/_2$ $12^1/_2$.

DEBENTURES[1]. — East London (Third Charge, Four per Cent.) ADVANCED 2 to 29 31; and ditto (Fourth Charge) 1 to 18 20.

AMERICAN. — East Tennessee, Virginia, &c. (Common), FELL $^1/_2$ to $9^1/_2$ $10^1/_2$.

CURRENCY BONDS[2]. — Louisville (Mortgage Bonds) ROSE 1 to 116 18; and Wheeling and Lake Erie 1 to 96 8. Mexican Central (Three per Cent. Income Bonds) FELL 1 to 20 2.

FOREIGN. — A RISE of 3 in Central Argentine to 209 11; 1 each in ditto (Shares) to 36, 7, Recife and San Francisco to 104 7; $^1/_2$ in Nitrate to 29 30; and $^1/_4$ each in Buenos Ayres Great Southern (1890 Extension) to $19^1/_4$ $^3/_4$, and ditto (1892) to $17^1/_2$ 18. A FALL of $^1/_2$ in Conde d'Eu to 15 16; 1 in Buenos Ayres and Ensenada Port to 161 5; and $1^1/_2$ in North-Western of Uruguay (First Preference) to 75 7.

BANKS. — London of Mexico and South America ROSE $^1/_4$ to $5^1/_2$; and Bank of Australasia FELL 1 to 92 4.

BREWERIES, &C. — Distillers ROSE $^1/_4$ to $13^3/_4$ $14^1/_4$, and Nalder and Collyer (Preference) $^1/_4$ to 12-$^1/_2$. New Westminster FELL $^1/_4$ to $5^1/_4$ $^3/_4$.

DOCKS. — Sharpness (Four-and-a-Half per Cent.) ROSE 2 to 99 102, ditto (Four per Cent.) 2 to 82 7; Milford (A) $1^1/_2$ to 94 8; and Hull 1 to 31 4.

COMMERCIAL. — A RISE of 1 in Primitiva Nitrate to $36^1/_2$ $7^1/_2$; $^1/_2$ each in Colorado Nitrate to 10 11 and San Pablo Nitrate to $13^1/_2$ $14^1/_2$; $^1/_4$ each in Assam Railways, &c. (Preferred), to $6^3/_4$ $7^1/_4$, Hotchkiss to $10^1/_4$ $^3/_4$, and James M'Ewan to $11^1/_2$ 12; and $^1/_8$ in New Explosives to $6^1/_4$ $^1/_2$. A FALL of $^1/_4$ each in Anglo-American Brush Light (fully paid) to 5-$^1/_2$, National Dwellings (Preferred) to $4^1/_2$ 5, Spratt's to $9^3/_4$ $10^1/_4$, and ditto (Russia) to $2^1/_4$ $^3/_4$.

COLONIAL CORPORATION. — Melbourne Harbour (Four-and-a-Half per Cent. Bonds) ROSE 1 to 111 13.

FINANCIAL. — Canada North-West Land Company FELL $^1/_8$ to $2^7/_8$ $3^1/_8$.

FINANCIAL TRUSTS. — General and Commercial Investment (Four per Cent. Perpetual Debenture Stock) ROSE 1 to 104 6. Investment Trust Corporation FELL 1 to 100 2.

GAS. — Gas Light and Coke (A) ADVANCED $1^1/_2$ to 246 50. San Paulo FELL $^1/_2$ to $15^1/_2$ $16^1/_2$.

MINES. — Don Pedro ROSE $^1/_8$ to 1 7-16 9-16, and United Mexican $^1/_8$ to $3^1/_8$ $^3/_8$. Day Dawn FELL 1-16 to $^5/_8$ $^3/_4$.

TELEGRAPHS. — African Direct ROSE 1 to 99 101, and West Coast of America $^1/_2$ to 9-$^1/_2$.

TRAMWAYS. — Belfast Street ROSE $^1/_4$ to $13^1/_2$ 14.

WATER. — Tarapaca ROSE $^1/_2$ to 14 15[3].

PUBLIC INCOME AND EXPENDITURE.

The following are the receipts into and payments out of the Exchequer[4] between April 1st, 1888, and November 10, 1888 : —

1. *Debentures,* obligations. — 2. *Currency bonds,* obligations papier-monnaie. — 3. Nous omettons ici le reste des valeurs de bourse dont la lecture n'offrirait ni plaisir ni instruction à nos lecteurs. — 4. *The Chancellor of the Exchequer* est le ministre des finances en Angleterre. Cette institution remonte pour le moins à la conquête normande et, dès son origine, fut regardée comme un contrôle des fonctions du grand trésorier (*Lord High Treasurer*) et comme une protection tant pour la couronne que pour les sujets. Depuis George Ier (1714-1727) le Grand Trésorier s'appelle *the First lord of the Treasury,* lequel est presque toujours Premier ou Président du Conseil, et rarement ministre des finances. Le mot *Exchequer* vient,

Revenue and other Receipts.

—	Estimate for the year 1888-89.	Total Receipts into the Exchequer from April 1, 1888, to Nov. 10, 1888.	Total Receipts into the Exchequer from April 1, 1887, to Nov. 12, 1887.
Balance, April 1st, 1888	£	£	£
Bank of England[1]	—	6,631,669	4,977,880
Bank of Ireland	—	1,015,403	972,227
REVENUE.		7,647,072	5,950,107
Customs[2]..	19,925,000	12,116,000	11,935,000
Excise[3]	25,505,000	15,280,000	15,433,000
*Stamps	11,780,000	7,821,000	7,451,000
Land Tax and House Duty	2,936,000	625,000	645,000
Property and Income Tax	12,250,000	3,691,000	4,327,000
Post Office	8,800,000	5,545,000	5,225,000
Telegraph Service	2,000,000	1,225,000	1,240,000
Crown Lands	390,000	205,000	185,000
Interest on Purchase Money of Suez Canal Shares[4], Sardinian Loan, &c. ..	241,000	14,257	22,013
Miscellaneous..	3,000,000	1,693,725	1,622,260
Revenue..	86,827,000	48,115,982	48,085,273
Total, including balance		55,763,054	54,035,380
OTHER RECEIPTS.			
Advances, under various Acts, repaid to the Exchequer.:—			
Bullion[5], &c.		370,743	504,987
Local Loans Fund Adjustments		—	1,510,790
Temporary Advances not repaid, for Deficiency		1,800,000	—
Totals..		57,933,797	56,051,157

*A transfer of £150,000 in respect of Probate Duty[6] has been made to the Local Taxation Account.

dit-on, du mot *échiquier*, parce que les sessions de la *Cour de l'Échiquier* se tenaient devant une table quadrangulaire, recouverte d'un tapis divisé en carreaux, où les comptes se faisaient avec des jetons, en mettant à des places différentes ceux qui désignaient les livres, sous, deniers, vingtaines ou centaines de livres. Le ministre des finances lui-même est contrôlé, quant aux dépenses et aux recettes, par un officier appelé contrôleur et auditeur général. Celui-ci ne peut pas être membre du Parlement; il ne saurait non plus être destitué que sur la demande des deux Chambres du Parlement. — 1. Ce sont les Banques d'Angleterre et d'Irlande qui sont chargées de la perception des impôts pour le compte du gouvernement. — 2. *Customs*, douanes. — 3. *Excise*, droit d'accise, contributions indirectes (spiritueux et tabacs). — 4. *Canal Shares*. Ce sont les actions du canal de Suez, au nombre de 177 000, achetées en 1875 au khédive d'Égypte, et qui donnent au gouvernement anglais le droit de prendre part au conseil d'administration du canal. Une partie de ces actions ne rapportera de l'intérêt qu'en 1894, mais ce sera alors une augmentation de £ 570 000 ou de 14 millions 250 mille francs. — 5. *Bullion*, or et argent non monnayés. — 6. *Probate duty*, taxe sur les testaments et les héritages.

EXPENDITURE AND OTHER PAYMENTS.

—	Estimate for the year 1888-89.	Total Issues out of Exchequer to meet Payments from April 1, 1888, to Nov. 10, 1888.	Total Issues out of Exchequer to meet Payments from April 1, 1887, to Nov. 12, 1887.
EXPENDITURE.	£	£	£
Permanent Charge of Debt	26,000,000	18,813,858	16,494,088
Interest, &c., on Exchequer Bonds (Suez) and Cape Railway Bonds	214,000	108,750	108,678
Other Consolidated Fund Services	1,647,000	1,090,935	1,100,672
Supply Services	58,753,944	32,568,589	33,976,198
	86,614,944		
Expenditure		52,582,132	51,679,636
OTHER PAYMENTS.			
Payments in connexion with the Conversion of the Debt		1,292,308	—
Advances, under various Acts, issued from the Exchequer :—			
Bullion, &c.[1]		400,000	505,000
Local Loans Fund Adjustments		—	1,469,977
Treasury Bills[2], more paid off than issued..		645,000	1,046,000
Exchequer Bills, more paid off than issued		52,000	8,800
Surplus Income applied to reduce Debt		1,500,000	—
		56,471,440	54,709,413
Balances.. .. Bank of England		1,064,723	933,545
Balances.. .. Bank of Ireland..		397,634	408,199
Totals..		57,933,797	56,051,157

Treasury, Nov. 13.

COURSE OF EXCHANGE, Nov. 13.

Amsterdam and Rotterdam, 12 $1^3/_8$ to 12 $2^3/_8$
D°., three months, 12 $3^3/_8$ to 12 $3^7/_8$
Antwerp and Brussels, d°., 25 $62^1/_2$ to 25 $67^1/_2$
Hamburg, 20 58 to 20 62
Berlin and German Bank Places, 20 58 to 20 62
Paris, cheques, 25 $28^3/_4$ to 25 $33^3/_4$
D°., three months, 25 $56^1/_4$ to 25 $61^1/_4$
Marseilles, d°, 25 $57^1/_2$ to 25 $62^1/_2$
Austria, d°, 12 $36^1/_4$ to 12 $38^3/_4$
St. Petersburg, d°, $24^1/_8$ to 24 3-16
Moscow, d°, 24 1-16 to 24 3-16
Genoa, d°, 25 90 to 25 95
Leghorn, three months, 25 90 to 25 95
Naples, &c., d°, 25 90 to 25 95
Barcelona, three months, 46 1-16 to 46 3-16
Cadiz, d°, 46 1-16 to 46 3-16
Madrid, d°, 46 1-16 to 46 3-16
Seville, d°, 46 1-16 to 46 3-16
Malaga, d°, 46 1-16 to 46 3-16
Valencia, d°, 46 1-16 to 46 3-16
Valladolid, d°, 46 1-16 to 46 3-16
Santander, d°, 46 1-16 to 46 3-16
Bilbao, d°, 46 1-16 to 46 3-16
Lisbon, d°, $52^3/_4$ to $52^7/_8$
Oporto, d°, $52^3/_4$ to $52^7/_8$
Copenhagen, d°, 18 35 to 18 40
Christiania, d°, 18 37 to 18 42
Stockholm, d°, 18 39 to 18 44

1. *Bullion*, voir note 5, p. 102. — 2. *Treasury bills, Exchequer bills*, bons du Trésor, dont on a racheté plus qu'on en a émis.

Royal College of Surgeons of England. — The following passed the first professional examination for the diploma of Fellow[1] at a meeting of the board of examiners on the 12th inst., viz. : — Messrs. John Michael Harding Martin, student of Edinburgh University and Liverpool; William Thomas Freeman, of St. Bartholomew's Hospital; Robert Caldwell, of Westminster Hospital; Wilfred Martin Barclay, of Guy's and Bristol; and John Edwards, of Ledwich School, Dublin, and Yorkshire College, Leeds. Eleven candidates were referred back[2] to their professional studies for six months.

City of London College[3]. — We are requested to state that, owing to the engagements of the Lord Mayor, who will preside on the occasion, the date of the distribution of prizes to the students of the City of London College by Lord Justice Bowen has been altered from the 4th to the 11th of December.

LATEST INTELLIGENCE.

(From our Correspondents.)

THE EAST AFRICAN QUESTION[4].

BERLIN, Nov. 13.

The Anglo-German exchange of notes with reference to the blockade of the East African coast is published here to-night in the official *Gazette*, simultaneously with its presentation to the English Parliament.

According to the *Post*, the double-screw despatch-boat[5] Pfeil (*i. e.*, Dart), now lying at Wilhelmshaven, has been commissioned for service on the East African coast, and is being prepared for speedy departure. The Pfeil, a new vessel, built entirely of steel, has a displacement of 1,328 tons, with a horse-power of 2,700, a *maximum* speed of 17 knots[6], an armament of five heavy guns and as many revolver-guns, and a crew of 127 men. It is thought that one or two other vessels may be detached from the Mediterranean Squadron for the same special service.

1. *Fellow*, agrégé. — 2. *Referred back*, ajourné. — 3. *City of London College*, City of London School. — 4. La question de la Côte orientale d'Afrique ou de la Côte de Zanzibar, vis-à-vis de l'île de ce nom. Une compagnie commerciale allemande s'y était établie, mais comme les agents de la compagnie traitaient par trop durement les noirs, ceux-ci, aidés d'ailleurs par les trafiquants d'esclaves arabes, ont massacré quelques Allemands et quelques missionnaires. Le gouvernement allemand a résolu de secourir les colons de ce pays et, prétextant de son désir de supprimer la traite et d'empêcher le commerce des armes, a invité les Anglais à l'aider dans cette entreprise. Les Anglais y ont consenti et le blocus de la côte s'est fait par les navires des deux nations. — 5. *Despatch-boat*, aviso. — 6. 17 *knots*, 17 nœuds par heure. Le *nœud* répond à un mille nautique équivalant à une distance de 1852 mètres.

To-day there is concurrent testimony from opposite sides to the effect that the German East African Company is gradually nearing the end of its financial tether[1], and is altogether in a very bad way. The company began its career with a nominal capital of 3,500,000m.[2], in shares of 10,000m., but of these three-and-a-half millions it is not known how much was paid up. The drain upon its resources has been steady and heavy, nor has it profited much, if at all, by its short and troubled lease as farmer of the Sultan's Customs[3]. In order to obviate confusion of ideas, it will be well to remember that the company has tried to take root in East Africa in the double quality of proprietor and tenant—proprietor, so to speak, in the region of Usagara and thereabouts, where its existence is to a certain extent guaranteed by an Imperial *Schutzbrief*, or protective charter, and tenant-farmer without such a charter on the Customs coast line belonging to the Sultan of Zanzibar, whom it there owns as Suzerain.

It will thus be seen that the company's claims on the Empire are not the same in respect of both these regions, but at the present moment so impenetrable are the designs of the Government even to the home officials of the company that it is impossible to say to what extent Prince Bismarck means to go in helping it to regain its lost footing[4]. His assistance, however, will be substantial; and perhaps those are right who suspect that this naval demonstration, in which he has so skilfully induced England to share, was partly devised as a means of making Parliament open its purse when it meets next week. The *Cologne Gazette* pleads earnestly for the co-operation of England with Germany in the interior of Africa as well as on the coast; but its arguments will find little acceptance across the water[5]. At the same time it is becoming clearer and clearer to people here that a mere blockade of the coast, without supplementary operations of some kind on land, will simply leave the African question and the slave question pretty much where they were.

" How long, " it is asked here, " do the Powers co-operating on the sea mean to keep up the effective blockade? In the accomplishment of their object a single year would count as nothing; and do they fancy that when they raise the blockade, one, or two, or three years hence, even supposing they could remain before the coast in permanence all that time, the export of slaves would not vigorously commence afresh, as a wound begins to flow again when its bandage is removed? "

The fact of the matter is that there is no one here who pretends to have

1. *Its financial tether*, ses ressources financières; *tether*, attache, corde (qui empêche la chèvre de brouter plus loin). — 2. *m.*, *mark;* le *mark* vaut 1 fr. 25. — 3. *Customs*, douanes. — 4. *Its lost footing*, la position qu'elle a perdue. — 5. *Across the water*, de ce côté-ci de l'eau.

the faintest inkling[1] how the blockade is likely to achieve the various ends in view—suppression of the slave-trade, reinstatement of the East African Company, &c. — or what it will all end in; and therefore it is, in default of forecasts[2] and explanations from official quarters here, that the Germans are primarily looking to the British Parliament for light on a dark and perplexing subject.

ZANZIBAR, Nov. 13.

The Agamemnon has arrived here, all well.

*ROME, Nov. 13[3].

The Commander of the Italian cruiser Dogali, which arrived at Zanzibar yesterday, has received orders to consult with the British and German Commanders, in order to co-operate with them in the blockade.

*BERLIN, Nov. 13.

It is stated that the German East African Society will be reconstituted under a fresh board of directors.

THE UNITED STATES.

PHILADELPHIA, Nov. 13.

The demoralization of stockholders, owing to the cutting of trunk line rates[4], continued to-day, but it was checked in the afternoon, and the market closed steady at a lower range of prices. Each of the leading railroad companies blames some other for originating the cut, but the prevalent belief is that the Pennsylvania Railroad Company began it, in order to force the Vanderbilt interests out of the rival South Pennsylvania project. There is much criticism of what has been done from investors, who will begin to doubt the value of trunk line stocks if these quarrels continue.

THE EUROPEAN SITUATION.

VIENNA, Nov. 13.

Diplomatists and politicians have ceased to pay much attention to the periodical attacks of the German semi-official Press on France, but the last article in the *North German Gazette,* which retorts upon some Chauvinist remarks in the Paris *Rappel*, gave a slight shock to the Bourse to-day. Financiers can never calmly read these articles, because there is no saying when war may come, and when it does come it will probably be heralded by a newspaper controversy.

The signs of a new onslaught[5] by the German Press upon Russian secu-

1. *The faintest inkling*, la plus faible idée. — 2. *Forecasts*, prévisions. — 3. L'*astérisque* désigne les dépêches directement envoyées par l'agence Reuter. Cette agence joue en Angleterre le même rôle que l'agence Havas en France. — 4. *The cutting of trunk line rates*, la diminution des tarifs des grandes lignes. — 5. *Onslaught*, attaque.

rities are also producing uneasiness, as the Vienna market is nervous of the political consequences which may result from Russia being driven to look to Paris instead of Berlin for money. The optimism of the Berlin *Post,* which argues that the taking up of a Russian loan in France would add to the guarantees of peace, seems here to be a little overpitched[1]. There is rather a fear in Vienna that if the French subscribe freely to a Russian loan, whether from confidence in Russian credit or out of Chauvinist enthusiasm, the circumstance must tend to draw France and Russia closer together, and may induce Germany to precipitate events[2]. It must be added that the situation in the Balkans is far from being reassuring. A few months ago it appeared absolutely certain that in the event of a war Roumania and Servia would co-operate with Austria-Hungary; but the late elections in Roumania and the Constitutional crisis in Servia, which may end by bringing an anti-Austrian Radical Cabinet to office with a strong majority, have, in the opinion of the most sanguine, considerably altered the aspect of affairs. Even the Progressists themselves admit that they can scarcely carry more than 200 seats out of 628 at the forthcoming Servian elections. The Russophil Liberals hope to win about 150, and it is generally expected that about 400 will fall to the Radicals. The bulk of the Radical party is neither Russophil nor Austrophil, but the leaders are decidedly on the Russian side.

A rumour was telegraphed yesterday evening from Budapest[3] that an attempt had been made on Prince Ferdinand's life. This has in no way been confirmed, but this evening the *Correspondance de l'Est* announces that a few days ago a Captain Hertzberg, formerly in the Austrian army, but now in the Turkish police, arrived at Sophia and gave the Prince information of a plot that was being hatched against him by some Bulgarian conspirators at Constantinople.

As a matter of historical interest, it may be noted that the Austrian fortresses in Bohemia and Moravia are to be " unclassed " — that is, struck off the list of war citadels, which is a sign that Austria-Hungary contemplates no possibility of a war with Germany for an indefinite time to come.

PARIS, Nov. 13.

In the Chamber to-day M. Alfred Kœchlin, General Boulanger's colleague in the Nord, read a long maiden speech, criticizing French foreign policy as being too timid. He approved circumspection, but France, he said, should herself be strong, letting friends and enemies know that whoever whetted the sword against her would find her prepared for all duties and all sacrifices. M. de la Ferronays, a Royalist, remarked that in existing

1. *Overpitched,* exagéré, qui va trop loin. — 2. Cet emprunt russe a eu lieu le 10 décembre 1888. — 3. *Budapest, Buda-Pesth,* capitale de la Hongrie, formée de deux villes, *Bude* ou *Ofen* et *Pesth,* séparées seulement par le Danube.

circumstances patriotism forbade any attack on the Minister whose duty it was to uphold French dignity and maintain an honourable peace. This was loudly applauded by the Republicans. M. Goblet, in reply, said :—

" The foreign situation certainly warrants all possible vigilance; but we can watch it with composure. France threatens nobody. Engaged with her domestic difficulties and preparing for the Exhibition, she has no schemes of foreign adventure or of conquest calculated to excite foreign susceptibilities. Wherever she plainly has rights she intends to exercice them firmly, no doubt, but also with the prudence and moderation befitting a great, pacific nation. He who has the honour of managing your foreign affairs should have a lofty sense of his dignity and of the interests of France; but he should also remember that the maintenance of peace is the supreme interest of this as of all civilized nations. " (Loud applause.)

The Foreign Office estimates[1] were then passed, that for the Embassy to the Vatican, which was warmly defended by M. Goblet, being carried by 307 votes to 217.

ROUMANIA[2].

VIENNA, Nov. 13.

The Roumanian Government is about to introduce a Bill reorganizing the National Bank of Roumania and establishing gold as the standard of currency. By an alteration in the statutes of the bank silver will cease to be a legal tender beyond the sum of 20f. The present time is a good one for this important change, as the late excellent harvest brought up the value of the silver coinage to par. The national Debt of Roumania amounts to about £20,000,000, the interest of which has to be paid, mostly to foreign holders of scrip, in gold, and it is expected that about 11,000,000f. a year will be saved by the general adoption of the gold standard.

The Government has also prepared a Bill for the sale and grant of State lands in allotments of from five to ten *Jochs* to peasants, according to the number of members in a family. The *Joch* is about three-quarters of an

1. *The Foreign Office estimates*, le budget des affaires étrangères. — 2. La Roumanie, jeune royaume, au nord-est du Danube, composé des principautés de Valachie et de Moldavie qui s'unirent en proclamant toutes les deux le prince Couza. Elle payait un tribut à la Porte jusqu'en 1877, année de la guerre russo-turque. Son armée s'unit alors à celle de la Russie, lui fut d'un grand secours, notamment à Plevna, et lors du traité de Berlin, en 1878, la Roumanie fut reconnue complètement indépendante, avec le prince Charles Ier comme prince souverain. En 1881, celui-ci fut proclamé roi. La province de la Dobrutcha fut annexée à la Roumanie, un peu malgré elle, en échange de la Bessarabie rétrocédée à la Russie par le traité de Berlin (1878). Outre les 5 millions d'habitants de ce royaume, on compte 2 millions de Roumains en Transylvanie, 800 000 en Bessarabie et 200 000 en Macédoine. Les Roumains sont regardés comme étant de race latine; ils sont descendus des colonies militaires romaines établies dans ce pays par Trajan et ses successeurs, pour sauvegarder l'Empire contre les Barbares. Leur langue, en effet, est proche parente de la langue latine, comme le prouve du reste leur nom de *Roumains*.

acre[1]. The grantees[2] will be chosen from among the poorest of the peasantry. Grants of land were made to the peasantry in 1864, but, as the Code Napoléon is in force in Roumania, the lands were divided and subdivided for equal distribution among the children of the successive owners, till it has come to pass that many have slips of earth which do not yield enough to support a single man. The subdivisions and over-cultivation have, moreover, in many districts completely exhausted the land.

BUCHAREST, Nov. 13.

The new Roumanian Legislature was opened by the King in person today. His Majesty being attended by the Ministers, the other State dignitaries and the members of the Diplomatic body.

In the Speech from the throne King Charles stated that Roumania's relations with all foreign Powers were absolutely satisfactory, owing to the prudent policy which an enlightened patriotism had suggested to all political parties.

"This," continued His Majesty, "proves that Roumania is a powerful element of peace and security. This correct attitude is a sure guarantee that we shall continue to enjoy the confidence of the great Powers, and the sincere friendship of our Balkan neighbours."

After announcing the introduction of various Bills the speech alluded to the sequestration of the Czernowitz-Jassy Railway, and stating simply that the Government, having taken in hand the working of the Itzkany-Jassy line, will be able by a less expensive administration to effect considerable retrenchment as compared with the past.

AUSTRIA-HUNGARY.

VIENNA, Nov. 13.

The Emperor of Austria will go to the Castle of Miramar, near Trieste, on December 1, and spend the 40th anniversary of his accession alone with the Empress.

A Bill was introduced into the Austrian Reichsrath[3] to-day making it illegal to purchase large estates for the purpose of reselling them in small holdings. The object of the measure is to prevent the creation of a "peasant proletariate."

---

1. C'est-à-dire environ 30 ares 35. — 2. *Grantee*, concessionnaire. — 3. *The Reichsrath*, c'est-à-dire le Conseil de l'Empire ou Parlement, se compose de deux Chambres, la Chambre des seigneurs (*Herrenhaus*) et la Chambre des députés (*Abgeordnetenhaus*). C'est le Parlement de la Cisleithanie ou de l'Autriche qu'il faut distinguer du Parlement de la Hongrie ou Transleithanie. La Leitha est une rivière d'Autriche qui coule entre les deux parties de l'empire austro-hongrois.

THE SIEGE OF SUAKIN[1].

SUAKIN, Nov. 13.

The fire from the enemy's guns is increasing daily, and displays greater accuracy of aim. Many shells fall into Suakin, doing considerable damage to the houses and shops in the outer town. The Arabs also keep up a heavy rifle fire from the trenches. Many persons have had narrow escapes from being hit by the shells, nearly all of which now burst. The number of those in the trenches is believed to have been much strengthened.

A small quantity of rain fell to-day and much more is expected shortly, which it is hoped will destroy the trenches to a great extent. The Racer and Starling fire numbers of shells daily, which, it is reported, are producing considerable effect. The gunners in the ships and forts, however, cannot dismount the enemy's pieces, as they are unable to ascertain their exact position.

EGYPT.

ALEXANDRIA, Nov. 13.

The Government has decided to extend the railway system largely by concessions to private companies. The railway systems of Upper and Lower Egypt will probably be connected by a bridge over the Nile at Embâbeh, near Cairo.

General Dormer, writing to the Sirdar, expresses great satisfaction with the very efficient state of the Egyptian army and the Nile frontier defences, which reflect the highest credit on Colonel Wodehouse and other English and native officers.

The rice crops in the Delta are proving unsatisfactory.

THE PRADO TRIAL.

PARIS, Nov. 13.

Maître Comby, the counsel for Prado, in his speech for the defence today, maintained that there was no direct proof of the guilt of the accused. If the prisoner's name were known it would produce all over Europe a deep impression of surprise and sympathy. Prado was an adventurer, a gambler, a receiver of stolen goods, but he was not a murderer. There was no trust-

1. *Souakim* est un port fortifié sur la côte ouest de la mer Rouge, appartenant à l'Égypte. Il était assiégé par les derviches, c'est-à-dire par les partisans du Mahdi, et défendu par quelques troupes égyptiennes avec des officiers anglais, et par deux petits vaisseaux de guerre de la marine britannique. Au mois de janvier 1889, le général Grenfell, ayant reçu des renforts de troupes anglaises, attaqua les derviches, les mit complètement en déroute et détruisit tous leurs retranchements. Depuis lors le gouvernement anglais a retiré ses troupes, et la garnison n'est plus composée que de troupes nègres, disciplinées et instruites par des officiers anglais.

worthy evidence that hè was the assassin of Aguétant. The counsel attributed the course taken by Forestier in making her declaration to two motives—first, the vengeance of a jealous mistress, and, secondly, the desire of notoriety. He concluded by appealing to the pity of the jury for the child of Prado.

The defence of Forestier by Maître Canet followed. It is expected that the verdict will be given to-morrow.

Telegrams received from Dax, in the Landes, state that Prado is not, as was supposed, the son of M. Castillon, who owns a small property at Magesq.

FRANCE.

PARIS, Nov. 13.

The Queen of Portugal and her son to-day visited the Pasteur Institute, and M. Pasteur explained his process. M. Carnot will be present at the formal opening of the Institute to-morrow.

There are dissentients among the Royalists. M. Baudry d'Asson has publicly protested against an alliance with Boulangism, and a meeting of the Royalist Senators convened for to-day was countermanded for fear of discord.

Miss Kathleen O'Meara, whose death *The Times* has announced to-day, was the author of an account of Madame Mohl (Mary Anne Clarke), and was latterly, I believe, Paris correspondent of the *Guardian*.

SPAIN.

MADRID, Nov. 13.

The students of Valladolid and Barcelona imitated yesterday the demonstrations made here against senor Canovas del Castillo. Madrid continues quiet. Nearly all the prisoners captured during the riots proved to be of the lower classes, and are not students.

*Through Reuter's Agency[1].

FOREIGN AND COLONIAL NEWS.

We have received the following telegrams through Reuter's Agency :—

ITALY AND CHINA.

ROME, Nov. 13.

An agreement has been come to between the Italian and Chinese Governments to the effect that Italians belonging to religious orders, residing or

1. Voir note 3, p. 106.

travelling in the Celestial Empire, who have up to the present carried French passports, must henceforth be provided exclusively with those issued by the Italian authorities.

ISHAK KHAN.

ST. PETERSBURG, Nov. 13.

A despatch from Kerki announces the arrival at that place of M. Tsarykoff, the Russian Agent, from Bokhara. It is stated that Ishak Khan[1], who was lately staying in the Kerki district, has re-entered Afghan Turkestan, and that the number of his adherents increases daily.

A Russian telegraph station was recently opened at Kerki.

THE ROYAL VISITORS TO GREECE.

ATHENS, Nov. 13.

The Duchess of Edinburgh and Prince George of Wales brought their visit here to a close to-day. Their Royal Highnesses proceeded by train to Corinth.

Subsequently the English Royal visitors embarked on Board Her Majesty's ship Surprise, which then left for Brindisi.

THE JOURNEY ACROSS GREENLAND.

COPENHAGEN, Nov. 13.

The following letter from Dr. Fridtiof Nansen, the Arctic explorer, dated from Godthaab, is published here : —

" After cruising about under difficulties among the ice-floes[2] for twelve days, during which we were much hindered by whirlpools, we at length reached land to the north of Cape Farvel, in lat. 61. On August, 15, we began our journey over the ice at Umivik, but were compelled to take a line 60 miles south of where we intended to cross. We reached Godthaab on October, 3, and are all in good health. "

THE KING OF WURTEMBERG.

STUTTGART, Nov. 13.

The *Official Gazette* announces that Messrs. Woodcock and Savage and their companions[3] have left the *entourage* of King Charles of their own free

1. Ishak Khan se souleva contre l'émir Abdurrahman ; mais il fut défait et a dû se tenir tranquille depuis. Il est probable que Ishak Khan est ou se croit encouragé par les Russes. — 2. *Ice-floe*, masse (*ou* île) de glace flottante. — 3. Ce sont des Américains qu'on accusait d'avoir circonvenu le roi de Wurtemberg et que celui-ci avait en effet comblés d'honneurs, excitant ainsi la jalousie des Wurtembergeois. MM. Woodcock et Savage avaient même reçu des titres de noblesse.

will, and that His Majesty will always bear in mind the services which the first-named rendered him during his illness in 1884. The *Gazette* declares further that Baron Woodcock never took part in spiritualistic experiments, and denies that the Ministers ever sent in their resignations or contemplated taking such a step.

On the other hand, they informed the King that an application had been made for legal proceedings against the disseminators[1] in Munich and Stuttgart of the false reports referred to, and requested His Majesty's views as to how they should act in this matter. The King, in reply, ordered them to abstain from legal proceedings.

HUNGARIAN FINANCE.

PESTH, Nov. 13.

The Lower House of the Diet to-day passed the Conversion Bill[2] by an overwhelming majority.

LORD DUFFERIN[3].

SIMLA, Nov. 13.

Lord Dufferin has started on a tour prior to his departure from India. His Excellency received an enthusiastic ovation on leaving this place.

MR. CHAMBERLAIN[4].

WASHINGTON, Nov. 13.

Mr. Chamberlain arrived here yesterday evening.

PERU.

NEW YORK, Nov. 13.

Advices from Panama dated the 5th inst. announce that the President and Cabinet of Peru and the representative of the British bondholders have agreed to a proposal embodying the basis of the Grace-Arambar contract, to be submitted to Congress[5] in an extra Sessión to assemble after the present Session which expires at the end of November.

1. *The disseminators of*, ceux qui avaient répandu.... — 2. *The Conversion Bill*, la loi pour la création d'un milliard de rentes nouvelles à 4 p. °/₀, qui devaient naturellement remplacer d'autres rentes à un taux plus élevé. — 3. Lord Dufferin, qui était à cette époque vice-roi des Indes. *Simla*, ville de la présidence de Bombay, près du Sutledj, résidence ordinaire des vice-rois de l'Inde. — 4. M. Chamberlain, chef du parti radical modéré en Angleterre, membre du Parlement et conseiller privé. C'est un des grands adversaires de M. Gladstone dans la question irlandaise. En 1887, il fut nommé commissaire du gouvernement britannique à Washington pour l'arrangement du différend entre le Canada et les États-Unis sur la question des pêcheries, mais le traité qu'il y conclut a été rejeté par le sénat américain. — 5. La république du Pérou a une constitution imitée de celle des États-Unis d'Amérique (président élu pour quatre ans, et Congrès composé de deux assemblées, le Sénat et la Chambre des

AMERICAN MARKETS.

NEW YORK, Nov. 13.

Wheat opened weaker at $\frac{1}{4}$c. decline[1], and prices fluctuated immediately with early sales as follows : — December, 110$\frac{1}{4}$, 110$\frac{3}{8}$, and 110$\frac{1}{2}$, and May[2] 117. “ Bears[3] ” sold somewhat freely early in the day, but afterwards covered, causing the market to advance, and though the export demand was small, the closing is barely steady with values $\frac{3}{8}$c. higher. On the curb[4], May was quoted at 117$\frac{7}{8}$.

Corn was unchanged at the opening and afterwards declined, mainly owing to “ bears ” selling. Outsiders[5] have sold somewhat freely. There was only a moderate export business, and the closing tone is weak at $\frac{1}{2}$c. to $\frac{5}{8}$c. decline.

Lard has been rather an irregular and inactive market, with “ bulls ” showing less disposition to operate. The cash demand was restricted, and the closing is weak at 1 to 5 points decline.

Coffee opened steady. Early in the day December changed hands at 13 40, and March and June at 13 15. The market afterwards reacted[6] on “ bulls ” operating. There was only a moderate business transacted, and the closing is weak at a decline of 5 to 10 points.

Cotton has been somewhat inactive with, however, some demand to purchase near deliveries. The market leaves off easier, unchanged to 2 points down.

Petroleum Pipe-Line Certificates[7] opened unchanged at 86$\frac{3}{4}$, and have varied but little during the day. The closing is steady at 86$\frac{3}{4}$.

Copper has been less active, owing to buyers and sellers being widely apart. The closing quotation for December delivery is 17 40.

PRICES FOR FUTURE DELIVERY.

Wheat. — November, 110; December, 111. 1889.—January, 112$\frac{3}{4}$; May, 117$\frac{3}{8}$. Receipts, Atlantic ports, 40,000 bushels[8]; same day last year, 133,468 bushels. Clearances[9], Atlantic ports, 10,000 bushels.

---

représentants). Ce pays a été presque ruiné par la guerre désastreuse avec le Chili (1881-1883), auquel il a dû céder les îles de guano, avec une clause prescrivant qu'une petite portion du produit de ces îles serait remise aux créanciers du Pérou. — 1. *At* $^1/_4$ *c. decline*, avec une baisse de $^1/_4$ de cent. Le *cent* vaut 0 fr. 05. — 2. Livrable en décembre, en mai. — 3. *Bears*, les baissiers, les vendeurs à la baisse. *The bear* est celui qui s'engage à livrer des actions ou des marchandises à un jour nommé et à un certain prix, en opposition avec *the bull*, qui s'engage à les prendre. L'intérêt du premier veut que les prix baissent dans l'intervalle entre la vente et la livraison, comme l'ours (*the bear*) tire en bas avec ses pattes, et celui du second veut que les prix haussent, comme le taureau (*the bull*) lance en l'air avec ses cornes. — 4. *On the curb*, sur le trottoir, c'est-à-dire en dehors du marché. — 5. *Outsiders*, ceux qui ne spéculent pas, les vendeurs ordinaires. — 6. Il y eut ensuite une réaction dans le marché par suite des spéculations des haussiers. — 7. *Certificates*, actions. *The Pipe-Line Association*. Les grands puits de pétrole, dans les États de Pensylvanie et de l'Ohio, ont été reliés à la côte par une ligne de tuyaux (*pipe-line*) longue de 434 kilomètres. — 8. *The bushel* (boisseau) vaut 36 lit. 3. Voy. Gramm. Elwall, p. 204. — 9. Déclarés au départ par les ports américains de l'Atlantique.

Corn. — December, 50. 1889.—January, 49; May, 48. Receipts, Atlantic ports, 180,000 bushels; same day last year, 168,676 bushels. Clearances, Atlantic ports, 110,000 bushels.

Lard. — November, 8 49; December, 8 36. 1889.—February, 8 39; March, 8 40; May, 8 45.

Coffee. — November, 13 60 to 13 65; December, 13 45 to 13 50. 1889. —January, 13 35 to 13 40; February, 13 30 to 13 35; March, 13 25 to 13 30; April, 13 25 to 13 30; May, 13 25 to 13 30; June, 13 25 to 13 30; July, 13 25 to 13 30; August, 13 25 to 13 30.

Cotton. — November, 9 65; December, 9 70. 1889.—January, 9 83; February, 9 96; March, 10 07; April, 10 16; May, 10 24; June, 10 33; July, 10 40.

CHICAGO, Nov. 13.

Wheat was weaker at the opening at 1/8c. decline, but later in the day the market improved owing to "shorts[1]" covering, and the closing tone is steady at 3/8c. to 1/2c. advance. On the curb[2], May was quoted at 115 1/4.

Corn opened unchanged and afterwards became depressed on "bulls[3]" realizing, and the final tone is weak at 1/8c. to 7/8c. decline.

Lard opened weaker and 2 1/2 points down. The market continued to decline owing to more speculative sales, and the closing is weak with rates unchanged to 5 points down.

Pork has ruled somewhat irregular. There has been some demand to purchase current month, and the market closes steady at the quotations.

Ribs have been in less demand, and close 2 1/2 points down; tone steady.

Bacon, a steady market with values unchanged. Light hogs are 5 points down and heavy hogs are unchanged.

The Provision Market has ruled steady.

PRICES FOR FUTURE DELIVERY.

Wheat. — November, 112 1/2; December, 113 1/2. 1889.—January, 111 3/8; May, 114 1/2. Receipts, Western points[4], 330,000 bushels; same day last year, 842,643 bushels.

Corn. — November, 40 1/4; December, 38 7/8. 1889.—January, 37 1/2; May, 38 7/8. Receipts, Western points, 260,000 bushels; same day last year, 214,235 bushels.

Lard. — November, 8 17 1/2; December, 8 07 1/2. 1889.—May, 8 22 1/2.

Pork. — November, 14 57 1/2; year, 14 57 1/2. 1889.—January, 14 67 1/2.

Ribs. — November, 7 45. 1889.—January, 7 45.

Bacon. — Halves, clear middle, 7 80; light hogs, 5 35; heavy hogs, 5 50.

Hogs. Receipts, Western cities, 64,000; same day last year, 90,000; ditto, Chicago, 21,000; same day last year, 43,541.

1. *Shorts*, son mêlé avec de la grosse farine. — 2. Voyez note 4, p. 114. — 3. Voyez note 3, page 114. — 4. *Western points*, des États de l'ouest.

THE WEATHER.

METEOROLOGICAL REPORTS.

WEATHER CHART, TUESDAY, NOV. 13, 6 P.M.[1].

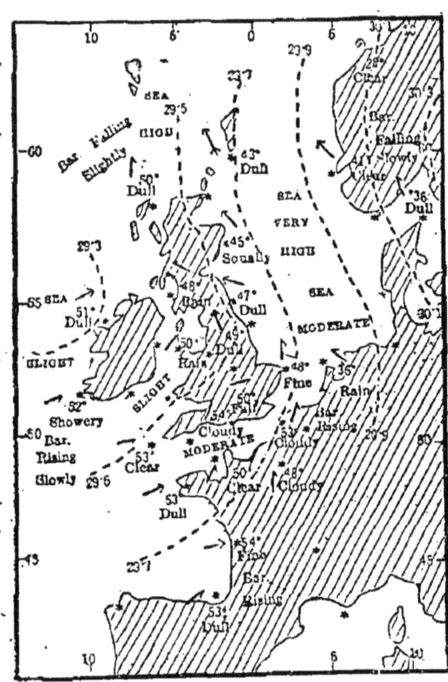

Explanation of the Chart.

In the above chart the dotted lines are "isobars" or lines of equal barometrical pressure, the values which they indicate being given in figures at the end, thus—30·4. The shade temperature[2] is given in figures for several places on the coast, and the weather is recorded in words. The arrows fly with the wind, the force of which is shown by the number of barbs and feathers, thus:— ⟶, light; ⟶, fresh or strong; ⟹, a gale; ⟹, a violent gale; ⊙ signifies calm. The state of the sea is noted in capital letters. The * denotes the various stations.

Remarks (8 30 p.m.).

The depression noticed off the west of Ireland on Monday evening appears to be dispersing over the Atlantic, and the wind has veered to the south-westward on our western and southern coasts, with improving weather. A small secondary disturbance is, however, moving northwards over Great Britain, and south-easterly gales are still reported in the north and east of Scotland, with squally, threatening weather and a very high sea. At 6 o'clock this evening pressure was highest, 30·4in.[3] and upwards, in the south of Sweden; lowest, 29·3in. and less, in a depression lying off the north-west of Ireland. Temperature was highest, 54deg.[4] at Hurst Castle[5], Jersey, and Rochefort, and 53deg. at Scilly, Dungeness[6], Brest, and Biarritz; lowest, 28deg. at Christiansund, 34deg. at Stockholm, 36deg. at Skagen and the Helder, 41deg. at Skudesnaes, and 43deg. at Sumburgh Head. Wind was light or moderate from the south-westward in the west and south of our islands and also at the French stations; strong to a gale[7] from south-east over the North Sea and the north and north-east coasts of Great Britain. Weather was fine at most of our southern and the French stations,

1. 6 *P. M.*, 6 heures du soir. P. M., *post meridiem*, après midi.—2. *Shade*, à l'ombre. La température est calculée d'après le thermomètre Fahrenheit, en usage dans tous les pays de langue anglaise. Voy. Grammaire Elwall, page 204, ou le *Dictionnaire français-anglais* du même au mot "thermomètre". Ce thermomètre marque 32° à 0 et 212° au point d'ébullition, de sorte que 9° Fahrenheit = 5° centigrades. — 3. 30.4 *in.*, c'est-à-dire 30 *inches*, 4 *tenths of an inch*, 30 pouces 4, ou environ 759mm. — 4. 54° Fahrenheit, voy. note 2. — 5. *Hurst castle*, dans l'île de Wight. — 6. *Dungeness*, cap au sud-est de l'Angleterre, dans le comté de Kent. — 7. *Strong to a gale*, ventant grand frais, presque grand vent.

dull over the northern parts of the kingdom, with rain at Ardrossan and Holyhead[1] and passing showers in the west of Ireland. A solar halo has been seen at Hurst Castle. The amount of bright sunshine registered at Westminster to-day has been about an hour. Sea was very high off the north and east of Scotland and high at Shields[2], but moderate or slight elsewhere. The barometer is at present rising steadily in the south and west, and although the general appearance is still very unsettled, it is possible that a short interval of fair weather will be experienced over the southern parts of the kingdom. The gale in the north is likely to subside gradually.

FORECASTS OF WEATHER FOR WEDNESDAY, NOV. 14.
(ISSUED AT 8 30 P. M. ON THE PREVIOUS DAY.)

0[3]. SCOTLAND, N. — South-easterly and southerly winds, moderating gradually; weather improving, but still showery.

1. SCOTLAND, E. — Same as No. 0.

2. ENGLAND, N. E. — Southerly winds, moderate or fresh; changeable, some showers, with bright intervals.

3. ENGLAND, E. — Same as No. 2.

4. MIDLAND COUNTIES. — Same as No. 5.

5. ENGLAND, S. (London and Channel). — South-westerly and southerly winds, moderate or fresh; changeable, some showers.

6. SCOTLAND, W. — South-easterly and southerly winds, moderate; fair to unsettled, and some rain.

7. ENGLAND, N. W. (and N. Wales). — Same as No. 6.

8. ENGLAND, S. W. (and S. Wales). — Southerly or south-easterly winds, force doubtful; unsettled, some rain.

9. IRELAND, N. — Same as No. 6.

10. IRELAND, S. — Same as No. 8.

WARNINGS. — The south cone has been lowered[4] this evening in districts 3 and 5. The signals are now down on all coasts.

By order, ROBERT H. SCOTT, Secretary.

---

1. *Ardrossan*, ville d'Écosse sur "the Forth of Clyde"; *Holyhead*, port au nord du pays de Galles, destiné à devenir très important; c'est le port d'où partent les steamers pour Dublin. — 2. Ville du nord de l'Angleterre, dans le comté de Durham. — 3. Les côtes britanniques sont divisées en onze districts (0 à 10), dont 6 pour l'Angleterre, 3 pour l'Écosse et 2 pour l'Irlande. Chaque district est surveillé par des gardes-côtes sous les ordres d'un capitaine de la marine royale, et se trouve en communication télégraphique constante avec les autres districts du moment que la mer devient menaçante. — 4. *The south cone has been lowered*, le cône du sud a été mis la pointe en bas. *The south cone* est un grand cône en bois noir dont se servent les gardes-côtes (sémaphore), dont la pointe tournée en bas (*the south cone*) indique qu'une tempête vient du sud, et dont la pointe tournée en haut (*the north cone*) indique qu'une tempête vient du nord. Il ne faut pas croire que ces prévisions du temps ainsi publiées tous les jours ne servent qu'aux marins et aux pêcheurs; elles sont tout aussi utiles aux fermiers et aux horticulteurs. Il n'est que juste d'attribuer au moins les principes de cette utile science à *Mathew Fontaine Maury* (1806-1873), mort commandant de la marine

BEN NEVIS OBSERVATORY[1],

THE TIMES OFFICE, 2 A.M.[2].

READINGS OF THE JORDAN GLYCERINE BAROMETER (CORRECTED FOR TEMPERATURE AND REDUCED TO MEAN SEA LEVEL), TAKEN AT INTERVALS OF TWO HOURS DURING THE PAST TWENTY-FOUR HOURS.

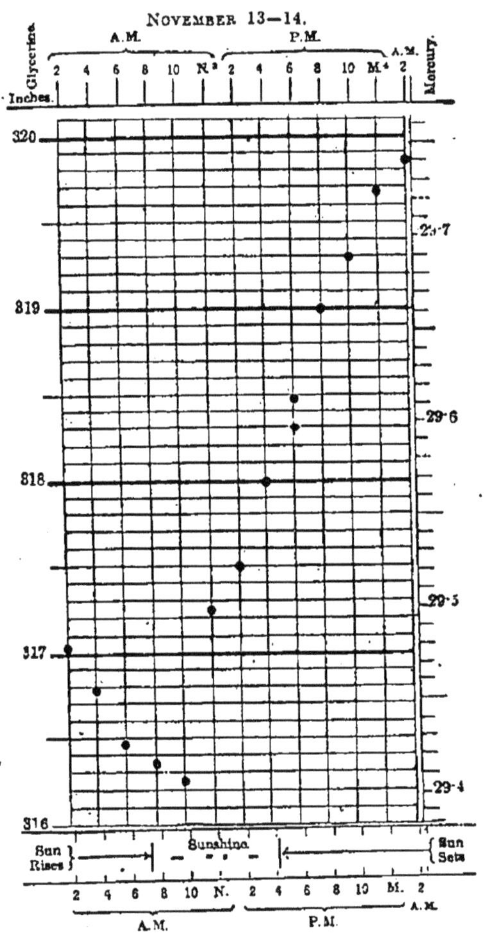

Sunshine is recorded by a Jordan's Photographic Recorder. Intensity varies with the thickness of the line. Broken lines show intermittent sunshine.

des États-Unis, auteur de la *Géographie physique* et de la *Météorologie de la mer*. Maury était descendu d'une famille de huguenots chassée de France par les dragonnades de Louvois. — 1. *Ben Nevis Observatory*, observatoire établi en 1883 sur le sommet de Ben Nevis, montagne au nord de l'Écosse (1330 mètres). Voici bien des années que les météorologistes cherchent à établir des observatoires à la plus grande hauteur possible. La France en a deux au Pic du Midi (2877 m.) et au Puy de Dôme (1465 m.); les États-Unis en ont également deux : *Pike's Peak* (4300 m.) et *Mount Washington* (environ 2000 m.). Il y en a aussi en Suisse et en Autriche et dans beaucoup d'autres pays. — 2. *A. M.*, *P. M.*, voy. note 3, p. 19, et note 2 page 31. — 3. *N.*, *noon*, midi. — 4. *M.*, *midnight*, minuit.

Nov. 13.

	Barometer.	Temperature.		Wind.		Cloud.	
	At 32°.	Dry Bulb.	Wet Bulb[1].	Direction.	Force 0 to 6.	Species.	Amount 0 to 10.
	In.	Deg.	Deg.				
9 A.M.	24·944	32·4	Sat.[2]	S.E.	3	Mist	10
9 P.M.	24·920	32·1	Sat.	S.E.	2	Mist	10

For the 24 hours.

Maximum, 32·6; *minimum*, 29·8. Ozone—morning, 4; night, 4. No sunshine recorded. Rainband[3], 4. Mist all day. Gale from east-south-east, force 4 to 5, till 2 a. m.; moderating gradually till 7 a. m.; and strong south-easterly breeze, force 2 to 3, since. Temperature rising till 10 a. m., and pretty steady since. Air saturated. Barometer falling till 2 a. m., rising till 5 p. m., and steady or rising a little since. Showers of snow, hail, and sleet fell during last night, and continual light drizzle from the mist during the day. Total fall ·0389in.

Temperature and Hygrometric Condition of the Air in London.

November 13 — 14.

Hours of Observation.	Temperature.		Tension of Vapour.	Weight of Vapour in 10 cubic feet of air.	Drying Power of Air (per 10 cubic feet).	Humidity (Saturation = 100).
	Air.	Dew Point.				
	Degrees.	Degrees.	Inches.	Grains[4].	Grains.	Per Cent.
Noon ..	51	41	·257	29	13	69
9 p.m. ..	51	45	·299	34	8	81
2 a.m. ..	49	45	·299	34	6	85

Minimum Temperature—49 deg. Maximum Temperature—55 deg.

Explanation.

The Dew Point is obtained directly by the use of a Dines's Hygrometer.

The Hygrometric values are calculated by using a modification of Glaisher's[5] Hygrometric Tables, 6th edition.

The "Drying Power" of the air is the weight of vapour which 10 cubic feet of air were still capable of absorbing at the time of observation.

The Humidity of the air (saturation = 100) is what is commonly known as "Relative Humidity".

---

1. *Dry bulb, wet bulb,* cuvette sèche, cuvette humide, c'est-à-dire baromètre métallique, baromètre à mercure. — 2. *Sat.*, saturated. — 3. *Rainband*, ligne de pluie. — 4. *Grain*, grain; 15 grains 4 valent un gramme. — 5. James Glaisher, né en 1803, fameux aéronaute. En 1865, il a remplacé l'amiral Fitzroy à la direction du département météorologique du *Board of Trade.* Il est président de la *Royal Astronomical Society.*

Heavy rain storms are reported from Wales, Cheshire, and Herefordshire. The rivers are reported to have overflowed their banks, much loss has been done to crops and live stock, and many houses are flooded. A severe gale is also reported as raging on the north coast of Scotland. The floods of Monday night did considerable damage to farming stock in the Culme Valley, East Devon. The river Culme overflowed its banks in many places and carried away the ballasting of the Culme Valley Railway near Uffculme, with the result that early traffic had to be suspended during the repair of the permanent way. Two men who were journeying home to Uffculme at a late hour lost their way and were drowned in the stream. The heavy fall of rain at Sherbone, Dorset, has flooded the west end of the town. At Westbury the street is like a river, and in some places the water is 3ft. deep. The silk factory there is flooded and has had to be closed. Near the station some cottagers are obliged to enter their houses through the bed room windows. At Boys Hill, about six miles from Sherborne, a horse and wagon were found yesterday morning stuck in the river without the driver, who, it is feared, has been drowned.

BERLIN, Nov. 13. — Clear and cold. Temperature at noon 1deg. (Réaumur) above zero. Barometer 766·5mm.

VIENNA, Nov. 13. — A cold day with strong east wind. Thermometer at noon 7deg. (Réaumur). Barometer 744mm.

IRELAND.

DUBLIN, Nov. 13.

To-day the Court for Crown Cases Reserved sat to hear the arguments in the case of " The Queen v. Dr. James Cormac Smyth, " who was convicted at the recent adjourned assizes in Wicklow of participation in the Belfast insurance frauds. Mr. Justice O'Brien, who tried the case, sentenced the traverser[1] to six months' imprisonment for conspiracy, at the same time reserving for argument the following query — " Whether the evidence was such as to sustain in law the inference of conspiracy. " In other words, whether the principle that was usually laid down of inferring the conspiracy from separate acts tending to a common object in the absence of other evidence, could be applied to the case of a false opinion given by a medical man, in the course of what was otherwise an ordinary professional act not brought about by himself. The traverser was one of several medical referrees who examined lives for the Equitable Company, and it was alleged that he conspired by signing false reports. In the result the Lord Chief Justice

---

1. *The traverser,* médecin examinateur pour une compagnie d'assurances.

delivered the unanimous judgment of the Court, upholding the conviction, and confirming the sentence of six months' imprisonment.

CORK, Nov. 13.

The Public Health Committee of the Cork Corporation to-day received an application for leave of absence from Mr. Burrell, city analyst. The Mayor thought Mr. Burrell should be asked to appoint a substitute, for he had been summoned by *The Times*[1] as a witness, and *The Times* should pay the substitute. M. Galvin, sanitary officer, thought it right to state that Mr. Burrell was going absolutely against his will, and had written to him that *The Times* would not be very glad when they got him over. It was decided to grant the application if a substitute were appointed.

TRALEE, Nov. 13.

To-day at Killarney Mr. Sheehan, M. P.[2], was convicted by the full bench of six magistrates, composed by Mr. Roche, R. M.[3], The M'Dermott, R. M., and Messrs. Colson, Herbert, Leahy, and Donovan, J. P.'s.[4], of abusive and threatening language towards the police in the execution of their duty. He was ordered to find sureties for his good behaviour, or in default to undergo one month's imprisonment. Mr. Sheehan refused to give sureties, and was lodged in Tralee Gaol. There was no excitement. Mr. Sheehan's conduct yesterday excited crowds, who hooted and followed the police, and had to be threatened with a charge before they would desist.

Plan of Campaign operations[5] on the Kenmare estate have been persistently attempted, but have been foiled by the police. Men have been going about the estate threatening the tenants, and taking one pound deposit from those afraid to resist as earnest[6] of their joining the Plan of Campaign. The tenants are very averse to the movement, but are in great dread of coercion by the agitators.

Mr. Gladstone, writing to a Belfast correspondent, says :—" I cherish hope that the opponents of Home Rule in Ulster[7] may be found progressively more and more disposed to resume the just and generous sentiments of their forefathers."

---

1. Dans le grand procès de *Parnell versus the Times*. — 2. *M. P.*, membre du Parlement. — 3. *R. M., resident magistrate*. — 4. *J. P.'s., justices of the peace*. — 5. *Plan of campaign operations*, les efforts pour obtenir des adhérents au " Plan de campagne ". Le *Plan* proposé par " the National League " (association instituée pour amener *the Home Rule* ou l'indépendance politique de l'Irlande et par là sa séparation d'avec l'Angleterre) n'est autre chose qu'une recommandation, ou plutôt un ordre, aux tenanciers de ne pas payer leurs fermages aux propriétaires, mais de remettre aux agents de la Ligue nationale ce que ceux-ci regarderaient comme *un loyer équitable*. La L. N. s'engageait à compter cette somme au propriétaire contre une quittance de *toute la somme due*. Ce mouvement est maintenant très diminué et limité aux districts écartés. — 6. *As earnest*, comme gage. — 7. Les habitants de l'Ulster, province du N. E. de l'Irlande, sont presque unanimement opposés à *the home rule*, préconisé par M. Gladstone.

THE MAILS.

The Royal Mail Company's steamer La Plata arrived at Southampton last night with the Brazil and River Plate mails, passengers, £3,763 in gold coin, one parcel of diamonds, and a full cargo.

The Nederlands[1] Company's steamer Soenda sailed from Southampton last night for Batavia and other ports in Java, *viâ* Marseilles, taking mails, passengers, Dutch troops, and a general cargo.

The Orient Line steamer Austral, from Sydney for London, left Adelaide on Monday.

The Hamburg-American steamer Australia, from the West Indies for Havre and Hamburg, passed the Lizard at 7 a.m. yesterday. The same line steamer Gellert, from Hamburg, arrived at New York on Monday.

The Cunard Line steamer Cephalonia arrived at Boston at 5 p.m. on Monday; all well.

A weekly service of mail steamers having been established between New Orleans, Belize, and Livingston, mails for British Honduras and Guatemala are now despatched from London every Wednesday evening by way of Queenstown[2], New York, and New Orleans; followed by supplementary mails every Saturday evening on the chance of their arriving at New Orleans in time. Mails are made up in Ireland on the following day in each case.

(FROM LLOYD'S[3].)

ADEN, Nov. 13.—The Queensland Line steamer Chyebassa, from Brisbane for London, has arrived here.

CALCUTTA, Nov. 13.—The P. and O.[5] steamer Mirzapore arrived here this morning.

COLOMBO, Nov. 12.—The P. and O. steamer Clyde left here this afternoon for Shanghai.

GIBRALTAR, Nov. 13.—The P. and O. steamer Sutlej, from London for Bombay, arrived here this afternoon.

KING GEORGE'S SOUND, Nov. 13.—The P. and O. steamer Paramatta, from London, arrived here this afternoon.

MONTEVIDEO, Nov. 12.—The Pacific Steam Navigation Company's steamer Galicia, from Liverpool for Chili, arrived here to-day. Messrs. Lamport and Holt's steamer Galileo, from Antwerp[6], arrived here to-day.

QUEBEC, Nov. 12.—The Dominion Line steamer Oregon, from Liverpool, arrived here to-day.

1. *Nederlands*, des Pays-Bas. — 2. *Queenstown*, port au sud-est de l'Irlande, dernier lieu de départ des paquebots pour l'Amérique. — 3. Voy. note 7, page 36. Toutes ces abréviations sont expliquées dans les premières pages du volume, où se trouvent également les explications géographiques. — 5. *The P. and O., Peninsular and Oriental Company*, voir note 3, page 34. — 6. *Antwerp*, Anvers.

(REUTER'S TELEGRAMS.)

BRISBANE, Nov. 13.— The Queensland Line steamer Dacca, from London, arrived here yesterday.

PORT SAID, Nov. 13.—The Queensland Line steamer Duke of Sutherland, from London for Brisbane, arrived here yesterday.

QUEBEC, Nov. 13.—The Allan Line steamer Circassian entered the River St. Lawrence to-day.

PRODUCE MARKETS.

TUESDAY EVENING.

SUGAR.—Crystallized by auction went at easier rates, 5,880 bags Demerara mostly sold, 16s. 6d. to 18s. 6d., fine 19s. 6d. to 19s. 9d.; and of 1,925 bags Trinidad, about half at 17s. 3d. to 17s. 9d. 29 tierces[1] 2,318 barrels and bags Demerara syrups sold chiefly at 12s. to 13s. 9d. 991 mats 1,797 bags Queensland about half sold, chiefly at 15s. to 16s. 3d.; and gray Muscovados, 11s. 3d. to 12s. 6d. 23 pockets Mauritius sold at 13s. 6d. 1,250 bags China bought in at 10s. 6d. per cwt. For beet[2] the market, after improving 3d. to 4 1/2d. since last Friday, is now less buoyant and closes at 13s. 3d., November. Refined has risen 3d. for pieces and 3d. to 6d. for dry goods. Tate's No. 1 cubes, 21s. 3d.; No. 2, 19s. 9d.; brushed, 18s. 6d.; Martineau's cut loaf, 20s. 9d.; titlers, 19s. 3d.; cubes, 19s. 9d.; pulverized, 19s. 3d.; and chips, 19s. 3d. Foreign loaves, 17s. 6d. to 18s. 3d. In the Clyde market a good business at fully firm prices.

TEA.—China.—To-day's public sales amounted to 7,356 packages, prices showing no change on previous rates. New Kaisow brought 7 3/4d. to 10 3/4d., Souchong 9 1/4d. to 11 3/4d., Moning 8d. to 10 1/2d., old Saryune brought 5d. Indian, Java, and Ceylon.—The sales to-day amounted to 6,171 packages. Indian were firm for teas "for price," but medium grades were easier. Ceylon and Java teas brought full rates.

COFFEE.—The limited quantity by auction went at nearly last weeks rates. 663 bags East India, mostly sold, small to medium Coorg, 80s. to 88s.; bold[3], 91s.; fine bold, 102s. 122 bags ordinary Jamaica, 71s. 440 bags New Grenada, middling to bold, 84s. 6d. to 88s.; pale and gray, 76s. to 83s. 52 bags Guatemala, new crop, 79s. to 85s. 400 bags pale to good bold Porto Rico, 80s. to 88s. 47 bags Vera Paz ranged up to 96s. for fine bold. 1,008 bags Rio, quay terms, part sold, 66s. 6d. to 68s. 1,512 bags Santos, sound, withdrawn, damaged sold 65s. to 67s. 6d. per cwt. The terminal markets show a decline.

COCOA.—Small public sales went without much change. 517 bags Tri-

1. *Tierces*, tierçons, petits fûts. — 2. *Beet*, sucre de betterave. — 3. *Bold*, qualité de café.

nidad, part sold, 82s. to 85s.; lower grades, 64s. to 70s. Part of 222 bags Grenada, ordinary, 59s. to 62s.; good to fine, 68s. to 69s. Part of 149 bags Ceylon, 82s. 6d. to 88s. Of the foreign 92 bags Caracas sold 57s. to 63s., and a small part of 460 bags Venezuela at 68s. to 90s. Other foreign, including 934 bags Guayaquil, bought in or withdrawn.

RICE.—Business has been done in new crop Burmah. Exact prices not known.

SPICES.—Zanzibar cloves continue firm. No business in pepper.

SHELLAC[1].—The public sales have gone at fully last auction's rates to 1s. higher for orange and 2s. for button. Of about 900 chests offered nearly 600 chests sold. B. S. L. S., 70s.; F. O. S., 61s.; J R diamond and S K double triangle, 56s. to 57s.; other second marks, 53s. to 55s.; one lot A.C. garnet, 46s.; blocky, 42s. 6d. to 43s.; fine third to fair second button, 57s. to 61s. per cwt. Since the end of last week sales of T. N. second orange for arrival, January shipment, at 67s., and A. C. garnet on the spot at 46s. per cwt.

GAMBIER[2].—For arrival 150 tons have sold at last week's decline, part November-January at 24s. 6d. to 24s. 9d. In auction 194 bales sold without reserve at 28s. and 490 bales cubes bought in at 40s. to 43s. per cwt.

JUTE[3].—A strong market. About 1,600 bales have sold to arrive at full to rather dearer rates. R. F. C. up to £16 5s.; rejections, £11 10s. to £12 5s. per ton.

LEATHER.—There is a quiet trade in most descriptions of leather, without any change in prices. English shoulders[4] are in very good request, and also cheeks and faces. Good heavy dressing hides, calf-skins, and horse hides are wanted. Market Hides.—A very small number of hides at market again this week, although there is an increase in the import of American cattle. Prices remain about the same.

METALS.—Tin easier. Straits sold at £101 5s. to £101 cash, sellers, three months, £102; English ingots, £104. Copper unchanged—G. M. B., £78 2s. 6d. cash[5]; £79 three months: English tough, £81; best selected, £82; strong sheets, £86. Lead dull. Spanish, sellers £13 7s. 6d. Spelter[6] unchanged. Silesian ordinary, £18 12s. 6d. to £18 15s.; special brands, £18 15 s. to £18 17s. 6d. Quicksilver flat, sellers £8 13s. second hand, £9 10s. first.

OILS.—Linseed, spot, London, 19s. 6d.; English brown rape, 29s. 3d. to 29s. 6d.; American spirit of turpentine, 35s. 3d. per cwt. Petroleum, $6^{6}/_{8}$d. per gallon.

1. *Shellac*, ou *Shell-lac*, laque en feuilles. — 2. *Gambier* ou *Gambir*, cachou, catechu. — 3. *Jute*, jute, chanvre de l'Inde. — 4. *English shoulders*, cuirs tirés des épaules de bétail anglais. — 5. *Cash*, comptant. — 6. *Spelter*, zinc.

DESTITUTE CHILDREN'S DINNERS SOCIETY.

TO THE EDITOR OF THE TIMES.

Sir,—This society is now entering on its 23rd year of labour on behalf of the destitute children of our vast metropolis. The necessity of providing some additional sustenance for the children of the poor has become as manifest to thoughtful persons in the present age as the necessity for their school instruction, so that the task of so doing has been taken upon all sides, and halfpenny dinners, self-supporting penny dinners, are such familiar incidents in our daily life that most people would scarcely credit that 30 years ago there was an entire absence of any such organization, although the need of it had attracted the attention of the thoughtful. It was not until the *Guernsey Star* narrated the success of the private effort of M. Victor Hugo in feeding a number of poor children once a fortnight with a good meat meal that a similar plan in 1864 was instituted in London, which, in 1866, became well known as the Destitute Children's Dinners Society. This society is now entering on its 23rd year of labour and has provided weekly during the last season between 17,000 and 18,000 meat dinners, making up a total of 343,301, in 64 dining rooms located among the poorest districts of our vast metropolis, such as Bethnal-green, Whitechapel, Isle of Dogs, London Docks, Hackney, Shoreditch, Bermondsey, Victoria-park, etc.— in fact, wherever the poor congregate. Each child contributes one half-penny towards the expenses of its dinner, these half-pennies during the past season amounting to the large sum of £713 3s. 3d., so that our children have done their part, and show how greatly these meat dinners are cherished. It should be borne in mind that the fundamental rule of the society is to allow each child a quarter of a pound of meat in each dinner provided. The last two seasons have greatly drained the resources of the society, mainly from its continuing its operations later than heretofore; it was difficult to close its hot kitchens against the starving children during the biting spring and to reject the small fee held out by eager hands. Although the cash in hand was only one-fourth the amount required to open all our dining rooms, we have opened them, having faith in the kindness of the public and with a firm hope that the many benevolent persons always on the look-out to soften distress may be induced to visit our dining rooms and see the children waiting for their dinner and realize what it would be to them should the doors be closed. Although the committee has, with insufficient means, risked opening the existing dining rooms, they dare not comply either with requests for increased grants to these or to open fresh centres of food for the children without a large increase of help. Will you give us the opportunity of making our wants known? One pound, it is calculated, will enable us to provide a dinner for 120 children, and we are confident many would aid us who look every day with pity on the scantily-clad and pinched-up faces of the school children swarming into our grand looking schools, whose kind-hearted teachers are ever earnestly calling out to us to provide some sustenance for the bodies whose empty stomachs neutralize the efforts made to feed the minds and improve the well-being of the little scholars. We would also earnestly seek to entreat any who may be willing and have the time to join us in the work of visiting and superintending the dinners (an oversight[1] absolutely necessary for the proper working of the society). They will find much to repay them in any little effort of sacrifice it may occasion, and in years to come they will find comfort and pleasure in the remembrance of the time they may have spent in one of our dining rooms.

Any one wishing to engage in such work may ascertain particulars by writing to the secretary, Mr. H. Norton Carr, 89, St. George's-square, S. W., and the subscriptions and donations which we most earnestly hope may result from this appeal on behalf of the destitute, hungry little children would be thankfully received by the treasurers, Lord Kinnaird, 1, Pall-mall east, and Mr. William Fuller, Stoughton-grange, Guildford, and by the secretary.

We are, Sir, yours faithfully,

BURDETT-COUTTS.
KINNAIRD.
E. Y. W. HENDERSON.
EBURY.
November, 10. WILLIAM FULLER.

PARLIAMENT.

HOUSE OF LORDS.

TUESDAY, NOV. 13.

The LORD CHANCELLOR[2] took his seat on the woolsack[3] at five minutes past 4 o'clock. There was a fair attendance of peers.

NEW PEER[4].

LORD SAVILE, introduced by LORD LAMINGTON and LORD WIMBORNE, took the oath and his seat, with the usual formalities, as Baron Savile, of Rufford, in the county of Nottingham.

1. *An oversight*, surveillance. *Oversight* signifie aussi « négligence, omission ». — 2. *The Lord Chancellor*, voy. note 3, page 63. — 3. *The woolsack*, le sac de laine, siège du *Lord Chancellor* à la Chambre des Lords. — 4. Lors de la présentation d'un pair nouvellement créé, les pairs siègent en robes, ce qui n'a lieu que lors de cette cérémonie et lors de l'ouverture du Parlement par la reine en personne. Le nouveau pair est présenté par deux autres pairs, ses parrains, accompagnés du comte maréchal (charge héréditaire du duc de Norfolk) et du grand chambellan, tous revêtus de leurs robes, par Garter, roi d'armes, et par l'huis-

PETITIONS.

The EARL of HARROWBY presented petitions from inhabitants of London, Brighton, Dover, Tunbridge Wells, Liverpool, Plymouth, Torquay, and Finchley against the Oaths Bill[1].

The EARL of MEATH presented a petition from inhabitants of Rochester, in favour of a well-considered scheme of voluntary State colonization.

The DUKE of RUTLAND presented a petition from Market Harborough, in favour of the Sunday Closing Bill.

The DUKE of BUCKINGHAM and CHANDOS presented a petition from the Mayor of Buckingham, as chairman of a public meeting, against the sale of intoxicating liquors on Sunday.

LORD BRAMWELL presented a petition from the Liverpool Land and Houseowners' Association, against the Bill for the Amendment of the Public Health Act.

The BISHOP of CARLISLE presented petitions from Staveley and from Preston Patrick, in favour of stopping the sale of intoxicating liquors on Sunday.

VICTORIA UNIVERSITY BILL.

On the motion of EARL GRANVILLE, this Bill was read the third time and passed.

OATHS BILL.

EARL SPENCER, on rising to move the second reading of this Bill, expressed his deep regret that his noble and learned friend Lord Herschell was unable to do so in consequence of his absence from England. His noble and learned friend had, therefore, requested him to take charge of the measure. In one sense the measure was full of legal points, and it might be of legal technicalities, and he wished the charge of it had fallen into the hands of some legal member of their lordships' House. On the other hand, there were many points in regard to which any one who took an interest in public affairs had a right to express his views. There was one happy circumstance upon which he might congratulate himself— viz., that during the last year a very marked change had taken place with regard to public opinion on this measure. A few years ago this question of oaths, particularly as it applied to the Houses of Parliament, was a matter of bitter controversy, and was taken up with great violence and great sincerity, perhaps, by men of both parties in the State; but in the early part of this Session a marked change appeared, and this measure passed through the other House without any display of those regretful feelings. Both sides then took up the measure, and the Solicitor-General[2], although, no doubt, in his individual capacity, assisted in

sier de la Verge-Noire. La procession entre, salue trois fois avant d'arriver au "sac de laine" (voy. note 3); le nouveau pair s'agenouille et présente l'acte de sa nomination au lord chancelier. Le greffier lit l'acte, le pair prête serment et signe. On le conduit à sa place, ses introducteurs et lui saluent trois fois le chancelier qui lui adresse alors ses félicitations. — 1. C'est un projet de loi autorisant toute personne à refuser le serment en justice par motif de conscience, et décrétant des peines sévères pour toute déclaration reconnue fausse. Après avoir passé à la Chambre des Communes, le projet doit être lu et discuté trois fois dans la Chambre des Pairs. — 2. *The Solicitor-General*, l'avocat général, un des grands conseillers de la couronne en matière de lois.

framing the clauses and in helping the measure to pass. He trusted that in his remarks he should do nothing to increase and draw out party feeling. First of all he desired to say a few words on the general subject of oaths, and he hoped he should not weary their lordships by doing so. He should like to refer to two of the principal objects to which oaths had been prescribed by Parliament—he meant originally as a test of loyalty, and also with regard to obtaining the greatest guarantee of the truth of evidence in Courts of justice. Oaths of allegiance affected in great measure the Houses of Parliament. Had they been effectual in their object? He could hardly do better than quote the report of the minority in a Blue-book delivered in 1867 on the question of oaths. They said: —

"Oaths of allegiance have seldom, if ever, been found to be of any practical benefit to the persons or the institutions whose safety and stability it has been sought to maintain by imposing them. In peaceful and prosperous times they are not needed. In times of difficulty and danger they are not observed. Contemporary history affords abundant proofs of the inefficiency of political oaths, whether taken by the people to their rulers or by rulers to their people."

Again, had oaths been effectual in obtaining the greatest amount of truth in Courts of justice? The same minority report said: —

"Oaths taken on important occasions have been violated by persons of all ranks, ecclesiastics as well as laymen, sometimes with the connivance or even with the approval of the authorities whose duty it was to watch over their fulfilment. They have been taken under circumstances which could hardly fail to bring them into contempt, and in various ways have been treated as unmeaning forms by those to whose opinion or example the public have been disposed or accustomed to defer."

Great weight was due to these opinions of distinguished men, including Mr. Robert Lowe (now Lord Sherbrooke), Dr. Milman, Dean of St. Paul's, and Lord Lyveden. There was a curious example of the inefficiency of oaths given in the same report: —

"Jeremy Bentham cites an oath taken by the Irish Bishops previously to investiture, in which each promises 'to see that in every parish within his diocese a school of a certain description shall have place.' 'Of the aggregate of these oaths,' he says, 'what in the year 1825 was the aggregate fruit? Performances, 782; perjuries, 480.'"

The late Sir John Mellor, justice of the Court of Queen's Bench, who had had a vast experience in Courts of law, thus expressed his opinion of the value of oaths: —

"The Legislature has enabled even atheists to depose without any obligation of taking an oath; but at the same time making them liable to punishment for false testimony, as if they had committed perjury. Profoundly convinced, by a long judicial experience, of the general worthlessness of oaths, especially in cases where their falsity cannot be tested by cross-examination or be criminally punished, I have become an advocate for the abolition of oaths as the test of truth; but I would retain the punishment for false declarations wherever at present the law prescribes a penalty for a false oath."

As far as his own individual opinion went, he should wish to see an affirmation take the place of the oath of allegiance. He could not say that he went so far as to wish to see all oaths dispensed with in Courts of justice, for he was afraid we had not yet arrived at such perfection of human nature that an oath would not assist the due administration of the law. During the last 60 years Parliament had been endeavouring to diminish the number of oaths. In 1829 the disabilities[1] which had been imposed on the Roman Catholics were removed. Then came the Act enabling Quakers to affirm[2]. This was followed by a statute enabling Jews to take an oath according to their own religious belief. The 3 and 4 William IV., c. 49, gave the option of affirmation in Courts of law to Quakers and Moravians[3]. This was followed by the Act of 1854, which allowed a witness in a civil case to affirm if he stated that the taking of an oath was not in accordance with his religious belief. Mr. Locke King's Act of 1861 extended the provisions of the last mentioned statute to criminal cases. Then the Act of 1867 extended to jurors in civil and criminal cases the relief given by Mr. Locke King's Act. These Acts referred to those who, having religious belief, could not lawfully take the oath. Then there were the two Acts of 1869-70 which dealt with those who objected to take the oath, or had been objected to as persons incompetent to take the oath. But it depended upon the presiding Judge to decide whether the oath would have a binding effect upon the witness's conscience. These were the Acts relating to persons who had no religious belief. He believed he was correct in saying that these two Acts did not refer to Scotland, and the curious result followed that if in Scotland a murder were seen by a man who was afterwards proved to be a disbeliever the murderer would escape scot-free. The Sheriff of Aberdeen had in a recent case called attention to this unsatisfactory condition of the law. He believed these two Acts only referred to evidence, and did not extend to jurors and the oath of allegiance, except in the case of Quakers, Moravians, and Separatists. Serious hinderance to the administration of the law was thereby caused, and there might be a positive breakdown[4] of justice if it were proved that a juror or magistrate was a disbeliever. The Court of Appeal, consisting of the Master of the Rolls[5] and Lords Justices Cotton and Lindley, recently affirmed the decision of Lord Coleridge and Justices Grove and Huddleston that a person without religious belief, or who, having re-

1. Les incapacités imposées par la loi. De 1688 à 1829, il était défendu d'employer les catholiques au service de l'État. Dès 1800 le second Pitt avait voulu les émanciper, mais Georges III s'y refusa obstinément, et c'est le duc de Wellington qui fit passer la loi d'émancipation des catholiques. — 2. *To affirm*, faire une affirmation, au lieu de prêter serment. — 3. *Quakers and Moravians*, les Quakers et les Moraves, deux sectes religieuses. Les Quakers, ou plutôt, comme ils s'appellent eux-mêmes, la Société des Amis, ne reconnaissent point de pasteurs et croient à l'enseignement et à la direction du Saint-Esprit. Leur nombre et leur austérité va en diminuant (environ 55 000 dans la Grande-Bretagne, et 70 000 aux Etats-Unis et au Canada) depuis qu'on a cessé de les persécuter; leur costume ne diffère guère plus du costume ordinaire et même le tutoiement tend à disparaître. — Les Frères Moraves, association chrétienne, débris des Hussites (1457), retirée en Moravie en 1722. C'est cette association qui, la première, fonda des missions au Cap de Bonne-Espérance, aux Antilles et au Labrador. On les nomme quelquefois les Quakers de l'Allemagne. Ils sont fort unis entre eux, s'assemblent souvent pour des repas en commun ou pour des cérémonies religieuses, se distinguent par une piété douce, une grande austérité, et un amour prononcé pour l'ordre et la paix. Ils portent un costume uniforme, d'une couleur foncée, et ont plusieurs établissements en Allemagne, à Londres, en Russie et aux États-Unis. On en compte environ 70 000. — 4. *A positive breakdown of justice*, un véritable manque de justice. — 5. Voy. note 4, page 64.

ligious belief, did not believe in a future state of rewards and punishments, was incapable of taking the oath. He believed that this decision had caused considerable difficulty in the position of men in the House of Commons who had, unfortunately, no religious belief. The time had, he hoped, now come when without party strife they might go further in removing disabilities. The present Bill[1] proposed that every person objecting to be sworn, upon stating the grounds of that objection—either that he had no religious belief, or that the taking of an oath was contrary to his religious belief—might be capable of affirming in all places and circumstances where an oath was now required by law. It was both just and equitable that we should extend the law in this country. First of all, the present law[2] was inoperative. There were many men who had entered the Houses of Parliament, or who had taken part in public business either as justices or solicitors, who, although practically under a disability, had been sworn. In the interests of religion itself it was not right to do that which was wrong and inequitable, and it was wrong and inequitable that a citizen should be prevented from taking part in many of the most important duties of the State because of his conscientious opinions. He sincerely trusted, therefore, that their lordships would give a second reading to this Bill, and that it would eventually pass into law and put an end to the difficulties which had so long been experienced from our present law. He must, however, confess that he should like to have extended the measure to Scotland, but he did not propose to alter the Bill, as it came from the other House in a shape which practically represented a compromise. He should be glad to consider any amendments which might be proposed, and begged to move the second reading of the Bill.

The LORD CHANCELLOR[3], speaking for himself and not for the Government, regarded the Bill with considerable jealousy. He did not, however, propose to move its rejection. It was not that he thought there was no necessity for amendment in the law relating to evidence; but he could not help observing that if the noble earl had had the courage of his convictions the Bill would have been very different from what it was, as the greater part of the noble earl's argument was directed against the existence of oaths altogether, and the quotation he gave from the distinguished minority of a distinguished committee that oaths of allegiance were ineffectual tended in the same direction. How could a committee or anybody else say that they were ineffectual? No doubt there were persons who disregarded their obligations in this as in other respects. Two totally different questions were mixed up in this Bill. It was one thing to say that religious objections of every kind should be considered. It was a totally different thing to relieve persons from the profession of religious belief, whatever office or duty they might have to perform. Personally he believed that the operation of the oath in Courts of justice was very considerable indeed, and it was a common thing for a man to avow that he had spoken falsely when not on oath, but must speak the truth wen sworn. (Hear, hear.) That was an

1. *The present Bill,* le projet de loi à présent en considération. Ne pas confondre *Bill* avec *Act* ou *law; an act,* c'est une loi votée. — 2. *The present law,* la loi telle qu'elle existe actuellement. — 3. *The Lord Chancellor,* président de la Chambre des pairs, prend part aux discussions. Il n'en est pas de même du *speaker,* président de la Chambre des Communes, qui ne fait que diriger les débats.

almost universal experience of Judges. The noble earl's remarks on the question of evidence were, no doubt, very weighty, and it was a consideration of that kind which induced the present Mr. Justice Denman to introduce the Bill to which the noble earl had referred. A dreadful murder had been committed, and there was a witness who had seen the act, but evaded giving evidence by professing religious disbelief. It was, however, a very different thing to apply this principle to the ordinary duties of citizens, such as that of sitting on a jury. He did not think that one who professed to have no religious belief was a proper person to sit in judgment on his fellow citizens, it might be in a case of life or death. He should endeavour, if the question were open when they went into Committee[1], if he could do so without absolutely destroying the Bill, to move such an amendment as would prevent the Bill from having such an operation as this. The state of the law applicable to oaths was not satisfactory, but for different reasons from those expressed by the noble earl. He thought the obligation of an oath was so solemn and serious in most minds that the objection was that it was too lightly taken. But he was not disposed to dissociate religious belief from any judicial function whatever. The only argument which had been urged in favour of that course was the old one—from the abuse of a thing to take away the use[2]. Speaking only on his own behalf he should conclude by stating that he did not propose to move any amendment on the second reading.

The EARL of CARNARVON said he supposed they must regard this as the close of a very long controversy, which had gone on during the whole of his Parliamentary life, and perhaps the lives of nearly every one in that House. When he first came into the House there were tests and subscriptions of some form or another existing everywhere. No doubt if these had been more reasonable they would have existed longer; therefore, he did not want to offer any captious objections to this Bill. But at the same time he shared the opinion of the noble and learned lord on the wool-sack to this extent—that he did not specially approve the objects which the promoters of the Bill had in view. The laws of a country must rest on some religious foundation, and if they departed from that they must take up ground that was very much lower. But this had been the doctrine up to the present generation. It was accepted in the time of the Reformation. It was the view of both parties in the time of the civil wars, and so on; and he knew no period in British history when that idea was not uppermost in the minds of men. The highest minds always recognized the sanctity of the oath. It did seem to him that this Bill went very near indeed to announcing the doctrine that legislation and religion were to be divorced. He said very near; it did not go the whole way. The object of an oath in a Court of law was first and last and essentially to get the truth. If for that purpose an affirmation could be made sufficient, then, on principle, he might be fairly satisfied. As regards the Parliamentary oath, that stood on a somewhat different footing, but it might be cast into something like the same category. But, conceding all this, he thought the phraseology of this Bill was dangerously loose. Their lordships would observe that every person on objecting to being sworn may

1. *To go into Committee,* passer à la discussion des articles. — 2. Il ne faut pas user crainte d'abuser.

state that he has no religious belief. He supposed that meant no belief in the existence of a Supreme Being. He was at a loss to understand how the want of such belief distinguished a man from being an atheist. Well, the Bill then went on to say that " he shall be permitted to make a solemn affirmation ". What was a " solemn affirmation "? He could understand an affirmation under the circumstances, but a solemn affirmation seemed to him to be absurd if there was any meaning at all in the words. (Hear, hear.) Solemn meant a deep sense of awe of some supernatural power. Their lordships would remember that the Quakers by Act of Parliament were able to make a solemn affirmation; but the solemn affirmation was accompanied by the words " in the presence of Almighty God ". (Hear, hear.) In this Bill the word solemn has no sense whatever. His first objection was that they were going under this Bill to create, for the first time, a class of persons who had no religious belief, whereas hitherto they had allowed men to make an affirmation, not because they had no religious belief, but because their religious belief was such that it precluded them from taking the oath. In the second place, those who were to take this affirmation were to describe themselves as having no religious belief. He had some doubt about the Bill, but at the same time he observed that the Bill was intended to close a long dispute. Reluctantly, and with sorrow, he should give his assent to the second reading of the Bill.

LORD ADDINGTON said it was interesting to observe the action of the member who refused to take the oath and insisted on making an affirmation. Having refused to take the oath and claimed to make an affirmation, with the utmost inconsistency, having been rebuffed by the House at every stage during that Parliament, he came forward in a new Parliament and walked up quietly to the table and took the oath[1], and there he had been seated ever since. He should, therefore, argue that there was no practical necessity for pressing on a Bill of this kind. The noble lord opposite had alluded to the perfunctory way[2] in which the oath was taken by some hon. members in another place; but that was entirely a matter for themselves, and the House itself was entirely exonerated from any participation in that proceeding. Oaths had been connected with the history not only of this country, but of the whole world since its commencement, and they had been inseparably incident to all the conditions under which civilization had endeavoured to bring home to the individual the sense of personal responsability. Looking at the terms of the Bill, it seemed to him to go beyond the necessities of the case. If the House of Commons chose to say that oaths should not be compulsory there, and that affirmation should suffice, in that case it would be better to leave out the word " solemn ". It was absurd to ask a man who had no belief in a Supreme Being to regard his making of an affirmation as a solemn act. In that connexion there was, he pointed out, all the difference in the world with regard to the admission of unbelievers and the relief given to Quakers and Moravians; but the Bill in effect said that henceforth

1. Lord Addington fait ici allusion à *M. Bradlaugh*, membre du Parlement pour Northampton, qui d'abord refusa de prêter serment, puis qui, réélu, consentit à le prêter. C'est M. Bradlaugh, du reste, qui introduisit et fit passer "*the Oaths Bill*" dans la Chambre des Communes. — 2. *The prefunctory way*, la manière légère.

every person, from the Monarch on the throne down to the humblest person in the witness-box[1], who chose to say he had no religious belief might be exempt from taking the oath. Now, he did not believe that oaths taken in Courts of justice were detrimental to the interests of truth; on the contrary, it was the commonest experience of magistrates to find persons who would not mind telling a lie, but who, nevertheless, would not swear a lie. He trusted, therefore, that if the Bill was read a second time it would undergo material changes in Committee.

The BISHOP of CARLISLE, who was the only occupant of the bench reserved for the Bishops, trusted that one conclusion might be drawn from the absence of his right rev. prelates—namely, that this Bill was not regarded generally by them as being a concession to unbelief, as it had been represented to be. No doubt that was an aspect in which it might be regarded, and he did not at all wonder that reference had been made to the genesis of the Bill and the unfortunate kind of origin it had had in another place[2]. He had endeavoured to keep his own mind as far as possible clear of any such consideration, because he felt that one was apt to have his judgment biased if he looked to unhappy circumstances, and did not look upon the great points which were at issue[3]. It seemed to him that they were by the force of circumstances put in a certain position out of which it was not possible to escape. They were face to face with a great difficulty—namely, that there were certain persons who, owing to a variety of causes, objected to take an oath; and he was not disposed to look at the Bill merely in the light of a concession of privilege to certain persons who might be aggrieved by the want of that privilege or from the necessity there was of getting evidence in the best way possible. It had been pointed out that it might be possible for a man, simply by the fact of saying it was contrary to his conscience to take an oath, to fail to give evidence which might involve a question of life or death. But he looked at the matter from two broad points of view. There were two cases in which they had oaths, and in which they had been defended. There was one with regard to the future, and another with regard to the past. As to the first, it was common to put a person chosen for a certain office upon his oath that he would faithfully discharge the duties thereof, and in such cases possibly an oath so taken was not of much avail. On the other hand with regard to the past, he entirely agreed that the oath was of very great value. The noble lord on the wool-sack had put a case of a man who would give one kind of evidence on oath and another kind if not sworn. He had seen a case the other day in the newspapers of a witness who had intended giving evidence before the Royal Commission, and had expressed his intention to give evidence of a different character from a statement he had already made, and explained that by saying that when he made his statement he was not sworn, but when he gave his evidence he would be on his oath. He did most earnestly believe that true evidence might be got in Courts of Justice by putting a man

1. *In the witness-box*, sur le banc des témoins. *Box*, loge, compartiment. — 2. Voyez note 1, page 132. *In another place;* il est d'usage de ne jamais citer dans une Chambre ce qui a été dit dans l'autre. On se tire d'affaire en disant : *dans un autre endroit.* — 3. *At issue*, en litige, en considération.

upon his oath, which would not be otherwise obtainable; but looking at the thing broadly, it did seem to him that it was a more important thing to obtain the truth in the way in which a man was prepared to give it, rather than to adopt a plan which made it impossible for some persons to give evidence at all, and put others in an entirely false position. (Hear, hear.) Whether in respect to offices or in Courts of Justice, he thought there was a great deal to be said in favour of substituting a solemn affirmation. He thought, however, that "solemn" was an unfortunate word, as he did not himself see how a declaration could be solemn if a man believed neither in God nor Devil; but that was not a matter for discussion on the second reading. What he rose for was to say that he intended to vote for the second reading of that Bill, and he did not think he was false to his God or his Saviour in so doing. He thought the Bill was required for the settlement of a most unfortunate state of things, and he would, therefore, vote for the second reading. (Hear, hear.)

The EARL of DERBY pointed out that all that was proposed by the Bill was that certain persons whose objections to take an oath were insuperable, and who, whether they[1] liked it or not were now, undoubtedly, a very numerous class, should not be exempt from the obligation to give their evidence where it might be of very great importance to third parties. The person who objected to take the oath was not, as a rule, or even often, the person who suffered by his evidence not being taken. The case had been mentioned of a man who would tell a lie, but would not swear a lie. His objection, however, might not be a conscientious one, because if he swore falsely he would subject himself to the penalties of perjury. He thought there was some force in the verbal objections which had been taken to the Bill. He did not think it desirable to call upon a man to say in so many words that he had no religious belief. In the first place, it was not very easy to say in what religious belief consisted. He should have thought that, instead of calling upon him to make that declaration, it would have been simpler to make him say that the taking of an oath was repugnant to his conscience. (Hear, hear.) That would be at once a less offensive form of words to some people, and as to others it would avoid the ambiguity of the present phrase. He did not believe in the value of promissory oaths or affirmations. He did not believe that they had ever induced any man to do his duty who would not have done so without them. (Hear, hear.) He hoped their lordships would pass the Bill without material alteration.

EARL GRANVILLE said it appeared clear to him that their lordships did not intend to reject the Bill on the second reading, and it would, therefore, be expedient for him to reserve a great deal that he had to say for the Committee stage[2]. As he understood his noble friend who moved the second reading, he said he thought it was not desirable to remove the oath in the case of witnesses in Courts of Justice. That had some bearing on the criticism of the adjective "solemn" as applied to the affirmation. He thought such an adjective was of no use; but practically it was found that an uneducated person attached considerable importance to the form in which he promised or swore to speak the truth,

1. *They*, c'est-à-dire *the Peers*. — 2. *For the Committee stage*, lors de la discussion des articles.

and on that view it would be just as well to retain the word. He did not imagine that the Bill was, in the opinion of any one present, an ideal Bill. He knew that there were amendments which he and some of his friends behind him would like; but his noble friend in moving the second reading had pointed out that the Bill was very much in the nature of a compromise. In that view he should be excessively anxious not to disturb the arrangement by moving any amendments which might be objected to, although he might think them an improvement to the Bill. He hoped, if he and his friends avoided pressing amendments they would like to make, that, on the part of the Government, it was not intended to support amendments in a different direction.

The MARQUIS of SALISBURY[1] said he had been asked to say that he would not support any amendments which might be made in an opposite direction. In an opposite direction to what? He proposed to follow the time-honoured custom of seeing the amendments before passing judgment upon them. He had no knowledge of what amendments his noble friend on the wool-sack, in his individual capacity, proposed to move. That was not a Bill which divided the two parties. It belonged to a class to which he was afraid the noble lord opposite had great objections—namely, the class of open questions[2]. He had always thought that there were a great many oaths which not only added no solemnity to the occasion on which they were made, but were a direct invitation to profanity and irreverence. (Hear, hear.) In reference to oaths of persons whose convictions, or whose want of religious belief, made them unfit to take an oath, he agreed that there was very little difference of opinion. As had been rightly stated by the noble earl opposite, the person who was injured by the throwing of difficulties in the way of evidence was not the person who was unable to take the oath, but the person on whose case evidence was wanted. He should not think of rejecting evidence adduced by persons whose convictions he did not approve. It was a practical illogicality to do so. It was a survival from ancient governments which had run into our law, and which undoubtedly, now that attention had been drawn to it, had become a practical inconvenience. Beyond those questions, however, he waited to see the amendments before he passed judgment upon them. He could imagine that the zeal of reformers might have gone too far in the clauses which they wished to introduce in the Bill, and he certainly could not undertake to make any deliberate engagement against all possible amendments in any possible direction such as the noble earl desired. (Hear, hear.)

EARL GRANVILLE was understood to explain that he gathered from the Lord Chancellor's observations that the noble and learned lord was inclined to go in an opposite direction from that of the noble earl who moved the second reading, and that he would have liked certain improvements made in the Bill.

The MARQUIS of SALISBURY said he might also explain that he did not know in what direction that was. (Laughter.)

1. *Prime Minister*, Président du Conseil. On remarquera que les ministres ne parlent que dans la Chambre dont ils font partie. En France, les ministres parlent dans les deux Chambres. — 2. *Open questions*, des questions ouvertes, c'est-à-dire des propositions sur lesquelles chaque ministre a le droit d'avoir sa propre opinion et de voter à son gré.

The Bill was read a second time, the Committee stage being fixed for that day fortnight.

The House adjourned at ten minutes to 6 o'clock.

HOUSE OF COMMONS.

TUESDAY, NOV. 13.

The SPEAKER took the chair at 3 o'clock.

PETITIONS.

Petitions in favour of Sunday closing of public-houses were presented, by Mr. J. C. STEVENSON, from School Boards, Methodists, Good Templars, and others, of Halifax, South Shields (3)[1], Sheffield, Gosforth, Salisbury, and other places; by the MARQUIS of GRANBY, from Stathern; by SIR F. FITZWYGRAM, from Porchester; by Mr. S. EVERSHED, from Burton-on-Trent; by CAPTAIN HEATHCOTE, from Tunstall; by Mr. A. R. HEATH, from Tetney and from Holton-le-Clay; by Mr. G. W. BALFOUR (7), from Leeds and New Wakefield; by Mr. MORRISON (2), from Skipton; by Mr. RENDEL (3), from Newtown and other places; by Mr. H. S. CROSS, from Bolton; by Mr. M. MAC INNES, from Dalton, Newborough, Hexham, and other places; by MAJOR RASCH, from Tilbury; by Mr. C. KENNY, from Barnsley; by Mr. W. SIDEBOTTOM (4), from Furness Vale, New Mills, and other places; by Mr. DONKIN (2), from North Shields; by Mr. A. H. D. ACLAND, from Rotherham, Mexborough, and other places; by ADMIRAL FIELD, from Seaford; by Mr. T. FIELDEN, from Wuerdle and Wardle; by Mr. C. A. V. CONYBEARE, from Gwennap; by Mr. W. BECKETT, from Misterton; by Mr. HANBURY-TRACY, from Llanidloes and Llanfyllin; by SIR J. SWINBURNE, from Tamworth, Glascote, and other places; by LORD BARING, from Lidlington; by Mr. JOHN ELLIS, from Hucknall Torkard; by Mr. H. STEWART, from Lincolnshire; by Mr. HERMON-HODGE, from Accrington; by SIR W. LAWSON, from Salford; by SIR S. CROSSLEY, from Oulton; by Mr. C. ACLAND, from Launceston, Copthorne, and other places; by Mr. F. PARKER, from Henley-on-Thames.

Petitions for the prevention of cruelty to animals were presented by Mr. J. MORLEY, from Neath and Penrith; by Mr. C. T. MURDOCH, from Reading; by Mr. J. C. STEVENSON, from Limehouse and Poplar; by Mr. FULLER, from Trowbridge; by Mr. S. HOARE, from South Heigham, Norwich; by Mr. W. SIDEBOTTOM, from Hayfield; by SIR G. ELLIOT, from Newport; and by Mr. RENDEL, from Llanfyllin.

Petitions for the total prohibition of vivisection were presented by Mr. A. B. WINTERBOTHAM, from Cirencester[2]; by COMMANDER BETHELL, from Bridlington Quay and neighbouring place; and by Mr. E. HARDCASTLE, from Salford.

Petitions were also presented, by Mr. RANKIN, from clergy of rural deanery of Weobley, praying that the Tithe-rent Charge Bills[3] introduced by the Government

1. Les chiffres indiquent le nombre de pétitions. — 2. Prononcez : ci'-cis-ter. — 3. Loi proposée par le marquis de Salisbury ordonnant le payement des dîmes par le propriétaire. Il a été décidé que la dîme serait payée par le tenancier qui la déduirait du montant de son loyer.

should be passed into law during the present Session; by Mr. BALLANTINE, from master bakers and confectioners of Coventry, against Weights and Measures Bill; by Mr. C. H. WILSON, from the Hull and East Riding Women's Liberal Association, in favour of women who pay rates and taxes having votes for Parliamentary elections; by Mr. G. CURZON, from Southport and neighbourhood, for repeal of Irish coercion laws; by SIR J. COLOMB, from Rochester, in favour of voluntary state colonization; by Mr. C. ACLAND, from Highway Board, Callington, in favour of van and wheel tax; by SIR R. LETHBRIDGE, from public meeting in Ladbroke-hall, North Kensington, in favour of the Licence Suspension Bill; and from Sons of Phœnix and West London Good Templars to the same effect; by SIR D. CURRIE, from the Road Trustees of the county of Perth, for alteration of sections 42 and 133 of the Police and Sanitary Administration (Scotland) Bill.

ALEXANDRA-GATE, HYDE PARK.

SIR A. BORTHWICK asked the First Commissioner of Works whether his attention had been called to the inadequacy of Alexandra-gate, Hyde Park, for the accommodation of the present traffic, and whether he was prepared to take steps for increasing the facilities of egress and ingress at that gate.

Mr. PLUNKET. — I agree with my hon. friend that the approaches of the Alexandra-gate, Hyde Park, are very inconvenient, and I propose to remedy the inconvenience by setting back the gates about 18ft. and rounding off the corners of the approaches. I have applied for the consent of the Vestry of St. Margaret's and St. John's, Westminster, who have charge of the roads outside, and I now only await that consent.

GLASGOW BOUNDARIES COMMISSION.

Dr. CAMERON asked the Lord Advocate whether he proposed before the end of this Session to produce the promised Bill carrying out the recommendations of the Glasgow Boundaries Commission.

The LORD ADVOCATE said that the recommendations of the Commissioners were still under the consideration of the Government, and he was not yet able to give a definite answer to that question.

ADDITIONAL GUNS FOR THE NAVY.

Mr. DUFF asked the Secretary to the Admiralty whether he would state to the House the names of the firms alluded to in his speech at Liverpool on the 25th of October to whom orders had been given for additional guns for the Navy, and whether the orders referred to included guns over 9in.[1] in diameter.

Mr. BRODRICK. — The firms alluded to by my hon. friend are those of Messrs. Vickers and Co., Sir W. Armstrong and Co., and Sir J. Whitworth and Co. The orders referred to do include guns over 9in. in diameter.

Mr. DUFF. — Will the guns in question be paid for out of the Estimates of the year, or will they cause a Supplementary Estimate?

Mr. BRODRICK. — The guns in question will be paid for out of the Estimates for the year, but if the payments falling due should prove to be in excess of the Estimates the balance will be provided by a Supplementary Estimate.

1. 9 *inches* = 228 millimètres.

THE TRUCK ACT[1].

Mr. BRADLAUGH asked the Secretary of State for the Home Department whether he would reconsider the approval given to the refusal of the Chief Inspector of Factories to prosecute under the Truck Act where fines had been deducted from workmen's wages, and whether he would cause fresh instructions on this head to be issued to the inspectors of mines and inspectors of factories.

Mr. MATTHEWS. — I will promise the hon. member to consult the law officers on the point of law raised by him; and I will act on their opinion when I have received it.

THE METROPOLITAN POLICE.

LORD H. BRUCE asked the Secretary of State for the Home Department whether the police force in the overcrowded districts of London was in the same numerical proportion to the number of residents as it was in less populated and wealthier districts, and whether he had any reason to believe that the force itself was overworked and undermanned[2], and thereby unable to cope as efficiently as it might do with its present multifarious duties.

Mr. MATTHEWS.—I am informed by the Commissioner that the police in the metropolis are located according to the wants of each particular district, and not according to numerical proportion or to rates. I have no reason to think that the police are overworked and undermanned as far as their ordinary duties are concerned. Occasionally there is, no doubt, a great pressure of work with which it is more difficult to cope[3], but the extra duties which sometimes become necessary are always cheerfully undertaken by all members of the force.

THE NEW COUNTY ELECTORAL DIVISIONS.

Mr. WARDLE asked the President of the Local Government Board whether, seeing that the new county electoral divisions covered in many instances three and in some cases part of four polling districts, he would, in order to avoid the practical disfranchisement of great numbers of the labouring population, advise the returning officers[4] to adopt as far as practicable the polling districts[5] formed under section 47 of the Corrupt and Illegal Practices Prevention Act, 1883.

Mr. RITCHIE.—It is the duty of the returning officer, when he deems it necessary, to divide an electoral division into polling districts, but each polling district must be an area or a combination of areas for which separate parts of the register of electors are made out. I do not doubt that the returning officers in determining as to the polling districts will have regard to the reasonable convenience of the electors, so far as the circumstances in connexion with the lists of voters admit; but the matter is not one in which I could give any instructions to the returning officers.

---

1. *The Truck Act* fait partie du *Factory and Workshop Act*, '78, qui consolide une série de statuts pour la réglementation du travail dans les fabriques et les ateliers. Le *Truck Act* réglemente la nomination et les fonctions d'inspecteurs et de médecins, fixe les amendes et stipule leur recouvrement devant un tribunal de juridiction sommaire. — 2. *Undermanned*, trop peu nombreux. — 3. *To cope with*, lutter. — 4. *The returning officer*, le commissaire chargé de l'élection. — 5. *The polling districts*, les divisions d'un comté ou d'un bourg, afin de rendre plus facile le vote.

THE ROYAL NIGER COMPANY[1].

Mr. PICTON asked the Under-Secretary of State for Foreign Affairs whether the Secretary of State had received a memorial adopted at a public meeting in Lagos, and sent to him through the Governor, protesting against any extension of the charter of the Royal Niger Company; whether he could say what answer had been given; and whether he would consent to lay upon the table a return for the year ending August 31, or any other recent date, showing the revenue raised by the above company by means of export and import duties and trade licences, and likewise showing the items of expenditure to which such revenue was applied.

SIR J. FERGUSSON.—The memorial has been received. It has not been answered, as no decision has yet been taken. The wishes of the principal traders in the Oil Rivers, as well as the interests of the shipping firms and of the neighbouring colonies, are being consulted and will receive the fullest consideration. As the whole question of the revenue and administrative expenditure of the company is undergoing investigation, it would be premature and perhaps misleading to lay papers which could give only imperfect information on the subject.

PENSIONS TO THE POLICE.

Mr. C. GRAHAM asked the Secretary of State for the Home Department whether he would consider the advisability of allowing members of the Metropolitan Police Force permanently injured and rendered incapable of work through injuries received on duty the privilege of full pension, irrespective of length of service.

Mr. MATTHEWS.—Under the scale of pensions authorized by the Secretary of State in 1873 the cases of police officers whose injuries received in the execution of their duty wholly incapacitate them from earning a livelihood are specially considered, and they may be granted a full pension, irrespective of their length of service, if the circumstances are considered of a character to justify such an award. Pensions of a lesser amount are granted to officers whose injuries may partially but not wholly prevent them from earning a livelihood.

CROFTER EMIGRATION[2].

Dr. CAMERON asked the First Lord of the Treasury, with reference to his statement that he proposed to bring on the supplemental vote of £10,000 for

1. Les districts du Niger, sous le protectorat de la Grande-Bretagne, s'étendent sur tout le delta du fleuve depuis le Rio del Rey et en remontant le fleuve jusqu'au Tchadda ou Binué, affluent très important à l'est. Depuis 1887, ce territoire s'est agrandi de la côte entière depuis Lagos jusqu'au Rio del Rey et de certains territoires dans le bassin du Niger acquis par la Compagnie royale du Niger pour y faire le commerce. Dans le Haut Niger, la France cherche à fixer sa domination par la Sénégambie. — 2. Les *Crofters* (petits fermiers; *croft*, ferme) sont les descendants d'anciens clans écossais habitant surtout les îles des Hébrides, puis certaines contrées montagneuses de l'Écosse et même les îles d'Orkney et de Shetland. Ils vivent bien pauvrement du produit de leurs fermes et de la pêche. Avant la rébellion de 1745, ils étaient co-propriétaires avec leurs chefs de clan, mais depuis les chefs se sont regardés comme seuls possesseurs du sol. Ils y ont établi d'abord de grands pâturages, et les *crofters* ont été relégués sur les bords de la mer très peu productifs; puis aux pâturages ont succédé de grandes étendues de terre pour la préservation des daims et des *grouse* (coqs de bruyère). Les *crofters*, qui sont à peu près au nombre de 70 000, ont été réduits à une grande misère. Une commission a été nommée pour les soulager, notamment

crofter emigration during the present Session, whether he would consult the convenience of Scottish members by taking it immediately before or after the other Scotch votes.

Mr. W. H. SMITH.—I shall be quite ready to consult the convenience of Scotch members as to the time at which the vote for crofter emigration will be taken.

THE POLICE AND THE SALVATION ARMY[1].

Mr. COBB asked the Secretary of State for the Home Department whether he was aware that recently in different parts of the country the police had interfered with and warned, and in some cases prosecuted members of the Wesleyan and Primitive Methodist bodies, and of the Church and Salvation Armies and other religious communities, under the Highway Act, for causing a general obstruction of public highways, but without alleging or proving any particular instance of the obstruction of any individual, or of inconvenience to any particular person; whether his attention had been called to the case of a member of the Salvation Army at Rugby who, on the 9th of October, was summoned before the county Bench and fined for obstruction in holding a service in Sun-street, at its junction with Cambridge-street, in that town, although all the inhabitants (with one exception) in Sun-street and Cambridge-street signed a memorial in favour of such services being held, and no person complained of being annoyed or obstructed by them; whether he was also aware that on the 23rd of October the captain of the Rugby Salvation Army was convicted and fined (or in default three days' hard labour) upon the sworn evidence of the police that he took part in the service, although, as a fact, he was not present, but ill at home; and whether the Government would take steps to amend the law so that in future prosecutions it should be necessary to prove an actual and particular case of obstruction of some individual.

Mr. MATTHEWS[2].—There are no papers in the Home Office which enable me to say positively whether the facts alleged in the first paragraph of the question are true. I have obtained a report from the Rugby justices as to the two cases quoted. In the first case the memorial was not entertained by the Bench, on the ground that, in the opinion of the Bench, the persons signing had no right to authorize an obstruction of a public thoroughfare. In the second case, I am informed that the defendant was defended by counsel, and that nothing was said in the hearing of the Bench, or as come to their knowledge since, that he was ill at home. There was no attempt to prove an *alibi*, and the Bench were satisfied with the evidence that the defendant was present. I cannot give the hon. member any pledge as to an amendment of the law relating to obstruction.

THE SHAN[3] STATES.

Mr. CHANNING, for Mr. S. SMITH, asked the Under-Secretary of State for

---

par la réduction de leurs fermages et par l'émigration d'un certain nombre de familles dans la Colombie anglaise, mais cela n'a réussi que partiellement. — 1. *The Salvation Army*, l'armée du Salut, association *militante* pour la propagation des sentiments religieux. Cette association est très active dans tous les pays, elle est commandée militairement, et malgré ses excellentes intentions elle cause souvent du scandale. — 2. Ministre de l'Intérieur (*the Home Office*). — 3. *The Shan tribes*, les tribus Shan, peuplades presque indépendantes, sont

India whether it was true that the Indian Government contemplated the annexation of some of the Shan States on the eastern side of the Salween River.

SIR J. FERGUSSON.—Her Majesty's Government, as the successor, of the late Government of Ava, have retained the control of some small trans-Salween States which were subject to Burmah at the time of the recent annexation.

THE LAND PURCHASE (IRELAND) ACT[1].

Mr. JOHN ELLIS asked the Chancellor of the Exchequer what amount of the £39,720 of interest and instalments under the Land Purchase (Ireland) Act, 1885, which fell due on May, 1, 1888, remained unpaid on November 1; and what sum of interest and instalments fell due on November 1 and had been paid.

The CHANCELLOR of the EXCHEQUER.—Of the £39,720 due on May, 1, 1888, £1,538 remained unpaid on November 1, but these arrears have since been reduced. The total arrears of interest and instalments on all payments previous to the 1st of this month now amount to £1,332. The amount due on November 1 is £58,300. With regard to the payments then due, the receivable orders issued in respect of them are not yet returnable.

" CRIMINAL LITERATURE. "

Mr. CHANNING, for Mr. S. SMITH, asked the Secretary of State for the Home Department whether his attention had been drawn to the report that the two boys who were now waiting their trial for murder in Maidstone Gaol had been addicted by their own confession to the reading of such books as " Dick Turpin," " Varney the Vampire, or the Feast of Blood, " and " Sweeney Todd, " and that one of them told a correspondent of the *Tunbridge Wells Advertiser* that he was prepared for his fate now he had made his name known ; whether he was aware that there was an enormous circulation of criminal literature among the young, and that about 25 English newspapers had recently been publishing the lives of Charles Peace, William Palmer, the Rugeley poisoner, and the murders of Burke and Hare ; whether he was aware that those stories attractively written were widely circulated and read by enormous numbers of children, and instigated many of them to the commission of crime ; whether any check could be put upon the circulation of those pernicious works ; and whether a record could be kept of the class of books or papers found on the persons of youthful criminals when arrested, as a guide to future legislation on the subject.

Mr. MATTHEWS. — I have seen the statement referred to, and I have instructed the Prison Commissioners to ascertain whether the statement emanated

---

les unes tributaires de la Chine, les autres de l'empire Birman ou d'Ava. Ce dernier empire dont la partie méridionale (cap. Rangoun) fut cédée aux Anglais en 1826 et en 1853, appartient maintenant (depuis 1888) tout entier à l'Angleterre. Il y a cependant encore quelques tribus au nord qui résistent, surtout parmi les Shans. L'Empire Birman est situé au nord et à l'ouest du royaume de Siam qui le sépare de l'Annam (le Tonkin au nord, l'Annam au centre et la Cochinchine au sud, aujourd'hui possédés par les Français ou sous leur protectorat). —

1. Cette loi agraire, passée en 1881, donnait aux Irlandais ce qu'on a appelé les trois F., c'est-à-dire *Fixity of tenure* (bail assuré), *Free sale* (liberté de vendre son bail) et *Fair rent* (loyer équitable). Cette loi, renouvelée et étendue encore en 1887, a fait beaucoup pour la pacification de l'Irlande, et aurait réussi encore mieux sans l'opposition acharnée des *politiciens* irlandais, les Parnellistes et partisans du Home Rule.

through the prison officials, as reported. The hon. member may be quite justified in supposing that there is a large circulation of demoralizing literature; and I stated last night to the House that the Government have taken, and are prepared to take, such steps as prudence dictates and the law enables them to take in order to check this circulation. I will undertake to give careful consideration to the last paragraph of the hon. member's question.

THE COST OF ROADS.

Mr. H. DAVENPORT asked the President of the Local Government Board when the arrears of the Treasury contributions towards the cost of roads[1] would be paid to the county highway or other local authorities; whether that contribution would be given as heretofore for the year ending March 31, 1888; and, if so, when the local authorities would receive that payment; and whether, under section 121, sub-section (2)—(1), of the Local Government Act, the local anthorities would be entitled to claim a contribution from the Treasury for the year ending March 31, 1889, calculated on the expenditure of the previous year; and, if so, whether the local authorities were to make that calculation and to send in that claim to the Treasury during the current financial year.

Mr. RITCHIE. — The payments to local authorities in respect of the current financial year on account of main roads[2] will be made by the Local Government Board on the same principles as the Parliamentary grants for main roads have hitherto been distributed. The payments for the current year will be based on the expenditure repaid by the county authorities to the highway authorities during the year ended March 25, 1888, on account of the expenditure of those authorities during the year ended March 25, 1887. The payments on this basis have been commenced, and these are the only payments to which the highway authorities are entitled for the year ending March 31, 1889. The local authorities will have no other claims in respect of that year. In the next financial year the cost of the maintenance of the main roads will be undertaken by the county councils.

THE VAN AND WHEEL TAX[3].

Mr. KELLY asked the Chancellor of the Exchequer whether he would inform the House if there was any truth in the very positive statements published in several newspapers quite recently, to the effect that he had decided upon proceeding no further with the Excise Duties (Local Purposes) Bill, at any rate so far as the proposed taxes upon carts and vans might be concerned.

The CHANCELLOR of the EXCHEQUER. — There is absolutely no foundation for the statements made in the Press with regard to the question of the hon. member. I wish hon. members kindly to understand that I consider myself pledged by the declarations I have made, and I do not consider myself in a position to withdraw from them.

---

1. Frais pour la construction des routes. — 2. *Main roads*, les grandes routes, c'est-à-dire les routes nationales. — 3. *Van and wheel tax*, impôt sur les tapissières, les fourgons et les roues, comprenant aussi les chevaux de luxe et les chevaux de course. M. Goschen, malgré sa résolution, a dû remettre cet impôt à la session suivante.

BALLYCOTTON PIER[1].

Mr. LANE asked the Secretary to the Treasury whether he had yet received a report from Mr. J. Wolfe Barry on the condition of Ballycotton Pier; and whether he had any objection to place a copy of the correspondence which had taken place between the Grand Jury of the county of Cork and the Board of Works, between the Rev. M. P. Norris, C. C., of Ballycotton, and the Board of Works, and between the Board of Works and the Treasury in reference to that pier, upon the table of the House before the estimates for the Irish Board of Works were submitted to Parliament.

Mr. JACKSON. — I have not yet received Mr. Barry's report. As regards the correspondence, my right hon. friend the Chancellor of the Exchequer has pointed out the inconvenience of giving inter-departmental correspondence, and the purport of the remainder is pretty well known through the medium of the public Press.

CIVIL SERVICE ESTIMATES[2].

Dr. CLARK asked the Secretary to the Treasury whether he would give a return of the sums voted in Civil Service Estimates for England, Ireland, and Scotland, and the sums chargeable on the Consolidated Fund for the present year (in continuation of the return of February 14, 1868).

Mr. JACKSON. — I have referred to the return of 1868, mentioned in the question. It does not appear to me to be, either in form or in substance, of much value. But if the hon. member is very desirous of having it I should not object to its being prepared, but it would probably be sufficient for his purpose that a manuscript copy should be placed in the library.

THE RESIGNATION OF SIR C. WARREN[3].

Mr. MATTHEWS. — In order to avoid misunderstanding as to the grounds of Sir C. Warren's resignation, which I announced yesterday, I ask the leave of the House to make a statement. On November 8, I directed the following letter to be written to Sir C. Warren : —

" Sir, — Mr. Secretary Matthews directs me to state that his attention has been called to an article signed by you in this month's number of *Murray's Magazine*, relating to the management and discipline of the Metropolitan Police Force. He desires me to forward to you the enclosed copy of a Home Office circular which was duly communicated to the Commissioner of Police in 1879, and to state that the directions in that circular were intended to apply to the Metropolitan Police and to every officer in the force from the Commissioner downwards. I am accordingly to request that, in the future, the terms of this order may be strictly complied with."

The following is the Home Office minute : —

" The Secretary of State, having had his attention called to the question of allowing private publication, by officers attached to the department, of books on matters relating to the department, is of opinion that the practice may lead to

1. *Ballycotton Pier*, jetée de Ballycotton, dans le comté de Cork, en Irlande. — 2. *Estimates*, budget des dépenses. — 3. Commissaire, commandant la police de la ville de Londres.

embarrassment and should in future be discontinued. He desires, therefore, that it should be considered a rule of the Home Department that no officer should publish any work relating to the department unless the sanction of the Secretary of State has been previously obtained for the purpose."

I received on the same day the following reply : —

"Sir, — I have just received a pressing and confidential letter, stating that a Home Office circular of May 27, 1879, is intended to apply to the Metropolitan Police Force. I have to point out that, had I been told that such a circular was to be in force, I should not have accepted the post of Commissioner of Police. I have to point out that my duties and those of the Metropolitan police are governed by statute, and that the Secretary of State for the Home Department has not the power under the statute of issuing orders for the police force. This circular, if put in force, would practically enable every one anonymously to attack the police force without in any way permitting the Commissioner to correct false statements, which I have been in the habit of doing, whenever I found necessary, for nearly three years past. I desire to say that I entirely decline to accept these instructions with regard to the Commissioner of Police, and I have again (Lord R. Churchill and other members. — 'Again!") to place my resignation in the hands of Her Majesty's Government."

I answered this letter on November 10 in the following terms : —

"Sir, — I beg to acknowledge your letter of the 8th inst. In that letter, after contending that the Secretary of State has not the power under statute of issuing orders for the Metropolitan Police, you decline to accept his instructions that the Commissioner and all officers of the force should comply with the Home Office minute of May 27, 1879, by which officers attached to the Home Department were enjoined not to publish any work relating to the department without the previous sanction of the Secretary of State, and you place your resignation in the hands of Her Majesty's Government. In my judgment the claim thus put forward by you as Commissioner of Police, to disregard the instructions of the Secretary of State, is altogether inadmissible, and accordingly I have only to accept your resignation. At the same time, I am glad to acknowledge the services which you have rendered to Her Majesty's Government during the course of your administration of the police force."

The Government accepted the resignation of Sir Charles Warren on the ground stated in the correspondence I have read, and on no other ground. The failure of the police to discover recent crimes in the metropolis and the differences of opinion between Sir C. Warren and Mr. Monro had nothing to do with the action of the Government in parting with an officer so distinguished and so zealous in the discharge of his office as Sir C. Warren has been. I wish to add, in justice to Mr. Monro and Mr. Anderson, that since Mr. Monro's resignation he has not interfered in any way with the conduct of the business of the Criminal Investigation Department, nor has he been consulted by myself or by any one else, to my knowledge, on that subject. The advice which I have sought from Mr. Monro was confined to the general question of the organization proper for the department in the abstract, without any reference whatever to the daily current business of the department.

Mr. GRAHAM.—I should like to ask the right hon. gentleman what the word "again" refers to in Sir Charles Warren's letter. Are we to understand that this is not the first time that Sir Charles Warren has tendered his resignation?

Mr. MATTHEWS.—There have been previous differences of opinion which led to Sir Charles Warren tendering his resignation.

Mr. GRAHAM.—When did this occur?

Mr. MATTHEWS.—I do not think it necessary to enter into that matter.

Mr. LABOUCHÈRE.—What is the precise position which Mr. Monro holds now? He has been consulted by the Home Secretary.

Mr. MATTHEWS.—He holds no office of any kind, and is in no way connected with the department.

Mr. STUART.—Will the correspondence read by the Home Secretary be laid upon the table?

Mr. MATTHEWS replied that it would.

Mr. CONYBEARE asked whether the report in the *St. James's Gazette* was true, that the post of Police Commissioner had been offered to the hon. member for Sheffield (Mr. Howard Vincent).

Mr. MATTHEWS.—The statements in the newspapers upon this subject are always, so far as I have seen them, without any foundation in fact.

NEW MEMBER.

Mr. PRITCHARD MORGAN took the oath and his seat for Merthyr Tydfil, in the room of Mr. H. Richard, deceased.

SUPPLY[1].

CIVIL SERVICE ESTIMATES.

The House went into Committee of Supply on the Civil Service Estimates.

On the vote of £408,315 for the Supreme Court of Judicature.

Mr. JENNINGS rose to move the reduction of the vote by £500. He said that this was altogether one of the most remarkable of the Civil Service Estimates. It had been specially investigated frequently, certain parts of it had been condemned, and yet they still remained. It must be remembered that the most highly-paid offices of the Supreme Court were filled by nomination, and not by competition. There was a good deal to be added to this vote, for there were charges on other votes amounting to £129,000, on the Consolidated Fund[2] of £150,000, and for pensions and compensations £78,000, making a grand total of three-quarters of a million. The permanent secretary to the Lord Chancellor received £1,500 a year. This was a recent advance of £300; and in 1873, before the Select Committee on the subject, Mr. Blackwood admitted that £1,200 a year was much too large a salary for the post, which the committee thought might be adequately filled for £900 a year. This was one illustration of the fact that commissions and committees on the subject had laboured in vain. The third lucky man on this vote was the Secretary of Presentations, who had £400 a year;

1. *Supply*, fonds votés pour le budget du service civil. *The civil service* comprend toutes les personnes qui servent la reine (l'Etat) dans une fonction civile en opposition avec l'armée et la marine. Il y a probablement environ 500 000 fonctionnaires civils. — 2. *The Consolidated Fund*, les fonds consolidés. Ce sont des fonds votés une fois pour tout de bon par le Parlement et qui sont payés sans avoir besoin d'être votés de nouveau chaque année. Ces fonds comprennent la dette nationale, la liste civile de la reine et de la famille royale, certains traitements et certaines pensions.

but in addition to this he had a salary as a clerk in the office of the Clerk of the Parliaments, with a salary rising by £20 to £600. The committee of 1874 reported that it would be a matter for consideration whether a change should not be made on the first opportunity; and it was still a matter for consideration. Then there was a Purse-bearer and Clerk of the Chamber at £400 a year, whose post there was reason to believe was a sinecure that appeared to have been bestowed for the abolition of other sinecures of "Chafe-wax[1]" and "Deputy chafe-wax," whose duties no one now living could explain. The gentleman who took charge of the Great Seal got £334, and £200 was paid to a train-bearer, who might be relieved of his functions by mechanism. (Laughter.) The Judges of the Queen's Bench required 22 clerks, who absorbed £8,700 a year. There were 16 Masters[2], at from £1,500 to £2,000 a year. The committee of 1874 reported that the number of Masters might be reduced, and Lord Selborne's committee made a similar report in 1887; and the evidence was even stronger than the report as to many of the duties of the Masters being such as could be performed by ordinary clerks. Yet there were attached to these offices 85 clerks, receiving salaries of from £250 to £700 a year. Even some of the highly paid clerks were admitted to be doing the duty of mere copyists. Five clerks who were redundant[3] drew £3,000 a year, and they had been redundant since 1881, while there were seven other clerks who were practically redundant. The redundant clerks were in receipt of full pay for doing nothing. In the railway clearing-house[4] if a clerk was found to be redundant he had his contributions to the pension fund returned to him and was sent away. Why should not the State be served on similar terms? One reply had been that a very small number of persons comparatively were allowed to share the big prizes of the Government service. Private secretaries of Ministers were made Treasury clerks at good salaries. No attempt had been made to conduct the business of the country on the same footing as that of large firms. On the contrary, the more worthless a man was, and the less he did, the greater seemed to be his reward. Was it conceivable that the redundant clerks who were paid for doing nothing were such bad bargains that they could not be transferred to any other department? (Hear, hear.) The whole system had been condemned over and over again. In his evidence before the Royal Commission on Civil Service Pensions Sir T. H. Farrer had said:—"I should be very glad to see a much larger transfer of men from one office to another than has hitherto taken place." Such transfer would do away with the system of paying clerks £600 or £700 a year for doing nothing, and it would be exactly in accordance with the resolution passed by the House in June last. The Select Committee of 1873 had reported very strongly in favour of the transfer of redundants to other

1. *Chafe-wax*, chauffe-cire. Ce terme désignait autrefois un fonctionnaire chargé de tenir prête la cire pour sceller les mandats, etc. — 2. *Masters in chancery*, ce sont des avocats de grande expérience, choisis par *the Lord Chancellor*, et dont les fonctions sont indiquées au cours de cette discussion.—3. *Redundant*, de trop, superflu. *Clerks*, employés, commis. —4. Ici *clearing-house* signifie simplement bureau de comptabilité. En général, *clearing-house* est une salle où les commis des différents banquiers se réunissent toutes les semaines pour échanger les traites tirées sur leurs différentes maisons et pour en payer la différence. De cette façon il suffit de très petites sommes d'argent pour solder des valeurs considérables. Exemple : B. a quatre traites montant à £5 960 tirées sur C.; C. a aussi des traites sur B., d'une valeur de £5 930 ; les deux commis échangent leurs traites respectives et C. paye à B. la balance, c'est-à-dire £30.

departments, and the Royal Commission had adopted the same view and condemned the system as the outcome of the old order of things. In spite of these reports, however, the redundants still made their appearance on the Estimates, and the Committee were now asked to vote them £3,000. The whole of the clerks in this department were extravagantly overpaid and absurdly underworked. (Hear, hear.) The office hours were nominally from 11 to 5 or from 10 to 4 o'clock. One of the clerks examined before Lord Selborne's Committee had stated that most of the clerks really left at 4, and not at 5, the *ennui* of the place being so great that few of them could stand it after 4 o'clock. (Loud laughter.) Asked if the clerks were punctual in the morning, the witness had replied, after hesitation, that when they had any private work to do they were not always at the office by 11 o'clock. (Laughter.) Some eminent persons, apparently of sound mind and judgment, thought that this system was destined to last for ever; he believed that it was destined to drag down with it every one who tried to support it. (Hear, hear.) Mr. Aldridge, another clerk examined before the Committee, had stated, in reply to a suggestion from the Lord Chief Justice, that a book of the times of arrival and departure of the various clerks should be kept, that he was sure there would be a very strong feeling against this among the clerks. (Laughter.) It would hurt their feelings. These clerks, who attended the office between 11 and 3 to exchange anecdotes, received salaries of £600 a year, and were allowed six weeks' holiday. Then, in the Chancery Division there were 12 chief clerks costing £17,400, 24 with nearly £600 a year, 18 with £300 or £400 a year, a First Registrar[1] with £2,000, three other registrars with £5,400 between them, four others with £6,000 between them, and a host more. (Hear, hear.) The Probate, Divorce, and Admiralty Division was another haven of peace and plenty[2]. The Senior Registrar of the Probate Registry[3] received £1,600 a year, with £8 16s. 9d. a year as late Proctor[4] and a compensation allowance of £1,863 8s. 6d. charged on the Consolidated Fund[5]. When this gentleman had been provided with a post worth £1,600 a year, why had he not been called upon to give up the compensation allowance for the sinecure office which he had formerly held? (Hear, hear.) It would probably be said that such things must exist on account of vested interests[6], but for his own part he would make short work of them[7]. He could not see that a gross "job" perpetrated years ago improved by age. (Hear, hear.) Then there was the Registrar of the Admiralty Registry, who drew £1,500 a year as salary and £608 12s. from the Consolidated Fund. It would be found, too, on the Estimates that the man who looked after the ushers in the Courts of Justice received £600 a year, that the person who gave out the pens and ink received £300 a year, and it was on the same prodigal scale that all the charges in the Estimates seemed to be based. (Hear, hear.) He would urge that the power of the Commissions and Committees had been expended on the vote in vain, and it must now be perfectly clear that the only hope of dealing

1. *Registrar*, greffier. — 2. *Another haven of peace and plenty*, un autre asile de paix et d'abondance. — 3. *The Probate Registry*, bureau pour l'enregistrement des testaments et héritages. — 4. *As late Proctor*, comme ancien procureur. *Compensation allowance*, sommes accordées à ceux qui ont rempli des fonctions aujourd'hui abolies. — 5. Voy. note 2, page 145. — 6. *Vested interests*, droits acquis. — 7. *He would make short work of them*, il y mettrait bien vite fin.

with it was by a direct vote of the House of Commons. (Hear, hear.) There certainly was a number of persons who obtained extravagant salaries for practically doing nothing, and the time had come when some decided protest ought to be entered. No doubt it would be said that inconvenience would be caused by reducing the vote, but the only way the Committee could show its opinion on this subject was to accept a motion for a small reduction of the vote such as be had proposed, and he therefore hoped such motion would be accepted. (Hear, hear.)

Mr. BRADLAUGH called attention to the utter uselessness of the office of Queen's Remembrance[1]. (Hear.) Its survival could not be accounted for on any principle of utility; yet it cost about £3,400 a year. He would support the motion for the reduction of the vote.

Mr. LAWSON asked why certain officers who had been transferred to other duties on the abolition of their former office were allowed to receive their full compensation for abolition of office in addition to the salaries of their present offices?

Mr. HALDANE complained of the present system of appointing clerks in the Chief Clerks'[2] department. Instead of these appointments being made from within the office by those who had knowledge of the aspirants, they were made in accordance with outside influence by the Lord Chancellor. The Chief Clerks' duties were most important, and the manner in which their offices were manned was also a matter of no little consequence. (Hear, hear.) A small sub-committee ought to be appointed to inquire into this subject.

Mr. COZENS-HARDY pointed out that the number of Official Referees[3] was unnecessarily large. There were four, who received each £1,500 a year, with £200 a year for a clerk. They were first appointed in 1873 under the Judicature Act, but of late business which they had to discharge had greatly fallen off. It was not large in 1879, and since then there was a gradual decrease of work till, in 1885-1886, there was not two-thirds of the work of 1879-1880. While the present Government had been in office there had been two vacancies, one of which was filled by the appointment of Mr. Ridley in January, 1887, and the other by Mr. Hemming in November of last year. He did not wish to say a word against these gentlemen personally, for he had no doubt that Mr. Ridley was an able and competent man, and he knew that Mr. Hemming was. But their appointment, under the circumstances, was wholly unnecessary and unjustifiable. There was scarcely work enough for even one Official Referee. During the present sittings Mr. Ridley only sat on one day and disposed of one case; Mr. Hemming sat on four days and disposed of four cases; Mr. Dowdeswell sat on four days and disposed of three cases; and the remaining Referee sat on six days and disposed of two cases. At present £6,000 a year was being paid to these gentlemen, besides £800 a year to their clerks, and there was no work done which in any way justified such an expenditure. (Hear, hear.)

Mr. BRADLAUGH read an extract from a letter which he had received, to

1. Le greffier archiviste de la reine. M. Bradlaugh est le promoteur de *the Oaths Bill*, discuté plus haut dans la Chambre des Pairs. — 2. *Chief Clerks'*, chefs de division dans une administration. — 3. *Official Referees*, référendaires officiels. *A referee* est un homme de loi nommé par un tribunal pour entendre les parties dans une cause et en rendre compte.

the effect that the Registrar's clerks in Chancery had a statutory rise in salary no matter how incompetent or overhanded[1] the staff might be; that though there was no instance recorded of absence on account of sickness or pleasure of the Masters, the clerks, or the registrars, nevertheless the Masters and clerks were able to absent themselves and did absent themselves.

LORD R. CHURCHILL[2] said that the subject under the consideration of the Committee illustrated in a manner most useful to the public the advantages and disadvantages of the Committee of Supply[3] and the defect of their mode of proceeding with regard to any effective control over the public expenditure. His hon. friend the member for Stockport[4], though he had not been many years in the House, had distinguished himself by having already forcibly arrested the attention of the House by the disclosures which he had made, and he could not have done it so forcibly if he had not devoted the greatest possible time, labour, and care to the subject. (Hear.) But his hon. friend had outdone himself on the present occasion. Never since the Committee of Supply began to sit in modern times had such a state of things been disclosed with regard to the expenditure of public money. Scarcely would a parallel be found in the pages of Dickens[5] or Thackeray when those eminent satirists were dealing with the Government of their day. A state of things amounting to more than a public scandal, amounting to a national disgrace, had been laid before the Committee. Some 80 or 100 members were present listening to this account of the absolute malversation of the public money on a large scale. If the Committee of Supply divided at the present moment they would not assent to this vote; they could not possibly do so. But what would occur? To the 80 or 100 members who had followed the discussion would be added 150 or 200 members who did not know what had been going on, and this vote, amounting to three-quarters of a million, would be carried on a division in spite of the disgraceful disclosures laid before the Committee of Supply by his hon. friend. (Hear, hear.) There was another matter also in connexion with this vote, and that was the tactics of Her Majesty's Government. He dit not blame Her Majesty's Government personally for the tactics pursued any more than he blamed any other Government. They were what he might call the hereditary tactics of that bench[6] with regard to getting votes from the House. It was more or less deluding or humbugging and baffling the House of Commons in matters amounting to an outrage on the taxpayer. (Hear, hear.) Pursuing the hereditary tactics of the Treasury bench, which he had no doubt had been pursued by the right hon. member for Mid Lothian and the right hon. member for Wolverhampton, the Government allowed other members to get up on the good chance

1. *Overhanded*, trop nombreux. *The staff*, le personnel. — 2. Lord Randolph Churchill, fils cadet du duc de Marlborough, né en 1849, est le chevau-léger du parti conservateur, et attaque presque autant son propre parti que le parti de l'opposition, les gladstoniens. C'est un brillant orateur, qui semble appelé à être un jour un des grands ministres de l'Angleterre. C'est un conservateur-démocrate, et il fera certainement parler de lui. — 3. *The Committee of Supply*, la commission du budget (les fonds à voter). — 4. Mr. Jennings, l'orateur qui a parlé le premier, nommé député en 1885. — 5. *Dickens* et *Thackeray*, deux romanciers anglais connus de tout le monde, même en France, qui, d'après l'exemple donné par Goldsmith dans le *Vicaire de Wakefield*, se sont servis avec succès du roman pour signaler et pour corriger les abus. — 6. *That bench*, ce banc, c'est-à-dire le banc des ministres, que l'orateur appelle plus loin le banc de la Trésorerie.

that specific statements would be made which Ministers would be able to overthrow, and thus conceal the effective attack made by his hon. friend and get the vote passed. His advice to the Committee of Supply was that whenever an hon. member after great care and labour had produced a really sound indictment against expenditure no other member should rise to address the Committee until a representative of the Government had answered the indictment. ("Hear, hear," and a laugh.) But no matter what answer the Government might give, it would be impossible for them to pass this vote without the aid of members who were lying in ambush in various parts of the House. (Hear, hear.) The responsibility would not rest with the Committe of Supply then present. The Government could not with decency ask the Committee of Supply to assent to the principle of paying the private secretary of the Lord Chancellor £1,500; they could only do so in face of the fact that either a House of Commons or a departmental Committee had reported that £900 a year would be ample remuneration for that official (hear, hear), and that report had been accepted for the last nine or ten years. He did not see how the Committee of Supply could vote a salary of £1,000 a year to the Secretary of Presentations after the statement of the hon. member for Stockport. Again they were confronted with the fact that 14 years ago a Committee reported against the continuation of the office. The same observation would apply to the Purse bearer of the Lord Chancellor. Then there was the Carrier of the Great Seal, who was paid £300 a year. It was not that those officials were worth the attention of the Committee of Supply, but it was that the existence of officials who had nothing to do was an illustration of our whole system. If members were to examine other votes as his hon. friend had examined this they would find the existence of the same scandals. Last year they had a debate, and the right hon. member for Wolverhampton[1] was indignant because it was said that there was a superabundance of lawyers in the House. He had himself asked a private secretary of the right hon. gentleman the member for Mid Lothian[2] whether he did not think great reductions could be made in the Civil Service Estimates[3] and he said he did not know about that, but he was sure immense reductions might be made in Class III. (Hear.) The right hon. member for Wolverhampton had before now talked of the manner in which the landed interest had influenced the legislation of this country. He would ask the Committee to mark how the lawyers had affected our legislation. Their numbers and the extravagance of their salaries amounted to absolute brigandage on the taxpayers of the country. (A laugh.) Last night they saw it gravely put forward by an hon. member opposite that a great department should be created consisting only of lawyers. (A laugh.) What was the use of appointing Committees and Commissions to examine into the expenditure of the country if Government after Government paid not the smallest attention either to the evidence they extracted or the recommendations which they made? He would ask the First Lord of the Treasury, who had been long in the public service and was actuated by a great desire for economy, whether the reports of these Committees and Commissions had been ever brought

1. On se rappellera qu'il n'est pas permis quand on parle d'un membre du Parlement en séance de l'appeler par son nom. On le désigne toujours par le nom de la circonscription qui l'a élu. — 2. M. Gladstone, Premier (*premier ministre*) d'avril 1880 à juin 1885, et de janvier à juillet 1886. — 3 Crédit

to his notice. It was very seldom they got the opportunity of drawing the attention of the country in a manner which would excite the imagination to the scandals connected with the expenditure on the public service. What he wanted to impress on the Committee was that if, as he assumed, the Government were unable to upset the facts stated by his hon. friend, they should refuse the vote. He did not say they could refuse to pay people what must be paid them in justice and fair play, but what they should do was to refuse to vote the money until the Government pledged themselves to introduce before next year such reforms as would obviate that scandal. (Hear, hear.)

The ATTORNEY-GENERAL[1] assured the Committee that it was from no hereditary guile that he had not risen before to address them. He had been sincerely interested, and also amused, by the speech of the hon. member for Stockport, and he thought that lawyers might learn a great deal from the hon. member's criticisms. The noble lord[2] had spoken of exciting the imagination of the country on that subject. If the noble lord used the language with which he had that evening embellished his remarks he might excite the imagination of the country, but would hardly appeal to its calm judgment. The noble lord had spoken of the malversation of public money, of the brigandage practised on the taxpayer, and of officials doing nothing but deluding and humbugging. If the noble lord had followed the example of the hon. member for Stockport and examined the question for himself, no doubt he might have pointed out, as the hon. member for Stockport had done, parts of the system in respect to which reforms were urgently called for, and would have endeavoured to abstain from seeking to excite the imagination or the prejudice of the country. The Government had been charged with not wishing to reply to the hon. member for Stockport. That was an entire mistake. They wished to hear the observations of hon. members in order that they might answer them together instead of answering them separately. No one could read the report which had been referred to without seeing that a number of the details of those offices required overhauling[3]; but no Government could all at once make a reduction of a particular amount, and very little attention to the report would show that to be impossible. The hon. member for Stockport was very severe on the permanent secretary to the Lord Chancellor, and said that a Committee 14 years ago reported that a clerk or officer could be found who would perform the duties then performed by the then private or principal secretary of the Lord Chancellor at £900 a year. He accepted that as substantially being the statement of the Committee. But what happened afterwards? That matter was most carefully considered by the Government of the right hon. member for Mid Lothian[4], when Lord Selborne was Lord Chancellor, and the whole state of things was placed on an entirely different basis. It was

1. *The Attorney-General*, le procureur général, principal conseiller de la couronne en matières légales, aux appointements de 175 000 francs. C'est aujourd'hui sir Richard Webster qui occupe ce poste. *The Attorney-General* est libre de plaider dans les affaires particulières. C'est lui qui plaide pour le *Times* dans le grand procès de *The Times v. Parnell*. — 2. *Lord Randolph Churchill* n'est lord que par courtoisie. Ce titre se donne ainsi aux fils *cadets* d'un duc ou d'un marquis. Les fils *aînés* prennent ordinairement le second titre de leur père. *Le marquis de Hartington* est fils aîné du duc de Devonshire, encore vivant. Il n'est pas pair d'Angleterre, et, par conséquent, peut siéger dans la Chambre des Communes. — 3. *To require overhauling*, demander à être examiné. — 4. M. Gladstone, voyez note 2, p. 150.

not his duty now to say whether that basis was right or wrong, but to say that successive Governments had refused to adopt the recommendation to reduce the salary to £900 was to shut one's eyes to the facts. In 1877 the amount was fixed at £900; but it was raised to £1,000 distinctly in consideration of the duties in that year. Subsequently, when the whole office was reorganized, a permanent secretary was appointed, and to the office were attached a number of fresh duties. In 1884 on the principal secretary being appointed the salary was fixed at £1,500, but was to be reduced to £1,200 until certain duties were transferred. In 1885 the office of the Clerk of the Crown in Chancery was abolished, and its duties were transferred to the permanent secretary of the Lord Chancellor, there then being a saving to the country, and the salary was fixed at a *maximum* of £1,500 on the taking over of those fresh duties. There was a distinct bargain made by a previous Government. That gentleman, now a Queen's Counsel, was first given the office at a salary of £1,200; then further duties were added on another office being abolished, and the salary was raised to £1,500, to which sum that officer was entitled by the sliding scale[1] existing at the time of his appointment. He could speak from personal knowledge of the very confidential, onerous, and responsible duties performed by the permanent secretary of the Lord Chancellor. (Lord R. Churchill asked what were the duties?) Among them were attending committees in reference to the rules of the Courts of justice, communicating constantly with the Judges as to alteration of the circuits, and as to any reforms that were necessary for rearrangement of the practice of the Courts. He had also duties of a confidential character under the Lord Chancellor in relation to questions of law reforms. The holder of the office must be a barrister of ten year's standing[2], and must devote the whole of his time to the duties of the office. He had further to attend to all lunacy business under the Lord Chancellor, to draft[3] and revise all orders relating to the Supreme or the County Courts[4], and to call attention to all matters connected with the administration of the law which required the consideration of the Lord Chancellor. He thought that if hon. members really understood the nature of the duties performed by the gentlemen in question they would not suggest that a salary of £1,500 was an excessive salary. An attack had been made upon the Secretary of Presentations, an office now held by Mr. Thesiger. This gentleman held the position of a clerk in the House of Lords, for which he received a rising salary of £600, and in addition he received £400 as Secretary of Presentations. He did not suppose that the noble lord the member for Paddington, or any other member, would suggest that they should cut down the salary of Mr. Thesiger. As Secretary of Presentations, Mr. Thesiger conducted all the Lord Chancellor's correspondence on ecclesiastical matters, and he could assure hon. members that the work connected with that office was of a very responsible character, and it was now performed by a gentleman who had had very great experience in connexion with the delicate duties of the office. The noble lord member for Paddington said that £1,000 a year was too much.

1. *The sliding scale*, l'échelle de proportion. — 2. *A barrister of ten years' standing*, un avocat ayant dix ans d'exercice. — 3. *To draft*, rédiger. — 4. *The County Courts*, les cours de comté, correspondant à peu près aux tribunaux de première instance français, avec des pouvoirs moins étendus.

LORD R. CHURCHILL.—My point is this—that salaries are paid for duties performed by lawyers five or six times in excess of salaries paid to laymen[1] for performing precisely the same duties.

The ATTORNEY-GENERAL thought it would be convenient to keep to the argument immediately before the Committee. He was dealing with the Secretary of Presentations, and he understood that the hon. member for Stockport attacked the salary of the gentleman who held that office. He replied that the work done was of a very confidential and important character and that it was performed by a gentleman who had held the office for a great many years, and who, they hoped, would continue to hold it. The proper way to deal with these matters was to attack the system rather than to attack the salary of a particular official who received that salary because he had to work a great deal more than the ordinary clerks of the establishment. He would now refer to the Purse Bearer and the Train Bearer. It was quite easy to say that there should be no official of this kind in connexion with the office of the Lord Chancellor. He was not aware that the hon. member for Stockport objected to the office of Train Bearer of the Speaker of the House of Commons. He quite agreed that these officials were perhaps more ornemental than useful. A great part of their time was not occupied in the performance of very heavy duties. He might say that the Purse Bearer was a confidential clerk to the Lord Chancellor and conducted that part of his correspondence which did not require to pass through the hands of the superior secretary. He also discharged the duties of Purse Bearer on ceremonial occasions and attended the Lord Chancellor in the House of Lords and on all public occasions. It was true that they might abolish the office; but it did not advance the discussion very much simply to refer to an official because he performed certain duties. All he could do in replying to the suggestions that had been made was to point out as briefly as possible what the duties were which the officials performed. Then, with regard to the Carrier of the Great Seal, this official was a messenger[2] in connexion with the office of the Lord Chancellor. The question was whether there was to be a messenger or not. If hon. members said that the Lord Chancellor could do without a messenger, well and good; but he would point out that this official had certain duties to perform as a messenger whenever the Lord Chancellor was out of town, and on other occasions, and no one would say that there were not very important documents which it was necessary to send to the Lord Chancellor when he was away from London. He did not want to go into details; but it was essential to mention these matters. If they thought that £324 was a larger salary than a messenger of this kind ought to receive, the matter might be considered when a fresh appointment was made; but they could not say to an official, " We will pay you this year a lower salary than we paid you last year. " He was very sorry to hear the observations made by the hon. member for Stockport with regard to the Masters. If the hon. member knew as much about the Masters as he did, he would not have made those observations.

---

1. *Laymen*, laïques, a ici un sens plus limité et signifie des employés n'ayant pas fait d'études de droit. — 2. *Messenger*, courrier.

Mr. JENNINGS said that they were not his observations. He quoted the words of the Committee, and of Sir Frederick Pollock. (Hear, hear.)

The ATTORNEY-GENERAL understood the hon. member to say that two of the Masters scarcely ever went to their office at all. He was well acquainted with the passage to which the hon. member had referred. The hon. member for Stockport had done a great injustice to the Masters [1] by the construction he had put upon some of the answers of witnesses. Many of the Masters were appointed at a time when they were required to attend only from 11 to 4. That was a statement of fact which could be made without implying that in the future they might not be called upon to attend from 10 to 6. The fact as to the past affected the manner in which the Government could be called upon to deal with the question. If the superiors of the Masters chose to say to them, "You ought to come earlier or stay later" by all means let it be done; but the Government could not say to the Masters, "We will reduce your salaries unless you attend longer". The salaries of the Masters averaged from £1,200 to £1,500 a year; and they had to hear arbitrations upon matters referred to them involving knowledge of the law; they had to tax costs, which required experience and knowledge of practice; they had to hear summonses on interlocutory applications; they had to inquire into the conduct of solicitors and others against whom charges were made; and the lightest part of their duty was to attend Court *in banc* [2]. The statement as to their duties being discharged by clerks referred only to a small part of their duties and did not refer generally to their duties as Masters. When he was a junior at the Bar some of the Masters were earning large professional incomes, and they were therefore men of experience who were doing judicial work of a responsible character and doing it well. He did not believe that any lawyer would make any attack upon the Masters with reference to the discharge of their duties. Of course no one would pretend that they were all equally efficient. It was quite possible that the number might be reduced as vacancies occurred; but still you could not obtain men to do the work without paying them substantial salaries; and you could not now suddenly reduce the salaries of men who had been doing the work for 20 years. There was no foundation for the suggestion that the Masters of the Queen's Bench were not to be found in their offices, unless absent on account of illness, or that they neglected their duties. The question of the "petty bag [3]" was one in which some interest had been taken by the hon. member for Northampton [4]. Unfortunately for the suggestion of the hon. member for Stockport that it was waiting to be filled up, it had been abolished and the duties were performed by other clerks (laughter); there was no intention of restoring the office or in any way re-establishing it; and the hon. member ought to have congratulated them upon its disappearance. The hon. member was under a singular misapprehension as to the Registrars of the Probate and the Admiralty Divisions. A long time ago a monopoly was enjoyed by Proctors of Doctors' Commons, and in 1854 or 1856 it was abolished and the practice thrown open to

1. *The Masters*, voyez page 146, note 2. — 2. *In banc*, pendant les sessions. — 3. "*The petty bag*," le petit sac, c'est la bourse du chancelier, qu'un officier porte devant lui. — 4. M. Bradlaugh.

solicitors. The compensation agreed to be paid to those who relinquished the monopoly was the yearly payment of one-half of the amount they had derived from the last year of their practice. This was all done under Parliamentary sanction; and he did not think the right hon. member for Wolverhampton would say that in this matter the right hon. member for Mid Lothian had laid himself open to the accusation of a gross job. With a great part of the hon. member for Stockport's[1] observations he heartily concurred. He fully recognized the importance of making searching inquiry and strenuous efforts in order to remove redundant clerks, and carrying out such transfers as would best utilize the labour for which payment was made. Already something had been done in this direction, and it ought to be borne in mind that the report of the Commission was only issued in March, 1887, and that practically nothing could have been done in the interval which could have had any effect on the present Estimates. He could assure the Committee that Her Majesty's Government fully recognized their duties in this matter; but there were many changes that could not be carried out without Parliamentary sanction, and so far there had been no time since the publication of the report to obtain such sanction. Any fairminded person, who addressed himself to this subject, not with a view to excite the public imagination, but to guide the public judgment, must admit this. The hon. member had spoken of what he termed many instances of gross favouritism. But what did he exactly mean by this? It was very unfair to make such a charge unless he had instances to support it. Would he mention any cases of gross favouritism for which the present Government were responsible, or even the Government of the right hon. gentleman the member for Mid Lothian? They were not now dealing with what took place in years gone by. Then the hon. member spoke of many instances of sinecures. Where were they? If he meant that clerks only working from 10 till 4 were cases of sinecures, of course there were many such. But if he meant cases of real sinecures, would he mention what they were? The hon. gentleman had referred to the salary paid to the person charged with looking after the stationery; but in the absence of intimate knowledge of what the duties were, he was not prepared to say that £300 a year was too large a salary, as to fill the office a thoroughly reliable man was required. (Hear.) The hon. member for Northampton had referred to information he had received as to unauthorized absences of clerks in the Masters' department. He did not much like the evidence of informers[2] (loud ironical cheers and laughter from the Irish Home Rule members); but if the hon. member gave him specific instances he would make inquiry. As to the Queen's Remembrancer, it was not accurate to say that there were no duties attached to the office; but such duties as did exist were now discharged by the Senior Master, who receives £300 a year in respect thereof. With regard to the remarks of the hon. member for Paddington[3], respecting appointments to the Chief Clerk's offices, he knew there had been of late some feeling aroused on the subject by a recent appointment, but he was led to believe that it was rather a personal question than one for

1. M. Jennings, qui a ouvert le débat.—2. *Informers*, délateurs. En Irlande, l'administration est bien obligée de chercher ses renseignements un peu partout. — 3. Lord Randolph Churchill.

which the Government could be responsible. Respecting the official referees, he admitted that the first appointments to that office were not very fortunate, and that a consequent lack of confidence in that tribunal had arisen. Still, with the present occupants he hoped that full confidence would return, and that there would be more work for them to do. There certainly were many cases at present tried out before a Judge which, dealing as they did with figures and details, would be much better tried before an official referee, and in such cases it was far cheaper for the litigants to try before an official referee than before arbitrators whom the parties themselves had to pay. With regard to the last two appointments, he thought that the hon. member for North Norfolk was not quite accurate in stating that at the time of those appointments there was a falling-off in the business before official referees. He was informed that the Lord Chancellor on each occasion carefully considered the subject, and after inquiry as to the increase of work that had been done, and the further increase that was expected, came to the conclusion that it was desirable to fill up both the vacancies. But, however this might be, what were the Government to do? These gentlemen had been appointed, and they could not be turned out, and it was the duty of the Government, therefore, to provide their salaries. He feared he might not have answered all the points that had been raised to the entire satisfaction of the noble lord the member for Paddington (Lord R. Churchill.—No), or the hon. member for Stockport; but he could assure the Committee that Her Majesty's Government were thoroughly desirous of making such rearrangements as would, while doing no injustice to present holders of offices, lead to economy and efficiency. (Hear, hear.)

Mr. CHILDERS[1] thought that the House ought to be much obliged to the hon. member for Stockport for his statement. (Hear.) A strong case had been made out for inquiry and for an expression of the opinion of the House. For the first time since 1873 the question of the general expenditure of this department had been fully brought up in Parliament. In 1873 a very important debate had taken place on the subject, and the result of the debate had been the appointement of a Committee over which he had presided, and which had sat during the whole Session. That Committee had found a large expenditure which it was absolutely necessary to scrutinize rigorously, and the Committee had spent four or five months upon the subject. As a result of their examination the Committee had recommended that a Royal Commission should be appointed with two objects—first, to look minutely into the great amount of the expenditure which was technical and which no Committee of the House of Commons could efficiently scrutinize; and, secondly, to consider by whom this expenditure of over £800,000 was to be controlled. Both the Committee and the Commission had pointed out very great extravagances with regard to this expenditure, very great want of system, and very great imperfection of classification. The Royal Commission had, by a majority of four to two, declared that the control of the Treasury over this department was not effective; and that it would be proper to trust some department of the Government directly responsible to Parliament

1. M. Childers, membre du Parlement depuis 1860, représente actuellement Édimbourg. C'est un des fidèles de M. Gladstone.

with powers to administer and organize these affairs, so as to secure the greatest amount of efficiency and economy. The Commission had then discussed how this could best be done, and had concluded that the Lord Chancellor in practice exercised but little actual control over the department. They saw no difficulty in placing all questions having relation to the numbers, duties, administration, organization, cost, and responsibility for estimates of the legal offices in the hands of a member of the Government, reference being made to Judges in questions where they were personally concerned. That position remained to the present day. The Lord Chancellor could not possibly spare the time to act as a Minister of Justice, and he did not sit in the House of Commons. Again, with the greatest respect for the ability of the Attorney-General, he ventured to assert that the right hon. gentleman could not by any possibility, with his ordinary duties, be responsible for the administration of the offices; and therefore it was absolutely necessary, if that vigilant eye were to be kept upon the establishments which could alone check their yearly increase, to give the control into the hands of some member of the Government responsible to Parliament. (Hear, hear.)

Mr. JENNINGS pointed out that scarcely any fact which he had laid before the Committee had been conclusively refuted. The Attorney-General had denounced him for speaking of "jobs[1]" without specifying which were the jobs. But he declared that everything he had mentioned was a gross and infamous job. The right hon. gentleman had taken no proper notice at all of the statement about the clerks drawing £700 a year who had never crossed their offices since 1881. (Hear, hear.) With regard to the question of the Masters he knew nothing about them, but simply quoted the statement of Sir F. Pollock, to the effect that their duties could be performed by any competent clerk.

The ATTORNEY-GENERAL.—The hon. gentleman will pardon me; Sir F. Pollock did not say that with regard to the duties of the Masters, but only with regard to one particular duty. The question was as to the Masters attending in the Court of Appeal and the duties they had to perform, and the answer was that there was nothing which a competent clerk could not do as well as a Master.

Mr. JENNINGS said that not one of the material facts which he placed before the Committee had been touched. It was an injustice to the taxpayers to pay those redundant clerks, and a gross injustice that new clerks should be taken into the departments while those redundant clerks were walking about doing nothing. It was true that the Committee could not reduce the salaries at the present moment, but by assenting to a substantial reduction of the vote they could strike a decisive blow at the system. He hoped his hon. friends about him who were as anxious for reforms as he was, and who had addressed their constituents on the subject, would not refuse to censure a system under which there were clerks with £500 a year who never crossed the threshold of their offices.

Mr. LABOUCHÈRE[2] was afraid that the hon. member would not meet with very much support from hon. gentlemen on the other side, who were fond of

1. *Jobs*, tripotages. — 2. M. Labouchère, membre radical.

making general speeches about economy, but when the necessity for economy was proved by one of their own friends would not follow him into the lobby[1]. He had listened with great pleasure to the speech of the Attorney-General. We had heard a great deal about the Tory democracy of late years, but here was a fine old crusted speech[2] which Lord Eldon[3] himself might have made. (A laugh.) He did not think that lawyers were worse than other people, but it so happened that there were more places which lawyers could get. Because purse-bearers and train-bearers had received excessive salaries for years, the Attorney-General thought they had established a right to eat into the Exchequer, and that it would be monstrous not to allow them to continue to do so during their lives. The hon. member for Stockport would probably not be in favour of cutting away these salaries at once. But why should persons receive £800 or £900 a year for doing nothing because they had received it for a number of years? The Attorney-General thought they might congratulate the Government on doing away with the Petty Bag. But it was he whom they might congratulate, because he had brought forward the subject year after year. They had got rid of this man now, and they would take care that he did not come back. The complaint as to the permanent secretary to the Lord Chancellor was that he was not receiving £1,500 a year, whereas formerly he received £900. The Attorney-General said that the gentleman had extra functions to perform, but did not tell the Committee what they were. We had a right to get from our officials seven hours' work *per diem*, and if this official could do the extra work within the seven hours he ought not to receive an extra salary, . The hon. and learned gentleman went on to explain about the Secretary of Presentations. That gentleman was a clerk in the House of Lords; he received £600 per annum for doing his work there, and £400 per annum for being Secretary of Presentations to the Lord Chancellor. The Attorney-General said that the functions were most important and that a man could not do the work under £400 a year. But these important functions consisted in replying to persons who asked the Lord Chancellor to give some of their friends a Lord Chancellor's living[4]. (A laugh.) He had never asked the Lord Chancellor to give him a Lord Chancellor's living. (A laugh.)

The ATTORNEY-GENERAL explained that the Secretary of Presentations had to conduct the correspondence with respect to nearly 700 livings.

1. *Would not follow him into the lobby*, refusaient de le suivre dans le couloir, c'est-à-dire ne voulaient pas voter avec lui. Au moment du vote, "*the speaker*," le président, prie ceux qui veulent voter pour la proposition de dire "*Aye*," oui ; puis ceux qui sont contre de dire "*No*," non. En cas de doute, il y a division. Le *speaker* prie ceux qui sont *pour* de sortir par le couloir (*lobby*) de droite, ceux qui sont *contre* par celui de gauche. En rentrant dans la salle, les *Tellers* (compteurs-scrutateurs) les comptent, et, d'après leur rapport, le *speaker* proclame le vote. On voit que de cette façon les *absents* ne peuvent pas voter, comme dans la Chambre des députés en France, lorsque le scrutin à la tribune n'est pas demandé. Dans les questions importantes, quand un membre du Parlement est forcé de s'absenter, il cherche un membre du parti opposé qui veut également s'absenter, *they pair off*, c'est-à-dire ils s'engagent à ne pas voter, et de cette façon la distribution des votes n'est pas altérée. Dans la Chambre des députés en France, 120 membres présents votent souvent pour 500. — 2. *Old crusted speech*, discours bien conservé. La métaphore est empruntée aux bouteilles de vieux vin de Porto, dont la croûte atteste que le vin est vieux. — 3. *Lord Eldon*, Grand Chancelier d'Angleterre, 1801-1827, au beau temps des abus. Fils d'un marchand de charbon, il s'est élevé jusqu'au rang de *Lord Chancellor*. — 4. Le Lord Chancelier dispose d'un grand nombre de bénéfices, et en général de beaucoup de bonnes positions. *Living*, cure paroissiale.

Mr. LABOUCHÈRE asked how many members of the House of Commons were in the habit of asking the Lord Chancellor for a Lord Chancellor's living? Not that they would get anything unless they were relations of the Lord Chancellor. (A laugh.) In fact the country had to pay an official £400 a year for refusing livings to members of the House of Commons. (A laugh.) Then the Lord Chancellor had three private secretaries who had two clerks to do their business. As to the Purse-bearer and Train-bearer, the hon. and learned gentleman said that the Lord Chancellor ought to appear in State on some occasions. Would the right hon. member for Bury say how many times the Lord Chancellor had been in the Court of Chancery during the last three years? Not half a dozen times. The Purse-bearer did the work of the secretary when the secretary was away, and the Train-bearer did the work of the Purse-bearer when the Purse-bearer was away, and the bearer of the Great Seal did the work of the Purse-bearer and the Train-bearer when they were away. (A laugh.) It was one man tumbling over another. These gentlemen were there because the Lord Chancellor had the patronage, and his lordship was not likely to recommend that the offices should be done away with. Unless the House gave a strong expression of opinion on the matter Lord Halsbury[1] would, as soon as a vacancy occurred in any of these offices, proceed to fill it up. The Committee wanted to have a distinct and pacific pledge that some of these offices, at least, should not be filled up. The Attorney-General unquestionably defended these offices, and did not hold out the slightest hope that they would not be filled up when vacancies occurred. The hon. and learned gentleman had referred to the Masters in Chancery.

The ATTORNEY-GENERAL.—The Masters of the Queen's Bench.

Mr. LABOUCHÈRE said he would simply call them the Masters. He asked whether the Attorney-General would lay upon the table a return of the public companies of which any particular Masters were directors. Would the hon. and learned gentleman also present a return showing how often these gentlemen attended as paid directors at times when they ought to be performing their official duties? He knew as a fact that a considerable number of these gentlemen, at times when they ought to be performing their official duties, acted as directors of public companies and received fees for doing so.

The ATTORNEY-GENERAL pointed out that this had never been mentioned before. The Masters in Chancery were not referred to. If the hon. member brought to his knowledge the fact that any of the officials in the Chancery or the Queen's Bench Division were in the habit of attending the meetings of public companies and being paid for their services, he would give to the House any information he might obtain on the subject.

Mr. LABOUCHERE further asked whether the hon. and learned gentleman would place on the table a list of the relatives of the Lord Chancellor who had been appointed to offices. There never had been such a jobber[2] since the time of

1. *Lord Halsbury*, actuellement Grand Chancelier, doit sa position entièrement à ses connaissances légales. Il ne siège pas à la Chambre des Communes; mais quelques jours plus tard, il fit dans la Chambre des pairs une vigoureuse et brillante réponse à cette attaque de M. Labouchère. — 2. *Jobber*, tripoteur.

Lord—well, he would not mention any particular Lord Chancellor. (Laughter.) The hon. and learned gentleman suggested that a few redundant clerks should be cut off. What they complained of was that the Government cut off the salaries of the humblest individuals, while these gentlemen with large salaries remained untouched. For instance, there was the hon. gentleman opposite (Mr. Ashmead-Bartlett), who was a Civil Lord of the Admiralty. What did he do for his £1,500 a year? He went about the country and made Tory speeches. This was the sort of thing that was done by a Conservative Government. They would not put down any offices by which the classes benefited. In his opinion, the offices bestowed upon friends and toadies of the Government ought to be done away with.

Mr. R. COOKE hoped that the First Lord of the Treasury or some other Minister of the Crown would give the Committee some assurance less vague than that given by the Attorney-General. If a satisfactory assurance were given, the supporters of the right hon. gentleman would be able to follow the Government into the lobby without breaking any of the pledges which they had given to their constituencies with regard to economy in the public service.

Mr. H. FOWLER said he would not dwell on the method by which the last speaker endeavoured to reconcile his loyalty to his party with his professions of economy. It would be a great pity if the Committee were diverted from what he might call a judicial consideration of this vote by a few isolated cases of special extravagance which had been adduced this evening. He agreed with the hon. member for Northampton that the Government possessed a consummate advocate in the Attorney-General. The hon. and learned gentleman did not answer the case of the hon. member for Stockport, and still less that of the noble lord the member for Paddington[1], but he conducted the defence with marvellous ability and carefully avoided the strong points in his adversaries' case. The noble lord said the members of the House who belonged to the legal profession were in the habit of voting money and of promoting the extension of offices in order to secure their own professional aggrandizement. Last night there arose an interesting discussion which was likely to result in a large saving in one branch of Government business. Well, that was the result of the labours of a Committee presided over by his right hon. friend the member for Bury, and in which he was associated with another lawyer who was a member of that House.

LORD R. CHURCHILL did not think he was imputing any interested motives in regard to any vote given by any lawyer in that House. He was merely referring to the stamp[2] which lawyers of former days had left on legislation, greatly to the advantage of the lawyers of the present day. (Hear, hear.)

Mr. H. FOWLER thought the noble lord was right. The debate last night showed that those members who were most familiar with this branch of the public service were not disposed to advocate economy. This vote involved a question of £760,000, and the sum devoted to the Supreme Court of Judicature did not cover all the branches of judicial administration. Every item of the vote was fixed on a most liberal scale. There were more officers than there ought to be,

1. M. Jennings et lord Randolph Churchill. — 2. *The stamp*, l'empreinte.

and those officers were paid upon the highest scale of any branch of the service; and according to the reports of the various committees which had sat, that amount of service was not rendered which ought to be rendered. With respect to the very expensive class of Masters, the committee on which sat Lord Coleridge, Lord Justice Bowen, Mr. Justice Mellor, the present Mr. Justice A. L. Smith, and Sir Horace Davey, reported that the Masters were not obliged to attend, like the Judges, from 10 to 4 or 10.30 to 4, but that absence was of almost uniform recurrence; that the seven Masters appointed under the Act of 1879 had not been called upon to undertake the general duties of Masters, and they recommended that the different Masters should be called upon to participate to the best of their ability in the duties of their office, and, if any of them should be unwilling to do so, that they should retire with the pension to which their services entitled them; and that the Masters should distribute their work among themselves during office hours. He should be glad to know whether the Government were prepared to carry out this report and embody its recommendations in the future administration of the legal department. He was not quite prepared to agree with the hon. member for Stockport on the question of vested interests. But when the Government paid a man for the whole of his time, they ought to get the whole of his time. Then there was the question of the hours of service, which the Attorney-General said could not be dealt with in a rapid manner. But the Royal Commission presided over by the right hon. member for Blackpool, a few days before the recess, reporting upon the whole of the Civil Service, expressed a hope that steps would be taken to carry out the recommendations of their first report, among which was one that the hours of service should be fixed at seven. This question lay with the Treasury. He did not know what the Treasury would do, but the Inland Revenue Department, under the guidance of Sir Algernon West, had already carried out this recommendation. He hoped also that a record of hours would be kept in every department by which, as in the Bank of England, the highest and lowest should be alike bound. The vote should be grappled with as a whole by the Government, and it was to strengthen the hands of the Government, and from no party motive, that he hoped the amendment would be carried. (Hear, hear.)

Mr. JACKSON[1] desired to explain some errors into which the hon. member for Stockport had fallen. The hon. member was apparently still under the impression that the payment made to the Registrar of the Admiralty on the abolition of certain rights which he possessed was in the nature of salary. The fact was that the payment made was in return for something which had been taken away from him, and he was as much entitled to that compensation as if his house or other property had been compulsorily acquired by the Government. There was no longer a monopoly of practice in the Courts in which he had formerly practised, but he was free to go into the world and do the best for himself; and the Government appointed him to this position because they considered him the best man available for that purpose. The hon. member for Stockport had again referred to the five redundant clerks, with reference to whom he applied

1. Membre ministériel pour la cité de Leeds, secrétaire de la Trésorerie. C'est la Trésorerie qui a le contrôle de tout maniement de fonds, des recettes et des dépenses.

the term job. Now a job had been defined as the corrupt use of patronage. But these gentlemen held their positions under statutable authority—viz., the Act of 1879, which it was not in the power of the Government to override[1]. Parliament deliberately preserved to those men who were then in office all the salaries and rights which they then possessed, and it was absolutely out of the power of the Government to dispossess them. They had complied with the wish of the House of Commons, and they had avoided in every case in which it was possible the retirement of comparatively young men on pensions. He need not go further into the clauses of the Act dealing with the matter. The individuals were protected by the Act of 1879 in all the remuneration to which they were entitled, to the right of compensation for the loss of chances of promotion, and the right of payment of fees to which they were entitled. Therefore he ventured to say when his hon. friend spoke of these jobs the most that could be said of it was this, that they allowed men to continue in office who had a statutable right to these salaries, and had not called upon them or compelled them to retire on abolition terms. But he would tell his hon. friend that the Government need not be neglectful of the views which he had himself expressed. As far as he was concerned—and he spoke the opinion of every member of the Government—as time permitted, as opportunity offered, it was their bounden duty to get rid of these useless offices. As to the five redundant clerks, they had been called upon to resign. (Lord R. Churchill.—Compelled?) They had no power to compel them, but they had been called upon. The committee in concluding their report stated that it remained for them to submit that the reorganization of the department and the retirement of unnecessary officers should be effected as soon as possible, and that officers incapacitated by age or infirmity or other cause should resign on pension. The committee did not recommend that any violent course should be taken, but suggested additions to the pension list, and that when vacancies occurred the Government should avoid filling them up. He thought he was entitled to say that the Government would pursue that course. A case occurred last week in the Chancery Pay Office, where the office of deputy assistant paymaster became vacant by the death of the gentleman who held the office. That position had been filled up only on the condition of the permanent abolition of the office, to the saving of a permanent clerkship at the rate of £800 a year. The member for Wolverhampton spoke, he thought, in reasonable terms, and he agreed with much that he said. He agreed that all Government offices ought to be made into seven-hour offices, and he believed that would be carried out in every case where it was practicable. But he would point out that it had been the custom hitherto in changing from six to seven hours to compensate the officials by additions to their salaries. (Laughter, "Oh, oh," and "Why?") He was very glad indeed to obtain from the House of Commons an expression of its views that the Government would be justified in adding one-sixth more labour without any addition to their salaries. ("Oh, oh.") If the House considered that right it would strengthen their hands considerably; but the Government had been under the impression that a contract made with men (voices, "Where, where?")—a contract made with a man—(The same voices.—"Where?" and

1. *To override*, méconnaître.

another voice,—" Their whole time.") An hon. member said that they ought to give their whole time. Did he mean the whole 24 hours? (An hon. member.—No, a working day.) Yes, but that was decided at the time they took the office. Where the office hours had been made seven from six the practice had been to make an increase. (Mr. C. Parker.—Was that the case in the Inland Revenue?) Yes, it was. He could assure the Committee that the Government would abolish useless offices as vacancies arose, and that was the course they were pursuing. (Hear, hear.)

LORD R. CHURCHILL said, with reference to the argument of the hon. member that the Government were doing all in their power to reduce offices, he quite agreed that they exerted their powers to the uttermost, but there were cases where the Government were absolutely powerless to abolish an office which was useless, because of the opposition of the Lord Chancellor. This was the office of official referee. The Treasury was strongly of opinion—he himself was strongly of opinion at the time—that the office was unnecessary, but they were overridden[1] by the Lord Chancellor, who filled the office, in the teeth of the Treasury. (Loud Opposition cheers.) This only showed how desirable it was that the House should strengthen the hands of the Government. In fact, the hon. gentleman seemed to invite that course, and he was sure that was the only course which would check needless expenditure. (Hear, hear.)

Mr. H. FOWLER pointed out that the difference between six-hour and seven-hour offices was the difference between £80 and £95. The Secretary to the Treasury's own colleague, Sir R. Welby, stated distinctly in his evidence that there would be no breach of faith whatever if the State were to insist upon seven hours' work a day instead of six from the Civil Service clerks. There was no contract in the matter further than the statement to a clerk on entering the office that the hours were so and so.

Mr. W. H. SMITH[2] said that he had listened to the debate with great interest. He had uniformly welcomed, and the Government welcomed, the assistance of the House of Commons in dealing, or attempting to deal, with extravagance or abuse of any kind whatever, with the view of obtaining both efficiency and economy. But the Government had to consider also the responsibility which rested on any Government in relation to maintaining good faith and recognizing statutable rights and claims. He was sure it was not the desire of the House of Commons arbitrarily to deprive any man in the public service of any right he possessed under statute or ordinance or contract entered into with him. He might claim for himself that during the last two years he had not filled one single office unless he had first satisfied himself that the office was necessary in the public service, and he had abolished many, and those not inferior clerkships alone. Such was the principle the Government proposed to follow. He would undertake on the part of the Government that the whole question of the report of the Royal Commission, which had been so much referred to, should be examined.

1. *Overridden*, contraint de céder. — 2. M. W. H. Smith, premier Lord de la Trésorerie. On se rappellera que c'est le Chancelier de l'Echiquier, M. Goschen, qui est ministre des finances. M. Smith est *the Leader* ou chef du parti ministériel dans la Chambre des Communes. Dans ces fonctions il a montré la plus grande énergie, mais s'est attiré la haine et les attaques les plus virulentes des membres du parti irlandais.

The Government had already made some progress in dealing with the principles upon which offices which had become vacant should not be filled up, and if it appeared necessary to get further authority from Parliament in the work they would not hesitate to ask for such authority. He was not prepared to make a definite answer to the point put by the right hon. member for Edinburgh; but the Government recognized that it was their duty to find an officer, a Minister who should be responsible that none of the appointments now the subject of question should be filled up unless he was satisfied that the duties to be discharged were necessary in the public interest, also that the pay was not more than was adequate and reasonable. The Government were prepared to give effect to the report as a whole, the whole object and aim of the report being such as met with their entire and cordial concurrence. The debate had undoubtedly strengthened and assisted the Government. They gave the most unqualified assurance to the House that they were in cordial agreement with the spirit and object of the right hon. gentleman and his noble friend and others in seeking to reduce useless expenditure and to remove all abuses. They took that responsibility upon themselves, and they trusted the House would accept that assurance.

Mr. JACKSON desired to make a personal explanation. The right hon. member for Wolverhampton appeared rather to challenge a statement of his with reference to the increase of pay given on the change of office from a six hours to a seven hours' office. The right hon. gentleman's explanation arising from the evidence of the Commission related only to the Higher Division; he did not challenge in any way his statement as regarded the Lower Divison. Now he had said, and he ventured to repeat, that the increase of pay on the change of office was a contract, and it was a contract defined, he believed, by an Order in Council. He only wished to make it clear that there was no actual difference between the right hon. gentleman's statement and his own.

SIR J. SWINBURNE referred to the case of the official referees, and repeated the complaints made by Mr. Cozens-Hardy.

Mr. MOLLOY said that in making two appointments to the office of official referee in 1887, when he had before him returns showing that the previous referees did only 50 days' work in the year, the Lord Chancellor had been guilty of an absolute job.

The Committee divided and the numbers were—

For the reduction of the vote	129
Against	148
Majority	—19

Mr. BRADLAUGH urged that great inconvenience, delay, and cost to suitors, and especially to the metropolitan public, was caused by the continued absence of the Judges from London, owing to their being occupied while on circuit[1] with a class of work which they need not perform. The Judges sat in London in full strength rather less than five months in each year, and that fact arose

1. Les juges du banc de la reine (voyez note 3, page 66) sont chargés d'aller en province présider les assises et juger les causes les plus importantes; M. Bradlaugh se plaint que depuis quelque temps ces magistrats jugent des causes peu importantes et que c'est là une source de grandes dépenses.

mainly from the circuit arrangements which had prevailed for a considerable time. The legal year began on October 24, the Judges went on assize, and about November 24 they were all back in London. Thus one month was swept away. At Christmas they rose; after Christmas all the Judges of the Queen's Bench Division went on circuit, leaving only sufficient Judges to form the Divisional Court[1], and it was near the middle of February before they all returned. They then sat about six weeks till Easter, and after the Easter vacation there was another circuit, leaving at best one month's full strength to Whitsuntide. After the Whitsuntide vacation they sat in full strength about one month. Then the Judges went on the summer assize, and did not sit again in London until after the Long Vacation, making practically a total of about four and a half months' full strength sittings in London in the year, and even those four and a half months were not devoted solely to metropolitan cases. The Judges, he submitted, took while on circuit criminal business, which ought really to be dealt with at quarter sessions[2]. In a letter which appeared in *The Times* of that day from Mr. Lofthouse, honorary secretary of the Bar Committee[3], it was stated that " the average number of quarter sessions cases[4] dealt with at the assizes when Easter falls neither early nor late is about 1,700 a year. This year, by reason of the autumn assizes being retarded by a month, the number will be about 2,000." It was a waste of the valuable time of the Judges to occupy them with the trial of cases which would be better tried under the superintendence of a chairman of quarter sessions. In every assize there were a number of eminent Queen's counsel who were put upon the commission, and formerly two or three Queen's counsel often sat in separate courts trying those cases which he called quarter sessions cases. That cost the country nothing, because, by the etiquette of the Bar, that work was done by Queen's counsel for nothing. It was not a bad training for the Judicial Bench[5], to which those eminent gentlemen were often subsequently raised, that they should try those cases. But that practice had been departed from in more recent times. There was a suggestion —he did not say it was a well-founded one—that the allowance of £7 10s. per day which was made to them during circuit might have allayed the desire of the Judges to get through the business by other help than their own. There were instances in which Judges had stayed three weeks or even a month in one assize town with only a few serious cases to be tried, the bulk of the cases being such as ought to be dealt with at quarter sessions. From time to time the cry was raised that the delays in litigation arose from the need of more Judges; but what was really required was a better distribution of their judicial power, and that the Judges of the Supreme Court ought not to be employed in trying those petty cases. The Judges should be induced to revert to the old practice, which was attended with great advantage to the country, of using for the trial of those cases the Queen's counsel whose names were on the commission, and

1. *The Divisional Court*, la chambre qui siège pendant les vacances. — 2. *At quarter sessions*, aux tribunaux de première instance, où siègent des magistrats résidents (*Justices of the Peace*, etc.) que préside un *Queen's Counsel*, conseiller de la reine, désigné par le *Lord Chancellor*.— 3. *The Bar Committee*, le comité du barreau, association des avocats. — 4. *Quarter sessions cases*, causes qui ressortissent aux tribunaux de première instance. — 5. Ce n'était pas un mauvais stage pour ceux qui aspiraient à siéger au banc des juges.

who were often sitting in the court. He desired to say that in making this motion he did not wish to personally attack any one of the Judges. What he attacked was the system which had grown up within the last 20 years or so. He hoped the law officers of the Crown would be able to give the Committee some assurance that the Government would pay attention to the question. The present system cost hundreds of thousands of pounds every year not only in the delay of the settlement of matters under litigation, but also in the piling up of costs to an extent never dreamt of 25 or 30 years ago. (Hear, hear.)

Mr. ADDISON said that the hon. member for Northampton had on this matter accurately represented the strong feeling of members of the legal profession on both sides of the House. He hoped that the Solicitor-General would take the speech of the hon. member as a speech which was re-echoed by nearly every member of the legal profession in the House of Commons. (Hear, hear.) The Judges were undoubtedly doing their very best to arrange the circuit business. They had a great deal of business to attend to, and the House should consider the best means of facilitating the circuit work without increasing the number of the Judges. (Hear, hear.) The grievance of which they complained had really arisen within the last ten years. Before the change took place magistrates committed to the sessions prisoners who were ordinarily tried there, and committed to the assizes prisoners who were triable there. It seemed to have occurred to some Judges about ten years ago that it was their duty to clear the gaols, and in Lancashire they actually altered the form of the commission for the purpose of trying quarter sessions prisoners, and the effect was that 10 or 12 serious cases and 60 or 70 sessions cases came before them for trial. The Judges tried these sessions cases without any advantage to the public, because there were no tribunals in England that tried these cases better than the courts of quarter sessions, whose sentences were very regular and just. (Hear, hear.) The trial of these cases had been taken away from quarter sessions for no other purpose, it would appear, than that of wasting the time of the Judges by taking them away from London. There was a Bill before Parliament which provided that the prisoners triable at quarter sessions should be tried there and not elsewhere, except under special order made by a Judge in Chambers. He hoped the hon. member for Northampton and his friends would support that Bill when it came before the House next session, and that he would have that influence with the Government which their most faithful supporters were unable to secure[1]. (Hear, hear.)

The SOLICITOR-GENERAL[2] said that this was no doubt an interesting and important subject. The question of the rearrangement of circuits[3] was, however, one of some difficulty. Not very long ago there was a great movement in favour of having more frequent circuits all over the country, and there was an expression of public opinion in favour of grouping the counties, and holding assizes in different centres for the trial of prisoners. No doubt there had been much that was experimental in the arrangement of the circuits during the last

1. M. Addison est conservateur, ami du ministère. — 2. *The Solicitor-general*, l'avocat général est le subordonné du procureur général et le second conseiller légal de la couronne. — 3. *Circuits*, les districts judiciaires que se partagent les juges du banc de la reine.

few years. The experiment of having four circuits in the year had proved not to be satisfactory, and had not produced the results which were expected; and he was extremely glad to say that the experiment which was made of grouping counties had been practically abandoned. (Hear, hear.) It was an experimen which he was very sorry to see made, because in the administration of criminal justice it seemed to him of the first importance that the trial of criminals should take place as close as possible to the spot where the offence was alleged to have been committed. (Hear, hear.) It was certainly essential to the interests of the poorer prisoners—and most prisoners where poor—that their trial should come off near to the place where they and their friends lived. He quite recognized the importance of the specific matter to which attention had been directed —namely, the extent to which the time of the Judges had been taken up by trying small cases which ought properly to be tried at quarter sessions. He would not say that there was no advantage in that system. He had a very high opinion of the way in which most quarter sessions discharged their duties; but still it was a good thing that, from time to time, these bodies should see how the cases were dealt with by the Judges. There was thus some counter-balancing advantage; but it did not at all counter-balance the mischief which had been spoken of, and it was much to be regretted that the time of the Judges should be so fully occupied in trying quarter sessions cases. He was a little surprised that his hon. and learned friend should speak of the Government in this matter as being insensible to his blandishments, and as being likely to capitulate to the assault of the hon. member for Northampton. (Laughter.) The Government, in any course they might take, would not deal with the question in consequence of anything that had taken place that evening. He could now discuss the proposals of the Bill by which the Government hoped to do something to relieve Judges from trying sessions cases, and so set them free for more important work. It had been the custom for Judges to appoint Commissioners when there were more prisoners than the Judges could try within the time allotted to one place; but he should be sorry to see the appointment of Commissioners resorted to continually. If the measure commended itself to the judgment of the hon. member for Northampton, the Government would hope to receive his assistance in carrying it.

Mr. BRADLAUGH said he certainly should support the Government in any such scheme, but he did not understand whether the object was to be attained by preventing quarter sessions cases being heard by Judges except under an order of the Court in special cases.

The SOLICITOR-GENERAL said he could not enter into details; but the intention of the Government was to cause a transfer to be made to quarter sessions of cases which, under present arrangements, were tried by Her Majesty's Judges. Whether this would be done by forbidding the trial of them at assizes, or by facilitating the trial of them at quarter sessions, he could not now say.

Mr. BRADLAUGH said it seemed to him that it would require something more than to facilitate trials at sessions; it would require hinderance to the possibility of sessions cases being tried at the assizes.

Mr. AMBROSE said the difficulty began with Mr. Justice Watkin Williams taking the point that was the duty of Judges on circuit not to leave any prisoners in gaol, as they might have to do when sessions came just after the assizes. The Judges deferred to what they believed to be a public demand rather than to their own judgment of the necessity for their trying sessions cases; and they would only be too glad if they could only be relieved of this sense of an imposed obligation.

M. BRADLAUGH said, after what had fallen from the Solicitor-General, he should be acting wisely if he asked leave to withdraw his motion.

The amendment was by leave withdrawn.

Mr. E. ROBERTSON said it was desirable that he should again call attention to the unclaimed funds in Chancery, which were advertised as amounting to a fabulous sum by persons who practised on the public credulity and obtained fees from persons of the same family names as those whose property was vested in the Court. Since exposures had been made in Parliament and in Court, the advertising in leading papers had fallen off; but it still went on largely in the provinces and abroad. These fraudulent agencies still kept up the lying advertisements about the 90 millions unclaimed in the English Court of Chancery. There was, of course, nothing like that amount. Little was known about it, but once in every three years a list was published, consisting of thousands of names. But he believed there was no single fund of more than £15,000, and the whole amount unclaimed was not more than a million. He ventured to suggest to the Secretary to the Treasury that all the information should be made known.

Mr. JACKSON thought the hon. and learned member for Dundee had done a public service in calling attention last year to this question, when he had promised to look into it. He had examined the matter and consulted those who knew more about it than he did. But he found that it was not possible to carry out the hon. and learned member's suggestion without raising other and more serious difficulties. It could not be too strongly emphasized that this fund was far from being so large as it was represented to be by enterprising agents, who were misleading the public for their own advantage. The fact that the hon. member had last year called the attention of the public to this matter had already done good, and he hoped to-night's conversation would be of further benefit.

Mr. ROBERTSON suggested that the amount unclaimed should be placed after each of the names in the lists published.

Mr. JACKSON said that he would see whether that could be done [1].

The vote was agreed to.

On the vote to complete the sum of £12,680 for the Wreck Commission.

Mr. SHAW-LEFEVRE[2] desired to know what were the intentions of the Government with regard to the important post of Wreck Commissioner[3]. It was now some four or five months since the death of Mr. Rothery, who had presided

1. On a supprimé ici une portion des débats peu intéressante. — 2. M. Shaw-Lefèvre, né en 1832, est membre du Parlement depuis 1864. Il a été secrétaire de l'Amirauté et commissaire principal des travaux publics. Il est partisan des idées de M. Gladstone sur l'Irlande. — 3. *The Wreck Commissioner*, le commissaire des naufrages, aidé de deux assesseurs, marins, experts, ou ingénieurs de marine, est chargé, à la demande du bureau du commerce, de s'enquérir des causes de la perte ou de l'abandon d'un navire, ou de tout accident en mer. Il peut suspendre ou retirer les certificats des capitaines au long cours, des patrons et des seconds.

over the Court with so much ability. The post, which was of considerable importance, was created in 1875 or 1876 in consequence of the agitation aroused by Mr. Plimsoll[1]. The Wreck Commission had performed very good work, and the Royal Commission over which he presided two years ago reported that the Wreck Commissioner's inquiries had been conducted with great benefit and had thrown a great deal of light on the causes of the loss of ships and of life at sea.

Mr. JACKSON said that no definite steps had been taken for filling up the post vacant by the death of Mr. Rothery. He believed he was right in saying that representations had been made to the Lord Chancellor to hold his hand with regard to this appointment for the time being to enable very serious consideration to be given to the report of the Commission on Saving Life at Sea. In the meantime, he was told that no inconvenience arose from not filling up the office. He believed the Commission which sat on the question of saving life at sea rather leant to the view that it was desirable to hold those inquiries by means of inspectors. Apparently legislation would be necessary to give effect to some of the recommendations of the Commission, and it seemed desirable to the Board of Trade[2] that some time should be allowed in order to enable them to see how they would proceed.

Mr. SHAW-LEFEVRE remarked that from time to time there must be considerable loss of life at sea, and the Royal Commission were certainly of opinion that the office should be continued.

Dr. CLARK thought that the trained assessors could themselves do the work, and that it was superfluous to give £3,000 to the Wreck Commissioner.

The vote was then agreed to.

Upon the vote to complete the sum of £17,743 for Police-courts[3] (London and Sheerness).

Mr. PICKERSGILL moved the reduction of the vote by £100, as a protest against the present system, which did not provide female attendants or warders to look after female prisoners in the police-court cells. Convicted females had this privilege and unconvicted had not, which was a very unjust anomaly. (Hear, hear.)

Mr. STUART-WORTLEY said that since the report of Mr. Justice Will's

---

1. *M. Plimsoll, M. P.*, a consacré une grande partie de sa vie à prévenir les naufrages de la marine marchande anglaise. Grâce à la manière dont se font les assurances au Lloyds, individuellement et non par compagnies, les *underwriters* ou assureurs maritimes ne prenaient que 1/8 ou 1/16 ou même 1/24 de la valeur chacun ; dès lors certains armateurs pouvaient envoyer en mer des navires *unseaworthy*, incapables de résister à un gros temps ou beaucoup trop chargés. Il en résultait des naufrages sans nombre et une grande perte d'existences. On était certain qu'il y avait eu fraude, mais les dépenses pour prouver les fraudes étaient trop considérables pour que la perte encourue par chaque assureur partiel et individuel engageât aucun d'eux à entreprendre un procès. M. Plimsoll, membre du Parlement, chercha à mettre fin à cet état de choses. Il étudia les faits, les exposa devant la Chambre, et fit établir une inspection de tout navire marchand avant qu'il lui fût permis de quitter le port. Les marins anglais et la nation anglaise tout entière doivent beaucoup aux efforts courageux et désintéressés de M. Plimsoll. — 2. *The Board of Trade;* le bureau du commerce, fondé en 1786, a des pouvoirs très étendus et s'occupe du commerce en général, des récoltes, des faillites, de toutes les voies de communication, des pêcheries, des ports, des phares etc., et a pleine autorité sur les navires marchands, sur les marins et sur la réserve de la marine royale. — 3. *Police-courts*, tribunaux de police. Il y en a 14 dans les différents districts de Londres.

Committee the attention of the Government had been directed to the great congestion of prisoners in police-court cells, but before spending money in enlarging the cells an attempt was being made to remedy the evil in other ways. Hitherto the van from Holloway, where the remanded prisoners[1] were lodged, had brought them down at 10 o'clock, and they had then been placed in the same cell with the prisoners arrested on night charges[2]. An arrangement had now been made whereby the remanded prisoners were brought down later, at an hour when the night charges had mostly been disposed of. In the case of six of the metropolitan police-courts there were police stations attached, and it was intended to utilize the cells of those police stations as much as possible, so as to relieve the police-court cells. As to the question of female attendants, this was a matter of great importance, and depended, to a certain extent, on structural improvements. He was engaged in inquiring into the matter as to the food for untried prisoners. He was in hopes of being able to meet that recommendation, and there were prospects of speedily carrying the recommendations into effect.

Mr. MOLLOY feared that the statement of the hon. member would not satisfy the public. The statements which had been laid before them as to the mixing of the sexes, the contamination of innocent women and youths, and the horrible insanitary condition of the cells demanded immediate attention. He was sure any vote which might be asked for such a purpose would be readily passed by that House. (Hear, hear.)

Mr. C. GRAHAM spoke as a specialist on this matter, having spent a night and a portion of a day in Bow-street police cells. It was that day year—the day they called " Bloody Sunday " — that he was confined. On one side of him were two drunken prostitutes, on the other three Whitechapel boys, and their language was " painful, frequent, and free, " to quote Bret Harte[3]. He had to listen to all this filth and obscenity the whole night long. What he wished to plead for—it was an unusual thing for a Radical to ask—was a little outlay[4] of public money in order to remove the reproach that did exist in our London police-courts, and place them upon a level with Paris and other cities. He had made a public charge in reference to the treatment of certain prisoners by the police on this very night of last year. He repeated, and he was ready to go into a Court of justice and declare upon oath, that he heard men groaning and scuffling in a cell close to his, and he heard also these words — " You needn't give a fellow such a doing. " Of course, he could not say what passed, but he did see in the morning men led past his cell with their heads bandaged up who, he was sure, showed no wound or injury when they were committed to the cells the previous afternoon. That was a most serious accusation for a member of

1. *The remanded prisoners*, les accusés écroués jusqu'à une nouvelle audience. Toute personne arrêtée doit paraître dans les 24 heures devant un magistrat. Celui-ci ou bien l'acquitte, ou l'admet à caution, ou la renvoie (*remands*) en prison pour paraître à une nouvelle audience. — 2. *Arrested on night charges*, arrêtés pour délit pendant la nuit précédente. — 3. *Bret Harte*, auteur humoristique, né à Albany (États-Unis) en 1839. A l'âge de 15 ans, il passa en Californie, y travailla dans les mines, se fit ensuite apprenti typographe, puis instituteur et enfin journaliste. Nommé consul des États-Unis à Glasgow en 1880, il publia une édition complète de ses œuvres, des contes pour la plupart, en 1882. C'est un écrivain original, et les scènes qu'il nous présente ne sont pas celles auxquelles nous sommes accoutumés ici. 4 somme à dépenser

Parliament to bring before the House of Commons; and he appealed to the Home Secretary[1] to let the House and the country know whether he was in a position to relate any facts relating to those occurrences, in order that men who might be falsely accused might not, perhaps, be exposed to insult and abuse in the secrecy of a police-court, and have no redress whatever through lack of witnesses.

Mr. MATTHEWS did not think he need detain the Committee[2]. ("Oh.") He hoped it would not be supposed that in saying that he was lacking in interest in the subject. On the contrary, he was warmly interested in it, and he entirely agreed with what had fallen from more than one hon. member. Where it was proved that an evil existed the evil must be removed, even though it involved some considerable outlay of public money. It would be observed that the Committee emphatically referred to this point, and remarked that in some of the courts much might be done to relieve the cells by some arrangement for removing the prisoners in batches as soon as their cases were disposed of, and they suggested that, instead of putting different classes of prisoners all together, the remanded prisoners should be brought up at a later hour, when the night charges were disposed of, taking away the night charges, and so avoiding the accumulation of both classes of prisoners in the same cells. But more than a rearrangement was required; additional accommodation in many cases was absolutely necessary. It had been a difficult and complicated subject to investigate fully, but they had now arrived at a fairly adequate result. There was no notion of observing an undue or shabby economy in the matter. The cost of constructing an improved cell was about £68; that was the estimate in the report. At most of the stations, in order to provide additional cells, land would have to be acquired, and this would be a matter of time and difficulty. He could assure the Committee, however, that there was not the slightest intention of shelving[3] or postponing the work.

Mr. STUART said he wanted to give one fact in respect to that matter. The population of the metropolis had increased during the last ten years by 20 per cent.; the cost of the Metropolitan Police Force during that time had increased by 44 per cent., and the money laid out for destitute prisoners awaiting trial had increased 14½ per cent. These figures were taken from the annual police returns, and he believed them to be correct. Where there had been such large increases, he thought an increase necessary for the welfare of the poorer classes might well be granted more rapidly than the Home Secretary seemed to contemplate. The hon. member was proceeding to deal with the treatment by some of the police-constables of prisoners awaiting trial, when

The CHAIRMAN[4] pointed out that that subject came more properly under the vote for the police.

1. *The Home Secretary*, le ministre de l'intérieur, M. Matthews, qui ensuite va prendre la parole. — 2. Le Comité, c'est la Chambre tout entière; celle-ci siège *en comité* lors de la discussion des articles, et en Chambre des Communes, quand il s'agit de la *discussion générale* des lois. Ce n'est plus dans le premier cas *the speaker* qui préside, mais le président de la commission du budget. — 3. *To shelve*, mettre sur une planche, serrer, c'est-à-dire laisser de côté, négliger. *Voy. Dict. angl.-franç. Elwall.* — 4. *The Chairman*, le président, non *the speaker*, voy. note 2 ci-dessus. *The speaker* n'a pas le droit de prendre part aux discussions générales, ni

Mr. H. FOWLER[1] said he did not agree with the recommendation of the Committee with respect to the structural changes. No doubt the inquiries mentioned by the Home Secretary were necessary, but he should like to know when they would come to an end. (Hear.) He happened when he was at the Home Office to have the whole of that question under his consideration, and he formed the opinion that it was absolutely absurd to attempt the reconstruction of the metropolitan police-courts in a haphazard, piecemeal fashion, extending over a number of years. If any of the other large towns were concerned, they would not think of taxing the people in any one year for such alterations, but would raise the sum necessary for the whole and spread the cost over a number of years. That was what should be done in the present case.

Mr. STUART-WORTLEY[2] said he had very strong reasons for believing that the right hon. gentleman was referring to what was going on when he was in office with regard to the cells of the police-stations in London. That policy had been carried out, and a sum of £200,000 was authorized in 1886, and it was treated as a matter of capital expenditure[3]. Of course the Home Office would not scruple to propose the structural changes should they prove to be necessary, but he did not anticipate that they would be very large.

Mr. PICTON did not think the promise of the Home Secretary quite satisfactory with regard to the very necessary reform as to female attendants.

Mr. J. ROWLANDS said that if the Government had not already powers to take the land necessary for structural alterations compulsorily they ought to bring in a Bill for the purpose.

Mr. LABOUCHÈRE[4] had no doubt that those police cells were now in a very bad state; but the question was, who was to pay for improving them? No one had ever been able to give a valid reason why the country should pay for the London police-courts, and he desired to test the sincerity of those metropolitan members who said that the people of London were ready to be taxed for purposes that concerned the metropolis only.

The CHAIRMAN pointed out to the hon. member that a motion had been made to reduce the vote on a special matter.

Mr. LABOUCHÈRE said he was rather in difficulty, as he wanted to explain why he was not going to vote for the proposed reduction, because he wished to protest against the entire vote. (A laugh.)

The CHAIRMAN said that the hon. gentleman could do so afterwards.

The question having been then put and a division challenged[5], Mr. Labouchère walked out of the House amid some laughter.

The Committee divided, and the numbers were —

---

même de voter, excepté quand le nombre des votants est égal des deux côtés ; il n'en est pas de même pour le *chairman* quand la Chambre siège en comité. — 1. M. H. Fowler, secrétaire des finances sous le ministère précédent de M. Gladstone. — 2. M. Stuart-Wortley, *under-secretary of the Home office,* sous-secrétaire d'Etat au ministère de l'intérieur. — 3. *Capital expenditure,* dépense de capital. — 4. Membre radical du parti de M. Gladstone, connu par ses réparties vives et spirituelles. Il est le directeur et le propriétaire du journal " *Truth,*" journal politico-satirique. — 5. *A division challenged,* vote compté (voy. note 1, p. 158). M. Labouchère quitte la Chambre sans voter, sachant bien que personne n'adopterait sa proposition humoristique.

For the reduction of the vote	91
Against it	150
Majority	—59

The vote was then agreed to.

On the vote to complete the sum of £583,520 for the Metropolitan Police.

Mr. BRADLAUGH[1] said that although the announcement made by the Government yesterday might be thought to deprive the motion of which he had given notice in regard to the Chief Commissioner's salary of some of its interest, yet the intimation made that day by the Home Secretary, that the resignation of Sir C. Warren was only in consequence of the attempt to enforce against him the order as to the publication of departmental matters, and that the Government accepted the responsibility for all the other questions which had been challenged, rendered it necessary that he should make a full statement to the Committee. During the last 25 years he had some opportunity of judging of the relations which existed between the people of the metropolis and the Commissioner of Police, and the alteration in those relations was now so great that those who, like himself, wished for fair and reasonable agitation on the part of the people regarded the state of things now existing with some alarm. (Hear, hear.) The Commissioners of Police had had, over and over again, to deal with very vast assemblies in the metropolis; and when it had been necessary for them to resort to physical force they had done this without revolting public opinion. The general disposition of the people had been to obey the law, and to regard those who had the control of the police with something like respect. That had now entirely changed, and it was due to the conduct of the Commissioner of the Police who had recently resigned[2]—conduct which, he understood, was endorsed and approved of by the Home Secretary. Although the motion was, in point of terms, obliged to be directed against the Chief Commissioner, he wished the Committee to understand that, in point of fact, it was directed against the Home Secretary, who was bound to accept responsibility for all the matters which he should challenge him upon that night. In the first place, he complained of the conduct of the police in the distribution of voting papers in connexion with the Marylebone Free Library[3]. In that case and in others the Commissioner had challenged him to make complaints and they should be inquired into; but whenever he had made complaints conditions had at once been annexed which had prevented the investigation being of the slightest value. In the case of the Marylebone Library, the charge was that the police, with the knowledge of the

1. On a déjà parlé de M. Bradlaugh, membre radical pour Northampton, le promoteur de "*the Oaths Bill*," discuté plus haut à la Chambre des pairs et aujourd'hui passé en loi. — 2. *Sir Charles Warren*, officier de l'armée anglaise de grande distinction et comptant les services les plus honorables, nommé *Chief Commissioner of Metropolitan police*, a été fort loué par les uns et fort blâmé par les autres à cause de la manière dont il a dirigé la police lors des réunions publiques au grand air, surtout à *Trafalgar-square*, dans Londres. Sir Ch. Warren donna sa démission par suite d'un blâme que lui avait infligé le ministre de l'intérieur (*the Home secretary*) à propos d'un article publié et signé par lui dans une Revue. — 3. *Marylebone* (Marie la Bonne, prononcez : Mar'-i-bonne), district de Londres. Par une loi passée en 1875-1877 et amendée en 1887, chaque commune a le droit de former une bibliothèque et de prélever un léger impôt pour la soutenir. Les directeurs sont nommés par les habitants du quartier payant l'impôt personnel.

Commissioner, had delivered voting papers as part of their duty, and with the voting papers other papers asking persons to vote in a particular fashion. The evidence on that matter was overwhelming, and he submitted it to the Home Secretary. He now wished to know what investigation was held, how it was held, who was permitted to be present, and what evidence, if any, was taken. It was absurd when complaints were brought against the police to hold hole-and-corner investigations [1], and then to taunt members of that House who brought the charges by saying that they had no evidence whatever to support those charges. He now came to more serious matters. He made, some time ago, charges against the police of having assaulted persons after they were in custody, and the right hon. gentleman thought it right to say that he had kept back the charges without disclosing their nature to the authorities, and that he had made those charges without the shadow of foundation. At that time the Commissioner of Police had sworn evidence of every one of the charges which he had made; and the Commissioner must have either wantonly and wickedly misled the Home Secretary, or the right hon. gentleman could not have sufficiently inquired into the matter submitted to him. The right hon. gentleman had himself laid on the table a return showing that in three of the cases which he had mentioned, in which he brought charges of assault by the police, sworn informations were filed [2] on December 3 last year. These informations were in the hands of the Solicitor to the Treasury, and the Commissioner was, to his knowledge, present in court when some of the depositions were made. It rendered the performance of a member's duties in that House exceedingly difficult when that member was held up by a responsible Minister of the Crown as one who had made charges " without a shadow of foundation ". The Home Secretary undertook to make an investigation if he would furnish a statement of the charges which he had made; but when he furnished that statement, outlining the evidence which he proposed to bring forward, the right hon. gentleman made a stipulation that there should be no specific charges dealt with that had not been before a legal tribunal. The right hon. gentleman knew that every one of the cases had been before a magistrate, and he offered him the barren privilege of not being able to prove any one of the allegations which he had made in that House, and which the right hon. gentleman described as having " not a shadow of foundation ". He contented that the conduct of the Commissioner was to be measured, with reference to the conduct of the police, by the description given by the Home Secretary in that House of the statements which he had made. The Home Secretary had spoken of the police getting out of hand [3]. He might speak of them as getting out of hand when they were charged on oath with striking prisoners in custody in the police-station. One of the cases to which he had referred was that of Police-constable Greenwood, who was charged with striking a prisoner at Bow-street [4], and yet the Home Secretary in that House held him up as making a charge without a shadow of foundation. He now wished to know where this matter

---

1. *Hole-and-corner investigation*, une enquête dans un coin. — 2. *Were filed*, produits devant le magistrat et enregistrés. — 3. *To get out of hand*, n'être pas bien exercé, avoir perdu la main. Ce n'est certainement pas dans ce sens que *the Home secretary* a employé la phrase. — 4. *Bow-street*, un des tribunaux de police dans Londres (voy. note 3, p. 169).

was investigated, by whom, and whether it was a public or private investigation. He had not very much faith in police investigations. (Hear, hear.) He had brought to the notice of the Home Secretary the case of the man Schumacher, who before he was released from custody was compelled to sign a statement. The answer of the right hon. gentleman was that Schumacher had signed some voluntary statement, but that it was not put to him as a condition of his release. Had the Home Secretary before him the minute of what took place at the investigation at Scotland-yard[1]? He would undertake to prove before a Select Committee of that House that this question was put to the police officer—" Did you ask Schumacher to make this statement, " and that the answer of the police official was, " Yes ". It would not do to tell the Committee that charges without a shadow of foundation were made in that House for outside purposes. Then there were the charges against Police-constable Frederick Goodwin. Sworn depositions in these cases were in the hands of the Treasury Solicitor, and yet the right hon. gentleman the Home Secretary charged him with making statements without any foundation. He trusted that now at the eleventh hour some reparation would be made by the Home Secretary for the injustice he had done. He had with him office copies of the depositions to which he referred. What kind of discipline, he asked, must there be in the police force when it became necessary to assault prisoners when they were in custody? It was not the habit some years ago. There was then on the side of the police an exhibition of good temper, good feeling, and forbearance. He[2] had tried their temper sorely himself when heading the masses he had brought together; he remembered that his task was a difficult one, but the police, superiors and inferiors, did nothing to aggravate it. Occasionally a policeman might have magnified his office, but generally the conduct of the police was good. Until this last year or two Chief Commissioners had done nothing to provoke a breach of the peace. He should have expected that a Minister charged with responsibility for the police would have exhausted every means to investigate the charges that had been made, instead of dimissing them because witnesses were in custody. He would not discuss whether the people were right or wrong in going to Trafalgar-square[3], but, supposing they were wrong, it was the duty of Chief Commissioners to exhaust all means of securing obedience before resorting to brute force. Could the Home Secretary say the Chief Commissioner did this? Marching through the streets was legal; was the same law applied to clubs and to the Salvation Army; and yet the police, under the order of Sir C. Warren, who presumably, acted under the orders of the Home Secretary (Mr. Matthews nodded assent), rode down men in the public streets; many were bruised and badly beaten, and some were since dead. For 50 years no such indictment had been made against the Home Secretary. The police rode down upon the processionists and broke their drums and instruments. This was not the way people were dealt with in

1. *Scotland-yard*, quartier général de la police de Londres. — 2. *M. Bradlaugh* lui-même, député radical et grand agitateur. — 3. *Trafalgar-square* est regardé par le gouvernement comme n'étant pas un lieu de réunion publique, et cette opinion a été confirmée par les tribunaux. Aussi la police, sous sir Charles Warren, s'est-elle opposée à une grande réunion en cet endroit. La foule a résisté et beaucoup de personnes ont été blessées, tant du côté de la police que de la foule.

England; this country, at any rate, was not Ireland. (Opposition cheers.) He never felt so tempted to break the law as he did when he had the sufferers before him. Seeing that brutal force was intended to be used, he had advised people not to go to Trafalgar-square, but to submit to wrong for a time. He always took pains to verify facts before making statements in the House, and he expected Ministers to be equally candid. Until now public demonstrations in London had been orderly, although sometimes attended with ebullitions of feeling. Never before within living memory had there been the outrages on public liberty that had occurred while the right hon. gentleman had been at the Home Office; and he impeached the right hon. gentleman before Parliament and before the people of England. When it was said that charges made were not true he demanded to know who made the investigation. It was known that the charges that were made were dismissed only because the necessary witnesses were in custody and could not be produced. He had put several questions to the Home Secretary on the subject, and when the right hon. gentleman saw that he had been misled by the Solicitor to the Treasury, or by the Chief Commissioner, or by both, he expected that the courtesy and kindness which the right hon. gentleman had shown in other matters would have induced him to have been reasonably fair in a matter of this kind.. But at present he stood with a charge of falsehood made against him by the right hon. gentleman in keeping back facts which the Home Secretary either did know or ought to have known, because he had in the Home Office the very documents which bore out the opposite of what the right hon. gentleman was then stating.

Mr. MATTHEWS.—Will the hon. member give me the date?

Mr. BRADLAUGH said it was in the course of the Trafalgar-square debate, which lasted two nights. He quoted from "Hansard"[1] the reply of the right hon. gentleman, which gave him great pain, and which he had tried to challenge in every respect. In moving the reduction of the vote, he asked the Committee, without regard to politics, to express its opinion that the irritated state of public feeling in the metropolis has been aggravated, first, by the conduct of Sir C. Warren, who imagined himself to be a military commander in London (hear, hear) instead of a civil officer, who imagined he had the duty of suppressing the people instead of protecting them; and, secondly, he asked it to condemn the Home Secretary as endorsing that policy. (Cheers.)

Mr. MATTHEWS, who was received with Ministerial cheers, said the speech of the hon. member had made this discussion a personal debate against him. He assured the hon. member that nothing was further from his wish, even in debate, than to let drop the least expression which could give pain to any hon. member. He could not find the passage containing words of the offensive character quoted by the hon. member; but all he could say was that if he did use words imputing to the hon. member that he made charges which he knew to be unfounded, then he without the slightest qualification retracted any language of that kind and apologized to the hon. member. That was not the purport of the charge which he intended to make against the hon. member. The hon. member

1. *Hansard.* La publication des débats du Parlement par l'imprimerie Hansard est regardée comme officielle.

mentioned certain names of police-constables who had been guilty of assaulting prisoners in the cells. Those names were new to him at the time of the debate, and the complaint which he made was this. He protested against the police having such charges brought against them in the House without notice, when the hon. member for Northampton had weeks and months in which he might have brought them forward in a Court of justice, at the same time pledging himself even then if the hon. member would bring a *primâ facie*[1] case against the conduct of the police that the matter would be thoroughly inquired into by the Director of Public Prosecutions. That was the language which he used; but if the hon. member believed that he used such language as that which had been quoted, again he said that he sincerely regretted it. As to the substance of this matter, he must again say what he had said before—that the only reasonable way in which charges of this grave kind could possibly be investigated was before a magistrate. The hon. member had referred to the return[2] of a later period, in which, no doubt, the name of Colman appeared as having not filed information[3], not having lodged a deposition, but simply of having obtained a summons against Police-constable Greenwood.

Mr. BRADLAUGH.—I put a question to the right hon. gentleman with reference to that. I asked him whether on the 2nd or 3rd of December four depositions were not filed in support of the charges—Colman, White, Crawford, another—and whether office copies of those documents were not taken by the Treasury on the following day. The names of Crawford, White, Colman, and another were all used by me in debate in this House.

Mr. MATTHEWS said the names used by the hon. member were Colman, Ellis, Morris, Sullivan, Cruickshank.

Mr. BRADLAUGH.—Those are the witnesses to the assaults.

Mr. MATTHEWS.—No; I have the hon. member's speech before me. The hon. member cited those persons as persons who had been assaulted by the police, as having been cuffed and kicked by constables at the station. There were three distinct charges which had never been investigated before a magistrate or a Court of justice, and he told the hon. member at the time that if he would bring before him anything like a *primâ facie* case with regard to any one of those men he would instruct the Director of Public Prosecutions to prosecute the policemen who were charged with conduct of this kind. (Cheers.) What other satisfactory inquiry could he offer? He was continually obliged to address inquiries to the chief constables and superintendents of police, and to take the best information upon them; but those were not satisfactory inquiries. They were hole-and-corner inquiries, and were conducted by men animated by a feeling of *esprit de corps*, who wished to stand by their subordinates, and who did not admit that there had been any misconduct at all. In proportion to the gravity of the charge must be the satisfactory character of the inquiry establishing it. This was why, when the hon. member brought forward these charges, he had told him, perhaps with too much warmth, that this was not the

1. *A primâ facie case*, une accusation avec une certaine apparence de probabilité. — 2. *The return of a later period*, le rapport plus récent. — 3. *To file information*, faire une dénonciation.

way to have these charges investigated, but that the proper course to pursue was for those who brought the charges to apply to a magistrate for summonses[1]. (Hear, hear.) In the case at Bow-street which was dismissed with heavy costs upon the parties not being there to adduce any evidence in support of their charges, these heavy costs were imposed by the magistrate to indicate his opinion of the conduct of those who brought charges such as these against the police, so as to raise a prejudice against them, but without any evidence or even intention to support them. (Hear, hear.) He quite agreed with the hon. member that the conduct of the police was a matter to be keenly scrutinized, and that any brutality on their part ought to be sternly put down (hear, hear), but in proportion to the gravity of the charge was the importance of having a full, fair, and public inquiry before one of the magistrates of the land. (Hear, hear.) He hoped that the hon. member, who was a fair-minded[2] man, would regard this as a satisfactory answer to the point he had raised. (Hear, hear.) He did not propose to follow the hon. gentleman into a discussion of the Trafalgar-square incidents of last year. They had already, he thought, been adequately discussed. He had nothing to retract from what he formerly said on the subject, and he fully accepted the responsibility for what was then done. No one regretted more than he did certain circumstances that then occurred. But it was absolutely necessary to restore order (hear, hear), and he rejoiced greatly in the admirable good sense shown by the great majority of the inhabitants of London with regard to this matter, who set their faces against the proceedings that were then taking place and becoming both a danger and a nuisance. It was satisfactory to reflect that now means had been found of keeping Trafalgar-square in a peaceful and orderly state. (Hear, hear.) With these few remarks he would pass to other and less stirring points raised by the hon. member. Complaint had been made of the police in regard to the distribution of voting papers under the Free Libraries Act. It ought to be borne in mind that this was no part of the police, but it had been undertaken for the sake of convenience. The explanation of the circumstance to which the hon. member referred appeared to be that a ratepayers' association sent round boys or men to deliver hand-bills, urging a certain view as to the advisability of free libraries, and these men or boys frequently accompanied the constable and delivered the hand-bill at the same time as he delivered the voting paper. If, in some cases the constable did himself deliver both, this was really a very insignificant matter. The hon. member for Northampton told him that Schumacher was compelled by the police to sign a statement, and asked why he had denied it. He called for a report from the local inspector, in whose presence the paper was signed, and it appeared that there was not the slightest ground for saying that the man was forced to sign the paper, after which he was released. The man was released not for having signed the statement, but because he had given an explanation of an apparently suspicious circumstance. The man made the explanation, and the police asked him whether he would sign it, and he did so.

Mr. BRADLAUGH observed that when the charge was entered it should have

1. *Summons*, mandat de comparution. — 2. *Fair-minded*, loyal.

gone before the magistrate in a proper way, and the police should not have released the man upon a statement signed by him.

Mr. MATTHEWS said he quite agreed with the hon. gentleman, and the inspector was reprimanded for what had been done.

Mr. MONTAGU explained the circumstances under which he desired the inspector of police at Leman-street Police-station to offer a reward of £100 on his behalf for the discovery of the criminal who had committed four or five atrocious murders in his constituency[1][5] He made his offer on the 10th of September, and it was not until the 17th that he received a letter from the Assistant Commissioner of Police, Scotland-yard, informing him that the Home Secretary did not consider it advisable that a reward should be offered. He complained of the delay which had occurred, and thought that if a reward had been promptly offered it might have been attended with good results. There was no doubt that this wild beast[2] had a lair, and somebody might have seen him going to it.

Mr. LAWSON said that the Home Secretary, in his reply to the hon. member for Northampton, had dealt with occurrences of the past. What was wanted was information about the policy of the future, especially in view of the resignation of Sir Charles Warren. Londoners wished that the police should be a civilian force under civilian head; but during the last two or three years it had been more and more militarized. There had been a systematic attempt to separate the police from the people, and much friction had been caused between the head of the force and the local authorities. Attempts had been made to lodge constables in barracks, and rules for enlistment had been made which practically excluded from the force any but old soldiers.

Mr. FIRTH agreed with the last speaker as to the necessity of a change in regard to the control of the police of the metropolis.

Mr. C. GRAHAM rose to make some remarks, but

It being now 12 o'clock, progress was reported in accordance with the standing order, and the House resumed.

REPORT OF SUPPLY[3].

The report of Supply was brought up and agreed to.

PLACES OF WORSHIP SITES BILL.

This Bill was withdrawn.

The House adjourned at five minutes past 12 o'clock.

Mr. Bryce, M. P., who has gone to India, has paired with[4] Mr. W. H. Hornby, M. P., for the autumn Session.

---

1. *M. Montagu* est membre du Parlement pour la ville de Londres dans le district de Whitechapel. — 2. *This wild beast,* cette bête sauvage, c'est-à-dire le meurtrier de Whitechapel. — 3. *The Report of supply,* le rapport sur les subsides votés. — 4. *Has paired with,* a annulé son vote contre celui de. Nous avons dit plus haut que dans le Parlement anglais il n'est pas permis aux membres présents de mettre dans l'urne un bulletin de vote au nom d'un membre absent. Quand un membre du Parlement est obligé de s'absenter et qu'il ne veut pas que son absence fasse du tort à son parti par l'absence de son vote, il cherche un membre du parti opposé également désireux de s'absenter, et ils s'engagent tous les deux à s'abstenir de voter pendant un temps déterminé. Cela s'appelle *pairing off,* s'en aller à deux. 5 ses commettants. son district électoral. sa circonscription.

PARLIAMENTARY NOTICE.

HOUSE OF COMMONS, WEDNESDAY, NOV. 14.

ORDER OF THE DAY.

Supply,—Committee.

COURT CIRCULAR.

BALMORAL[1], Nov. 13.

The Queen and Princess Beatrice, attended by the Hon. Ethel Cadogan and the Hon. Marie Adeane, drove yesterday through Braemar to Allan-a-Quoich.

MR. CRICHTON BROWNE[2]. — A telegram from Tangier announces that Mr. Crichton Browne, who was left by Mr. Joseph Thomson at Casablanca on October 14, reached Fez on October 30, safe and well. All was quiet on his route, and he neither saw nor heard anything of the rumoured disturbances in the Forest of Mamora, through which he passed.

HYDERABAD[3]. — It is stated that the Nawab[4] Mehdi Hasan, Chief Justice of Hyderabad, has been offered by telegraph and has accepted the important post of Home Secretary of the State[5]. The Nawab is now in this country representing the Nizam's Government in the negotiations respecting the Deccan mining concession[6]. The Home and Financial portfolios rank next to the Prime Ministership.

EDUCATION IN SCOTLAND. — A meeting of the Committee of Council on Education in Scotland was held yesterday at Dover-House, Whitehall. There were present the Lord President, the Marquis of Lothian, K. T. (Vice-President), the Chancellor of the Exchequer, the Right Hon. Sir Francis Sandford, K. C. B., the Lord Advocate, and Mr. Henry Craik, C. B. (Secretary).

DEATH OF SIR RICHARD BAGGALLAY.

The Right Hon. Sir Richard Baggallay, who sat as Lord Justice of Appeal till the latter part of the year 1885, and then resigned his seat, owing

1. Propriété et séjour favori de la reine en Écosse. — 2. Voyageur anglais dans le Maroc. — 3. *Hyderabad*, capitale des États du Nizam, roi dans le Dekkan septentrional. Les Anglais y tiennent garnison et y sont représentés par un résident. — 4. *Nawab*, vice-roi *ou* administrateur. — 5. *The State*, l'Etat du Nizam. — 6. *The Deccan mining concession*, la commission chargée d'examiner la concession des mines faite par le Nizam, concession qui a donné lieu à beaucoup de scandale à la Bourse de Londres. C'est un agent hindou, Abdul Nuck, qui a été la cause principale de ce scandale ; il a dû rembourser au Nizam toutes les actions et tout l'argent qu'il avait indûment reçus, et le gouvernement du Nizam a promis de maintenir la concession.

to ill-health, died yesterday morning at Brighton at the age of 72. The late Lord Justice suffered from weakness of the heart, which was, as usual, accompanied by other internal disorders; had gone to Brighton for the sea breezes, and had there lain ill for some time, but the end came unexpectedly. He will be generally deplored as a most courteous, kindly, and careful Judge, whose amiability and fine sense of justice made him generally beloved by his learned brethren and by those who practised before them.

THE WHITECHAPEL MURDERS.

In the Holborn casual ward[1] yesterday the police arrested a man who gave the name of Thomas Murphy. He was taken to the police station at Frederick-street, King's-cross-road, where, on being searched, he was found to have in his possession a somewhat formidable looking knife with a blade about ten inches long. He was therefore detained in custody on suspicion, and the police proceeded to make inquiries into the truth of his statements. The task was rendered very difficult by the confused and contradictory accounts which Murphy gave of himself, and the man was still in custody at 6 o'clock yesterday evening. Murphy is about 5ft. 6in. in height, and has the general appearance of a sailor. His hair and complexion are fair. He is dressed in a blue jersey[2] tucked underneath his trousers, and his coat and trousers are of a check pattern.4

Another man was arrested late yesterday afternoon in the neighbourhood of Dorset-street, but was released on inquiries being satisfactorily answered.

The funeral of the murdered woman Kelly will not take place until after the arrival from Wales of some of her relatives and friends, who are expected to reach London this evening. If they be unable to provide the necessary funeral expenses, Mr. Wilton, of 119, High-street, Shoreditch, has guaranteed that the unfortunate woman shall not be buried in a pauper's grave[3]. Any person, however, who may be desirous of sharing the expense with Mr. Wilton can communicate with him. The remains, according to present arrangements, will be interred either on Thursday or Friday at the new Chingford Cemetery.

The following statement was made yesterday evening by George Hutchinson, a labourer: —

" At 2 o'clock on Friday morning I came down Whitechapel-road into

1. *In the Holborn casual ward*, dans la salle des accidents de l'hôpital de Holborn (Londres). — 2. *Jersey*, vareuse. — 3. *In a paupers grave*, dans la fosse commune. 4 Dessin à carreaux

Commercial-street. As I passed Thrawl-street I passed a man standing at the corner of the street, and as I went towards Flower and Dean-street I met the woman Kelly, whom I knew very well, having been in her company a number of times. She said, 'Mr. Hutchinson, can you lend me sixpence?' I said I could not. She then walked on towards Thrawl-street, saying she must go and look for some money. The man who was standing at the corner of Thrawl-street then came towards her and put his hand on her shoulder and said something to her, which I did not hear, and they both burst out laughing. He put his hand again on her shoulder, and they both walked slowly towards me. I walked on to the corner of Fashion-street, near the public house. As they came by me his arm was still on her shoulder. He had a soft felt hat on, and this was drawn down somewhat over his eyes. I put down my head to look him in the face, and he turned and looked at me very sternly, and they walked across the road to Dorset-street. I followed them across and stood at the corner of Dorset-street. They stood at the corner of Miller's-court for about three minutes. Kelly spoke to the man in a loud voice, saying, 'I have lost my handkerchief.' He pulled a red handkerchief out of his pocket and gave it to Kelly, and they both went up the court together. I went to look up the court to see if I could see them, but could not. I stood there for three-quarters of an hour, to see if they came down again, but they did not, and so I went away. My suspicions were aroused by seeing the man so well dressed, but I had no suspicion that he was the murderer. The man was about 5ft. 6in. in height, and 34 or 35 years of age, with dark complexion and dark moustache turned up at the ends. He was wearing a long dark coat trimmed with astrachan, a white collar with black necktie, in which was affixed a horse-shoe pin. He wore a pair of dark spats[1] with light buttons over buttoned boots, and displayed from his waistcoat a massive gold chain. His watch chain had a big seal with a red stone hanging from it. He had a heavy moustache curled up, and dark eyes and bushy eyebrows. He had no side whiskers, and his chin was clean shaven. He looked like a foreigner. I went up the court and stayed there a couple of minutes, but did not see any light in the house or hear any noise. I was out last night until 3 o'clock looking for him. I could swear to the man anywhere. The man I saw carried a small parcel in his hand about 8in. long and it had a strap round it. He had it tightly grasped in his left hand. It looked as though it was covered with dark American cloth. He carried in his right hand, which he laid upon the woman's shoulder, a pair of brown kid gloves. He walked very softly. I believe that he lives in the neighbourhood, and I fancied that I saw him in Petticoat-lane on Sunday morning, but I was not

1. *A pair of dark spats*, des guêtres de couleur foncée.

certain. I went down to the Shoreditch mortuary to-day and recognized the body as being that of the woman Kelly, whom I saw at 2 o'clock on Friday morning. Kelly did not seem to me to be drunk, but was a little bit spreeish[1]. After I left the court I walked about all night, as the place where I usually sleep was closed. I am able to fix the time, as it was between 10 and 5 minutes to 2 o'clock as I came by Whitechapel Church. When I left the corner of Miller's-court the clock struck 3 o'clock. One policeman went by the Commercial-street end of Dorset-street while I was standing there, but not one come down Dorset-street. I saw one man go into a lodging-house in Dorset-street, and no one else. I have been looking for the man all day."

The description of the murderer given by Hutchinson agrees in every particular with that already furnished by the police and published yesterday morning.

At a late hour last night the man Murphy was still in custody, and he will be detained until the result of police inquiries into his antecedents, which are being conducted at Gravesend, Woolwich, and other places, is known.

BOULEVARDS[2] FOR LONDON.

Every one who knows London is familar with long stretches of road faced on either side by rows of houses of three or four stories, built of London brown brick, and standing behind gardens or fore-courts, some thirty or forty feet in depth. Such rows of houses and gardens are a leading feature of some of the main thoroughfares out of London—for example, the Brixton and Clapham roads; they are to be found again in the long reaches of the Euston and Marylebone roads; and they formerly abounded in many streets where they no longer exist. Too often, their history might thus be told. As London spread, and smoke, dirt, and noise increased, they were forsaken by private residents, and the gardens which were once trim with grass-plots, flower-beds, and shrubs, became neglected weed-beds or well-worn play-grounds. Then some one ran out a shop on the ground floor, to the edge of the pavement. His example was soon followed, and, before long, the row of houses looked down upon shop-roofs instead of garden ground. For some time the old line was preserved in the upper stories. But after a while, as space became more valuable, houses and projecting shops were,

1. *Spreeish*, mot populaire, signifiant gai. — 2. Sauf peut-être la magnifique voie connue sous le nom de *The Thames Embankment*, et malgré les routes magnifiques qui passent entre les deux parcs, Londres ne possède pas de *boulevards* proprement dits, c'est-à-dire de larges voies d'une grande longueur et bordées de chaque côté par de belles maisons et de riches magasins.

one by one, replaced by buildings rising some forty or fifty feet from the footway. The road, in consequence, instead of passing as formerly between two open spaces, now runs in a comparatively narrow channel between high walls. The airy thoroughfare has become a close street.

That the process of evolution is so gradual is probably due in great part to certain provisions of the Metropolis Management Acts. The question is, whether these provisions cannot and ought not to be used to make the transformation altogether impossible. Even before the present reign, which has seen the infancy, if not the birth, of local government, precautions existed against undue interference with the uniformity of the street line. The first Act which constituted the Metropolitan Board[1], thirty-three years ago, laid down a definite rule on the subject. But these provisions were not considered sufficient. In 1862 they were repealed, and it was enacted, that no building, structure, or erection should, without the consent in writing of the Metropolitan Board of Works, be erected beyond the general line of buildings in any street, place, or row of houses, where the distance of such line of buildings from the highway does not exceed 50ft. Where the distance is greater, 50 feet from the highway is to be kept clear; and where there is a doubt as to where the general line of buildings runs, the superintending architect of the Board is to decide where it is. As if to show clearly that the rule is to apply to such rows of houses as we have described, the reference to the line of building is explained by the following phrase, of somewhat curious grammar, " notwithstanding there being gardens or vacant spaces between the line of buildings and the highway ". Further the Board is empowered, if it should give its consent to any advance upon the general line, to annex any condition to the enjoyment of such permission; and a recent Act (passed in 1882) especially authorizes the Board to require that the owner who seeks to use up the air-space previously enjoyed by wayfarers shall, as the price of the desired permission, dedicate a part of his land to the public. If, for example, allowed to advance his building ten feet, he may be required to throw the remaining twenty or thirty feet of the old garden into the highway. Finally, the fullest powers are given both to the Metropolitan Board and to the vestry, or district board, of the neighbourhood to enforce the line of frontage, and to require the fulfilment of any prescribed conditions.

Few provisions could be better adapted for preserving the airiness of London streets, and securing the formation of noble boulevards. But to

1. *The Metropolitan Board of works,* la direction des travaux de la métropole. Cette commission, établie en 1855, qui cessa d'exister le 31 mars 1889, a fait de grands travaux à Londres et a grandement embelli et assaini la ville. Mais une enquête faite devant une commission royale a ébranlé, jusqu'à un certain point, la confiance qu'on avait dans son administration. La direction des travaux de la ville est confiée désormais au *London County Council,* auquel on a alloué de grands pouvoirs d'administration.

what use have they been put? They have been employed, as we have seen, to retard the advance of the building frontage; but that is all. They have led to that curious projection of shops from the lower floors of private houses which we have described, and for a time they have preserved a certain cubic space of air over the shop-roofs. They never seem to have been used to keep back permanently the whole building line, nor to bring about the formation of a broad leafy thoroughfare[1]. Private interests have weighed with the Board more heavily than the claims of that impersonal suitor, the public. While money has been spent in acquiring parks and laying out gardens, a means of securing, at little or no expense, a large area of open land in the most frequented districts, has been wholly neglected. Certain private persons have been endowed with so many additional square feet of building land, the value of which has probably, through deterioration in the character of the road, been reduced in proportion to the area gained; and London has been deprived of fresh air and has lost what might have been handsome avenues, keeping the town sweet and giving pleasure alike to the resident and the passer-by.

But the mischief is not yet beyond repair[2]. There are still some roads of importance, notably the Euston and Marylebone roads, where the general line is for long distances that of the old houses. In the Euston-road one or two excrescences have, unhappily, been allowed in the neighbourhood of St. Pancras Station; but from this point until we approach Gower-street the old gardens still exist. Their depth on either side must be nearly 40ft., and the road is further broken by Euston-square. Between Gower-street and Portland-street, where the old lines of building can still be seen to have been set back like those already passed, shops have been run out and buildings advanced till every particle of green has vanished, and the road, departing from its original design, has been converted into an ill-formed and unattractive street. Park-crescent comes as a pleasant contrast, and, beyond, the road again assumes its leafy character, which it preserves in the main till it loses itself in Oxford and Cambridge terraces. Thus, with a single break of ill-arranged bricks and mortar, the northernmost of London's three arterial thoroughfares[3] still runs between trees and gardens. But if it is to be saved from degradation no time must be lost. In St. Pancras the houses have already ceased to be occupied as private residences. Some appear to be let out in tenements[4], and others are occupied for business purposes. It is just the time in the history of such roads, when the Board is besought to recognize the change in the character of the neighbourhood

1. *A broad leafy thoroughfare*, une voie large bordée d'arbres. *Leaf*, feuille. — 2. *Beyond repair*, sans remède, ce qui ne peut être réparé. — 3. *The northernmost of London's three arterial thoroughfares*, la plus septentrionale des trois grandes artères de Londres. — 4. *To be let out in tenements*, être loué en appartements séparés.

and to allow shops to be run out. It is even rumoured that a public institution—and such are often the worst sinners against the public weal—has already obtained leave to run up a lofty building far in advance of the general line. If such an encroachment is allowed to pass without protest, the difficulties of maintaining and improving the character of the road will be greatly increased.

On the other hand, what an opportunity exists for the formation of a handsome boulevard! The Board has only to exercise the powers confided to it, and no building can be protruded into the eighty feet of open land through which the road passes. One of two things must then happen. Either the houses will be occupied as private residences and the gardens used by the occupants, in which case the public will enjoy the sight of trees and shrubs and the free circulation of air; or the owners and occupiers, being anxious for business purposes to bring their buildings to the edge of the footway, will come to terms with the Board. The garden ground being comparatively worthless as private property, the Board will be able to secure the whole or the greater part of it at a nominal price. Thirty or forty feet on either side of the road will give room for a double row of trees, with seats and broad sideways. It is difficult to see why London should not have its boulevards equally with Paris and other capitals. At present there is scarcely a street to which the name can be properly applied, for the Thames Embankment is not a street, and though there are trees in the Northumberland-avenue, the houses on either side have been suffered to run to such a height that what ought to have been a handsome approach to the "finest site in Europe" is dwarfed into a lane. There is now an opportunity for a new departure. The situation and character of the Euston and Marylebone roads render them especially suitable for treatment as a boulevard. In position they resemble the outer ring of boulevards in Paris. They are, and must always be, much used, not only as a thoroughfare from east to west, but as an approach to the termini of the great railways of the north. Properly treated they would provide a broad line of trees separating central London from the thickly peopled suburbs of the north, and circulating fresh air between the two camps. When widened by the additional land contained in the gardens on either side they will be of a sufficient breadth to defy the pernicious effects even of the highest buildings. But they are only specimens of many roads which might be similary treated, if the central authority of London determines to use boldly and wisely its power of preserving existing building lines. It is late in the day for the Metropolitan Board to enter upon the task; to the County Council[1] will belong the opportunity of purifying and beautifying London by the

1. Voyez note 1, page 184.

formation of handsome tree-lined ways. In the meantime, the Metropolitan Board may be reasonably expected to keep things *in statu quo*, to turn a deaf ear to applications for leave to break building lines, and to hand over to its successor the broad spaces which edge so many roads and serve to keep them fresh and sweet. And it may be hoped that the societies which care for open spaces will aid the Board and its successor in securing the best results from the exercise of their powers for the protection of London streets.

THE GROSVENOR CLUB[1], 135, New Bond-street, W.[2].

This Club, which is proprietary and on a non-political basis, numbers 1,100 members. There are the usual club rooms, recently redecorated and lighted throughout by electricity. To meet the expenses of further proposed improvements by an influx of members, the Committee has resolved to temporarily suspend the entrance fee[3].

Members have free admission to the galleries during the Exhibition[4].

All members have the privilege of subscribing to the large circulating library, for the use of their families, at a reduced rate. For reading in the Club, books are supplied free of expense to members.

The Club reference library[5] is exceptionally fine.

High-class smoking and other concerts have been successfully inaugurated.

The long association of the Grosvenor Gallery with Art should render this Club attractive to artists, as well as to professional, literary, scientific, and other gentlemen.

Great attention is paid to the cuisine and to the wines.

The subscription is five guineas for town, three guineas for country members, and one guinea for residents abroad, whether military or civilian. Subscriptions paid after 1st October, 1888, will hold good until the 31st December, 1889.

The following names have recently been added to the Committee: — The Earl of Crawford and Balcarres, Lord Wantage of Lockinge, V. C., K. C. B.[6], etc., Sir Coutts Lindsay, Bart.[7], Sir Charles H. Stuart Rich, Bart., Rev. A. Wellesley Batson, Mus. Bac. Oxon[8], Edmund Yates, Esq., Joseph Barnby, Esq., Chas. Wyndham, Esq., and F. C. Burnand, Esq.

Applications for membership should be addressed to the Secretary.

THE EXCHANGES CLUB[9], 43 and 44, Albemarle-street, Piccadilly, W.

Committee. — Mr. Deputy Beard, C. C.[10] Julius E. Beerbohm, Geo. Cutt, Henry Forbes, Henry Garle, Colonel Hartnell, A. Honricks, Herbert W. Mayhow, Fred W. Munk, Walter Pallant, W. H, Pannell, C. C., W. P. Pattenden, J. Banks Pittman, H. B. Simonson, L. Sokoloski, Percy Wallace, T. L. Willis, D. Mackway Wilson.

1. *Club*, en anglais, veut dire *cercle*, et n'a pas le sens du mot *club* tel qu'on l'emploie en France, c'est-à-dire une assemblée publique s'occupant de questions politiques. — 2. *W.*, *Western postal district*. — 3. *The entrance fee*, le droit d'admission. — 4. *The Exhibition*, l'Exposition (annuelle) de peinture, qui a lieu dans les galeries du club. — 5. *Reference library*, bibliothèque de renseignements et de recherches. — 6. *V. C.*, *K. C. B.*, *Victoria Cross, Knight Companion of the Bath. The Victoria Cross* ne s'accorde qu'aux militaires. *The Order of the Bath*, l'ordre du Bain, fondé en 1399 par Henri IV, lors de son couronnement. — 7. *Bart.* c'est-à-dire *baronet*. — 8. *Mus. Bac. Oxon*, bachelier en musique de l'Université d'Oxford. — 9. *The Exchanges Club*, le Cercle des Bourses. — 10. *C. C.*, *common councillor*, conseiller municipal.

The object of the club is to promote the social intercourse and foster the interests of the members of the various London and Provincial Exchanges, merchants, and others engaged in commercial enterprise.

Many of the above committee are members of the recognized exchanges.

400 original members now joining without entrance fee.

Annual subscription—Town members, five guineas; country members, three guineas.

For particulars and application forms address the Secretary.

ASSOCIATION of IMPERIAL OTTOMAN BONDHOLDERS[1], Group 1.—The present Association is formed to enable the holders of the Converted Bonds of the Ottoman Debt, Group 1, to reap the full benefit of the arrangements made by the decree of the Imperial Ottoman Government issued in 1881, under which the Turkish securities known as Groups 1, 2, 3, and 4 were created.

Full particulars and forms of adhesion may be obtained at the office, 3, Throgmorton-avenue, London, E. C.

CITY of MONTREAL THREE per CENT. LOAN. — Messrs. Baring, Brothers and Co. are prepared to deliver part-paid SCRIP CERTIFICATES[2] of the above in EXCHANGE for LETTERS of ALLOTMENT[3].

BOROUGH of SHEFFIELD. — The Corporation of Sheffield are prepared to RECEIVE LOANS of £100 and upwards on mortgage at £3 per cent. per annum, subject to six months' notice.

Applications to be made to

BENJAMIN JONES, Borough Accountant. 8

Bridge-street, Sheffield, July 27, 1888.

CITY of LIVERPOOL. — Loans of Money.—The Corporation of Liverpool are prepared to receive LOANS on MORTGAGE for periods of three or five years at 3 per cent. and seven years at 3¼ per cent. Interest payable half-yearly by coupons. Communications to be addressed to the City Treasurer, Municipal offices, Liverpool.

By order,

GEORGE J. ATKINSON, Town Clerk.

Liverpool, October 5th, 1888.

THE MERSEY DOCKS and HARBOUR BOARD[4] are prepared to issue PERPETUAL ANNUITIES, having the effect of Permanent Stock, and also to receive Loans of Money on the security of their Bonds, for various periods at the option of the lenders.

For particulars apply to the Treasurer, Dock office, Liverpool.

By order of the Board,

EDWARD GITTINS, Secretary.

SWANSEA HARBOUR TRUST[5]. — FOUR per CENT. STOCK. — The Swansea Harbour Trustees are now issuing at par[6], in sums of £50 and upwards, a further allotment of SWANSEA HARBOUR STOCK, bearing fixed interest at four pounds per centum per annum, and redeemable at par on the 1st day of July, 1946. The interest is payable half-yearly, by warrants posted to the stockholders. The object of this issue is to replace terminable Debentures[7] now current, and about to be redeemed in pursuance of the Swansea Harbour Act, 1886.

Further particulars and forms of application may be obtained from the undersigned,

FRANCIS JAMES Clerk.

Harbour offices. Swansea.

---

1. *Bondholders,* porteurs d'obligations. — 2. *Part-paid scrip certificates,* des certificats.... du payement partiel d'actions souscrites. — 3. *Letters of allotment,* les lettres qui annoncent la répartition. — 4. *Board,* les administrateurs de. — 5. *Trust,* la commission. — 6. *At par,* au pair, c'est-à-dire à 100 livres argent pour 100 livres rentes. — 7. *Terminable Debentures,* obligations amortissables. 8 agent comptable.

THEATRE ROYAL, DRURY-LANE.
Augustus Harris, Lessee and Manager.
THIS EVENING, at 7.30. THE ARMADA : Misses Winifred Emery, Bruce, James, Neilson, and Maud Milton; Mssrs. Leonard Boyne, Lablache, Gardiner, Stevens, Beaumont, Loraine, Dawson, Dallas, and Harry Nicholls.
The unanimous praise bestowed upon this historical drama and grand spectacle by the leading Press[1] of the country is nightly endorsed[2] by crowded audiences.

HAYMARKET THEATRE.
Lessee and Manager, M. H. Beerbohm Tree.
TO-NIGHT, at 8.30, CAPTAIN SWIFT : Mr. Tree, Mr. Macklin, Mr. Kemble, Mr. Fuller Mellish, Mr. Allan, Mr. Harwood, Mr. Harrison, and Mr. Brookfield; Lady Monckton, Miss Rose Leclercq, Miss Cudmore, and Mrs. Tree. At 7.50, THAT DREADFUL DOCTOR.
Box-office[3] opened 10 to 5. No fees[4].

ADELPHI THEATRE.
A. and S. Gatti, Sole Proprietors and Managers.
THIS EVENING, at 8, THE UNION JACK[5] : Mr. William Terriss, Messrs. C. Cartwright, J. D. Beveridge, J. L. Shine, L. Cautley, D. Somers, H. Russell, etc.; Miss Millward, Mesdames D. Dene, L. Brandon, D. Drummond, E. Bufton, and C. Jecks. At 7.15, THE LOTTERY TICKET. The Theatre lighted entirely by electricity.

PRINCESS'S THEATRE.
Lessee, Miss Hawthorne : Manager, Mr. W. W. Kelly.
THIS EVENING, at 8, HANDS ACROSS THE SEA : Messrs. Henry Neville, Robert Pateman, E. W. Garden, W. L. Abingdon, Julian Cross, Bucklaw, Gurney, Morell, Grace, Mayeur, etc.; Misses Webster, Barnard, Vizetelly, and Mary Rorke.
Morning performance[6] of HANDS ACROSS THE SEA on Saturday next Nov. 17 at 2.30.

LYCEUM THEATRE.
Sole Lessee, Mr. Henry Irving.
THIS EVENING, at 8.45, PRINCE KARL : Mr. Richard Mansfield, Messrs. Crompton, Burrows, Parry, Frankau, and Vivian; Madame Carlott Leclercq, Miss Sheridan, Miss Emerson, and Miss Beatrice Cameron. At 8, ALWAYS INTENDED.

Mr. HENRY IRVING, Miss MARION TERRY[7] and Lyceum company. GRAND THEATRE, LEEDS, TO NIGHT, FAUST. Prince of Wales's Theatre, Birmingham, Nov. 19.

1. *The leading Press*, les principaux journaux. — 2. *Endorsed*, confirmé. *To endorse a bill*, endosser un effet (de commerce). — 3. *Box-office*, bureau de location. — 4. *No fees*, pas de frais accessoires, c'est-à-dire sans frais de location. — 5. *The Union Jack*, le drapeau national (pour la marine). — 6. *Morning performance*, matinée. On se rappellera que pour les commerçants, les légistes et les employés, il y a toujours congé en Angleterre le samedi à partir de deux heures, sauf naturellement pour le commerce en détail de l'alimentation. — 7. M. Irving et Miss Terry sont aujourd'hui les plus grands acteurs tragiques en Angleterre. Ils viennent de jouer *Macbeth* à Londres avec une grande fidélité historique, une magnificence extraordinaire de décors et un talent hors ligne.

CRYSTAL PALACE THEATRE.

THIS EVENING, at 7.30. IT'S NEVER TOO LATE TO MEND[1]. Messrs. James Fernandez, Percy Lindal, Royce Carleton, T. C. Bindloss, Basset Roe. W. E. Blatchley, William Herbert, Perceval Clark, Reuben Inch, J. Aylmer; also F. W. Irish and J. G. Grahame; Miss Minnie Inch and Miss Fanny Enson. Seats 1s. to 5s. 1,000 seats at 1s.

GAIETY THEATRE.

THIS EVENING, at 7.40, "LOT 49." At 8.30, FAUST UP TO DATE[2] : Miss Florence St. John, Miss Fanny Robina, Miss Jenny M' Nulty, Miss Lillian Price, Miss E. Broughton, Miss M. Jones, Miss F. Levey, Miss A. Young, Miss E. Greville, Miss M. Love; Mr. E. J. Lonnen, Mr. H. Parker, Mr. C. Maude, Mr. W. Lonnen, and Mr. George Stone.

GLOBE THEATRE.

Lessee and Manager, Mr. John Lart.

TO-NIGHT, at 8.30, THE MONKS' ROOM : Messrs. E. S. Willard, Hermann Vezin, Forbes Dawson, Stephen Caffrey, Ivan Watson, Edward Rose, A. J. Byde, Edwin Shepherd, etc.; Mesdames Alma Murray, Helen Leyton, Marion Lea, E. H. Brooke, May Whitty, De Sola, etc. At 8, THAT TELEGRAM.

VAUDEVILLE THEATRE.

TO-NIGHT, at 8.30, JOSEPH'S SWEETHEART. At 7.45, THE BROTHERS. Mr. Thomas Thorne, Messrs. W. Rignold, F. Thorne, Maude, Blythe, Buist, Grove, Gillmore, and Mr. H. B. Conway; Mesdames K. Rorke, G. Homfrey, M. A. Giffard, Banister, B. Harrison, R. M'Neill, Bowman, Adlercron, Maunders, G. Arnold, etc.

SAVOY THEATRE.

Sole Proprietor and Manager,
R. D'Oyly Carte.

TO-NIGHT, at 8.15. THE YEOMEN[3] OF THE GUARD : or, The Merryman[4] and his Maid : Messrs. George Grossmith, Richard Temple, W. H. Denny, Shirley, W. A. Brownlow, and Courtice Pounds; Mesdames Geraldine Ulmar, Jessie Bond, R. Hervey and Rosina Brandram. At 7.20. MRS. JARRAMIE'S GENIE.

TOOLE'S THEATRE.

Lessee, Mr. J. L. Toole.

TO-NIGHT, at 8-15, PEPITA : Mesdames Wadman, Kate Cutler, Alma Stanley: Messrs. Horace Lingard, Frank Wyatt, Walker Marnock, Frank Seymour, Lytton Grey, etc. Conductor, Mons. Aug. Van Biene.

OPERA COMIQUE.

TO-DAY, at 2.30 and 8.15, CARINA : Mesdames C. d'Arville, J. Findlay, A. Dores, J. Dene, B. Murray, F. Wilmos, and A. Lethbridge; Messrs. Durward Lely, G. H. Snazelle, E. D. Ward, W. Guise, Eric Thorne, H. Halley, and C. Collette. At 7.30, THE BLACKSMITH'S DAUGHTER; For cast[5] see under clock.

COURT THEATRE.

Proprietors, Mrs. John Wood and Mr. Arthur Chudleigh.

TO-NIGHT, at 9, MAMMA[6], Mr. John Hare, Mr. Charles Groves, Mr. Eric Lewis, and Mr. Arthur Cecil; Miss Annie Hugues; Miss Filippi, Miss Caldwell, Miss Brough, and Mrs. John Wood. Preceded, at 8, by COX AND BOX : Mr. Deane Brand, Mr. Lugg, and Mr. Eric Lewis.

1. *It's never too late to mend*, " il n'est jamais trop tard pour se corriger ", pièce tirée d'un roman du même nom par Charles Reade, où l'auteur expose les abus qui peuvent exister dans les maisons de santé (pour les fous). — 2. *Faust up to date*, Faust comme il serait de nos jours. — 3. *The yeomen*, les soldats. — 4. *The Merryman*, le bouffon. — 5. *For cast*, pour la distribution des rôles. — 6. *Mamma*, maman, pièce tirée des *Surprises du divorce*, jouée au Vaudeville en 1888.

COMEDY THEATRE.

THIS EVENING, at 9, UNCLES AND AUNTS : Messrs. W. S. Penley, T. G. Warren, Wilfred Draycott, W. F. Hawtrey, Walter Everard, and W. Lestocq; Misses Cissy Grahame, Maria Daly, Caroline Elton, Kate Lee, Miss Scarlett. Preceded, at 8.10, by BARBARA.

ROYALTY THEATRE.

FRENCH PLAYS.—Sole Manager, Mr. M. L. Mayer.

THIS EVENING, at 8.30, CLARA SOLEIL : Mdlle. Aimée Martial, Mdlle. Charlotte Raynard, Mdlle. Dick; MM. Dalbert, Schey, Dolnay, Feroumont, Lagrange, and Charton.

CRITERION THEATRE.

Lessee and Manager, Mr. Chas. Whyndham.

THIS EVENING, at 8, BETSY : Messrs. W. Blakeley, H. Standing, A. Maltby, A. Boucicault, Cecil Bartir, and Geo. Giddens; Mesdames Rose Saker, F. Robertson, M. Viney, F. Moore, E. Penrose, and Lottie Venne. Preceded by, at 8.10, THE DOWAGER. Doors open at 7.45.—N. B. Stage and auditorium[1] lighted entirely by electricity.

AVENUE THEATRE.

Manager, Mr. H. Watkin.

THIS EVENING, at 8.15, NADGY : Miss Giulia Warwick, Miss Clara Graham, Miss Florence Melville, Miss Sallie Turner, and Mdlle. Vanoni; Mr. J. J. Dallas, Mr. Joseph Tapley, Mr. Alec Marsch, Mr. Leon Roche, and Mr. Arthur Roberts. Preceded by QUITS.

PRINCE OF WALES' THEATRE.

Sole Lessee and Manager, Mr. Horace Sedger.

TO-NIGHT, at 8.30, DOROTHY : Mdmes. Marie Tempest, Florence Perry, H. Coveney, F. Neville, and Amy Augorde; Messrs. Bell Davies, Furneaux Cook, Arthur Williams, John Le Hay, S. King, and C. Hayden Coffin. At 7.40, WARRANTED BURGLAR PROOF[2].

The safest theatre in London, constructed entirely with concrete[3] and iron. Absolutely fire proof. Lighted throughout with electricity.

TERRY'S THEATRE.

Sole Lessee and Manager, Mr. Edward Terry.

TO-NIGHT, at 8.30, SWEET LAVENDER : Messrs. Edward Terry, Alfred Bishop, Brandon Thomas, F. Kerr, H. Beeves Smith, Sant Matthews, Prince Miller; Mesdames M. A. Victor, Carlotta Addison, Maude Millett, and Blanche Horlock. Acting Manager, Mr. H. F. Brickwell.

SHAFTESBURY THEATRE.

Proprietor, Mr. John Lancaster.

THIS EVENING, at 8, AS YOU LIKE IT[4] : Miss Wallis, Mesdames Annie Rose, Kate Fayne, Edward Saker; Messrs. William Farren, Mackintosh, A. Stirling, Crauford, Seymour Jackson, C. Cooper, J. Buckstone, Allen Thomas, Matthew Brodie, C. Arnold, S. Harcourt, Fenwick, and Forbes Robertson.

SHAFTESBURY. THE LADY OF LYONS[5], will be played on Saturday evening next and following evenings at 8.15.

1. *Stage and auditorium,* la scène et toute la salle. — 2. *Warranted Burglar proof,* Garanti à l'épreuve des voleurs. — 3. *Concrete,* béton. — 4. *As you like it,* "Comme il vous plaira," comédie de Shakespeare. — 5. *The Lady of Lyons, or Love and Pride,* La Dame de Lyon, ou l'Amour et l'Orgueil, par lord Bulwer Lytton, célèbre romancier et auteur dramatique, père de lord Lytton, l'ambassadeur actuel de l'Angleterre, connu également comme poète et écrivain distingué. *The Lady of Lyons* est une histoire tirée des événements de la Révolution française, que nos jeunes gens trouveront d'une lecture fort agréable.

NOTICES.

THE LOCAL GOVERNMENT ACT[2]. — *Now ready, the Series of Explanatory Articles which have recently appeared in The Times, price 6d., bound in cloth.*

THE SPECIAL COMMISSION. — Now ready, Parts I., II., and III. of The Times Report of the Proceedings before the Special Commission[3], *price 6d. each.*

PARNELLISM AND CRIME[4]. — *Reprints of the Two Series of Articles published under this title, of the Facsimile Page from the Irish World of the alleged Facsimile Letter of Mr. Parnell on the Phœnix Park Murders, and of the articles entitled " Behind the Scenes in America, " are now on sale, and may be had by application to the Publisher, price 1d. each. Also the above in one volume, bound in cloth, price 1s.*

O'DONNELL v. WALTER[5]. — *A Full Report of this case, reprinted from The Times, is now ready, price 2d.*

A VISIT TO THE STATES. — The Two Series of Letters under this title are now ready, bound in cloth, price 1s. each volume.

THE TIMES PARLIAMENTARY DEBATES, arranged in a convenient form for binding, will be issued every Monday during the sitting of Parliament. Price 1s., or 25s. per annum, post free. Annual subscription for bound volumes — half bound in morocco leather, £3 10s.; cloth, lettered, £2 10s. Vols. I. and II. of the Lords, and Vols. I., II., III., IV., V., VI., VII., VIII., and IX. of the Commons, are now ready.

1. *Antiope*, reine des Amazones, épouse de Thésée, et mère d'Hippolyte. — 2. Voy. note 3, page 54. — 3. Le procès de Parnell contre *the Times*. Voy. note 1, p. 55. — 4. Ce sont les articles du *Times* où ce journal accusait M. Parnell, chef du mouvement pour l'indépendance de l'Irlande (*the Home Rule*), d'avoir encouragé les assassins de lord Cavendish, vice-roi d'Irlande, et les Parnellistes d'avoir organisé un système de coercition et d'intimidation en Irlande, soutenu et mis à exécution par le " boycottage, " l'assassinat et la violence. — 5. *O'Donnell v. Walter*, le procès de *O'Donnell*, membre du Parlement, contre *Walter*, propriétaire du *Times*, à la suite duquel le *Times* a été acquitté et O'Donnell a été condamné aux frais.

THE TIMES WEEKLY EDITION, price 2d., is issued every Friday morning, containing all that is of special or lasting interest in the editions of The Times of that and the five previous days, and printed in a form suitable for binding as an annual volume, or for postal transmission abroad.

THE MAIL, a reproduction of the substance of The Times, with the Latest Intelligence, appears on Monday, Wednesday, and Friday in each week. Price 2d.

Advertisers are requested not to send stamps. Post-office orders to be made payable to Mr. GEORGE EDWARD WRIGHT, at the Chief Office.

News Agents in the country can be supplied with papers from this Office, carriage paid to their railway stations, on condition of their selling at 3d. per copy.

The Times is sold for 3d. per copy at all railway bookstalls in England and Wales. Persons who cannot obtain it at that price are requested to communicate with the Publisher.

The Times will be forwarded by Inland Post to subscribers desirous of receiving it through that channel[1] on payment of £1 quarterly in advance. Subscribers residing within the London Postal District have *The Times* delivered to them by the first post. Applications should be addressed only to the Publisher at *The Times* Office.

TO CORRESPONDENTS.

No notice can be taken of anonymous communications. Whatever is intended for insertion must be authenticated by the name and address of the writer, not necessarily for publication, but as a guarantee of good faith.

We cannot undertake to return rejected communications.

LONDON, WEDNESDAY, NOVEMBER 14, 1888.

In the House of Lords last evening[2],

LORD SAVILE (SIR JOHN SAVILE) took the oath and signed the roll on his elevation to the peerage.

On the motion of LORD GRANVILLE the Victoria University Bill was read a third time and passed.

LORD SPENCER, in moving the second reading of the Oaths Bill, remarked on the great change which had occurred in public opinion in respect of oaths since the comparatively recent date when the subject of the oaths taken by members of Parliament was one which gave rise to great agitation. The Bill now before their lordships was introduced on the Opposition side[3] in the House of Commons, but the SOLICITOR-GENERAL of the present Government—in his individual capa-

1. *Through that channel*, par cette voie. — 2. Les deux articles qui suivent sont le résumé des séances de la Chambre des Pairs et de la Chambre des Communes données tout au long pages 126 à 179. On se rapportera aux notes données à ces mêmes pages. — 3. Par M. Bradlaugh.

city, it was true—assisted in passing it through that House by framing clauses and otherwise assisting the promoters. There was a great weight of authority in favour of the proposition that oaths of allegiance were of no value, and that oaths intended to secure truth had not altogether fulfilled the object for which they had been designed. He would abolish oaths of allegiance, though he was not prepared to go the length of abolishing oaths in Courts of Justice. The Bill did not go that length, but it provided that any person who objected to take an oath should be allowed to make a solemn affirmation instead of it in all cases where an oath was now required.

The Lord Chancellor believed that in Courts of Justice the oath was of great importance. Experience in these Courts showed that there were many persons who would not take an oath to an untruth which they would utter when not on oath. He proposed to move certain amendments. He viewed with jealousy the provision to enable persons to make an affirmation instead of an oath on their statement that they were of no religious belief; and on his own responsibility he would frame an amendment to prevent that in the case of jurors[1].

Lord Carnarvon concurred with the Lord Chancellor that the Bill required amendment. The affirmation to be taken under Clause 1 was a " solemn affirmation ". How could such a term as " solemn " be applied to an affirmation to be made by persons who had no religious belief?

Lord Addington regarded the Bill as a concession to unbelief and held that the country was not called upon to legislate for the relief of persons who had no religion.

The Bishop of Carlisle did not regard the measure in the light in which Lord Addington viewed it. He thought that promissory oaths by persons on their appointment to office were useless. But he agreed with the Lord Chancellor that oaths as to things past were often of importance in Courts of Justice when taken by witnesses. On the other hand, the exemption from giving any evidence at all of persons who professed no religion was frequently detrimental to justice. He would vote for the second reading.

Lord Derby looked on the Bill as one to provide that a person should not be exempted from giving evidence and from the consequences of giving it because he had no religious belief. He thought, however, that the words of Clause 1 might be altered with advantage.

Lord Granville hoped for an intimation as to the intentions of the Government with respect to the Bill after the announcement of the Lord Chancellor that he proposed to move amendments.

Lord Salisbury would follow the time-honoured custom of waiting to see the amendments which his noble and learned friend in his individual capacity had expressed his intention of moving. For himself, he had long thought that in some cases oaths were a direct invitation to profanity and irreverence.

The Bill was then read a second time, and Lord Spencer said he proposed to take the Committee on that day fortnight.

The House rose at ten minutes to 6 o'clock.

---

1. *Jurors*, jurés, membres du jury.

The House of Commons was in Committee all the evening on the Civil Service Estimates, Class III. (Law and Justice), beginning with the vote of £408,315 for the Supreme Court of Judicature.

MR. JENNINGS[1] called attention to the large number of officials in the department, and especially complained of the salaries paid to many of them, which he regarded has unnecessarily extravagant. He referred in particular to the permanent secretary and other officers of the Lord Chancellor's department, to the Principal Registrar of the Court of Probate, and to the Masters of the High Court, who, he contended, were overpaid and underworked, and to emphasize his objection to the present system, which he characterized as a gross scandal, moved the reduction of the vote by £500.

In the course of a prolonged discussion,

LORD R. CHURCHILL[2], who remarked that the "hereditary tactics" of the front bench in Committee of Supply were to delude and to humbug the House, maintained that MR. JENNINGS's statement showed that there was an absolute malversation of public money on a large scale, which he characterized as brigandage on the taxpayers of the country, and a scandal which the Committee ought not to continue. He insisted that the Government of the day ought to take notice of an act upon the reports of Commissions making economical recommendations in regard to the Estimates, and he urged the Committee to refuse the vote until the Government undertook to remedy the abuses complained of.

The ATTORNEY-GENERAL, dealing categorically with all the complaints made, blamed LORD R. CHURCHILL for the strong language he had used, which he denied was justified by the facts. The salary of the Lord Chancellor's permanent secretary had been increased, he said, because his duties had been increased, and he insisted that, having regard to the nature of those duties, he was not overpaid. He also defended the Masters at some length, and, as regarded all the complaints made, he contended that the first question to consider was whether the officers in question were required or not. If they were not needed the House should say so, but if they were needed he was satisfied that they were not overpaid, having regard to the character of the work they had to perform.

After some remarks from MR. CHILDERS and MR. LABOUCHÈRE, MR. COOKE appealed to MR. W. H. SMITH[3] to give an assurance that the subject should be inquired into, and MR. H. FOWLER, denying that the ATTORNEY-GENERAL had substantially answered the complaints made, repudiated the suggestion that the lawyers in the House were in the habit of voting exceptional sums to their own class, although he admitted that the whole vote was on a very liberal basis.

MR. JACKSON promised that useless offices should be abolished, and Mr. W. H. SMITH, remarking that the Government welcomed the assistance of the House in securing economy and efficiency, gave an assurance that none of the offices referred to should be filled on vacancies occurring unless the Government were satisfied that they were required.

On a division MR. JENNINGS's amendment was negatived by 148 to 129.

Among other subjects discussed were the holding of four assizes a year and

1. Voyez note 4, page 149. — 2. Voyez note 2, page 149. — 3. Voyez note 2, page 163.

the sending of prisoners for trial to quarter sessions; and ultimately the vote was agreed to.

On the Wreck Commission vote of £12,680, MR. JACKSON, replying to MR. SHAW-LEFEVRE, who asked what course the Government proposed to take with regard to the vacant office of Wreck Commissioner, said that no definite decision had been arrived at, but the Lord Chancellor had been asked not to fill the vacancy pending the consideration of the report of the Committee on the Saving of Life at Sea. The vote was then agreed to, as were also the votes for County Courts (£438,030), the Land Registry (£2,796), and Revising Barristers (£20,370).

On the vote for Police Courts (£17,743) a discussion arose with regard to the cell accommodation in the Metropolitan police stations, in which MR. GRAHAM, MR. STUART, MR. J. ROWLANDS, and others took part. MR. PICKERSGILL moved a reduction of the vote, but it was negatived on a division by 150 to 91, and the vote was agreed to.

The vote for the Metropolitan Police (£583,520) was under discussion at midnight, when the Committee adjourned until to-day.

The report of Supply was brought up and agreed to, and the remaining orders having been disposed of, the House adjourned at five minutes past 12 o'clock.

Before the House of Commons[1] went into Committee of Supply yesterday, the HOME SECRETARY[2] made a statement explaining more fully the circumstances of SIR CHARLES WARREN'S resignation[3]. It appears from the correspondence which MR. MATTHEWS read that the late COMMISSIONER of POLICE resigned because he declined to submit to the rule prohibiting all officials connected with the Home Department from publishing any comments or criticisms on departmental matters. Indeed, SIR CHARLES WARREN directly challenged the validity of the rule, contending not only that it was opposed to the spirit of the statutes regulating the Metropolitan Police, but that it would, if enforced, leave the Commissioner and those under his command at the mercy of any irresponsible calumniator. The resignation tendered on these grounds was accepted, with not a little alacrity, by the HOME SECRETARY. It is, however, evident that the disagreement between SIR CHARLES WARREN and MR. MATTHEWS was not confined to this point. There are traces in the correspondence of earlier friction, and attention was drawn in the House to the fact that a previous offer to resign was mentioned. The country will not be satisfied if it should be shown that SIR CHARLES WARREN, a very able and energetic public servant, who has maintained the peace in London during a most critical time, has been sacrificed not so much to the exigencies of official punctiiio as to a vicious system of dual government. Later in the evening MR. BRADLAUGH revived the old charges against SIR CHARLES WARREN and the Home Office, alleging that the attempts to hold meetings in Trafalgar-square had been suppressed with brutal violence, and that in other respects the police had been encouraged to depart from their ordinary course of duty. MR. MATTHEWS declined to go into the matter, which, he said,

1. Cet article et le suivant sont un résumé et un commentaire des séances de la Chambre des Communes et de la Chambre des Lords déjà données pages 136 à 179. — 2. *The Home Secretary*, le ministre de l'intérieur. — 3. Voy. note 2, page 173.

ought to have been investigated, if there was any charge of wrong-doing, before the Courts of law. The debate was adjourned before the division was taken on MR. BRADLAUGH'S proposal to reduce the vote for the Commissioner's salary. Meanwhile a great deal will depend upon the apointment of SIR CHARLES WARREN'S successor. Of course rumour is already prematurely busy with this or that name and speculations are ventured upon, in some quarters, in very confident and positive language. The HOME SECRETARY, however, declared yesterday that the statements he had seen upon the subject were " without any foundation in fact". It will be necessary, before any new appointment is made, to determine whether the Chief Commissioner is to be subjected to the disability against which SIR CHARLES WARREN protested, and whether he is or is not to remain responsible, not only for the force he actually controls, but for the semi-independent organization of the detective department.

The discussion of the Civil Service Estimates[1] was resumed in Committee of Supply, and the most important question considered arose on the vote of £408,315 for the Supreme Court of Judicature, which was attacked in a lively and vigorous speech by MR. JENNINGS. In the brisk debate which followed, LORD RANDOLPH CHURCHILL emerged from his retirement and laid about[2] him, in the character of a reformer and economist, with an energy that recalled to mind the days when he sat below the gangway on the Opposition side and made it his business to trouble the repose of Liberal Ministers. LORD RANDOLPH CHURCHILL has done good service in bringing to light the waste of public money and public time that is allowed to go on in too many of the departments. His extravagance of language, however, tends to spoil an excellent case, especially when, as happened yesterday, he has imperfectly mastered the facts, and is driven by lack of matter to indulge in vague and violent generalities. To justify the assertion that there existed in the expenditure[3] on legal offices " a public scandal amounting to a na- " tional disgrace", that the " hereditary tactics" of the Government consisted in " humbugging and baffling the House of Commons", and that the salaries of legal officials was " absolute brigandage on the taxpayers of the country", something more was needed than a few scraps of evidence pieced together from MR. JENNINGS'S speech. Of the latter we can speak with a good deal more respect. MR. JENNINGS undoubtedly was able to show in detail that a number of useless offices or extravagant salaries are maintained, and the ATTORNEY-GENERAL'S defence of some of them, such as those of the permanent secretary to the LORD CHANCELLOR, the Clerk of Presentations, the Purse-bearer, the Train-bearer, and so forth, does not strike us a remarkably cogent. We must, at the same time, point out that, though MR. JENNINGS made out a strong case, some at least of the remedies he suggested are of more than doubtful expediency.[4] Take for instance the case of " redundant" clerks. Unquestionably some means ought to be devised to prevent this waste of money and time. It is monstrous that men in any branch of the public service should be left with nothing to do but to kick their heels and draw their salaries. But the proposal that such redundant clerks should be treated, as MR. JENNINGS suggests, like the superfluous *employés* in a railway clearing-house[5] who are simply sent away when the work is reduced, shows a grave misconception of the conditions under which the Civil Service exists. Permanence of tenure is one of the chief compensations held

1 Crédit. 2 tapait à droite et à gauche de tous les côtés. 3 Dépense. 4. à-propos
5. salle de réunion pour la balance des comptes entre les banquiers d'une ville

out by the State to its official servants to be set against very moderate pay, and it is indispensable if a high standard of honour and integrity is to be maintained. The remedy must be sought in another direction. In the opinion of SIR THOMAS FARRER, which MR. JENNINGS quotes with approval, what is needed is a much larger power of transfer from one office to another. This, however, would involve a considerable curtailment of the independence of the department and the establishment of some controlling and regulating authority. With regard to many of the officials referred to by MR. JENNINGS, it seems clear enough that when they were originally appointed, some of them several years ago, the best bargain was not made in the interests of the taxpayers. But as they have been made, the country must keep its faith. MR. JENNINGS, indeed, contended that a job perpetrated years ago " has not improved by age ". The sarcasm, which MR. LABOUCHÈRE improved upon with characteristic boldness, strikes at the root of the doctrine of prescription, which may be said to be one of the corner-stones of civilized society.

The ATTORNEY-GENERAL'S defence of the legal appointments was sufficiently uncompromising, but it did not enter very thoroughly into some of the most important of the charges referred to in the debate. Thus it is difficult to say what can really be said in favour of the recent nominations of two official referees by the LORD CHANCELLOR when the persons previously appointed had not enough of work to do. But MR. LABOUCHÈRE was not content to leave the case where MR. JENNINGS had placed it, or even to join in LORD RANDOLPH CHURCHILL'S peremptory cry for reform. He turned aside from the discussion of the vote to attack the Government for keeping up political salaried offices. He asked what the Civil Lord of the Admiralty, MR. ASHMEAD-BARTLETT, did for his salary. " He went about the country and made Tory speeches " — which is, we suppose, what junior members of every Government under the party system are in the habit of doing; nor, we presume, did MR. LABOUCHÈRE ever object to it, say, in the case of MR. HERBERT GLADSTONE[1], when his own party was in power. For a comprehensive and thoroughly useless proposition it would not be easy to find anything to excel MR. LABOUCHÈRE'S contention that " the offices bestowed " upon friends and toadies of the Government ought to be done away with ". Fortunately, the debate was brought back to its proper subject by MR. HENRY FOWLER, who argued in favour of putting into force the recommendations of the Royal Commission and especially of increasing the daily working time in all the departments to seven hours, a change already carried into effect in the revenue departments. The SECRETARY of the TREASURY frankly recognized the moderation and the practical character of MR. FOWLER'S criticisms and avowed that he was himself in favour of the seven hours system, but, he argued, when contracts were entered into with the existing clerks the working day was fixed at six hours or less. Here we are met with the question whether such a contract, if it exists, can be or ought to be varied without the consent of the parties. The same difficulty presents itself in an even more serious form in the case of the " redundant clerks ", who have a statutory right to their salaries, even when their work has dwindled to nothing, who cannot be compelled to retire, and whom there is,

1. M. Herbert Gladstone, fils de M. William Gladstone, voy. note 1, p. 4, et note 2, p. 150.

apparently, no power of transferring to other employment. This is an unfortunate state of things, but the present Government cannot be held responsible for it, and it is in no sense the result of a "job[1]". Mr. Jennings and Lord Randolph Churchill weaken their case by misusing this term of reproach. Nevertheless, there is a growing feeling that, apart from "jobs", the interests of the taxpayers are too often neglected, and arrangements allowed to come into force, for no good reason, which tie the hands of the Government, obstruct plans of administrative reform, and make economy impossible and efficiency improbable. The discontent on the Ministerial side was apparent in the speech of Mr. Cooke, who begged the Government to give such assurances as would enable Conservative economists to vote against Mr. Jennings's amendment. Mr. W. H. Smith[2], in reply to this appeal, pledged himself that the Government would give effect to the recommendations of the report of the Royal Commission. The division was, nevertheless, a narrow one. The proposal to reduce the vote was supported by 129 members, while 148 went into the lobby with the Government. The issue was not a party one, but the Government ought to understand that, if the subject is neglected, it may hereafter furnish ample materials for envenomed party attacks.

The Oaths Bill[3] was read a second time yesterday in the House of Lords without a division. It was not very favourably received by some speakers, and the general sense of the House was probably expressed by Lord Carnarvon when he said that he should give his consent to the second reading, reluctantly and with sorrow, but should give it, nevertheless, because it was intended to close a long dispute. The Lord Chancellor, speaking for himself and not for the Government, announced his intention of moving certain amendments in Committee[4], apparently with the purpose of preventing persons who declare they have no religious belief from acting as jurors. We may follow the example of the Prime Minister[5] in saying that it will be time enough to consider these amendments in detail when we know their exact scope and purport; but it is necessary to point out at once that the Solicitor-General[6] — who, together with Mr. Bradlaugh, is responsible for the form which the Bill has now taken— argued strongly in the House of Commons against a proposal analogous to that foreshadowed[7] by the Lord Chancellor. The Lord Chancellor said that "he did not think that one who professed to have no religious belief was a proper "person to sit in judgment on his fellow-citizens". The amendment of Mr. Tomlinson, which was discussed in the House of Commons, and rejected by a majority of 191 to 97, only went so far as to give either party in a civil suit and the accused in a criminal suit the right to challenge a juror who declares that he has no religious belief. "It would be an outrageous thing," said the Solicitor-General, "that those who honestly declared themselves to be atheist should be "marked as a class who were not to come into a jury-box, while the atheist who

---

1. *Of a job*, de tripotages. — 2. *The Home Secretary*, le ministre de l'intérieur. — 3. Voy. note 1, page 127. — 4. *In Committee*, lors de la discussion des articles. — 5. Lord Salisbury, chef du parti conservateur. — 6. Voy. note 2, page 127. — 7. *Foreshadowed by the Lord Chancellor*, qu'a fait prévoir le chancelier.

"had not the honesty to declare it was to have that privilege." To this we may add that the office of juror is not always regarded as a privilege. It is not expedient to give men the opportunity of evading its duties by declaring that they have no religious belief. We cannot, therefore, think that the amendment on this point which the LORD CHANCELLOR foreshadowed yesterday is either expedient in itself or likely to prove acceptable to the House of Commons or even to the House of Lords.

Two distinct questions and two distinct forms of oath are involved in the Bill as it stands at present. If the sole object of the measure were to remove the difficulty which arose in the Parliament of 1880, there would be no serious objection to the more general form of relief which was contained in the Bill as originally introduced by MR. BRADLAUGH. The operative clause then ran, "Every "person, upon objecting to being sworn, shall be permitted to make his solemn "affirmation instead of taking an oath." But inasmuch as, with a view to the more general and final settlement of the question, the Bill was made applicable, not merely to promissory oaths, oaths of service, oaths relating to the future as the BISHOP of CARLISLE called them yesterday, but to oaths in courts of justice which require a witness to tell the truth concerning the past, it was obvious, and was admitted by MR. BRADLAUGH, that the more general form quoted above involved a dangerous laxity, which might, and probably would, tend to defeat the ends of justice. It is now generally acknowledged that promissory oaths are of no great value. A man is not constrained to obedience in such cases by his oath, but by his conscience and the legal sanctions involved; and if these will not constrain him, the oath adds little or nothing to their force. But the case of oaths of testimony is quite distinct. It is a matter of common experience that there are men who will tell a lie but will not swear a lie. It would never do to relax the hold of justice on people of this kind. If a man could relieve himself from the obligation of telling the exact truth in the witness-box by simply saying that he objected to being sworn, and thereby escaping the necessity of making oath, it is certain that perjury and false witness would be far more common in courts of justice than they are at present. For this reason MR. BRADLAUGH, very properly in our opinion, consented to introduce after the words "objecting to being sworn" the words "and stating, as the ground of "such objection, either that he has no religious belief, or that the taking of an "oath is contrary to his religious belief", and these words, though strenuously resisted by many speakers in the supposed interests of religious liberty, were ultimately accepted in the House of Commons by a narrow majority[1]. Thus the Bill stands as a compromise. MR. BRADLAUGH loyally adhered to his understanding with the SOLICITOR-GENERAL, and steadfastly resisted the pressure of those who professed to be more earnest in the cause of religious liberty than himself. If the objection to being sworn is to be based, as the interests of justice require it to be based, on scruples which can be honestly and honourably avowed, the words accepted by MR. BRADLAUGH seem to contain a complete and exhaustive enumeration, by way of dichotomy[2], of the legitimate grounds of such objec-

1. *By a narrow majority*, par une petite majorité. — 2. *Dichotomy*, division par paires. M. Bradlaugh a donné deux raisons opposées l'une à l'autre.

tion. They are necessary for two purposes—to bind the conscience of the witness, and to secure the admission of his testimony. The second is even the more important purpose of the two, because as, was pointed out in the debate, the evidence of a witness who has no religious belief is at present inadmissible in certain cases, although its absence may defeat the ends of justice even in a matter of life and death. It is not merely for the relief of conscience, therefore, that it is expedient to extend the power of making affirmation in lieu of taking an oath to persons who have no religious belief. As the PRIME MINISTER said, the person who is injured by the throwing of difficulties in the way of evidence is not the person who is unable to take the oath, but the person in whose case evidence is wanted. This is a practical inconvenience which it is necessary to remove. Some doubts were expressed in the course of the debate as to whether the words employed are sufficient or appropriate for the purpose. The word " solemn", it was urged, as applied to an affirmation has no meaning in the case of a person without religious belief. We should hesitate to go as far as this. A person without religious belief is not necessarily without a sense of the solemnity of certain acts and occasions, and it is clearly expedient that the obligation to tell the truth in a Court of justice should be invested in all cases with the utmost solemnity that the mind of the witness is capable of understanding and appreciating.

On the other hand, the words accepted by MR. BRADLAUGH are perhaps in some respects less appropriate to the case of promissory oaths. Unlike the oath of testimony, the promissory oath [1] is now acknowledged to be of little value. " There were a great many oaths," said LORD SALISBURY, " which not only added " no solemnity to the occasion on which they were made, but were a direct in- " vitation to profanity and irreverence." In such cases the more logical and, perhaps, the more reverent course would be to dispense with the oath altogether, and this is what LORD SPENCER, who introduced the Bill in a very temperate and conciliatory speech, expressed his own willingness to do. But the Bill is a compromise [2], and its painful history illustrates the expediency as well as the prudence of not attempting too much at once. We have no sympathy with those who complain that to ask a man on proper occasion to declare that he has no religious belief is an infringement of religious liberty. It is far more manly to say, with MR. BRADLAUGH, that those who have no religious belief are ready to fight their own battles in the open [3], and have no desire to evade the confession so long as it carries no civil disabilities with it. But if the declaration were, as is alleged by some, calculated to create a prejudice against the persons who make it, it would perhaps be as well to seek for some form of words which might mitigate the prejudice as far as possible. That would be easy enough if the Bill

1. *The promissory oath* regarde l'avenir, tel qu'un serment de fidélité, de bien s'acquitter des fonctions qu'on accepte, etc., etc. ; *the oath of testimony*, c'est celui qu'on prête comme témoin devant une cour de justice. — 2. *The Bill is a compromise*, le projet de loi est une transaction. Il en est presque toujours ainsi en Angleterre où l'esprit est plus pratique que logique. Une réforme complète peut paraître nécessaire, mais certaines opinions, certains intérêts en seraient lésés ; on améliore, on ne réforme pas complètement, persuadé que l'on est qu'un peu plus tard l'amélioration bien démontrée entraînera la réforme. — 3. *To fight their own battles in the open*, de combattre au grand jour.

dealt with promissory oaths alone. But it is not easy, so long as promissory oaths and oaths of testimony are dealt with in the same Bill, to relieve the scruples of those who are now required to take promissory oaths without enabling dishonest witnesses in a Court of justice to secure an unrestrained liberty of lying. LORD DERBY, who spoke on the Bill with his usual frigid common sense, said that he should have thought that, instead of calling upon a man to make the declaration required by the Bill, it would have been simpler to make him say that the taking of an oath was repugnant to his conscience. For promissory oaths this is certainly all that is really needed, though there are some, no doubt, who hold that conscience can have no meaning for a man who has no religious belief. But as regards oaths of testimony the words suggested by LORD DERBY are open to the fatal objection that the Courts of law have held that conscientious objections mean religious objections, and that, therefore, no man who is devoid of religious belief can plead conscientious objections. On the whole, when we consider the history of this painful question, and the long controversy which the Bill is designed to close, we cannot but share the hope expressed by LORD DERBY, that the House of Lords will pass the Bill without material alteration. It is avowedly a compromise, and, like most compromises, it is distasteful to those who hold extreme views on either side. But it substantially effects two objects which are well worth securing. In the interests of justice it renders valid the testimony of witnesses who have no religious belief; and in the interests of public morals and public decency it renders impossible for the future such scenes as were enacted in the House of Commons when MR. BRADLAUGH first attempted to take his seat. If it is possible to render the settlement more complete and more durable without infringing the terms of the compromise or wounding the legitimate susceptibilities of either party to the dispute, so much the better; but we should regard it as a serious misfortune if, in the attempt to make the Bill more perfect, the settlement itself were made more remote.

SPORTING INTELLIGENCE[1].

DERBY NOVEMBER MEETING, TUESDAY.

QUORNDON PLATE[2] of 100 guineas. About six furlongs[3] straight[4].

Mr. Brydges Willyams's Harlow, by Plebeian[5] — Lady of the Lea, 3 yrs, 9st. 6lb.[6] (Watts)[7] 1
Mr. J. Hammond's Aintree, 4 yrs, 10st. (Rickaby) 2
Mr. D. M. O'Connor's Countess Macaroni, 3 yrs, 9st. 2lb. (North) 3

1. *Sporting intelligence*, nouvelles des courses, etc., « le Turf ». Il ne faut pas confondre ces courses d'automne, qui ont lieu à Derby, chef-lieu du comté de Derby, au centre (vers le nord), avec la course pour le Grand Prix du Derby, courue à Epsom, à 22 kilomètres de Londres, et qui est ainsi appelé parce qu'il a été fondé par le comte de Derby, en 1780. Il est bon de se rappeler que le nom patronymique de la famille des comtes de Derby est Stanley. — 2. *Plate*, pièce de vaisselle plate; c'est le prix décerné au cheval gagnant. — 3. *Six furlongs*, 1206 mètres. — 4. *Straight*, piste droite. — 5. *By Plebeian*, par Plébéien. *Plebeian* est le nom du père. — 6. *Three years*, âgé de trois ans; *nine stones, six pounds*, soit 60 kilog. 141; c'est le poids du jockey; le *stone* est 6 kilog. 349. — 7. (*Watts*). Le nom entre parenthèses est le nom du jockey.

Betting. — 85 to 40 on Harlow, and 5 to 2 agst[1] Aintree.

The favourite made all the running[2], and won easily by three lengths; bad third.

PRICRY NURSERY HANDICAP[3] PLATE of 200 sovs.[4]; winners extra.
About five furlongs, straight. 50 entries[5].

Mr. Abington's Master Bill, by Carnelion—Sword Knot, 8st. 10lb. (Watts) ... 1
Mr. A. Spalding's Grouse, 6st. 6lb. (G. Chaloner) 2
Mr. J. Waugh's Negligent, 6st. 6lb. (Bradbury) 3

Thirteen ran.

Betting. — 9 to 2 agst Choufleur, 6 to 1 agst Master Bill, 100 to 15 agst Blair Hope, 8 to 1 agst Gaillarde, 100 to 12 agst Drayton, and 10 to 1 each agst Camballina, Grouse, Negligent, and Gloucestershire.

Won easily by a length; bad third. Drayton was fourth, Blair Hope fifth, and Erfurt last.

PRINCE OF WALES'S HANDICAP STEEPLECHASE[6] of 250 sovs.; winners extra.
About three miles.

His Royal Highness the Prince of Wales's Magic, by Berserker, aged, 11st. 3lb. (A. Hall). 1
Mr. H. T. Fenwick's Bertha, 4 yrs, 10st. 11b. (Barker) 2
Captain Childe's Merry Maiden, 6 yrs, 10st. 6lb. (W. Nightingall) 3

Six ran.

Betting. — 7 to 4 agst Magic, 4 to 1 agst Merry Maiden, 6 to 1 agst Bertha, 100 to 14 agst Forest King, and 10 to 1 each agst Bay Comus and M. F. H.

Won, after a most exciting finish, amid loud cheering, by a neck. Merry Maiden was a very bad third, and the others did not pass the post.

MATCH[7], 500 sovs., 100 ft. Five furlongs.

Lord Penrhyn's Noble Chieftain, by Fitz James — Village Belle, 3 yrs, 9st. 7lb. (T. Cannon) 1
Lord Durham's Brooklyn, 3 yrs, 8st. (Rickaby) 2

Betting. — 5 to 4 on Noble Chieftain, who waited on Brooklyn to the distance, when he came away[8], and won at his ease by a length.

ALLESTREE PLATE (Welter Handicap) of 200 sovs., by subscription of 5 guineas each. 3 ft.; winners extra. The Straight Mile[9].

Mr. D. Henty's Whitelegs, by Albert Victor — Flora M'Ivor, 3 yrs, 8st. 8lb. (T. Cannon) 1
Mr. John Dawson's Greenwich, 6 yrs, 8st. 13lb. (Watts) 2
Mr. G. E. Paget's Marioni, 3 yrs, 7st. 7lb. (car.[10] 7st. 8lb.) (S. Loates) ... 3

1. *Betting*, les paris; *agst*, *against*. — 2. *Made all the running*, mena le jeu tout le temps, c'est-à-dire garda toujours la tête. — 3. *Pricry Nursery*, écurie de Pricry. *Handicap* s'appelle de même en français. C'est une course où les meilleurs coureurs doivent porter une surcharge, que désigne un expert appelé juge du Handicap, *the Handicapper*. Le mot vient probablement du tirage au sort par les jockeys de la place qu'ils doivent occuper sur la ligne avant le départ; chacun mettait sa main (*hand*) dans la toque ou *cap* contenant les numéros d'ordre. — 4. *Sovs.*, c'est-à-dire *sovereigns*. — 5. 50 *entries*, cinquante chevaux inscrits. — 6. *Steeple-chase*, course aux clochers, c'est-à-dire course à travers pays, en ligne droite, sautant tous les obstacles. — 7. *Match*, match, course entre deux chevaux. — 8. *Waited on*, accompagna; *came away*, s'en éloigna, c'est-à-dire le distança. — 9. *The Straight Mile*, la piste droite d'un mille (1609 m.). — 10. *Car.*, *carried*; n'oublions pas que c'est un Handicap. Voy. note 3.

Twelve ran.

Betting. — 3 to 1 agst Greenwich, 6 to 1 agst Queen Bee, 100 to 14 agst Whitelegs, 8 to 1 agst Easington, 100 to 12 each agst Warlaby and Volga, 10 to 1 agst Titterstone, 100 to 8 agst Tyrant, and 20 to 1 agst any of the others.

Whitelegs won somewhat cleverly by three-quarters of a length; Marioni was a bad third, Warlaby fourth, and Titterstone last.

Chatsworth Plate (handicap) of 500 sovs., by subscription of 5 guineas each, the only forfeit if declared[1], or 10 guineas in addition if left in; winners extra Five furlongs, straight.

Mr. G. Cleveland's Albertus, by Albert Victor — Velindra, 3 yrs, 6st. 9lb. (Wall) 1
General Owen William's Harpagon, 3 yrs, 6st. 12lb. (5lb. all.) (Hibberd) ... 2
Mr. H. E. Beddington's Betelgeux, 3 yrs, 6st. 9lb. (Blake) 3

Fifteen ran.

Betting. — 7 to 2 agst St. Symphorien, 5 to 1 agst Betelgeux, 8 to 1 agst Nina, 10 to 1 agst Saucy Lass, 100 to 9 agst The Gloamin and Wise Man, 100 to 8 each agst Dog Rose and Albertus, 100 to 7 agst Harpagon, 100 to 6 each agst Cataract and Southhill, 20 to 1 each agst Castlenock, Bullion, and Ice, and 25 to 1 agst April Fool.

Won in a canter[2] by five lengths.

Foston Selling Plate[3] of 150 sovs.; about a mile and a half.

Mr. A. James's Andrassy, by Van Amburgh — Toretha, 5 yrs, 10st. 7lb. (Watts) 1
General O. Williams's Symphony, 2 yrs, 7st. 8lb. (S. Loates) 2
Mr. T. Green's Lente, 2 yrs, 7st. 8lb. (G. Chaloner) 3

Eight ran.

Betting. — 7 to 4 agst Symphony, 100 to 30 agst Lente, 5 to 1 agst Andrassy, 6 to 1 agst Banana, and 20 to 1 agst any of the others.

Won easily by a length and a half; three lengths separated the second and third. The winner was sold to Mr. Jarvis for 300 guineas, and Mr. T. Green claimed Symphony for Mr. W. R. Marshall.

Doveridge Stakes[5] of 550 sovs., by subscription of 5 guineas each, the only forfeit if declared; colts 8st. 10lb.; fillies and geldings[4] 8st. 7lb; winners extra; maidens allowed 5lb.; the second to receive 50 sovs. out of the stakes; the Straight Mile.

Mr. Abington's Pioneer, by Galopin — Moorhen, 8st. 5lb. (S. Loates)... ... 1
Duke of Westminster's Prebend, 8st. 5lb. (T. Cannon, jun.) 2
Mr. Milner's Australia, 8st. 2lb. (E. Martin) 3
Mr. T. Jennings's George, 8st. 5lb. (M. Cannon)... 0

Betting. — 5 to 4 agst Pioneer, 2 to 1 agst Australia, and 11 to 2 each agst Prebend and George.

1. *The only forfeit if declared*, la seule amende si on le retirait. — 2. *In a canter*, au petit galop. — 3. *Selling Plate*, prix à réclamer, c'est-à-dire que le gagnant est à vendre après la course au plus haut enchérisseur. 4 cheval hongre 5 prix

The favourite waited on his field until nearing the distance when he came to the front, and eventually won by three-parts of a length; a similar distance separated the second and third.

ORDER OF RUNNING THIS DAY.

	H.M.		H.M.
Belper Hurdle Handicap	12 40	Queen's Plate	2 10
Selling Handicap	1 10	Elvaston Castle Selling Plate ..	2 40
Chaddesden High Weight Handicap	1 40	Derby Handicap	3 10
		Osmaston Nursery	3 40

LATEST SCRATCHING[1].

OSMASTON NURSERY[2]. — Marcus.

FOOTBALL[3].

MARLBOROUGH COLLEGE V. WELLINGTON COLLEGE. — The annual match between these public schools under Rugby Union rules was played yesterday on the College-ground at Marlborough. The home fifteen[4] proved the stronger team, and Wellington were beaten by one goal and three tries[5] to nothing.

THE RIFLE BRIGADE V. ROYAL MILITARY ACADEMY. — This match, arranged to be played at Woolwich to-day, has been postponed, owing to the funeral of Colonel Buller, of the Rifle Brigade.

ROWING.

CAMBRIDGE UNIVERSITY COLQUHOUN SCULLS.

The annual race for the Colquhoun Sculls began yesterday afternoon. In the first heat, A. L. R. Gaddum, First Trinity, won by 80 yards from A. Hardie, Trinity Hall, who then ceased rowing, and B. W. Crump, Jesus[6], finished second. Time, 9min. 19sec. In the second heat, S. D. Muttlebury, Third Trinity (the light blue president), won as he pleased from H. W. Smyth, Third Trinity. Time, 9min. 13 2-5sec. In the third heat, P. E. Shaw, Lady Margaret B. C., won by three dozen yards from A. G. Cooke, Lady Margaret B. C. Time,

1. *Latest scratching*, dernier cheval retiré. — 2. L'écurie Osmaston. — 3. *Football*, grosse vessie gonflée et revêtue de cuir, très dure, qu'on pousse avec le pied. Bien que ce soit un jeu violent et brutal et même dangereux, *the football* jouit d'une grande popularité dans le Royaume-Uni et ses colonies où il se joue école contre école, ville contre ville, comté contre comté, et même pays contre pays, l'Angleterre contre l'Écosse, par exemple, ou celle-ci contre l'Irlande ou contre le Pays de Galles. Des indigènes Maoris sont même venus de la Nouvelle-Zélande lutter au *football* avec les Anglais pendant l'hiver 1888-1889. Le Royaume-Uni est partagé en divisions, chacune ayant le droit de nommer un conseiller, et les divisions comprennent des associations, elles-mêmes composées de cercles, tout en étant dirigé par un conseil général. On essaye d'introduire le jeu de *football*, comme celui du *cricket*, dans les lycées et les colléges de France. C'est un jeu qui demande de l'adresse et du coup d'œil, mais qui offre du danger. — 4. *The home fifteen*, les quinze joueurs de Marlborough, qui étaient chez eux. — 5. *One goal and three tries*, un but touché et trois points. *A try*, une tentative, un essai. Ce sont surtout les règles dressées par l'école de Rugby qui dirigent ce jeu. — 6. C'est-à-dire *of Jesus College*.

8min. 35sec. The final heat will take place to-day between Muttlebury, Shaw, and Gaddum.

Colonel C. Grove, C. B.[1], East York Regiment, has been appointed Assistant Adjutant-General at headquarters vice Colonel Ardagh, C. B., R. E.[2], Mr. G. Fleetwood Wilson succeeds Colonel Grove as private secretary to the Right Honourable Edward Stanhope, M. P., Secretary of State for War.

THE PRINCESS OF WALES[3]. — The Princess of Wales, Prince Albert Victor, and Princess Victoria passed through Hamburg last night *en route* to Copenhagen.

CONSCIENCE MONEY[4]. — The Chancellor of the Exchequer acknowledges the receipt of the remaining half of a £20 note from " M. D. S. ".

THE LONDON COUNTY COUNCIL. — A correspondent, who is himself a man of mark, writes : — " It may be well to inform you that the article in your paper has suggested to certain influential inhabitants of South Kensington the determination to form a committee for the purpose of selecting two persons of distinction to represent South Kensington on the county council. We should be glad if you could notice this fact in order to prevent the ratepayers promising their votes. "

DISASTERS AT SEA.

Our Plymouth Correspondent telegraphed last night : — There is no doubt whatever that the collision between the Cunard Line steamship Nantes, Captain Simpson, and the German ship Theodore Ruyer, Captain Meyer, which took place off the Lizard[5] on Tuesday last, proved more disastrous than was previously reported. The Nantes was bound from Liverpool to Havre with a crew of 28 all told. The Theodore Ruyer was running down Channel with all sails set. There was a strong east-south-east breeze blowing, with a heavy sea running. The ships sighted each other some miles distant, but owing to circumstances at present unexplained the German ship came into collision with the Nantes, crashing into the port side. Two of the crew of the Nantes jumped on board the German ship as the vessels were locked, and thus saved their lives. The Theodore Ruyer was

1. *C. B., Companion of the Order of the Bath.* — 2. *R. E., Royal Engineers,* du génie. — 3. La princesse de Galles est fille du roi de Danemark. — 4. On appelle *conscience money* de l'argent envoyé sous le voile de l'anonyme au chancelier de l'Echiquier en payement d'impôts évités par fraude et que peut-être on n'avait pas le moyen de payer lors de la perception régulière. Pour assurer la réception, l'expéditeur coupe un billet de banque en deux moitiés et envoie chacune par une voie différente. — 5. *Off the Lizard* ou *Lizard Point,* au large du cap Lizard, à la pointe sud-est du comté de Cornouailles.

found after the collision to have her bows smashed in, and fears were entertained from the first that she would founder. Sixteen of the crew, together with the two men who had jumped on board from the Nantes, got into the life-boat, and had barely pushed off when the vessel made a heavy plunge forward and sank with the captain and mate and fully 12 of the crew. In the meantime the crew of the Nantes had prepared themselves for the worst. They had put lifebelts[1] on and taken off their boots. Four or five hours elapsed before the heavy seas filled the engine room, and then signals of distress were fired. No vessel came near, and from what can be gathered from one of the three survivors out of the total crew the Nantes sank suddenly at 6.30 on the following morning in deep water. The captain, second mate, and a number of the crew went down with the vessel. Those who rose to the surface wearing their lifebelts were for the most part overwhelmed by the terrific seas. The chief mate and second engineer were seen to sink within ten minutes of each other, and shortly after were followed by other members of the crew who had escaped the suction of the Nantes. The boat containing 16 of the crew of the Theodore Ruyer and two of the Nantes was picked up by the steamer Antrim four hours after the collision. Robert Parkinson, able seaman, who had two lifebelts on, was picked up by the Dutch vessel Rotterdam off Start Point[2], having been carried by the tide at least a dozen miles. He states that the Theodore Ruyer struck the steamer on the port quarter[3], crushing into her to the extent of several feet. The port boats were smashed, and the funnel of the Nantes fell over the starboard side, carrying away the forward life boat. The other boat was slightly damaged, but she was got ready for any emergency. When the Nantes showed signs of foundering several of the crew took to the boat, and they had just got clear of the ship when she sank. The captain and second mate, with several of the crew, went down with her. Several, however, floated, including the chief officer and seven or eight seamen. These, however, disappeared one after the other.

Mr. G. C. L. Glubb, county coroner[4], held an inquest to-day at Talland on the body of a man unknown. George Bidduck, coastguard, proved finding the body on the rocks. A telegram was found on the body directed to J. C. Mayer, captain of the Theodore Ruyer. His gold watch was found wrapped up in a kid glove, and he wore a gold ring bearing the initials " T. C. " and the date " 31st of October, 1855. An open verdict[5] was returned. Mr. Glubb afterwards held an inquest at Launcells into the cir-

1. *Lifebelt*, ceinture de sauvetage. — 2. *Start Point*, cap au sud de l'Angleterre, au-dessous de Plymouth. — 3. *On the port quarter*, à bâbord. — 4. *The coroner*, le coroner. C'est un magistrat nommé par la couronne, qui a pour mission de s'informer des causes de toute mort subite ou arrivée par accident, à l'aide d'un jury réuni à cet effet. — 5. *An open verdict*, c'est un verdict qui constate la mort sans accuser personne de l'avoir causée.

cumstances attending the death of a man whose body was found on the beach. Bidduck said he found the body, which was much tattooed. Close by the body was found a bottle containing the following sentence, written in German : — " Theodore Ruyer ran into by steamer[1]. — J. C. Mayer. " A similar verdict was returned.

Yesterday the brig Granite, Captain Leng, of West Hartlepool, while endeavouring to enter the Tees[2], grounded upon Seaton North Gare. The Seaton lifeboat, and subsequently the Middlesbrough lifeboat, went to the rescue. The position was so perilous that, although repeated and desperate attempts were made to get alongside, the vessel went to pieces before this could be done, drowning her crew of eight in sight of a large crowd of spectators, one of whom, Miss Strover, was dreadfully excited and dropped dead on the sands. Most of the crew belong to Hartlepool and Whitby[3]. Captain Leng leaves a widow and three children.

Lloyd's agent[4] at Mossel Bay telegraphs that the British Duke has gone ashore west of Cape Francis and has become a total wreck. Part of her cargo may be saved. Her crew were picked up by the Anglian, from Cape Town, and landed at Mossel Bay. The British Duke sailed from Calcutta Sept. 2, for London. She was an iron vessel of 1,464 tons, built at Barrow in 1875, and owned by the British Shipowners' Company, of Liverpool.

A Reuter telegram, dated Falmouth, Nov. 13, says : — " The Galatea, bound for Las Palmas, arrived here last night, and reports that on the 6th inst., when between the Start and the Eddystone Lighthouse[5], she saw about midnight distress rockets being fired from a steamer. She got within hailing distance, and was informed that the steamer was in a sinking condition, that her boats were smashed, and that she required assistance. The fearful state of the weather which prevailed prevented the Galatea from launching her boats, but she remained close by all night until 5.40 a. m., when a heavy squall struck both vessels, and on the weather clearing about 6 o'clock the steamer had sunk. The Galatea cruised about for three hours, but could see nothing but wreckage floating about. "

LATEST SHIPPING INTELLIGENCE.

(FROM LLOYD'S.)

WRECKS AND CASUALTIES.

Lloyd's agent at Santiago de Cuba telegraphs that the Mary Elizabeth, British barque, lying at anchor off La Guayra, lost an anchor and chain and came into

1. *Ran into by steamer*, abordé par un vapeur. — 2. *The Tees*, rivière du N. E. de l'Angleterre, dans le comté de Durham, qui se jette dans la mer du Nord. — 3. *Hartlepool and Whitby*, petits ports de mer sur la même côte. — 4. *Lloyd's agent*, l'agent de Lloyd's, voy. page 36, note 7. — 5. *The Eddystone Lighthouse*, le Phare d'Eddystone, construit sur les *roches*

collision with the Dunphaile Castle. The former is badly damaged; the latter slightly damaged.

Lloyd's agent at Napier, N. Z.[1], telegraphs that the Langstone, British ship, with a full outward cargo on board, took fire in port, and the fire was not extinguished until much damage was done to the vessel and cargo.

Lloyd's agent at Malta telegraphs that the Delbeattie, steamer, from Taganrog[2], reports having fallen in with the Saxon Briton, steamer, with crank shaft[3] broken on Nov. 10, 20 miles east of Malta. The Delbeattie took her in tow from 6 a. m. to 10 p. m., but was obliged to abandon her on account of the hawser parting and a strong gale blowing from the west.

A telegram from Muchall's Coastguard Station[4] reports that the Isabella, schooner, of Banff, from Sunderland, with coal, went ashore on Scatraw at 8.20 a. m. yesterday. The crew were saved by lines from the pier.

The Dunrobin Castle, barque, of Aberdeen, official No. 17,960, laden with timber, has arrived in Cromarty Roads with loss of deck cargo and vessel leaking badly.

Lloyd's agent at Batavia telegraphs that the Pertha, Dutch barque, from Rotterdam for Batavia, was burnt at sea on Nov. 9, south of the Straits of Sunda[5]. Her crew were picked up by the Johanna.

A Sundswall telegram states that the Norwegian barque Olaus, for Poole, with deals, has been cut through by ice, and towed in waterlogged. She must discharge.

A Hamburg telegram states that two steamers and one barque are aground off Finkenwaeder[6]. The German mail steamer Bohemia, thence for New York, and the British steamer Harrogate are aground off Schulau[6]. The German mail steamer Marsala, from Hamburg for New York, is aground off Finkenwaeder.

FOREIGN ARRIVALS.

AKASSA, Nov. 7. — Clydesdale, st.[7].

ALEXANDRIA, Nov. 11. — Pera, st., Newport.

CAPE TOWN, Nov. 9. — Cwmdonkin, Garston.

GALVESTON[8], Nov. 11. — Crete, st., Swansea.

GIBRALTAR, Nov. 10. — Heathmore, st., Sulina for London. — Craigmore, st., the Danube for Sharpness. Nov. 11. — Jesmond, st. — Ardoe, st.

MONTEVIDEO, Nov. 9. — Croma, st., Birkenhead.

SUEZ CANAL, Nov. 13. — At Port Said. — Marco Minghetti, st., Savona. — Knight Companion, st., Cardiff for Colombo. — Kairos, st., Cardiff for Bombay.

SYDNEY, Nov. 8. — Skelmorlie, London.

---

d'Eddystone (roche au tourbillon), au sud de l'Angleterre, entre Plymouth et Falmouth. Le Phare construit d'abord en 1696, reconstruit en 1708, y est depuis 1759 remplacé par un phare modèle dû à l'architecte Smeaton. — 1. *N. Z.*, New Zealand. — 2. *Taganrog*, port de commerce de la Russie d'Europe, au fond de la mer d'Azof, près de l'embouchure du Don. — 3. *Crank shaft*, arbre (de la machine). — 4. Station des gardes-côtes, au N. O. de l'Écosse. — 5. *The Straits of Sunda*, le détroit de la Sonde, dans la mer des Indes, entre les îles de Sumatra et Java. — 6. Non loin de l'embouchure de l'Elbe. — 7. *St.*, steamer, bateau à vapeur; les navires à voiles ne sont l'objet d'aucune désignation. — 8. Port du Texas (États-Unis), sur le golfe du Mexique.

The Times.

FOREIGN SAILINGS.

AKASSA, Nov. 11. — Fortescue, st., United Kingdom.

CRONSTADT, Nov. 11. — Black Head, st., Belfast.

GIBRALTAR, Nov. 10. — Roumania, st., London. Nov. 12. — Rubens, st., Leith.

PORT AUGUSTA[1], Nov. 12. — John Rennie, London.

HOME ARRIVALS.

LIVERPOOL, Nov. 12. — Rippling Wave, Villa Nova. — Moselle, Bay Verte. Nov. 13. — Cherbourg, st., Constantinople.

LONDON. — Passed Gravesend[2], Nov. 13. — Cadiz, st., Cadiz, &c. — Matilda, Dordt. — Daphne, Charleston. — Persian, Trinitad. — Caroline, st., Treport. — Twickenham, st., Nicolaieff. — Duchess, st., Taganrog. — Gogo, st., Huelva. For East India Dock. — Otago, Canterbury, N. Z. For London Dock. — Bodvar, Drobak. — Birkhall, st., Ergasteria. For Millwall Dock. — Divina, st., St. Petersburg. For Surrey Commercial Dock. — Aberlady Bay, st., Sulina. — George Linck, Quebec. — Drammenscren, Saguenay. For Fresh Wharf. — Pizzaro, st., Dordt. — Columba, st., Patras.

HOME SAILINGS.

LIVERPOOL, Nov. 13. — Nepthis, st., Alexandria. — Tafna, st., Galveston. — Rallus, st., Rotterdam. — Velox, Brevig. — Alice, Matanzas. — Cape Wash, Calcutta. — Genl. Elliot, st., Gibraltar. — Jane Jolliffe, St. Vincent. — Britannia, st., Constantinople.

LONDON. — Passed Gravesend. — Swallow, st., Ostend. — Grebe, st., Bordeaux. — Ilios, st., Rosario. — Gozo, st., Riga. — Houghton Tower, Sydney. — Archimedes, Copenhagen. — Carne, Mandal. — Cadiz, st., Cadiz, &c. — George Linck, Quebec. — Ilios, st., Rosario. — Vesta, Aarhuus.

HIGH WATER AT LONDON-BRIDGE THIS DAY[3].

Morning .. .. .. 7 min. after 11 | Evening .. .. 38 min. after 11

THE QUEEN AND THE GLASGOW EXHIBITION[4]. — In reply to a telegram sent by Sir Archibald Campbell, president of the Glasgow Exhibition, to the Queen, announcing the successful closing of the Glasgow Exhibition,

1. *Port Augusta*, capitale du Maine (États-Unis d'Amérique). — 2. *Gravesend*, sur la Tamise, à 12 lieues de Londres. C'est là que l'eau commence à être salée. — 3. La marée ne cesse de se faire sentir qu'un peu au-dessous de Londres. — 4. *Exposition internationale de Glasgow*, ouverte le 8 mai 1888 par le prince et la princesse de Galles et visitée par la reine le 22 août, était consacrée surtout à tout ce qui regarde la construction des navires et le génie maritime, à toutes les applications du fer et de la houille et à toutes les industries de la ville de Glasgow, métropole du commerce du nord. Les industries manuelles des femmes, les dentelles, l'art de tresser la paille, la ganterie, etc., y furent très bien représentés. Le Canada, les Indes, l'île de Ceylon y prirent une part remarquable, malgré la distance. La France et les autres contrées de l'Europe y tenaient également une place des plus honorables.

the following message was received in Glasgow yesterday : — " The Queen thanks you for your telegram, and rejoices to hear that the Glasgow Exhibition has been so successful."

THE PRINCE OF WALES IN DERBYSHIRE. — The Prince of Wales paid his second visit to Derby races yesterday, and again met with a most enthusiastic reception. The Prince having been entertained with a distinguished assemblage overnight at Doveridge-hall, near Uttoxeter, by Lord and Lady Hindlip, it had been arranged that his Royal Highness should be driven to Derby early yesterday morning, to attend a meet of the South Notts[1] Hunt, under the mastership of Lord Harrington, but, unfortunately, the unpropitious state of the weather upset the programme. The Royal party left Uttoxeter Station yesterday morning at 11.45, and travelled in two first-class saloon carriages, three composite carriages, and the Royal saloon. The special arrived in Derby at 12.15, and the Prince, accompanied by Lord and Lady Hindlip, at once proceeded to their carriages and drove off to the race-course. At the conclusion of the races, his Royal Highness and party again left Derby for Doveridge. The Prince having intimated, through Colonel Teesdale, that he would visit Derby School at noon to-day, arrangements have been made to suit his Royal Highness's pleasure. The Prince will arrive at the Great Northern Station in Derby at 11.50, and will be conveyed direct to the school along Friar-gate, Ford-street, and St. Helen-street. After briefly inspecting the class-room in the wing known as the Prince of Wales's building, which his Royal Highness formally opened 15 years ago, he will proceed to the race-course, *viâ* Bridge-gate and Nottingham-road. The Prince will conclude his visit to Derbyshire to-morrow morning, and, after visiting Allsopp's brewery at Burton, will proceed to London.

THE SPECIAL COMMISSION[2].

ROYAL COURTS OF JUSTICE, Nov. 13.

(*Before the Right Honourable* SIR JAMES HANNEN, MR. JUSTICE DAY, *and* MR. JUSTICE A. L. SMITH, *Commissioners.*)

The Special Commission held their 13th sitting to-day at half past 10 o'clock in No. 1 Probate Court of the Royal Courts of Justice.

1. *South Notts*, South Nottinghamshire. — 2. La commission spéciale instituée par la reine pour examiner les accusations du *Times* contre M. Parnell (voy. page 55, note 1). Le principal témoin, un nommé Pigott, ayant avoué qu'il avait lui-même forgé les lettres et surpris la religion du *Times*, ce journal, sans abandonner ses autres accusations, a loyalement fait des excuses publiques à M. Parnell. Tous ceux qui n'approuvent pas le rôle politique de M. Parnell et qui regardent le *Home-rule*, s'il était adopté, comme l'affaiblissement, sinon la destruction du Royaume-Uni, sont néanmoins

The counsel representing *The Times* were the Attorney-General (Sir R. Webster, Q. C.), Sir H. James, Q. C., Mr. Murphy, Q. C., and Mr. W. Graham, of the English Bar, and Mr. John Atkinson, Q. C., and Mr. Ronan, of the Irish Bar.

Mr. Parnell was represented by Sir C. Russell[1], Q. C., and Mr. Asquith; and other members of Parliament, against whom charges and allegations have been brought, by Mr. R. T. Reid, Q. C., Mr. F. Lockwood, Q. C., Mr. Lionel Hart, Mr. A. O'Connor, and Mr. A. Russell, of the English Bar, and Mr. T. Harrington, of the Irish Bar. Mr. Hammond (solicitor) represented Mr. Chance. Mr. Biggar, Mr. Davitt, and Mr. T. Healy appeared in person.

Mr. Bucknill, Q. C., appeared for the Marquis of Clanricarde[2].

On the Commissioners, taking their seats,

The PRESIDENT said: — At our last sitting our subject of discussion was the admissibility of certain evidence. It was proposed to ask certain employers whether any and what reports had been made to them by persons in their employment concerning property in charge of those persons. We took time to consider, and I now have to state the conclusion at which we have arrived. The questions were addressed to employers of herds[3] as to what reports they made on the subject of the property which was in their charge. I am satisfied, speaking for myself, that there was a misunderstanding between the Court and counsel on the subject. The arguments of counsel were addressed to showing that hearsay[4] evidence would not be proof of the facts alleged to have taken place. It never was the intention of the Court to lay down anything contrary to that. The question on which I expressed an opinion — I believe with the concurrence of my colleagues — was this — that the fact that a particular report had been made by a person in discharge of his duty was admissible in evidence, not that the contents of that report should be taken as evidence of the facts to which it related. Let me illustrate it in this manner. Suppose that instead of its being the employer, the employed had been called to state the facts. He might have been asked, " Did you report that to your employer at the time? " And in the same way the employer may be asked the fact whether he as employer received that report. The bearing of such evidence is not to prove the facts. It has this bearing: — If the person employed were to say " I made no such report, I intended to say nothing about it to my employer," that

heureux de voir M. Parnell acquitté de toute complicité avec des assassins. Pigott, le faussaire, s'enfuit aussitôt de Londres et s'est suicidé à Madrid, le 2 mars 1889, au moment où il allait être appréhendé en vertu de la loi de l'extradition. — 1. C'est sir C. Russell qui, par son habile interrogatoire, a arraché à Pigott l'aveu du faux. — 2. *Lord Clanricarde*, grand propriétaire en Irlande, dont les procédés contre certains de ses tenanciers ont irrité extrêmement la Ligue nationale en Irlande. Ses fermes ont été *boycottées* et son principal agent assassiné. — 3. *Herds*, bouviers, bergers. 4. [illegible]

would have a tendency to discredit the fact of such a thing having happened. On the other hand, the fact that the report was made in the discharge of his duty at the time is admissible in evidence. If the matter rested there, without there being any other evidence of the facts except that contained in the report, that could not be regarded as evidence of the facts by the Court. That is the opinion at which we have arrived. There is another point that has been raised, as to certain claims which were made by employers for compensation. It was clear that these claims were in writing, and we at once said, at an early stage of the inquiry, that the writing must be produced. Still, if the writing were produced, the objection taken by Sir Charles Russell was that the claims themselves were not admissible. Upon that we are of opinion that they are admissible. Again, it turns out that there is a broad distinction between a thing being merely admissible in evidence and its being taken as proof of the facts alleged. Of course, the fact of a man making a claim does not prove the ground on which the claim was made, but it is admissible in evidence on the ground that he made the claim at the time, and that it is an essential part of the *res gestæ*[1]. On these grounds we think these two branches of evidence admissible.

MR. JUSTICE A. L. SMITH. — I have nothing to add, except that I agree entirely in what Sir James Hannen has said, and for the grounds which he has given.

The PRESIDENT. — With regard to the documents, I cannot say that absolutely every document has come under our eyes, because in some instances we have thought specimens of the class to which they belonged were sufficient. With that reservation, we have examined every document, and we are of opinion with regard to some of them that they ought to be disclosed. I refer particularly to some documents which are alleged to have come into the possession of Mr. Soames[2], purporting to be written by certain persons, among whom are those against whom the charges and allegations are made. They appear to be admitted to be spurious, and were rejected by Mr. Soames because he thought so. I think from his point of view he was justified in not including them in his affidavit of documents; but we have a larger discretion to exercise. We are of opinion that some of these documents should be disclosed in this trial. It is alleged on the side of those charged that certain documents are forgeries, and we think that they are entitled to the assistance which it is conceivable they might derive from the examination of those documents, because after examination it might be found that the documents produced to Mr. Soames and rejected by him might be shown to be in the same handwriting as those documents which are said to be in the handwriting of Mr. Parnell. I only threw this out as

1. *Res gestæ*, choses ayant lieu. — 2. *M. Soames*, l'avoué du *Times*.

an illustration. We are therefore of opinion that these ought to be disclosed[1]. We have also found that some of the documents are in the handwriting of Mr. Davitt, and we are of opinion that in fairness to Mr. Davitt they ought to be disclosed. It is unnecessary to point out the bearing of these documents, because I may observe generally with reference not only to those documents in which Mr. Davitt is interested, but to those also in which others are interested, that the fact of our directing that they should be disclosed to the other side does not make them evidence, but if it should be sought hereafter to use them in evidence their admissibility will depend upon other considerations than those to which I have referred. With regard to other documents, of which there is a large mass, we have examined them, and we find in them nothing inconsistent with the statements which were made on oath with regard to them. They appear to us to be documents which relate exclusively to the case of the defendants in the action of "O'Donnell v. Walter[2]." They do not in any way tend to assist the case of the other side, and we are of opinion that they are not documents which the persons charged are entitled to inspect. It has occurred to us that with regard to many of them there might naturally arise this sort of observation on them, "We know nothing about these documents," and that that might be a ground for delay in dealing with them. But I must say that, considering this question of disclosure of documents, we cannot fail to see that the disclosure of them would show who were the witnesses about to be called, and that is not a thing to which the other parties are entitled. We must be careful that in our search for the truth we do not obstruct the sources of truth. There is some reason to fear that the mention of names might be an impediment to justice, and this is illustrated by the fact that I myself, several days ago, received a threatening letter.

Sir C. Russell. — I have received two or three, my Lord.

The President. — The fact that any one should venture to threaten a member of this Court makes it not improbable that other means of intimidation might be brought to bear upon the witnesses. On these grounds, therefore, we do not think that any other documents than those mentioned should be submitted for inspection.

Sir C. Russell. — We have no opportunity of knowing what the documents are which it would be convenient or inconvenient that we should see; might I suggest to your Lordships that the Secretary to the Commission,

1. *Disclosed*, c'est-à-dire montrés aux parties accusées. — 2. *O'Donnell v. Walter*. C'est un procès qui a précédé celui de *Parnell v. the Times*, où M. O'Donnell, autrefois membre de la Chambre des Communes, où il siégeait parmi les Parnellistes, accusait de calomnie le *Times* dont Walter est le principal propriétaire. O'Donnell fut débouté de sa demande; mais les accusations produites en public contre certains des Parnellistes émurent l'opinion, et c'est pour en rechercher la vérité ou la fausseté que le gouvernement a institué la commission spéciale.

under your Lordships' direction, should make some kind of schedule as to the class of documents we are entitled to see?

The PRESIDENT. — Yes.

SIR C. RUSSELL. — Or, at all events, some kind of description such as your Lordships has given.

The PRESIDENT. — Yes; I will endeavour to have it done. I am not able at once to decide the point, but whatever can be done shall be done.

The ATTORNEY-GENERAL. — I would make only one observation. With regard to the documents which are to be seen of course there is no difficulty; these can easily be scheduled. But with regard to the others your Lordships previous judgment is that they are fairly within the protection, on oath, of Mr. Soames. Therefore, that being so, my learned friend would not be entitled to anything that would give him further information with regard to them.

SIR C. RUSSELL. — If my learned friend had been listening he would have seen that your Lordships made one exception with respect to certain classes of documents. Your Lordships came to the conclusion that they relate exclusively to the case of "O'Donnell v. Walter," and have no bearing upon the issues in this case. So far as that exception is concerned I at once admit we can make no claim, but with regard to that exception I have not been able to appreciate that there should be any further extension. Your Lordship said that in discovery a party is not entitled to know the names of witnesses. I agree; but he is not to be precluded from his right of discovery of certain documents merely because that might put him in possession of information as to the witnesses who were to be called on the other side. I do not desire to prolong this discussion, but I contend that we are entitled to such description as your Lordships may think proper of the documents which we are not entitled to see.

The PRESIDENT. — You must remember that it was agreed that we should inspect the documents and judge. That puts the matter in a different position than would have been the case if the request had not been made. I have given the reasons why we do not consider that you are entitled to inspection—because from our examination of them there appears nothing inconsistent with the statement made upon oath by Mr. Soames. We have given reasons why, in the exercise of our discretion, we have said what documents you are entitled to inspect and what might impede the course of justice, and we will use our discrimination in the matter.

The ATTORNEY-GENERAL. — There are certain other documents which have been handed in. We have just seen ——

The PRESIDENT. — Yes. I had forgotten to mention those. We are of opinion that there is nothing in them which calls for disclosure[1].

---

1. *Which calls for disclosure*, qui exige que ces documents soient communiqués.

Mr. Bucknill, Q. C. — Will your Lordships allow me to make an application on behalf of the Marquis of Clanricarde[1], with reference to some correspondence that passed between him and his agent, Mr. Blake?

The President. — No order has been made as to that. If an order had been made I am not sure that you have any *locus standi*[2] here.

Mr. Bucknill. — If no order has been made I am afraid I have no *locus standi* to make an application; but it has been understood by Lord Clanricarde, and it has been generally gathered from the report of the proceedings before you in the newspapers, that an order was made by your Lordships, or something amounting to an order, there being no objection on either side.

The President. — Oh, no. No order has been made. I suppose you desire to be heard against such an order being made?

Mr. Bucknill. — If your Lordships tell me that no such order has been made, I will not trouble your Lordships with any observations. I will only remind you that Mrs. Blake, the widow of the murdered agent of Lord Clanricarde, was asked by my learned friend, Sir Charles Russell, whether she had in her possession certain letters showing her husband's recommendation to Lord Clanricarde that a reduction should be allowed on the rents on certain parts of his estate. The answer was to the effect that she had them.

The President. — I really cannot see what *locus standi* you have. I do not mean that I am going beyond that; but I really do not see that anybody who may suppose himself to be affected by our proceedings can on that ground come before us.

Mr. Bucknill. — My argument is of a very limited nature, because Lord Clanricarde, on my advice, does not propose to offer any opposition to the jurisdiction of this Court; he admits the power of your Lordships to direct that any correspondence relative to the matters before you should be produced, even the letters which passed between him and his agent. But the application I have to make is this—and I think you will see the justice of it. This correspondence was of a strictly private and confidential nature between Lord Clanricarde and his agent, and a Court of competent jurisdiction in Ireland has for good reasons directed in the case before it that the correspondence should not be published; yet, if that correspondence can be shown to throw light on any matters now before your Lordships, of course that correspondence will be forthcoming. Lord Clanricarde, acting on my advice, will make no objection; but what I ask on his behalf is this—that, although such of this correspondence as is relevant[3] should be produced,

1. Voyez note 2, page 212. — 2. *Locus standi*, droit d'intervenir. — 3. *Such of this correspondence as is relevant*, la partie de la correspondance qui pourra avoir rapport au procès.

there is a mass of correspondence which passed during the agency of Mr. Blake which, as I have said before, is of an entirely private and confidential nature, and could in no way throw any light on the matters your Lordships are asked to decide. On the other hand, there may be some letters which your Lordships may think relevant to the matters before you, and my application on behalf of Lord Clanricarde is that you will be good enough to look at that correspondence yourselves, which is now in Ireland, and to say what you think should be produced and what should not. Unless such an order is made the whole of the correspondence will be handed in to my learned friends, on the one side and the other, to deal with in any way they may think fit, and, although I am sure they would not do anything which might be improper or unjust to Lord Clanricarde, it is possible that an effect might ensue which would be unjust and cruel to him. Therefore I ask your Lordships to look at the correspondence and to ascertain what is relevant and what is not relevant.

SIR C. RUSSELL. — Perhaps, my Lords, I may be allowed to say that, so far as we are concerned, we shall not make any such application as my learned friend has foreshadowed without giving full notice of our intention to do so. As to the suggestion of my learned friend, I must say that I think it would be a highly inconvenient course, on several grounds. In the first instance, your Lordships would be in possession of a number of documents which will make an impression on the minds of those who read them—an impression which might or might not be injurious to one side or the other. I would therefore respectfully submit that your Lordships will not be in a position to judge of the relevancy[1] of the whole or any part of this correspondence until you have heard the case as represented by those on either side.

MR. BUCKNILL. — I can hardly think that my learned friend is serious in his contention that the perusal of the correspondence may affect the minds of those to whom it is produced. He has not dealt with my point, which is this—that the Court will not direct by what I may call a wholesale[2] order that the correspondence, all the correspondence, that has ever passed between Lord Clanricarde and Mr. Blake should be handed in, in a matter of this description, by the widow of the late Mr. Blake, to be dealt with by my learned friends as they may think fit.

The PRESIDENT. — Yes; I am in possession of your point. We will deal with the matter presently.

The subject then dropped.

SIR H. JAMES. — With permission of your Lordships, I will re-call Sergeant Langford in order that he may be examined as to a document which,

1. *Of the relevancy*, du rapport avec ce procès. 2 en gros

in his evidence on Friday, he said was a copy made immediately after he had seen the original of a certain letter.

Mr. LOCKWOOD[1]. — Sir Henry James has handed this document to me pinned down,[2] and I understand from my learned friends that the only portion of it which relates to the matter before your Lordships is now exposed. I would ask your Lordships kindly to look at the document. (The document was handed to the Court.) Your Lordships will remember the circumstances in which this document was produced. Sergeant Langford stated that immediately after reading it he took out his tablet and copied it. Will your Lordships allow me to put a question to Sergeant Langford with reference to this document?

The PRESIDENT. — Certainly.

Sergeant Langford was recalled.

Mr. LOCKWOOD. — I understood you to tell their Lordships on the last occasion that you wrote this copy of the letter in the station immediately after you had seen the original? — Yes.

Can you tell me from any documents in your possession on what date you saw the letter first? — I believe it to have been about the last days of September, 1880.

Is it not a fact that after you had seen the letter you endeavoured to obtain the original on a subsequent date, about the end of October? — I endeavoured to obtain the original letter.

Was not that about the end of October? — I really do not know.

Did you ever write down your recollection of that letter until you found that you could not obtain the original? — I wrote it at the station. I wrote it in my tablets first.

Take that document in your hand. Is that what you call the tablet? — No.

Do you mean to suggest that your recollection of the letter has not been quickened from any other source? — The document was copied from the small tablet.

Look at the letter as you have written it there with the alterations? — Yes.

Do you mean to say that that is copied from something else? — I do.

Let me read the document. You begin here, on October 28, by stating that you had endeavoured to get the original letter. You say: — "I beg to state that I have been to see Mr. O'Flaherty on this day, and I endea-

1. M. Lockwood est avocat d'un des Parnellistes compris dans l'accusation du *Times*. Devant les tribunaux anglais, ce n'est pas le président qui interroge les témoins, ce sont les avocats des deux parties. Dans les procès *criminels*, le président ne demande à l'accusé que son nom, âge, etc., et s'il plaide coupable ou non coupable. L'accusé n'est pas chargé de prouver son innocence. C'est l'affaire de l'accusation d'établir la culpabilité. M. Lockwood est aussi membre du Parlement. 2 attaché avec une épingle.

voured, but unsuccessfully, to get the letter from him. I give underneath some of the words as I recollect them from reading the letter." You go on : — "Sir, I have heard you are about taking a grass farm at Ross. You know our rules are against it." Then you write, "To give it up," and then some words are scratched out, and then you say, "If you take it I shall be obliged," and then other words are put in and crossed out. Then you go on — "reluctantly to bring you before the public." Now is not that simply written from recollection? — I believe still that I took a copy from Mr. O'Flaherty when I spoke to him.

Mr. LOCKWOOD. — I think the document speaks pretty well for itself. There are some other documents produced by this witness, I think.

SIR H. JAMES. — It is for the Court to decide what shall be done with them. They relate to confidential matters which are not relevant to the matter before the Court.

The SECRETARY of the COMMISSION. — I will have a facsimile copy made of the entry in the diary.

The PRESIDENT. — With the alterations.

Mr. LOCKWOOD (to witness). — Were you acquainted with the family of Mr. O'Flaherty? — Yes.

Before this incident? — Yes.

Did you say that you were in the chapel on the Sunday when Father Coyne alluded to the O'Flaherty family? — No.

You have no report of that? — No.

Had you heard that the Bishop of the diocese had censured a member of the family on some previous occasion for something not connected with the taking of land? — No.

Did you hear that after this incident at the chapel Father Coyne received a threatening letter? — I never did.

You have never heard anything as to the Bishop of the diocese having censured one member of the family on a previous occasion? — I never heard of it.

SIR H. JAMES. — You have given the Court the best information you can as to the contents of the letter? — Yes.

The incident, we know, occurred eight years ago? — Yes.

Mr. Davitt. — May I, my Lords, be allowed this afternoon to inspect the documents that are said to have been written by me? May I inspect them with Mr. Lewis?

The PRESIDENT. — I cannot say that it will be possible this afternoon, but probably it will. At any rate you shall inspect the documents as speedily as possible.

Patrick Kennedy, examined by Mr. ATKINSON. — Where do you live? — I object to that.

To tell where you live? — Yes.

Where you live in London or where you live in the country? — Where I live in the country[1].

Did you take a farm from a woman named Katherine Dempsey?

SIR C. RUSSELL. — Wait a moment; we want to have this case in some way localized.

The ATTORNEY-GENERAL. — There will be no difficulty. There is no difficulty as to the farm. The question which he does not wish to answer is where he is living now.

Mr. ATKINSON (to witness). — Did you take a farm from which a woman named Katherine Dempsey had been evicted[2]? — Yes; that farm was in Kylebeg, county Galway. At that time I lived at some distance from there. There is a village called Mullagh near that farm. There was no Land League established in Mullagh at the time I took the farm. I took it in April, 1879. I lived near the village of Carrol at that time. I know a man named Martin Halloran; he lives, I believe, about seven miles from Mullagh; it is not near the place where I resided. Martin Halloran is a wheelwright. I know a man named Cunningham, a reporter on the papers; I also know a man named John Farrell, a railway clerk. These three men came and had an interview with me in October, 1880. I have since ascertained that these men were members of the Land League.

SIR C. RUSSELL. — How has he ascertained that?

Witness. — I cannot account for that.

Mr. ATKINSON. — Have you attended any Land League meetings? — I have only attended one, in November, 1880.

Were these men present at the meeting? — There were two of them present, Cunningham and Halloran. It was held at Kylebeg on this farm, which formerly belonged to Mrs. Dempsey. One Hogan, a man I knew, was present at the meeting. Neither Mr. Mat Harris nor Mr. Sheehy was present. There were three or four speeches delivered in my presence. I heard a man named O'Sullivan speak, but I do not remember much of what he said. He said he hoped the grass might wither beneath my feet. Halloran said he had come there all the way from Newinn to evict the land-grabber[3] and to re-instate the widow Dempsey and her five orphans. There were about 600 or 700 persons, or over, present at that meeting. Halloran had had an interview with me in October. He was on the farm at this meeting, and made a speech. When he came to me on the first oc-

1. Le témoin évidemment hésite à faire connaître sa résidence à la campagne, c'est-à-dire en Irlande, de peur que les nationalistes ne se vengent de lui. — 2. *The Land League*, la Ligue agraire, défend de prendre à bail les fermes d'où d'autres ont été évincés, et ceux qui les prennent sont toujours maltraités et très souvent assassinés. — 3. *The landgrabber*, le voleur de terre : c'est le nom qu'on donne à ceux qui prennent les fermes de ceux qu'on a évincés.

casion in October, Cunningham was with him. I met them going to visit the farm Mrs. Dempsey had been evicted from. They talked to me about the way the widow Dempsey had been evicted and said they were going to reinstate her, and that if I did not give up the farm I should meet with so and so.

Did they say what they meant by "so and so?" — Those were the words they used. I said "Very good," and they left me. The meeting was held in November, 1880. On the day of the meeting some people came to me. I believe they were on the platform at the meeting. They said if I gave up the land it would not be any loss to me, and that there would be no man in the country more thought of. In the following spring I sent a communication to the central office of the Land League in Dublin and received a reply to it. I gave the letter to a member of the Mullagh Land League. A branch of the League had been established at Mullagh in 1881. Mat Ryan's son was the president or the secretary. I cannot say whether the parish priest, Father Bodkin, was the president of that branch of the League. I went to Father Bodkin's house with the letter. On leaving his house I gave the letter to some person, either the secretary or to some member of the local League. On a Sunday shortly afterwards I saw Mat Ryan about the letter, and he talked about paying my losses if I would give up the land. He said that there would be some delay in writing backwards and forwards to the central office, and he gave me directions to go up to Mat Harris in Dublin. He said that Mat Harris was the only person who could arrange in cases of this kind. I did not go to Dublin to see Mat Harris. A few days after I tilled the land, and a short time after I was put under police protection. That was in the latter end of April, 1881.

Do you know what being boycotted is? — I do, Sir.

From April, 1881, were you boycotted? — I was, slightly. After some time the League ceased at Mullagh. I got no annoyance from my neighbours between 1883 and 1886. I believe that the Land League had been suppressed during those years. I saw no meetings of the Land League during those years. I had no knowledge of a branch of the National League being established at Mullagh in 1884. A branch was, I believe, established there in July, 1886, when the annoyance recommenced. I then noticed a change in the demeanour of the people towards me. In that month I attended an auction of hay at Lisstuff and was declared the highest bidder, but when the auctioneer heard my name he would not let me buy the hay[1]. The auctioneer gave no reason for his conduct. In November, 1886, I received a notice through the post that a public meeting of the National League would be held at Kylebeg. It was a printed notice, and I

1. C'est un effet du boycottage.

gave it to Sergeant Hennessy. After the receipt of that notice a meeting was held on my farm—that was on the 21st of November. I did not attend the meeting, because I had notice that I was to give up the farm. Two men came to me and asked me to give up the farm. I saw the persons assembled on my farm. I was some distance from them. I saw my stock all right that day. The next day I examined my stock, and I missed eight or nine cattle and about 30 sheep. I looked for them the next day, and I could not get anybody to tell me where they were. I ultimately found them about a mile and a half from the farm. I was living with my brother at the time. My brother was boycotted. A few days afterwards a messenger came to me from the League.

Was he a member of the League? — I believe he was.

What was his name? — I object to give his name.

Why? — Because there might be ill-feeling towards me.

What did he say? — He advised me to give up the land. He talked of how they spoke at the meeting. He told me it was said that I would be found dead one day. I had had police protection some time before, but it had then been taken off. It was removed in January, 1882, and from that time until 1886 I lived without protection. I had nothing but two dogs for protection. After receiving that message I went to the parish priest at Mullagh, Father Bodkin. I told him I would remove the stock if I could get leave to find other grass. Father Bodkin said nothing to that. I tried to get other grass for the purpose of transferring my stock to it, but I did not succeed at that time, because I had not the consent of the League. I remember passing the house of Derwin, the secretary of the League, at Tynagh. I lived at Tynagh, but my farm was at Mullagh. Mrs. Derwin came out and spoke to me as I was passing. I went back with her to her house.

There was a meeting being held in the house? — There was.

Did you go into the meeting? — I did.

Who were at the meeting? — Pat Weyland, Thomas Lawless, and a stranger.

Did your subsequently ascertain that the stranger was Mr. David Sheehy, the member of Parliament? — I was told so subsequently.

Was anybody else present? — Yes, Mat Harris. He was presiding.

Was your brother with you? — He was.

Did your brother say anything as to what brought him there? — Yes; he wanted to explain how I came to take the land, but Mr. Sheehy said he did not want to hear about that at all. What he wanted to know was whether I was going to give up the land. I said I would give up the land if I could get leave to get grass for my stock.

From whom were you to get the leave? — From the League.

Did Mat Harris say anything? — He said that if I would give up the farm I would get leave to get the grass. I said I would not give up the farm until I had got the leave. I told him I would give up the land to the person I got it from—to the agent.

Some time after that did any person come to you from the Tynagh branch? — Yes, the same night Ford came to my house.

Was Ford a member of the Tynagh branch of the National League? — I suppose he was. I cannot exactly say. As far as I understood he was a member of it.

Did Ford give you any message from the Tynagh branch of the National League as to whether they were satisfied with you? — Yes, he told me that Harris knew nothing about the matter, and that if I would give up the land to the landlord they would be satisfied. In consequence of what he said I attended a meeting of the Mullagh branch of the League when the committee was sitting. Pat Dillon, the secretary, and Michael Garvey were present. The parish priest was there. I told them the reasons why I did not give up the farm and they said they would give me handwriting for it if I gave up the farm.

Handwriting for what? — For permission to remove my stock—to get grass.

What were you to do if you got the grass? — I was to clear the farm.

What were you to do with the farm when you had cleared it? — I was to give it up to the landlord.

Was any time fixed for you to give it up? — Yes, on the 8th of January, after Ballinasloe Fair, when I could dispose of my cattle.

Did Dillon say anything to you? — Yes, he said he did not like me. (Laughter.) I asked him what was the reason, and he said because I was a land-grabber. I asked him what did he know about a land-grabber in 1879, when I took the farm. As I was leaving, Dillon said, "This arrangement will do us a great deal of good." I said to him, "I suppose it is not for the benefit of widow Dempsey you are doing it?" and he said, "No, it is only to benefit ourselves," or "to save ourselves".

On getting that authority did you take grass? — I did, and I put sheep upon it. I was still boycotted. I took the grass from a Mrs. Kelly, who is a farmer, and who keeps a grocer's shop. After I took the grass Mrs. Kelly's customers were boycotted. I thereupon gave her the leave I got from the League.

Why? — To avoid the boycotting[1]. I had afterwards to remove my sheep from her land.

1. *The boycotting*, le boycottage. Les mots *boycotter* et *boycottage* sont maintenant admis dans l'usage. Ils sont tirés du nom du capitaine *Boycott*, propriétaire irlandais, à qui cette mesure fut appliquée pour la première fois.

Some time afterwards did you get the authority back again from Mrs. Kelly? — I did.

What became of it? — I put it in my pocket and it fell to pieces. Sergeant Hennessy took a copy of it. I went to the agent in January to give up the land, but he refused to take it without my notice to surrender. I still continued in possession up to March or April, 1887. I then got a letter from the League. (Letter produced.)

"Mullagh Branch.

"I am instructed by the committee to communicate with you with regard to widow Dempsey's farm. We are informed you are still in possession of the farm. If you do not send us a satisfactory account on or before next Sunday, we shall be brought to the disagreeable necessity of declaring you still a land-grabber.

"By order,

"PATRICK DILLON, Assistant Secretary."

There is no date on the letter, but I received it in March or April, 1887, After that I received a second letter. (Letter produced.)

"Mullagh Branch, April 4, 1887.

"Sir, — I am directed by the committee of the above to communicate with you with regard to widow Dempsey's farm, to give some satisfactory answer whether you have given up possession or not. Waiting your reply by return of post,

"I am your obedient servant,

"PATRICK DILLON."

Now in June of that year did you see stock on your land? — I did.

Were they yours? — No; I believe they were Mrs. Dempsey's. In the following month hay was cut on my land, but not by me. I was told it was the Dempseys. Later on it was removed off the land. I attended Wicklow Assizes for the trial of some of the men who had removed the hay. I told the same story then—at least part of it; as much as I was asked—and I do not know whether any one was called to contradict me. After giving evidence at the trial I was still boycotted.

Now, up to 1879 were you on good terms with your neighbours? — Yes, I was.

And there was no reason for the change except taking up this land? — No, I never did anything to make them on bad terms with me. I had police protection in 1881.

Cross-examined by SIR C. RUSSELL. — Who was Hennessy? — He was a sergeant of police at Tinagh. I cannot tell you about what time he came; I have no knowledge of it. He might have been there five years off and on.1

How long ago? — I object to the question. (Laughter.)

1 à des reprises différentes, à bâtons rompus.

Who told you to object to the question?—No one; I could not tell you the time exactly, or about how long ago it was.

Where do you live? — With my brother.

Where? — I object to the question.

Why do you refuse to say where you live? — So many people know where I live. I know there will be an ill-feeling against me when I go back.

You had police protection, you say; people must have known where you lived? — In Ireland.

You do not want people in London to know where you live? Now, answer a straightforward question. Where did you live at the time you took Mrs. Dempsey's farm? — With my brother.

Where? — In the county of Galway, in the parish of Tynagh. I had no land; I was not farming land with my brother, but I was with him. I was not with him as a labouring man; I had no gains from the land.

How were you earning your bread? Come, speak out. — I got it from my father.

Had you a share of the land? — No.

A share of his means? — Aye.

Living on his money? — I was living with my brother.

Were you living on your father? — No, I was in the house with my brother.

Do you mean he gave you bite and sup[1]? — I was supporting the house.

The PRESIDENT. — Do you say you were supporting the house. What were you living on?

SIR C. RUSSELL. — Come, Sir, give an answer.

Witness. — How can I answer you? I was living with my brother and working on the land. I was helping him on the land. I am not married.

How long were you living with your brother? — I could not exactly tell you.

About how long? (Witness did not answer.)

Come, do not keep us here all day. — I cannot tell you; I am not going to answer such a question, because I cannot tell the exact time. Since my father died.

When did your father die? (Witness again hesitated.)

Come, Sir, none of this nonsense; when did your father die? — About 12 or 13 years ago, but I could not exactly say.

When was widow Dempsey evicted? — In April, 1879.

1. *Bite and sup*, le boire et le manger.

I guess from her description she was a widow? — I suppose she was.

Had she a family? — Yes.

How many acres of land had she? — Twenty-eight acres 39 perches. The landlord was Mr. Trench, and the agent Mr. Allen.

What rent did she pay? — I cannot tell.

What rent were you paying? — £36.

You say she was evicted in April, 1879. When did you take the land? — About the 18th or 19th of April.

Did you clear up any arrears on getting the land? — No, I only took it for six months.

You only took it for six months, from April to October, 1879?

The Attorney-General. — As your Lordship is aware, tenants have six months to redeem.

Sir C. Russell. — Yes, we understand that. (To witness.) Was it understood that if she did not redeem you would continue the farm? — I do not know. I took it for the six months.

There was no arrangement that you were to stay on it if she did not redeem? — Well, no such word was used at the time. If she wished to redeem I would have gone out.

Where did Mrs. Dempsey go when she was evicted? — To Clontubber.

How far was that from the evicted farm? — About an English mile.

Who put her there? — I do not know whether it was the landlord or the agent.

Do you think it was one or the other? — I do not know; I cannot account for it.

A few days after Mrs. Dempsey went out, did you go to the agent? — I went to the agent; the farm was put up to bidding.

When was the first Land League, to your knowledge, established in Mullagh? — There was no branch up to November 15, 1880.

In 1881? — There was in March, 1881.

Is that the nearest date you can fix? — Well, it did not trouble me.

Was there one in Tynagh? (Witness hesitated for some time.) Come, wake up and answer the question. — I do not know in March; in November, 1881, there was no branch established.

When was the first branch established in Tynagh? — I could not exactly tell you; it did not trouble me; I do not want to hear about it.

As nearly as you can? — I have no knowledge of it.

Do you tell my Lords that you do not know when the first branch was established in Tynagh? Do you hear my question? — Yes, I object to answer.

The President. — I thought he gave an answer.

Sir C. Russell. — He said that it was not before November, 1881.

(To witness.) Why do you object to answer that question? — I cannot give a particular account of it.

I want to know as nearly as you can about what time. You say it was not there in November, 1881? — I did not say 1881; I said 1880.

I am sorry you should contradict me so rudely, Kennedy; you said 1881. — To the best of my belief there was not a branch in 1881.

Who was the president of the Mullagh branch? — I had no knowledge; I believe Father Bodkin was, but I could not exactly say.

In the spring of 1881 you say you wrote to Dublin and got an answer? — Yes.

Did you show your answer to the police? — I cannot say whether I did or not.

Will you swear you did not tell the police you had written to Dublin and got an answer? — I could not tell you.

Have you not since 1881 been in constant communication with the police, informing them of these meetings and when you were attending them? On your oath? — I did not tell them half of what passed. (Laughter.)

Answer me; have you not since 1881 been in constant communication with the police, telling them what you were doing and the meetings you were going to? — I went to no meetings since 1881.

You have told us of several. Have you not been in constant communication with the police and told them practically all of what took place at the meetings, and the names of the parties attending them? — I have no recollection; but I was at a Star Chamber[1] Court; it was held at Killamore. I do not know when that was. It was not in 1882.

The PRESIDENT. — I suppose " Star Chamber " is a nickname?

The ATTORNEY-GENERAL. — Yes, a court of secret inquiry.

Cross-examination continued. — When was this? (Witness did not answer.) Come, you are not treating me—and, what is more important, the Court—respectfully. — It was some time in 1887. I do not know exactly what time it was.

I am not asking you the exact time; about what time? — I do not know what time; I believe some time in 1887. Mr. Joyce was the magistrate.

Do you swear that that was the first time you made any communication to the police? — I had nothing to do with them to the time when I had protection.

1. *The Star Chamber*, la Chambre étoilée ou plutôt la Chambre des actes était une salle du palais de Westminster où les Juifs, sous les rois normands, étaient admis à déposer, pour sûreté, leurs actes, obligations (*starrs*) et les reconnaissances de leurs débiteurs. Plus tard elle devint le siège d'un tribunal, dont Charles Ier (1629-1640) abusa en faisant juger devant " la Chambre étoilée " tous les délits punissables d'amendes. Dans le but d'enrichir le trésor royal, ces amendes furent augmentées d'une manière indigne et les actes de la Chambre étoilée furent une des grandes causes de la révolution de 1640, par laquelle l'Angleterre revendiqua et conquit sa liberté.

I ask you again, do you swear that in 1881 you were not in communication with the police, informing them as to meetings you were going to? — I will.

Did you tell the police you wrote to Dublin? — I cannot exactly say. I could not tell you.

Did you show them the answer you got? — I cannot say whether I did or not.

Will you swear that you did not? — I could not say whether I did or not.

You say that you gave that letter to some one to give it to the Mullagh branch; who was it? — A man named Kennedy.

A relation of yours? — Yes, a cousin.

Now, I ask you, did you not show that letter to the police before you gave it to your cousin Kennedy? — I could not say whether I did or not.

Did I understand you to say that you said when you attended the meeting that you would give up the land if you were paid for your loss? — Yes.

When did you say any annoyance began? — No annoyance began till November, 1880.

What was the annoyance? — They held meeting on my land.

Anything else? — They boycotted me.

How? — When I went to the fair to buy a cow a man would ask me a price I would not give, and when he knew who I was and I came back he put another £1 on.

Anything more? — I cannot tell you anything more.

I want you to tell me everything. Was there anything more? (No answer.)

Come, Sir, anything more? — They used to shout and groan after me.

Who, the children? — And the men. There was an understanding among them.

Has there been more than one meeting on your land? — Yes, the first on November, 1880, and the last in November, 1886.

When you attended the meeting you were called to at Mrs. Derwin's did you say that you would clear off the land by January, 1887, if you got leave to get grass somewhere else? — Yes.

Did you mean it? — Yes.

Did you afterwards go to Constable Hennessy and tell him what had taken place? — I did not go to him.

Did he come to you? — He was in the house when I came back. (Laughter.)

Did you tell him what took place? — He asked me about it.

Did you intend to keep your promise about giving up your land? — I did.

In order to avoid trouble? — Yes.

And to get on good terms with your neighbours? — I suppose so.

Did the constable tell you not to give up the land? — He did not.

Why did you give it up? — Because he would not take it from me.

Did you give notice? — No, I went to him.

When did you go? — On January 10.

Did you ever give notice to give it up? — No.

I understand you to say you have a letter from Secretary Dillon authorizing you to get grass elsewhere? — It was not from him, but from Andrew Cahill I had it.

Did you show that to the head constable? — He was in the house when I got home.

Did I understand you to say Sergeant Hennessy took a copy of it? — He did.

In your house? — Not in my house; in my brother's house.

You continued to live with your brother? — Yes.

With reference to what took place in respect of the hay cut by Mrs. Dempsey there was a prosecution of a number of people, was there not? — Yes, about 11.

How often was Mrs. Dempsey sent to gaol? — I cannot say.

About how often[1]? — Only once—about the meeting in 1880.

Cross-examined by Mr. LOCKWOOD. — Mrs. Derwin is some relation of mine. I do not know whether she had been to see Mr. Harris to ask him to use his influence for me. I did not want to go to Mrs. Derwin's at all, but she called me in when I was passing. After being there I had no communication with the police. I had no communication with the police that day. I could not exactly say when I next had any communication with the police, but it might have been the next day.

Just tell me the names of some of the police you have communicated with since 1881? — No answer.

The question was repeated, and still no answer was given.

Are you afraid to give me the names of the police you have communicated with since 1881? — No answer.

The PRESIDENT. — We cannot wait here all day for your answer. What is your answer to this question? It is a very simple question.

The witness. — Sergeant Hennessy is one of them.

1. On remarquera combien ces questions posées par l'avocat de la contre-partie et les remarques qui l'accompagnent sont faites pour faire perdre son sang-froid à un témoin. Celui qui voudrait en avoir une idée joyeuse ferait bien de lire le procès de M. Pickwick dans les "Papers of the Pickwick Club" par Dickens.

Mr. Lockwood. — Now give us the rest of the names? — Sergeant Burns.

When did you first communicate with him? — I could not exactly tell you. It might have been 1881.

Do you mean to say on your oath that you cannot give me the names of any other men besides the two you have mentioned? Answer me this. What did you get for your communications to the police since 1881? — Nothing.

Do you swear that? — Yes.

From 1881 to 1888? — Nothing. I have been more at a loss than I have gained by it.

But I want to know what you gained; then we can judge? — Don't I tell you I got nothing?

Not up till to-day? — Yes.

Who is keeping you now?

The witness not answering, Mr. Lockwood asked again. — Do you know or don't you? — I suppose *The Times* is keeping me now.

Cross-examined by Mr. Biggar. — Did you never know of cattle and sheep straying from the land in parts where there is no ill-feeling among tenants and neighbours? — I have heard of cattle straying.

Has land-grabbing always been unpopular, so far as you know? — I do not remember much of it.

Had there not been a great deal of land-grabbing in the county Galway long before 1879? — I do not know. I never heard of such a name as "land-grabbing" until 1880.

But do you not know that land-grabbing means the taking of land over people's heads, and from those who have been unfairly evicted?—There was no objection to my taking the land.

Was land-grabbing ever a popular practice? — I never heard the word mentioned at all till 1880.

Was it ever popular to take land over people's heads, or from which tenants had been unfairly evicted? — I did not see many cases of that kind.

Did you ever think it a popular thing? — A man could not let the land go idle.

Was it a popular thing to take land from which a widow had been evicted? — It was often done. I do not know whether it was popular or not.

You told us that you took the land for six months; did you make a fresh arrangement at the end of the six months? — Yes. I gave £20 as security and £20 to give to Mrs. Dempsey.

Mr. Lockwood. — There is one other question I should like to ask, my

Lords. (To witness.) You have spoken of the Star Chamber tribunal before which you appeared. Did you make any statement of your evidence to any one apart from the statement you made before the Star Chamber? — (The witness made no reply.)

The PRESIDENT. — Has your evidence been checked by somebody? — Yes, it has.

Mr. LOCKWOOD. — When? (No answer.)

Question repeated.

The PRESIDENT (to witness). — Why will you not answer the question? — (The witness continued to be silent.)

Mr. LOCKWOOD. — Where did you make any statement of your evidence? (No answer.)

The PRESIDENT. — Will you not answer? You told us you had made a statement; do you remember that? — I do.

Well, then, you must remember where you made the statement? — In Killamore.

Mr. LOCKWOOD. — Before whom? — Mr. Joyce.

Is that the only statement you have made? (No answer.)

Can you tell me of any statement you have made besides that to Mr. Joyce? (Witness made no reply.)

The ATTORNEY-GENERAL[1]. — Just look at this gentleman, Mr. Shannon. (Mr. Shannon here stepped forward.) Did that gentleman ask you any questions? — Yes.

When you came to London? — Yes.

Did you see anybody writing down? — Yes.

When you took over this land what did you tell Mr. Allan? — I told him I would have nothing to do with the land if the widow Dempsey was able to hold it. He told me he could get many to take it if I did not.

In reply to further questions, witness said, — I gave Mr. Allan £20 as security and £20 to give to the widow Dempsey. I held about 30 Irish acres. I lived in my brother's house and had my meals with him. My brother did not pay me any money and I wanted none. I had some money from my father, and I was looking out for land. I had been two or three years helping my brother before I took the widow Dempsey's farm. The police gave me protection without my asking for it. So far as I know, no one interfered with me except the Land League. I mean by the Star Chamber a Crimes Act inquiry. I got the name from hearing it so called by a solicitor at Loughrea, who appeared for the defence of the prisoners there. It had never happened to me before not to get information as to where my cattle had strayed.

---

1. Le procureur général, avocat du *Times*, vient ici au secours du témoin.

Sergeant Michael Hennessy, Royal Irish Constabulary, examined by the Attorney-General, said, — In 1880 I was stationed at Tynagh; in 1882 I went to Portumna; and in 1884 I went back to Tynagh, and have been there ever since. I know the last witness Kennedy. After the meeting on his farm in December, 1880, I found he was protected by patrols. In April, 1881, he was under special protection. That was because his life was in danger. I think at that time that special protection was necessary. I believe that the Land League at Tynagh was established in December, 1880. In the early part of 1881 Land League meetings were held there. The officers of the Land League in Tynagh were John Derwin and Thomas Lawless. That is all I am positive about. Special protection was accorded to Kennedy from April, 1881, to January, 1882. He refused to take two men of the auxiliary force when the police left him. In 1882 the Land League[1] at Tynagh was suppressed. The National League was established in 1885, and its principal officers were John Derwin and Thomas Lawless, the same as for the Land League. On the night of December 5, 1886, I went to Kennedy's house, and he showed me a letter which he said he had received from Mr. Patrick Dillon at Mullagh. The letter was as follows : — " 5th Dec., 1886. — Mullagh Branch. — Mr. Patrick Kennedy, the man in possession of the widow Dempsey's farm at Kylebeg, has appealed to the committee of the above, asking time until January, 1887, in order to dispose of his cattle, and we have come to the conclusion that any person would be justified in exchanging dealings with him. By order of the committee." I have no doubt that letter referred to the National League. I knew from Kennedy at that time that he was trying to get grass for the cattle upon his farm. From what he told me I knew that he had difficulty in doing so. Kennedy arranged to put his cattle on Mrs. Kelly's farm. Mrs. Kelly kept a bakery, and had a large farm besides. I do not know whether anything happened to her when Kennedy's cattle were on her farm. Previous to November, 1886, I saw a notice posted calling a meeting at Kylebeg. It called upon the people to meet on Kylebeg farm, which was the one occupied by Kennedy. I do not recollect by whom the notice was signed. I remember a meeting afterwards taking place. I was not there. I do not know whether the people I have mentioned were there. I remember receiving two notices from Kennedy. They were sent to him by Patrick Dillon. I received the first on March 9. I happened to be in Kennedy's house on the day when he came in and he gave me the notice. I got the other one from him subsequently, in a similar manner, on April 14. At

1. *The Land League*, c'est la Ligue agraire ; supprimée en 1882 par le ministère de M. Gladstone, elle a été remplacée par *la Ligue nationale* avec le célèbre Plan de campagne, que M. Gladstone, ayant changé d'avis, ne désavoue pas. Le but de la Ligue nationale est d'obtenir la quasi-indépendance de l'Irlande, c'est-à-dire " *the Home Rule* ".

this time patrols were looking after Kennedy—not special protection; and when a man is being looked after by patrols it is our duty to visit his house from time to time.

Cross-examined by SIR C. RUSSELL. — Was there any looking after Kennedy from December, 1880, to January, 1882? — Yes, he had special protection part of that time, and after that was withdrawn he was protected by patrol. From December, 1880, to April, 1881, he was protected by patrol.

Were you in communication with Kennedy during the whole time you were in the neighbourhood? — Not much, because he was some time under special protection. When I returned in October, 1884, he was neither under patrol nor special protection. He told me he was willing to give up his farm.

You have no doubt, I suppose, in your mind that the cause of ill-will towards him was the having taken this farm? — I believe there was no other reason.

What countryman are you? — I am a native of Kerry.

You know there is a very strong feeling against any one who takes an evicted farm? Was it a popular thing to do? — I never knew any ill-feeling being caused by it before the time of the League, except among the parties evicted.

Were you present in London when Kennedy's evidence was taken? — I was—that is, when his evidence was taken down by Mr. Shannon. It was taken down in Mr. Soames's office. There were present three clerks, Mr. Shannon, and two others whom I did not know.

Had Mr. Shannon a printed paper before him? — No.

Do not answer without thinking. Had he a copy of the evidence taken before what has been called the "Star Chamber" inquiry before Mr. Joyce? — I do not know. I did not see one. My evidence was taken down at the same time. I brought Kennedy over. I was not examined at that inquiry.

Who instructed you to bring Kennedy over? — My superior officer, Mr. Somerville. He is a district inspector.

Did you get money to bring Kennedy over? — Yes, I got money, but I handed it to Mr. Somerville.

Re-examined by the ATTORNEY-GENERAL. — Sir Charles Russell has asked you about this unpopularity of taking evicted farms. Now, before 1879, if land was vacant in the district in which you were stationed, was it generally taken up by another tenant? — It was. There were always people ready to take the land. Apart from any ill-feeling entertained by the man turned out against the man who went in, I never knew it to be regarded as an offence to take an evicted farm or to pay rent. I never

1 fermage

knew of land-grabbers being denounced before League meetings, and until the League was established I never knew of any meetings being held to prevent people taking farms, nor heard of persons being punished for paying their rent. I have been in the force about twenty years and four months, and have been stationed in Tipperary and Galway.

Did Kennedy give his evidence at Wicklow Assizes? — He did. I was present in Court at the time. He gave more evidence than he has given to-day. Matthew Harris was also in Court.

Were any of the other people whose names you have mentioned present in Court? — Yes, John Derwin was there. He was attending the assizes as a witness.

Was any witness called to contradict the story Kennedy told? — No. Father Bodkin was a witness for the defence, but I cannot say whether he was sitting in Court while Kennedy gave his evidence.

Sergeant Roughan, examined by Mr. Ronan, said, — I was formerly in the Constabulary, and had charge of the Mullagh sub-district from April, 1883, to November, 1887. A branch of the National League was started in Mullagh in March, 1884. I was present at the meeting, at which Matthew Harris and Father Bodkin were present. I remember on August 1 attending a committee meeting of the League in the chapel yard at Mullagh. I know a man named John Donellan. He was a member of the committee. He said there was a land-grabber in the district. A member of the committee asked him who it was, and Donellan said it was Kennedy. The committee on that occasion decided to take no action, but appointed three members to attend a public meeting which was to be held at Loughrea on August 8 to consider the matter. I remember a committee meeting being held on October 24, 1886. I know Michael Garvey. He was present on that occasion, and introduced the name of Kennedy. He said that some action ought to be taken in the matter. I remember a League meeting being held on November 21, 1886, at Kennedy's farm, at which Mr. Sheehy, M. P., was present. He made a speech. I am aware that immediately after that meeting Kennedy had to send away his stock. I remember getting some information in April, 1887, that people were to attend to till the farm. In consequence of that I went to the farm with two of my men. I saw a man named Andrew Hardiman. I had a conversation with him. I asked him why they were sowing potatoes. There were eight police there altogether, and in consequence of their presence the people did nothing on the farm. I remember going to the farm on July 8, when I saw a man mowing the grass. That man was Michael Dempsey. During the months of July, August, and September I saw Mrs. Dempsey and her two sons and two daughters on the farm. Ten loads of hay were removed from the farm on September 21. The police pursued the people, who took the hay to Loughrea. They were brought up at the Wicklow Assizes and charged. Four of the men were convicted of conspiracy in connexion with Kennedy's farm.

Cross-examined by SIR C. RUSSELL. — These committee meetings were held in the chapel yard in the open air and were above-board[1]. I was present at them. I took no part in the proceedings.

You did not move any resolution? — Oh, no. (Laughter.) The majority of the people about there were members of the League. They made no objection to my presence and treated me civilly.

By Mr. REID[2]. — Was any police reporter present at the meeting at which Mr. Sheehy spoke? — Yes, a note was taken by a shorthand reporter, Constable Noble.

Mr. RONAN[3]. — That is a speech we shall put in.

Mr. REID. — I am much obliged. That is what I wanted to know.

Re-examined by the ATTORNEY-GENERAL. — The people were asked to subscribe to the League. I saw subscriptions handed in at some of these meetings.

The Court here adjourned for luncheon.

James Mannion was next called, in answer to Mr. ATKINSON, said, — I am a farmer and live in the county of Galway, in the west, near Letterfrack. I remember the Land League being established in Letterfrack. It was established by members of the League. Among them were Pat Ruane, of Tully, who was a money collector or treasurer, and a man named James Varilly. I do not remember exactly when the League was established, but it was some time in 1880. These two men were most active in establishing it.

In addition to these two men were there any others who collected money for the League? — There was another man named Michael Cawley. He was another collector. There were also Michael M'Donnell, Pat M'Kerran, and Michael Coyne. I was myself a member of the League for a while. I attended meetings of the League. These meetings were held in Letterfrack, in the house of a Mrs. Walsh, one of whose sons was hanged for the murder of Lyden[4]. Meetings were very often held there. The meetings were held about once a fortnight, but there was no special day for meeting. I was also a member of the Fenian Society[5]. I was sworn into it by Pat Ruane,

---

1. *And were above-board*, et n'avaient rien de caché. — 2. Avocat du côté Parnell. — 3. *M. Ronan*, avocat irlandais pour le *Times*. — 4. Toujours pour la cause agraire. — 5. *The Fenian Society*, société secrète fondée primitivement aux États-Unis pour obtenir l'indépendance absolue de l'Irlande et sa séparation complète du reste du Royaume-Uni. Recrutée surtout parmi les immigrants irlandais qui avaient servi en Amérique pendant la guerre de

in 1880, I think. Varilly was a member of the Fenian Society. All the men whom I have mentioned as collectors for the Land League were members of that society. All the men who attended the meetings at Mrs. Walsh's house were members of the Land League. I am not aware that there were any persons present who did not belong to it. The members of the Fenian Society had a sign by which they could know one another. I joined the Land League first. I was asked to join it by James Varilly. I did not collect for it. I did not get money from those who collected, but sometimes drink. At the meetings in Mrs. Walsh's house drink was distributed, and I believe it was the League that paid for it. Ruane used to pay for it. After I had been sworn in by Ruane I received a notice from John Faherty, who was a member of the League and a Fenian. In consequence of that notice I went to a place called Tully with John Faherty. On the way to Tully we stopped at James Varilly's house. From there we went on with Edward Varilly and Patrick Walsh. At the Tully cross roads we met Pat Ruane, Michael M'Donnell, and others. Altogether 60 or 70 people assembled. From there we went a mile further off to Anthony Coyne's house. Ruane gave M'Donnell certain orders. Up to that time he had been in command, but he then left M'Donnell in command. After this we approached Coyne's house. When we had reached it M'Donnell told us to break open the door and pull Coyne out of bed. We had been told that Coyne was going to evict an under-tenant of his named Lyden. The circumstances had been discussed at a meeting at Mrs. Walsh's house before the expedition. It had been arranged at that meeting that Coyne should be given a good beating, and that he should be asked for a copy of the processes[1].

Had any of the party fire-arms with them? — Yes. Michael Cawley had a pistol, Pat Walsh had a rifle, and M'Donnell had a revolver. I could not say who broke open the door of Coyne's house. John Faherty and a couple more pulled Coyne out of bed. There was no light in the place. He was dragged into the kitchen and warned not to exercise the law against Lyden, and he was asked for a copy of the processes. He swore that the process-server[2] in Clifden had them and that they were not in his possession. He was very much beaten and received a great kicking. Shots were fired through the roof of the house. Afterwards we scattered and went home, each to his own place. I went back to Letterfrack. No one was apprehended for this outrage. It occurred, I guess, in 1880, very soon after I was sworn in[3]. I think I was sworn in in the month of November.

---

la sécession, elle comptait à un certain moment un grand nombre d'associés et avait de nombreuses succursales en Irlande. — 1. *The processes,* les procès-verbaux d'éviction. — 2. *The process-server,* le distributeur des avis d'éviction. — 3. *I was sworn in,* après que j'étais devenu membre de la Ligue.

After this business at Coyne's house did you receive notice to attend a meeting? — I did. Edward Varilly gave me notice to attend at Mullaghglass, but I did not go. Subsequently I attended a meeting at which there was a discussion about Mr. Graham's tenants. The meeting was held at Letterfrack, in Pat Ruane's shop. It was in 1881, seven or eight months after Coyne's affair. The hour was about 9 o'clock. There were only five or six persons present. Pat Ruane was there himself. I happened to be in his shop that evening, and he told me to wait, as he wanted me.

Tell us what occurred with reference to Mr. Graham's tenants? — I was one of his tenants myself. Ruane said that the tenants would ruin the country by paying rent, and I replied that Mr. Graham and his tenants were on good terms, that he had given good reductions, and that we were all satisfied. It was then said that Mr. Graham or somebody belonging to him should be shot.

Was anything more done that night? — No. Our party gave the tenants notice not to pay any more. I went myself and posted notices on two tenants' doors.

What was the substance of the notice? — That no rent must be paid, and that any man who should pay would be found out and shot. Other notices were posted by others on other doors.

After that did the tenants pay? — They paid by stealth, not openly.

Were proceedings taken? — No, the tenants paid on the sly[1].

Do you remember after that having a conversation with Ruane about a Mr. Joseph M'Donald? — Yes, I received a message telling me to be at Letterfrack at 4 o'clock. I met Pat Ruane and five or six others at a place near Letterfrack where three roads meet. Ruane called me aside and said, " I am told that Mr. M'Donald is going to dine this evening with Mr. Graham, and I want you to find out at what time. "

Did he say what Mr. M'Donald had done? — He did not. Mr. M'Donald was Mr. Graham's agent.

Did he state why he wanted to ascertain whether Mr. M'Donald was to dine with Mr. Graham that night? — Yes, he wanted to know, because Mr. M'Donald was to be shot, adding that anybody who would shoot him would be well paid for the work.

Did you go to Mr. Graham's? — I did. I asked the butler, who was a great friend of mine, whether Mr. M'Donald was going to dine that night, and he told me that Mr. M'Donald would be there. Then I went back and told Ruane that Mr. M'Donald would not be there, and that Mr. Graham was going to dine at Mr. Brown's.

That was not true? — No.

1. *On the sly*, en cachette.

Why did you say it? — Because I knew the gentleman, and did not want to have a hand in it.

According to the rules of the Fenian Society, are you obliged to do what you are ordered? — Certainly; if you do not you will be shot if you are found out.

Was anything done to Mr. M'Donald? — No, except that a great number of his sheep were taken.

What was done with the sheep? — They were taken to Mrs. Walsh's farm at Letterfrack. We wanted to boycott Mr. M'Donald out of his farm. He had succeeded to it, and we determined to boycott him. That was discussed at a meeting held at Mrs. Walsh's house. We resolved to boycott him, and we determined to take his sheep. They were taken at intervals, five or six at a time, to Mrs. Walsh's. Both her sons were alive at this time.

Did you know the Rev. Canon Fleming, of Ballinakill? — Yes. I remember once working in the quarry near his house. John Faherty was working with me. Young Mr. Fleming passed us, and Faherty, speaking in the Irish language, said that he should not like to be in the canon's shoes.

Was canon Fleming subsequently fired at? — Yes.

Had you attended a meeting in Mrs. Walsh's house with reference to this outrage? — No, I knew nothing about that.

The PRESIDENT. — Was Faherty a Fenian and a Land Leaguer? — Yes, my Lord.

Mr. ATKINSON. — Do you remember a meeting at Cawley's Mountain? — Yes, I guess it was in 1881. It was a large meeting, attended by 200 people. They wanted to boycott Mrs. Blake, of Ryndvale, and another lady, Mrs. Prior. The meeting was held at night between 12 and 1 o'clock, by the moonlight. Ruane was there; all the members of that locality were there. All those persons were members of the Land League; they were also Fenians. As far as I was concerned, I did not know any difference between the members of the two bodies; the members of the one were members of the other. I remember the time that the Lydens were murdered. Before that day a meeting was held in Mrs. Walsh's house. Her son Pat was present; he was the son who was hanged for Lyden's murder. Michael was also present. There were also present Edward Varilly, Mike Cawley, John Faherty, and others. I do not remember all. A good many were there. I got notice to attend from Ruane. Ruane himself was not there, but his brother Johnny Ruane was. He was both a Land Leaguer and a Fenian. There was a discussion about the Lydens. It was said that they ought to be shot on account of herding for[1] Mr. Graham on part of the

1. *On account of herding for*, parce qu'ils avaient gardé des troupeaux pour.

farm from which the Walshes had been evicted. It was arranged that a party was to go to the Lydens for the purpose of shooting them, and Ruane said he would send for them. This meeting was the second meeting, and about six of us went to the house, about a mile or a mile and a half away—John Faherty, John Ruane, Pat Walsh, Edward Varilly, and myself—and I forget the name of the other man, but there were six. They were named by Ruane and Pat Walsh. Pat Walsh was the boy who was hanged for Lyden afterwards. We went within 50 yards of Lyden's house. We had fire-arms. Mike Cawley had one, and Walsh had a revolver. I had none, but Edward Varilly had a revolver. When we arrived at the house there was a light in it. There were cattle about the house when we arrived. The cattle were about 50 yards away from the house, and because the light was there we did not make any appearance, and one said that the best plan was to drive the cattle about the house, so that Lyden might come out and drive them away; but he did not come out. The dogs were barking, and they did not get the chance of shooting. The party then dispersed. Afterwards Lyden was shot. I was not there when that took place, and did not know it until the following morning. Between the time of this visit till the time he was shot I did not attend any meeting. I got notice from time to time to attend these meetings at Mrs. Walsh's house, but I could not attend. I have been at many of these meetings, but I did not attend one out of a hundred of those which were held. I know what moonlighting[1] means, and I have sometimes been moonlighting. The Land Leaguers were the moonlighters. I do not know any moonlighter who was not a member of the Land League.

When the moonlighters go to a man's house to visit him, what do they do to him? — Well, Sir, perhaps they might beat him, or shoot, or commit outrage on him.

For what offences? — That depends on what he was doing out of the way[2].

What do you mean, "out of the way"? — It depends, Sir, whether he was paying rent.

SIR C. RUSSELL. — I object, my Lords, to these general statements.

The PRESIDENT. — He has been moonlighting, and he will tell us what that means.

Mr. ATKINSON. — Have you yourself engaged in any moonlighting? — Nothing, except paying rent or taking an evicted farm.

SIR C. RUSSELL. — My Lords, I object. It is most unfair to make any statement of that sort.

---

1. *Moonlighting*, sortir au clair de lune pour attaquer quelque personne ou quelque maison désignée par la Ligue agraire. — 2. *Out of the way*, qui n'est pas dans les règles.

Mr. ATKINSON. — Have you yourself moonlighted a man for paying rent?

SIR C. RUSSELL. — No, no; I object again.

Witness. — I have left a notice at a man's door that he was not to pay any rent.

Mr. ATKINSON. — Some of the men you have mentioned, were they tried? Ruane, for instance; where is he? — In America.

Were some of the others tried? — Some of them were tried for conspiracy to murder.

Who were tried? — Conneally, Joyce, Varilly, and John Faherty were all tried for the Lydens' murder. I was present in court at the trial for conspiracy to murder. I was examined before the grand jury. I made a deposition before a magistrate in the presence of these men, and they pleaded guilty.

Cross-examined by SIR C. RUSSELL. — Are you a Ribbon man[1]? — I do not understand you, Sir.

Did you ever hear of the Ribbon Society? — I did not, Sir.

Never? — Never.

When did you first hear of Fenianism? — I never knew anything about it until I was a Land Leaguer down in that country of ours. I never heard of it before.

Have you lived in Letterfrack all your life? — Yes, Sir.

Have you been in America? — No; I never left the country except to come to London.

With whom did you come to London? — I came by the train.

With whom? — There was any amount of persons with me, but I do not know who they were.

Not even policemen? — I saw some policemen in the society that I had seen in Galway.

Were you charged yourself with having anything to do with the murder of Lyden? — Yes, Sir.

How long were you in gaol? — Something about three or four months.

How did you come to be let out? — I was let out because they could not find much against me.

Did you make any statement before you were let out? — Not to my recollection, Sir.

Think. — Well, if I did, Sir, I don't remember.

Did your mind give way at all when you were in prison? — Yes, Sir; I got a little excited.

---

1. *The Ribbon Society*, dont les membres sont appelés *Ribbon men*, est une société secrète opposée aux Orangistes ou Protestants.

You think you have got back your recollection quite clear? — Oh, yes; I guess so, now.

What was it that excited you? — I don't know, Sir.

How long was your mind affected? — About five or six weeks.

Where were you at that time?—I was in an institution at Ballinasloe.

In gaol?—No, in an asylum. I was removed from the gaol to the lunatic asylum, and I was there five or six weeks.

And after that five or six weeks, what then?—I came home. I was let out. The doctor said he would not want me any more.

Had you been released before you went to the lunatic asylum?—No; I was a prisoner at the time I was removed to the asylum.

Did you make any statement before you left the lunatic asylum?—No.

Or before you left the gaol?—No.

What age are you?—I cannot exactly tell you, Sir, but I think I am about 28 or 29.

On this particular night, when you went with five other men to Lyden's house, you went to murder Lyden if you got the chance, and you knew that when you went?—I did.

And when you went to Coyne's house you knew you were going to commit an outrage on that man, and you went?—Yes.

Except those two outrages and the posting of these notices, have you taken part in anything else?—Certainly, Sir, I have not taken part; but I went with the others.

Have you taken part by going with the others? If so, where?—I do not understand you, Sir, well.

You have told us of two or three outrages. Have you taken part in other outrages?—Well, yes, some more.

Upon whom?—Well, I just went when Mr. M'Donald—but I did not go——

Will you tell us what you know? You say that you put the other murderous men off the scent?—Yes, Sir.

Is there any other that you have taken part in?—Well, I have seen some of those sheep of Mr. M'Donald's taken away.

On your oath do you say you never heard of Fenianism before 1880?—I swear I did not. I swear I never heard of it or knew anything about it.

Is it not the fact that secret societies existed in that part of Galway, and to your knowledge?—Not to my recollection.

Have you heard them spoken of?—I knew nothing about them until I had seen the Land League started. I have heard of them since.

Have you heard since that they existed before your childhood in that part of the country?—Well, I heard something about it afterwards.

Were these meetings at Walsh's Fenian meetings?—I do not see how I could call them Fenian meetings because they were Land League meetings.

Was there any one there who was not a Fenian ?—I would not know what to call them. I call them Land Leaguers.

Was there any one there that was not a Fenian ?—No.

Do you allege—be cautious in your answer—that people who were members of the Land League there were all Fenians ? Take care, now, before you answer.—I do not know, Sir. I did not know much about them at the time, but just attended them sometimes.

Did you know the clergy of the district ?—I did, Sir ; the parish priest is down there now.

Do you know that he is a Fenian ?—I do not, Sir.

Do you say that he was a member of the Land League ?—I do not know, Sir.

You do not know if he was president of the Land League ?—I do not, Sir.

Do you know Father O'Connor ?—Yes, Sir.

Was he a Fenian ?—I do not know anything about the rev. gentleman.

Was he connected with the Land League ?—I do not know.

If he was the secretary of the Land League you never knew anything about him ?—I did not, Sir.

We have been told by another witness that he was the secretary ?—Well, he might know a little more than I do, Sir. (Laughter.)

Were any of these meetings that were held at night at the widow Walsh's house Fenian meetings and nothing else ?—I would not call them so, Sir. The Fenians are the people who would not kill cattle or anything else ; they would have gone up and shot their man.

Have you any reason except that for suggesting that these were not Fenians ?—That is my belief.

All these men, then, that you did meet in the dead of the night at widow Walsh's were Fenians ?—I would not call them Fenians. I would call them Land Leaguers.

But you have told the learned counsel that every one of them was a Fenian. Is that true or not ?—Well, I might, Sir.

Is it true or not what you have sworn ?—They were sometimes called Fenians and sometimes Land Leaguers.

Is it true or not that you have sworn that each one of the persons that attended these night meetings at the widow Walsh's, that they were to your knowledge Fenians ?—I guess they were both parties ; that is as far as I could go.

Do you now say that no persons attended at widow Walsh's that were not Fenians ?—They called themselves both parties—they were both Fenians and Land Leaguers.

Do you now swear that no one attended these night meetings at Mrs. Walsh's who was not a Fenian? If so, name one. Come, Sir, answer. —I call them——

I am not asking you what you call them; I am asking you, will you swear that any whom you saw at these night meetings of widow Walsh's were not Fenians?—There were some women in the house.

I am not talking of the women and children. Were the people who went there Fenians? Did you know them by a secret sign?—Yes, Sir.

Was it true that, knowing these men by secret signs, each of them was a Fenian?—Yes, that is true.

Well, we have got it at last. Are you a Land Leaguer?—I was, Sir.

Had you a card?—I got one, Sir.

Had you a card?—Yes, Sir.

Who gave it to you?—Ruane, Sir, about six or seven years ago. I got it at Letterfrack.

Where? Letterfrack consists of several houses at least.—He gave it to me at Mrs. Walsh's on Sunday. There were no meetings on that day.

Whose name was signed to it?—I cannot read, and I do not know.

Did you ever get a card signed, as membership cards are signed, by the president and secretary of the Land League?—I cannot read, and I do not know.

There was a card, and you did not know what it was?—"Here is a card for your being a Land Leaguer," he said.

Have you got it?—I do not know whether it is in the house or not.

What house?—Ireland, at Letterfrack.

I suppose you could get it?—Well, it may be, Sir.

Well, I wish you would try. Who asked you to be a member of the Land League?—The members of the Land League.

That is no answer. Who asked you, if any one, to join the Land League?—Pat Ruane and James Varilly. James Varilly is at Letterfrack. When I saw the whole of them joining it, they asked why was not I going to do it.

When?—I cannot understand what you mean.

When were you asked to join the Land League?—About the same time that I had been sworn being a member of the Fenian Brotherhood, or whatever they call themselves. I was joining the Land League before that.

When were you asked to join the League; what year?—I guess it was in 1880.

Will you swear it was in 1880?—As far as I can go it was.

Will you swear there was any League in Letterfrack in 1880?—As far as my opinion goes that was the time. I cannot exactly swear.

In reference to this man Lyden, did you come over with poor Mrs. Lyden, the wife of the murdered man? — I have not seen her for the last six years.

You were a tenant of Graham's, were you?—My father was.

And was Mrs. Walsh, at whose house these night meetings were held, any relation to the person who was evicted by Graham?—I do not understand, Sir.

Do you know there was a tenant named Walsh evicted by Graham? You know that Lyden went in to take care of the land?—Yes.

Was Mrs. Walsh, at whose house these night meetings were held, any relation to the evicted tenant?—No.

Was she herself the evicted tenant?—Yes, Sir. (Laughter.)

Why did you not tell me?—I did not understand you.

And the man who was hanged for the murder was her son?—There was one, Sir, hanged. Yes.

And he was not one of the six that went on the night when you went as one of the murderous party?—He was, Sir.

You did not mention that?—I did, Sir.

Pat Walsh was one of the party?—Yes.

Were you examined at any inquiry—at any secret commission?—I do not know. Yes, I was examined before the grand jury in Galway. I was not before any other Court. I was not examined at the trial.

Who came to you at Letterfrack about giving your evidence?— I was arrested by the police at Letterfrack.

Who came to you about giving your evidence here?—Oh, I do not know the gentleman that handed me the summons.

Cross-examined by Mr. REID.—You told us you were a Fenian; are you a member of any other secret societies?—No. I never heard of any other secret society in Ireland except the Fenians.

By Mr. LOCKWOOD.—Do you remember anything of the oath you took in 1880?—I do not; it was very hard, and I cannot remember it. I repeated it, but I cannot remember it now.

Do you remember the Rev. Mr. Ryder being shot at?—I do not know that gentleman. Yes, I remember he was fired at. I guess that was about 1880 or 1881.

Do you remember the incident? Do you suggest that it was after the Land League was established in the neighbourhood?—I do not know about that gentleman.

You have heard the question; now, I ask you whether you mean to suggest that took place after the Land League came into existence?—I never heard a word about him.

Yes, you said he was shot at in 1880 or 1881.—Do you mean Lyden?

I understood you to say that Mr. Ryder was shot at in 1888 or 1881.

Now, with regard to this Mr. Ryder, a Protestant clergyman?—I know a certain gentleman, a Canon Fleming.

Leave Canon Fleming alone for a short time. (Laughter.) Do you know in that neighbourhood a Protestant clergyman called Ryder?—I never heard of him.

Do you suggest that Canon Fleming was shot at in 1880 or 1881?—Yes, he was fired at, but I forget which year. I thought you were asking me aboutLyden.

By Mr. Biggar.—Do you know anything about the evidence given at the trial of Walsh?—I do not know anything except what I told the gentleman at the trial.

Do you remember the evidence given for the defence?—I do not know anything about Pat Walsh's evidence.

Re-examined by SIR H. JAMES.—I understand that you became a Land Leaguer and a Fenian; which were you first?—A Land Leaguer.

Mr. REID.—That is a flat contradiction of his own evidence.

The PRESIDENT.—No; I took it exactly as he says it now.

Cross examination continued.—I paid a shilling to James Varilly, and then I received a card from another person—I think it was Pat Ruane. I do not know whether I have kept that card or not. After paying that money and receiving the card I attended meetings at Mrs. Walsh's.

Did you attend those meetings before paying the money and receiving the card?—I was there before to get a card of the meeting.

Had any one spoken to you about becoming a member of the Land League before you paid the money?—Yes, Ruane said I would have to be a member of the League.

Did he ask you that before you went to Mrs. Walsh's or after?—Before.

You knew of Canon Fleming being shot at?—Yes.

But not about Mr. Ryder?—I never heard of the gentleman.

Peter Flaherty, examined by Mr. MURPHY, said,—I am a farmer, and live at Ardnagreeva. I am a tenant of Mrs. Blake. I remember being asked to join the League. James Hanna asked me. I agreed to do so and paid money.

At that time were there any secret societies in the neighbourhood to your knowledge?—Not at that time.

After you joined the Land League did you attend any of the meetings?—I did.

Can you give me the date when you joined?—I could not give you the exact date, but to the best of my belief it was in 1880. The men I remember to have taken part in the Land League when I first joined were the two Ruanes, Mulcarran, John M'Donnell, and Michael Cawley.

1 Deposition

After you had become a member of the Land League, do you remember joining some other society?—I do, Sir. A party of men came to my house, and I was sworn in my own house. They got me out of bed. I did not know who they were at the time. I was sworn not to pay any rent and to be true and loyal to the Irish Republic[1]. There were about thirteen men. I did not know who they were that night, but I afterwards got to know them. I got to know the names from Hanna on the night of the outrage on O'Neill's sheep. Hanna was the man who swore me in[2].

You have spoken of the outrage at O'Neill's farm. I want to ask you a little about that. Had there been a meeting the night before this outrage? —There was, Sir. It was held on some townland[3] on Mrs. Blake's property, between 12 and 1 o'clock at night. There were some eighty men present. To my knowledge there were a good many Land Leaguers present. It was decided at that meeting to banish O'Neill's cattle and sheep from the farm, and that if after notice O'Neill did not take them away, they should be destroyed.

What had O'Neill done?—Nothing at all, Sir. He was a very good man. They wanted him to give up his land. He was at that time a tenant of Mrs. Blake's, and she was boycotted. The two head men in this affair, that I knew of, were Ruane and Mulcarran. I went to O'Neill's farm on the night of the outrage. Pretty near ninety men went, I suppose. I was appointed, with ten other men, to go and watch at the herd's house[4]. If he or any of his family were disturbed we were not to allow them to come outside. If they attempted to do so we were to destroy them.

Had some of the men got guns with them?—One had a revolver. The sheep were drowned, I believe, but I was not present. Five or six weeks after that I remember attending another meeting at Derryherbert, at which about sixty men were present. It was held at between 1 and 2 o'clock in the night. Ruane made a speech at that meeting. He told us to repeat what he said after him, and to hold up our right hands while we did so. We did as he told us. I do not remember the substance or the form of the oath. When I became a member of the Land League I paid the money to Hanna. He collected money for both societies. I attended another meeting which was held at the sacristy of the chapel at Tully.

What sort of a meeting was that? Was it of the Land League or of the secret society?—It was a meeting of evicted tenants on Mrs. Blake's property. They were expecting to get more or less money from the priest, and he told them that it was not right at all to give the League money to the landlords for rent.

1. Les Fénians voulaient établir la République en Irlande. — 2. *Who swore me in*, qui me fit prêter serment. — 3. *Townland*, terrains communaux. — 4. *The herd's house*, la demeure du surveillant des bestiaux.

Who was the priest?—Father O'Connell. Mr. Robinson, the agent, was to come and collect the rents, and Pat Mulcarran swore by God to make it his business to go and watch Mrs. Blake's house that day, and if any one went to pay his rent we should know it. The priest had then gone out. On another occasion, when I came out of the chapel, in the square of the chapel Michael Cawley read out of a letter that any one who settled with Mrs. Blake would not get any money from the Land League.

Mr. REID.—I really must submit, my Lords, that this is not admissible in evidence.

The PRESIDENT.—First of all, who is Michael Cawley?

Mr. MURPHY (to witness).—Who is Michael Cawley?—He was connected with the Land League.

The PRESIDENT.—Assuming that the letter was read at the meeting, surely it would be admissible?

Mr. REID.—I apprehend that that would be so.

Mr. MURPHY (to witness).—Did he read the letter out loud to you?—He read it when there were 12 or 13 standing by.

The PRESIDENT.—From whom was the letter?—I could not tell you from whom it came.

Mr. MURPHY.—On whose land were the secret meetings held?—On Michael Cawley's land.

Is Pat Mulcarran in the country now?—No, he went away to America for fear of arrest. That was after Cawley and the rest were tried for conspiracy.

Cross-examined by Mr. REID.— You took part in the moonlighting at O'Neill's?—Yes.

You went there to watch the herd's house and to shoot the herd. You were quite prepared to do it, of course?—We were.

Did you take part in any other outrages?—In only that one. I had nothing to do with any other outrage. I knew that outrages were committed, but I had nothing to do with them.

You took care to be absent yourself? — I was not asked to join in them.

You have said that you joined a society and took an oath in favour of the Irish Republic?—I did.

Do you mean to say that you did not know the nature of that society?—I did not know what it was.

Have you never heard of the Irish Republican Brotherhood?—I have not.

Do you say that you do not now know what it was you swore to join?—I do not, Sir.

You too kanother oath at another meeting?—I did.

Do you know what it was for?—We were sworn in to be moonlighters, I suppose. That is what I understood by it.

And you were perfectly prepared to go moonlighting whenever requested? —Yes; whenever I was called upon to go.

How long did you remain in that frame of mind?—Not very long—a year or a year and a half, between 1880 to 1882.

In what form did repentance come, or did you repent?—No, Sir; they accused me of things I was not guilty of, and then I turned against them.

There was no repentance, then, on your side?—There is not, Sir.

And you would be ready to do it again?—I would do it again.

Why?—Because they treated me badly.

How came you to quarrel with these moonlighters?—They accused me of saying things which I did not say, and then on one occasion Mulcarran seized me by the collar and threatened me and fired a shot at me. Then I gave information to the police.

When was that?—In 1882.

Did you complain that you had been shot at yourself?—I did.

Was the man tried for it?—He was.

Was he convicted?—He escaped to America.

Since then have you been constantly giving information to the police? —Never since.

Did you ever see Mannion, the last witness, at any meeting?—No.

You saw Ruane?—Yes.

Where did these meetings generally take place?—On the mountain.

Were you ever at a meeting held in any building?—No.

When were you first asked to give evidence in this inquiry?—Last Thursday, about 8 o'clock, I was served with a summons.

By whom?—I do not know. I had had no communication with the gentleman before.

You received a subpœna[1]?—Yes.

You came to London?—I did, Sir, and made a statement.

Whom did you travel with?—Mannion, the last witness.

Any one else?—There was another woman along with me. (Laughter.)

Cross-examined by Mr. Biggar.—Were all the tenants prosperous on Mrs. Blake's farms in 1880?—They were better off than now.

Do you know whether the tenants were getting relief from the relief funds?—There were some of them.

How many?—Every one got more or less, but the poorest class of them got it three or four times.

1. *A subpœna*, une citation de comparaître (sous peine d'amende).

Was Mrs. Blake's brother-in-law one of the committee appointed to distribute the relief?—He was.

In spite of the fact that her tenants were prosperous and that she was giving no reductions, her brother-in-law was distributing relief among a large number of the tenants?—Yes.

Re-examined by SIR H. JAMES.— How far does Mannion live from you? —About nine miles.

Were you examined in May, 1883, in Galway?—I was, before the grand jury and in Sligo.

Now, you were asked by my learned friend whether you were ashamed, and you told us you were not ashamed, because you had been ill-treated. What was it you were not ashamed of?—I was not ashamed to be a Crown witness, because they ill-treated me.

The PRESIDENT.—I so understood it.

Mr. REID.—I think he went on to say that he would do it again. Of course, we may have been at cross purposes. I hope I have not made any unfair suggestion.

The PRESIDENT.—No, no. Nothing can be fairer than your mode of cross-examination.

Mr. REID (to witness).—As I understand, you were prepared to join in moonlighting affrays whenever required until 1882?—Yes, I should have gone.

And you were prepared to commit murder in these moonlighting affrays, if necessary?—Yes, I should take hand and part with them.

In 1882 you quarrelled with your confederates, you say?—Yes.

And thereupon became a Crown witness?—Yes.

Was it not from anger or revenge that you left the confederacy?—If there had not been an attempt to shoot me I should never have left it.

And you would have been prepared to continue moonlighting and to commit murder, if held to be expedient?—Yes, I should.

Your ideas upon murder have not altered?—Well, I do not want to murder anybody.

SIR H. JAMES.—Before you went out on these expeditions, had you taken an oath?—I had.

How many people were present when you took the oath?—About 13.

What was the oath? What did you undertake to do?—I was to be true and loyal to the Irish Republic. That is all I understood.

Was there any oath taken binding you to obey orders or to commit outrages?—I do not understand.

The PRESIDENT.—I understood him to say before, "I was sworn not to pay rent and to be true and loyal to the Irish Republic."

Witness.—I was sworn, first, not to pay any rent; and on the mountains I was sworn to be true and loyal to the Irish Republic.

Sir H. James.—Did you receive any summonses to take part in moonlighting outrages after taking these oaths?—No, but Hanna used to tell me what was going on, and I used to go with him. Hanna told us that if one refused to go out when called upon, one would be killed on the following night.

And having taken the oath, you did go out?—Yes.

The Court then adjourned.

NAVAL AND MILITARY INTELLIGENCE.

The Commander-in-Chief has appointed Colonel F. G. S. Curtis, C. M. G.[1], half-pay, to command the troops in Natal, in succession to Colonel Stabb, deceased.

The following appointments were made at the Admiralty yesterday :—Commander Archibald J. Pocklington, to the Hercules, to date November 23; Lieut.[2] Claude A. W. Hamilton, Lieut. Amherst C. H. Pearson, and Lieut. Lawrence A. Tawney, to the Linnet; and Lieut. Henry H. Stileman, to the Mariner, all to date November 19; Lieut. William P. Lodder, and Lieut. John Nicholas, to the Mariner, undated; Lieut. George W. Gubbins to the Shannon, to date November 19; Lieut. George W. Smith, to the Rover, to date November 13; Lieut. George J. S. Warrender, to the Duke of Wellington, to date October 27; and Lieut. Hugh Talbot, to the Excellent, to date November 13; William Rabbidge, chief engineer[3], to the Pandora, to date November 13; William B. Clark, paymaster, to the Wrangler, to date October 16; Ernest F. Ellis, engineer, to the President; Henry J. Walker, engineer, to the Beagle; William Whittingham, engineer, to the Amphion; James M. Simpson, engineer, to the Cossack; James A. Roye, engineer, to the Neptune; Henry T. Knapman, engineer, to the Ajax; and William D. Chope, engineer, to the Devastation; Henry J. Little, acting assistant engineer[4], to the Hercules; John E. Mortimer, acting assistant engineer, to the Hotspur; and Septimus Ham, acting assistant engineer, to the Invincible; and Thomas H. Turner, probationary[5] assistant engineer, to the Belleisle, all to date November 13.

UNIVERSITY INTELLIGENCE.

CAMBRIDGE, Nov. 13.

Mr. Francis Darwin, M.A., M. B.[6], of Trinity College, has been appointed Reader in[7] Botany in succession to Dr. Vines.

1. *C. M. G., Companion of the Order of Saint Michael and Saint George. Half-pay,* à demi-solde. — 2. *Lieutenant.* — 3. *Engineer,* mécanicien. — 4. *Acting assistant engineer,* pour faire fonctions d'aide mécanicien. — 5. *Probationary,* pour faire un stage comme. — 6. *Master of Arts, Bachelor of Medecine.* — 7. *Reader in,* professeur de.

Mr. Edward Henry Douty, M. A., M. R. C. S.[1], L. R. C. P.[2], of King's College, has been appointed Senior Demonstrator[3] in Anatomy. Mr. William Stanley Melsome, B. A., Fellow of Queen's College, and Mr. Robert William Michell, B. A., of Gonville and Caius College, have been appointed Junior Demonstrators of Anatomy.

Dr. Routh has been appointed Chairman of the Examiners for the Mathematical Tripos[4] Part II.

MR. GOSCHEN[5].—Mr. Goschen is expected to arrive in West Bromwich at 4 o'clock to-day, when he will be received at the Town-hall by about 100 delegates, with addresses from the various local Liberal Unionist[6] and Conservative organizations. At the evening meeting Mr. Alderman Farley will preside and will move a resolution of welcome to Mr. Goschen and of confidence in the Unionist Government. After Mr. Goschen's reply, Mr. Kenrick, M. P., will propose, and Mr. George Salter, chairman of the Conservative Association, will second a vote of thanks to Mr. Goschen for his address.

THE IRON TRADE.—Business at Middlesbrough was very quiet yesterday, and prices of pig-iron were less strong than last week, for, though 34s. 3d. was generally quoted for early deliveries of No. 3, 34s. would readily be taken by a few merchants, and buyers even hesitated about giving that. There is no buying for forward delivery[7] at present. Middlesbrough warrants were 33s. 7½d. Grey forge has dropped to 33s. Makers not so firm in their prices, and several would be glad to get 34s. 6d. for No. 3. They are put to considerable inconvenience in delivering, owing to want of trucks. Finished iron prices very stiff at last week's rates, but steel rails rather cheaper, £4 being taken.

SUPPOSED MURDER AT THE EAST-END.—On Friday last William Wood, a waterman, was in his boat on the river Thames, off Wapping-stairs[8], when he noticed the body of a woman dressed in good clothing floating down the river. He secured the body and took it ashore. Wood communicated with the police and they removed the body to the mortuary[9]. The deceased woman

---

1. *Member of the Royal College of Surgeons.* — 2. *Licentiate of the Royal College of Physicians.* — 3. *Senior Demonstrator*, premier chef d'anatomie. — 4. Le *Tripos* est une liste divisée en *trois* classes des candidats reçus avec honneur à l'Université à l'examen de sortie, en Lettres, en Sciences, et en Mathématiques. — 5. M. Goschen. Le très honorable George J. Goschen, membre du Parlement, conseiller privé et actuellement chancelier de l'Échiquier (ministre des finances). C'est un des plus puissants adversaires des projets de "Home Rule" en Irlande soutenus par M. Gladstone, bien qu'il soit d'accord avec ce dernier sur presque toutes les questions. C'est un orateur des plus éloquents et des plus véhéments, et un excellent ministre des finances.(α) — 6. *The Liberal Unionists* sont ceux des libéraux qui se sont séparés de M. Gladstone, quand, après l'avoir longtemps combattu, celui-ci est devenu le promoteur du *Home rule.* — 7. *For forward delivery*, pour des livraisons à terme. — 8. *Off Wapping-stairs*, près du débarcadère de Wapping, au-dessous de Londres. *The East End* est l'est de Londres. — 9. *The mortuary*, la morgue. 3) saumon de fer (masse de fer telle qu'elle est sortie de la fonte) 11 camion

(α) C'est un Juif -

was fully dressed with the exception of hat and shoes, which were missing. Inquiries were at once made by the police, and it was ascertained that the body was that of Frances Annie Hancock, who had been missing since October 21. On that day she was seen in the Strand, in company with a tall, fair gentleman with a heavy moustache. She was wearing a gold necklace, and that was the last time she was seen alive. When the body was recovered the necklace was missing. Deceased resided at Prusom-street, Brixton, where, it is stated, she was supported by some gentleman at present unknown. At an inquiry held on Monday evening at the Vestry-hall, Shadwell, by Mr. Wynne E. Baxter, the coroner[1] for the South-Eastern Division of Middlesex, on the body of deceased, only evidence of identification was taken. Owing to the mysterious nature of the case and the supposition that the deceased woman has met her death by foul means, the coroner adjourned the inquiry in order that a *post mortem* examination[2] might be made on the body and to give the police an opportunity of fully inquiring into the facts of the case.

FOREIGN COMMERCIAL INTELLIGENCE.

(REUTER'S TELEGRAMS.)

PARIS, Nov. 13, 10 p. m.—Business was done on the Petite Bourse this evening as follows :—Three per Cent. Rente, for account[3], 82f. 95c. ; Five per Cent. Italians, 96f. 77½c. ; Imperial Ottoman Bank, 530f. ; Egyptian Unified 410f. ; Turkish, Group IV., 15f. 47½c. ; Rio Tinto shares, 678f. 75. ; Four per Cent. Spanish, 73¼ ; Panama Canal shares, 253f. 75. ; Four per Cent. Hungarian Gold Rente, 85⅛.

BERLIN, Nov. 13.—The Bourse was weak under the influence of realizations and speculative sales. Leading international stocks[4] all declined, Russian and Egyptian losing ½ to fully ¾ per cent. ; other descriptions were about ¼ per cent. easier. Short exchange[5] on London easier at 20 34, and three months' bills at 20 22. Bills on St. Petersburg fell to 206, and roubles to 209 75 for money, and 209 50 for the account. Private discount 3¼ per cent. The subscriptions to the New Turkish Loan[6] were so numerous that the list was closed early to-day.

VIENNA, Nov. 13.—The stock market was very dull, and home funds declined ⅛ to ¼ per cent. Lombards and Lemberg shares were both 1fl.[7] easier, but the principal banking and financial shares remained steady and unchanged. Sight exchange[8] on London firmer at 122, and sovereigns rather dearer at 12 16. The closing prices at the Evening Bourse to-day were as follows :—Four per Cent. Hungarian Gold Rente, 100 90 ; Lombardo-Venetian Railway, 102 ; napoleons, 9f. 67.

1. *The coroner*, voy. page 207, note 4. — 2. *A post mortem examination*, une autopsie. — 3. *For account*, à terme. — 4. *Leading stocks*, les fonds principaux. — 5. *Short exchange*, chèque à courte date. — 6. *The New Turkish Loan*, le nouvel emprunt turc. — 7. *Fl.*, florin ; le florin autrichien vaut environ 2 fr. 15. — 8. *Sight exchange*, chèque à vue.

MADRID, Nov. 13.—Four per Cent. Interior, 72 80; Four per Cent. Exterior, 74 75; Exchange on London (three months), 25 50.

FRANKFORT, Nov. 13.—A decidedly weak tendency prevailed on to-day's Bourse and quotations of leading foreign stocks, of Lombards, Credit Anstalt, and other speculative descriptions were all lower. Short exchange on London 20 36. Private discount 3 3/8 per cent.

NEW YORK, Nov. 13.—Stocks opened very weak, and a sharp decline[1] in prices ensued. Later the market recovered and left off dull, but firm. Money easy. Petroleum firm, but quiet. Flour steady. Sugar strong. Tin quiet. Iron quiet but steady.

	Quotations.		
	Nov. 13.	Nov. 12.	Nov. 10.
Call Money, U. S. Government Bonds[2] ..	2 p.c.	2 p.c.	1 1/2 p.c.
D° Other Securities	2 p.c.	2 p.c.	1 1/2 p.c.
Exchange on London, 60 days' sight	4 84 1/2	4 84 1/2	4 84
Cable Transfers	4 88 1/4	4 88 1/4	4 88 1/4
Exchange on Berlin, 60 days' sight	95 1/8	95 1/8	95 1/8
Exchange on Paris, 60 days' sight..	5 23 1/8	5 23 1/8	5 23 1/8
Four per cent. United States Funded Loan.	127 5/8	127 1/2	127 1/4
Western Union Telegraph Shares	84 5/8	84 3/8	85 1/8
RAILWAYS.			
Canadian Pacific	54	55 1/4*[3]	55 1/8
Canada Southern..	52 3/8	53	53 1/2
Central of New Jersey	90 1/4	90	90 3/4
Central Pacific	35	36	36 1/2
Chicago, Burlington, and Quincy	110 1/4	111	110 1/2
Chicago, Milwaukee, and St. Paul, Com.	65 3/8	65 3/4	66 1/2
D°, Preferred[4]	105 3/4	106 1/2	106 3/4
Chicago, and North-Western	109 7/8	110 3/4	111 1/2
D°, Preferred Shares	141 1/2	142 1/2	142
Delaware, Lackawanna, and Western	136 1/2	137 1/2	138
Denver and Rio Grande	17 1/2	18 1/2	18 3/4
Illinois Central	115 5/8	116	116 1/8
Lake Shore and Michigan Southern	99 7/8	101 3/4	103 1/8
Louisville and Nashville..	57 1/2	58 3/8	59 3/4
Michigan Central..	86	87 1/2*	88 3/4
Missouri, Kansas, and Texas	13	12 3/4	13
New York Central and Hudson River	108 3/8	109 1/8	109 3/4
New York, Lake Erie, and Western	27 1/8	28	28 3/4
D°, Second Mortgage Bonds[5]	99 3/4	100 7/8	101
New York, Ontario, and Western	15 1/2	16	16 3/8
Norfolk and Western Preferred	50 7/8	51 3/4	52 1/4
Northern Pacific	28 3/8	26 1/2	27
D°, Preferred	60 3/8	60 7/8	61 5/8
Ohio and Mississippi..	22 1/8	23	22 3/4
Oregon & Transcontinental Common	30 1/8	30 1/2	31 3/8
Philadelphia and Reading	47 3/4	48 1/8	49 1/4

1. *A sharp decline*, une forte baisse. — 2. *Call money, United States Bonds*, obligations du gouvernement des États-Unis payables au gré du gouvernement. — 3. L'astérisque ici est un renvoi, dont l'explication se trouve page 254 : **Price asked*, c'est-à-dire prix demandé. — 4. *Preferred*, actions privilégiées, qui passent avant les actions ordinaires, quand les affaires de la compagnie ne suffisent pas pour payer des dividendes sur toutes les actions. Les actions ordinaires deviennent alors des *deferred shares*, actions à dividende différé. — 5. *Mortgage bonds*, obligations hypothécaires. 6 Ditto = idem. the same

	Quotations.		
	Nov. 13.	Nov. 12.	Nov. 10.
St. Louis and San Francisco	$25\frac{1}{2}$	$25\frac{5}{8}$	$26\frac{7}{8}$
D°, Preferred	66	$65\frac{1}{2}$	$67\frac{3}{8}$
D°, First Preferred	110	$111\frac{3}{4}$	113
Union Pacific	$63\frac{3}{4}$	$64\frac{1}{4}$	$65\frac{1}{8}$
Wabash, St. Louis, and Pacific..	$13\frac{1}{8}$	14	$14\frac{1}{2}$
D°, Preferred	27	27	$27\frac{1}{2}$
Coffee, fair Rio	$15\frac{1}{2}$	$15\frac{1}{2}$	$15\frac{1}{2}$
D°, good Rio	$15\frac{3}{4}$	$15\frac{3}{4}$	$15\frac{3}{4}$
Copper, December delivery	17 40	17 $47\frac{1}{2}$	17 $47\frac{1}{2}$
Corn, new Western	$50\frac{1}{4}$	$51\frac{3}{8}$	$52\frac{1}{4}$
Cotton, day's receipts at U. S. ports, bales[1].	48,000	46,000	37,000
D°, day's export to Great Britain	12,000	18,000	29,000
D°, day's export to the Continent	22,000	10,000	6,000
D°, middling upland	10	9.15-16	10
Flour, extra State shipping brands[2]	3 80. 4 00	3 80 4 00	3 80 4 00
Freight for grain, steamer to Liverpool, per bushel..	$5\frac{3}{4}$d.	$5\frac{1}{2}$d.	5d.
D°, steamer to London, per bushel	6d.	6d.	$5\frac{7}{8}$d.
D°, for cotton to Liverpool	$\frac{1}{4}$d.	$\frac{1}{4}$d.	$\frac{1}{4}$d.
D°, petroleum to U. Kingdom, per brl.[3].	3s. 9d.	3s. 9d.	3s. 9d.
D°, d°, to arrive	—	—	—
Iron, Coltness, No. 1..	21 50	21 50	21 50
Lard[4], Wilcox's	8 85	8 90	8 95
D°, d°, futures, December delivery	8 80	8 85	8 85
D°, Fairbank's..	8 85	8 90	8 95
Petroleum, crude[5]	$6\frac{5}{8}$	$6\frac{5}{8}$	$6\frac{5}{8}$
D°, Pipe Line Certificates[6]	$86\frac{3}{4}$.	$86\frac{3}{4}$	$85\frac{3}{8}$
D°, standard white	$7\frac{3}{8}$	$7\frac{3}{8}$	$7\frac{3}{8}$
Spirits of Turpentine	$45\frac{1}{2}$	$45\frac{1}{2}$	$45\frac{1}{2}$
Steel Rails..	$28\frac{1}{2}$	$28\frac{1}{2}$	$28\frac{1}{2}$
Sugar, fair refining muscovados	$5\frac{1}{8}$	5	5
Tallow, prime city	6	6	6
Tin, Straits	22 35	22 50	22 50
Wheat, red winter	$111\frac{1}{4}$	111	113
D°, spring, No. 2, Chicago	116	$113\frac{1}{4}$	114

*Price asked.

Sales on the New York Market.—Wheat, futures[7] (bushels), 4,128,000; ditto, spot[8], 18,000; corn, futures (bushels), 448,000; ditto, spot, 147,000; coffee (bags), 20,700; cotton (bales), 96,100; lard (tierces), 2,000; petroleum (barrels), 1,557,000; ditto, Pipe Line Runs, 564,000; ditto, shipment from regions, 141,000.

PHILADELPHIA.

	Nov. 13.	Nov. 12.	Nov. 10.
Pennsylvania Railroad Shares	$52\frac{5}{8}$	$53\frac{1}{4}$	$53\frac{5}{8}$
Petroleum, standard white	$7\frac{1}{4}$	$7\frac{1}{4}$	$7\frac{1}{4}$

1. Nombre des balles (de coton) reçues aux ports des États-Unis. — 2. *Extra State shipping brands*, marques extraordinaires de l'Etat pour exportation. — 3. *Per brl.*, per barrels. — 4. *Lard*, saindoux. — 5. *Crude*, non raffiné. — 6. Voyez page 114, note 7. — 7. *Futures*, à venir. — 8. *Spot*, pour *on the spot*, sur-le-champ, actuellement sur le marché.

NEW ORLEANS.

	Nov. 13.	Nov. 12.	Nov. 10.
Cotton, middling..	9 5/8	9 9/16	9 9/16

RAILWAY AND OTHER COMPANIES.

A general meeting of the EAST and WEST INDIA DOCK[1] Company was held yesterday at the Dockhouse, Billiter-street, under the presidency of Mr. H. H. Dobree. The chairman stated that the meeting was a special one, convened in accordance with the London and St. Katharine and East and West India Docks Act[2], 1888, the provisions of which, so far as that day's business was concerned, had been placed before the proprietors in the official circular addressed to them by the secretary. Under these provisions they had three matters to deal with—to settle the number of directors to be elected on to the board, the *maximum* authorized by the Act being 18 and the *minimum* 12; to elect a new body of directors; and to determine the remuneration of those members of the joint committee who would represent the company on such committee. The directors had invited the committee who were associated with them in the action which led to the passing of the Act to confer with them as to what recommendations should be made to the proprietors in regard to the number of directors to be elected on the new board, and also as regarded the number of the old directors to be selected to serve on that board. The result of the conference was the circular which had been issued by the committee, of which M. John Coles had acted as chairman. With the recommendations in that circular the directors concurred, and the proxies[3] they had received showed that the recommendations were approved by a very considerable body of the ordinary stockholders. The circulars and proxies were issued at the expense of the committee, acting quite independently of the directors. He might state that the committee and the directors together had received 254 proxies, representing 277 votes; while by Mr. C. H. Stewart, Sir Richard Nicholson, Mr. Mead, and Mr. Bartley 55 proxies had been received, representing 49 votes. The directors had always advocated a large board, on the ground that as members of the principal firms importing produce into the City of

1. On sait que les *Docks*, à Londres, sont de grands bassins sur les bords de la Tamise, entourés d'énormes magasins ou entrepôts (*warehouses*), hauts de six ou sept étages. Les navires de commerce de long cours entrent dans ces bassins pour y charger ou pour décharger leurs cargaisons, et aussi pour y être réparés. Les principaux Docks de Londres sont *the London, the Saint Katherine* et *East and West India Docks*. — 2. C'est une loi qui permet aux trois compagnies des Docks de Londres d'être administrées par un comité de direction dont les membres sont choisis parmi les directeurs des trois compagnies; ce qui diminue les effets de la concurrence. Avant que cette loi fût passée, les Docks de Londres et de Sainte Katherine s'étaient déjà associés sous le titre de "*the London Docks Company*". — 3. *The proxies*, les procurations, c'est-à-dire les autorisations de voter pour des membres absents.

London they were able to influence a large business to the company. That had been the principal ground which they had urged upon the committee, and which he now urged on the proprietors, for electing the *maximum* number of directors that could be elected under the Act. Last year the charges actually paid by firms[1] represented on the board amounted to £80,000, and he believed that for warehouse accommodation for those goods another £80,000 was paid. He might state that the action of the proprietors in the St. Katharine Company in rejecting some of the directors who were on the house list of that board had already begun to bear fruit, for he had been told that they were taking their business elsewhere; and if the proprietors in the East and West India Company turned out all the influential members of the old board it would be extremely difficult for the new board to get sufficient business to make a remunerative return to the shareholders. Immense competition still prevailed in the City of London, and they must look for that competition to continue until, he hoped, a Dock Trust[2] was brought about for London, the same as prevailed in Liverpool. He was quite sure that if the twelve old directors whose names were before the meeting that day for election on the new board were appointed, the retiring directors would continue to influence as much business as they could to their late colleagues. Some very arduous duties had also to be performed by the directors during the next few months—he alluded particularly to the scheme of arrangement with the creditors of the company, and in connexion with that matter they would require all the influence they could possibly have. With regard to the six new directors who were proposed for election, he thought it only fair that there should be an infusion of fresh blood into the new board. He concluded by moving a resolution reducing the number of the directors to eighteen. Mr. R. A. Hankey seconded the motion, which was supported by Mr. John Coles and Mr. J. Edwards. Mr. Mead admitted that the proprietors were deeply indebted to Mr. Coles and his committee for their action in bringing about the passing of the London and St. Katharine and East and West India Docks Act, 1888; but he could not speak so highly of their work as a selecting committee, for which, moreover, they were not appointed by the proprietors. He was strongly of opinion that their affairs would be far better managed by a small board on twelve than by a board of eighteen directors. The idea that they influenced business was, he maintained, an exploded fallacy[3]; and he held that it was the old

1. *By firms*, par des maisons de commerce. — 2. *Dock Trust*, à ce sujet, M. Broadbank, secrétaire de l'*East and West India Docks Company*, nous transmet les renseignements suivants : " ... the object of the trust is that the Docks should be worked for the benefits of « the Port rather than for the benefits of a section of the trade of the Port; at the same time « a fair rate of interests is guaranteed to the shareholders of the undertaking. The adminis- « tration of the Docks is, I believe, under the control of gentlemen who are elected represen- « tative of the city of Liverpool. " — 3. *An exploded fallacy*, une illusion qui ne trompait plus personne. *Exploded*, décrié, discrédité.

directors who had reduced the rates. They would not for eight years derive the full benefit of the working union with the St. Katharine Company; and he reminded them that at the recent meeting of that company the proprietors decided, by an overwhelming majority, to adopt the *minimum* number of directors for their new board. That was an example which it would be wise for the proprietors in the East and West India Docks Company to follow. He objected to the proportion of twelve of the present directors to six new members for their future board; or, with Colonel du Plat Taylor, thirteen old to five new men. He also protested against the short time which had been given to the proprietors within which to organize any effective opposition to the proposals of the board. The circular had reached them only six days before the meeting, and proxies had to be at the offices 48 hours before the meeting. He proposed an amendment to the effect that the number of directors constituting the new board should be twelve. M. C. H. Stewart seconded the amendment. Mr. Bartley, M. P., Mr. S. Copping, Sir R. Nicholson, and Mr. E. Kimber also addressed the meeting, generally supporting the views expressed by Mr. Mead. The chairman put the amendment, which he declared lost on the show of hands, his ruling, however, being dissented from[1], Mr. A. Lawrie demanded a poll[2], which was at once taken, the result being afterwards declared by the chairman as follows :—For the amendment 83 votes, against it 300 votes. Mr. Mead again protested against the short time which the directors had allowed the proprietors for taking any effective action. The chairman replied that it was perfectly well known to the great majority of the proprietors that the Act decided that the new board should be elected before the 15th inst., and therefore they had months in which to take any action. He afterwards put the original motion for reducing the number of the directors to eighteen, and on the show of hands he declared it carried by 30 to 26. Objection was taken to the directors voting, but the chairman said that they were perfectly entitled to vote as proprietors on any question. After some further discussion and the disposal of certain amendments, the following twelve members of the old board were elected directors of the new board :—Sir H. D. Le Marchant, and Messrs. C. W. Cayzer, J. J. Hamilton, R. A. Hankey, J. S. Hill, A. Lawrie, F. F. Lidderdale, W. Milburn, jun., M. R. Pryor, J. H. Tod, C. H. Wigram, and J. Willis; and subsequently Messrs. E. Boyle, T. F. Burnaby-Atkins, J. L. du Plat Taylor, C. B., Sydney G. Holland, David Powell, and E. Wagg were also appointed directors. A resolution was next passed fixing at £1,150 per annum the remuneration of the directors representing the company on the joint committee[3]; and at a subsequent extraordinary

1. *His ruling, however, being dissented from*, sa décision, cependant, ne rencontrant pas l'approbation générale. — 2. *To demand a poll*, demander un vote par scrutin. — 3. *On the joint committee*, dans la commission générale des Docks de Londres.

meeting the remuneration of the directors of the company was fixed at £3,250 per annum.

The report of the MONTEVIDEO WATERWORKS Company (Limited) for 1887 states that the gross revenue amounted to £71,090, an increase of £13,525, as compared with the previous year. Out of an available balance of £31,901 the directors recommend a dividend at the rate of 5 per cent. on the share capital, placing £12,000 to the special reserve fund, and carrying forward £2,391.

TRAFFIC RECEIPTS[1].

The total traffic receipts of the Manchester, Sheffield, and Lincolnshire Railway Company's railways and canals (exclusive of joint lines) from the 1st of July to the 4th of November, 1888, amounted to £671,425, as compared with £682,802 from the 1st of July to the 6th of November, 1887. The total expenses, including rents, toll, duty, &c. (exclusive of joint lines), were £376,847, as against £361,520. As the receipts and expenses for the corresponding period of 1887 include two days more than the current period, it will be necessary, in order to make a correct comparison for an equal number of days, that the figures for the two days named should be added to those above shown for 1888, which may be estimated at £11,000 for receipts, and £5,500 for expenses. On this basis the revenue will show a decrease of £377, and the expenses an increase of £20,827, making a net decrease of £21,204, as compared with a net decrease of £15,284 shown a fortnight ago.

The traffic receipts of the Bengal Central Railway for the week ended October 6 show an increase of Rs. 13,119[2], October 13, an increase of Rs. 12,110; Bengal and North-Western (October 13), an increase of Rs. 4,505; Bengal-Nagpur (October 20), an increase of Rs. 2,649; Chicago, St. Paul, and Kansas City (November 7), an increase of $[3]8,175; Cincinnati and Washington (November 7), a decrease of $8,000; Mexican (November 10), an increase of £1,700; New York, Ontario, and Western (November 7), a decrease of $812; Rohilkund and Kumaon (October 13), an increase of Rs. 1,472; Southern Mahratta (October 13), an increase of Rs. 25,231; and Southern Mahratta (Mysore State), an increase of Rs. 23,344. Those of the Swedish Central Company for September amounted to £3,005, against £2,629, or an increase of £376.

The receipts of the Demerara[4] Railway for the fortnight ending the 20th of October were $7,956, against $6,417 for the corresponding period of 1887.

1. *Traffic receipts*, recettes des chemins de fer, etc. — 2. *Rs.*, *rupees*. La roupie vaut 2 fr. 25. *A lack of rupees* (100 000 r.) vaut £10 000 ou 250 000 francs. — 3. $, *dollars*; le dollar vaut 5 fr. 20 et se divise en *cents*, le *cent* valant 5 centimes. — 4. *Demerara*, nom donné à la Guyane britannique, au nord-est de l'Amérique du Sud.

The traffic receipts of the Alabama Great Southern Railroad Company for October were $139,000, against $154,000; Cincinnati Southern Company (October), $330,000, against $328,000; New Orleans and North-Eastern Company (October), $88,000, against $84,000; Vicksburg and Meridian Company (October), $51,000, against $66,000; and Vicksburg, Shreveport, and Pacific Company (October), $69,000, against $77,000.

The net earnings[1] of the Cleveland, Columbus, Cincinnati, and Indianapolis Railway for nine months were $232,200, against $230,548.

The gross earnings[2] of the Norfolk and Western Railway for September were $430,210, against $404,724; the expenses were $262,477, against $218,418, leaving a net earning of $167,733, against $186,305. The gross earnings for nine months were $3,594,398, against $3,004,303, and the net earnings for that period were $1,398,553, against $1,210,296.

The approximate gross earnings of the Mexican Central Railway for the first week in November on the main line were $78,774, against $98,533; and Guadalajara line $7,878.

The traffic receipts of the Suez Canal on Monday amounted to 160,000 f., against 150,000 f.

The traffic receipts of the Glasgow Tramways for the past week show an increase of £1,424; Provincial, £647; Belfast, £196; London Street, £110; Edinburgh Street, £85; North Metropolitan, £82; North London, £79; Southern of Paris, £66; Leicester, £58; Sheffield, £43; West Metropolitan, £31; Wolverhampton, £27; London Southern, £8; North Staffordshire, £3; and Tramways Company of France, £2. Those of the Southwark and Deptford Company show a decrease of £7; Southampton, £10; Calais, £13; Burnley and District, £14; South London, £15; Stockton and Darlington, £23; Hull Street, £24; and Germany, £81. The receipts of the Railways and Metropolitan Omnibus Company for last week amounted to £221, against £210.

ELECTION INTELLIGENCE.

DEWSBURY.—Seven meetings in favour of Mr. Arnold-Forster's candidature were held on Monday and addressed by Mr. Cameron Corbett, M. P., Mr. Penrose-Fitzgerald, M. P., and Mr. Sinclair, M. P.; and two women's meetings, convened by Mrs. Arnold-Forster have been held. Lord C. Beresford has written to Mr. Arnold-Forster a letter of encouragement. Yesterday the Liberal Unionist cause was advocated at five meetings, with the result that in almost every instance Mr. Arnold-Forster's popularity was

1. *The net earnings*, les profits nets. — 2. *The gross earnings*, les recettes brutes.

distinctly manifested. A Liberal Unionist[1] meeting was held in the drill shed[2] at Batley last night, and was addressed by Mr. Milvain, M.P., and Mr. Corbett, M.P. A resolution in favour of the candidature of Mr. Arnold-Forster was carried almost unanimously. The Separatist candidate[3] had meetings yesterday both in Dewsbury and Batley, in the programme of which the names of Mr. T. Fry, M.P., Mr. Winterbotham, M.P., and Mr. T. P. O'Connor, M.P., were conspicuous.

Aston Manor.—With reference to a contradiction of the report that Mr. Kynoch intends to resign his seat for Aston Manor, *The Birmingham Daily Post* of to-day says :—" We do not withdraw our announcement, and are willing to allow our accuracy to be judged by the event. Mr. Kynoch has paired[4] for the remainder of the Session, and has gone to South Africa on private business, and Mr. R. P. Yates is also away from the country. Mr. Yate's absence naturally delays the announcement of Mr. Kynoch's resignation, but that announcement only waits for a convenient moment. Meanwhile the canvass-books[5] on both sides are being prepared."

The Russian Navy.—In consequence of the Neva being closed to navigation by ice, the launch of the new Russian ironclad Emperor Nicholas has been postponed till the spring.

The Late Colonel Buller.—A solemn military pageant was witnessed at Woolwich yesterday. The melancholy death of Colonel Buller, commandant of the 2d Battalion, Rifle Brigade, which occurred at the Dockyard station of the North Kent Railway on Thursday last, under circumstances already reported, has evoked profound sympathy in the garrison ; and when it was decided that the interment should take place in Staffordshire, measures were adopted for paying all possible honour to the deceased in the course of removal. It was also arranged that the funeral service should take place in the garrison church of St. George, and opportunity was thus afforded to many of Colonel Buller's friends and comrades for taking part in the proceedings, among them being Lord Chelmsford, under whom the deceased officer served in Zululand. The body was taken on a gun-carriage from the Cambridge barracks to the church, and from the church to the Arsenal railway station, the entire route being lined with troops, mounted and on foot. Three hundred of the Rifle Brigade led the *cortège* with arms reversed, followed by the band of the regiment and the Royal Artillery band, playing solemn music. General Williams, R. A.[6], commanding the

---

1. *The Liberal Unionists*, les libéraux qui se sont séparés de M. Gladstone sur la question de l'Irlande. — 2. *The drill shed*, la parade couverte. — 3. *The separatist candidate*, le candidat séparatiste (partisan de l'indépendance de l'Irlande). — 4. Voyez page 158, note 1. — 5. *The canvass books*, les registres des votants à visiter. *To canvass*, parcourir le pays pour solliciter les votes des électeurs. — 6. *R. A.*, *Royal Artillery*.

district, Colonel Pemberton, A. D. C.[1] representing the Duke of Cambridge, and other staff officers[2] were among the chief mourners. The coffin was loaded with wreaths and other symbols of condolence. All the troops available were employed either in the procession or in keeping the thoroughfare, from which the traffic was temporarily diverted, and people thronged the sidewalks for the whole distance. Arrived at the railway station, the coffin was placed in a special carriage, draped with black and decked with flowers, and conveyed to its destination.

ENGLAND AND GERMANY IN EAST AFRICA.

The following correspondence respecting the suppression of the Slave Trade in East African waters was issued last night as a Parliamentary paper :—

Memorandum communicated by Count Leyden[3], October 8, 1888.

(Translation.)

The exchange of views which has hitherto taken place between the Cabinets of Berlin and London on the existing disturbances in East Africa and the position of the Sultan of Zanzibar has happily shown the existence of a full understanding between the two Governments in the main points of their policy in those regions. The Chancellor has seen with special satisfaction that Lord Salisbury unreservedly recognizes the community of German and English interests in Zanzibar, and shares the conviction that it is only by mutual co-operation, founded on reciprocal trust on the part of the two Powers, that the task of Christian civilization in East Africa can be satisfactorily fulfilled.

The German and English Goverments are united in the opinion that the first thing to be done is to restore and uphold the authority of the Sultan of Zanzibar against the insurrectionary movement on the mainland. The disturbances which, according to the later information, appear to have arisen in the districts around the sources of the River Rovuma and the Lake Nyassa, and then to have spread northwards, have no doubt been long prepared, and brought forward principally by the Arabs who are interested in the slave trade. The Sultan of Zanzibar's own forces are not strong enough for a forcible suppression of the insurrection. His rule over the mainland appears to have been entirely broken up. It is therefore to be considered how the authority of the Sultan can be supported, and the agitation of the fanatical and stranger-hating Arab element can be withstood.

It appears doubtful to the German Government whether military expedi-

1. *A. D. C.*, aide de camp. — 2. *Staff officers*, officiers de l'état-major. — 3. Secrétaire de l'ambassade allemande auprès de S. M. britannique.

tions into the interior are suited for such a purpose. Besides the extent and pathlessness[1] of the land, the enemy, who knows the country, will always be able to avoid the shock of a superior force and renew the struggle at places and times of his own choosing. Standing garrisons[2] of European troops could be maintained in the interior only, if at all, with the heaviest sacrifice of men and money. Under these circumstances, it appears desirable to confine the joint action of Germany and England in support of the Sultan at first to maritime action, and for this purpose, perhaps, to establish a blockade of the coast of the mainland of Zanzibar between Kipini and the River Rovuma by German and English ships in co-operation with the Sultan of Zanzibar. The object of such a blockade would be to cut off all traffic with the insurgent coast districts, and especially that in slave vessels and the carriage of arms and ammunition.

In order to arrive at this last object the Portuguese Government must also be pressed to forbid the export of munitions from their neighbouring East African possessions, as otherwise the insurgents in the southern ports of the Sultanate of Zanzibar could supply themselves through their connexion with the Arab traders in Mozambique. So far as the blockade is concerned, it is principally the Arab sailing vessels which carry on the trade between the mainland ports and Zanzibar which will be affected by it. Notification of the blockade to all the Powers interested in the trade in those parts could be carried out in the name of the two allied Governments and the Sultan.

The Imperial Government is desirous of learning the views of Her Majesty's Government on the foregoing proposals. In the event of an understanding in principle being come to, the more particular instructions necessary for carrying out the common programme of action could then be drawn up and communicated to the German and English representatives in Zanzibar.

German Embassy, London, October 8.

Count Hatzfeldt[3] to the Marquis of Salisbury[4].
(Received November 3.)

(Translation.)

London, November 3.

The undersigned Ambassador of Germany near the Court of St. James, has the honour, by order of his Government, to make the following communication to his Excellency the Marquis of Salisbury, Her Britannic Majesty's Minister for Foreign Affairs :—

1. *Pathlessness*, absence de routes frayées. — 2. *Standing garrisons*, des garnisons permanentes. — 3. Ambassadeur d'Allemagne à Londres. — 4. Premier ministre d'Angleterre.

In view of the increasing extent of the hostility that the slave-traders of Arab nationality oppose to the suppression of the slave trade and to the legitimate commerce of Christian peoples with the natives of Africa, the Imperial Government propose to Her Majesty's Government to blockade, in common and with the consent of the Sultan of Zanzibar, the coasts of East Africa forming part of the territory of that Sovereign, in order to suppress the exportation of slaves and the importation of arms and munitions of war. The details for carrying out this blockade shall be arranged in concert between the German and English Admirals at Zanzibar.

In order to make the blockade effective against the slave trade, it will be necessary that the vessels of war of both nations should visit and, in case of need, arrest any suspected vessel under whatever flag she may be sailing.

The Government of His Majesty the Emperor are ready in common with that of Her Majesty the Queen to take the requisite steps with other Powers in this sense.

As the traffic in slaves and arms and the hostility of the slave merchants extend to the Portuguese coast line adjoining Zanzibar[1], it will be useful and desirable to obtain the co-operation of Portugal and her consent to the extension of the blockade to the portion of the coast belonging to that Power.

In begging the Marquis of Salisbury to be so good as to inform him as soon as possible whether Her Majesty's Government agree to the proposal which be has the honour to submit to it, the undersigned takes &c.

V. HATZFELDT.

The Marquis of Salisbury to Count Hatzfeldt.

Foreign Office, November 5.

M. l'Ambassadeur,—In view of the increasing prevalence of the slave trade on the East Coast of Africa, and of the disturbances and impediments to legitimate trade which it produces, Her Majesty's Government accede to the proposal of the Imperial Government to establish, with the assent of the Sultan of Zanzibar, on the shores of His Highness's continental dominions, a blockade against the importation of munitions of war and the exportation of slaves.

The programme for the execution of the blockade is to be settled by the English and German Admirals in concert, and the blockade shall continue until either Power gives notice of the intention to discontinue it.

That the blockade may be effective for the above-mentioned purposes, it is essential that the ships of war of the two Powers should have, within the area of the blockade, the right of visiting and, in case of need, detaining any suspected ship, under whatever flag she may be sailing. The Govern-

1. Au sud de Zanzibar.

ment of Her Majesty will associate itself with the Government of the Emperor in urging upon other Powers to agree to the arrangements necessary for this purpose.

As the slave trade, and the preparations of the traders who conduct it, extend to the neighbouring Portuguese dominions, it would be advantageous and desirable to obtain the co-operation of Portugal and the consent of that Power to the extension of the blockade to the Portuguese coast.

I have, &c., SALISBURY.

The Marquis of Salisbury to Sir E. Malet.

Foreign Office, Nov. 5.

Sir,—I enclose to your Excellency a copy of a note which I have received from Count Hatzfeldt, and the note which I have addressed to him in reply.

The lamentable events which have taken place upon the East Coast of Africa have been attributed by the German Government to the increasing strength and audacity which has been displayed in recent years by the Arabs who carry on the slave trade. In their view, it is the apprehension of the effects which German colonization may have upon the exportation of slaves that has induced them to undertake a resistance which has terminated so calamitously for the German Company; and they are of opinion that the most effective way of punishing the authors of the attack upon the German merchants, and of depriving them of strength for similar enterprises in the future, will be to destroy the slave trade, which is the object for which their organization exists and the industry from which their resources are drawn.

It is possible that too large a share in the rising of the coast tribes against the German Company is attributed to the slave-traders. Much of it is no doubt due to the errors which have been committed by the German Company themselves. Their experience of Oriental habits and character has been insufficient, and in the measures they have taken they have allowed too little for the difference between the conditions to which they are accustomed in Europe and those with which they have had to deal on the African coast. But though much may be said, and said with justice, of the evil results of the precipitate action and of their disregard of native character and religious customs, I am disposed to think that there is considerable foundation for their belief that the apprehensions and the resentment of the slave-traders have been a potent cause of the disturbances which have taken place. There can be little doubt that the efforts which have been made to expel Europeans from Lake Nyassa on the south and from Suakin in the north at this time have been due to the action of the slave-trading Arabs. The testimony of Mr. Cameron and of Cardinal Lavigerie combine to establish the fact that there has been a formidable increase in the activity of this hateful traffic during the last few years. There can be no doubt that it has been attented with cruelty and desolation far in excess of any that we have ground for believing that it produced in former times, and there is no other cause to which we can attribute this deplorable phenomenon except the increased destructiveness of the firearms which commerce has been able in recent times to place in the hands of the Arab adventurers who conduct these exterminating raids. At the same time, the extension during the same period of French influence in Madagascar and the Comoro Islands has added another element to the causes by which the slave trade has been stimulated. The French are as anxious as any other Christian nation to destroy this traffic, but the naval force by which they are represented in those seas is very small, and they have always refused to give to other nations that right of arresting and searching suspicious vessels which is essential to prevent the French flag from being used for the purpose of covering it. Our cruisers, therefore, have been obliged to look on while Arab dhows[1], flying[2] the French flag and evidently carrying slaves, have passed outwards under their guns with impunity. Under the influence of these causes, there is no doubt whatever that the slave trade, both by land and sea, has recently undergone a considerable revival; and I think it probable that that circumstance has borne its share in the disturbances which have been so fatal to the German Company.

The German Government appear inclined to confine their action to the prevention of the importation of arms by which the slave raids are rendered possible, and the exportation of slaves which provides the principal motive for them. It is impossible, however, that they should conduct this operation upon the coast of Zanzibar, which is subject to German influence, without the co-operation of Her Majesty's Government; for unless a similar policy is pursued upon that portion of the coast which is subject to British influence, the only result of the German action might be to transfer to the British ports the importation of arms and the exportation of slaves. They, therefore, have applied to Her Majesty's Government for their co-operation. The request is too much in harmony with the policy which Great Britain has uniformly pursued[3] to be refused by us. Even if there were no special motive for acceding to it, we should welcome the assistance of a powerful nation like that of Germany in the enterprise which this country has pursued through good and evil report, and at the cost of great sacrifices, for three-quarters of a century.

But there has been, in the present instance, a special reason which has weighed heavily with Her Majesty's Government in inducing them to

1. *Dhow* [daou], navire côtier arabe. — 2. *Flying*, déployant. — 3. C'est l'Angleterre qui, la première, a aboli l'esclavage dans ses colonies.

comply with the wishes of the German Government in this matter. It has been possible, in view of the present exigencies, to remove for the first time the most formidable obstacle which exists to the suppression of the present slave trade, namely, the refusal of France to agree to a mutual right of search. The French Government, though unwilling to grant the right of search on all occasions and in all cases, has consented that it shall be looked upon as one of the incidents of a blockade.

There is no question but that the rights which arise under this state of things confer a facility in conducting the operations against the slave trade which this country has never possessed before. It furnishes, therefore, an additional reason for taking advantage of the co-operation offered by Germany, and gives fair ground of expectation that the measures now contemplated may result in closing the last outlet[1] at the command of this detestable trade.

The blockade will be strictly limited to the two objects I have named. It will be conducted by the British and German naval forces in co-operation, and the necessary arrangements in detail will be left to be settled by the two Admirals on the spot. It is of course to be carried on with the assent and by the authority of His Highness the Sultan of Zanzibar, whose sanction has already been obtained, and the restoration of his legitimate authority is not the least among the advantages which it is hoped this measure may bring about. I am, &c.,

SALISBURY.

The FALL of a HOUSE in MARYLEBONE[2].

Yesterday afternoon, the Coroner[3] for Central Middlesex, Dr. George Danford Thomas, opened his investigation as to the serious occurrence of the falling of a newly-erected house in Great Titchfield-street, on the afternoon of Friday last.

The jury were impanelled as to the deaths of WILLIAM MORSDALE, aged 36 years; THOMAS PHILIP WATKINS, aged 27; ALFRED BLOXHAM, aged 21; CABEL TOMBS, aged 38; RICHARD HENRY CONABER, aged 37; and ALEXANDER WAIN, aged 44, the six unfortunate workmen who were killed, while some 15 or 16 others were seriously injured by the collapse of the building in question. The court was densely crowded by professional men, architects, builders, and others. Mr. Edwin F. Tadman, solicitor, attended to watch the case on behalf of Messrs. Oldrey and Co., the builders, of 4, Gray's-inn-place, Gray's-inn; Mr. William Whitfield, solicitor, of Finsbury-

1. *The last outlet*, le dernier débouché. — 2. *Marylebone* [mar'-i-bonne], corruption de « Marie la bonne », paroisse et district de Londres. — 3. Voyez page 207, note 4.

pavement, represented the friends of William Morsdale and of the other deceased persons; and Mr. Cuthbert, Chief Inspector of the D division, watched the proceedings for the police. The jury having viewed the bodies, which lay in the parochial mortuary adjacent, and the bodies having been identified,

The first witness called was Mr. Montague Tench, one of the medical officers of the Middlesex Hospital, who deposed that the deceased, Alexander Wain, had died in the hospital, 16 hours after admission, from internal injuries.

John Clements Richards, general foreman to Messrs. Oldrey and Co., builders, said that the old buildings at the corner of Titchfield-street and Riding-house-lane were entirely pulled down, and the new buildings were chiefly composed of bricks, stone, and iron. They commenced the work of rebuilding about nine weeks ago. They had 32 men employed on the works, which were to be completed within a given time. The work comprised two houses, 53 and 55, Titchfield-street, but that to be reinstated was only one house, and the one that fell was No. 53. They had completed the house as far as construction, and they were being carried out under the supervision of an architect, Mr. Miller, and he considered the whole of the work was proceeding very satisfactorily. On Friday morning he was on the works and he noticed nothing dangerous. Iron work was used in the building, and the materials generally were good and sound. The roof was put on to the house 55 about a quarter to 4 on Friday afternoon. Witness continued:—I was in No. 55, in my office, when a clerk came to speak to me, and said I was wanted. On going out of the door, with the intention of going up to the roof of 53, I heard a rumbling noise and thought that it might be that the large tank on the top scaffolding might have fallen. The bricks and the mortar and all the materials were good; but we had a great deal of wet weather. When the building fell I was at the door of 55. I could not tell the cause of the collapse. The works were being carried out under the supervision of the architect, who acted also as clerk of the works, and they were carried out in accordance with the specifications he had drawn. I could not form any opinion as to the cause of the accident. The district surveyor visited and inspected the works, I should think, about once a week. I believe I have seen him there seven or eight times. The witness, in a severe cross-examination, stated that they had a foundation of 3ft. of concrete and it was bound by girders[1] to the adjacent houses in Riding-house-lane. The mortar was properly mixed with lime and sand. The materials were good. He worked from the architect's specifications and not from any ideas of his own. He did not consider that the mortar

1. *Girders*, poutres (en fer), traverses.

was of such an inferior character that on being pressed in the fingers it crumbled like dirt. Mr. Miller, the architect, had a clerk named Freeman. He might have been more frequently there than Mr. Miller himself. The party wall[1] of the adjacent house in Riding-house-lane was underpinned before the footings of the new buildings were put in.

George Winter, a bricklayer, said he had been working on the fallen premises for a month or six weeks. He understood the character of mortar. That used in this building was good mortar. He neither heard of nor saw anything wrong in the construction of the building. At the time of the fall of the building he was at work at the top of the house 53, at a chimney. The house suddenly collapsed, and he came down with the chimney to the bottom. He was but very slightly injured. The whole place seemed to collapse in a moment. He could give no explanation whatever as to the cause of the collapse. He heard no complaint or remark whatever among the men as to the character of the building. He had been for 15 years a bricklayer, and would know if the materials were good or bad. He looked upon the building materials at this place as good. He had no idea of how this occurrence took place.

Thomas Robinson, a cheesemonger, residing in Great Titchfield-street, said he was looking out of his window at the time of the fall. He had watched the building day by day, and on Friday afternoon it seemed as if it was nearly finished, when all at once it gave a sort of quiver and suddenly collapsed. In less than a minute the entire building fell. All the men were at work, and when he saw what had happened he rushed down stairs and sent his sons for cabs to take the poor fellows away to the hospital. He was not a builder, but he thought it must have been one of the girders gave way. A police-constable and some other witnesses having given evidence as to seeing the building suddenly collapse, but without being able to give any evidence as to the cause.

The Coroner said he should adjourn the inquiry and have the plan, the specification, and the *debris* of the building practically and professionally examined with a view, if possible, to arrive at the conclusion as to the real cause of the accident. He pointed out, however, that the magistrates made no allowance for such a purpose, and he had on previous occasions to pay for this professional aid out of his own pocket. On this occasion, however, he was pleased to say that a professional gentleman, Mr. Collins, had kindly undertaken to perform the duty without remuneration.

The inquiry was ultimately adjourned till the 28th inst.

---

1. *The party wall*, le mur mitoyen.

THE ASSIZES.

OXFORD CIRCUIT[1].

Yesterday, at Reading, before Mr. Justice Field, George Martin, described as a retired officer, was indicted for stealing the visitors' book from the Royal Tapestry Works at Windsor. Mr. Rose Smith prosecuted ; and Mr. E. R. Turton (specially retained), defended. The prisoner who was said to have served in a West Indian regiment had, in the early part of October, taken the cottage which forms part of the court-yard of the works, and used frequently to go into the central-hall where there is a billiard table, on which the prisoner was invited to play. In the hall was kept in a desk the visitors' book, containing autographs of the Queen and other members of the Royal Family. This book was missed on October 28, and a search warrant[3] having been obtained, the prisoner's house was searched, when he produced the book, alleging that the manager had told him he might borrow it when he wished, which was denied. It was stated that the prisoner had been in the habit, for the last three years, of taking enormous quantities of morphia and chloral, but Mr. Turton admitted that his medical evidence would not go the length of proving that the effect of this constant use morphia had, at the time the book was taken, so unhinged[4] the prisoner's mind, as not to make him criminally responsible, but urged that there was no felonious intent. The jury found him guilty and two other charges of larceny were not proceeded with. His Lordship, in passing sentence, said it was the worst case he had tried for a long time, and sentenced the prisoner to 15 months' imprisonment.

1888.

LONDON SCHOOL BOARD ELECTION[2] (Westminster Division).

F. Cavendish Bentinck, Esq.
The Rev. A. Gerald Bowman.
The Lord Colchester.
Major-General C. A. Sim.
William Winnett, Esq.

The following General Committee has been formed to promote the return of the above Candidates on November 26th :—

---

1. On a vu plus haut que les juges du cours du Banc de la Reine vont tenir les assises dans différentes parties de l'Angleterre, divisée à cet effet en *circuits*, ayant chacun pour chef-lieu une des grandes villes du pays. Les juges y sont reçus avec un grand cérémonial; l'un des juges préside aux affaires criminelles, l'autre aux civiles. — 2. La loi sur l'éducation élémentaire adoptée en 1870 a ordonné la création d'un bureau de direction de l'enseignement primaire composé de 55 membres élus et non payés pour les onze différentes sections de la ville de Londres, dont Westminster fait partie. Jusqu'en 1839, l'instruction primaire était donnée par des écoles privées ou par des sociétés religieuses. Dès 1832, le gouvernement

3 autorisation [illegible] 4 [illegible]

His Grace the Duke of Norfolk, E.M.[1], K.G.[2].
His Grace the Duke of Richmond and Gordon, K.G.
His Grace the Duke of Northumberland, K.G.
His Grace the Duke of Westminster, K.G.
His Grace the Duke of Buccleuch, K.T.[3].
His Grace the Duke of Abercorn, C.B.[4].
The Marquess of Bath.
The Marquess of Lothian, K.T.
The Marquess of Hartington, M.P.[5].
The Marquess of Waterford.
The Earl Beauchamp.
The Earl Percy.
The Earl of Onslow, K. C.M.G.[6].
The Earl of Jersey.
The Earl of Harrowby.
The Earl of Erne.
The Earl of Limerick.
The Viscount Halifax.
The Viscount Cranbrook, G.C.S.I.[7].
The Viscount Cross, G.C.B.
The Viscount Barrington.
The Viscount Midleton.
The Viscount Pollington.
The Lord Francis Hervey, M.P.
Colonel Lord Eustace Cecil.
The Lord Bishop of London.
The Lord Clinton.
The Lord Dorchester.
The Lord Norton, G.C.M.G.
The Lord Brabourne.
The Lord Hillingdon.
The Lord Magheramorne.
The Lord Addington.
The Lord Colville of Culross, K.T.
The Hon. Sydney Holland.
The Right Hon. G. J. Goschen, M.P.
The Right Hon. G. A. F. Cavendish Bentinck, M.P.
The Right Hon. W. H. Smith, M.P.
The Right Hon. G. Cubitt, M.P.
Sir Walter Farquhar, Bart.[8].
Sir Alfred Slade, Bart.
Sir Trevor Lawrence, Bart., M.P.
Sir James Paget, Bart., F.R.S.[9], D.C.L.
Sir W. Bowman, Bart., F.R.S., LL.D. 14
Sir Thomas W. Evans, Bart.
Sir John Tilley, K.C.B.[10].
Sir J. Beilby-Alston, K.C.M.G.
Sir J. Pender, K.C.M.G.
Sir William Harman.
G. R. T. Bartley, Esq., M.P.
H. Cosmo Bonsor, Esq., M.P.
W. L. A. Burdett-Coutts, Esq., M.P.
F. D. Dixon Hartland, Esq., M.P.
Colonel Makins, M.P.
J. G. Talbot, Esq., M.P.
W. E. Tomlinson, Esq., M.P.
Colonel C. E. Howard Vincent, C.B., M.P.
His Eminence Cardinal Manning.
The Bishop of Emmaus.
The Very Rev. the Dean of Westminster.
The Ven. Archdeacon Farrar, D.D.[11], F.R.S.
The Rev. Canon Furse.
The Rev. Canon Capel Cure.
The Rev. Prebendary Kempe.
The Rev. Prebendary Harry Jones.
The Rev. Henry Wace, D.D.
The Rev. J. F. Kitto.
The Rev. T. Teignmouth Shore.
The Rev. W. M. Sinclair.
Major-Gen. Francis Barry-Drew, C.B.
Vice-Admiral Leveson E. H. Somerset.
Colonel Francis Haygarth.
Colonel Thomas W. Ogilvy.
C. M. Clode, Esq., C.B.
R. C. Antrobus, Esq., Chairman of Executive Committee.
A. B. Kempe, Esq., F.R.S.
Dr. Lionel Beale, Esq., F.R.L.?
Colonel Scrivener.
Dr. George Johnson, F.R.S.
J. Lowe, Esq., M.D.
J. Wickham Legg. Esq., M.D.
Colonel Bruce, C.B.
T. Bond, Esq., F.R.C.S.[12].
W. S. Savory, Esq., F.R.S.
John Bonthron, Esq., M.B.W.[13].
Lieut.-Colonel Fitzgerald.
Surgeon-Major Elkington.

avait accordé 500 000 francs pour favoriser les progrès de l'instruction élémentaire ; les subventions, qui ont été toujours en s'augmentant, avaient atteint, en 1870, 7 millions de francs. Depuis 1870, l'enseignement primaire, qui n'est pas gratuit, excepté en cas de nécessité absolue, mais dont la rétribution varie de 10 c. à 60 c. par semaine, est soutenu par des impôts locaux fixés par le *school-board.* Le *school-board* non seulement soutient ses propres écoles, mais aussi les écoles volontaires qui se soumettent à ses instructions. Le *school-board* est chargé de veiller à la présence régulière des élèves, et il y a une école spéciale pour ceux qui persistent à faire l'école buissonnière ; la discipline y est tellement stricte que ceux qui y sont envoyés perdent le goût du vagabondage. *The school-board* réclame des parents dans ce cas la rétribution scolaire. — 1. *E. M., Earl Marshal.* — 2. *K. G., Knight of the Garter.* — 3. *K. T., Knight of the most ancient and most noble order of the Thistle,* établi en 1540 par Henri VIII et constitué à nouveau en 1703 sous la reine Anne. Il ne compte que 21 chevaliers. — 4. *C. B., Companion of the Bath,* ordre de chevalerie fondé en 1399, au couronnement de Henri IV ; reconstitué en 1815 par le prince régent. Il comprend trois classes et se décerne aux militaires et aux civils en récompense de services distingués. — 5. *M. P., Member of Parliament.* — 6. *K. C. M. G., Knight Commander of Saint Michael and Saint George.* Cet ordre, fondé en 1810, a été reconstitué en 1887 par la reine Victoria ; il sert à récompenser des services dans l'administration coloniale et dans la diplomatie. Le duc de Cambridge en est le grand-maître. — 7. *G. C. S. I., Grand Commander of the most Exalted Order of the Star of India,* ordre établi en 1861 et reconstitué en 1878, accordé pour services rendus dans l'Inde. Il existe aussi un *Imperial Order of the Crown of India,* fondé en 1878 et accordé aux princesses de la maison royale et impériale, aux princesses indigènes des Indes et aux femmes et parentes des gouverneurs de l'Inde. — 8. *Bart.,* baronet, c'est le dernier titre de noblesse *héréditaire* conféré en Angleterre. — 9. *F. R. S., Fellow of the Royal Society* (*for the pursuit and spread of Science*) ; cette société, fondée en 1662 par Charles II, se compose de 450 membres anglais et 50 étrangers. Son grand prix annuel de Copley est décerné à des membres nationaux ou à des étrangers ; il est fort recherché. M. Chevreul a été lauréat de ce prix. — 10. *K. C. B., Knight Commander of the Bath,* voy. note 4. — 11. *D. D., Doctor of Divinity,* docteur en théologie. — 12. *F. R. C. S., Fellow of the Royal College of Surgeons.* — 13. *M. B. W., Member of the Board of Works,* membre du Conseil général.

14. Legum Doctor. 15 Doctor of Civil Law.

J. S. Burroughes, Esq.	Miss Bramston.
Captain Probyn.	T. J. White, Esq., M.B.W.

G. T. Miller, Esq.	H. A. Cameron, Esq.	M. Isaacs, Esq.
B. B. Mansfield, Esq.	G. W. Tallents, Esq.	W. Boore, Esq.
H. H. Seymour, Esq.	H. S. Freeman, Esq.	Messrs. Ravenscroft.
J. S. Virtue, Esq.	J. Fergusson, Esq.	R. Reid, Esq.
L.W. Hiscox, Esq.	G. Jupp, Esq.	T. P. Beckwith, Esq.
J.A. Sarsons, Esq.	F. G. Rest, Esq.	E. Laing, Esq.
J.H. Bishop, Esq.	H. Deedes, Esq.	Eales, Esq.
F. Rose, Esq.	P. Finch, Esq.	W. B. Challice, Esq.
W.M. Power, Esq.	H. A. Hunt, Esq.	J. Thynne, Esq.
W.M. Scudamore, Esq.	H. Hardcastle, Esq.	A. W. Dixey, Esq.
F.J. Tucker, Esq.	W. M. Trollope, Esq.	H. F. Dickins, Esq.
T. Adams, Esq.	J. Taylor, Esq.	A. L. Liberty, Esq.
G. L. Berry, Esq.	A. Taylor, Esq.	F. Walker, Esq.
W.H. Baker, Esq.	E.J. Chapple, Esq.	W. Manning, Esq.
T. Lane, Esq.	G. F. Trollope, Esq.	W. Silk, Esq.
A. Fitzgerald, Esq.	G. A. Spottiswoode, Esq.	J. Sinclair, Esq.
W. Dawis, Esq.	Z. King, Esq.	W. Sayne, Esq.
H. O. Hamborg, Esq.	J. Burman, Esq.	A. Neale, Esq.
H. D. Erskine, Esq.		G. Slatter, Esq.[1]

Central Committee Rooms, 35, King-street, Westminster, October, 1888.

MR. ERIC STUART BRUCE, M.A. Oxon, F.R.M. et Soc., on "Electricity, The Coming Power, " Literary Institute, Edinburgh, TO-NIGHT. Lecture communications to E. Bruce, Esq., 10, Observatory-avenue, Kensington, London, W.

Patron—The QUEEN.

THE PEOPLE'S PALACE for EAST LONDON[2].—BEAUMONT TRUST. Bankers—London and Westminster Bank, Whitechapel.

One and a-half millions of people have visited the People's Palace during the last twelve months.

FUNDS to complete the building, and donations of books for the library, are urgently NEEDED.

EDMUND HAY CURRIE, Chairman of Trustees.

The People's Palace, Mile-end-road, E.

ROYAL IRISH CONSTABULARY[3]. — DONATIONS for the QUEEN'S JUBILEE FUND[4] of the Royal Irish Constabulary, to provide for the necessitous orphans of members of this Force.

Amount subscribed by members of the Force and from Royal Irish Constabulary Depôt Funds at Jubilee period	£2,495	7	10
Donations already acknowledged, including £500 from Henry Whiting, Esq., and £1,000 from Robert Mackay Wilson, Esq.	2,150	2	7

1. On voit par la liste nombreuse qui précède l'intérêt que les personnes d'une certaine position dans le monde prennent au développement et à la bonne direction de l'enseignement primaire. Ce n'est pas le gouvernement qui dirige cet enseignement, mais la société tout entière. Le gouvernement y contribue par ses subventions. — 2. *Le Palais du Peuple pour les districts est de Londres* a été ouvert par la reine Victoria en mai 1887. Il fournit à la vaste population pauvre de l'est de Londres une grande salle de concerts, de représentations de toute espèce, une bibliothèque et des salles de lecture, des salles et des appareils de gymnastique, des bains de natation, des salles de réunions sociales, des salles pour certains jeux, des buffets, des boutiques et des écoles prsfessionnelles (*technical schools*). Ces dernières écoles, bâties et équipées aux frais de la corporation des drapiers en 1888, ont coûté 500 000 francs, et sont regardées comme devant former un facteur social d'une grande importance. Du reste, le palais tout entier a été construit et aménagé par souscriptions publiques. Il y a eu pendant l'année 1888 des fêtes, des concerts, diverses expositions, sans compter une exposition de tableaux et une fête d'automne qui ont duré six semaines et qui ont attiré 310 000 visiteurs, payant chacun 0,10 c. (*a penny*). Cette institution est un agrandissement de l'institution philosophique de Beaumont, fondée, il y a un demi-siècle, dans cette partie de Londres. — 3. C'est le corps royal de police en Irlande. — 4. On sait que le jubilé de la Reine ou la célébration de sa cinquantième année de règne (21 juin 1887) a donné naissance à un grand nombre d'institutions charitables dont le Palais du Peuple n'est pas la moindre. Les présents personnels faits à la Reine de toutes les parties du monde étaient d'une richesse extrême.

The Committee of the Property Defence Association, per Lord Courtown..	£100	0	0
E. T. Hudman, Sion Mills .. '..	1	0	0
Colonel Penefather, Clonmel	2	0	0
Miss Darley, Dublin...	1	0	0
C. Wilkinson, London, E. C.	10	10	0
Lord Dartrey	10	0	0
Admiral R. Coote, Shales Bitterne	3	0	3
F. N. Blackburne Daniell, Shalden Manor.	2	0	0
A. H. Wynne, Collon.	1	10	0
J. G. Butcher, Hyde ..	2	0	0
W. G. Williamson, Adjutant R. I. C.[1] (annual)	2	0	0
Thomas Hayes, C. I. R. I. C.	5	0	0
G. E. Newland, late A. I. G. R. I. C. . ..	5	0	0
Sir Edward C. Guinness, Bart.	500	0	0
John Jackson, Dublin..	5	0	0
J. R. Fowler, Bray.. ..	2	0	0
Lord Ardilaun	300	0	0
Lieut. W. H. Vicars, Pachmarhi, India.. ..	1	0	0
W. J. Paul, R. M. (annual)	3	0	0
R. C. Dobbs, Greystones.	0	10	0
Hugh Wilbraham, Westport	2	0	0
H. Cleghorn, M.D., Strathvithie	1	0	0
J. W. Murland, Nutley, Booterstown	10	0	0
H. Mansergh, late R. I. C., per W. Fry	5	0	0
A. Sympathizer, per D.I. Hurst Ferbane	1	0	0
H. P. Truell, Clonmannon	10	10	0
Lord Dunsany	10	0	0
T. K. Duncan, Belfast.	£1	1	0
Subscriptions of officers and men of R. I. C. for months of August and September, 1888.	262	16	5

Effort is being made to raise the capital of the Fund to £10,000, towards which a sum of upwards of £6,000 has been subscribed.

Donations will be received by Andrew Reed, Inspector-General Royal Irish Constabulary, Dublin Castle.

PROPOSED VAN and WHEEL TAX[2]. — A public MEETING in opposition to the above will be held at Cannon-street Hotel, at 8 p.m., TO-DAY. Chairman, R. K. CAUSTON, Esq., M. P., supported by Sir Geo. Baden-Powell, M. P., Sir Henry Roscoe, M. P., W. Winterbotham, Esq., M. P., J. Richards Kelly, Esq., M. P., and many other members of Parliament and influential delegates from Provincial Committees.

CHURCH of ENGLAND YOUNG MEN'S SOCIETY. — LADY HALSBURY will OPEN the BAZAAR at the Leopold Rooms, 3, St. Bride-street, THIS DAY, on behalf of H. R. H.[3] the Duchess of Albany.

CHARING-CROSS HOSPITAL. — The TRIENNIAL FESTIVAL DINNER, in AID of the FUNDS of the Hospital, will be held on Wednesday, 21st. November, in the White-hall Rooms of the Hôtel Métropole, the Right Hon. the EARL of DERBY, K. G.[4] (Vice-President of the Hospital), in the chair.

The musical arrangements will be under the superintendence of Mr. J. Monro Coward.

A list of those who have kindly promised to act as stewards[5] will be found in Saturday's paper. Gentlemen wishing to attend the dinner will kindly send their names to the Secretary at the Hospital.

---

1. *R. I. C., the Royal Irish Constabulary.* — 2. C'est un impôt proposé par M. Goschen sur les voitures légères, mais la proposition a été retirée avant la fin de la session. — 3. *H. R. H., Her Royal Highness.* — 4. *K. G., Knight of the Garter.* — 5. *As stewards,* comme commissaires.

Donations and subscriptions will be thankfully received by
ARTHUR E. READE, Secretary.

VICTORIA HOSPITAL[1] for CHILDREN, Queen's-road, Chelsea. — Notice. — A QUARTERLY COURT of the Governors of this Charity will be held in the Board Room of the Hospital on Wednesday, November 21st, at 5 p. m., to receive a report of the financial and general state of the Hospital from the Committee of Management; to elect Governors; and transact such other business as shall be brought up for consideration.

Special business — To elect Trustees for General Fund.

By order, W. C. BLOUNT, Secretary.

BRITISH ORPHAN ASYLUM, Mackenzie-park, Slough. — Instituted 1827. — The NEXT ELECTION of ORPHANS of those once in prosperity will take place at the Cannon-street Hotel, on Tuesday, the 8th January, 1889, when ten boys and eight girls will be elected.

The poll will open at 12 and close at 2 o'clock.

ALFRED MACKENZIE, Secretary.
Offices, 30, Finsbury-circus, E. C.

ROYAL ALBERT ORPHAN ASYLUM. — Notice is hereby given, that the HALF-YEARLY ELECTION to the benefits of this Asylum will take place in the offices as undernamed on Friday, 30th inst., when ten boys will be elected.

The application for girls to be elected, not having exceeded the vacancies, the Committee have resolved that they would accept all the candidates, amounting to 17, subject to the Doctor's examination and other regulations.

By order, RICHARD WITHERBY, Secr.
No. 62, King William-street, E. C.

ORPHAN WORKING SCHOOL (instituted May 10, 1758).

Senior children at Maitland-park, N. W.[2].

Junior children at Alexandra Orphanage, Hornsey-rise, N.

Sickly children at Convalescent Home, Harold-road, Margate.

635 orphan and other necessitous children from infancy to 14 years of age are now maintained and cared for by this National Charity. Founded more than a century and a quarter ago. More than 4,000 have been benefited.

President — H. R. H. the DUKE of CAMBRIDGE, K. G.

The NEXT ELECTION of CHILDREN will take place on Wednesday, January 30th, 1889.

Children of both sexes, between infancy and 11 years of age, are eligible from all parts of the Empire.

Forms of nomination of candidates must be in the hands of the Secretary completed on or before November 30th.

The need of FUNDS is most urgent.

Contributions sent now will entitle the subscriber to vote at the forthcoming election.

Treasurers { BASIL WOODD SMITH, Esq., J. P., D. L.[3], WILLIAM HOLT, Esq., V. P.[4].

JONADAB FINCH, Secretary.
Offices, 73, Cheapside, E. C.

WORKING LADS' INSTITUTE, Whitechapel, E. (opposite the London Hospital). — The TWELFTH ANNUAL MEETING will be held in the Lecture Hall on Monday, November 19th, 1888.

The President, the Right Hon. the LORD MAYOR, will take the Chair at 7 o'clock.

---

1. On se rappellera que la plupart des hôpitaux en Angleterre sont soutenus par des souscriptions et des dons. Il y a un dimanche dans l'année où tout l'argent recueilli dans les quêtes est distribué entre les hôpitaux. On l'appelle *Hospital Sunday*. En 1888, la somme recueillie s'est élevée à près d'un million et demi de francs. — 2. *N. W., North West postal district.* — 3. *J. P., Justice of the Peace; D. L., Deputy Lieutenant (of the county).* — 4. *V. P., Vice-President.*

The Times.

The following gentlemen are expected to be present: — Samuel Montagu, Esq., M. P., Rev. J. B. Heard, Rev. William Tyler, D. D., F. A. Bevan, Esq., Treasurer, Henry Hill, Founder and Hon. Sec.[1].

The prizes for progress at the evening classes and a swimming challenge cup[2] will be presented by the Lord Mayor. During the evening there will be a gymnastic display by the Institute Club. Admission free by ticket.

HENRY HILL, Hon. Sec., 38, Bow-lane, E. C.

ROYAL HOSPITAL for INCURABLES,
West-hill, Putney-heath.
Seaside-house[3]. — 95, Marina, St. Leonard's-on-Sea.
Patron — His Royal Highness the PRINCE of WALES, K. G., &c.

The THIRTY-FOURTH ANNUAL MEETING and the AUTUMNAL ELECTION will be held *on Friday*, 30th of November, 1888, at the Cannon-street Hotel, E. C.

JOHN DERBY ALLCROFT, Esq., F. R. A. S.[4], Treasurer, in the Chair[5].

The Annual Meeting will commence at 11 o'clock, when the annual report and financial statement will be presented, and the usual business transacted.

Thirty Candidates will be elected.

The Elections will commence at 12 o'clock, and close at 2 precisely.

An annual subscriber has one vote for half-a-guinea, and an additional vote for every additional half-a-guinea.

A life subscriber has one vote for life for five guineas, and an additional vote for life for every additional five guineas.

Subscriptions received at the office, 106, Queen Victoria-street, by the Secretary, Mr. Frederic Andrew, to whom all orders should be made payable; by the Treasurer; by Messrs. Glyn, Mills, and Co.[6], No. 67, Lombard-street; and Messrs. Coutts and Co.[6], 59, Strand.

FREDERIC ANDREW, Secretary.

Offices, 106, Queen Victoria-street, E. C., November, 1888.

CLAPHAM HOME for INCURABLES. — Miss E. Warner, of 61, Gloucester-terrace, Hyde-park, is sincerely grateful to all the kind friends who aided her in getting LOUISA J. WOODS elected as an inmate of the above Home on Friday last.

CHRISTMAS PRESENTS and GIFTS for the POOR. — The Countess of Harrowby and the Committee of the SOCIETY for PROMOTING FEMALE WELFARE invite inspection of the INDUSTRIAL WORK of their affiliated Institutions, which will be on SALE at their Central office, 22a, Devonshire-street, W.[7], on Tuesday, Wednesday, and Thursday, the 4th, 5th, and 6th December, between 12 and 5 o'clock.

THE TIMES COLUMN OF NEW BOOKS and NEW EDITIONS.

⁂ This column is restricted to Books published during the last three months.

HURST and BLACKETT'S NEW LIST, to be had at all Libraries: —

Now ready, in 2 vols. demy 8vo., with upwards of eighty original Illustrations, by Alfred Bryan and W. H. Margetson, price 30s.

REMINISCENCES of J. L. TOOLE the COMEDIAN[8]. Related by Himself and Chronicled by JOSEPH HATTON.

---

1. *Honorary Secretary.* — 2. *A swimming challenge cup*, un prix (coupe d'argent) de natation. — 3. *Seaside house*, succursale au bord de la mer. — 4. *Fellow of the Royal Astronomical Society.* — 5. *In the chair*, président. — 6. Maison de banque. — 7. *West postal district of London.* — 8. Comédien encore vivant, connu pour son observation de la nature dans tous ses rôles.

NEW YORK. — Now ready, in 1 vol. demy 8vo., with 12 full-page Illustrations, price 12s.

SCOTTISH MOORS and INDIAN JUNGLES : Scenes of Sport in the Lews[1] and India. By CAPTAIN J. T. NEWALL, late Indian Staff Corps, Author of "Eastern hunters".

Mrs. LYNN LINTON'S NEW NOVEL. Now ready, at all the Libraries, in 3 vols., crown 8vo.,

THROUGH THE LONG NIGHT. By Mrs. E. LYNN LINTON, Author of "Patricia Kemball," "Paston Carew," &c.

NEW NOVEL by DORA RUSSELL. Now ready, at all the Libraries, in 3 vols., crown 8vo.,

THE TRACK of the STORM. A Novel. By DORA RUSSELL, Author of "Footprints in the Snow," &c.

NEW NOVEL by GERTRUDE FORDE 3 vols. crown 8vo.,

HUGH ERRINGTON. By GERTRUDE FORDE, Author of "In the Old Palazzo," "Driven before the Storm," &c. "The story is pleasantly told, and we think it will add to the authoress's popularity." — Literary World.

THE DEATH SHIP : a Strange Story. By W. CLARK RUSSELL, Author of "The Wreck of the Grosvenor". 3 vols. crown 8vo. "The best of all the author's novels, both in conception and in execution." — Graphic.
Hurst and Blackett, Limited, 13, Great Marlborough-street.

MESSRS. HATCHARD'S NEW BOOKS : —

Crown 8vo., with 50 Illustrations, cloth, 6s.,

A SHORT LIFE of CHRIST, for Old and Young. By CUNNINGHAM GEIKE, D. D., Author of "The Life and Words of Christ".

The GIFT BOOK of the SEASON. With nearly 400 Illustrations, imp. 8vo., cloth extra, 8s.,

ATALANTA, 1888, and Papers by the following popular Authors : — H. Rider Haggard, Grant Allen, F. Anstey, Archdeacon Farrar, Walter Besant, Mrs. Molesworth, Miss Thackeray, L. B. Walford, Miss Yonge, L. T. Meade, &c.

Crown 8vo., cloth extra, 5s.,

THE ADVENTURES of a MIDSHIPMITE[2]. By ARTHUR LEE KNIGHT, Author of "Ronald Halifax," &c. With twelve Illustrations by Rowland Holyoake.

Fcp.[3], 8vo., cloth extra, 2s. 6d.,

THE FISHERMAN'S DAUGHTER. By FLORENCE MONTGOMERY, Author of "Misunderstood".

Just published, oblong, 2s. 6d.,

TUNES for TOTS[4]. By the Hon. Mrs. FINCH HATTON. With an Illustrated Cover by Franck Dicksee.

Just published, 4to. vellum, cover, 3s. 6d.,

HISTORICAL TABLEAUX. An Evening's Entertainment. By RICHARD COMBE MILLER. Illustrated by Wm. Wontner.
London, Hatchards, 187, Piccadilly, W.

MESSRS. BELL'S NEW PUBLICATIONS :—

Fcp., 4to., £1 1s.,

THE HISTORY of HAMPTON COURT PALACE. Vol. II. In Stuart Times. Profusely Illustrated with Copper-plates, Etchings, and Engravings. By ERNEST LAW, B. A., Barrister-at-law.

1. *The Lews,* les landes d'Écosse. — 2. Familier pour *midshipman,* aspirant de marine. — 3. *Fcp., foolscap,* papier minute. — 4. Airs pour les tout petits.

1. Albert Dürer, né à Nüremberg, mort en 1528, célèbre peintre et surtout graveur. — 2. Docteur ès lettres (à l'étranger). — 3. Docteur ès lois, docteur en droit. — 4. Charles Lamb, poète ami des Lakistes, Wordsworth et Coleridge, mais surtout prosateur ; auteur des Essais d'Elia et de la touchante histoire de Rosamund Gray ; mort en 1834. Nous recommandons à nos jeunes lecteurs de lire dans le texte anglais les *Tales from Shakspeare*, écrits dans une langue simple et facile à comprendre.

GEORGE PHILIP and SON'S LIST of NEW BOOKS :—

This day, at all Libraries,

THE UNKNOWN HORN of AFRICA; an Exploration from Berbera to the Leopard River. By F. L. JAMES, M.A., Author of " Wild Tribes of the Soudan ". With 23 Full-page Plates and numerous Text Illustrations. Demy 8vo., square, price 21s. N.B.—A limited number with hand-coloured Illustrations of Fauna, price 28s., and 14 large-paper copies (sur Japon). Price on application.

Just published, large 8vo., illustrated cover, price 7s. 6d.,

PICTURES of NATIVE LIFE in DISTANT LANDS. A series of 12 beautifully Coloured Plates, size 15in.[1] by 13in., by H. Leuteman, affording life-like representations of the Life and Pursuits of the Principal Races of Mankind. Each plate accompanied by explanatory letterpress. A suitable gift book. George Philip and Son, 32, Fleet-street, London.

REMINGTON'S NEW BOOKS :—

Just published, ENGLISH EDITION of

MEMOIRS of DUKE ERNEST of SAXE-COBURG-GOTHA. Period 1818-1850, with Portraits of Prince Albert and Duke Ernest. 2 vols. demy 8vo., 30s.

THE MAPLESON MEMOIRS, 1848-1888. Second edition. 2 vols. demy 8vo., 30s. " The best book of the year."—People. " The book of the season. "—Newcastle Leader. " Will be read by every one. "—Graphic. " A never-failing stream of anecdote. " —Vanity Fair.

LOVE LETTERS of FAMOUS MEN and WOMEN. Edited by J. T. MERYDEW. 2 vols. demy 8vo., with 28 Portraits, 30s. " These handsome volumes are full of amusement and interest. "—Standard.

THE SOUDAN.—'83 to '87 in the SOUDAN, with an Account of Sir William Hewett's Mission to King John of Abyssinia. By A. B. WYLDE. Two vols., 30s. " One of the newest and most readable books about Africa. "—Manchester Guardian.
Remington and Co., Henrietta-street, Covent-garden.

W. B. WHITTINGHAM and CO.'S NEW LIST :—

Second and Cheaper Edition, 452 pages, post 8vo., price 7s. 6d.,

CHRISTIANITY, ISLAM, and the NEGRO RACE. By EDWARD W. BLYDEN, LL.D. Mr. R. Bosworth Smith, in the " Nineteenth Century ", says :—" It is in the pages of Mr. Blyden's book that the great dumb, dark, continent has at last begun to speak, and in tones which. . . .even those who most differ from his conclusions will be glad to listen to and wise to ponder. . . "

Five Maps, Appendices of Distances, and other Handbook Information. 400 pages, post 8vo., price 2s. 6d.,

GOLDEN SOUTH AFRICA; or, the Goldfields re-visited. By EDWARD P. MATHERS, F. R. G. S.[2]. The " Morning Post" says :—" The book contains much information and sound advice. " The Financial News says :— "Will be eagerly studied by shareholders in the different mines. "

Monthly, 3d. ; annual subscription, 3s., post free,

THE PHOTOGRAPHIC ART JOURNAL, high-class Illustrated Monthly[3], contains the Photographic and Fine Art News for the Month, informa-

1. *Fifteen inches by thirteen,* 0 m. 380 sur 330. — 2. *Fellow of the Royal Geological Society.* — 3. *Monthly,* revue mensuelle.

tion on modern Progress in Photography for Professional and Amateurs, Correspondence, Reviews, &c. A Series of Articles on Practical Amateur Photography, by Mr. Buchanan Wollaston, commenced in the September, 1888, number.

---

212 pages, post 8vo., Eight Illustrations, price 7s. 6d.,

LUX BENIGNA. Being the History of Orange-street Chapel, otherwise called Leicester-fields Chapel. By REV. RICHARD FREE, M. A.

91, Gracechurch-street, London.

RICHARD BENTLEY and SON'S LIST :—

Now ready,

THE LIFE of RICHARD, LORD WESTBURY, Lord High Chancellor of England. By THOMAS ARTHUR NASH, Barrister-at-Law. In 2 vols. demy 8vo., with Two Portraits, 30s.

Now ready,

JOHN FRANCIS and the ATHENÆUM[1] : A Literary Chronicle of Half a Century. By JOHN C. FRANCIS. In 2 vols. crown 8vo., with Two Portraits, 24s.

Now ready,

THE HORSE, and HOW to BREED and REAR HIM. The Thoroughbred, Hunter, Carriage Horse, Cob, Farm Horse, Dray Horse, Pony, &c. By WILLIAM DAY, Author of " The Race Horse in Training, " &c. In demy 8vo., 16s.

Now ready,

THE MIDLAND RAILWAY : its Rise and Progress. By FREDERICK S. WILLIAMS. A new edition, in crown 8vo., with numerous Illustrations, 6s.

Now ready,

A SPORTSMAN'S EDEN[2]. A Season's Shooting in Upper Canada, British Columbia, and Vancouver. By CLIVE PHILLIPPS-WOLLEY, Author of " Sport in the Crimea and Caucasus ", &c. In demy 8vo., 9s.

Now ready,

OUR IRON ROADS : their History, Construction, and Administration. By FREDERICK S. WILLIAMS. A new edition, in demy 8vo., 8s. 6d.

Richard Bentley and Son,
New Burlington-street, Publishers in Ordinary to Her Majesty the Queen.

WM. CLOWES and SONS' NEW BOOKS :—

This day, third edition, revised and enlarged, demy 8vo., cloth, 15s.,

CHASTER'S POWERS of EXECUTIVE OFFICERS. Mr. Gladstone to the Author :—" I am much obliged by your kindness in sending me what appears, so far as I can judge, to be a work of great value and convenience. " " A compendium of the liberties of Englishmen. "—Bristol Times and Mirror.

Just published, demy 8vo., cloth, 7s. 6d.,

FRAUD and MISREPRESENTATION. A Short Treatise on the Law Relating to Fraud and Misrepresentation. By SYDNEY HASTINGS, B. A., of the Inner Temple, Barrister-at-Law, Author of " A Treatise on the Law of Torts, " and "The Law Relating to Riots. "

Now ready, crown 8vo., cloth, price 5s.,

MATRIMONIAL LAW and the GUARDIANSHIP of INFANTS. An Annotated Edition of the Ten Matrimonial Causes Acts. With Rules, Forms, and Scales of Costs. By DOUGLAS M. FORD, Solicitor and Notary

---

1. *The Athenæum,* le plus important des journaux littéraires publiés en Angleterre. — 2. Le Paradis des chasseurs.

Public, Author of " Solicitors as Advocates ".
London, Wm. Clowes and Sons (Limited), 27, Fleet-street.

Now ready, demy 8vo., cloth, price 20s.,

THE ELECTION of COUNTY COUNCILS[1] UNDER the LOCAL GOVERNMENT ACT, 1888, with Especial Reference to the First Elections in January, 1889. By FRANK R. PARKER, Solicitor and Parliamentary Agent, Author of " The Parker's Election Agent and Returning Officer" &c. London, Knight and Co., 90, Fleet-street, E.C.

Just published, Second Edition, royal 8vo., cloth. 7s. 6d.,

COUNTY COUNCILS, The LAW RELATING to : being the Local Government Act, 1888, County Electors, Act, 1888, the Incorporated Clauses of the Municipal Corporations Act, 1882, and a Compendious Introduction and Notes. By C. NORMAN BAZALGETTE and GEORGE HUMPHREYS, Barristers-at-Law. Stevens and Sons, Law Publishers, 119, Chancery-lane, London.

Handsomely bound, price 10s. 6d.,

TADEMA, MEISSONIER[2], HOOK. The LIVES and WORKS of. With 15 full-page Etchings or Engravings and about 120 Illustrations. London, J. B. Virtue and Co. (Limited). No. 26. Ivy-lane.

THE TIMES SECOND COLUMN OF
NEW BOOKS and NEW EDITIONS.
*** This column is restricted to Books published during the last three months.

SAMPSON LOW, MARSTON, and CO.'S NEW BOOKS :—

NEW ZEALAND of TO-DAY, 1884 to 1887. By JOHN BRADSHAW, late Chairman of the Canterbury Farmers' Co-operative Association, Author of " New Zealand as It Is ", " Raphael ben Isaac ", &c. With Maps. Demy 8vo., cloth, 14s.

TENT LIFE[3] in TIGER LAND : being Twelve Years' Sporting Reminiscences of a Pioneer Planter in an Indian Frontier District. By the Hon. JAMES INGLIS (" Maori "), Author of " Our New Zealand Cousins ", &c. 1 vol. royal 8vo., with 18 Coloured Illustrations, cloth, 18s. " His stories outdo in graphic power and exciting adventure anything that Mr. Rider Haggard has imagined. "—Pall Mall Gazette.

THE KINGDOM OF GEORGIA : being Notes of Travel in a Land of Women, Wine and Song; to which are appended Historical, Literary, and Political Sketches, Specimens of the National Music, and a compendious Bibliography. By OLIVER WARDROP. With numerous Illustrations and Map. Demy 8vo., cloth, 14s.

YOUNG SIR HARRY VANE. By PROF. JAMES K. HOSMER, of Washington University, St. Louis, Mo.[4], Author of " The Life of Adams " in "The American Statesmen Series ". With a Portrait of Vane engraved on wood. In 1 vol. 8vo., 500 pages, cloth extra, 18s.

THE LAND of the MOUNTAIN KINGDOM[5] : a Narrative of Adventure in the Unknown Mountains of Thibet. By D. LAWSON JOHNSTONE. Numerous Illustrations. Crown 8vo., cloth extra, 5s.

1. Voyez page 184, note 1. — 2. Nous n'avons pas besoin de faire ici l'éloge de Meissonier. *Tadema* et *Hook* sont deux peintres anglais. — 3. La vie sous la tente. — 4. *Mo.*, abr. pour *Missouri* (États-Unis). — 5. On remarquera le grand nombre de livres de voyages, d'explorations, de chasses lointaines, qui se publient tous les ans en Angleterre.

NEW YORK by JULES VERNE,

THE FLIGHT to FRANCE; or, the Memoirs of a Dragoon. A Tale of the Days of Dumouriez. By JULES VERNE, Author of "The Clipper of the Clouds," &c. Crown 8vo., with 34 full-page Illustrations. 7s. 6d.
London, Sampson Low, Marston, Searle, and Rivington, Limited.

MR. MURRAY'S LIST :—

Portrait, 2 vols. 8vo., 36s.,

THE LETTERS and PRIVATE CORRESPONDENCE of the late DANIEL O'CONNELL[1], M. P. Edited, with Notices of his Life and Times, by WM. J. FITZPATRICK, F. S. A.[2].

8vo., 7s. 6d.,

INTERNATIONAL LAW. Being the Whewell Lectures delivered before the University of Cambridge in 1887. By the late SIR H. SUMNER MAINE.

8vo., 12s.,

THE INFALLIBILITY of the CHURCH. A Course of Divinity Lectures. By GEORGE SALMON, D. D., Provost[3] of Trinity College, Dublin.

Two vols. crown 8vo., 24s.,

LIVES of TWELVE GOOD MEN. By JOHN W. BURGON, B. D., late Dean of Chichester.

Vol. XXIV., Part 2, 8vo., 498 pp., 6s.,

ROYAL AGRICULTURAL SOCIETY'S JOURNAL. Principles of Forestry—Farming in Channel Islands—The Herbage of Old Grass Lands—Food for Stock—Fruit Evaporation—Barley from a Maltster's Point of View—The Hay and Straw Press Competition—The Horse's Foot and the Principles of Shoeing.

Post 8vo., 2s. 6d.,

A BROKEN STIRRUP-LEATHER. By CHARLES GRANVILLE, Author of "Sir Hector's Watch".
London, John Murray, Albemarle-street.

CHATTO and WINDUS'S NEW LIST :—

2 vols. demy 8vo., 24s.; and at every Library,

PLAYERS and PLAYWRIGHTS I HAVE KNOWN. By JOHN COLEMAN. "Mr. Coleman's book is lightness and brightness itself—vivaciously chatty[4] eminently readable. It appeals alike to the general reader and to the earnest playgoer."—Globe.

JULIAN HAWTHORNE'S NEW NOVEL.—Crown 8vo., cloth extra, 3s. 6d.,

THE SPECTRE of the CAMERA; or, The Professor's Sister. By JULIAN HAWTHORNE, Author of "Dust", &c.

Cheap edition, crown 8vo., cloth extra, 3s. 6d.,

HERR PAULUS: his Rise, his Greatness, and his Fall. By WALTER BESANT, Author of "All Sorts and Conditions of Men". With a New Preface.

Crown 8vo., cloth extra, 6s.,

THE EULOGY of RICHARD JEFFERIES. By WALTER BESANT. With Photograph Portrait and Fac-simile Autograph. "This 'Eulogy' is at least as interesting as Mr. Besant's most interesting novels."—Daily News.

Cheaper edition, with 17 Illustrations, crown 8vo., cloth extra, 3s. 6d.,

IN PERIL and PRIVATION. By JAMES PAYN, Author of "By Proxy".[5]

1. Voyez note 9, page 3. — 2. *Fellow of the Society of Antiquaries.* 3 proviseur 4 Babillard
5 par procuration

THE HYGIENE of the SKIN : a Complete Code of Rules for the Management of the Skin, Diet, and Baths. By J. L. MILTON, Senior Surgeon to St. John's Hospital for Diseases of the Skin, Lecturer on Diseases of the Skin, &c. Third edition, revised, 1s.; cloth, 1s. 6d.

London, Chatto and Windus, Piccadilly, W.

MESSRS. RIVINGTON'S NEW LIST :—

EASY SELECTIONS from PLATO. Forming a Greek Reading Book for the use of Middle Forms of Schools. By A. SIDGWICK, M. A., Fellow and Tutor of Corpus Christi College, Oxford, and late Assistant Master at Rugby School. Crown 8vo., 3s. 6d.

LATIN SYNTAX. For the use of Upper Forms. By the REV. E. C. EVERARD OWEN, M. A., Fellow of New College, Oxford, and Assistant Master at Harrow School. Crown 8vo., 4s. 6d.

SELECT PASSAGES from FRENCH and GERMAN POETS, for Repetition. With English Metrical Renderings, and Elocution and other Notes. Compiled by CLOVIS BEVENOT, Assistant Master at Clifton College. With a Preface by J. M. WILSON, M. A., Head Master of Clifton College. Crown 8vo., 3s. 6d.

TEACHING as a CAREER for UNIVERSITY MEN. By J. J. FINDLAY, M. A., late Scholar of Wadham College, Oxford, and recently Head Master of Queen's College, Taunton. With a Prefatory Note by ARTHUR SIDGWICK, M. A., Fellow and Tutor of Corpus Christi College, Oxford. Crown 8vo., 1s. 6d.

GERMAN EXERCISES. Including Specimens of Correspondence. By G. J. R. GLUNICKE, B. A., Assistant Master at Bedford Grammar School. Crown 8vo., 6s.

PROGRESSIVE GERMAN DIALOGUES. With a Synopsis of German Construction, a Collection of Idioms indispensable for Conversation, and Notes. For Schools and Private Study. By A. an der HALDEN, German Master, Gordon's College, Aberdeen. 16mo., 2s. 6d.

Rivingtons, Waterloo-place, Pall-mall, London.

GARDNER, DARTON, and CO.'S LIST :—

A never-failing help with children.

SUNDAY.—The New Volume, now ready, contains 416 pages, well illustrated with 250 Engravings drawn on purpose for this ever-popular volume. Daintily coloured paper boards, 3s.; cloth elegant, gilt edges, 5s. "Well printed, well illustrated, well written." —Morning Post. "Deservedly a favourite."—Saturday Review.

The FIRST BISHOP of ADELAIDE[1].

AUGUSTUS SHORT. The Story of a Thirty-four Years's Episcopate. By CANON WHITINGTON. With Portrait, crown 8vo., cloth boards, 7s. 6d.

The NEW BOOK by the Author of "Ethne",

BRYDA. A Story of the Indian Mutiny. By Mrs. E. M. FIELD, Author of "Ethne". "Mixed Pickles," &c. With numerous Illustrations by A. FORESTIER. Large crown 8vo., cloth boards, 3s. 6d.

The NEW BOOK by the Author of "Honor Bright," &c.

GILLY FLOWER. By the Author of "One of a Covey," "Peasblossom," "M. or N.," &c. Illustrated by Gordon Browne. Large crown 8vo., cloth, 3s. 6d.

---

1. Capitale de l'Australie du Sud ; 120,000 habitants.

Dedicated, by permission, to be Bishop of Rochester.

THE PARISH GUIDE. A Handbook for the Use of the Clergy and Lay Helpers. Edited by the REV. THEODORE JOHNSON. Demy 8vo., cloth boards 6s. "One of the most marvellous and most useful handbooks we have ever met with."—John Bull.

22nd edition, with Appendix.

PASTOR in PAROCHIA. By the BISHOP of WAKEFIELD. Fcp. 8vo., cloth, 3s. 6d.; leather, 5s.; calf or morocco antique, 10s. 6d. A most valuable help to the clergy and district visitors.

Gardner, Darton, and Co., Paternoster-buildings, E. C.

MR. GEORGE REDWAY'S LIST :—

GRAMMAR of PALMISTRY[2]? By KATHERINE ST. HILL. With 18 Illustrations. 1s.

BACON, SHAKESPEARE, and the ROSICRUCIANS. By W. F. O. WIGSTON. With 2 Plates. 7s. 6d.

LIVES of ALCHEMYSTICAL PHILOSOPHERS. By A. E. WAITE. With a Bibliography. 10s. 6d.

DREAMS and DREAM STORIES. By ANNA KINGSFORD, M.D. Edited by E. MAITLAND. 6s.

CHRISTIAN SCIENCE HEALING: its Principles and Practice. By FRANCES LORD. 8s. 6d.

THE WHITE KING; or, Charles the First and the Men and Women, Life and Manners, Literature and Art, of England in the First Half of the 17th Century. By W. H. DAVENPORT ADAMS. 2 vols., 21s.

George Redway, York-street, Covent-garden.

GRIFFITH, FARRAN and Co.'s BOOKS :—

Just out,

JAPANESE FAIRY TALES. A Series of 16 Little Volumes by Japanese Artists, exquisitely produced in original style by Japanese printers, on Japanese crêpe paper. The stories in English.

CHRISTMAS in MANY LANDS. Four quarto books, in paper cover. Price 1s. each. In one vol., cloth elegant, bevelled boards, price 3s. 6d. By FLORENCE SCANNELL. Illustrated by EDITH SCANNELL.

Fun and Figures for the Little Ones.

MARMADUKE MULTIPLY'S MERRY METHOD of MAKING MINOR MATHEMATICIANS. A New Edition of an Old Favourite. In three vols., miniature 4to, 24 pp. each. Coloured Cover and Frontispiece. Price 4d. each.

Crown 4to., cloth, bevelled boards and gilt edges, price 6s.,

WHEN I'M A MAN; or, Little Saint Christopher. By ALICE WEBER. Profusely Illustrated by W. H. GROOME.

Crown 4to., cloth, bevelled boards and gilt edges, price 6s.,

BIRDIE: A Tale of Child Life. By HARRIET CHILDE-PEMBERTON. Profusely Illustrated by W. AINEY.

Small 4to., paper boards, price 2s. 6d.; or boards, price 3s.,

THE STORY of the MERMAIDEN[3]. Adapted from the German of Hans Andersen by E. ASHE, Author (in part)

---

1. Voyez page 275, note 3. — 2. *Palmistry*, chiromancie. — 3. *The Mermaiden*, les Sirènes.

of "Twilight Shadows and other Poems". Profusely Illustrated by LAURA W. TROUBRIDGE. Griffith, Farran, Okeden, and Welsh, London.

Just published, 8th Edition, demy 12mo[4] cloth, 2s. 6d., per post, 2s. 8d.,

PALMERS SHAREHOLDERS' and DIRECTORS' LEGAL COMPANION : a Manual of every-day Law and Practice for Promoters, Shareholders, Directors, Secretaries, Creditors and Solicitors of Companies. With an Appendix on the Conversion of Business Concerns into Private Companies. By F. B. PALMER, Esq., Barrister-at-Law. Stevens and Sons, Chancery-lane.

THE NATIONAL REVIEW. November. Possible Remedies for the Sweating System[1]. Arthur A. Baumann, M. P. — Red Deer Shooting. James Munro.—Waist Belts and Stays. C. S. Roy, M. D., and J. G. Adam—French Clergy Exiles in England. Rev. F. G. Lee, D. D.—The Oratory of the House of Commons. C. W. Radcliffe-Cooke, M.P.— The Income of a University. Rev. Professor G. F. Browne, B. D.[5] &c. London, W. H. Allen and Co.

Second edition, price 1s.,

THE CURSE UPON MITRE-SQUARE, A. D. 1530-1888. By JOHN FRANCIS BREWER. "Lose no time in securing it."—St. Stephen's Review. "'Tis indeed a well-written booklet."—The Gentleman. "It cannot be denied that Mr. Brewer has written a clever and a blood-curdling book."—Evening Post. London : Simpkin, Marshall, and Co.

Mr. HURLBERT'S BOOK on IRELAND.—Second edition, 2 vols., 15s.,

IRELAND UNDER COERCION. "Incomparably the most able, inpartial, and interesting contribution to the discussion of the great problem of the government and social condition of Ireland which has been given to the world." — Edinburgh Review[2]. Edinburgh, David Douglas; and all Booksellers.

Now ready, Second Annual Issue. 7th edition, royal 8vo., cloth 20s.,

WILSON'S PRACTICE of the SUPREME COURT of JUDICATURE, containing the Acts, Orders, Rules, and Regulations relating to the Supreme Court. With Practical Notes. By CHAS. BURNEY, a Chief Clerk of the Hon. Mr. Justice Chitty; M. MUIR MACKENZIE; and C. ARNOLD WHITE, Barristers-at-Law. Stevens and Sons, 119, Chancery-lane, London.

The EMPEROR FREDERICK'S DIARY[3], in fcp. boards, price 1s.,

THE EMPEROR'S DIARY of the AUSTRO-GERMAN WAR, 1866, and the FRANCO-GERMAN WAR, 1870-71. To which is added Prince Bismarck's Rejoinder.[6] Edited by HENRY W. LUCY. George Routledge and Sons, Broadway, Ludgate-hill.

SIMS REEVES: His LIFE, by himself. The famous tenor's book is full of interest."—Dramatic Review.

---

1. *The Sweating System.* Cet odieux système, sur lequel une commission royale poursuit son enquête dans toute l'Angleterre, est le suivant : des sous-traitants entreprennent l'exécution d'ouvrages de tailleur chez eux ou dans de petites boutiques, et engagent d'autres ouvriers pour ce travail, trouvant un profit pour eux-mêmes dans la différence qui existe entre les prix d'adjudication et le salaire qu'ils payent à leurs aides. Le but du sous-traitant étant son propre gain, la tendance de ce système est d'amener l'ouvrier à travailler au prix le plus bas possible. — 2. Revue trimestrielle fondée le 25 octobre 1802. Son premier éditeur fut J. Jeffrey, plus tard Lord Jeffrey. Parmi les rédacteurs, dont beaucoup furent célèbres, on compte Sidney Smith et lord Brougham. — 3. *Diary*, journal. C'est la publication posthume de ce journal qui, il y a quelques mois, faisait naître une polémique dans la presse, et appelait une réponse du prince de Bismarck.

" Mr. Sims Reeves is an admirable narrator." — Morning Advertiser. " His name is familiar to the lips as household words." — Observer. One vol. demy[1] 8vo., 10s. 6d. London Music Publishing Company (Limited). 54, Great Marlborough-street, W.

FIRE.—The Committee of the BOYS and GIRLS' INDUSTRIAL HOMES, Forest-hill, S. E., are URGENTLY in NEED of FUNDS for carrying on the good work of sustaining these Homes for the rescue of poor helpless children. To add to the anxieties of the Committee, a fire has occurred, caused, it is supposed, by an incendiary, resulting in the total destruction of the stable connected with the Homes and the burning to death of the pony and donkey used for carting the work made by the boys to residents in the neighbourbood. The building and animals were, unfortunately, not insured. Will some kind friends assist to make good the loss? The late Lord Shaftesbury was President of the Homes, which he himself opened, and to which he kindly gave his own name. Subscriptions will gladly be received by the Secretary,
T. G. LITCHFIELD, Boys and Girls' Industrial Homes, Shaftesbury-house, Perry-rise, Forest-hill, S. E.

J. WHITE—SECOND EXHIBITION of

J. WHITE—NOVELTIES for the SEASON,

J. WHITE—THIS DAY,

J. WHITE—and FOLLOWING DAYS.

J. WHITE—DRESSES, Ball and Dinner.

J. WHITE—COSTUMES, Morning and Visiting.

J. WHITE—MANTLES, Sealskin and Fur-lined.

J. WHITE—BOAS, Muffs, Rugs, &c.

J. WHITE—MILLINERY[2], Flowers, Lace, Fans.

J. WHITE—TEA GOWNS, Children's Dresses.

J. WHITE—TROUSSEAUX and LAYETTES.

J. WHITE—HOSIERY, Jerseys, Gloves.

J. WHITE—REGENT-STREET and ARGYLL-STREET.

FRY'S PURE CONCENTRATED COCOA.—Thirty-eight Prize Medals awarded to the firm.

FRY'S PURE CONCENTRATED COCOA.—Sir C. A. Cameron, M. D., President of the Royal College of Surgeons, Ireland, &c.— " I have never tasted Cocoa that I like so well, and I strongly recommend it as a substitute for tea for young persons."

FRY'S PURE CONCENTRATED COCOA.—Dr. N. C. Whyte, Coroner[3] for the City of Dublin.—" There are innumerable varieties of Cocoa, but to my mind incomparably the best is Fry's Pure Concentrated Cocoa. I have been using it myself for some time with manifest advantage.

1. *Demy*, papier coquille. — 2. *Millinery*, modes ou articles de modes. — 3. Le *Coroner* est, en général, un fonctionnaire dont les attributions sont à la fois administratives et judiciaires. Sa principale fonction est de réunir et de présider un jury ou commission d'enquête chargé de vérifier les causes du décès de ceux qui meurent subitement. Voy. aussi page 207, note 4.

FRY'S PURE CONCENTRATED COCOA. — E. Bucknill, M.D.[1] — "Your Pure Concentrated Cocoa is so extremely nice that I have ordered it for family use, and I shall certainly recommend it to my patients."

FRY'S PURE CONCENTRATED COCOA.—W. H. R. Stanley, M.D. — "I consider it a very rich, delicious Cocoa. It is highly concentrated and therefore economical as a family food. It is the drink par excellence for children, and gives no trouble in making."

FRY'S PURE CONCENTRATED COCOA.—Be careful to ask for this Cocoa.

J. S. FRY and SONS, Bristol; 252, City-road, London, E. C.; and Sidney, N. S. W.

COOPER COOPER and Co.

COOPER COOPER and Co.'s TEAS. One Shilling and Fourpence a pound.

COOPER COOPER and Co.'s TEAS. Possessing strength and character.

COOPER COOPER and Co.'s TEAS. Such value is not offered by any other house in the kingdom.

COOPER COOPER and Co.'s TEAS. The finest Tea the world produces at 3s. a pound.

COOPER COOPER and Co.'s TEAS. Strong and goodly Teas at 1s. 6d. and 1s. 8d. a pound.

COOPER COOPER and Co.'s TEAS. Also a Tea mighty in power at 2s. a pound.

COOPER COOPER and Co.'s TEAS. The finest Tea the world produces at 2s. 6d. and 3s. a pound.

COOPER COOPER and Co.'s TEAS. Ceylon Teas at 2s., 2s. 6d., and 3s. a pound.

COOPER COOPER and Co.'s TEAS. Samples and Price List free by post.

CHINA, INDIA, and CEYLON TEAS.

COOPER COOPER and Co.'s TEAS. The best Tea ever offered at the prices.

CHIEF OFFICE—50, King, William-street, London-bridge, E. C.

Branches—

LONDON :—63, Bishopsgate-street, within, E. C.
268, Regent-circus, W.
85, Strand, W. C.
21, Westbourne-grove, W.
334, Hgh Holborne, W.C.
98, Sporeditch High-street, E.
266, Westminster-bridge-road, S. E.

BRIGHTON :—20 and 21, East-street.

NESTLE'S FOOD.—An Entire Diet[2] for Infants.

NESTLE'S FOOD.—An Entire Diet for Infants. Supplies all the elements necessary for the complete nourishment and growth of the human frame.

NESTLE'S FOOD, being partly composed of milk, is complete and entire in itself, and requires simply the addition of water to make it instantly ready for use. It is not merely an auxiliary, like other infants' foods, which require milk to be added in preparing for use.

NESTLE'S FOOD for INFANTS.—Recommended by the highest me-

1. *M. D.*, docteur en médecine. — 2. *Diet*, ici nourriture.

dical authorities as the nearest equivalent to mother's milk.

CAPPERS.—WINTER COSTUMES and MANTLES. Newest designs. Colourings exquisite.

VELVET FINISH HABIT CLOTH, 24s. 6d. the full dress of seven yards. 48in. wide.

CAPPERS. — DUNOON SERGES, Navy and Black, pure wool, 1s. 2½d. per yard. 27in. wide.

SILK and WOOL COMBINATION ROBES, with ample material, 39s. 6d. the full dress.

CAPPERS.—REDINGOTES and ULSTERS, Furs, Boas, Capes, and Muffs.

BLANKETS, Flannels, Quilts, and Rugs, at net wholesale prices for charitable purposes.

CAPPER, SON, and Co. (Ld.), 63 and 64, Gracechurch-street, City. Established in the year 1779.

GOLDSMITHS' ALLIANCE (Limited),

NOS. 11 and 12, CORNHILL, London, E. C.

JEWELLERY.—The GOLDSMITHS' ALLIANCE (Limited) respectfully solicit an inspection of their extensive STOCK, which contains a beautiful assortment of the following articles :—

Bracelets, from..	£6	to	£200
Brooches, from ..	£2	to	£200
Lockets, from ..	£2	to	£200
Earrings, from ..	£1	to	£200
Pendants, from ..	£2	to	£500
Chains, from..	£3	to	£50
Pins, from ..	£1	to	£50
Studs[1], from..	£1	to	£50

To obviate the difficulty which is so often experienced in choosing suitable gifts, the Goldsmiths' Alliance (Limited) have prepared a new edition of their Illustrated Pamphlet, and will be happy to forward the same gratis and post free on application.—11 and 12, Cornhill, London, opposite the Bank of England.

RINGS.—THE GOLDSMITHS' ALLIANCE (Limited) respectfully solicit an inspection of their magnificent and carefully-selected stock of RINGS :—

Diamond Half-hoop rings, from	£7	to	£500
Emerald Half-hoop Rings, from	£15	to	£500
Ruby Half-hoop Rings, from..	£15	to	£500
Sapphire Half-hoop Rings, from	£20	to	£500
Opal Half-hoop Rings, from..	£5	to	£50
Pearl Half-hoop Rings, from ..	£2	to	£30
Coral Half-hoop Rings, from ..	£2	to	£30
Turquoise Half-hoop Rings, from	£2	to	£20

Single-stone, Three-stone, Cluster, and Gipsy Rings of every description, and at various prices, always ready for immediate selection. Drawings and every information forwarded on application.—11 and 12, Cornhill, London.

DIAMONDS. — GOLDSMITHS' ALLIANCE (Limited), 11 and 12, Cornhill, London.—DIAMOND NECKLACES, bracelets, brooches, earrings, crosses, lockets, half-hoop and single-stone rings, &c., in great variety, at fixed net prices for cash.

LICENSED APPRAISERS[2].

VALUATIONS MADE for PROBATE.

GOLDSMITHS' ALLIANCE (Limited),

NOS. 11 and 12, CORNHILL, London, E. C.

1. *Studs*, boutons doubles. — 2. Experts patentés.

HYAM and Co.'s CLOTHING, 136 to 140, Oxford-street, W., for gentlemen and their sons, ready-made and to order, now on view at their extensive establishments. The various new styles and materials introduced by them at most moderate prices. Public inspection of the same is respectfully solicited.

HYAM and Co.'s GENTLEMEN'S CLOTHING.

HYAM and Co.'s BOYS and YOUTHS' CLOTHING.

HYAM and Co.'s HATS, Caps, and Umbrellas.

HYAM and Co.'s HOSIERY, Shirts, and Collars.

HYAM and Co.'s GENTLEMEN'S BOOTS and SHOES.

HYAM and Co.'s BOYS' BOOTS and SHOES.

HYAM and Co.'s LADIES' BOOTS and SHOES.

HYAM and Co.'s LADIES' COSTUMES.

HYAM and Co.'s LADIES' JACKETS, ULSTERS, RIDING HABITS, &c.

HYAM and Co.'s SERVANTS' LIVERIES.

CAUTION.—HYAM and Co. (Limited) beg specially to notify their only establishments are :—London—130 to 140, Oxford-street, W.; and at Birmingham, Wolverhampton, Leede, and Dewsbury.

DE JONG'S PURE SOLUBLE COCOA, the Acme of all pure Cocoas.

DE JONG'S PURE SOLUBLE COCOA makes hot or cold Cocoa or Chocolate in one minute.

DE JONG'S PURE SOLUBLE COCOA. Dr. Hehner, the well-known public analyst, says :—" I found

DE JONG'S PURE SOLUBLE COCOA to be of absolute purity and of the highest excellence. It surpasses in delicacy of aroma and richness of taste the best kinds of Cocoas which have hitherto been offered to the public."

DE JONG'S PURE SOLUBLE COCOA. —2oz. sample tins, containing sufficient for 15 breakfast cups, free of charge and postage paid, may be had by addressing the

CHIEF DEPOT of DE JONG'S COCOA, 6 and 7, Coleman-street, London, E.C. (All rights reserved.)

JENNER and KNEWSTUB (Limited), 33, St. James's-street, and 66, Jermyn-street, S.W.

JENNER and KNEWSTUB'S STERLING SILVER GUINEA PRESENTS.

JENNER and KNEWSTUB'S BAG of BAGS. Ladies' and Gentlemen's Bags Fitted silver and ivory, £4 14s. 6d.

JENNER and KNEWSTUB'S GEM JEWELLERY, at half-price. Merchants supplied at less than wholesale prices.

JENNER and KNEWSTUB'S GEM RINGS, from £1 1s. to £300. Brooches, Earrings, Head Ornaments, Necklaces, &c., equally cheap.

JENNER and KNEWSTUB'S BRACELETS, from £1 1s. to £1,000; Pendants, Scarf Pins, Sleeve Links, Studs, &c., at less than manufacturers' cost.

JENNER and KNEWSTUB'S magnificent collection of GEM JEWEL-

From the LONDON GAZETTE[2], *Tuesday, Nov.* 13.

WHITEHALL, Nov. 12.

The Queen has been pleased to direct Letters Patent to be passed under the Great Seal of the United Kingdom of Great Britain and Ireland, granting the dignities of an Earl and Marquess of the said United Kingdom unto Frederick Temple, Earl of Dufferin[3], Knight Grand Cross of the Most Honourable Order of the Bath, Knight of the Most Illustrious Order of Saint Patrick, Grand Master and First and Principal Knight Grand Commander of the Most Exalted Order of the Star of India, Knight Grand Cross of the Most Distinguished Order of Saint Michael and Saint George, Grand Master and First and Principal Knight Grand Commander of the Most Eminent Order of the Indian Empire, Viceroy and Governor-General of India, and the heirs male of his body lawfully begotten, by the names, styles, and titles of Earl of Ava, in the Province of Burma, and Marquess of Dufferin and Ava, in the county of Down and in Burma aforesaid.

The Queen has been pleased to give and grant unto Thomas Cecil Farrer, Esq., Her Royal licence and authority that he may accept and wear the Insignia of the Third Class of the Order of the Medjidieh, which His Highness the Khedive of Egypt, authorized by His Imperial Majesty the Sultan, has been pleased to confer upon him in connection with his services whilst actually and entirely employed beyond Her Majesty's Dominions in the inspection of Egyptian railways.

ADMIRALTY[4], Nov. 9.

Engineer Joseph Langmaid has been promoted to the rank of Chief Engineer in Her Majesty's Fleet.

1. C'est à Noël que se fait en Angleterre l'échange de présents qui se fait en France à l'occasion de la nouvelle année. — 2. Fondée en 1642, ensuite transportée en 1665 à Oxford, où s'était retirée la cour pour échapper aux dangers de la peste. C'est l'organe officiel, propriété du Gouvernement, où sont publiées toutes les nouvelles d'intérêt public; il paraît deux fois par semaine. — 3. Le comte (Earl) de Dufferin succéda à Lord Ripon comme vice-roi des Indes, et donna sa démission en 1888. C'est un descendant de Sheridan. — 4. Ami-

In accordance with the provisions of Her Majesty's Order in Council of Feb. 5, 1872 : — Chaplain and Naval Instructor the Rev. Arthur Castell Wright, M.A., has this day been placed on the retired list at his own request.

ROYAL MARINE LIGHT INFANTRY.

The undermentioned gentlemen to be Second Lieutenants : — Mr. Charles Stanbrough Watson, Mr. Wilfred Hugh Moore Smith, Mr. John Raymond Garrett, Mr. Charles Walter Tribe, Mr. Charles Edwin Collard, Mr. Edward Frederick Kempson Sorsbie.

The undermentioned Second Lieutenants to be Lieutenants : — Charles Stanbrough Watson, Wilfred Hugh Moore Smith, John Raymond Garrett, Charles Walter Tribe, Charles Edwin Collard, Edward Frederick Kempson Sorsbie.

NOVEMBER 10.

The undermentioned Gunners[1] have been promoted to the rank of Chief Gunner in Her Majesty's Fleet : — Henry J. Metters; Alfred Smith; William Pearce.

NOVEMBER 12.

In accordance with the provisions of Her Majesty's Order in Council of Feb. 22, 1870 : — Lieut. Albert John O'Rorke has been placed on the Retired List, with permission to assume the rank of Commander.

WAR OFFICE[2], PALL MALL, Nov. 13.

1st Life Guards. — Capt. George L. Holford has been seconded on appointment as Extra Equerry to Field-Marshal his Royal Highness the Prince of Wales, K.G., K.T., K.P., &c.

1st Dragoon Guards. — Cap. George Wentworth Forbes has been seconded for service as an Adjutant of Auxiliary Forces.

Royal Artillery. — The four promotions of Officers to the rank of Major in the Royal Artillery which were notified in the " Gazette " of November 6, 1888, are vice Officers promoted "Lieutenant-Colonels" on half-pay, and not as therein stated.

REGIMENTAL DISTRICT.

Lieut.-Col. and Col. William Lowry Auchinleck, commanding the 35th Regimental District (the Royal Sussex Regiment), has been placed on half-pay.

Col. R. F. Butler, from Lieutenant-Colonel, half-pay, to be Colonel, to command the 35th Regimental District (the Royal Sussex Regiment), vice Col. W. L. Auchinleck, who has vacated that appointment.

LINE BATTALIONS.

The Suffolk Regiment. — Second Lieut. G. R. D. Stoddart has been seconded for service with the Indian Staff Corps.

The Prince Albert's (Somersetshire Light Infantry). — Second Lieut. Robert William C. Keays has been seconded for service with the Indian Staff Corps.

---

rauté, administration de la marine. Il y a un Conseil de l'Amirauté composé de *Lord Commissioners*, dont le premier *Lord* est ministre de la marine. — 1. *Gunner*, canonnier; *chief gunner*, maître canonnier. — 2. Ministère de la Guerre.

The Times.

The Prince of Wales's Own (West Yorkshire Regiment). — Second Lieut. Henry Tweddell has been seconded for service with the Indian Staff Corps; Lieut. Ward Sausmarez Carey, from the 4th Battalion, the Cheshire Regiment, to be Second Lieutenant, in succession to Lieut. J. C. Yale, promoted.

The Cheshire Regiment. — Capt. Henry S. Marshall has been seconded for service as an Adjutant of Auxiliary Forces.

The East Lancashire Regiment. — Lieut. Frederic George Lucas has been seconded for service with the Indian Staff Corps.

The Black Watch (Royal Highlanders). — Sergeant Charles Herbert Philip Carter, from the 4th Dragoon Guards, to be Second Lieutenant, in succession to Lieut. W. G. Wolrige-Gordon, appointed Adjutant.

The Essex Regiment. — Capt. Charles Edward Orman has been seconded for service as an Adjutant of Auxiliary Forces. — Sergeant Edward Dalton Fawkes, from the Cameronians (Scottish Rifles[1]), to be Second Lieutenant, in succession to Lieut. T. G. Hopkins, promoted.

The Royal Irish Rifles. — Lieut. Fitz Roy E. P. Curzon, from the Cameronians (Scottish Rifles), to be Captain, in succession to Lieut.-Col. and Col. S. Flower, placed on retired pay.

Staff.—Lieut.-Col. F. T. C. Du Vernet, from half-pay, to be a Deputy Assistant Adjutant-General, vice Major E. A. W. S. Grove, the Queen's Own (Royal West Kent Regiment), whose period of service in that appointment is about to expire.

Royal Military Academy.—Lieut. A. J. Breakey, Royal Artillery, to be a Lieutenant of a Company of Gentlemen Cadets, vice Capt. A. M'N. C. Cooper-Key, Royal Artillery, who vacates that appointment on promotion.

Ordnance Factories[2].—Lieut.-Col. M. T. Sale, C. M. G., from half-pay, is continued in his appointment as Superintendent of Building Works.

Chaplain's Department [3].—The Rev. George Wylde, M. A., Chaplain to the Forces, First Class, retires on retired pay; the Rev. Willoughby Charles Haines to be Chaplain to the Forces, Fourth Class, dated Nov. 6, 1887, such antedate not to carry back allowances.

Commissariat and Transport Staff.—Deputy Assistant Commissary-General, with the honorary rank of Captain, George Thomas Colebrook, half-pay, has been placed on retired pay, on account of ill-health.

Medical Staff.—Surgeon-Major William Henry Garde is granted retired pay.

Army Pay Department[4].—The undermentioned Staff Paymasters and Honorary Majors to be granted the honorary rank of Lieutenant-Colonel :—Frederic Treffry, John Johnson Tuck. Capt. Edward Loftus Roche Thackwell, the Royal Fusiliers (City of London Regiment), having resigned his combatant commission, to be Paymaster, with the honorary rank of Captain in the Army.

MEMORANDA.

Supernumerary General and Colonel Commandant Sir John Lintorn Arabin Simmons, G. C. B., G. C. M. G., Royal Engineers, has been placed on the retired list under the provisions of Article 89 of the Royal Warrant of Nov. 15, 1887; Lieut.-Col. S. Bradburne, the Leicestershire Regiment, to be Colonel.

1. *Rifles*, carabiniers. — 2. Fabriques d'armes. — 3. Division des aumôniers militaires. — 4. Division de la trésorerie de l'armée. *Paymaster*, trésorier.

Capt. H. W. Lovett, the Prince Albert's (Somersetshire Light Infantry), has been granted the local rank of Major while employed as Deputy Assistant Adjutant-General to the Colonial Forces in South Australia.

Capt. H. B. Lassetter, the South Staffordshire Regiment, to have the local rank of Major while employed with the local Forces in New South Wales.

ARMY MEDICAL RESERVE OF OFFICERS.

Surgeon and Hon. Surgeon-Major Cornelius Scamp Hall, 1st Volunteer Battalion the Border Regiment, to be Surgeon-Major, ranking as Lieutenant-Colonel.

Commissions signed by the Lord Lieutenant of the county of Devon.—Sir William Robert Williams, Bart., William Rennell Coleridge, Esq., and Francis Drummond Fulford, Esq., to be Deputy Lieutenants.

PARTNERSHIPS DISSOLVED[1].

J. J. Marcel, J. H. Blow, A. C. Dunlop, and H. G. Dunlop, Bishopsgate-street, City, Southampton, Paris, and Manchester, under the style of George Dunlop, and Co., and Havre under the style of Marcel and Co., shipping agents and commission merchants; as far as regards H. G. Dunlop.—Bamber and Mills, Manchester, designers[3] and stamp makers.—L. Fossett and Co., Regent-street, hatters.—M' Dougal Brothers, Mark-lane, City, Millwall Docks, Manchester, and Chadderton, near Oldham, manufacturing chemists, wood pulp manufacturers, corn millers, and flour dealers; as far as regards John M'Dougall.—G. E. Bowring and J. D. Jamieson, St. Leonard's Wharf, Bromley St. Leonard's, and Great St. Helen's, City, wharfingers[2], W. and A. J. Smout, Mount-street, Grosvenor-square, under the firm of Scarlett and Co., and Connaught-street, Hyde-park-square, under the firm of Groves and Co., butchers.—Aspinall, Aspinall, and Co., Brayard's-road, Peckham, enamel paint manufacturers.—Eadington and Scarr, Bradford, coachbuilders.—Lees and Cliffes, Brighouse, Yorkshire, stone merchants; as far as regards Joseph Cliffe.—Walls and Fall, Great-Driffield and Kilham, Yorkshire, general drapers.—Whitehead and Gravestock, Northampton, milliners.—Robinson, Elias and Co., Manchester, manufacturers' agents and merchants.—J. Williamson and Son, Darwen, grocers and tea dealers.—P. Ward and Son, Bolton, cotton waste dealers.—Humphrey and Sons, Hove and Crowborough, Sussex, grocers and oil and Italian warehousemen, and wine, coal, and general merchants.—N. and C. Lamacraft, Otterton, Devonshire, millers.—Ruben and Isaacs, Great Grimsby, pawnbrokers.

DECLARATION OF DIVIDEND.

(Under the Bankruptcy Act, 1889.)

Griffiths, G., Stockton-cross, Kimbolton, Herefordshire, cattle dealer — first and final div. of 10 1-3d., any day, Mr. M. J. G. Scobie's, 2, Offa-street, Hereford.

SCOTCH SEQUESTRATIONS.

J. Anderson, deceased, Bainsford, Falkirk, draper, Nov. 20, at 12 30, Crown Hotel, Falkirk.—W. Davidson, Pulteneytown, Wick, fish curer, Nov. 20, at 2,

---

1. Dissolution de société. — 2. *Wharfingers*, maîtres de quai, propriétaires d'entrepôt.

3 Dessinateur. 4 Prêteur sur gage

Sinclair's Auction Rooms, Wick.—W. Davidson, jun., Pulteneytown, Wick, fish curer, Nov. 20, at 2, Sinclair's Auction Rooms, Wick.—A. Davidson, Pultneytown, Wick, fish curer, Nov. 20, at 2, Sinclair's Auction Rooms, Wick.—J. Davidson and Sons, Mauchline, box manufacturers, Nov. 19, at 12, George Hôtel, Kilmarnock.—R. Grieve, Dalbeattie, Kirkcudbright, printer, clog caulker, shoe, heel, and toe plate manufacturer, Nov. 16, at 3 30, Maxwell Arms Hotel, Dalbeattie.—T. F. Gilmour, Glasgow, physician and surgeon, Nov. 22, at 12, Faculty-hall, Glasgow.—R. Peddie and Son, Leith and Edinburgh, painters and paperhangers[1], Nov. 19, at 2, Dowell's Rooms, Edinburgh.—T. Creighton, Gotterbie, Lochmaben, Dumfriesshire, farmer, Nov. 19, at 11, Queensberry Hotel, Dumfries.

THE BANKRUPTCY (DISCHARGE AND CLOSURE) ACT, 1887[2].

Application for Debtor's Discharge.

Ormerod, James (trading as James Ormerod and Co.), Leeds, chemical manufacturer.—Dec. 6, County Court-house, Leeds.

Orders Made on Applications for Discharge.

Charnock, Joseph, Birkenshaw, Yorkshire, carrying on business with M. Sharp, at Bowling, Bradford, under the style of M. Sharp and Co., worsted spinner and manufacturer—absolute.

Yeo, John, and Yeo, Daniel Joseph, Lyneham, Wiltshire, timber merchants and farmers—absolute discharge.

THE BANKRUPTCY ACT, 1883.

Receiving Orders[3].

In London.

Appleby, Walter, George-yard, Aldermanbury, late of Aldermanbury, City, traveller, late trimming manufacturer.

Evans, Charles Watkyn De Lacy, Portland-road, Notting hill, lately carrying on business at Davies-street and Brook-street, Grosvenor-square, surgeon.

Frankcom, Edward James, and Hickmann, John William (trading as E. J. Frankcom and Co.), Holloway-road, timber merchants.

Leon Brothers and Co., Union-court, Old Broad-street, and Lenthall-road, Dalston, merchants.

Morgan, George Joseph, Canterbury-road, Kilburn, Willesden, boot dealer and draper.

Pilgrim, Abel, Plaistow, Essex, builder and publican[4].

Turner, William Edward Bennett, Cheltenham-terrace, Chelsea, no occupation, late a sub-inspector of police (metropolitan).

---

1. *Paperhangers*, tapissier. — 2. *The Bankruptcy (Discharge and Closure) Act*, 1887, fournit le moyen de décharger du chef de banqueroute d'après l'Acte de Banqueroute abrogé, et de mettre fin aux poursuites d'après l'Acte de 1869. L'Acte de 1869 supprimait l'emprisonnement pour dettes, tout en réservant les cas de fraude pouvant être imputés au failli. — 3. *Receiving orders*, ordonnance de sequestre. L'ordonnance de sequestre n'a pas les effets de la déclaration de faillite, *adjudication of Bankruptcy*. Elle ne dessaisit pas le débiteur et ne le soumet pas aux incapacités que la faillite entraîne. Le séquestre officiel est appelé à jouer à peu près le rôle du juge-commissaire nommé en France, si la faillite vient à être déclarée. — 4 *Publican*, aubergiste.

In the Country.

Akerman, Thomas Martin, French's Farm, near Andover, Hampshire, farmer.

Barrat, William, Birmingham, jet ornament manufacturer.

Baskcomb, William Richard, New Clee, Lincolnshire, fisherman.

Bennett, Joseph, Stockport, candlewick spinner.

Berry, James, trading as James Berry and Sons, Manchester, nurseryman and seedsman[1].

Blinman, Samuel, Dundry, Somersetshire, farmer and hay dealer.

Bowden, John, Uppermill, Saddleworth, Yorkshire, rolling board manufacturer.

Bowen, Alfred, formerly of Kidderminster, now of Radstock-street, Battersea, coachbuilder.

Bowen, Richard, Pontyeasts and Penygwiter, Llangendeirne, Carmarthenshire, licensed victualler, grocer, and farmer.

Butler, Thomas Edward, late of King's-hill, Wednesbury, Staffordshire, now of Darlaston and Wednesbury, builder and carpenter.

FIRST MEETINGS AND PUBLIC EXAMINATIONS.

In London.

Alexander, William Wilson, Martin's-lane, City, late of Ashchurch-grove, Hammersmith, now of Boscombe-road, Hammersmith, machinery and hardware merchant — first meeting, Nov. 20, Bankruptcy-buildings, Portugal-street, Lincoln's-inn; public examination, Dec. 5, 34, Lincoln's-inn-fields.

Burrows, William, Chariton-crescent. High-street, Islington, and Britannia-street, Gray's-inn-road, late of Pentonville-road, and Gray's-inn-road, lamp manufacturer; Nov. 20, 33, Carey-street, Lincoln's-inn; Dec. 5, 34, Lincoln's-inn-fields.

Clarke, Samuel, Godalming, glass and china merchant—Nov. 21, No. 16, Room, 30 and 31, St. Swithin's-lane, E. C. Dec. 13, Town-hall, Guildford.

Cooper, William John, High-road, formerly known as Manchester-terrace, Kilburn, butcher—Nov. 20, 33, Carey-street, Lincoln's-inn; Dec. 6, 34, Lincoln's-inn-fields.

Freeman, James, Hertford-road, Kingsland, and Cropley-street, Hoxton, furrier —Nov. 20, 33, Carey-street, Lincoln's-inn; Dec. 7, 34, Lincoln's-inn-fields.

Hambly, William Henry, Ventnor, Isle of Wight, ironmonger — Nov. 22, Chamber of Commerce, 145, Cheapside; Nov. 24, Court-house, Newport, Isle of Wight.

In the Country.

Adcock, John, Radford and new Lenton, Nottingham, Jacquard card puncher[2] —first meeting, Nov. 20, Official Receiver's offices, Nottingham; public examination, Dec. 7, County Court-house, Nottingham.

Akerman, Thomas Martin, French's Farm, near Andover, Hampshire, farmer — Nov. 23, Star Hotel, Andover; Dec. 7, Council-house, Salisbury.

Baldwin, William Edmund, formerly of Guisely, now of Leeds, formerly woollen manufacturer, afterwards draper, now out of business—Nov. 22, Official Receiver's offices, Leeds; Dec. 4, County Court-house, Leeds.

1. *Nurseryman and seedsman*, pépiniériste et grainetier. — 2. Fabricant de cartons Jacquard.

Bleasdale, Benjamin, Great Harwood, Lancashire, butcher—Nov. 21, County Court-house, Blackburn; Dec. 4, County Court-house, Blackburn.

Bowden, John, Saddleworth, Yorkshire, rolling board manufacturer—Nov. 21, Official Receiver's offices, Oldham; Dec. 7, Town-hall, Oldham.

DAY APPOINTED FOR PUBLIC EXAMINATION.

Graham, Walter, now a prisoner in Her Majesty's Convict Prison, Milbank, previously a prisoner in Her Majesty's Prison, Pentonville—High Court of Justice, Nov. 20, 34, Lincoln's-inn-fields.

ADJUDICATIONS.

In London.

Boss, Isaac (trading as T. Boss and Co.), Commercial-road east, fancy goods importer[1].

Evans, Charles Watkyn De Lacy, Portland-road, Notting-hill, late of Davis-street and Brook-street, Grosvenor-square, surgeon.

Freeman, James, Hertford-road, Kingsland, and Cropley-street, Hoxten, furrier.

Glenie, George Richard, Strand, confectioner.

Smith, Jane, Devonshire-street, Marylebone, and Lansfield-street, glass and china[2] dealer.

Tester, T. W., Gordon-road, Peckham, builder.

In the Country.

Akerman, Thomas Martin, French's Farm, near Andover, farmer.

Baskcomb, William Richard, New Clee, Lincolnshire, fisherman.

Bates, Peter, Kingston-upon-Hull, fishing smack owner[3].

Berry, James (trading as James Berry and Sons), Manchester, nurseryman and seedsman.

Burton, William Collard, West-place, Putney, late of Upper Richmond-road, Putney, builder and decorator.

Butler, Thomas Edward, Darlaston, and King's-hill, Wednesbury, builder and carpenter.

Christmas, Walter, Stedham, Sussex, licensed victualler and brick-layer.

Crookes, Brocklesby, Woodhall Spa, Lincolnshire, late of Childer's-drove, Spalding, Lincolnshire, Robin Hood's Bay, Yorkshire, and Nottingham, joiner and builder.

Cupper, John, Comhampton, Ombersley, Worcestershire, labourer and fruiterer.

ORDERS ON APPLICATIONS TO APPROVE SCHEMES[4].

Bennett, William (trading as Bennett Brothers), Old Swan, near Liverpool, and Liverpool, ironfounder and general dealer—scheme approved.

Curnow, Matthew, Bristol, grocer—composition of 6s. by two instalments of 3s. each, at two and six months. Receiving order rescinded.

1. Importateur (d'articles) de fantaisie. — 2. *China*, porcelaine. — 3. *Smack*, sorte de grand sloop, employé pour le cabotage et pour la pêche (*fishing smack*). — 4. Arrêtés relatifs à des demandes d'approbation de projets.

NOTICES OF DIVIDENDS[1].

In London.

Banks, Thomas James, Queen's-road, Buckhurst-hill, Essex, draper—first div.[2] of 8s. 6d., Nov. 19, Mr. J. D. Viney's, 99, Cheapside, London.

Burdett, George Edward Hunt, Darmouth-road, Forest-hill, late of Westow-street, Upper Norwood, printer and publisher—first and final div. of 5d., Nov. 26, 109, Victoria-street, Westminster, S.W.

Fletcher, Elliott (trading as Fletcher and Co.), Cobham-street and Bath-street, Gravesend, timber merchant—third div. of $5^1/_4$d., Nov. 26, 57, Gracechurch-street, E. C.

Hart, William (trading as W. Hart and Co.), Blackfriars-road, Southwark, coffin furniture dealer—first and final div. of 1s. 8d., any day except Saturday, Chief Official Receiver's offices, 33, Carey-street, Lincoln's-inn.

In the Country.

Allatt, Frederick Thomas, Frizington and Cleator Moor, Cumberland, chemist and druggist—first and final div. of 2s. 4d., any day, Official Receiver's office, Whitehaven.

Burton, Alexander, Radcliffe, Lancashire, stonemason and contractor—first and final div. of 2s. 5d., Nov. 22, 79, Mosley-street, Manchester.

Collingbourne, Edwin (trading as W.E. Collingbourne), Horsforth and Leeds, twine and cordage merchant—second and final div. of 2d., Nov. 20, Official Receiver's office, Leeds.

Davies, Robert, Sarn, Meilltyrne, Carnavonshire, draper—second and final div. of $6^1/_4$d., Nov. 24, Crypt-chambers, Chester.

Dresel, Siegfried (formerly trading as Dresel and Co.), Canton and West Bute Dock, Cardiff, formerly fruit and potato merchant, now out of business—first and final div. of 1s. $4^3/_4$d., any day, Official Receiver's office, Cardiff.

Fletcher, Robert Richard, late of Manchester, now of Salford, botanic beer dealer and licensed broker—first and final div. of 6 1-10d., any day, Official Receiver's offices, Manchester.

APPLICATION FOR DEBTORS' DISCHARGE.

In London.

Marshall, Edward Reeve, Picton-street, Chiswell-street, and Elmington-road, Camberwell, wholesale manufacturing confectioner—Dec. 13, High Court of Justice in Bankruptcy.

Morewood, G. E., St. Michael's-house, Cornhill, City, insurance broker[3]—Dec. 13, High Court of Justice in Bankruptcy.

Sharp, Willmer James, Kingsland-road, and Lincoln-road, Ponders End, builder and decorator—Dec. 11, High Court of Justice in Bankruptcy.

In the Country.

Davies, Richard, Penrhiw, Bethesda, Carnarvonshire, quarry overlooker—Dec. 10, Court-house, Bangor.

---

1. Avis de répartition des dividendes. — 2. *Div., dividend.* — 3. *Insurance broker*, courtier d'assurances.

Eliot, Samuel (trading as Lucombe, Pince, and Co.), Alphington and St. Thomas, Devonshire, nurseryman—Dec. 6, the Castle, Exeter.

Griffith, Lewis, Braichmelyn, Bethesda, Carnarvonshire, quarryman—Dec. 10, Court-house, Bangor.

ORDERS MADE ON APPLICATIONS FOR DISCHARGE.

Bootle, William, Wigan, insurance and house agent—discharge suspended for three years.

Dynes, Frederick Thomas, Bedford, currier, leather seller, and boot manufacturer—discharge suspended for two calendar months.

Emmett, Alfred, Kenton-lodge, near Exeter, hotel proprietor—discharge suspended for five years.

Farrant, George Herbert Sweet, Bemerton, Wiltshire, corn merchant and woolstapler—discharge suspended for three years, &c.

French, Edmund Oliver (trading as Messrs. J. H. and B. French), Coventry, and Finham, near Coventry (as executor of Benjamin French, deceased), commission agent, silk broker, and farmer—discharge suspended for fourteen days.

TERRY'S THEATRE[1].

Farcical comedy has of late exhibited symptoms of decline, but it will probably receive a new lease of life from the bustling, good-natured, entertaining piece which was produced at Terry's Theatre yesterday under the title of *The Balloon.* The authors of *The Balloon,* Messrs. Darnley and George Manville Fenn, are practised hands[2]; and have learnt the art of inventing numerous situations without having recourse to the familiar motives of the French stage. In the present instance they have depicted the troubles of a medical man who, being led by an ingenious train of circumstances to believe that he has poisoned a patient, jumps into a balloon in despair and is carried off. He lands safely some hours afterwards, and comes home in a terrible plight, his clothes having been torn off his back; but, as the wreck of the balloon has meanwhile been picked up at sea, he is believed to be drowned, whence a string of complications that the experienced playgoer can very well imagine. Mr. Glenny played the doctor with the intense earnestness and conviction that the part demanded; and another humorous character sketch was given by Mr. Charles Groves, as an amiable but blundering friend who had unconsciously committed bigamy. The cast[3] also included Mr. Forbes Dawson, Miss Florence Wood, who is becoming a very useful *ingénue,* Miss Goldney, and Miss Susie Vaughan.

INDUSTRIAL EXHIBITION.—Yesterday afternoon Mr. John Aird, M.P.,

1. Ce théâtre est situé dans le Strand et a pour directeur Edward Terry, acteur qui acquit une grande célébrité à Manchester dans certains rôles des drames de Shakspeare; le rôle où il eut le plus de succès fut celui du "clown" de *Antoine et Cléopâtre.* Il a depuis créé plusieurs rôles dans des comédies modernes. — 2. *Are practised hands,* sont gens d'expérience. — 3. *The cast,* la distribution des rôles.

accompanied by his daughter, Mrs. Basil Ellis, opened the seventh annual industrial exhibition at the London City Mission-hall, Kilburn-park-road. Lady Knutsford was to have performed the ceremony, but was unable to attend. The exhibition, which contains many objects of interest, will remain open to-day and to-morrow. A number of entertainments are included in the programme.

A HOSPITAL BUILT BY VERDI[1].—The *Gazzetta Musicale* of Milan contains an interesting account of the hospital recently opened at Villanova, and entirely built and supported by Verdi, the composer. Villanova is situated about 20 miles from Piacenza, and in close vicinity to the Villa di Sant' Agata, the country seat which Verdi has made his home, and where he lives in the manner of a farmer, abandoning all music from his thought, and without so much as a piano in his house. The new hospital, an unpretentious but large building, lies in a commanding situation overlooking the Po and with a distant view of the Appenines. There are two wings, one for women, the other for men, and a separate ward is set aside for contagious cases; there is also a hydropathic establishment[2] and most elaborate arrangements have been made for the disinfection of linen and other sanitary purposes. An efficient staff of nurses and attendants is also provided, and Signora Verdi has made the housekeeping department her special care. The large sums required have been contributed by Verdi, who has also deposited sufficient funds for the maintenance of the hospital. The munificence of the great composer is only equalled by his modesty. The opening ceremony, which took place on the 6th inst., was of the simplest kind, only Verdi and his family, the physician, and the Sindaco of Villanova being present. No speechifying was allowed, Verdi remarking that the only inauguration necessary was the admission of the sick and ailing, 12 of whom were received then and there. The Sindaco proposed that the new building should be called "Verdi Hospital", but to this also the donor objected, and the name "Hospital of Villanova" was finally adopted.

EXECUTION AT NEWGATE[3].—At 8 o'clock yesterday morning Levi Richard Bartlett, who was convicted at the last sessions of the Central Criminal Court[4] of the wilful murder of his wife and condemned to death, suffered the extreme penalty of the law within the walls of Newgate, where he had been confined since his conviction. Bartlett was a man, 66 years of age, who lived at Poplar, and it will be remembered that he caused his

1. Giuseppe Verdi, célèbre compositeur italien, né en 1814, à Raucola dans le duché de Parme. Son père était aubergiste. Il fit ses études à Milan. Ses opéras les plus connus sont *Il Trovatore* et *La Traviata*. — 2. *Hydropathic*, hydrothérapique. — 3. *Newgate*. C'est la prison centrale qui reçoit les criminels de Londres et de tout le comté. Son nom lui vient d'une grande porte flanquée de donjons qui date de 1218. C'est à Newgate que sont renfermés les condamnés à mort et qu'ont lieu les exécutions. — 4. *The Central Criminal Court*, la Cour d'assises.

wife's death by striking her about the head with a heavy hammer, after which he inflicted a wound upon his own throat. Since his condemnation Bartlett expressed contrition for the crime. Efforts were made to obtain a reprieve[1], but, after due consideration, the Home Secretary intimated that he was unable to see any grounds for interfering in the matter. There were present yesterday morning the under sheriffs, Messrs. Metcalfe and Halse, Colonel Milman, Governor of Newgate and Holloway prisons, the Rev. H. G. Duffield, M. A., the Ordinary of Newgate, Dr. Gilbert, the surgeon of Holloway, and the usual officials. Bartlett, who preserved his composure to the last, was supported on his way to the scaffold by warders. Berry was the executioner. On arrival at the place of execution the operation of adjusting the rope to the convict's neck and placing the white cap over his face was quickly performed. At 8 o'clock the signal was given, and the trap-door fell. Death was instantaneous, a suitable drop being allowed[2]. After hanging the usual time the body was cut down, and the customary inquest subsequently held. A small crowd assembled in the precincts of the prison to witness the hoisting of the black flag.

POLICE.

At the MANSION-HOUSE[3], yesterday, ALEXANDER JOHNSTON attended before Mr. Alderman Evans on a summons charging him with unlawfully pretending to be a solicitor. Mr. C. O. Humphreys, solicitor, who conducted the prosecution on the part of the Incorporated Law Society[4], explained that on September 17 the defendant wrote a letter to Mr. Hughes, an advertisement contractor[5], in which he said he was instructed by Miss Elizabeth Hughes, of Clapham-road, to take proceedings against him for debt, and he gave him notice that unless an account which he enclosed was paid to his client or to himself in 14 days he should take proceedings to enforce payment. It was contended that that letter was written by the defendant with an intention to convey that he was a solicitor. On receiving the letter, Mr. Hughes searched the " Law List " and the roll of solicitors, but not finding the defendant's name he complained to the Incorporated Law Society, who instructed these proceeding to be taken against the defendant. The defendant said he simply acted as a friend at the request of Miss

1. Un sursis. — 2. La chute ayant été ménagée avec toute la précision requise. — 3. *Mansion-house.* C'est la résidence du Lord-maire. Ici il ne s'agit que du tribunal de police du quartier auquel la "Mansion-house" donne son nom. — 4. La corporation des avocats, le barreau. Fondée en 1827, officiellement reconnue en 1831, cette corporation des *solicitors* a pour devoir de veiller à la dignité et aux intérêts de la profession. Les bâtiments, contenant une bibliothèque de 30 000 volumes, sont situés dans *Chancery Lane.* On y a établi des conférences de droit et des examens donnant la garantie que tout *solicitor* aura fait une étude suffisamment approfondie de sa profession. — 5. Courtier d'annonces.

Hughes, and he did not receive any payment. Mr. Alderman Evans fined the defendant £5 and £1 1s. costs, to be paid by next Saturday, with the alternative of a month's imprisonment.

At the GUILDHALL[1], ERNEST CHAPMAN, a clerk in the service of Mr. Frank Blowfield, meat salesman, Metropolitan Market, was charged on remand with, embezzling money and falsifying the accounts. When charged he said to prosecutor, " I have been betting on horse racing and have been robbing you for some years ". The prosecutor was unable to go through the books as the day books were missing since 1886. The accused was committed for trial.

At WESTMINSTER, Inspector Brunning, B Division, reported to Mr. d'Eyncourt that a prisoner named Robert Stimpson, described as a general dealer[2], 35 years of age, charged with stealing a timepiece from an auctioneer's[3] premises and kicking an attendant who tried to stop him, had escaped from custody under somewhat remarkable circumstances. At the police-station the man either was or pretended to be very ill and the doctor who was called advised his removal to Chelsea Workhouse Infirmary. A constable took him there and he was put to bed in one of the wards, but shortly afterwards—about 10 o'clock at night—taking advantage of being unwatched he opened a window, got out, climbed over a wall, and dropped into the street attired only in a night shirt and wrapped round with a blanket. It was pouring with rain at the time, and a coachman on the spurt of the moment, not knowing how the man came in the street in such a plight, took off his great coat and lent it him. Prisoner then ran off, and the coachman thinking something was wrong gave an alarm, as also did a constable who had just before noticed what he thought to be a bundle wrapped in a blanket drop from the Infirmary premises. Mr. d'Eyncourt remarked that a warrant[4] would not be necessary to re-arrest the prisoner.

At WORSHIP-STREET, GEORGE BARTLETT, 36, described as a jeweller, with no fixed abode, was charged with the unlawful possession of a silver sceptre and other articles supposed to have been stolen. Detective-Inspector Reid, H Division, deposed that on the previous night, in Spitalfields, his attention was drawn to the prisoner, who was carrying a black shiny bag (produced). In appearance he somewhat answered the description circulated of a man who had been seen in the neighbourhood of the recent murders. He was followed, and in Brick-lane stopped and requested to give some account of himself, particularly as to what he had got in the bag. He displayed great objection to exhibit the contents, and the police found the bag secured with a padlock. The man was removed to the station in Commer-

1. Le Guildhall (salle des guildes ou corporations) est l'hôtel de ville de la Cité. Ici encore il ne s'agit que du tribunal de simple police du quartier de Guildhall. — 2. Représenté comme un trafiquant. — 3. Commissaire-priseur. — 4. Maudat d'arrêt.

cial-street and there produced the key of the bag. On opening it various articles were seen, consisting of handkerchiefs, a book, a screw driver, and the silver staff, described as a sceptre, in question, but no knives. In a back pocket of the prisoner's trousers there was also found a shell, silver mounted. The prisoner was charged with the unlawful possession, but during Tuesday it was found that the Church of Old St. Pancras had been broken into[1] and the articles, with others—one stated to be a cross given by the Duke of York—carried off. On the application of the inspector the prisoner was given back into his custody to be charged at Clerkenwell with sacrilege. The magistrate (Mr. Montagu Williams, Q. C.[2]), commended the inspector for the "intelligence and activity" he had shown in the capture.

At CLERKENWELL, a man named AVERY was charged before Mr. Bros with assault under the following circumstances:—Soon after midnight on Monday the prisoner, who had been drinking, seized a man in the street, as a practical joke, and called out to him, "I'm Jack the Ripper[3] and this is how I do it," at the same time running his hand up the front of prosecutor's clothes. The prosecutor said he was seriously alarmed, and struggled with the prisoner. A constable came up and took the prisoner into custody. The magistrate said that at a time like the present such outrages must be stopped, and he sent the prisoner to gaol for 14 days without the option of a fine.

At SOUTHWARK, Mr. EDWIN PALMER, cab proprietor[4], of Horseshoe-yard, Newington-causeway, was summoned for having, on or about the 15th of October last, maliciously published a certain defamatory libel concerning Edward Biletho and another. Mr. Besley prosecuted for the Cab-drivers' Mutual Aid and Protection Society[5], and Mr. Forrest Fulton, M. P., appeared for the defendant. Mr. Besley said the organization that had been mainly instrumental in instituting these proceeding was formed in July of last year, and was registered under the Trades Union Act on the 27th of August. It was a perfectly legal society, and was intended to benefit its members by combination. Mr. Palmer, the defendant, was the owner of a number of cabs plying for hire at the London-bridge and Victoria stations, and he required the men taking out his vehicles to pay a higher price than the owners of improved cabs supplied with the best class of horses. The result was that a reduction was asked for and refused. The men, supported by their society, decided not to take out his vehicles, and they all had their licences returned by registered letter. Then the defendant did what he

1. *To break into*, pénétrer avec effraction.—2. *Q. C.*, *Queen Councillor*.— 3. Jacques l'Éventreur, nom donné à l'homme, jusqu'ici resté inconnu, qui, par une série de crimes identiques et se suivant de près, a jeté et jette encore la terreur dans Londres. — 4. *Cab proprietor*, loueur de voitures. *Cab* (du français *cabriolet*), voir page 50, note 6. — 5. Société de secours mutuels des cochers.

would find he was not allowed to do by law. He sent out a lithographed list of the men who had been working for him to the cabowners in London, not only giving their names but their addresses and badge[1] numbers, and asterisks were affixed against the names of those who had been most active in the dispute. The result was that the men could not get work, and Mr. Besley contended that the issue of this document brought the defendant within the statute. He urged that the document on the face of it was a libel, and that the magistrate had no other course open to him than to commit the prisoner for trial. It would be proved that the defendant, when spoken to about the matter, boasted that he had "blocked[2] the men all over London" from getting work. The complainant was called, and gave evidence bearing out the statements of counsel, and he added that he could not get work for some time after leaving the defendant's yard on the 11th of October. A number of other men who had been in the defendant's employ were called, and gave similar evidence. Henry Paul Peacock, the defendant's manager, was called, and admitted that the circular was sent out to the various cabowners in London. Mr. Fulton urged that in no way no libel had been proved, but Mr. Slade said that, in his opinion, quite sufficient had been shown for him to send the case for trial.

At WANDSWORTH, SUZANNAH PRIDE, a young woman, living at 24, Wayland-street, Clapham Junction, appeared to answer a summons at the instance of the London, Brighton, and South Coast Railway Company for unlawfully making use of the means of communication to the guard of a train without reasonable or sufficient excuse. Alfred George Ethridge, a guard in the employ of the company, deposed that at midnight on the 13th ult. he was in charge of a train from Victoria to West Croydon, and before the train arrived at Clapham Junction the cord of communication was pulled by a passenger. On reaching the station he walked along the platform. The clerk.—Did you stop the train? Witness. — No; we were about a hundred yards from the station. Mr. Plowden (with surprise).—You really took no notice? That seems extraordinary. Supposing it was a case of life or death, would you have pulled up? Witness.—No; the train was too near the station. Mr. Plowden.—It might make all the difference to a man's life. The witness went on to say that the defendant complained of having been assaulted by a gentleman, and showed her wrist, which had a slight scratch, apparently caused by a pin. The gentleman denied the allegation and continued on his journey. Mr. Arthur Vivian, a gentleman residing at Wandsworth-common, the passenger accused of the assault, said on the night in question he entered the train at Victoria Station. The

1. *Badge*, médaille. Les cochers à Londres portent sur la poitrine une sorte de médaille numérotée à la façon des commissionnaires. — 2. *To block*, obstruer; *blockade*, blocus. Le mot signifie ici : empêcher de trouver du travail.

defendant and another woman entered the same compartment, but her companion left as the train was about to start. During the progress of the journey the prisoner, addressing him, said " Good evening ". He returned the compliment. The defendant then sat opposite him and demanded £5 from him, or she would prefer a charge of assault against him. He indignantly refused her demands, but she again asked for money and behaved like a mad woman, walking about the carriage and assuming threatening attitudes. He remained the whole of this time sitting in the corner, reading his newspaper. She seized hold of the bell-handle and pulled it out of the socket. In answer to questions, witness denied knocking her hat over her eyes and threatening to throw her out of window. He absolutely denied having used any violence towards her. Mr. Plowden.—How came she to ring the bell? Witness.—It was an attempt to extort money. Mr. Plowden.—That might be a reason for threatening to pull the bell, but she did it. After some further evidence Mr. Plowden said it was a most extraordinary case; one of two things was perfectly clear—either that the gentleman did assault her, or else she trumped up a charge in order to extort money. If her story were true she could have no more reasonable or sufficient excuse. It would be unfair for him to assume that the gentleman's story was true and the story told by the defendant false. He dismissed the summons, and expressed an opinion that the official was to blame for not stopping the train. It was obvious that the apparatus was meant to be used in cases of extreme emergency, so that the train might be pulled up at once and assistance rendered. This case might have been one of that character, and to delay stopping the train until it reached the station might have been to decide a matter of life or death.

The Poor-box[1].—At Wandsworth, £3 15s. was received from W. J. Carr; and at Clerkenwell, £1 from " Penalty ".

LAW NOTICES[2], *This Day (Wednesday)*, *Nov.* 14.

HOUSE OF LORDS, WESTMINSTER. — Their Lordships will not sit for judicial business to-day. The following causes are appointed for hearing to-morrow, at 10 30: — Mackill and others v.[3] Wright, Brothers, and Co. (further hearing).— F. W. Berk and Co. v. Lebi and others, ex parte (for hearing).

JUDICIAL COMMITTEE OF THE PRIVY COUNCIL[4], WHITEHALL. — At 10.30 :— Appeals. Rhaiya Rahidat Singh v. Maharani Indar Kunwar and others,

---

1. Tronc des pauvres. — 2. Annonces judiciaires. — 3. *V.*, *versus*, contre. — 4. Le Conseil privé. Ses membres ont pour attribution d'aider de leurs avis le souverain sur les questions de gouvernement. L'on en compte deux pour le Royaume-Uni, l'un pour l'Angleterre, l'autre pour l'Irlande.

part heard.—Shankar Baksh v. Hardeo Baksh and others, part heard.—Nandi Singh and another v. Sita Ram and another.

SUPREME COURT OF JUDICATURE. — COURT OF APPEAL.

APPEAL COURT I. — Before the LORD CHANCELLOR, the MASTER of the ROLLS and LORD JUSTICE BOWEN, at 11 : — For Judgment. — Johnson v. North-Eastern Railway Company. Before the LORD CHANCELLOR, the MASTER of the ROLLS, and SIR JAMES HANNEN. — For Judgment. — Brunton, Waywarden, &c., v. Highway Board of Langbaurgh West (Crown Side) (appeal of Highway Board). Before the MASTER of the ROLLS and LORDS JUSTICES FRY and LOPES. — Appeal Motions, ex parte[1] from the Queen's Bench and Admiralty Divisions. Original Motions. — Scoth Whisky Distillers (Limited) v. A. L. Elborough and others, and Same, v. Elborough and Co. (application of defendant C. E. Eden). — Weldon v. Smythe. Appeals from the Queen's Bench Division (Interlocutory List). — Re Metropolitan Buildings Act, 1855 : Straker, Brothers, and Co. v. Reynolds and Eason (2).—Robertson v. Gardiner.—Henry and Co. v. Portugal.—Smith v. Edwards.—Re Briton Medical, &c., Life Association and Companies Act, 1862, ex parte B. Boaler (appeal of B. Boaler).—Gill v. Lomer and Co. (13).

APPEAL COURT II. — Before LORDS JUSTICES COTTON, LINDLEY, and BOWEN, at 11 : — Lunacy Matter. — For Judgment. — Re Tompkins. Appeal Motions, ex parte, from the Chancery and Probate and Divorce Divisions. Appeals from the Chancery Division (Separate Interlocutory List). — Field v. Field (Divorce) (advanced by order). — American Braided Wire Company[2] and another v. W. S. Thomson and Co. — Re Apollinaris Company's Trade Marks and Patent, &c., Act, 1888 (appeal of A. Sexlehner).—Turncock v. Sartoris.—Re Missouri Railway and Iron Company and Companies Acts (appeal of W. Shephard, liquidator).—Corbett v. Corbett (Divorce)—White v. Hewitt (16).

HIGH COURT OF JUSTICE. — CHANCERY DIVISION.

CHANCERY COURT I. — Before MR. JUSTICE KAY, at 10 30 : — Adjourned Summonses[3]. — Re Collyer-Bristow and others and Re Greville's Settlement (taxation).—Re Equestrian and Public Buildings Company and Companies Acts.—Eardley v. Knight, and Knight v. Eardley.—Kelson v. Ellis.—Markby v. Tyringham.—Bedingfield v. D'Eye.—Bud v. Daubney.—De Caux v. Skipper, and Tee v. De Caux.—White v. Hall.—Knight v. Knight.

CHANCERY COURT III. — Before MR. JUSTICE CHITTY, at 10 30 : — Causes for Trial, with witnesses. — Re Dowley, deceased (Child v. Cavell[4]).—Sheffield and South Yorkshire Permanent Building Society v. Sheffield and Hallamshire Bank. —Gaine v. Abraham.—Cleverton v. Cleverton (3) (transferred from Queen's Bench Division), etc., etc.

CHANCERY COURT II. — Before MR. JUSTICE NORTH, at 10 30 : — Causes for Trial, with witnesses. — Surbiton Improvement Commissioners v. Mercalfe, part heard.—Day v. Woolwich Equitable Building Society.

1. *Ex parte*, voy. note 2, page 88. — 2. Compagnie américaine des fils métalliques tressés. — 3. Assignations ajournées. — 4. Child contre Cavell (*Child*, nom propre).

LORD CHANCELLOR'S COURT. — Before MR. JUSTICE STIRLING, at 10 30 : — Two Motions, by order. — Dodd v. Brown (in private), part heard[1].

CHANCERY COURT IV. — Before MR. JUSTICE KEKEWICH, at 10 30 : — Causes for Trial, with witnesses. — Osmond v. Osmond, part heard.— Commins v. Sampson.—Smith v. Crane.—Nicholl v. Eberhardt and Co.

QUEEN'S BENCH DIVISION.

LORD CHIEF JUSTICE'S COURT. — DIVISIONAL COURT. — Before the LORD CHIEF JUSTICE of ENGLAND and MR. JUSTICE WILLS, at 11 : — Crown Paper[2]. — Price v. Roberts, part heard (50). Ex parte Motions on the Civil Side. Opposed Motions on the Civil Side. — Hobbs v. Means.--Re H. Foskett, gent, one, &c. — Muir v. M'Mahon.

QUEEN'S BENCH COURT I. — DIVISIONAL COURT. — Before MR. BARON POLLOCK and MR. JUSTICE MANISTY, at 11 : —New Trial Paper[3]. — Redman v. King, Patten, and Co., part heard (27). Opposed Motion on the Civil Side. — Vernon v. Manchester, Sheffield, and Lincolnshire Railway Company, part heard (90).

QUEEN'S BENCH COURT III. —Before MR. JUSTICE DENMAN, at 10 30 : — Special Juries.—Jackson v. Carshalton Gas Company.—Williams v. Dutton.—Zaretsky, and Co. v. Arracan Company and another (225).

QUEEN'S BENCH COURT IV. — Before MR. BARON HUDDLESTON, at 10 30 : — Special Juries.—Weldon v. Rivière and others, part heard.—Pass v. East London Railway Joint Committee.—Harris v. Balfour (408).

QUEEN'S BENCH COURT V. — Before MR. JUSTICE HAWKINS, at 10 30 : — Common Juries. — Foskett v. Jacobs and others.—Warden v. C. Veale and Co. — Hamaton v. Swithinbank.—Kellond v. Thomas.—Daggatt v. Ratcliffe (134).

QUEEN'S BENCH COURT VIII. — Before MR. JUSTICE STEPHEN, at 10 30 : — Common Juries. —Churchill v. Gedney, part heard.—Ettridge v. Catchpole.— Esson v. Newcomb.—Summers and another v. Howard.—Lyall and another v. Seear and another (95).

QUEEN'S BENCH COURT IX. — Before MR. JUSTICE MATHEW, at 10 30 : — For Judgment. — Vale v. Mills, without Juries. —Kitchener v. West Metropolitan Tramways Company, part heard.—Salter v. Atwood, part heard.—Quick v. Hill.

QUEEN'S BENCH COURT VI. — Before MR. JUSTICE GRANTHAM, at 10 30 : — Without Juries.—Colborne v. Vander Byl.—Neel, Levy, and Co. v. Commercial and Industrial Association and another.—Crane v. Barclay and others.

The Court for Consideration of Crown Cases Reserved will sit on Saturdry, the 24th inst., to take the following Cases : — The Queen v. Dawson.—The Queen v. Tolson.—The Queen v. Adams.—The Queen v. Judd and others.

BANKRUPTCY.— At the Court, Lincoln's-inn. — Before MR. REGISTRAR GIFFARD. — First Court. — Public Examinations. — J. J. Baldwin, at 11.—H. G. Atwell, at 11.—J. Broom, at 11 30.—R. Bruce, at 11 30.—A. F. Bluett, at 12.—

1. (En particulier) cause entendue en partie. — 2. Dossier de la couronne. — 3. Dossier des causes nouvelles.

A. S. Brown, at 12.—W. C. Branford, at 12.—W. Corti, at 12.—E. Detmold, at 12 30.—E. Dealtry, at 12 30.—A. Bird, at 1.—J. Bertin, at 1.—E. H. Bedford, at 1. —E. Crickmay, at 1. Before MR. REGISTRAR LINKLATER. — Second Court. — Discharge. — J. C. Thorne-George, at 11. In Room 19. — Private Sitting. — Wood and Dixon, at 3. Before MR. REGISTRAR BROUGHAM : — In Room 20. — Motions, Section 55.—F. E. Hundley, at 11.—J. Gooch (2), at 11. Application, Section 53. — W. S. Hutton, at 11. Application. — D. Jones, at 11. Two petitions at 11 30, three petitions at 12, two petitions at 12 30, two petitions at 1, and five petitions at 2. To Settle Order[1]. — W. J. Luxmore, at 1.

MEETINGS OF CREDITORS. — Before the OFFICIAL RECEIVERS :— At Bankruptcy-buildings, Portugal-street, Lincoln's-inn. — First Meetings. — Morgan and Thumwood, at 11.—C. Murquardt, at 2 30. At 33, Carey-street, Lincoln's-inn.— First Meetings.—A. J. E. Dimma, at 11.—G. Julier, at 12.—E. J. Ward, at 2 30.

PROBATE[2], DIVORCE, AND ADMIRALTY DIVISION.

PROBATE, DIVORCE, AND ADMIRALTY COURT II. — Before MR. JUSTICE BUTT, with Trinity Masters, at 10 30 : — Admiralty. — Damage, with witnesses. — The West Stanley. At 12 : — Damage, with witnesses. — Saltburn.

LORD MAYOR'S COURT, GUILDHALL, at 10 30 :—Causes.—Ross v. Bourne.— Maltby v. General Steam Navigation Company.—Scott v. Clarke.—Stokes v. Smith. —Pressland v. House Property Insurance Company.—Brunton v. Berk.—Allison v. Rohrbach.—Waters v. Turner.—Lampord v. Robson.—Cockshott v. Bromfield. —Abbott v. Martin.—Jones v. Maclean.

COLLEGES, PUBLIC SCHOOLS, &c.

BEDFORD COLLEGE, London (for LADIES), 8 and 9, York-place, Baker-street, W.

Dr. SCHUDDEKOPF will BEGIN his GERMAN CLASSES at the half term, November, 15th.

The Art School is open daily from 10 to 4.

B. SHADWELL, Hon. Sec.

MALVERN COLLEGE. ENTRANCE SCHOLARSHIPS[3].

Examination on Tuesday and Wednesday, December 11th and 12th. One Scholarship of £99 for the first year and £87 for subsequent years, four of £50, five of £30. Names to be sent to the Head Master on or before December 10th. For further information apply to the Head Master or Secretary.

ISLE of WIGHT COLLEGE (Limited), near Ryde.

Visitor — The Right Rev. the LORD BISHOP of WINCHESTER.

President — The Right Hon. LORD ROLLO.

Chairman of Council — The ATTORNEY-GENERAL, SIR RICHARD WEBSTER, Q.C., M.P.

Vice-Chairman — LIEUT.-GEN. SIR HENRY DALY, K.C.B., C.I.E.

Head Master — REV. F. D. TEESDALE, M.A., New College, Oxon.

Eight assistant masters. Classical and modern departments. Army and Navy classes. Boarders are received by the Head Master and by three assistant masters, including the French master (in whose house French is exclusively spoken). Special arrangements for Indian boys. The College stands in 21

1. Pour arrêter l'ordonnance. — 2. *Probate court.* C'est la cour chargée d'examiner et d'enregistrer les testaments ; cour d'homologation. — 3. *Scholarship,* bourse.

acres, and enjoys all the advantages of a southern climate. Private chapel, gymnasium, racquet and fives courts[1] sea bathing, and boating.

For prospectuses apply to the Rev. the Head Master.

UNIVERSITY COLLEGE SCHOOL. LENT[2] TERM COMMENCES January 8th. The school is carried on in strict accordance with the principles laid down by the founders of University College, and is organized as a first grade modern school with a classical department.

For prospectus apply to the office, Gower-street, W.C.

J. M. HORSBURGH, M.A., Secretary.

LONDON B.A.[3].

A List of the Successfull Candidates at the above Examination will be sent post free on application to the Principal, Univ. Corr. Coll., Cambridge.

A copy of the B.A. Guide, containing the papers set at the recent examination and guide to books for 1889, will be sent on application to any intending candidate.

The UNIVERSITY CORRESPONDENCE COLLEGE Classes for B.A., 1889, Commence this week.

The Tutorial Series embraces over 60 works specially written for London Examinations.

Prospectuses and full particulars may be had from the Secretary, Univ. Corr. College, Cambridge.

CRONDALL SCHOOL, Farnham, Surrey. Invigorating country life. Healthiest district in England. See Registrar's report.

PREPARATION for PUBLIC SCHOOLS, Royal Navy, &c. French and German guaranteed. School farm, tennis, riding ponies. Address Principal.

ROCHESTER HOUSE, Ealing.

At last month's examination of Militia officers for Commissions in the Regular Army all sent up passed, viz. : — Lieut. C. Mackenzie, 4th ; Lieut. the Hon. C. B. F. Greville, 27th ; Lieut. T. A. Armstrong, 65th.

W. C. NORTHCOTT, M.A., L.L.M. ; W. W. NORTHCOTT, B.A., Captain, Yorkshire Regiment.

SOUTHBOROUGH, Tunbridge-Wells. — Mr. E. M. BLACKBURN, M.A.[4] (Winchester and C.C.C. Oxford) and Mr. C. E. FREEMAN, M.A. (Uppingham and Pembroke, Oxford), PREPARE BOYS for the PUBLIC SCHOOLS.

Scholarships at Westminster, 1886 and 1887.

Scholarship at Eton 1888.

PRIVATE TUITION in SWITZERLAND for SANDHURST[5], Woolwich, and other COMPETITIVE EXAMINATIONS.

F. H. SHAFTON MEREWETHER, B. A. Oxon.[6], PREPARES a limited number of PUPILS for above at Chalet de Lucens, Vaud, Switzerland. Individual attention. Mathematics under the direction of a Cambridge Wrangler and Oxford Honourman[7].

For prospectus, list of successes, &c., apply as above; or to Messrs. Askin, Gabbitas, and Killik, 38, Sackville-street, W.

OXFORD MILITARY COLLEGE, Cowley, Oxon.—TWO ENTRANCE

1. *Racquet and fives courts*, emplacement pour jeu de paume et balle au mur. — 2. *Lent*, carême. — 3. *B. A.*, *bachelorship of arts*, *London B. A.*, baccalauréat de l'Université de Londres, qui, ne recevant pas d'étudiants, ne fait que donner des grades. — 4. *Master of Arts*, docteur ès lettres. — 5. *Sandhurst* est l'école militaire correspondant à notre école de Saint-Cyr. *Woolwich* répond, au contraire, à l'école Polytechnique. — 6. *Oxon.*, *Oxonian*, c'est-à-dire de l'Université d'Oxford. — 7. *A Wrangler* est un élève qui, à l'Université, a obtenu une des premières places à l'examen de mathématiques. Le premier a le titre de *Senior Wrangler*. *Honourman*, lauréat des concours à l'Université d'Oxford.

SCHOLARSHIPS, of the value of £50 a year, each tenable for three years, will be offered for competition on the 18th December, to candidates for the Army or any other profession. Candidates, who must be under 16 years of age, must send in their applications not later than December 12th.

For particulars apply to the Head Master.

MISS CHREIMAN'S INSTITUTION of PHYSICAL CULTURE and REMEDIAL TRAINING[1], Portman Rooms, Baker-street, W. Branches—Town-hall, Kensington, Queen's-gate-hall, South Kensington, Norwood.

DEPARTMENTS.

1. Hygienic Bodily Training. By Musical Exercises, Respiratory and Voice Exercises, &c.
2. Remedial. By Adapted Exercises, Massage, and other Manual Treatment, &c.
3. For Training Teachers, for Direction of Physical Training in Schools and Families, and for organization of Country and Suburban Classes, &c.

WHAT to DO with YOUR SONS.—Journalism.—Mr. DAVID ANDERSON, 222, Strand, London, W.C., Author of "Scenes in the Commons," &c., from 1879, a principal leaderwriter, special correspondent, and critic of the Daily Telegraph, INSTRUCTS YOUNG MEN in the practical and literary branches of journalism. Splendid results. Prospectus free.

A trained journalist earns from £300 to £1,000 a year.

CHARITIES, &c.[2].

MIDDLESEX HOSPITAL, W., Cancer Wards.—FUNDS urgently NEEDED. F. C. MELHADO, Secretary.

ST. MARY'S HOSPITAL. Paddington, W.—FUNDS urgently NEEDED.—THOMAS RYAN, Secretary.

UNIVERSITY COLLEGE HOSPITAL, Gower-street, W. C. FUNDS urgently REQUIRED.—N. H. NIXON, Secy.[3].

KING'S COLLEGE HOSPITAL, W. C.—CONTRIBUTIONS urgently NEEDED.

T. MOSSE MACDONALD, Secretary.

NATIONAL HOSPITAL for CONSUMPTION, on the separate principle, Undercliff, Ventnor, Isle of Wight. FUNDS urgently NEEDED to maintain this recently-enlarged Hospital. Every bed occupied, and large numbers waiting.

Office, 34, Craven-street, W. C.

ERNEST MORGAN, Secretary.

EAST LONDON HOSPITAL for CHILDREN and DISPENSARY for WOMEN, Shadwell, E.—Many sad cases arise daily from the utter destitution of the unemployed in this neighbourhood, and the Committee make a special and urgent APPEAL for FUNDS in actual necessity.

ASHTON WARNER, Secretary.

WESTMINSTER HOSPITAL, Broad Sanctuary, S. W. Instituted 1719. The oldest unendowed hospital in London.—An earnest APPEAL is made for ADDITIONAL ANNUAL SUBSCRIPTIONS of 21s. and upwards. Expenditure, £12,500. Assured income, £2,600. S. M. QUENNELL, Secretary.

SEAMEN'S HOSPITAL (late Dreadnought), Greenwich.—Supported by voluntary contributions, and free to the whole maritime world.—FUNDS urgently NEEDED.

PIETRO MICHELLI, Secretary.

---

1. D'éducation physique et de traitement hygiénique. — 2. Œuvres de charité. — 3. *Secretary.*

LONDON FEVER HOSPITAL, Liverpool-road. N.—The Committee beg very gratefully to ACKNOWLEDGE the undermentioned SUMS received for furthering the great and useful work of this unendowed Charity :—

Messrs. A. Gordon and Co., annual subscription	£10	10	0
F. A. White, Esq., d°	10	0	0
Mrs. Joshua Williams, d° (new)[1]..	1	1	0
John White, d°..	5	5	0
E. M. C., d° (new)	1	1	0
Lt.-Col. Poë, C. B., d° (new).	2	2	0
Messrs. Chappell and Co., d°.	5	5	0
Mrs. Campbell Prinsep, d° (new)	3	3	0
Mrs. J. A. Clarke, d° (new)..	1	1	0
Chas. Sidey, Esq., d° (new)..	1	1	0
W. H. Brown, Esq., d° (new)	1	1	0
Gilbert Tonge, Esq., d° (new)	1	1	0
Chas. Sperati, Esq., d° (new)..	1	1	0
Sir Fredk. Halliday, K. C. B., d°..	3	0	0
Mrs. Code, "A thankoffering," d° (new)	1	1	0

&c. &c.

Close on 700 cases of diphtheria, scarlet, and other infectious fevers[2] have been treated in this Hospital since the beginning of the present year; each case a protracted and dangerous illness. Expenses are exceedingly heavy and additional help is earnestly asked.

A subscription of a guinea after the first year or a donation of ten guineas will secure prompt admission and free treatment for the servants of contributors.

Cheques should be made payable to the Secretary, at the Hospital.

MAJOR W. CHRISTIE.

Bankers—Messrs. Dimsdale and Co., 50, Cornhill, E. C.

METROPOLITAN PROVIDENT MEDICAL ASSOCIATION.—Object.—To provide efficient medical treatment and medicine for working-class families, by their own provident payments. 13 branches now opened; 55 medical officers; 26,000 members paying upwards of £3,000 per annum.

FUNDS urgently NEEDED to further extend the movement.

Bankers—Messrs. Hoare, 37, Fleet-street.

W. G. Bunn, Secretary, 5, Lamb's Conduit-street, from whom full particulars can be obtained.

ROYAL NATIONAL LIFEBOAT[3] INSTITUTION.—Supported solely by voluntary contributions.

The Committee earnestly APPEAL to the British public for FUNDS to enable them to replace a considerable number of their 299 lifeboats now on the coast by boats of the newest type, and possessing the latest improvements, as well as to maintain the service generally in the most perfect state of efficiency.

The institution has since its establishment granted rewards for the saving of nearly 34,000 lives from shipwreck on the coasts of the United Kingdom.

Annual subscriptions and donations will be thankfully received by the Secretary, Charles Dibdin, Esq., 14, John-street, Adelphi, W. C., and by all the Bankers in the United Kingdom.

DEAF and DUMB CHILDREN[4].—345 are being maintained and educated free of cost at the Asylums, Old Kent-road, S.E., and Margate, Kent. 4,902 have been admitted.

Every child capable is taught to speak.

Annual subscription—one vote, 10s. 6d.; two votes, £1 1s.

1. (*New*), c'est une souscription annuelle nouvelle. — 2. Et autres fièvres contagieuses. — 3. *Lifeboat*, bateau de sauvetage. Cette institution fut fondée en 1824. Elle a 299 bateaux ainsi répartis : 217 pour l'Angleterre, 45 pour l'Écosse et 37 pour l'Irlande. Depuis 1824, la Société a distribué, outre 97 médailles d'or et 996 médailles d'argent, la somme de £96,762 en récompenses. — 4. Enfants sourds et muets.

Life subscription—one vote, £5 5s.; two votes, £10 10s.

The Charity is in great need of help.

CONTRIBUTIONS most earnestly solicited.

T. LYNN BRISTOWE, M. P., Treasurer.
W. H. WARWICK, Secretary.
Office, 93, Cannon-street, E. C.

HOMES for LITTLE BOYS, Farningham and Swanley.

Treasurer—W. H. Willans, Esq.

In the Cottage Homes at Farningham, and the Orphan Homes at Swanley there are just Five Hundred Homeless and Orphan Boys.

They are taught trades, have technical education, and are fitted for a working life.

SUBSCRIPTIONS and DONATIONS earnestly solicited, and thankfully received by the Secretary,

BENJAMIN CLARKE.

Offices, Bank-buildings, Ludgate-circus, E. C.

FIELD-LANE REFUGES and RAGGED SCHOOLS[1].

President—the Right Hon. the EARL of ABERDEEN.

Treasurer—Wilfrid A. Bevan, Esq., 54, Lombard-street.

This Charity (founded in 1842) maintains constantly 260 destitute and homeless children and adults, and affords them the blessing of religious instruction and of industrial training.

Holds religious services on Sundays for outcast men and women, with an average attendance of 400.

Upwards of 800 children are in attendance at the Bible Ragged Schools.

The benefits dispensed among the poor exceed 3,500 weekly.

H. R. H. the Duke of Connaught has characterized this work as " a perfect network of charitable operations —an immense boon to the poor ".

The Institution being dependent upon voluntary contributions, the Committee plead for continued support.

About £2,000 is needed to meet expenses to December 31.

SUBSCRIPTIONS and DONATIONS thankfully received by the Treasurer; Messrs. Barclay, Bevan, Ransom, and Co., 54, Lombard-street; or by the Secretary, Vine-street, Clerken well-road, E. C. Bequests are also earnestly solicited.

PEREGRINE PLATT, Secretary.

CHARITY ORGANIZATION SOCIETY. Office of the Council, 15, Buckingham-street, London, W. C.

Bankers to the Council—Messrs. Coutts and Co., 59, Strand, W. C.

Additional FUNDS much NEEDED.

PUBLIC APPOINTMENTS.

THAMES CONSERVANCY[2].—Election of Four Conservators of the river Thames under the provisions of Thames Conservancy Act, 1864.

Notice is hereby given, that the Conservators of the river Thames have appointed that the ELECTION of FOUR CONSERVATORS under the above Act, viz. :—

A Representative of Shipowners[3],

A Representative of Owners of Lighters and Steam Tugs[4],

A Representative of Dockowners and Wharfingers[5],

A Representative of Owners of Passengers Steamers,

shall take place at the Thames Conservancy office, 41, Trinity-square, Tower-hill, London, on Friday, the 7th day of December next, to commence at noon.

Proxy papers[6] cannot be used at the Election unless they have been deposited at the Thames Conservancy office above-mentioned not later than 48 hours

---

1. École "déguenillée". C'est une école du dimanche pour les enfants abandonnés. — 2. Commission chargée d'empêcher les empiètements sur les eaux de la Tamise. — 3. *Shipowners*, armateurs. — 4. Gabares et remorqueurs. — 5. Voy. note 2, page 291. — 6. *Proxy papers*, bulletins de vote par procuration.

before the time appointed for the Election. JAMES H. GOUGH, Secretary.

Thames Conservancy office, 41, Trinity-square, Tower-hill,
London, E.C., 5th November, 1888.

NEW SOUTH WALES.—The Government of New South Wales intend to establish metallurgical works on a scale sufficiently large for determining, in bulk, the best methods of treating ores produced in the colony.

A SUPERINTENDENT is REQUIRED to erect, control, and direct these works. He must possess the highest qualifications and widest experience, and it will be his duty to introduce the best methods of treating ores, with a view to extract therefrom the metals and other substances possessing an economic value. He would also have to impart full instruction in the various methods of treatment, and to afford every facility to smelters[1] and miners for acquiring a practical knowledge of the processes employed.

Applications, stating candidate's age, accompanied by copies of testimonials, must be sent, on or before the 12th December, 1888, to the Agent-General for New South Wales, 5, Westminster-chambers, London, S.W.

SAUL SAMUEL, the Agent-General for New South Wales.

1st November, 1888.

TEACHERSHIP of[2] BENGALI.—The Board of Indian Civil Service Studies are PREPARED to APPOINT a TEACHER of Bengali, whose duties will commence on or about January 15, 1889. The appointment will be made in the first instance for one year only. The stipend is £100, with power to charge a fee of £3 3s. per term for a course of not less than three hours a week during eight weeks. Residence is desirable. Applications and testimonials should be sent to the Secretary, Sir Roland K. Wilson, Bart., Brookfield, Newnham, Cambridge, to arrive not later than Nov. 19.—November 5, 1888.

PUBLIC COMPANIES.

The Subscription List was Opened on Tuesday, the 13th November and will be Closed on or before Thursday, the 15th November, 1888.

THE MONTEVIDEO WATER-WORKS COMPANY (Limited)[3].

Capital—

20,000 shares of £20 each, £400,000, of which there has been issued..	£350,200
First Debenture Stock[4] £200,000, of which there has been issued	200,000
Second Debenture Stock £100,000, of which there has been issued..	100,000

Subscription at par for 13,350 shares of £20 each (£267,000), part of the share capital of £400,000.

DIRECTORS.

FREDERICK S. ISAAC, Esq. (Director Rosario Waterworks Company, Limited), Chairman.

J. H. Duncan, Esq. (Director River Plate Trust, Loan, and Agency Company, Limited)[5].

Thomas Farrell, Esq. (late of Montevideo).

William A. Jones, Esq. (Director, London Bank of Mexico and South America, Limited).

John Morris, Esq. (Chairman, River Plate Trust, Loan, and Agency Company, Limited).

William Wilson, Esq. (Director, North-Eastern of Uruguay Railway, Company, Limited).

Bankers—The London and County Banking Company (Limited), 21, Lombard-street, E. C.

Secretary—James Anderson, Esq.

Offices—61, Moorgate-street, E. C.

---

1. *Smelter*, fondeur. — 2. *Teachership of*, chaire de.... — 3. Société anonyme des eaux de la ville de Montevideo (dans l'Amérique du Sud). — 4. Premier lot d'obligations. — 5. Directeur du syndicat des prêts et commissions de la Plata.

The River Plate Trust, Loan, and Agency Company (Limited), No.61, Moorgate-street, London, offer for subscription 13,350 shares of £20 each (£267,000), part of the share capital of £400,000 of the Montevideo Waterworks Company (Limited), of which 2,490 shares represent the unissued capital of the Company, and the remaining 10,860 shares are the property of the River Plate Trust, Loan, and Agency Company (Limited), being part of the assets[1] taken over by them from the Mercantile Bank of the River Plate liquidation.

Price par, payable as follows :—

£1 per share on application,
£9 per share on allotment[2],
£10 per share on 31st December, 1888,
£20

The shares now offered will be entitled to the full dividend for the current year (1888).

Subscribers can pay up their shares in full on allotment, in which case a rebate will be allowed at the rate of 3 per cent. per annum. After the final instalment has been paid the shares will be passed to them, either by direct allotment or by transfer, and in the latter case free of expense.

Applications can be made on the form accompanying the prospectus, and lodged at the London and County Banking Company (Limited), 21, Lombard-street, London, with a deposit of £1 per share on the number of shares applied for.

If no allotment be made the amount paid on application will be returned in full. If default be made to payment of any of the instalments the amounts previously paid will be liable to forfeiture.

The Montevideo Waterworks were opened in 1871, and were acquired by the existing Company in 1879.

The water is supplied from the River Santa Lucia, about 33½ miles from Montevideo (being the nearest point at which a good supply of water could be obtained), and is thence pumped about 23½ miles to the service reservoirs at Las Piedras, about ten miles from Montevideo, from which it is distributed to the City by gravitation[3].

The population of Montevideo is about 100,000, and the number of houses about 20,000, of which not more than about 7,747 are as yet served by the Company, thus showing a large field for further development.

The steady growth of the Company's operations is shown by the following facts :—

(1) From 1882 to 1887 the number of services increased from 4,771 to 7,395.

(2) For the first eight months of the current year (1888) there was an increase of 352 in the number of services.

(3) The manager reports he has received orders to lay on supply to 600 new houses on one building estate alone.

(4) A second delivery main has just been laid all the way from Las Piedras to Montevideo, and filtering beds and storage reservoirs are now under construction at the Company's intake[5] at Santa Lucia, and are expected to be completed within the next six months.

These important additions to the Company's works will greatly improve the service, and cannot fail to add to the revenue.

The great distance of the source of supply having necessitated an unusually heavy expenditure, the National Government of Uruguay[4] granted to the undertaking a subvention of $55,200= £11,730 per annum for the term of the exclusive concession, which expires in 1891, after which the works still continue the property of the Company.

Experience has shown that competition is practically impossible, as regards

1. L'actif. — 2. A la répartition. — 3. *By gravitation*, descendant à la ville par son propre poids. — 4. République de l'Amérique du Sud, entre le Brésil, au N., l'État d'Entre-Rios, à l'O., le Rio de la Plata, au S., et l'Océan Atlantique, à l'E., entre 30° et 35° lat. sud, et 55° et 61° long. ouest. La capitale est Montevideo. 5 le point où les tuyaux prennent l'eau

the water supply of large towns, and more especially would that be so where the distance of the service supply is so exceptionally great as in this case, and where the water has to be pumped from the intake to the service reservoirs.

The following tabular statement[1] shows the balance of net income (including the Government subvention) for the past five years, after providing for working expenses and administration charges, viz. : —

	Net Income.	Dividend on Share Capital.	Annual Addition to Reserve.
1883	£32,756	2½ per cent.	£5,000
1884	36,053	2½ per cent.	5,000
1885	37,614	3 per cent.	5,000
1886	38,474	3½ per cent.	5,000
1887	50,423	5 per cent.	12,000
			£32,000

It will be seen that the amount (£12,000) placed to reserve for 1887 exceeded the amount of the Government subvention for that year (£11,730), and that consequently the dividend of 5 per cent. was earned out of ordinary income.

Waterworks shares, when the net income has been proved by actual experience, are regarded as sound investments, as shown by the high prices they maintain in the Official List, and especially is that so where, as in this case, there is every prospect of future development.

The Company has, since its formation in 1879, entered into numerous contracts, of which it would be practically impossible to give the particulars required by section 30 of the Companies Act, 1867. Applicants must therefore waive the right to a specification of the dates and names of the parties to contracts.

The concession, the memorandum and articles of association, and the last report and balance-sheet[2] of the Company can be seen at the Company's office, No. 61, Moorgate-street, London, E.C.

Prospectuses can be had at the offices of the Company; and of the River Plate Trust, Loan, and Agency Company (Limited), both of 61, Moorgate-street, London, E. C.; and of the London and County Banking Company (Limited), 21, Lombard-street, E. C.

12th November, 1888.

The List of Applications Opened on Monday, the 12th day of November, 1888.

COMPAGNIE GÉNÉRALE DES HANSOM CABS A PARIS (Limited). Registered under the Companies Acts, 1862 to 1886. Capital £100,000 (Frs. 2,500,000).—Present ISSUE[3] of £95,000, in 95,000 Shares of £1 each, the remaining 5,000 being allotted to the founders, in part payment, at par, of their expenses in connexion with the undertaking, payable as follows : — 5s. per share on application and 15s. on allotment.

DIRECTORS.

The Right Hon. the Earl of Shrewsbury and Talbot, Ingestre-hall, Staffordshire.

Sir John Morris, J.P., Bycullah-park, Enfield.

Colonel Gourley, M. P., Roker, Sunderland.

General W. T. Corrie, Braemar, Chiswick.

A. F. Wentworth-Gore, Esq., 33, Earl's-court-gardens, S. W.

Roger A. Gartside, Esq., Greenfield, Yorkshire.

Monsieur A. Duchemin, 35, rue de Naples, Paris.

Monsieur Jefferson de Castro, Proprietaire, 155, Avenue Wagram, Paris.

Banks—Messrs. Martin and Co., 68, Lombard-street, London, E. C.; Agents in Paris, Messieurs J. Allard et Cie, Place de la Bourse, Paris.

Broker—Mr. Franck S. Barnard, Crown-court, Old Broad-street, and Stock Exchange, London.

Auditors—Messrs. Woodthorpe, Gardner, and Co., Chartered Accountants, Leadenhall-buildings, E. C.

---

1. L'exposé du tableau ci-dessous. — 2. *Balance-sheet*, le compte de balance. — 3. L'émission actuelle.

Solicitors—Messrs. Thomas and Hick, 18, Walbrook, London, E.C.
General Manager—M. Jacques Mizraki, 28, Boulevard Pereire, Paris.
Yard Manager—C. S. Horne, Paris.
Secretary (Secretaire)—Mr. F. W. Stancomb.
Registered offices—120, Cannon-street, London, E. C.

ABRIDGED PROSPECTUS.

Messrs. Martin and Co., Bankers, and their Agents in Paris, Messrs. J. Allard et Cie, Bankers, will receive subscriptions on behalf of this Company, which has been formed for the purpose of carrying on the business of Cab Proprietors and Jobmasters in Paris, and ultimately, if deemed advisable, at other of the principal towns in the Republic of France.

Visitors to Paris cannot fail to be surprised at the heavy, uncomfortable, and ugly public vehicles plying for hire, and above all the inferior class of horses in the French metropolis. Residents and the French Press both join in this general chorus of complaint.

Having regard to the increasing number of English and American visitors to Paris and the enormous influx of visitors expected at the approaching Universal Exhibition of 1889[1], the present time is considered most opportune for effectually and substantially establishing the sound working of this company's undertaking.

It is the intention of the Directors to use English horses only.

The scheme of the Company has been very favourably received by many people in Paris, and the Prefecture has already approved of it and granted the required authorization to set on foot this most promising enterprise.

The cabs will be built by Messrs. Forder, Bros., and Co., of Longacre, London, and Wolverhampton.

A very careful estimate of the profit to be made on 300 cabs has been made by the Directors, which can be seen at the offices of the Company. The result shows, after payment of all expenses, and the utmost allowance for depreciation in value of stock and plant, a dividend of 14 per cent. per annum. It is obvious that a higher dividend could be declared after taking into consideration the profits to be derived from the sale of the noiseless types.

No Directors' fees will be drawn, but their remuneration left entirely in the hands of the shareholders, to be voted at the general meeting.

The contracts may be inspected at the offices of the Solicitors to the Company; and prospectuses, memorandum, and articles of association may be obtained of the Secretary to the Company.

Should no allotment be made, deposits will be returned in full.

Full prospectuses and forms of application for shares may be obtained of the Solicitors, of the Bankers, and at the offices of the Company.

27th October, 1888.

ORIENTAL GAS COMPANY (Limitd). — Notice is hereby given, that the ORDINARY GENERAL MEETING of the Shareholders of this Company will be held at the offices of the Company, 14, St. Mary-axe, London, on Wednesday, the 28th day of November instant, at half-past 12 o'clock precisely. The Directors who retire are Henry McLauchlan Backler and Henry Lawrence Hammack, Esquires; the retiring Auditors are Edward Garey and John Blacket Gill, Esquires. All are eligible for re-election and offer themselves accordingly.

By order of the Board,
A. HERSEE, Secretary.

No. 14, St. Mary-axe, E. C., 7th November, 1888.

N. B.—The Transfer Books[2] will be closed from the 19th instant to the 3rd proximo[3] inclusive.

---

1. L'Exposition universelle a été ouverte le 6 mai et fermée le 6 novembre 1889; elle a eu un succès immense. — 2. *The transfer books*, les Registres des transferts. — 3. Du 19 courant au 3 du mois prochain.

THE NAMAQUA[1] COPPER COMPANY (Limited).—Notice is hereby given, that at a Meeting of the Directors held this day it was RESOLVED,—

That a dividend of 2s. per share be and is hereby declared, payable to the shareholders registered in the books of the Company on the 13th day of November and to holders of share warrants to bearer[2], and that the same be payable on the 20th day of November. The warrant for the dividend upon the registered shares will be forwarded by post on the evening of the 19th instant.

Holders of share warrants to bearer will receive payment of the interim dividend on presentation of Coupon No. 2, either at the Company's office in London or at the Credit Lyonnais in Paris. Coupons for payment in London must be left two clear days previously for examination, and must be listed upon the Company's printed forms, obtainable at the Company's office. They can be deposited on and after the 16th inst. Coupons presented in Paris will be paid at the current rate of exchange.

By order of the Board,

C. LEWIS BENNETT, Secretary.

Office of the Company, 34, Leadenhall buildings, Gracechurch-street, London, E. C., 13th November, 1888.

GREAT EASTERN RAILWAY COMPANY[3].—Notice is hereby given, that the TRANSFER BOOKS of the METROPOLITAN, DEBENTURE, and RENT CHARGE STOCKS of the Company will be CLOSED on the evening of Monday, the 26th November instant, and all parties registered at the time of such closing of the transfer books will be entitled to the dividend payable on the 1st January, 1889.

The Transfer Books of the above Stocks will Reopen on Wednesday, the 28th November instant.

By order,

JOSEPH HADFIELD, Secretary.

Liverpool-street Terminus, London, 13th November, 1888.

CHEQUE BANK[4] (Limited). Established 1873.—

Agents in all parts of the world.

4, Waterloo-place, Pall-mall.

3, George-yard, Lombard-street, City.

THE LONDON and GENERAL BANK (Limd.[5]). Current accounts opened in accordance with the usual practice of London Banks. Deposits in sums of £10 and upwards received at rates varying with the length of notice. Terms on application.

No. 20, Budge-row, E. C.

G. E. BROCK, Manager.

THE DEBENTURE CORPORATION (Limited). Subscribed capital, £1,000,000. Offices, 75, Lombard-street, E.C.

Chairman—RICHARD BIDDULPH MARTIN, Esq.

The Corporation purchases or makes advances upon the debentures of limited companies, or guarantees the issue of the same to the public.

The tendency to convert trading and manufacturing firms into limited liability companies has created an active demand for loans on their debentures.[7] These securities are not readily saleable, being outside the ordinary business of banks and financial houses, and not being known to the private investor.

Even where the issue is of so large an amount as to obtain a Stock Exchange quotation[6], it has been found that companies are willing to dispose of their entire issue on moderate terms to insure their being placed without the

---

1. *Namaqua*, pays du sud de l'Afrique, le long de l'Océan Atlantique, depuis le Kuisip, au N., jusqu'à l'Orange, au S., annexé par les Anglais en 1878. — 2. Certificats d'actions au porteur. — 3. Réseau des chemins de fer de l'Est (Angleterre). — 4. *Cheque Bank*, c'est le nom de la Banque, littéralement Banque des Chèques. — 5. C'est-à-dire *limited*, anonyme. — 6. Une cote à la Bourse. 7 obligations

expense and risk attendant upon offering them to the public.

Deposits received for fixed periods.

The fullest information can be obtained on application to the Secretary, to whom proposals of business should be addressed. T. T. MOYES, Secretary.

BRITISH EMPIRE MUTUAL ASSURANCE COMPANY, New-Bridge-street, E. C. Funds £1,212,101.

GRESHAM LIFE ASSURANCE SOCIETY, St. Mildred's-house, Poultry, London, E. C.

LAW UNION INSURANCE COMPANY, 126, Chancery-lane.—Fire, Life, Mortgages[1], Reversions.

THE MUTUAL LIFE ASSURANCE SOCIETY (established 1834), 39, King-street, Cheapside, London, E. C.

THE LAW FIRE OFFICE (established in 1845),

No. 114, Chancery-lane, London.

GEORGE WILLIAM BELL, Secretary.

THE WHITTINGTON LIFE ASSURANCE COMPANY, 58, Moorgate-street, E. C. Established 1855.

All kinds of Life Assurance business transacted.

ALFRED T. BOWSER, Manager.

NORWICH UNION FIRE INSURANCE SOCIETY. Estd. 1797[2]. Head office—Surrey-street, Norwich. London offices—50, Fleet-street, and 18, Royal Exchange, E. C.

ATLAS ASSURANCE COMPANY (FIRE and LIFE). Estab. 1808. Funds exceed £1,800,000.

West-end office, 4, Pall-mall east.

Chief office, 92, Cheapside.

SAML. J. PIPKIN, Secretary.

BRITISH EQUITABLE ASSURANCE COMPANY, 4, Queen-street-place, E. C.

Accumulated Fund £1,206,570

WILLIAM SUTTON GOVER,
Managing Director.

EAGLE INSURANCE COMPANY, 79, Pall-mall, S. W. Establised 1807.

Interim Bonuses given[3].

Favourable rates for Endowment Assurances.

LIFE ASSOCIATION of SCOTLAND. Founded 1838 for Life Assurance and Annuities.

London, 5, Lombard-street, and 123, Pall-mall.

Edinburgh, 82, Princes-street.

PRUDENTIAL ASSURANCE COMPANY (Limited), Holborn-bars, London. Founded 1848.

Invested Funds .. £8,000,000
Claims Paid[4] £10,000,000

CLERICAL, MEDICAL, and GENERAL LIFE ASSURANCE SOCIETY, Established 1824, for the assurance of healthy and invalid lives. 15, St. Jame's-square, S. W., and Mansion-house-buildings, E. C.

B. NEWBATT, Actuary and Secretary.

LONDON ASSURANCE CORPORATION. Established by Royal Charter A. D. 1720[5]. No. 7, Royal Exchange, and 43a, Pall-mall.—Marine, Fire, and Life Assurances have been granted by the Corporation for more than a century and a half.

Funds in hand exceed £3,400,000.

WESTMINSTER FIRE OFFICE, 27, King-street, Covent-garden.

Founded A. D. 1717. Losses promptly paid.

---

1. *Mortgages*, hypothèques. — 2. *Estd.*, c'est-à-dire *established*, fondé en 1797. — 3. On accorde des bonis provisoires. — 4. *Claims paid*, échéances et sinistres payés. — 5. *A. D.*, en l'an (de grâce) 1720.

Insurances arranged by telephone, No. 3,692.
CHARLES ROUSE BROWNE,
Secretary.

THE NATIONAL FIRE INSURANCE CORPORATION (Limited). — Head office, 72, King William-street, London, E. C. TRUSTEES.
Sir Henry Arthur Hunt, C. B.
Charles Hoare, Esq. (Messrs. Hoare)
Sir Gabriel Goldney, Bart. (Chairman).
Manager—William Collis.

METROPOLITAN LIFE ASSURANCE SOCIETY, 3, Princes-street, Bank, London.
Established 1835. Assets £1,850,000.
No commission paid and no Agents employed.
Expenses only 4 per cent. of income.
No shareholders to participate in profits.
Whole world residence free after five years.

ROYAL EXCHANGE ASSURANCE. Incorporated A. D. 1720.
Funds, £4,000,000; Claims paid, £34,000.
Life, Fire, Sea, Annuities.
Modern and improved system of assurance.
Full particulars on application to chief office, Royal Exchange, E.C.; or to 29, Pall-mall, S.W.

BRITISH LAW FIRE INSURANCE COMPANY (Limited).
Offices—5, Lothbury, Bank, London, E. C.
Subscribed Capital, £500,000.
Applications for agencies may be made to H. FOSTER CUTLER,
Manager and Secretary.

BRITISH LAW FIRE INSURANCE COMPANY (Limited).
Head office, 5, Lothbury, Bank, E. C.
Notice is hereby given that the TRANSFER BOOKS[1] of the Company will be CLOSED on the 14th inst. until the 24th inst.
Dated this 10th day of November, 1888. By order of the Board,
H. FORSTER CUTLER,
Manager and Secretary.

NORTHERN ASSURANCE COMPANY. Established 1836.
London, 1, Moorgate-street, E. C.;
Aberdeen, 1, Union-terrace.
Income and Funds, 1887.

Fire premiums	£607,000
Life premiums	197,000
Interests..	143,000
Accumulated funds. ..	£3,421,000

The Original Society, established 1840.
THE GUARANTEE SOCIETY. Empowered by Special Act of Parliament.
Capital £100,000, fully paid up and invested.
Guarantees for fidelity granted for travellers, commission agents, cashiers, and others, and Bonds to the High Court of Justice, in Bankruptcy, and for Government officials.
No. 19, Birchin-lane, E. C.
AUGUSTUS MUZIO, Secretary.

REVERSIONS and LIFE INTERESTS in LANDED or FUNDED PROPERTY[2], or other Securities and Annuities PURCHASED, or Loans or Annuities thereon granted, by the EQUITABLE REVERSIONARY[3] INTEREST SOCIETY (Limited), 10, Lancaster-place, Waterloo-bridge, Strand. Established 1835. Capital £500,000. Interest on loans may be capitalized.
F. S. CLAYTON } Joint
C. H. CLAYTON } Secretaries.

ANNUITIES are granted by the NEW YORK LIFE INSURANCE COMPANY upon more favourable terms than by British offices. For full particulars address J. Fisher Smith, General

---

1. Registre des transferts. — 2. Propriétés foncières et rente sur l'État. rentes viagères

Manager, 76 and 77, Cheapside, London, E.C.

ACCIDENTS of ALL KINDS.—EMPLOYERS' LIABILITY[6] ASSURANCE CORPORATION (Limited).
84 and 85, King William-street, London, E. C.
GUARANTEES of FIDELITY.

ACCIDENT INSURANCE COMPANY (Limited),
No. 10, St. Swithin's-lane, E. C.

General Accidents.	Personal Injuries.
Railway Accidents.	Death by Accident.

C. HARDING, Manager.

AERATED BREAD COMPANY[1] (Limited). Incorporated Oct., 1863. Capital £250,000.—Bread by Dr. Daughlish's system is absolutely pure, all the nutritious and digestive elements of the wheat are preserved in the loaf.

It is the only system by which the mixing, kneading, and moulding[2] are done in hermetically closed vessels, entirely by machinery. In every other system the kneading and moulding are by hand or other objectionable form of manual labour.

Granulated Wheat Meal Bread made of the finest decorticated wheat. Its daily use is beneficial to health.

Depots in principal London districts. Offices, Eastcheap-house, No. 24, Eastcheap, E. C.

J. LEWIS MILLS and Co. (Limited), STOCK and SHARE BROKERS and DEALERS, 15, New Broad-street, London, E. C., open speculative accounts on 1 per cent. cover with no further liability. Immediate settlements. Telegrams free. Prospectus and telegraphic code[3] on application. West-end branch, No. 217, Piccadilly, W.

BONDHOLDERS will find the actual number of all bonds drawn given in the BONDHOLDERS' REGISTER. Only 6s. a year, post free. Offices, 2, Royal Exchange-buildings, E. C.

A SAFE 4½ per CENT.—For SALE, MORTGAGE DEBENTURES of £100 each, bearing 4 1/2 per cent. interest, forming a first charge on a brewery business. Apply to Vendor, R110, Address and Inquiry office, The Times Office, E. C.

INVESTORS.—Advertiser would be glad to hear from ladies and gentlemen willing to take SHARES in a financial company for the provinces. Dividends of 10 per cent. expected. Address Q. R. at Horncastle's Central Advertisement offices, London.

CONTRACTS, etc.

INDIA OFFICE,
Whitehall, 12th November, 1888.
INDIAN STATE RAILWAYS
By Order of the Secretary of State for India in Council.

THE Director-General of Stores for India is prepared to receive TENDERS[4] from such persons as may be willing to supply

1. STEEL RAILS;
2. Fishplates;
3. Fishbolts;
4. Spikes[5].

The conditions of contract may be obtained on application to the Director-General of Stores, India Office Whitehall, S.W., and tenders are to be left at his office, at any time before 2 o'clock p. m. on Tuesday, the 20th November, 1888, after which no tender will be received.

A. ABERCROMBIE JOPP,
Director-General of Stores.

---

1. Compagnie de panification "à l'air". Procédé où l'air atmosphérique remplace l'acide carbonique de fermentation. — 2. Le mélange, le pétrissage, et la fabrication. — 3. Code télégraphique, dictionnaire d'abréviations convenues, et où un mot traduit quelquefois toute une phrase. — 4. *Tenders*, soumissions (pour une adjudication). — 5. *Fishplates*, minces plaques en fer forgé pour unir deux rails; *fishbolts*, boulons en fer en usage aux chemins de fer; *spikes*, grands clous en fer. 6 responsabilité) portions d'obligations du trésor. . .
emplacements.

TRANSPORT DEPARTMENT, ADMIRALTY,

12th November, 1888.

THE Commissioners for executing the office of Lord High Admiral of the United Kingdom of Great Britain and Ireland do hereby give notice that they are prepared to receive TENDERS on the 20th instant for the TOWAGE of a SUBMARINE MINING VESSEL[1] from PORTSMOUTH to SINGAPORE, about the beginning or middle of December. Dimensions—69 feet, 6 inches long, 15 feet 2 inches broad, mean draught of water about 6 feet.

The tender must include the supply of approved hawsers[2] necessary for towing, and the provision of a crew of five hands on board the miner, including an engineer.

The Government will put a supply of coal on board the miner, to enable her to steam in the event of her being compelled to cast off[3], from bad weather or other cause; also a chronometer and charts.

Payment will be made by the Accountant-General of the Army, through the Director of Transports, in the following manner, viz. : — One half on the sailing of the vessel, and the remaining half on receipt of a notification, from the officer acting on behalf of the Transport Department at Singapore, of the due performance of the service, and of the delivery into his hands of the chronometer and charts.

All tenders must be enclosed in sealed envelopes addressed to the Director of Transports, and are to be delivered at the Admiralty, 57, Spring-gardens, S. W., before noon on the day above specified.

The name of the vessel offered must be stated in the tender, and tenderers may offer to tow from any other port in the United Kingdom than Portsmouth.

H. W. BRENT,
Director of Transports.

LEGAL NOTICES.

PURSUANT to an order of the High Court of Justice, Chancery Division made in the matter of the estate of Charles Smith deceased and in an action of Robson against Tidy, 1888 S 868, the CREDITORS of CHARLES SMITH late of Fox Lodge, No. 166, Brixton Road, in the County of Surrey, Gentleman deceased, who died in or about the month of April 1885, are on or before the 13th day of December 1888, to send by post prepaid[4] to Mr. John Hawthorne Lydall, of 37, John Street, Bedford Row, London, the Solicitor of the defendants the executors of the deceased, their Christian and surnames, addresses and descriptions the full particulars of their claims, a statement of their accounts and the nature of the securities (if any) held by them or in default thereof they will be peremptorily excluded from the benefit or the said order. Every creditor holding any security is to produce the same before Mr. Justice Chitty at his Chambers, the Royal Courts of Justice Strand, London, on Thursday the 20th day of December 1888, at 11 o'clock in the forenoon being the time appointed for adjudicating on the claims. Dated this 9th day of November, 1888.

W. TYNDALE MOORE,
26, Great Saint Helens E.C. Solicitor for the Plaintiff.

PURSUANT to an order of the High Court of Justice Chancery Division, made in the matter of the Estate of Ann Cresswell, deceased, and in an action Clarke against New and others The CREDITORS of ANN CRESSWELL, late of Gotherington in the Parish of Bishops Cleen, in the County of Gloucester, Widow who died in or about the month of December 1887, are on or before the 10th day of December 1888, to send by post prepaid to Messrs. F. and

1. Soumission pour le remorquage d'un vaisseau devant servir aux opérations de mines au fond de la mer. — 2. *Hawsers*, haussières. — 3. Filer le câble (se détacher du remorqueur). — 4. *Prepaid*, affranchi.

E. Griffiths, of 2, Crescent Place Cheltenham, the Solicitors of Sarah Mary New, the executrix of the said testatrix, their Christian and surnames addresses and descriptions, the full particulars of their claims a statement of their accounts and the nature of the securities (if any) held by them, or in default thereof they will be peremptorily excluded from the benefit of the said estate. Every Creditor holding any security is to produce the same before the Chief Clerk (Mr. Burney) at his Chambers, situated at the Royal Courts of Justice, Strand Middlesex, on Monday the 17th day of December 1888, at 11 o'clock in the forenoon, being the time appointed for adjudication on the claims. Dated this 9th day of November 1888.

CROWDERS and VIZARD, 55, Lincoln's Inn Fields, W. C. Agents for C. Llewellyn Griffiths of Cheltenham, Solicitor for the Plaintiff.

LUCY GLEDHILL decd. late of 432, Kings Road Chelsea, and 31, Wells Street Camberwell, and formerly of Roman-road Row, and 30, Crawford-street, Draper, and who died about June last. All persons having any CLAIM against the deceased are requested to send particulars of same on or before the 20th November instant to Messrs. Collison and Viney, 99, Cheapside, London.

RE PHILIP THOMAS FISH, Esq. deceased. All persons having CLAIMS against the ESTATE of the above named deceased late of No. 18, Highbury Terrace, in the County of Middlesex, are requested to send in full particulars addressed to the Executors at the Offices of the undermentioned as soon as possible. Dated this 13th day of November 1888.

H. CLIFFORD GOSNELL, 73 & 75, Finsbury Pavement, E.C. Solicitor for and one of the said Executors.

IN the Matter of the Companies Acts 1862 and 1867, and In the Matter of The VICTORIA GOLD COMPANY (Limited).— Notice is hereby given that CREDITORS of the above-named Company are required on or before the 6th day of December 1888, to send their names and addresses and the particulars of their debts or claims and the names and addresses of their Solicitors (if any) to the undersigned Shershew Powell Gilbert, of 5, Copthall Buildings, London, E. C. the surviving Liquidator of the said Company, and if so required by notice in writing from the said Liquidator are by their Solicitors to come in and prove their said debts or claims at such time and place as shall be specified in such notice, or in default thereof they will be excluded from the benefit of any distribution made before such debts are proved. Dated this 6th day of November 1888. S. P. GILBERT, 5, Copthall Buildings, London, E. C.

IN the HIGH COURT of JUSTICE, Chancery Division. — Mr. Justice Chitty.—In the Matter of the Companies Acts, 1862 and 1867, and in the Matter of the WENHAM LAKE ICE COMPANY (Limited).—The CREDITORS of the abovenamed Company are required, on or before the 10th day of December, 1888, to send their names and addresses and the particulars of their debts or claims, and the particulars of the securities (if any) held by them, and the names and addresses of their solicitors (if any), to Charles James Singleton, of 8, Staple-inn, in the county of Middlesex, the official liquidator of the said Company, and if so required by notice, in writing, from the said official liquidator, are, by their solicitors, to come in and prove their said debts or claims, at the Chambers of Mr. Justice Chitty, at the Royal Courts of Justice, Strand, London, at such time as shall be specified in such notice, or in default thereof they will be excluded from the benefit of any distribution made before such debts are proved. Monday, the 17th day of December, 1888, at eleven o'clock in the forenoon, at the said Chambers, is appointed for hearing and

adjudicating upon the debts and claims. — Dated this 31st day of October, 1888.
GEO. A. CROWDER, Chief Clerk.
STANLEY J. ATTENBOROUGH,
10, New-inn, W. C.,
Solicitor for the Official Liquidator.

THE BANKRUPTCY ACT, 1883. In the High Court of Justice. In Bankruptcy, No. 1265 of 1888. Re GEORGE WHITE of No. 21, Grove Mews Notting Hill Square, Middlesex, late Cab Proprietor and now Cab Driver :

Receiving Order made .. .. 24th October 1888.
Date of Order for Summary Administration .. 26th October 1888.
Date of Adjudication.. .. .. 31st October 1888.
Date and place of First Meeting. .. .. .. 21st November 1888.
at Eleven o'clock, at 33, Carey Street, Lincoln's Inn.
Date of Public Examination at Eleven o'clock, 27th November 1888.
Dated 13th November, 1888. R. P. HARDING, Chief Official Receiver.

SITUATIONS.

A LADY (experienced) desires a RE-ENGAGEMENT as RESIDENT GOVERNESS. Now or after Christmas. French and German acquired in Paris and North Germany, good music, drawing, and English. Address, W., 68, Chesterton-road, Cambridge.

A RE-ENGAGEMENT desired, as RESIDENT GOVERNESS. Thorough English, good French and music, singing, drawing, needlework[1]. Experienced, and fond of children. 3 1/2 years' excellent reference. — G., 2, King's-road, Brownswood-park, N.

AN ENGLISH VISITING GOVERNESS[2] desires AFTERNOON RE-ENGAGEMENT, or Private Lessons. English (literature, grammar, analysis), music, French, German (acquired abroad). —Miss A., 8, Shrewsbury-road, Talbot-road, Bayswater.

A SWISS-FRENCH CATHOLIC WANTS SITUATION with young ladies or children. Good French teaching, dressmaking[3] and good references. —B. G., 1, Vine-terrace, Holland-street, Kensington.

BOYS' GOVERNESS REQUIRES RE-ENGAGEMENT. Family or school. English, Latin, mathematics, music, drawing. Age 29. Reference, 10 years'. £40-£50.—D. W., Madame Aubert's, 166, Regent-street, W.

DAILY GOVERNESS.—A lady, an experienced teacher, desires RE-ENGAGEMENT in January (or earlier if required), to instruct pupils under 15 in English, French, music, elementary Latin. Good references. No agents.—Address A. M. W., No. 36, Richford-street, The Grove, Shepherd's-bush, W.

DRAWING and PAINTING.—Lady teacher REQUIRES RESIDENT RE-ENGAGEMENT for next term. Prepares successfully for examinations. Can assist with music. Excellent school housekeeper. Age 30. Reference, five years'. £50-£60.—L. H., Madame Aubert's, 166, Regent-street, W.

FRENCH PROTESTANT GOVERNESS. Good music, German, some drawing, arithmetic. Speaks English. Highly recommended. Diplômée. £50. —Mesdames Friede Lintot, Governess Agency (under high patronage), 205, Regent-street.

1. *Needlework*, travail à l'aiguille. — 2. *Visiting governess*, en opposition avec *resident governess*, c'est-à-dire institutrice donnant des leçons en ville. — 3. *Dressmaking*, bonne couturière en robes.

UNE DAME demande tout de suite une INSTITUTRICE FRANÇAISE, pour deux jeunes filles, 16 et 11 ans, pour quelques semaines, à la campagne, 1/2 heure de Paddington. Musique et dessin. On offre £5 pour six semaines. Si l'institutrice convenait elle pourrait rester.—S'adresser à Hon. Mrs. W., care of Steel and Jones, Advertising Agents, Spring-gardens, S.W.

AN ENGLISH GOVERNESS, with school experience, REQUIRED, for a Continental school. Can acquire French and German and have ample time for study. Apply, personally, Governess Agency, 17, Hanover-street, Hanover-square.

NURSERY[1] GOVERNESS REQUIRED. English, music, and needlework, French and drawing desirable. Age about 23. Personal reference. Apply, before 1 o'clock, to Mrs. S., 4, Albany-terrace, Regent's-park (opposite Park-crescent).

ORAL TEACHING for the DEAF and DUMB.—WANTED, a RESIDENT GOVERNESS, with certificate from Ealing, for a boy of nearly seven. Must have had experience in a family. Address Mrs. Archibald, Berkeley-lodge, West-hill, Putney.

ABLE LADY TEACHERS VISIT FAMILIES, and SCHOOLS for LESSONS in ENGLISH, French, German, Italian, Spanish, Latin, Greek, mathematics, science, elocution, music, singing, painting, &c. Pupils prepared for University, Civil Service, Army, Navy, and Diplomatic Examinations. Daily, Morning, and Afternoon Governesses for general education.—Madame Aubert, No. 166, Regent-street, W.

TO the NOBILITY and GENTRY. — The International Employment Company, 131, Regent-street, introduces well-recommended gentlewomen[2] as GOVERNESSES, Secretaries, Housekeepers, Companions, also superior Servants.

A NORTH GERMAN LADY is open to MORNING RE-ENGAGEMENT as CHAPERON or COMPANION. Highest references.—Fräulein A., 8, Shrewsbury-road, Talbot-road, Bayswater.

AN intelligent, refined GENTLEWOMAN (widow, 38) seeks a RE-ENGAGEMENT as TRAVELLING COMPANION, Chaperon, or Lady-Housekeeper—any position of trust requiring good abilities, energy, and practical experience in management and control of house and servants. Home or abroad[3]. Highest references.—S. S., R126, Address and Inquiry office, The Times Office, E. C.

COMPANION and NURSE[4] to INVALID LADY. — SITUATION WANTED. Accustomed to travel. Age 26. Salary moderate. Unexceptionable reference.—A. W., 14, Hunter-street, Brunswick-square.

COMPANION or LADY-HOUSEKEEPER — RE-ENGAGEMENT desired. Has had sole control of and great experience in well-appointed households. Well-educated. Good amanuensis[5]. Refined, energetic, cheerfull. Has travelled.—Miss Adams, 12, Kent House-road, Sydenham.

YOUNG LADY, Rector's daughter[6], desires immmediate ENGAGEMENT as COMPANION to lady

1. *Nursery*, chambre de la maison consacrée à l'éducation des enfants. — 2. *Gentlewomen*, féminin de *gentlemen*, c'est-à-dire des dames ou demoiselles de bonne famille. — 3. *Home or abroad*, en Angleterre ou à l'étranger. — 4. *Nurse*, nourrice et garde-malade ; le mot est employé ici dans ce dernier sens. — 5. *Good amanuensis*, bon secrétaire ou copiste. — 6. *A Rector*, pasteur protestant préposé à l'administration d'une paroisse.

going abroad. Apply to L., Tindall and Co.'s, Newmarket.

A LADY (age 28) desires an ENGAGEMENT in some light capacity. Tall, nice appearance. Very domesticated[1]. Musical. Excellent references. Small salary. — T. D., 7, Hereford-road, Bayswater.

MADAME GOBETTO, French Dressmaker, begs to announce that she MAKES-UP LADIES'OWN MATERIALS into COSTUMES, Jackets, evening dress, tailor-made dresses. Perfect fit and style guaranteed. Moderate charges. — 5, Great Titchfield-street, Oxford-street.

A LADY wishes to RECOMMEND her late MAID. Thoroughly experienced in all her duties, good dressmaker, packer[2], &c. Eight years' excellent reference. Age 38. — M. H., 5, Mansfield-place, Heath-street, Hampstead, N.W.

AS MAID (GERMAN). Thoroughly experienced. Good dressmaker, hairdresser, and packer. Address L. M. B., No. 29, George-street, Hanover-square.

A Ssuperior USEFUL LADIES'-MAID. Understands housekeeping, care of wardrobe and linen. Good dressmaker and manager, and trustworthy, willing, and obliging. 3 ½ years' good personal character. — C. E. H., Richard's Library, 42, Tachbrook-street, London, S.W.

SITUATION WANTED, by middle-aged person, as NURSE-ATTENDANT on elderly or invalid lady or gentleman. Has had long experience, and can be highly recommended. — M. M., Ladd's Library, 71, Bishop's-road, Bayswater.

A Superior MIDDLE-AGED LADY wishes to find a HOME. Nursing an invalid, care of a gentleman's household, education of children, or similar employment would suit. Good linguist. Moderate salary. Highest references. Address B. C., No. 13, Fopstone-road, Earl's-court.

A LADY wishes to RECOMMEND her HEAD NURSE. Been with her 6½ years. Good needlewoman. Thoroughly experienced and trustworthy. Age 36. Wages £30. Disengaged. — C. P. A., Fair View, Broomsleigh-street, West Hampstead.

NURSE (GOOD) WANTED, to children out of arms[3]. Three in nursery. Assistance given. Good needlewoman. Personal character. Personally or letter to Mrs. Dodd, Kimberley, No. 173, Tulse-hill, S. W.

NURSERYMAID, Under or Third[4]. — A lady RECOMMENDS respectable, strong girl of 16. — J. L., Mrs., Nelson's, 34, Bryanston-street, Bryanston-square, W.

A Respectable WIDOW would like the CARE of a LADY'S CHILD. Would take it from the month. Highest references given. — E. A. L., 19, Buxton-road, High-street, Walthamstow.

HOTEL. — RE-ENGAGEMENT WANTED, as BOOKKEEPER, or Assistant Housekeeper. Family hotel preferred. Address E. A., King's Head Hotel, Dover.

GENTLEWOMAN, middle-aged, experienced, active, cheerful, offers

1. C'est-à-dire bien habituée à une vie d'intérieur. — 2. *Packer*, emballeur, c'est-à-dire faisant habituellement les malles. — 3. *Children out of arms*, des enfants sevrés, *ou* qui commencent à marcher. — 4. *Under or third*, ne venant que comme seconde ou troisième servante.

services as LADY-HOUSEKEEPER or CHAPERON for refined home and nominal salary. Highest references. — Vera, 15, South-street, Thurloe-square, S.W.

LADY-HOUSEKEEPER. — A lady, who has had the care of a gentleman's house and family, desires a similar APPOINTMENT. Experienced, with excellent references. — N., 23, Valmar-road, Denmark-hill, S. E.

NO SALARY. — Widow lady, aged 36, seeks an ENGAGEMENT as LADY-HOUSEKEEPER to widower or single gentleman, thoroughly domesticated, excellent cook, and musical, who would give her services for a good home. References. — B. A., 11, Maitland-street, Bedford.

REQUIRED, a LADY to undertake the management of a nobleman's household (abroad), accustomed to good society, able to receive and entertain. Apply personally, in first instance, this week, Mrs. Thornton, 13, Stanhope-terrace, Hyde-park-gardens, W.

A RE-ENGAGEMENT WANTED, as HOUSEKEEPER[1] in hotel, club, or otherwise. Thoroughly experienced. Excellent hotel references. — E. H., 23, South-street, Manchester-square, W.

A LADY wishes to RECOMMEND a widow lady (50), who lived with her four years in a position of trust, as HOUSEKEEPER to a widower, with charge of children at school by day, or otherwise (would teach one or two under 12), or for any responsible position. She has very good health, is musical, active, cheerful, kind, and careful with children. Church of England[2]. Salary £30-£35. Address Mater, Public-hall, Tunbridge.

SITUATION WANTED, as COOK-HOUSEKEEPER to a gentleman, or lady and gentleman. Been five years in last situation. Left through death. Highest references. Age 40. Address C. S., 32, Roman-road, Barnsbury.

A Thorough COOK WANTED, for country. Kitchen and scullery[3] maids kept. State age, wages, character, to Mrs. Heywood, Bignor, Pulborough.

A Good COOK WANTED. Soups, entrées, game, creams, jellies, &c. Dairy.[4] Age about 30. State wages last received and full particulars to Mrs. G. Twentyman, Green-hill-park, New Barnet.

GOOD PLAIN COOK WANTED, to assist a little in housework. Must be an early riser and have good character from last situation. Apply, at first by letter, to 17, Bramham-gardens, Kensington.

A YOUNG WOMAN WANTED, not over 35, to cook and assist in the housekeeping. Housemaid kept, and girl for kitchen work. Small family. Wages begin £18. Letter to T., Davis's Library, King's College-road, South Hampstead, N.W.

AS HOUSEMAID (thorough), with assistance in the morning. Good needlewoman, and wait on lady if required. Age 27. Tall. One year and three months' personal character. Wages £21. — E. M. R., 4, Melrose-terrace, New-road, Buckland, Hants.

HOUSEMAID (thorough). — A lady wishes to RECOMMEND her HOUSEMAID, who has been with her nearly three years, and with whom she is only parting on account of a change in her

1. *Housekeeper*, gouvernante ou femme de charge. — 2. *Church of England*, c'est-à-dire appartenant par la religion à l'Église réformée d'Angleterre. — 3 laveuse de vaisselle — 4 laiterie

household arrangements. Reply, by letter, to Mary Chimer, 53, Gloucester-gardens, W.

GENERAL SERVANT (superior) WANTED, £18-£22; all except beer[1]. Family three, servants two. Suburbs. Or respectable girl to train. Address R 118, Address and Inquiry office, The Times Office, E.C.

BUTLER, about to marry, desires SITUATION in country. Present employer can confidently recommend him after eight years' experience. Address W., 20, Queen's-gate, London, S.W.

AS BUTLER and VALET (thorough), where two in livery or one and odd man are kept[2]. Country all the year round, near London, preferred. 3½ years present situation, two years at each previous. Good character. — H., 7, Sloane-square, S.W.

VALET and SERVANT. — A thorough VALET and SERVANT REQUIRED, by a gentleman living in chambers. Must be single and with unexceptionable references. Address, stating age, height, salary required, and enclose carte de visite[3], Valet, care of Messrs. Reynell and Son, 44, Chancery-lane, W. C.

VALET WANTED, immediately, for invalid gentleman, to go to Italy. — Colonel Neilson, Ringford, Kirkcudbrightshire.

REQUIRED, SITUATION as INDOOR SERVANT, Footman, or Valet. Italian, speaks French and English (not fluently). 18 months' good personal character. Age 26, height 5ft. 11in. — C. T., 21, Frith-street, Soho-square.

GROOM and COACHMAN. Single. A gentleman can strongly RECOMMEND. Sober, honest, and trustworthy. Apply F. Richards, 23, Coach and Horses-yard, Old Burlington-street, London, W.

GROOM-COACHMAN WANTED. Another coachman and groom kept. Must be smart, young, thoroughly understand team and tandem work, also shooting things. Apply, by letter only, with full particulars, to W. S., 39, Herne-hill, S. E.

GARDENER (HEAD)[4], age 30, single. The advertiser begs to offer his services to any lady, nobleman, or gentleman requiring a man as above. Has had sound practical experience in all branches of gardening. First-class references from present and previous employers. — Robert Petfield, Foreman, Welcombe-gardens, Stratford-on-Avon.

MADDOX-STREET AGENCY. — MALE SERVANTS only. High-class Butlers, Valets, Footmen, Pages, Coachmen, Grooms, Gardeners, &c., for town and country. Address Secretary, 9, Maddox-street, Hanover-square, W. Registration free in town.

A BARRISTER, M.A., Oxford (in high honours), very successful with his pupils, READS with gentelmen for Bar and Solicitors' Examinations[5]. Address Lex., care of Porter, New-court, Carey-street, Lincoln's-inn, London.

A CAMBRIDGE MAN VISITS and RECEIVES PUPILS. Has successfully prepared many for Army, Cambridge, London Matric, Medical and Law prelim.[6], &c. — A. J. Mainwaring, M. A., 115, Edith-road, West Kensington.

1. On ne fournit pas la bière. — 2. Où l'on emploie deux hommes de livrée ou un seul et un homme de peine. — 3. Envoyer en même temps carte de visite. — 4. *Gardener (head)*, jardinier en chef. — 5. Examens d'admission au barreau et à l'ordre des avoués. — 6. *And law*

ARMY TUTOR, Resident or Travelling. Successful in coaching[1] for Sandhurst and Militia Competitive Examinations. Experienced traveller and linguist. Address Coach, care of May's, 162, Piccadilly, W.

LESSONS or LECTURES in CLASSICS, English Literature, Logic, and Political Economy, by experienced teacher. First-class honours. Good testimonials. Address Rev. M. A., Rowley's, Stationer, 157, Gloucester-road, South Kensington.

SCHOLASTIC.—WANTED, English and Foreign MASTERS, for first-class schools in England and abroad. Salaries £30 to £200. Well-qualified tutors should apply at once to receive full particulars of good engagements from Messrs. Biver, 298, Regent-street. (Est. 30 years.) Telegrams, Biver, London.

SECRETARY, Accountant[2]. — Gentleman (27), well up in company work, varied experience and best references, desires RE-ENGAGEMENT at home or abroad. French, shorthand[3]. Address F. R. 440, Messrs. Deacon's, Leadenhall-street, E.C.

A GENTLEMAN, 28 years of age, who speaks and writes English, German, and French thoroughly, perfect accountant, who has managed the counting-house and financial part of a large business in London for the last three years, is desirous to accept a POSITION as SECRETARY, Managing Accountant, or Bookkeeper, or any other office of trust. Best references to his former employer, as well as many other highest recommendations. — R 119, Address and Inquiry office, The Times Office, E.C.

TO CONSERVATIVE MEMBERS of PARLIAMENT. — A Secretary, of experience, having good offices in close proximity to the Houses of Parliament and a highly efficient staff[4], is prepared to undertake SECRETARIAL WORK for the above. Address Parliament, care of Messrs. Walter Hill and Co., 69, Southampton-row, W.C.

EXCEPTIONALLY good opportunity offers for a gentleman wishing to invest £3,000 to £5,000 and desiring employment ta take POSITION of LONDON MANAGER and SECRETARY in connexion with a highly important company, or, if preferred, can join the Board. Money to be utilized in extending business and carrying out very important contracts. Process recommended by the Government. Specially suitable for retired officers, Royal Engineers, gentlemen home from the colonies, &c. Security given by mortgage or debentures. Only those with best references need apply, by letter in first instance, to W. J., 3, Westminster-chambers, London, S.W.

GENTLEMAN, aged 23, who has had considerable sea experience, REQUIRES SITUATION in any suitable office. Moderate salary. — A. Z., Temple-chambers, Temple-avenue, E.C.

HOTEL MANAGER and his WIFE, thoroughly experienced, with first-class testimonials, will be open to an ENGAGEMENT after Christmas. Apply R. H., R116, Address and Inquiry office, The Times Office, E. C.

H S., 26 years, is desirous of adapting himself to some business or calling wherein perseverance and integrity would assist him in obtaining a thorough knowledge and a chance of

prelim., c'est-à-dire *preliminary*, aux examens d'admission à l'Université de Londres, aux écoles de médecine, et aux épreuves préliminaires de l'école de droit. — 1. *In coaching*, à "chauffer", c'est un terme d'argot d'écolier. — 2. Comptable. — 3. *Shorthand*, sténographie. — 4. État-major très actif.

promotion. (Is now butler, having lived with present family about four years.) Would any gentleman kindly reply to 16, Lennox-gardens, Pont-street, S.W.?

TO BANKERS' CLERKS and others. — PERMANENT EVENING EMPLOYMENT, half-past 6 to 9 o'clock. Commencing salary £40 a year. Applicants must be accustomed to paying and receiving money, quick and accurate with figures[1], and able to give their day employer as a reference. Only those who have permanent day employment need apply. Apply, by letter only, stating nature of day employment, age, &c., to Cashier, care of Messrs. Street Brothers, 5, Serle-street, Lincoln's-inn, W. C.

THERE is a VACANCY for an ARTICLED PUPIL[2] in one of the oldest firms of Estate Agents in the Westend. Premium £150, and preference given to gentleman who can introduce business on liberal commission. Apply Hyde Park, R84, Address and Inquiry office, The Times Office, E. C.

TO PARENTS and GUARDIANS. — An Auctioneer, with branch office[3], wishes to dispose of same. Capital opportunity for young gentleman completing articles, as supervision could be arranged first year. Cash required £350. Apply Q106, Address and Inquiry office, The Times Office, E.C.

LAW. — WANTED, a GENERAL MANAGING CLERKSHIP[4], by a young Solicitor with good experience. Salary moderate. Could introduce business and find some capital if required. Address W., care of Messrs. Street, Brothers, 5, Serle-street, W. C.

PARTNERSHIP. — Solicitor (25), admitted June, 1886, and in practice, will invest £2,000 in the purchase of a JUNIOR PARTNERSHIP in an old-established London firm. No agents need answer. — R. G. M., R81, Address and Inquiry office, The Times Office, E.C.

PARTNERSHIP. — £10,000 to £12,000. — Excellent opening for an educated gentleman. Mechanical knowledge desirable. Old and safe business. Limited liability. Large profits, and pleasant occupation. Principals or solicitors only. Apply S. T. Biggs, Solicitor, 45, Lincoln's-inn-fields.

PARTNERSHIP. — Merchant, with old-established, large, and remunerative business, REQUIRES a suitable PARTNER with £7,000. Security will be given. Substantial income guaranteed. Fullest investigation. Excellent opportunity for young gentleman. Principals only to apply. Letters endorsed Partner, care of Messrs. Hoyle and Shipley, Solicitors, Newcastle-on-Tyne.

PARTNER WANTED, at once. A lady, having a handsomely-furnished house, in splendid position, close to Hyde-park, wishes to meet with a lady to join her in opening a high-class boarding house[5]. £300 required for half share of furniture that cost £1,000. All profits divided. Address Beta, care of Messrs. Murray and Son, Solicitors, 11, Langham-street, Portland-place.

A PROFESSIONAL MAN REQUIRES the LOAN of £250 from private source. Will pay 10 per cent. and deposit life policy for amount. Address Y. D., at Horncastle's Central Advertisement offices, London.

FORTUNE. — Any one with a few pounds can secure a large sum, probably a fortune. Though strange in appearance, this is genuine and bona

1. A calculer rapidement et avec précision. — 2. Élève apprenti. — 3. Qui a une succursale. — 4. Un emploi de clerc dirigeant. — 5. Une pension (hôtel) de première classe.

fide, as will be proved to all. Write, in first instance, C. W., May's Advertising offices, 162, Piccadilly.

INVESTMENT[1]. — A financial company will be prepared to pay 10 per cent. upon deposits of £50 to £500. Undoubted security. Address K. O., at Horncastle's Central Advertisement offices, London.

ONE HUNDRED POUNDS a YEAR for every £500 deposited, £8 6s. 8d. monthly. Similar interest on smaller or larger deposits. Particulars and Press opinions of Frederick Brooke, No. 13, Copthall-court, Throgmorton-street, London.

BOARD AND RESIDENCE, APARTMENTS, &c.

BOARD and RESIDENCE, in a well-appointed house, for a family, lady, or gentleman. Situation central. Apply 9, Woburn-place, Russell-square, W. C.

BOARD and RESIDENCE, Roseville, Gipsy-hill, Upper Norwood (five minutes from Crystal Palace and railways). Morning, bath, smoking, and spacious dining and drawing rooms.

BOARD and RESIDENCE (West-end), 73, Gloucester-place, Portman-square, near Baker-street Station and parks. Single room 30s., and double three guineas.

BOARD and RESIDENCE, 10, Duchess-street, Portland-place, close to the Langham Hotel, Regent-street. Mrs. Phillips receives ladies and gentlemen who desire a comfortable home where the society is select.

BOARD and RESIDENCE (superior), Grosvenor-house, Linden-gardens, Bayswater, W. Three minutes' from Notting-hill-gate Station and omnibus, close to Hyde-park and Kensington-gardens.

BOARD and RESIDENCE (first-class), near Exhibition and Museums. Most convenient for candidates for Army, &c., competitive examinations. — 3, Lexham-gardens, Cromwell-road, Kensington.

BOARD and RESIDENCE, highly commended, being select, cheerful, and home-like. Unequalled for appointments, table, &c. — Knaresborough-house, Collingham-place, Cromwell-road, S. W., close to Earl's-court Station.

BOARD and RESIDENCE WANTED, in the house of a medical man, for a young lady suffering from hysteria. Highest references required. Reply, by letter only, W.Z., No. 36, Guildford-street, Russell-square.

BOARD and RESIDENCE, with comfort and elegance (per day or week), at Thrale-hall, Streatham (London's healthiest suburb). Unequalled table d'hôte, experienced chef. Noble reception, reading, billiard, and recreation rooms; asphalted tennis court. Entertainments. Corridors warmed. Special winter terms.

BOARD and RESIDENCE en PENSION, at a mansion, handsomely furnished and decorated for the purpose of providing temporary or permanent accommodation to ladies and gentlemen, affording all the advantages of the largest English and Continental hotels at moderate expense. Fifty bed and sitting rooms, smoking room, and bath rooms (free), fitted with every modern appliance. Specially good table d'hôte and refined society, this being the only establishment in London combining all

1. *Investment*, placement (de fonds).

home comforts with the luxury and independence of an expensive hotel. Situate in the centre of the West-end, close to all fashionable places of amusement, clubs, exhibitions, parks, railway stations. Particulars, by letter (or personally, before 2 and after 5 o'clock, or between those hours by appointment), 8, Mandeville-place, Manchester-square, W.

TO INDIAN PARENTS, and others. — A lady, living in a very healthy country place, near Ross, Herefordshire, wishes to take CHARGE of three or four YOUNG CHILDREN. She has had many years' experience with children, and would give them every possible care. Good references. Terms moderate. — Miss Adams, Peterstow, near Ross, Herefordshire.

MEDICAL MAN (married) seeks a lady or gentleman patient as BOARDER. Could receive married lady for her accouchement. A City gentleman not objected to. Terms moderate. — W., 96, Kennington-park-road, S. E.

UNFURNISHED[1].— Excellent DRAWING-ROOM FLOOR (two rooms), in a private house in the best part of Kensington, two minutes' from High-street Station, to be LET. Moderate rent, including attendance. Apply Penning and Daniel, No. 19, Kensington-court-place, W.

UNFURNISHED APPARTMENTS WANTED, by a lady. Two sitting rooms, bed room, and box room[2], with good cooking and attendance, and where no other lodgers are taken. Earl's-court or Kensington, not West Kensington. Address E. J. C., Hobbins' Library, 154, Earl's-court-road, S.W.

UNFURNISHED, in Fellows-road, Swiss-cottage, high-class APARTMENTS—drawing room, dining room, and kitchen, first floor, and two bed rooms second floor, bath (hot and cold), pantry, coal cellar, garden, &c. Address, in first instance, Mrs. C., care of Boone, Stationer, Swiss-cottage, N. W.

FLAT[3], 9k, Hyde-park-mansions—eight rooms. Rent £130. Apply Manager, Hyde-park-mansions Estate office, No. 332, Marylebone-road.

FLATS, superior fireproof[4], healthiest situation in London, gravel soil, close to Kensington-gardens. Three reception, four to seven bed rooms, bath room, and excellent offices. Lifts[5] and all modern improvements. Apply Office, Palace-court-mansions, Bayswater-hill, W.

FLATS to be LET, Hyde-park-mansions, W.—first floor, eight rooms, £155; entrance floor, seven rooms, £135; ground floor, six rooms, £70; furnished flat, eight rooms, five guineas a week. Apply Manager's office, 332, Marylebone-road, Edgware-road, N.W.

FURNISHED FLAT (Albert-hall-mansions, S.W.), consisting of two reception rooms, seven bed rooms, bath room, kitchen, and pantry. South aspect, overlooking Horticultural-gardens. For particulars apply T. Hussey, office.

FIRST-FLOOR FLAT, artistically and comfortably furnished, light, airy, and in good sanitary order, near Albert-hall and Kensington-gardens, to be LET, from December or January, for several months. Two large reception, five bed rooms, dressing and bath rooms, good kitchen, and offices, two water-closets. Eight guineas per week,

---

1. Non meublé. — 2. Chambre de débarras. — 3. Appartement. — 4. Très bien construit, à l'épreuve du feu. — 5. Ascenseurs.

with use of piano and books. Address S, A., 3, Place-gate-mansions, Kensington.

OFFICES to be LET[1], best part of City. First, second, or third floors; front room, 21ft. 6in. by 17ft. 9in. Moderate rents. Apply to H. J. E. Brake, 34, New Bridge-street, E.C.

OFFICES.—To be LET, a capital GROUND FLOOR[2], with six rooms en suite, and lavatory and two water closets and cellars. One door from Victoria-embankment and near Temple Station. Also a Second Floor[3] of six rooms and waiting room en suite, and lavatory and water closet and cellar. Also Two Rooms on Third Floor. The above together or separately. Apply to Arding, Bond, and Buzzard, Surveyors, 22, Surrey-street, Strand.

OFFICES, in City, to be LET.—St. Dunstan's-house, Idol-lane—first and second floors, one office, or two, three, or four offices, en suite, with good light; 121, Cannon-street, near Terminus, South-Eastern Railway—first floor, a suite of three offices; 122, Cannon-street (corner of King William-street)—second and third floors, a suite of three or two offices, or one office, all very light : 124, Fenchurch-street, third floor, two offices, and small wine cellar and office. Inquire of Mr. E. Rogers, Messrs. Wm. Dawson and Sons', No. 121, Cannon-street, E. C.

CITY of LONDON.—Premises to be Let[4].—To Firms Requiring Premises for the New Year.—Messrs. Jones, Lang, and Co., of 3, King-street, Cheapside, E. C., have to LET LARGE and SMALL SUITES of OFFICES in all parts of the City; also light Warehouses of various sizes in the different wholesale districts. Messrs. Jones, Lang, and Co.'s printed list comprises all information. Apply at 3, King-street, Cheapside.

HOUSES, &c., WANTED.

FURNISHED COTTAGE WANTED, for six months, with six or seven bed rooms, stabling for four horses, and a few acres of grass preferred. Neighbourhood of Leatherhead, Cobham, or Claremont preferred. Moderate rent. Full particulars to A., 19, Bramham-gardens, South Kensington, S.W.

FREEHOLD PROPERTY, WANTED, to PURCHASE, in London, suitable for the investment of trust funds amounting to £50,000, which would be divided. Particulars to C., R122, Address and Inquiry office, The Times Office, E. C.

REQUIRED, to RENT, with option of purchase, SMALL HOUSE, with stables, garden, orchard, and some land. Standing high on gravel or sand, and with south aspect. Rent about £100. No agents need apply. Address H. Urmson, Kenley, Surrey.

REQUIRED, FURNISHED MANSION, for a year from the present time, South Kensington or Belgravia. Must be really handsomely furnished and clean, and accommodation ample. Stabling for 10 horses. Rent from 1,000 to 1,500 guineas. Replies treated in confidence if required. Address A. J. Best (for G.), Land and Estate Agent, 17, Sloane-street, S.W.

FREEHOLD LAND for STABLES[5].—WANTED to PURCHASE, in the neighbourhood of Whitechapel, about 3,000 or 4,000 square feet of LAND, upon which to build stabling. Address B. B., care of Messrs. Street and Co., 30, Cornhill, E.C.

1. Bureaux à louer. — 2. Un charmant rez-de-chaussée. — 3. Un deuxième étage. — 4. Local à louer. — 5. Propriété pour y bâtir des écuries.

HYDE-PARK and PORTMAN ESTATES.—Messrs. FREDERICK A. MULLETT, BOOKER, and Co.'s REGISTER of the principal select furnished and unfurnished RESIDENCES to be LET or SOLD may be inspected daily at their Auction and Estate Agency offices, Albion-house, Hyde-park-square (the corner of Albion-street), W.

PORTMAN-SQUARE and HYDE-PARK ESTATE OFFICES.—Mr. WALTER HOLCOMBE has on his REGISTER the most eligible furnished and unfurnished HOUSES throughout the fashionable area of the metropolis. —30, Orchard-street, Portman-square.

RENTS COLLECTED and DISTRAINTS LEVIED[1] by Mr. WOOD, 1, Great James-street, Bedford-row. Certificated to distrain under the new Act. No fees to landlords when rent over £20. References and prompt settlements. Advice free.

HOUSES, &c., TO BE LET AND SOLD.

TO be LET, with possession at once, a detached VILLA, in Holland-villas-road, Kensington, Garden back and front. House now being done up[2]. For terms, &c., apply to Messrs. Harrison and Son, 9, Russell-gardens, Holland-road, Kensington.

TO be LET, immediately, fully and comfortably Furnished, 46, BAKER-STREET, Portman-square, containing two lofty, handsome reception rooms, five bed rooms, kitchen, large hall, and good staircase. Rent five guineas a week.

TO be LET, unfurnished, 37, CHENISTON-GARDENS, Kensington. Four sitting rooms, seven bed rooms; perfect drainage; bath room (hot and cold water), speaking-tubes[3]. Rent £125. Apply to Marsh, House Agent, 12, Lower Phillimore-place, Kensington.

TO be LET, Furnished, for eight or nine weeks from now, a very nice, clean HOUSE, near Portman-square, with 10 bed rooms, large reception rooms, full basement, and two staircases. Apply to H. Grogan and Co., 101, Park-street, Grosvenor-square, W.

TO be LET or SOLD, FREEHOLD MANUFACTURING PREMISES, with fine wharfage on river Lea, nearly half an acre, at Bromley-by-Bow, London; two minutes' walk from Bromley Station. Apply Bingemann Bros., 4, Catherine-court, Seething-lane, London, E.C.

TO be LET, unfurnished, a charming, detached BIJOU RESIDENCE, in the main (Finchley) road, close to three lines of omnibuses and two railway stations, containing six bed rooms, bath room, two reception rooms, billiard room, and good domestic offices. Modern appointments. Excellent stabling. Apply to Geo. Head and Co., 7, Upper Baker-street, N. W.

TO be LET or SOLD, in choice parts of South Kensington, on moderate terms, the following high-class HOUSES, replete with every modern arrangement, all redecorated and ready for occupation, with highest sanitary certificates :—

HOUSE and STABLES, close to Natural History Museum; 10 or 11 bed rooms, five reception rooms, good basement; roomy stabling.

Fine HOUSE, within five minutes of Gloucester-road Station, with large reception rooms, full-sized billiard room, 11 bed rooms, and offices; stabling if wanted.

Charming RESIDENCE, near Cromwell-road; beautifully fitted; ground

---

1. M. Wood touche les loyers et opère les saisies. — 2. On décore la maison à neuf. — 3. Porte-voix.

floor reception rooms, 11 bed rooms; private garden; stabling optional[1].

Apply to Messrs. Rogers, Chapman, and Thomas, 78, Gloucester-road, South Kensington.

BRIGHTON SEASON.—Best furnished and unfurnished HOUSES in PARSONS and SON'S REGISTER (free)[2]. Special list by return on receipt of requirements. Offices, 9, Marine-parade, and 124, Western-road, Brighton. Telephone 88.

BRIGHTON.—WILKINSON and SON have all the best furnished and unfurnished HOUSES to LET and SELL. Lists free on application.—Offices, 168, North-street, Brighton, and 30a, Western-road Hove.

BRIGHTON.—Mr. RAWLINSON'S LIST contains nearly all the best FURNISHED HOUSES in the fashionable parts, some exceptionally moderate, two to 25 guineas per week.—Auction offices, 109, King's-road, Brighton.

CHEYNE-WALK (Nos. 7, 8, 9, 10, and 11), Chelsea facing the River and Embankment[9].—To be SOLD, these high class RESIDENCES, containing five reception rooms, billiard room 10 bed rooms, bath room, attic, large kitchen, housekeeper's room, butler's pantry, and complete domestic offices. They are exceptionally well-planned, having large central well-lighted halls (with fire-places) in which the principal staircase is placed, serving rooms with food lift[3] between morning and dining rooms, secondary staircase from basement to second floor, the dining rooms having large ingle nooks[4] fitted in the Old English style; gardens and entrance at front and back. Decorations left to suit purchasers. Apply on premises, or to J. T. Chappell, 149, Lupus-street, S.W.

QUEEN'S-GATE-TERRACE.—A Bargain[5].—To be SOLD, for 3,000 guineas, a RESIDENCE, comprising five reception rooms and 10 bed and dressing rooms. Agent, Mr. Chas. Saunders, 3, St. George's-terrace, Gloucester-road, S.W. (2,016.)

RUSSELL-SQUARE (south side).—The LEASE[6], with possession, of a FAMILY RESIDENCE to be SOLD. A considerable sum has recently been expended in improving and fitting it with bath and other modern conveniences. Apply to Mr. Robert Reid, 51, Great Marlborough-street, W.

REGENT'S-PARK (Park-square east).—To be LET on LEASE, in this convenient and favourite square, a SMALL, compact RESIDENCE, close to Portland-place, and within five minutes' walk of Regent-circus. Rent only £130. Small premium.—J. and R. Kemp and Co., the Regent's-park Estate Office, 27, Albany-street, N.W.

REGENT'S-PARK, Gloucester-gate.—A gentleman, going abroad for the winter, is willing to LET, to a careful tenant, at an almost nominal rent[7], his well FURNISHED detached RESIDENCE, containing good accommodation, conservatory[8]; large gardens, &c. Apply to J. and R. Kemp and Co., the Regent's-park Estate office, 27, Albany-street, N.W.

RICHMOND-HILL.—To be SOLD or LET, a gentleman's handsomely FURNISHED, detached RESIDENCE, containing, on two floors, nine bed rooms, bath room, and lavatory, with two lower rooms; on ground floor, three fine reception rooms, lavatory, and

---

1. *Stabling optional,* la location des écuries est facultative. — 2. Gratuit. — 3. Monte-plats. — 4. Grand renfoncement au coin du foyer. — 5. *A bargain,* excellente occasion. — 6. *Lease,* bail. — 7. Loyer presque fictif. — 8. *Conservatory,* serre de jardin. 9 Levée
10 attique (petit étage supérieur servant à dissimuler le toit d'une maison)

spacious hall; basement[1], housekeeper's room and good light offices. Lawn, with well-grown elm trees. Three-stall stable, coach-house, two rooms over, and loft. Sole agent, Mr. Pennington, Railway Station, Richmond.

SYDENHAM-HILL.—ONE of the choicest PROPERTIES in this most favoured spot in Surrey to be LET; 10 bed chambers, elegant reception rooms; conservatory, greenhouse, stabling, &c.; lovely views. Apply to Walford and Wilshin, House Agents, Anerley-road, near Cristal Palace, S. E.

SOUTH KENSINGTON.—Mr. WILLETT'S HOUSES and STABLES, all sizes. Good positions. Perfect construction. Moderate terms.—Office, Sloane-square, S.W. (opposite the Station). Telephone 3,184. Similar properties at Brighton.

SOUTH KENSINGTON, Earl's-court, and Neighbourhood.—Mr. C. W. Mayne has a large selection of RESIDENCES, furnished and unfurnished, in this favourite district. Selected list will be forwarded on application, stating requirements.—Auction and Estate offices, 158, Earl's-court-road, S.W. Close to station.

SUNNINGHILL, on high ground.—Attractive RESIDENCE. 12 bed and four reception rooms; stabling, &c. To be LET, for winter or longer. Agent, Mr. Chancellor, Sunningdale.

SUNNINGDALE, close to station.—Complete MANSION. 21 bed and bath rooms, four reception and billiard rooms; stabling for seven. To be LET or SOLD. Agent, Mr. Chancellor, Sunningdale.

SURBITON.—A very superior detached FAMILY RESIDENCE, in a favourite spot, to be SOLD. It contains 20 rooms. Excellent stabling, and large garden, greenhouses, conservatory, &c. Price for the freehold £6,000. Apply to Horncastle and Pember, 14, Billiter-street, E. C.

TOWN HOUSES for SALE.

IN the BEST POSITIONS.

AGENTS, ARBER, RUTTER, and WAGHORN.

ONLY OFFICES, 105, Mount-street, W. Established half a century.

PORCHESTER-TERRACE.—To be SOLD, ONE of these fine detached RESIDENCES, with gardens and good stabling. The reception rooms and billiard room are on the ground floor, and the bed rooms on floor above.—Messrs. Greatorex and Co., No. 11, Stanhope-terrace, Hyde-park-gardens, W.

HYDE-PARK (overlooking the Park).—Several first-rate MANSIONS to be LET or SOLD, at much reduced prices.—Greatorex and Co.

GLOUCESTER-TERRACE. — Rent £145 only.—Situated close to Kensington-gardens and Hyde-park, and having every modern convenience. Seven bed, bath &c.— Greatorex and Co.

HOLLAND-PARK.—Several of these detached RESIDENCES, with billiard rooms, to be LET, Sold, or to be Let, Furnished.—Greatorex and Co.

FURNISHED HOUSES.—A select LIST can always be obtained from GREATOREX and Co., 11, Stanhope-terrace, Hyde-park-gardens, of Residences to be Let in Mayfair, Belgravia, Hyde-park, and Kensington neigh-

---

1. Sous-sol. 2 mansarde

bourhoods. Rentals from three guineas to 30 guineas per week.

FREEHOLD MANSION for SALE, or to be Let on Lease, admirably situated in Chelsea, conveniently near the Houses of Parliament, seven minutes from Hyde-park-corner, nine from St. James's-street. The residence is unique, and was erected under the superintendence of an eminent architect for the occupation of the owner. It contains the comforts of a country house with the advantages of a London one. Beautiful reception rooms, which include a fine music room and billiard room, 15 or 16 bed rooms; perfect drainage; laundry[1], large stabling. Commands a beautiful view, and more light and fresh air than any other locality in London. Apply to Messrs. Marler and Bennett, 175 and 176, Sloane-street, Belgravia, S.W. (3,077.)

THIS DAY, SALE by AUCTION, at the Mart, Tokenhouse-yard, E.C., at 2 o'clock, the following:

No.23, ENNISMORE-GARDENS, S.W.

No. 12, LOWNDES-SQUARE, S.W.

No. 19, BRUTON-STREET, Berkeley-square.

ROBT. W. MANN and SON, Auctioneers, 12, Lower Grosvenor-place, and 32, Lowndes-street, S.W.

FOR SALE, splendid gentleman's RESIDENCE, near Bonn-on-the-Rhine, freehold property; 14 rooms; large park, hothouse, &c. This property may be had with or without the complete furniture, many valuable paintings, antiquities, and works of art. For further particulars apply to Mr. P. Friedheim, in Berlin, W. Kurfürsten Str. 166.

OFFICE of Me. GUIARD, Notary, Bordeaux (Gironde), France, 137, rue Ste Catherine. SALE by AUCTION, in the Chamber of Notaries, situated at Bordeaux, 5, rue Combes, Wednesday, 5th December, 1888, at 1 o'clock p. m., of various CHALETS, situated at Arcachon, viz. :—1. Villa Vides, upset price[2] 35,000f. 2. Fior d'Aliza, upset price 40,000f. 3. Villa Graziella, upset price 25,000f. 4. Villa Esperanza, upset price 45,000f. 5. A Chalet, without name, upset price 62,000f. 6. Villa Europe, upset price 40,000f. 7. Villa D'jali, upset price 10,000f. 8. Villa Haydn, upset price 12,000f. 9. Villa Luxembourg, upset price 40,000f. Negotiations can be made by mutual agreement up to date of sale. Apply for information to Me. Guiard, Notary, and for inspection to Mr. Duba, Villa Degaune, Arcachon.

WINTER QUARTERS.—Well FURNISHED, gentleman's HOUSE. Warm, cheerful, central. Close to Crystal Palace and trains to London-bridge and West-end. Address T., Miss Cottrell's, 21, Anerley-road, Upper Norwood.

COMMANDING POSITION, nine doors from Piccadilly.—SHOP, front 14ft., depth 40 ft., to be LET. Bold, double plate-glass windows, elegant show-cases, cabinets, looking-glasses, counter 16½ ft. with marble top, gas, electric lights (15 incandescent lamps), ceilings and walls lincrusta. — 9, Old Bond-street.

TO FAMILIES CHANGING RESIDENCE, or giving up Housekeeping.—FURNITURE REMOVED from house to house, in town or country, or stored in the warehouses. Terms and prospectus free.—The PANTECHNICON, Belgrave-square.

TRADES.

TEETH. — Messrs. ESKELL and SONS, 445, Strand (exactly oppo-

---

1. *Laundry*, buanderie. — 2. *Upset price*, mise à prix.

site Charing-cross Station), and 58, Ludgate-hill, City, the old-established Surgeon-Dentists. Their celebrated ENAMELLED TEETH supplied without pain while waiting, and are fixed by atmospheric suction. A tooth, 5s.; a set, £4. Consultations free. Established over 50 years. Pamphlet (explaining new painless systems) sent gratis and post free. Note.—Only Addresses.

AMERICAN DENTISTRY. — DR. PAGET, Surgeon Dentist, 445, Strand (opposite Charing-cross Station), the old-established Dentist.—SPECIALITIES in ENGLISH and AMERICAN DENTISTRY. The painless adjustment of artificial teeth entirely without plates or palates[1], also without springs or wires, by atmospheric pressure. Charges most moderate. See descriptive pamphlet, sent gratis and post free. Country patients supplied in one visit. Consultation free daily 10 to 5.

GOLD STOPPINGS[2].—DR. PAGET'S SYSTEM.—Teeth, no matter how badly decayed, can, by the aid of pure American gold, be retained in the mouth for years; in fact, many decayed teeth or apparently useless shells can be effectually restored to masticatory power without pain or discomfort.—Dr. Paget, Surgeon Dentist, 445, Strand (opposite Charing-cross Station).

SOUTH KENSINGTON LADIES DENTAL INSTITUTION and ASSOCIATION, Registered (vide Registration Journal), Sussex-house, 43, Sussex-place, Old Brompton-road, directly opposite London and Provincial Bank. Superior ARTIFICIAL TEETH, and high-class dentistry only, at moderate charges, especially to servants. All consultations free. No branches[3].

SOUTH KENSINGTON DENTAL ASSOCIATION. — Messrs. L. E. and C. ESKELL'S Dental Association, No. 2, Onslow-place, South-Kensington, established 1866, for the supply of their well-known artificial teeth at moderate charges. Ladies and gentlemen 10 till 6. Servants, reduced fees, daily, 8 a.m. till 9 p.m. All consultations free. To avoid all disappointment, note address, seven doors from South Kensington Station.

THE following are the ADDRESSES of the AMERICAN DENTAL INSTITUTE, Limited :—

No. 55, St. James's-street, S.W. (near Piccadilly).

No. 34, Thurloe-square, S. W.

No. 44, Finsbury-square, E. C.

And at 123, King's-road, Brighton.

Attendance at each address 9 till 6 daily.

Pamphlet free on application to the Secretary at each address.

FACE POWDER. — SAUNDERS' FACE POWDER, or Bloom of Ninon: retains its superiority over all other cosmetics for preserving the beauty and youthful freshness of the complexion. It is of delicate roseate hue, and perfectly harmless. Price 6d., 1s., 2s. 6d., 5s.; or by post for 7, 14, 33, or 63 stamps. The Pure White Face Powders, precisely the same preparation, but colourless. Only prices, 1s., 2s. 6d., and 5s.—J. Touzeau Saunders, 313, Oxford-street; and of all Chemists and Perfumers.

GOLDEN-HAIR. — ROBARE'S AUREOLINE produces the beautiful golden colour so much admired. Warranted perfectly harmless. Price 5s. 6d. and 10s. 6d. Of all principal Perfumers and Chemists throughout the world. Agents R. HOVENDEN and SONS, 31 and 32, Berners-street, London, W.

IMPERIAL HAIR DYE (Registered). One liquid—black, brown, light brown, or golden. Harmless, perfect,

1. Sans pièces ni palais (artificiels). — 2. Plombage à l'or. — 3. Pas de succursales.

permanent, and free from smell[1]. All clear, without sediment, 2s. 6d., 3s. 6d., 5s., and 10s. 6d.—J. BRODIE, 41, Museum-street, London.

SWEET SCENTS. — PIESSE and LUBIN'S OPOPONAX, Jockey Club, Patchouly, Frangipanni, Kiss-me-Quick, White Rose, and 1,000 others, from every flower that breathes a fragrance, 2s. 6d. each, or three bottles in a case, 7s. The above sweet scents in sachet powder, 1s. 6d. each, can be forwarded by post. Sold by the fashionable druggists and perfumers in all parts of the world.—Laboratory of Flowers, 2, New Bond-street, London, W.

PIESSE and LUBIN. — FLORIMEL of PALM, for the Prevention of Chapped Hands[2], Rough, Skin, Chilblains, Cold Feet, &c. The Florimel of Palm being rubbed over the skin, is to be removed with a little water, then dried, with a soft towel. Once used will convince the most sceptical that, if daily applied, too much cannot be said in favour of Florimel of Palm. In jars, 3s. 6d.—Laboratory of Flowers, 2, New Bond-street, London.

SULPHOLINE LOTION cures eruptions, pimples, redness, blotches, scurf, eczema, psoriasis, &c.; in a few days Sulpholine attacks old skin disorders, and totally destroys them, producing a clear, healthy, smooth, supple, natural skin. Bottles 2s. 9d. Sold everywhere.

PEPPER'S QUININE and IRON TONIC promotes appetite, strengthens the stomach, stopping sinking sensations, removes indigestion, heartburn[3], palpitation, cures dyspepsia, debility, and restores great bodily nerve, mental and digestive strength. Bottles 2s. 6d. Sold everywhere.

POWELL'S BALSAM of ANISEED. To persons who suffer from a chronic inflammatory condition of the mucous membrane, periodically assuming an acute aspect, in the form of catarrh, bronchitis, and asthma, will find POWELL'S BALSAM of ANISEED a friend indeed. Sold by Chemists throughout the world. Establisbed 70 years.

DR. STOLBERG'S VOICE LOZENGE, for throat irritations, imparting strength, richness, and endurance to the voice for singing and speaking. Over a thousand testimonials, including Patti, Trebelli, Patey, Santley, &c. Established 45 years. Sold by Chemists in boxes, 1s. 1½d. and 2s. 9d.

KEARSLEY'S WIDOW WELCH'S FEMALE PILLS have a reputation of over 100 years, and are the acknowledged leading remedy for female complaints. They restore a healthy hue to the complexion, in place of the deathly pallor so distressing to witness. May be obtained of all chemists, 2s. 9d. per box; or by post 34 stamps, from SANGER and SONS, 489, Oxford-street, London.

BLAIR'S GOUT and RHEUMATIC PILLS. The great Remedy for Gout, Rheumatism, Sciatica, Lumbago, and Neuralgia. The excruciating pain is quickly relieved and cured in a few days by this celebrated medicine. Sold by all chemists at 1s. 1½d. and 2s. 9d. per box.

ASTHMA and CATARRH CURED by CIGARETTES ESPIC. Oppression, cough, colds, neuralgia. From all chemists and wholesale stationers.—No. 20, rue Saint-Lazare, Paris. Ask on every cigarette the signature Espic.

ALEX ROSS'S NOSE MACHINE. — Applied to the nose for an hour

1. *Free from smell*, sans odeur. — 2. Empêchant les gerçures aux mains. — 3. *Heartburn*, cardialgie. 4 pellicules

daily, so directs the soft cartilage that an ill-formed nose is quickly shaped. 10s. 6d.; post free, 10s. 8d., secretly packed. Skin Tightener, a lotion for marks under the eyes; post 50 stamps. —21, Lamb's Conduit-street, near Holborn, London, Est. 1850.

T. W. STAPLETON and Co. invite attention to the undermentioned WINES and SPIRITS, imported direct :—

Sherries[1].—15s., 18s., 20s., 24s., 28s., 30s., 36s. per dozen.

Ports.—19s., 24s., 30s., 34s., 42s., 45s., 48s. per dozen.

Clarets[2].—12s., 16s., 20s., 24s., 30s., 36s., 42s. per dozen.

Champagnes. — 26s., 38s., 44s., 46s., 54s., 66s., 70s. per dozen.

Brandies, finest quality.—48s., 54s., 60s., 66s. per dozen.

Old Scotch and Irish Whiskies[3]. — 40s. per dozen.

Price lists on application.—203, Regent-street, W.

JOHN EXSHAW and Co.'s celebrated OLD BRANDY, so extensively used in India and the Colonies. Supplied in one dozen cases, as imported from France, 68s. per dozen.—T. W. STAPLETON and Co., 203, Regent-street, W.

FORTNUM, MASON, and Co. solicit attention to the following cheap and pure WINES : —

Sherry, 24s., 30s., 36s. per doz.
Port, 24s., 36s., 42s. per doz.
Hock[4], 24s., 36s., 42. per doz.
Claret, 18s., 21s., 24s. per doz.
Champagne, 36s., 42s., 48s. per doz.
Burgundy, 24s., 30s. per doz.
Cognac Brandies, Scotch and Irish Whiskies of the choicest quality, 5 per cent. discount for cash. — 182, Piccadilly, W.

GEO. ROE and Co. (Limited).—Finest DUBLIN MALT WHISKY, guaranteed six years old, and bottled as received from the distillery, can be obtained at any of the 96 branches of the VICTORIA WINE COMPANY, in quantities of one bottle or upwards, at the rate of 42s. per dozen, or one dozen sent carriage paid, bottles and case included, to any station in England or Wales, 44s. 6d. Post-office order to W. W. Hugues, head offices, 8 to 10, Osborne-street, London, E.

BEST HAVANA CIGARS at IMPORT PRICES. The great connoisseurs, the keenest buyers, the best juges of value now purchase their cigars at BENSONS'S, 61, St. Paul's-churchyard, London. Good foreign cigars, 12s., 16s., 20s., 22s. per cent. Samples five for 1s. (14 stamps). Cigars to suit the most delicate palate.

BORWICK'S BAKING POWDER — For Bread,

BORWICK'S BAKING POWDER — Cakes, Pies,

BORWICK'S BAKING POWDER — Puddings,

BORWICK'S BAKING POWDER — The best,

BORWICK'S BAKING POWDER — that money,

BORWICK'S BAKING POWDER — can buy.

COOK'S PATENT MEAL for PORRIDGE[5].—Dr. Richardson says :— " Oatmeal is too heating." Cook's Patent Meal is cooling, nutritious. It acts as an aperient ; is beneficial to the skin. Growing children, dyspeptics, and sufferers from constipation should take

---

1. *Sherries*, vins de Xérès. — 2. *Clarets*, vins de Bordeaux. — 3. *Whisky*, whiskey, nom donné à l'eau-de-vie de grains en Angleterre, en Écosse et en Irlande. — 4. Vin du Rhin. — 5. *Porridge*, bouillie.

this food daily. It contains the elements of life in due proportion. Of Grocers &c., 4d. per lb. packet; sample, 3½lb. bag, post free 1s. 6d., of the Manufacturer, C. A. Cook, Pewsey, Wilts.

POTATOES. — 112lb. Magnum Bonums[1], 2s. 6d.; selected, 4s. 6d. and 5s.; 56lb. 2s. 6d. Onions, beetroot, turnips, carrots, 6d. each 14lb. Carriage paid to suburbs. Cash delivery[2]. Weight and soundness guaranteed. — FIELD, 17, Gracechurch-street. Estab. 1874.

POTATOES at market prices, floury, 112lb. 3s. 6d.; Magnum Bonums, selected, 4s. 3d.; best, 4s. 9d.; 56lb., 2s. 6d.; turnips, carrots, onions, beetroot, 6d. each 14lb. Warranted sound, full weight, will keep. Carriage paid to suburbs. Cash delivery. — JAMES FARMER, 140, Leadenhall-street. Estab. 1870.

MOORE and MOORE. — PIANOFORTES from 16½ guineas. Vertical grands from 50 guineas; horizontal grands from 72 guineas. Hire-purchase system, from 10s. 6d. per month. American organs from seven guineas, at from 7s. per month on hire-purchase.

MOORE and MOORE. Established half a century. New, Illustrated PRICE LIST, with terms of the hire-purchase system[3], now ready, and sent, post free, to any address. Extensive warerooms, 104-5, Bishopsgate-street within, London, E. C. (near Bank of England).

MOORE and MOORE. — IMPORTANT NOTICE. — In supplying their admired instruments on the hire-purchase system, as invented by them in the year 1846. Messrs. Moore and Moore make no addition to the price, require no deposit, no guarantee, and make no charge for carriage or tuning.

PIANOS, 15s. per Month, on the Three Years' System, become the property of the hirer if the payments are kept up. There is no other house in London that offers such good pianos at 15s. per month on the three years' system as the Manufacturers, THOMAS OETZMANN and Co., 27, Baker-street, W.

THOMAS OETZMANN and Co.'s ANNUAL SALE of PIANOS returned from hire at the end of the London season. Nearly new pianos by Broadwood, Collard, and Erard, very cheap. Illustrated catalogues and lists post free. — Thomas Oetzmann and Co., 27, Baker-street, London, W.

ERARD, £35. — Genuine ERARD OBLIQUE PIANO, seven octaves and trichord throughout, in rich Italian walnutwood case. A magnificent instrument, and offered at one-third of its original cost. At the great sale of pianos at THOMAS OETZMANN and Co.'s, 27, Baker-street.

JOHN BROADWOOD and SONS, 33, Great Pulteney-street, London, W. — Gold Medal, Inventions Exhibition, 1885. Gold Medal, Society of Arts, 1885. — PIANOFORTES for SALE at from 25 to 250 guineas. Pianofortes for Hire.

CHALLEN and SON, Pianoforte Makers to H. R. H. Prince Albert Victor of Wales. Established 1804. Highest rewards at International Exhibitions for " good tone and touch, good general workmanship, and moderate price of pianos. " — Vide Jurors' Reports.

CHALLEN and SON'S HIRE PURCHASE SYSTEM is conducted upon the most liberal terms. Prices from £2 5s. per quarter, or a substantial

1. Nom d'une variété de pommes de terre. — 2. Livraison contre espèces. — 3. Avec les conditions du payement par versement périodique.

discount allowed for prompt cash. Illustrated list and terms post free. — 46, Oxford-street, London, W.

CRAMER'S NEW METAL-FRAME COTTAGE PIANOFORTES, unequalled in tone and unsurpassed in durability. Cash prices, from 50 guineas; pianettes, from 28 guineas. — J. B. Cramer and Co., Moorgate-street, E.C.

SEMI-GRAND and GRAND PIANOFORTES, in good order, powerful tone, admirably adapted for choral societies, large halls, institutions, or clubs. Prices vary from 22 guineas cash, or two guineas per quarter on the three years' hire system. May also be hired by the month or season. — J. B. CRAMER and Co., 40 to 46, Moorgate-street, E.C.

CRAMER and Co. have a large stock of HARMONIUMS, American Organs, and Pipe Organs of all sizes. Prices from 6 guineas to 300 guineas. — 46, Moorgate-street, E.C.

THE BLÜTHNER PIANOFORTES, Grand and Upright, hold their supreme position by a twofold title — (1) through their unrivalled merits resulting from the Blüthner inventions, and (2) by the verdict of public opinion, the instruments having the largest annual sale of any pianofortes in the world. Catalogues free on application.— Blüthner-house, 7 and 9, Wigmore-street, Cavendish-square, London, W.

COAL[1].— GEORGE J. COCKERELL and Co. Best 26s. Other prices see below. — 13, Cornhill.

COAL, 19s. — RUSSELL and Co.'s Stanley House — large and bright. — Belmont-wharf, King's-cross, N., and 97, Newgate-street, E.C.

COALS, 17s. 6d. — GREAT NORTHERN COAL COMPANY deliver their selected Wallsend (large and double screened[2]) at 17s. 6d. per ton; seconds at 16s. 6d. Cash. — C. Gordon, Agent, 175, Pancras-road, N.W. Prices will advance shortly.

COALS, 20s. — The NEWCASTLE COLLIERY[3] OWNERS, 123, Pancras-road, N.W., deliver their Best Handpicked Wallsends (one of the best coals brought to London) at 20s.; Newcastle Main Wallsends, 18s.; Best Bright House, 17s.; Close Range Cobbles[4], 16s. Cash. — F. Cross, Agent.

COALS. — The Marquis of Londonderry supplies the following SEABORNE COAL from his Durham Collieries : — Londonderry Wallsend, 25s.; Pittington Wallsend, 24s.; Primrose, 23s. per ton. Cash on delivery. — Seaham Wharf, Nine Elms-lane, Vauxhall. No agents.

COALS (best), 20s. 6d. — The GOOLE COLLIERY OWNERS are now delivering for Cash their Best WALLSEND (all large and double screened) at 20s. 6d. per ton. These splendid coals are unsurpassable for drawing-room or household use. Silkstone, 19s. 6d.; Brights, 19s. — Order office, 167, Pancras-road, N.W.

COALS, 18s. — WOMBWELL MAIN Co. (Limited). Silkstone and Elsecar Coal Owners' Co. — Wombwell (International Prize), 23s.; Silkstone, 24s.; Swaithe, 23s.; Derby, 22s.; Kitchen, 21s.; Nuts, 20s.; Cobbles, 18s. — Coal Department King's cross, N. Telegrams, Wombwell Main, London.

COAL. — NATH. PEGG and Co. (established 70 years). — Selected, 25s.; best Wallsend, 26s.; Silkstone,

1. L'Angleterre, chaque année, extrait 130 millions de tonnes de houille. — 2. *Screened*, charbons criblés; *to screen*, passer au crible. — 3. Houillères de Newcastle, dans le comté de Northumberland. — 4. Gaillettes.

24s.; Derby Brights, 22s.; Kitchen, 21s.; Nuts, 20s.; Coke, 13s.; Depôts : —Warwick-road, Kensington, W.; Clapham-road, S.W.; Maiden-lane, N.; Kew-bridge, W.; and Old Ford, E. Local prices at Forest-hill and Penge. Truck loads to any railway station.

COALS. — NEWTON, CHAMBERS, and Co. (Limited), Thorncliffe Collieries, Sheffield. — Selected, 25s.; best Silkstone, 24s.; Thorncliffe Main, 23s.; Brazils, 23s.; kitchen, 21s.; nuts, 20s.; bright cobbles, 19s.; Earl Fitzwilliam's Elsecar house, 22s.; Coke, 13s. — Coal Department, King's-cross, N., Clapham, West Brompton, Harringay, Tufnell-park, Brockley, &c.

COALS. — W. H. LEE and Co.'s celebrated Inland Wallsend, double screened, 24s.; seconds, 23s. 6d.; Silkstone, 23s. 6d.; second Silkstone, 23s.; Durham Wallsend, 26s.; Barnsley, 22s.; Derby, 22s.; kitchen, 21s.; cobbles for kitcheners, 19s.; hard cobbles, 18s.; steam, 19s.; nuts, 20s.; coke, 11s.; per 10 sacks. Discount 6d. per ton or two tons. — W. H. Lee and Co., 12, Pancras-road, N.W.; or 135, Tottenham-court-road, W. Terms — prompt cash.

COAL, 18s. — HERBERT CLARKE, Limited (Telephone No. 7,607), Great Northern Railway, King's-cross, Kensington, Bayswater, Holloway, Highgate, Crouch-end, Hornsey, Wood-green, Elephant, Clapham, Brixton, Nunhead, Herne-hill, Wandsworth, H. C.'s selected (all large), 25s.; best Wallsend, 26s.; best Silkstone, 24s.; New-castle, 24s.; New Silkstone, 23s.; Derby, 22s.; kitchen, 21s.; cobbles, 19s.; hard cobbles, 18s.; nuts, 20s.; coke, 13s.

COALS. — RICKETT, SMITH, and Co.'s selected COAL, 25s.; best Silkstone, 24s.; best Wallsend, 26s.; New Silkstone, 23s.; Derby Brights, 22s.; kitchen, 21s.; bakers', 20s.; hard steam, 20s.; nuts, 20s.; cobbles, 19s.; smokeless, Welsh, coke, &c. Cash, General offices, King's-cross, W.C.; Victoria-wharf, Grosvenor-road, Pimlico; City offices, 12, Devonshire-square, Bishopsgate; Elephant and Castle and Clapham Stations; Addington-wharf, Camberwell, and other depôts at local prices.

COALS.—PHILLIPS' DIRECT SUPPLY.

Class A best, 23s.

Class B Silkstones, 21s. and 22s.

Class C kitchen, 18s. and 19s.

Class D steam, 17s. 6d., 18s., 18s. 6d.

Phillips' best best, 24s. 6d.

Truck loads direct from the pits to any railway station in the United Kingdom. We are now making contracts to supply consumers for 12 months with any kind of coal, at 6d. per ton on our cost prices for house coals and 3d. on steam, by truck loads for cash.

Phillips and Co., Coal Brokers, 25, Coal Exchange, E.C., since 1851. Telephone No. 2,136.

LIBERTY — ART.

LIBERTY — ART FABRICS for Dresses and Furniture for the winter season. Beautiful and inexpensive. Patterns post free[1].

LIBERTY — VALLEY CASHMERE, warm, soft, and durable. In colours and black. Price 3s. 3d. per yard, 42in. wide. Patterns post free.

LIBERTY — CASHMERE; in Liberty colours and all shades. Soft, light, and durable. Price 21s. and 25s. per piece of 9 yards, 26 inches wide. Patterns post free.

LIBERTY — ART VELVETEEN. A perfect and rich material, in delicate and numerous new shades. Price 8s. 11d. per yard, every yard stamped

1. Échantillons francs de port.

LIBERTY ART VELVETEEN. Patterns post free.

LIBERTY SILKS, tough and light. For dresses or under garments[1]. Price 3s. 3d. per yard, about 30in. wide. Patterns post free.

LIBERTY — TAPESTRIES, for the winter season, in new and original designs and charming colourings, from 9d. per yard, 50 inches wide. Patterns post free.

LIBERTY — DAMASQUE WALL-PAPERS (Registered), resembling rich silken brocades, 1½d. a yard, per piece of 12 yards. Patterns post free.

FIVE HUNDRED INDIAN PALAMPORES[2], hand block printed, very effective for curtains and portieres, 4 yards long by 4ft. wide, 5s. each.

LIBERTY — 4ft. four-fold hand-painted JAPANESE DRAUGHT SCREENS[3], 6s. 6d. each; 4ft. 6in. four-fold Japanese Screens, gold embroidery, £1 5s. each; 5ft. 6in. four-fold Japanese Screens, silk embroidery, on black ground, decorated with birds and flowers, 37s. 6d. (Packing cases extra.) — Liberty and Co., Regent-street, W.

CLOSE of the ITALIAN EXHIBITION. — DEBENHAM and FREEBODY beg to announce that the whole of their EXHIBITS at the Italian Exhibition, consisting of Coloured Armures, satin Duchesse, Poult de Soie, Surat glacé, Fedora, black gros grains, Faille Française, plain Zoagli velvets, and a few short lengths of rich brocades and striped silks, together with silk coverlets, portières, curtains, table covers, and scarfs, will be offered during the next few days at prices varying from 25 to 50 per cent. below Exhibition prices. The collection is now on view at Debenham and Freebody's, Wigmore-street and Welbeck-street, W.

MARSHALL and SNELGROVE. — CARPET, FURNISHING, and LINEN DEPARTMENTS. — A Large and splendid Assortment of New Goods[4] will be found in each of the above-mentioned Departments.

Just added to our already large stock of Foreign Carpets, several bales of Indian carpets in different sizes. These will be sold under usual prices.

300 Indian carpets, size 9ft. by 6ft., at 48s.; 14ft. 1in. by 9ft. 10in., at £6. Other sizes in proportion.

Turkey Carpets, 14ft. 9in. by 10ft. 7in., £10 10s. All other sizes.

600 Thick Bangalore Rugs, 6ft. by 3ft. 3in., 9s. 6d. each.

Brussels Carpets, 12ft. by 9ft. 9in., 58s.

Pile Carpets, 12ft. by 11ft. 3in., £5 18s.; several hundred in different sizes to select from.

Floor-cloths, linoleums, cork carpets, &c. English and foreign rugs of every make and price.

Tapestry Curtains, 15s. 6d., 22s. 6d., 31s. 6d. and 42s. per pair.

Tapestry for curtains and furniture covering, from 3s. 3d. to 4s. 3d. per yard.

Tapestry table-covers, two yards square, 11s. 6d. and 15s. 6d. each.

Novelties in Hand-Painted and Embroidered Folding Screens; also leather-paper and other varieties of draught screens.

An immense Stock of Down Quilts in all sizes, covered with Turkey chintz, printed sateen, and printed and brocaded satin.

Occasional Folding Chairs, enamelled art colours, and covered plush, 13s. and 23s. 6d. each.

Anavato and Mantarli Embroidered Artis and Table Covers, 12s. 6d., 16s. 6d., 21s. 6d., 33s. 6d., and 42s. each.

1. Vêtements de dessous. — 2. Nom indien d'une espèce de coton. — 3. *Draught screens*, paravent. — 4. Un assortiment d'articles nouveaux.

Carriage Foot-warmers, 4s., 6s. 6d.; 8s. 9d., and 20s. each.

Linen Department.

The Stock of Goods for charitable purposes is now complete.

White Blankets, 6s.. 6s. 6d., 7s. 3d., 8s., 8s. 6d., 9s. 3d., 10s., 11s., 12s. 3d., 13s., to 16s. 6d. per pair.

Gray Blankets, 5s. 6d., 6s. 9d., 7s. 3d., 8s., 8s. 9d., and 9s. 3d. per pair.

Brown Blankets, 4s. 6d., 4s. 4d., 6s. 3d., and 7s. 3d. per pair.

Striped Blankets, 2s. 10d., 3s., 3s. 7d., 4s. 3d., 4s. 7d., 5s. 6d., 6s. 4d. and 7s. 3d. each.

Real Welsh White Flannel, 7d., 8d., 9d., $9\frac{1}{2}$d., $10\frac{1}{2}$d., $11\frac{1}{2}$d., and 1s. $0\frac{1}{2}$d. per yard.

Stout All-Wool Scarlet Flannel, 9d., 10d., 11d., 1s., and 1s. $3\frac{1}{2}$d. per yard.

Coloured Flannel, $5\frac{1}{2}$d., $6\frac{1}{2}$d., $7\frac{1}{2}$d., 8d., 9d., and $10\frac{1}{2}$d. per yard.

Gray Calicoes, from $2\frac{1}{2}$d. per yard.

White Calicoes, from 3d. per yard.

Marshall and Snelgrove having bought the entire London Stock of a Barnsley Linen Manufacturer, are now selling it much below ordinary prices.

The Stock consists of Linen Sheetings, Huckaback[1] and Roller Towellings, Glass and Tea Cloths, Dusters, &c.

Marshall and Snelgrove, Vere-street and Oxford-street, W.

FUR-LINED COATS[2]. — H. P. Truefitt (Limited), having purchased for cash the entire stock of one of the best manufacturers in Riga, are enabled to offer these seasonable garments at prices quite unprecedented in London. — 13-14, Old Bond-street, or Brighton.

TRELOAR and SONS.—CARPETS and FLOOR COVERINGS.—Treloar and Sons have just received a large consignment of real Turkey Carpets, which are offered at very low prices for cash. All sizes in stock. All the new patterns of Axminster, Wilton, Brussels, Tapestry; Shetland, Cheviot, and Paisley Carpets now in the warehouse. Cork Carpet, Linoleum, Matting, and Mats, all of the best quality. Prices and estimates free. Competent men sent to show patterns and take measurements free of charge. Old carpets taken up and beaten by steam machinery, altered, and relaid.—Treloar and Sons, 68, 69, and 70, Ludgate-hill (established 1832). Eleven prize medals.

AN EXHIBITION and SPECIAL SALE of rare and costly ORIENTAL CARPETS and RUGS is now being held at HOWELL and JAMES' ART GALLERIES. Prices from 10 shillings to 200 guineas; sizes from 6 feet to 40 feet. Suitable for drawing rooms, dining rooms, boudoirs, studios, ante rooms, corridors, atriums, &c. Rare Yaprak Carpets, worth 23 guineas, will be sold at 15 guineas; some handsome smaller Carpets, worth 7 guineas, will be sold at $3\frac{1}{2}$ and 5 guineas. One hundred Rienzi Art Carpets, suitable for bed rooms and breakfast rooms, will also be sold at 25s. to 60s. — Howell and James (Limited), 5, 7, and 9, Regent-street, and 10, Charles-street, Waterloo-place.

SUPERIOR SECOND-HAND FURNITURE. — L. SPILLMAN and Co., noted for the last 60 years for first-class second-hand furniture, invite an inspection of their large assortment in Chippendale, inlaid Sheraten, and carved oak. Complete sets of modern furniture by Gillow, Holland, and others. Large handsome sideboards, dining tables, bookcases, cabinets, overmantels, and bedroom suites, Turkey, Persian, and Indian carpets, and office furniture. All goods marked in plain figures[3], and sent home equal to new. Shippers supplied. Furniture exchanged. — 14 and 4, Newcastle-street, Strand.

1. *Huckaback*, grosse toile ouvrée. — 2. *Fur-lined coats*, vêtements doublés de fourrure. — 3. Prix marqué en chiffres connus.

COFFEE in PERFECTION.

ASH'S KAFFEE-KANNE, used in Her Majesty's Household, supersedes coffee pots, biggins[1], percolators, and the best of other contrivances for making coffee.

Block Tin, with stand complete.

One-and-a-half pint[2]	£0 6 6
Two pints..	0 8 6
Three pints	0 10 6
Four pints	0 12 6
Six pints	0 16 0

Electro-plate, handsome urn shape.

One pint	£2 0 0
Two pints	2 10 0
Three pints..	3 0 0
Four pints..	3 10 0
Five pints..	4 0 0

PISTON FREEZING MACHINE and ICE COMPANY, 301 and 303, Oxford-street, W., near Hanover-square-gate.

STOVES, TERRA COTTA PORTABLE, for COAL. — ROBERTS'S (IMPROVED) PATENT. Pure and ample heat, 24 hours for about 1d., without attention. For bed rooms, greenhouses, sitting rooms, damp rooms, or almost any purposes. Pamphlet, drawings, and authenticated testimonials sent. See in use, and order at Patentee's, T. Roberts, 112, Victoria-street, Westminster.

CLUB-HOUSE SPERM CANDLES[3], in all sizes, plain or pencilled ends, the best table lights, burn without smoke or smell, price 9d. per lb. All country orders forwarded carriage paid and in free cases. — MARCHANT and SON, 59, Berners-street, London, W.

HAMPTON and SONS.

FURNITURE and DECORATION.

CARPETS, CURTAINS, and

ORNAMENTAL OBJECTS.

DRAWING-ROOM FURNITURE of every description.

Inlaid Cabinets, of good design and finish, from £9 10s.

Easy Chairs, from 37s. 6d. Sofas and Couches, from 70s.

Easy Chairs.—Hampton and Sons' Shell Chair, registered design, covered in sateen, in three sizes, £3 15s., £4 5s., £4 15s.

Card, Centre, Writing, Occasional, and Coffee Tables in great variety.

DINING-ROOM and LIBRARY FURNITURE. Sideboards, new designs, from £6 15s.

Easy Chairs in morocco, from £5 10s.; Dining Chairs in ditto, from 30s.

Dining Tables, extending, with screw, with deal tops, from 30s.

SCREENS.

HAMPTON and SONS invite an inspection of their new stock of SCREENS for this season, which are not only an exceedingly fine assortment, but are cheaper even than last season, especially Japanese screens.

SCREENS. — JAPANESE, HAND-PAINTED, on paper, with decorated cloth backs, four-fold, 5ft. 6in. high, 12s. 9d.; superior ditto, 15s. 9d.

GOLD EMBROIDERED JAPANESE SCREENS, on black satin ground, with decorated cloth backs, four-fold, 5ft. 6in. high, superior quality, 25s., and in richer qualities from 35s. to £10.

A large quantity of rich silk and gold embroidered Screens, on special French satins, in beautiful shades and colourings, from 6s. to £30.

1. *Biggins*, brocs. — 2. *Pint*, mesure de capacité anglaise = 0 lit. 567. — 3. *Sperm candles*, bougies plus fines fabriquées avec du spermaceti ou *blanc de baleine* qu'on extrait de la tête du cachalot, *sperm whale*.

SCREENS. — New high RELIEF LEATHER PAPER four-fold SCREENS, sunk panels, brocaded borders, and decorated cloth backs, 6ft. high, from 35s.

JAPANESE CABINETS, carved satinwood, rich gold-lacquered decoration, inlaid ivory and pearl in relief. Several very fine specimens from £12 10s.

OLD CHINESE BLUE and WHITE WARE[1]. — Very rare old specimens, at exceptionally low prices.

Taizan Ware. — A new shipment of this novel decorative ware, in rich blended colourings and new forms.

ARTISTIC, STANDARD, ADJUSTABLE LAMPS, new and special designs, with improved self-extinguishing burners[2]. A splendid assortment in wrought iron and copper, brass and copper, and all polished brass, from 55s.

Table and Suspension Lamps, fitted with all the latest improvements.

A choice selection of lace lamp shades[3], in newest designs and shapes, from 6s. 9d.

BLACK and BRASS FENDERS and SET of IRONS, from 10s. 6d.

Brass Fenders and set Fire Brasses, from 25s.

Wrought Iron Curbs, pair of Rests, and set of Irons, from 75s.

Coal Boxes, in all woods, best make, 12s.

Coal Scuttles, Japanned, art colours, 3s. 9d.; Spark Guards, 1s. 6d.

HAMPTON and SONS' BED-ROOM FURNITURE.

WHITE ENAMELLED SUITES[4], from $3\frac{1}{2}$ guineas to 50 guineas.

ASH BED-ROOM SUITES, with bevelled-edge, silvered plate to wardrobe and toilet glass, tile back to washstand, complete, with pedestal, towel rail, and chairs. £5 18s. 6d.

LARGE BED-ROOM SUITES, in new woods, with 6ft. wardrobe with bevelled-edge silvered plate glass to centre door, from £17 10s.

IRON FRENCH BEDSTEADS, fitted with double wire-woven spring mattresses, wool mattress, bolster, and feather pillow, 36s. 6d.

BRASS FRENCH BEDSTEADS, fitted with double wire-woven spring mattress, hair mattress, feather bolster, and pillow, 90s.

BEDDING, manufactured on the premises from the purest materials, at the lowest possible prices. Bedding purified and re-made.

HAMPTON and SONS, Pall-mall east, Charing-cross, London.
Works—43, Belvedere-road, S. E.

WM. WALLACE and Co.'s NEW ART FURNITURE CATALOGUE (Illustrated), just published. The most artistic, explicit, and complete book of drawings ever issued to the public. Post free on application. Every one should see this unique book before placing their orders. Gentlemen are invited to inspect goods, which are all on show as per catalogue, without being importuned to purchase.—Wm. Wallace and Co., Wholesale House Furnishers, 151, 152, and 153, Curtain-road. Telephone No. 61.

HEWETSON, MILNER and THEXTON (Ltd.[5]), 200, 203, 204, 211, 212, 213, 214 and 215, Tottenham-court-road, London, W. Illustrated and descriptive catalogues post free. Established 1825.

1. *Ware*, faïence. — 2. Becs-éteignoirs perfectionnés. — 3. *Lace lamp shades*, abat-jour de dentelles. — 4. Mobilier émaillé ou en émail blanc. — 5. C'est-à-dire *limited*.

CARVED OAK FURNITURE, Second-hand; also reproductions from ancient designs. Dining-room sets in this effective style, £25, £39, £46, &c. Design on application.

CARVED OAK MANTEL-PIECES, Over-Mantels, bureaus, clocks, sideboards, chairs, bookcases, &c., dado[1] and ceiling panelling, &c. Catalogues free.

ORIENTAL CARPETS — Turkish (new colouring), Indian, Persian, Mirzapore, Ghiordes, Lahore, &c. Large Oriental rugs from 6s. 6d. each.

CARPETS, British manufacture—Axminster, Wilton, Brussels, Kalmuck, Burmese, art squares &c., and Rugs of every description. Special bordered Chenille Carpets, artistic and inexpensive.

DINING-ROOM FURNITURE. — Complete sets, finished in the most approved and artistic modern designs, in various woods, from £25. Designs on application.

DRAWING-ROOM FURNITURE, in satinwood, rosewood inlaid, white and gold, &c. Upholstered in the newest and most approved fabrics.

CHIPPENDALE, Sheraton, Hepplewhite CABINETS, Bureaus, Bookcases, China Cabinets, Tables, Wardrobes, Chairs, &c., in great variety, and well worthy the attention of artists and collectors of antiques, &c. Special designs free.

DECORATIONS (chaste in design), Plumbing, Painting, &c.—Sanitary work carefully and inexpensively carried out by experienced workmen in town and country. Estimates free. English and French paperhangings, &c.

HEWETSON, MILNER, and THEXTON (Limited), 200, 203, 204, 211, 212, 213, 214, and 215, Tottenham-court-road, London, W. Furniture removed and warehoused[2], &c. Established 1825.

CARPETS, British and Foreign manufacture. N. B. — Small cargo of antique Daghestan Rugs on sale at reduced prices.—HEWETSON, MILNER, and THEXTON (Ltd.), Tottenham-court-road, W. Entrance to carpet show rooms, No. 215, Established 1825.

WILLSON'S noted stock of first-class SECOND-HAND FURNITURE[3], 68, Great Queen-street, Lincoln's-inn-fields comprising noble sideboards, dining tables, chairs, bookcases, and bed-room suites by Gillow, Holland, and eminent makers. Office furniture of every description.

CHIPPENDALE CHAIRS, Sideboards Bookcases, Bureaus, &c., in great variety. Also some very fine examples by Sheraton, Adam, and Hepplewhite, including a complete mahogany dressing and bed room set inlaid with satinwood. — WILLSON'S, as above. Estab. 1818.

CAST-OFF CLOTHES[4] for EXPORT ONLY. — Mr. and Mrs. MAURICE, of 65, New Oxford-street, W. C., having been appointed purchasing agents by Messrs. Malcolm and Co., of Cape Town, are now giving 20 per cent. more than any other dealers for home consumption for any quantity of the above. Also Uniforms, Artificial Teeth, Jewellery, &c. Parties waited on by Mr. or Mrs. M. Parcels receive prompt attention.

CAST-OFF CLOTHES, &c. — Mr. and Mrs. EDWARDS, of 6, Middle-row, Albert-gate, S.W., require for imme-

1. *Dado*, dé en architecture : on appelle ainsi la partie carrée d'un piédestal ou la base cubique d'une colonne. — 2. Transport et garde de mobiliers. — 3. Meubles d'occasion. — 4. Des mises-bas ou vêtements usés.

diate export an unlimited quantity of LEFT-OFF WEARING APPAREL of every description. Uniforms, jewellery, artificial teeth, and all kinds of property bought for cash and full value given. Parcels receive prompt attention. Appointments attended by Mr. or Mrs. E..

CAST-OFF CLOTHES, Uniforms, &c. WANTED. — S. SOLOMONS, for many years Manager to the late Mr. and Mrs. Lewis Hart, No. 24, Newcastle-street, Strand, is giving the utmost trade value for every description of LADIES', Gentlemen's, and Children's CLOTHING, Jewellery, Artificial Teeth, and all Miscellaneous Property. Ladies and gentlemen waited on in town and country by Mr. or Mrs. S. free of charge. Address as above; on parcels being sent, post-office orders remitted same day. Terms cash.

MR. and Mrs. LEWIS HART, 15, Stockbridge-terrace, Pimlico, S. W., facing the Metropolitan Victoria Station, who will wait upon ladies and gentlemen at their own residences, in town or country, in the strictest privacy, paying for all goods before clearing them away. A private room for persons calling.

LETTERS and PARCELS receive the strictest attention, and all articles returned if price not approved of. Please address all letters, &c., to Mr. and Mrs. LEWIS HART, No. 15, Stockbridge-terrace, Pimlico, S.W., which is their only address. Bankers — The National Bank. Established 1820.

MR. and Mrs. HENRY LEWIS, 3, Upper Baker-street, W. — The old-established (1830) buyers continue to give the highest price for ladies' and gentlemen's CAST-OFF CLOTHING, jewellery, furniture, old teeth, &c. Boxes and parcels sent receive prompt attention. Ladies waited on by Mrs. Lewis.

OLD ARTIFICIAL TEETH, Jewellery, Plate, Household Furniture, Linen, Guns, Horses, Carriages, Harness, and every description of property purchased for cash, to any amount, by Mr. and Mrs. LEWIS DAVIS, 2, Crawford-street, Baker-street, W., the old-established buyers. Letters and parcels forwarded receive immediate attention. Established 1800.

WANT PLACES.—All letters to be post-paid.

NURSE (HEAD) to young children, or take a lady's first baby. Experienced. 3 years' character. Age 45.—G. B., 14, Torrington-mews east, Bloomsbury, W. C.

NURSE (HEAD). Experienced to take entire charge. Very good needlewoman. Not object to travel. Age 37. Please state wages and particulars.—A. R., Cooper's, Chislehurst, Kent.

NURSE to lady's first baby. 20 years' experience. Highly recommended. Age 40. Wages £25.—A. B., 22, Langley-road, Small-heath, Birmingham.

NURSE. German. Protestant. Highly recommended. Take infant from the month. Great experience. Age 35. Wages £24.—M. D., Adams' Library, Kensington, W.

NURSE (experienced) in a good family. Middle-aged. 2 years' personal character. Wages £25, all found. First baby preferred.—A. B., 96, Acklam-road, North Kensington, W.

NURSE (UNDER) in good family. Young person, age 17. Not been out before. Used to children.—A. Chapman. The Case Is Altered Hotel, Willesden.

CHILDREN'S-MAID, or Maid to two young ladies. Plain dressmaker.

Age 22. 6 months' personal character. 2½ and 3 previous.—E. C., 29, Craven-road, Lancaster-gate, W.

CHILDREN'S or PARLOUR MAID. Good needlewoman and waitress. Good references. Catholic.—M. J. B., 19, Haberdasher-street, East-road, London.

MAID to elderly lady. Plain dress-maker. Good needlewoman, packer. Many years' good character. Left through death[1].—C. B., 39, Carmichael-road, South Norwood, S. E.

MAID to one lady. Thoroughly understands her duties. 2½ years' good character. Town or town and country.—G. L., Wilson's Library, 40, Southwick-street, W.

MAID to one lady. Good dressmaker, milliner, and plain sewer. No objection to travelling. Age 25. Good character.—E. A. D., Ditchett's Library, Circus-road, N.W.

MAID (USEFUL), or Young Ladies'-maid. No objection to travel. Understands her duties.—L. Garnham, Bucklesham, Ipswich, Suffolk.

PARLOURMAID[2] in a small family where housemaid is kept. Leaving through family travelling. Age 21. Disengaged[3]. — B., 16, Glady-road, West Hampstead.

PARLOURMAID, by day or on a job. Thoroughly experienced. Excellent reference. Town or country.—Mrs. M., 37, Dartrey-road, West Chelsea.

HOUSEKEEPER (superior). Well educated. Thoroughly conscientious and trustworthy. Excellent, economical cook. Town or country.—A. E., Tamblyn's Library, 8, Ladbroke-grove-road.

HOUSEKEEPER to gentlemen, or place of trust where a servant is kept. Good reference. — G. L., 16, Crampton-road, Penge.

HOUSEKEEPER (WORKING). Good cook. Age 50. Where she could have her daughter, age 18, to assist. Good character.—S. S., 8, Little Queen-street, Edgware-road.

COOK (thorough FRENCH). Speaks English. Active. Age 40. Wages from £35 to £40.—F., 16, Charlton-street, Portland-place.

HOUSEMAID, or House-Parlourmaid. Wages £18.—T. E., 23, Campden-street, Kensington.

HOUSEMAID, Second or Single-handed. Town or country.—F. Wilson, 7, Euston-grove, N. W.

HOUSEMAID, Second of three or four or Upper of two. Tall, age 24, 2 years and 4 months' character.—E. P., Rendcomb-park, near Cirencester, Gloucestershire.

HOUSEMAID (SECOND) where three or four are kept. Good reference. Disengaged[3].—S. B., 1, Sydney-street, Fulham-road, South Kensington.

LAUNDRYMAID[4]. Head or Single-handed, where assistance is given.—M., Mrs. Jones's, Portmore-common, Lymington, Hants.

LAUNDRYMAID, school or private. Age 28. Please state wages.—J. N., 51, Kender-street, New-cross-road, London, S. E.

KITCHENMAID in a gentleman's family. Three years' personal character. State wages. Kensington pre-

1. Ayant quitté son ancienne place par suite de la mort de sa maîtresse. — 2. *Parlour-maid*, femme de chambre, chargée d'une partie du ménage; *house-maid*, bonne à tout faire. — 3. *Disengaged*, sans place. — 4. Chargée de la lessive.

ferred.—E. Adams, 174, Cromwell-road, London, S.W.

SCULLERYMAID, or China Maid[1], in hotel or club.—A. J., 33, Marshal-street, Golden-square, W.

SCULLERYMAID in nobleman's or gentleman's family. Tall, strong, well taught, and steady. Highly respectable references. Age 17.—A. Z., 119, Seymour-place, Bryanston-square.

A Most respectable, MIDDLE-AGED PERSON. Care of a lady's House, or any place of trust. References. Last engagement, nine months. — H. 19, Shrewsbury-road, Bayswater.

MAN and WIFE : Mental Attendant and Housemaid[2]; work of house or Caretakers[3]. Pugh, London-road, Staines.

MAN and WIFE : man as thorough In-door Servant, good valet; wife good Cook. Over 2 years' character. Both abstainers[4]. Town or country.—H. M., Chapel-street, Bicester, Oxon.

BUTLER[8] (thorough) where footman is kept, or Butler-Valet and Travelling Servant. Not object to Australia. Age 33. Height 5ft. 9. 7 years in last situation. — D. Mc Craw, Burnham, Bucks.

FOOTMAN,[9] Second or Single-handed[10] under a butler. Age 17, height 5ft. 5. 14 months' good personal character.[12] Leaving, family going abroad. H. S., 42, Holland-park, W.

PAGE BOY in a gentleman's family. Age 16. Good appearance. Can be highly recommended. Town or country. —A. P., 50, Upper George-street, Bryanston-square, W.

COACHMAN (thorough) in a gentleman's family. Knows town well. Understands hunters[5]. Married, no family. Age 30. Can be highly recommended.—A. B., 26, Sherwood-st., W.

COACHMAN (thorough). Married. Age 40, no encumbrance[6]. Town or country. Highly recommended by present employer.—J. M., 33, Heath-street, Hampstead, N.W.

COACHMAN (experienced). Pair or more. Age 38, married, no family. Town or country. Good personal character if required.—C. M., 8, Clanricarde-gardens, Bayswater, W.

COACHMAN. Thoroughly understands management of horses. 13 years' character. Age 47. No family. Wife good laundress.[13]—A. B., 4, Denmark-terrace, Vincent-road, Norbiton, Surrey.

GROOM, or Second Coachman. Single, age 25, weight 10st. 5 years' character. — J. Basford, Westdean-park, Chichester, Sussex.

GARDENER (HEAD WORKING). Scotch, age 36. Single at present. Thoroughly experienced in all branches. Well recommended.—C. T., Elmwood, Bickley, Kent.

GARDENER, Head or Single-handed. Thoroughly understands his duties. Married, age 40. 5 years' good character.—M. C., Walmer-hill-house, Haslemere, Surrey.

HOTEL PORTER, or Boots[7]. Age 30, single. First-class character from last and former places. Town or country. Thoroughly understands his work. E. O., New Quebec-street, Portman-sq.

1. Fille de cuisine ou laveuse de vaisselle. — 2. Garde auprès d'un aliéné; bonne à tout faire. — 3. Soins de ménage, ou fonctions de gardien. — 4. Tous deux buveurs d'eau. — 5. Sait soigner les chevaux de chasse. — 6. Point de charges de famille. — 7. Concierge d'hôtel ou homme de peine. 8 majordome 9 laquais 10 seul 12 [illegible] 13 [illegible]

WAITER (HEAD) in an hotel. Thoroughly experienced. English. Single, age 34, height, 5ft. 9in. Good appearance. Highest references.— H. H. 137, Blackfriars-road, S. E.

WAITER (HEAD). Experienced first-class London and country hotels. Excellent testimonials and character. Age 32. English. Good appearance. Sidney, East-cottage, Kemptown, Brighton.

SALES BY AUCTION[1].

In the High Court of Justice, Chancery Division. —Arnold v. Barreto, 1887, A 785.—Southend, Essex.—Valuable Freehold Property, known, as the Thames Farm, containing 73a. 3r. 36p., with immediate possession.

MR. G. A. WILKINSON will SELL by AUCTION, at the Mart[2] on Monday, November 19th, at 2, the very valuable FREEHOLD PROPERTY, known as the Thames Farm, in the parish of Prittlewell, and adjoining the town of Southend. It comprises a farmhouse, with six bed rooms, three sitting rooms, and good domestic offices, &c.; pleasure and kitchen gardens, extensive farm buildings, and arable and pasture lands: the whole containing together 73a. 3r. 36p.[3]. The proximity of the town renders this property which possesses frontages to main roads of about 3,230 feet, immediately available for building purposes. Particulars may be had of Messrs. Tolhurst, Lovell, and Clinch, Solicitors, Gravesend; of Messrs. Tolhurst, Lovell, Clinch, and Tolhurst, Solicitors, Southend; and in London, of Messrs. Sismey and Sismey, Solicitors, 11, Serjeants'-inn, Fleet-street; of Joseph Harwood, Esq., Solicitor, 90, Cannon-street; of Messrs. Watson, Sons, and Room, Solicitors, 12, Bouverie-street, Fleet-street; and of Mr. G. A. Wilkinson, Land Agent and Auctioneer, 7, Poultry, City.

Mitcham-hall, Surrey. — The bulk of the elegant and costly Contents of the Mansion, including a valuable collection of paintings and water colours; also a collection of old proof engravings after Raphael, Rubens, Titian, Correggio, also proof engravings after Landseer[4] and other eminent masters: a choice collection of old English and other china; also the contents of greenhouses and conservatory. By direction of the owner, who is removing to London.

MESSRS. E. and H. LUMLEY are favoured with instructions to SELL by AUCTION, on the premises, as above, on Wednesday, December 12th, 1888, and following days, at 12 o'clock precisely each day, the excellent HOUSEHOLD FURNITURE, comprising Brussels, Axminster, Persian, and Turkey carpets, chimney, pier, and console glasses in carved frames[5], suites of curtains, drawing-room suite in crimson velvet, buhl, tortoiseshell, and inlaid cabinets, Amboyna and other tables, collection of paintings in water-colours, including examples of

Buckley — Salvator Rosa
Lamb — Sherrin
Pearson — Koekkoek
Rowbotham — Nakhen
Alexander Johnstone, R. S. A. — Rayner
Weigall
Motham

and others; valuable collection of old line proof engravings after

Correggio — Rubens
Titian — Raphael

also proof engravings after

Rosa Bonheur — Landseer — Millais

&c.; an assemblage of old English and other china in Wedgwood, Leeds, Dresden, Berlin, Sèvres, and Oriental ware; marble statuary and columns; billiard table by Stevens and Sons, and appointments of rooms; also the contents of the greenhouses and conservatory, dairy, laundry, and a vast quantity of out-door effects. May be viewed

1. Ventes aux enchères. — 2. A l'Hôtel des ventes. — 3. 73 *acres*, 3 *roods*, 36 *perches*; 1 acre = 40 ares 4671; 1 rood = 10 ares 12; 1 perche = 0 are 25. — 4. *Landseer*, voy. note 2, page 28. — 5. Glaces de cheminée, miroirs à placer sur trumeaux ou au-dessus de consoles, à cadres sculptés.

Monday and Tuesday before the sale. Catalogues to be had of Lumleys, Land Agents and Auctioneers, St. James's, Piccadilly.

Telephone No. 3,707. Telegraphic address, Oxenhams, London.

OXENHAM'S AUCTION ROOMS, 187 and 189, Oxford-street (30 doors east of Regent-circus). Established 80 years. The largest, best situate, and most convenient in London.—TOOTH and TOOTH (late Oxenham). (Telephone No. 3,707.)

Friday next.—Oxenham's Auction Rooms, 187 and 189, Oxford-street.—An immense assemblage of capital Furniture, removed from 44, Longridge-road, Earl's-court; Grosvenor-chambers; Grosvenor-gardens, and various private residences; 23 grand and cottage pianofortes, and effects.

MESSRS. TOOTH and TOOTH (late Oxenham) will SELL by AUCTION, at their Rooms, as above, on Friday next, at 12 exact time, an immense assemblage of capital FURNITURE, in clean condition, comprising handsome drawing-room suites in various woods, the chairs, easy chairs, couches, and settees[1] covered in silks, satins, Genoa velvet, plush, and saddle-bag; expensive cabinets, centre, loo, and card tables[2], overmantels, etagères, 23 grand and cottage pianofortes by Collard, Erard, Broadwood, and other wellknown makers, American walnut-tree, brown oak, and mahogany dining-room suites covered in morocco, noble sideboards, a superior extending frame dining table opening 18 feet, several others of smaller dimensions, dinner waggons, bookcases, library tables, the appointments for ball and staircase, Turkey, Wilton pile, and Brussels carpets, fenders and fireirons, the appointments of 30 bed chambers in mahogany, walnut-tree, ash, pitch pine, and japanned woods, of wardrobes, garderobes, chests of drawers, washstands dressing tables, &c., iron and brass bedsteads and bedding, linen, blankets, china, glass, plated articles, and miscellanies. May be viewed Thursday, and catalogues had, or forwarded on application.

Hartlands, Cranford (11 miles of Hyde-park).

MESSRS. GIDDY and TURNER have received instructions to SELL by AUCTION, at the Mart, E. C., on Wednesday, November 21st, 1888, this substantially-built FREEHOLD MANSION, with six acres of finely-timbered old grounds, stabling, and outbuildings. Particulars on application at 121, Pall-mall, or at either of their branch offices, Guildford, Sunningdale, and Maiden-head.

Pall-mall.—This Day.—Old French and other Furniture, Clocks, Bronzes, Brocades, old china, and cabinet objects from abroad.

MESSRS. FOSTER respectfully announce for SALE by AUCTION, at the Gallery, 54, Pall-mall, THIS DAY (Wednesday), the 14th Nov., at 1 o'clock precisely, a large consignment of DECORATIVE EFFECTS, including several handsome carved cabinets, old French marqueterie cabinets and tables, a sculptured marble chimney piece, carved wood overmantels and panels, a Louis XVI, carved and gilt centre Ottoman, Empire, bronze, and or-moulu clocks, candelabra and wall lights, old Italian brocades and embroideries, old Oriental, Vienna, and Dresden china, miniatures, snuff-boxes, and other cabinet objects. May be viewed and catalogues had. — 54, Pall-mall.

MESSRS. KING and CHASEMORE, under instructions from Harry Tuppen, Esquire, at the Auction Mart, Tokenhouse-yard, London, E. C., on Thursday, Nov. 29th, 1888, at 2 o'clock in the afternoon, in two lots. Particulars, plans, and conditions of sale

---

1. *Settees*, causeuses. — 2. Tables de jeu; *loo*, jeu analogue à la Mouche dont parle si spirituellement Balzac dans *Béatrix*.

may be obtained of John Herbert Tuppen, Esquire, Solicitor, Lowfold, Wisborough-green; and of Messrs. King and Chasemore, Land and Timber Surveyors, Horsham, Sussex.

This day.—Without Reserve.—The capital Stock of a well-known London Gun Maker, removed from 166, Fenchurch-street, E.C.

MESSRS. ROBINSON and FISHER will SELL, at their Rooms, 21, Old Bond-street, THIS DAY (Wednesday), at 2,30 precisely, the capital STOCK, comprising double-barrel breech-loading[1] and other guns by Daw, Boswell, Blakemore, Leech; rook rifles, revolvers, and gun fittings, Spanish mahogany show cases, desks, partitions, &c. Catalogues of the Auctioneers.

No. 65, Oxford-street.—On Friday Evening next, November 16th, at 6 precisely, 300 lots of Pictures, by old and modern artists.

W. and F. C. BONHAM will SELL by AUCTION, as above, 300 lots of PICTURES, including works by and after

B. Foster	Rubens
D. Cox	Palma
Tadema	Morland
Creswick	Correggio
Broome	Ruysdael.
Lidderdale	Hobbema

and others; also water-colours, engravings, 25,000 chromos, frames, &c. On view morning of sale.

Well-secured Improved Ground-rent.

MR. H. J. BROMLEY will SELL by AUCTION, at the Mart, E. C., on Thursday, November 22d, 1888, at 1 o'clock, a well-secured improved GROUND-RENT of £32 per annum, payable out of the Robin Hood Tavern, Penge, in the county of Surrey. Further particulars may be had of Messrs. Burroughs and Bisdee, Solicitors, Forest-hill, S. E.; or at the offices of the Auctioneer, facing the Railway Station, Forest-hill.

Near Oxford-street. — Freehold Investment.

MESSRS. BRAY, YOUNG, and Co. will SELL by AUCTION, at the Mart, Tokenhouse-yard, Bank, London, E. C., To-morrow (Thursday), Nov. 15, at 1 precisely, the valuable FREEHOLD SHOP and DWELLING-HOUSE, No. 48, James-street, Oxford-street, near Marble-arch and Manchester-square, prominently situated in a busy trading thoroughfare. Let on lease, terminating in 1895, and now in the occupation of Mr. Edwin Dennis, Oil and Colour Warehouseman, at the very low rent of £65 per annum, but estimated to be well worth £80 per annum. May be viewed by permission of the tenant, and particulars and conditions of sale obtained of Messrs. Church, Rendell, and Co., Solicitors, 9, Bedford-row, London, W. C.; Thomas-Southall, Esq., Solicitor, Worcester; at the Mart; and of the Auctioneers, Messrs. Bray, Young, and Co., 6, Warwick-court, High Holborn, London, W. C., and High-street, Hampton Wick, Middlesex.

Public Sale of Wines and Spirits, without reserve, on Thursday, November 29th.

MESSRS. SOUTHARD and Co., Sworn Brokers, 2, St. Dunstan's-hill, will hold their Public SALES, as above, at the Commercial Sale Rooms, Mincing-lane. Particulars in due course.

1. *Breech-loading gun*, fusil se chargeant par la culasse (système Lefaucheux).

Printed and published by GEORGE EDWARD WRIGHT, Printer, of No. 2, Printing-house-square, at the offices in Printing-house-square and Playhouse-yard, in the Parish of St. Ann. Blackfriars, in the City of London. Wednesday, November 14, 1888.

INDEX DES NOMS CITÉS DANS LES NOTES.

Paris. — Imprimerie DELALAIN FRÈRES, rue de la Sorbonne, 1 et 3.

www.ingramcontent.com/pod-product-compliance
Ingram Content Group UK Ltd.
Pitfield, Milton Keynes, MK11 3LW, UK
UKHW020604230726
13926UKWH00005B/2196

9 782016 151167